Microsoft® Power Point®
2013 Bible

Microsoft® PowerPoint® 2013 Bible

Faithe Wempen

WILEY

Microsoft® PowerPoint® 2013 Bible

Published by
John Wiley & Sons, Inc.
10475 Crosspoint Boulevard
Indianapolis, IN 46256
www.wiley.com

Copyright© 2013 by John Wiley & Sons, Inc., Indianapolis, Indiana

Published simultaneously in Canada

ISBN: 978-1-118-48811-9
ISBN: 978-1-118-64715-8 (ebk)
ISBN: 978-1-118-68009-4 (ebk)
ISBN: 978-1-118-64708-9 (ebk)

Manufactured in the United States of America

10 9 8 7 6 5 4 3 2 1

For general information on our other products and services please contact our Customer Care Department within the United States at (877) 762-2974, outside the United States at (317) 572-3993 or fax (317) 572-4002.

Wiley publishes in a variety of print and electronic formats and by print-on-demand. Some material included with standard print versions of this book may not be included in e-books or in print-on-demand. If this book refers to media such as a CD or DVD that is not included in the version you purchased, you may download this material at http://booksupport.wiley.com. For more information about Wiley products, visit www.wiley.com.

Library of Congress Control Number: 2012924233

Trademarks: Wiley and the Wiley logo are trademarks or registered trademarks of John Wiley & Sons, Inc. and/or its affiliates, in the United States and other countries, and may not be used without written permission. PowerPoint is a registered trademark of Microsoft Corporation. All other trademarks are the property of their respective owners. John Wiley & Sons, Inc. is not associated with any product or vendor mentioned in this book.

To Margaret, who makes it all possible.

About the Author

Faithe Wempen, MA, is an A+ Certified hardware guru, Microsoft Office Specialist Master Instructor, and software consultant with over 120 computer books to her credit. She has taught Microsoft Office applications, including PowerPoint, to over a quarter of a million online students for corporate clients including Hewlett Packard, CNET, Sony, Gateway, and eMachines. When she is not writing, she teaches Microsoft Office classes in the Computer Technology department at Indiana University-Purdue University at Indianapolis (IUPUI), does private computer training and support consulting, and owns and operates Sycamore Knoll Bed and Breakfast in Noblesville, Indiana (www.sycamoreknoll.com).

About the Technical Editor

Glenna Shaw has been creating data visualizations in the form of presentations, project management tools, dashboards, demos, prototypes, and system user interfaces for nearly two decades. She is frequently sought out for her innovative information management solutions using SharePoint and Microsoft Office as well as her creative PowerPoint designs. She is the author, subject matter expert, and/or technical editor for many online courses, articles, and webinars on PowerPoint. She is a Microsoft Most Valued Professional (MVP) for PowerPoint and the owner of the PPT Magic and Visualology.net websites. Glenna is a Project Management Professional (PMP) and holds certificates in accessible information technology, graphic design, cloud computing, knowledge management, and professional technical writing.

Credits

Acquisitions Editor
Mariann Barsolo

Development Editor
Susan Herman

Technical Editor
Glenna Shaw

Production Editor
Christine O'Connor

Copy Editor
Judy Flynn

Editorial Manager
Pete Gaughan

Production Manager
Tim Tate

Vice President and Executive Group Publisher
Richard Swadley

Vice President and Executive Publisher
Neil Edde

Project Coordinator, Cover
Katie Crocker

Proofreader
Josh Chase, Word One New York

Indexer
Nancy Guenther

Cover Image
© Aleksandar Velasevic / iStockphoto

Cover Designer
Ryan Sneed

Acknowledgments

Thank you to the wonderful editorial team at Wiley for another job well done. You guys never fail to make me better.

Contents at a Glance

Contents

Contents

Contents

Contents

Contents

Preface

S ome books zoom through a software program so fast it makes your head spin. You'll come out dizzy but basically able to cobble together some sort of result, even if it doesn't look quite right. This is not one of those books.

PowerPoint® 2013 Bible is probably the only PowerPoint book you will ever need. In fact, it might even be the only book on giving presentations you'll ever need. No, seriously! I mean it.

As you probably guessed by the heft of the book, this is not a quick-fix shortcut to PowerPoint expertise. Instead, it's a thoughtful, thorough educational tool that can be your personal trainer now and your reference text for years to come. That's because this book covers PowerPoint from "cradle to grave." No matter what your current expertise level with PowerPoint, this book brings you up to the level of the most experienced and talented PowerPoint users in your office. You might even be able to teach those old pros a thing or two!

When you finish this book, you will not only be able to build a presentation with PowerPoint, you'll also be able to explain why you made the choices you did, and you'll deliver that presentation smoothly and with confidence.

If you are planning a presentation for remote delivery (for example, posting it on a website or setting up a kiosk at a trade show), you'll find lots of help for these situations too. In fact, an entire section of the book is devoted to various nontraditional presentation methods, such as live Internet or network delivery, trade show booths, and interactive presentation distribution on a disk or CD.

How This Book Is Organized

This book is organized into parts, which are groups of chapters that deal with a common general theme. Here's what you'll find:

- **Part I: Building Your Presentation.** In this part, you start building a robust, content-rich presentation by choosing a template, entering your text, and applying text formatting.
- **Part II: Using Graphics and Multimedia Content.** This part teaches you how to import and create various types of graphical and multimedia content including clip

art, diagrams, photos, charts, sound effects, movies, and music. You'll also learn here how to create movement with animation effects and transitions.

- **Part III: Interfacing with Your Audience.** This part helps you prepare your presentation for various delivery scenarios, including printing handouts for a live audience, running a live show on a computer screen, designing visual aids for user-interactive or self-running presentations, and sharing and collaborating with others.

- **Part IV: Project Labs.** This part provides four step-by-step walk-throughs that demonstrate how to create some of the most powerful and sought-after PowerPoint effects and projects, including creating navigation systems, classroom games, complex animations, and graphically presented text. Please visit www.wiley.com /go/powerpoint2013bible to download the files you need for the project labs.

Special Features

Every chapter in this book opens with a quick look at what's in the chapter and closes with a summary. Along the way, you also find icons in the margins to draw your attention to specific topics and items of interest.

Here's what the icons mean:

These icons point you to chapters or other sources for more information on the topic under discussion.

NOTE
Notes provide extra information about a topic, perhaps some technical tidbit or background explanation.

TIP
Tips offer ideas for the advanced user who wants to get the most out of PowerPoint.

CAUTION
Cautions point out how to avoid the pitfalls that beginners commonly encounter.

Good luck with PowerPoint 2013! I hope you have as much fun reading this book as I had writing it. If you would like to let me know what you thought of the book, good or bad, you can e-mail me at faithe@wempen.com. I'd like to hear from you!

Part I

Building Your Presentation

IN THIS PART

A First Look at PowerPoint

IN THIS CHAPTER

Who uses PowerPoint and why?

What's new in PowerPoint 2013?

Learning your way around PowerPoint

Changing the view

Zooming in and out

Displaying and hiding screen elements

Working with window controls

Using the help system and getting updates

PowerPoint 2013 is a member of the Microsoft Office 2013 suite of programs. A *suite* is a group of programs designed by a single manufacturer to work well together. Like its siblings — Word (the word processor), Excel (the spreadsheet), Outlook (the personal organizer and e-mail manager), and Access (the database) — PowerPoint has a well-defined role. It creates materials for presentations.

A *presentation* is any kind of interaction between a speaker and audience, but it usually involves one or more of the following: computer-displayed slides, noncomputerized visual aids (such as transparencies or 35mm slides), hard-copy handouts, and/or speaker's notes. PowerPoint can create all of these types of visual aids, plus many other types that you'll learn about as you go along.

Because PowerPoint is so tightly integrated with the other Microsoft Office 2013 components, you can easily share information among them. For example, if you have created a graph in Excel, you can use it on a PowerPoint slide. It goes the other way too. You can, for example, take the outline from your PowerPoint presentation and copy it into Word, where you can dress it up with Word's powerful document formatting commands. Virtually any piece of data in any Office program can be linked to any other Office program, so you never have to worry about your data being in the wrong format. PowerPoint also accepts data from almost any other Windows-based application and can import a variety of graphics, audio, and video formats.

In this chapter you'll get a big-picture introduction to PowerPoint 2013, and then we'll fire up the program and poke around a bit to help you get familiar with the interface. You'll find out how to use the tabs and panes and how to get help and updates from Microsoft.

Who Uses PowerPoint and Why?

PowerPoint is a popular tool for people who give presentations as part of their jobs and also for their support staff. With PowerPoint, you can create visual aids that help get the message across to an audience, whatever that message may be and whatever the format in which it is presented. Although the traditional kind of presentation is a live speech presented at a podium, advances in technology have made it possible to give several other kinds of presentations, and PowerPoint has kept pace nicely. The following list outlines the most common PowerPoint formats:

- **Podium.** For live presentations, PowerPoint helps the lecturer emphasize key points through the use of computer-based shows (from a notebook or tablet PC, for example) or overhead transparencies.
- **Kiosk shows.** These are self-running presentations that provide information in an unattended location. You have probably seen such presentations listing meeting times and rooms in hotel lobbies and as sales presentations at trade show booths.
- **CDs and DVDs.** You can package a PowerPoint presentation on a CD or DVD and distribute it with a press release, a marketing push, or a direct mail campaign. The presentation can be in PowerPoint format, or it can be converted to some other format, such as PDF or a video clip.
- **Internet formats.** You can use PowerPoint to create a show that you can present live over a network or the Internet, while each participant watches from their own computer. You can even store a self-running or interactive presentation on a website in a variety of formats and make it available for the public to download and run on a PC.

When you start your first PowerPoint presentation, you may not be sure which delivery method you will use. However, it's best to decide the presentation format before you invest too much work in your materials because the audience's needs are different for each medium.

▷ Need help structuring a presentation or planning for its delivery? See Appendix A, "What Makes a Great Presentation?"

Most people associate PowerPoint with sales presentations, but PowerPoint is useful for people in many other lines of work as well. The following sections present a sampling of how real people just like you are using PowerPoint in their daily jobs.

Sales

More people use PowerPoint for selling goods and services than for any other reason. Armed with a laptop computer and a PowerPoint presentation, a salesperson can make a good impression on a client anywhere in the world. Figure 1.1 shows a slide from a sample sales presentation.

FIGURE 1.1

PowerPoint offers unparalleled flexibility for presenting information to potential customers.

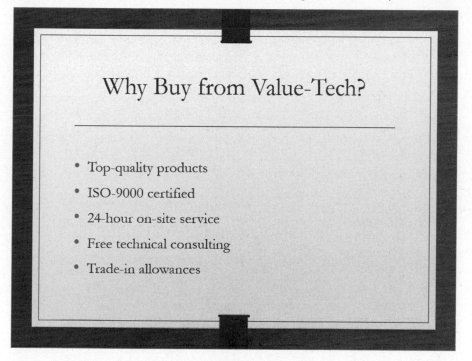

These are just some of the sales tools you can create with PowerPoint:

- Live presentations in front of clients with the salesperson present and running the show. This is the traditional kind of sales pitch that most people are familiar with.

- Self-running presentations that flip through the slides at specified intervals so that passersby can read them or ignore them as they wish. These types of presentations are great for grabbing people's attention at trade show booths.

- User-interactive product information demos distributed on CD/DVD that potential customers can view at their leisure on their own PCs. This method is very inexpensive because you can create a single presentation and distribute it by mail to multiple customers.

See Chapter 19, "Designing User-Interactive or Self-Running Presentations," to learn about controlling a live presentation. You create a self-running or user-interactive presentation in Chapter 20, "Preparing a Presentation for Mass Distribution."

Marketing

The distinction between sales and marketing can be rather blurred at times, but marketing generally refers to the positioning of a product in the media rather than its presentation to a particular company or individual. Marketing representatives are often called upon to write advertising copy, generate camera-ready layouts for print advertisements, design marketing flyers and shelf displays, and produce other creative selling materials.

PowerPoint is not a drawing program per se, and it can't substitute for one except in a crude way. However, by combining the Office 2013 clip art collection and drawing tools with some well-chosen fonts and borders, a marketing person can come up with some very usable designs in PowerPoint. Figure 1.2 shows an example. You learn about clip art in Chapter 11, "Working with Clip Art and Photos." You can also integrate video clips in PowerPoint presentations that can tell the story of your product; see Chapter 15 for more information.

FIGURE 1.2

PowerPoint can generate camera-ready marketing materials, although it can't substitute for the tools that professional advertising companies use.

Overwrought by technology?

Computer glitches giving you fits?

Don't despair!

Your Computer Friend can help. It's not easy being a computing beginner these days, but we can help you get up to speed with word processing, the Internet, or any other aspect of computing that you want to learn more about. We can even fix your current computer's ailments and recommend upgrades that will give you the most bang for your buck.

Your Computer Friend
123 Main Street
Franklin, IN 46062
317-555-8281

Human Resources

Human resources personnel often find themselves giving presentations to new employees to explain the policies and benefits of the company. A well-designed, attractive presentation gives the new folks a positive impression of the company they have signed up with, starting them off on the right foot.

One of the most helpful features in PowerPoint for the human resources professional is the SmartArt tool. With it, you can easily diagram the structure of the company and make changes whenever necessary with a few mouse clicks. Figure 1.3 shows an organization chart on a PowerPoint slide. You can also create a variety of other diagram types. Organization charts and other SmartArt diagrams are covered in Chapter 10, "Creating SmartArt Diagrams."

FIGURE 1.3

Microsoft's SmartArt feature lets you easily create organizational diagrams from within PowerPoint.

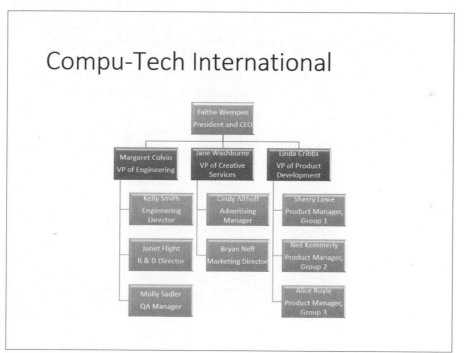

Education and Training

Most training courses include a lecture section in which the instructor outlines the general procedures and policies. This part of the training is usually followed up with individual, hands-on instruction. PowerPoint can't help much with the latter, but it can help make the lecture portion of the class go smoothly.

If you have access to a scanner, you can scan in diagrams and drawings of the objects you are teaching the students to use. You can also use computer-generated images, such as screen captures and video clips, to teach people about software.

PowerPoint's interactive controls even let you create quizzes that each student can take on-screen to gauge their progress. Depending on the button the student clicks, you can set up the quiz to display a "Yes, you are correct!" or "Sorry, try again" slide. See Figure 1.4. For details about this procedure, see Chapter 19 and Lab 4 in the Project Labs section at the end of the book.

FIGURE 1.4

Test the student's knowledge with a user-interactive quiz in PowerPoint.

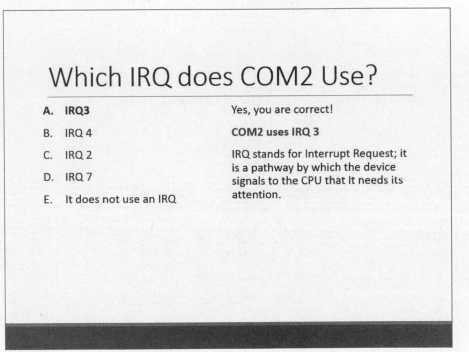

Hotel and Restaurant Management

Service organizations such as hotels and restaurants often need to inform their customers of various facts but need to do so unobtrusively so that the information will not be obvious except to those looking for it. For example, a convention center hotel might provide a list of the meetings taking place in its meeting rooms, or a restaurant might show pictures of the day's specials on a video screen in the waiting area.

In such unattended situations, a self-running (kiosk) presentation works best. Typically the computer box and keyboard are hidden from passersby, and the monitor displays the information.

You learn more about kiosk setups in Chapter 19.

Clubs and Organizations

Many nonprofit clubs and organizations, such as churches and youth centers, operate much the same way as for-profit businesses and need sales, marketing, and informational materials. But clubs and organizations often have special needs too, such as the need to recognize volunteers for a job well done. Microsoft provides a certificate template for PowerPoint that's ideal for this purpose. Figure 1.5 shows a certificate generated in PowerPoint. Another popular use for PowerPoint is to project the lyrics of a song on a big screen for sing-alongs at churches and meetings.

FIGURE 1.5

With PowerPoint, you can easily create certificates and awards.

What's New in PowerPoint 2013?

PowerPoint 2013 is very much like PowerPoint 2010 in its basic functionality. It uses a tabbed Ribbon across the top, rather than a traditional menu system, and employs dialog boxes and a Quick Access Toolbar in the same ways that 2010 did.

This doesn't mean that there aren't changes and improvements though! The following sections outline the major differences you will see when you upgrade from PowerPoint 2010 to PowerPoint 2013.

Cloud Integration

You can purchase Office 2013 (or the standalone PowerPoint 2013) either as a traditional boxed application or as a cloud-based subscription called Office 365. There are several benefits to the cloud version, including lower price, automatic updates, the ability to use Office on multiple PCs without paying extra (with some editions), and the ability to access your Office applications and files from multiple locations. The cloud-based version is marked primarily to businesses, but versions are also available for university students and home users too. See http://www.microsoft.com/en-us/office365/small-business-home.aspx for more information.

Start Screen

In earlier PowerPoint versions, you started up in a blank new presentation, which some beginners found intimidating. PowerPoint 2013 opens with a Start screen (Figure 1.6), providing easy access to both local and online templates as well as recently used files.

FIGURE 1.6

PowerPoint 2013 opens with a Start screen that offers links to templates and recent files.

Improved Shape Merging

If you have ever tried to create anything with the drawing tools in an Office app, you know that it can be frustrating because the shapes provided don't always match the shapes you want. Office 2013's drawing tools contain several new commands and capabilities that make the process of creating just the right shapes much easier. You can find the Merge Shapes button on the Insert Shapes section of the Drawing Tools Format tab when two or more shapes are selected. Clicking Merge Shapes opens a menu of merge types.

These new commands are all focused around merging two or more shapes into a single shape, using actions like Union, Combine, Intersect, Fragment, and Subtract. For example, suppose you want a shape that consists of a rounded rectangle with two arrows emerging from it. You could start with the three separate shapes shown at the left in Figure 1.7 and then use the Union command to join them into a single shape, as shown on the right.

FIGURE 1.7

Drawn shapes, before and after merging.

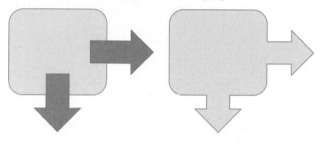

You will learn a lot more about these in Chapter 9, "Drawing and Formatting Objects."

Improved Smart Guides

PowerPoint 2013 makes it easier than ever to precisely align and evenly space objects with one another. When you drag an object to position it, dotted guidelines called Smart Guides appear, showing its relationship to other objects on the slide and allowing you to easily snap the object into precise alignment and spacing. Earlier versions of PowerPoint had alignment commands, but you had to specifically issue them; Smart Guides present themselves automatically whenever they might be needed. Figure 1.8 shows an example. Smart Guides are covered in Chapter 9.

You can also create permanent drawing guides on the slide masters, making it easier to position content on slide masters and layout masters. Chapter 4, "Working with Layouts, Themes, and Masters," covers modifying slide masters.

FIGURE 1.8

Alignment guides make it easier to align objects on slides.

Improved Comments

PowerPoint has included a Comments feature in the past, but it hasn't been very robust. In PowerPoint 2013, there is a Comments pane that you can use in Normal view to display and manage comments. See Figure 1.9.

FIGURE 1.9

The Comments pane helps you display and respond to comments.

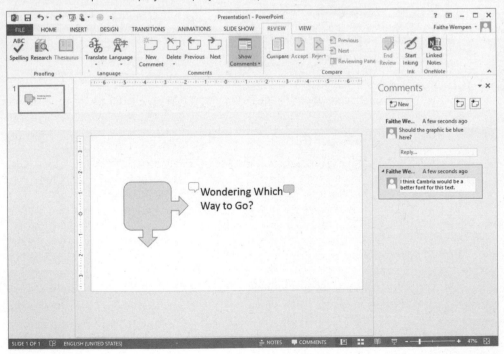

SkyDrive Integration

SkyDrive is Microsoft's online file storage service. Each user gets a certain amount of free space there (usually 2GB), and you can purchase additional space.

In Office 2013 apps, the logged-in user's SkyDrive is the default save location, making it as easy to save files to your SkyDrive as it is to save to any local folder on your hard disk. Files saved to SkyDrive are private and secure, and you can access them from any Internet-connected computing device, no matter where you are. For more information about SkyDrive, see Appendix B.

Online Pictures and Videos

PowerPoint 2013, like other Office 2013 applications, includes integration with online picture and video sharing services such as YouTube and Flickr, enabling you to easily access your own and other people's online content for use in your presentations.

Microsoft's clip art collection is now accessed entirely online from Office.com. You can also easily import pictures from your own SkyDrive and from a Bing image search. To help you avoid copyright problems, by default the Bing image search returns only results that are free to use under Creative Commons (a public user license).

For videos, you can embed video code from any website that provides it. (PowerPoint 2010 also allowed this.) But what's new now is that you can search for videos with Bing video search and select and embed clips directly from YouTube. See Figure 1.10.

FIGURE 1.10

You can insert or embed video content from online sources.

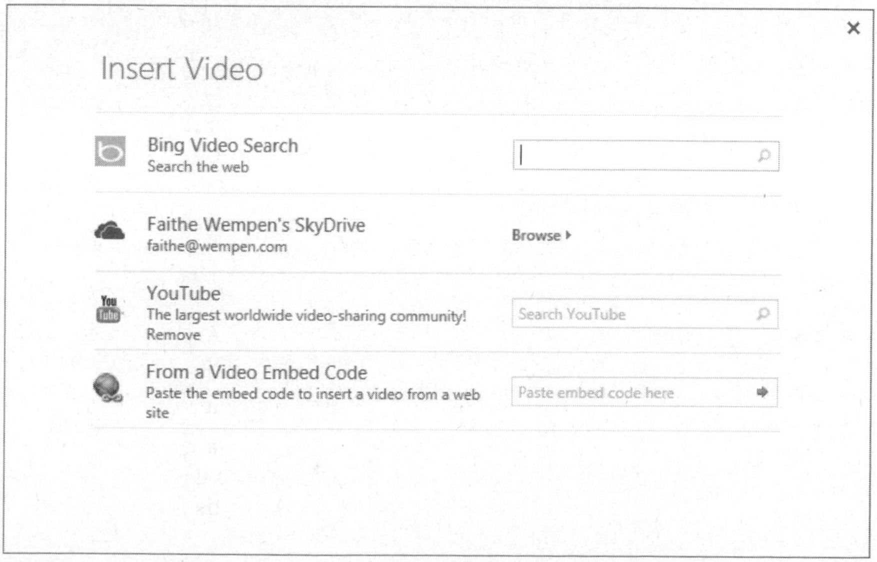

13

Improved Presenter Tools

PowerPoint 2013 improves on-screen presentation capabilities in several ways. First, the tools available to you in Slide Show view are now more robust, including the ability to zoom in on a particular area of a slide and to select a slide to jump to from an array of thumbnail images.

Presenter view can now be viewed on one monitor, allowing you to rehearse without connecting anything else. Presenter view has also been been enhanced, with extra display settings and easier-to-use slide controls. See Figure 1.11.

FIGURE 1.11

Presenter view is now easier to use.

...And Other New Features

Besides the features I've just outlined, there are plenty more nice surprises awaiting upgraders:

- **Theme variants.** For many years now, PowerPoint users have complained that the templates PowerPoint provides are not customizable enough. For example, what if a certain template has a perfect background graphic but the colors are all wrong? PowerPoint 2013 solves this by providing color variants for many of the built-in themes.

- **Touch controls.** All of the Office 2013 apps, including PowerPoint, are more easily controlled with touch screens than their predecessors. You can use PowerPoint 2013 in the traditional way, with a mouse, or by pointing, tapping, swiping, and dragging on a touch screen.

- **Eyedropper tool.** Some graphics programs enable you to use an Eyedropper tool to pick up a color from one object and copy that color to another object. Now you can do that in Office applications too. For example, you could pick up a color from a photograph on a slide and apply it to the text on the slide so that everything matches. This is great for matching colors for themes. You'll find the Eyedropper tool on the Shape Fill and Shape Outline buttons' menus on the Drawing Tools Format tab when working with shapes.

- **MP4 support.** PowerPoint 2010 was revolutionary in that it allowed users to create their own video versions of their presentations. However, only one video format was supported: AVI. PowerPoint 2013 adds MP4 support, making the resulting videos much more widely shareable because MP4 is one of the most common video formats for online use.

- **Welcome Back.** When you reopen a presentation that you were previously working on, the last slide you were editing automatically reappears.

Learning Your Way around PowerPoint

Now that you have seen some of the potential uses for PowerPoint and toured the new features, let's get started using the program.

PowerPoint is one of the easiest and most powerful presentation programs available. You can knock out a passable presentation in a shockingly short time by skimming through the chapters in Part I and Part II of the book, or you can spend some time with PowerPoint's advanced features to make a complex presentation that looks, reads, and works exactly the way you want.

Starting and Exiting PowerPoint

You can start PowerPoint just as you would any other program in Windows: from the Start screen (in Windows 8) or the Start menu (in Windows 7). Office 2013 runs only under those two operating systems.

In Windows 8:

1. **Press the Windows key, ⊞, on the keyboard to display the Start screen, or on a touch screen, swipe in from the right and tap Start.** The Start screen appears.

2. **Scroll to the right if needed to find the PowerPoint 2013 tile, and click or tap it.** The program starts.

In Windows 7:

1. **Click the Start button.** The Start menu opens.
2. **Click All Programs.**
3. **Click Microsoft Office.**
4. **Click Microsoft PowerPoint 2013.** The program starts.

When PowerPoint 2013 opens, a Start screen appears, as you saw back in Figure 1.6, offering help for opening existing files or starting new ones. If you want to bypass the Start screen and jump immediately to a new blank presentation (as in earlier versions of PowerPoint), just press the Esc key.

TIP

If you want quick access to PowerPoint from the Windows 8 Desktop, add a shortcut to PowerPoint to the taskbar. To do so, right-click the PowerPoint 2013 tile on the Start screen and click Pin to Taskbar. From then on, you can start PowerPoint by clicking the PowerPoint 2013 icon on the left end of the taskbar.

When you are ready to leave PowerPoint, click the Close (X) button in the top-right corner of the PowerPoint window. If you have any unsaved work, PowerPoint asks if you want to save your changes. Because you have just been playing around in this chapter, you probably do not have anything to save yet. (If you do have something to save, see Chapter 2, "Creating and Saving Presentation Files," to learn more about saving.) Click No to decline to save your changes, and you're outta there.

Understanding the Screen Elements

PowerPoint's interface is typical of any Windows desktop program in many ways, but it has some special Office-specific features as well. The PowerPoint window contains these elements, as shown in Figure 1.12:

- **Title bar.** Identifies the program running (PowerPoint) and the name of the active presentation. If the window is not maximized, you can move the window by dragging the title bar.
- **Ribbon.** Functions as a combination of menu bar and toolbar, offering tabbed "pages" of buttons, lists, and commands. The next section describes it in more detail.
- **File tab.** Opens the File menu (Backstage view), from which you can open, save, print, and start new presentations.
- **Quick Access Toolbar.** Contains shortcuts for some of the most common commands. You can add your own favorites here as well.
- **Minimize button.** Shrinks the application window to a bar on the Windows taskbar; you click its button on the taskbar to reopen it.

- **Maximize/Restore button.** If the window is maximized (full screen), it changes to windowed (not full screen). If the window is not maximized, clicking here maximizes it.

- **Close button.** Closes PowerPoint. You may be prompted to save your changes, if you made any.

- **Work area.** Where active PowerPoint slide(s) appear. Figure 1.10 shows it in Normal view, but other views are available that make the work area appear differently.

See the section "Changing the View" later in this chapter for details.

- **Status bar.** Reports information about the presentation and provides shortcuts for changing the view and the zoom and accessing the Notes and Comments panes.

FIGURE 1.12

The PowerPoint window is a combination of usual Windows features and unique Office elements.

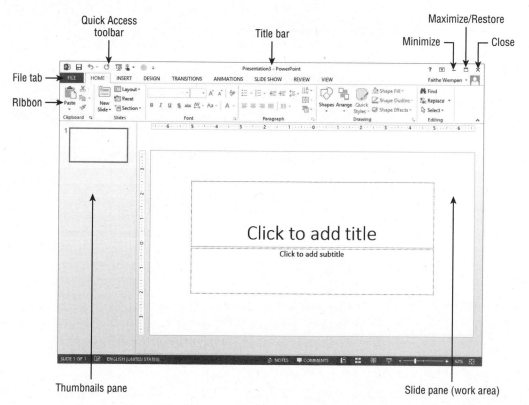

Working with the Ribbon

PowerPoint 2013's user interface is based on the Ribbon, which is a bar across the top of the window that contains tabbed pages of commands and buttons. Rather than opening a menu and selecting a command, you click a tab and then click a button or open a list on that tab.

Here are some important terms you need to know when working with tabs:

- **Ribbon.** The whole bar, including all of the tabs.
- **File tab.** A rectangular orange button that opens Backstage view (also called the File menu), from which you can choose to start a new presentation and save, print, and perform other file-related activities. See Figure 1.12 for this button's location.
- **Quick Access Toolbar.** A small toolbar adjacent to the Office button from which you can select commonly used commands.

TIP

To add a command to the Quick Access Toolbar, right-click the icon for it and choose Add to Quick Access Toolbar. To remove the command from there, right-click its icon and choose Remove from Quick Access Toolbar.

- **Tab.** A tabbed page of the Ribbon. Figure 1.13 shows the Home tab, for example.

FIGURE 1.13

The Ribbon is PowerPoint 2013's primary user interface.

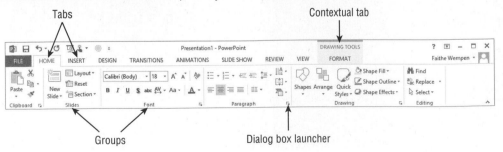

- **Contextual tab.** A tab that appears only when certain content is selected, such as a graphic or a chart. The context name appears above the tab name. In Figure 1.13, Drawing Tools is the context name for the Format tab.

- **Group.** A section of a tab. The Home tab shown in Figure 1.13 has the following groups: Clipboard, Slides, Font, Paragraph, Drawing, and Editing.

- **Dialog box launcher.** A small icon that is in the bottom-right corner of a group and from which you can open a dialog box related to that group.

NOTE

To find out what a toolbar button does, point the mouse at it. A ScreenTip pops up explaining it.

Working with Collapsible Tab Groups

Within a tab, groups can expand or collapse depending on the width of the PowerPoint window. When the window is large enough, everything within each group is fully expanded so that each item has its own button. When the window is smaller, groups start collapsing so that all groups remain visible. At first, large buttons get smaller and stack vertically; if that's not enough, then groups collapse into single large buttons with drop-down lists from which you can select the individual commands. Figure 1.14 shows the same tab in three different widths for comparison.

FIGURE 1.14

The size of the PowerPoint window determines how much the groups are collapsed or expanded on the Ribbon.

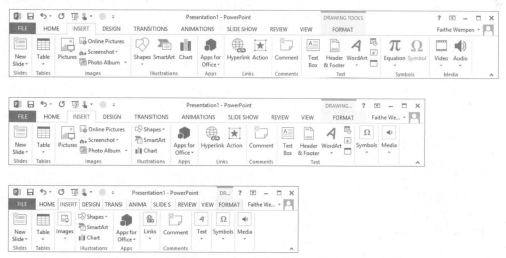

CAUTION

Because the Ribbon collapses, the exact steps for performing certain procedures depend on the active PowerPoint window's width. A small window may require an extra step of opening a button's menu to select a command, for example. For a large window, each command appears directly on the tab. This book assumes a PowerPoint app window size of 1024 x 768 pixels; if you run PowerPoint at a smaller resolution, you may occasionally have an extra step to access a command.

Working with Backstage View

When you open Backstage view by clicking the File tab, a multilayered menu system appears. Many of the commands along the left side of the screen are categories that open submenus when you click them. For example, in Figure 1.15, the Export command has been selected, revealing additional choices.

FIGURE 1.15

Backstage view is a hierarchical menu system; first select a category on the left, then a command in the middle, and then an option on the right.

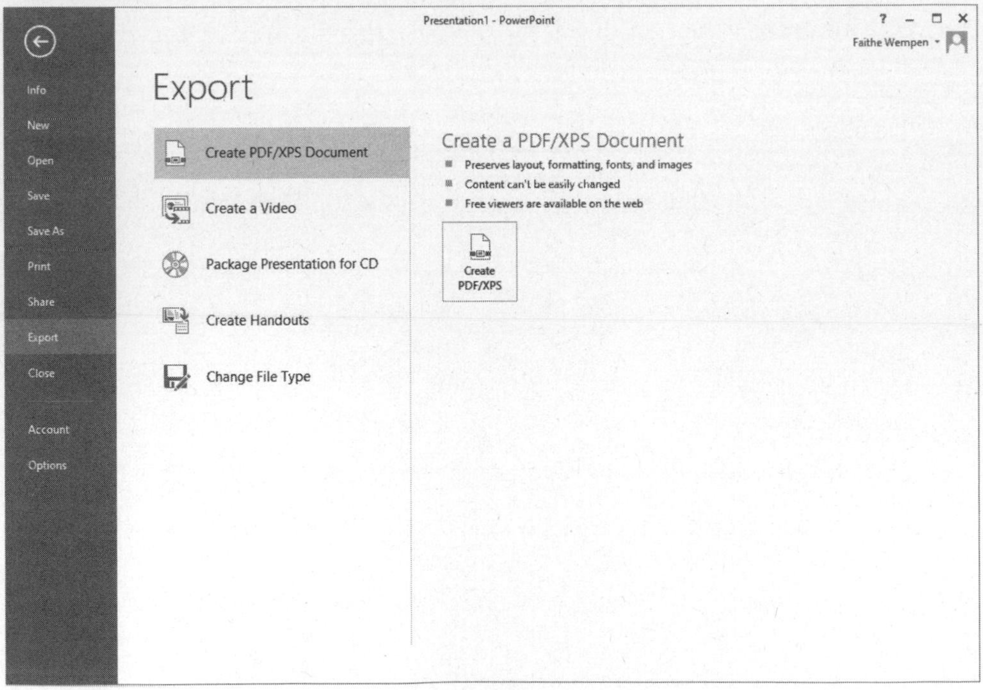

The top-level categories and commands in Backstage View are as follows:

- **Info.** Displays information about the current presentation, including its properties. Commands are available for working with versions, permissions, and sharing.

- **New.** Displays a list of templates available for starting a new presentation.
- **Open.** Displays the Open dialog box, from which you can select a file to open.
- **Save.** Saves the current presentation.
- **Save As.** Saves the current presentation and prompts you for filename and location information, even if the file has been previously saved.
- **Print.** Provides access to printing options, including setting a print range, choosing a printer, and specifying settings like color and collation.
- **Share.** Offers access to features for distributing the presentation via e-mail or fax, sharing it on your SkyDrive, presenting it online, or publishing slides to a SharePoint server.
- **Export:** Provides commands for creating PDF and XPS files, creating videos, exporting handouts to Word, packaging a presentation for CD, and changing the file type.
- **Close.** Closes the active presentation.
- **Account.** Enables you to see the user account information that you are logged in with and manage your connected services, such as your SkyDrive. You can also check for updates from here and view software version information.
- **Options.** Opens a dialog box where you can customize the interface, also described in Chapter 22, "Customizing PowerPoint."

NOTE

PowerPoint 2010 had an Exit command on the File menu, but PowerPoint 2013 does not. You can exit PowerPoint by clicking the Close (X) button in the upper-right corner of the app window.

Working with Dialog Boxes and Panes

PowerPoint sometimes uses dialog boxes to prompt you for more information. When you issue a command that can have many possible variations, a dialog box appears so you can specify the particulars.

Figure 1.16 illustrates some of the controls you may encounter in PowerPoint's dialog boxes:

- **Check box.** These are individual on/off switches for particular features. Click to toggle them on or off.
- **Increment buttons.** Placed next to a text box, these buttons allow you to increment the number in the box up or down by one digit per click. For example, the Size text box has increment buttons in Figure 1.16.
- **Drop-down list.** Click the down arrow next to one of these to open the list, and then click your selection from the menu that appears. For example, the Latin text font setting has a drop-down list.

- **Command button.** Click one of these big rectangular buttons to jump to a different dialog box. OK and Cancel are also command buttons; OK accepts your changes and Cancel rejects them.

- **Tabs.** Click a tab along the top of the dialog box to see a different page of options. In Figure 1.16, there are two tabs: Font and Character Spacing.

Dialog boxes that open or save files have some special controls and icons all their own, but you learn about those in more detail in Chapter 2, where you also learn to open and save your files.

FIGURE 1.16

The Font dialog box illustrates several types of controls.

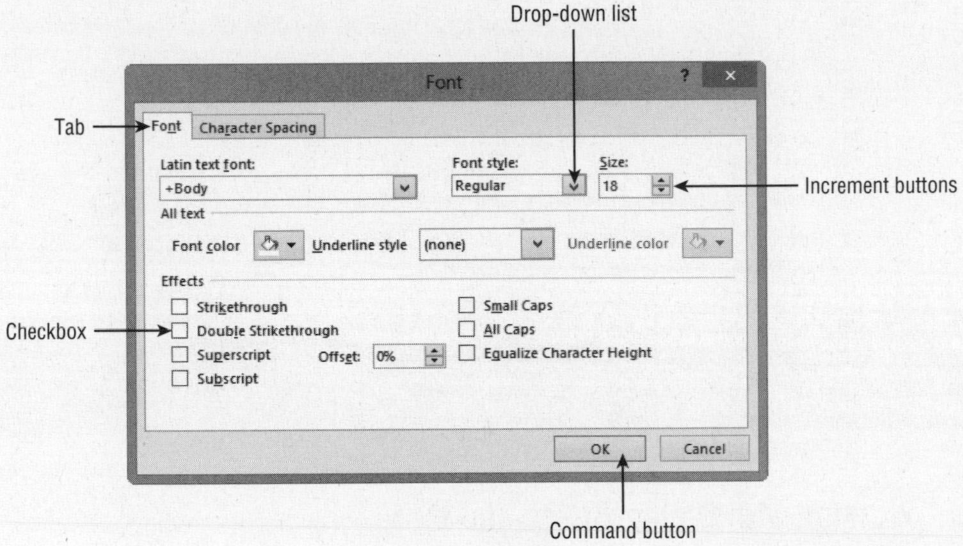

Office 2013 has moved away from using dialog boxes for some features; you may also encounter panes that ask for more information when you issue a command. A *pane* is a rectangular area along the left or right side of the screen, as shown in Figure 1.17. Notice that the Format Shape pane in Figure 1.17 has two tabs: Shape Options and Text Options. Click one or the other of those terms near the top of the pane to switch among the different pages of options. Beneath the selected tab are several icons; each icon shows a different page of options as well.

Some of the additional controls are shown in Figure 1.17:

- **Option buttons.** Option buttons are round, and operate in mutually exclusive groups. In Figure 1.17, under the Line heading, there are three Option buttons: No line, Solid line, and Gradient line. Option buttons are sometimes called radio buttons.

- **Slider.** A slider enables you to drag a bar to indicate a setting along a sliding scale. Transparency has a slider in Figure 1.17.

FIGURE 1.17

Some features use panes instead of dialog boxes.

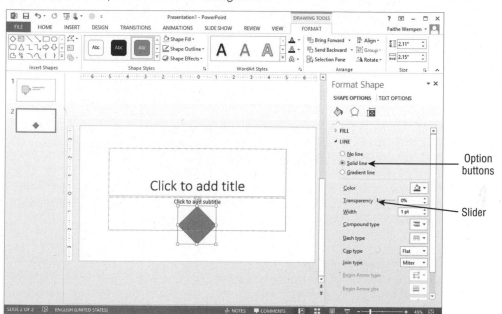

Changing the View

A *view* is a way of displaying your presentation on-screen. PowerPoint comes with several views because at different times during the creation process, it is helpful to look at the presentation in different ways. For example, when you add a graphic to a slide, you need to work closely with that slide, but when you rearrange the slide order, you need to see the presentation as a whole.

PowerPoint offers the following presentation views:

- **Normal.** A combination of several resizable panes so you can see the presentation in multiple ways at once. Normal is the default view.

- **Outline.** A variant of Normal view in which slide content appears as a text outline in the left pane rather than as graphical slide thumbnails. This view is available only from the View tab.

- **Slide Sorter.** A light-table-type overhead view of all the slides in your presentation, laid out in sections and rows, suitable for big-picture rearranging.

- **Slide Show.** The view you use to show the presentation on-screen. Each slide fills the entire screen in its turn. This view is not available from the View tab, but it is available in several other places, including in the status bar and in the Quick Access Toolbar.

- **Reading.** Similar to Slide Show view, except it's windowed and the status bar remains in view. You can use Reading view to check your work as if you were showing the slide show but still retain access to certain commands.

- **Notes Page.** A view with the slide at the top of the page and a text box below it for typed notes. (You can print these notes pages to use during your speech.) This view is available only from the View tab.

> This chapter covers only the presentation views (that is, regular views in which you can see the individual content of each slide). The master views are discussed in Chapter 4; master views enable you to make global changes to many slides at once.

There are two ways to change a view: Click a button on the View tab, or click one of the view buttons at the right end of the status bar at the bottom of the screen, shown in Figure 1.18. Not every view is available in both places.

FIGURE 1.18

Select a view from the View tab or from the viewing controls in the bottom-right corner of the screen.

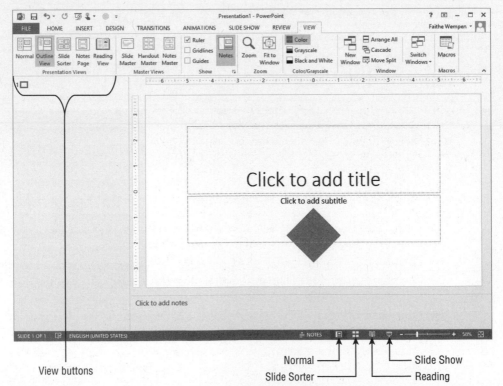

TIP

When you save, close, and reopen a file, PowerPoint opens it in the view in which you left the file. To have the files always open in a particular view, choose File ➪ Options ➪ Advanced, and in the Display section, click the drop-down arrow on the Open All Documents Using This View list and select the desired view. The options on this list include some custom versions of Normal view that have certain panes turned off. For example, you can open all documents in Normal – Slide Only to always start in Normal view with just the main editing pane open.

Normal and Outline Views

Normal view, shown in Figure 1.19, is a very flexible view that contains a little bit of everything. In the center is the Slide pane, where the active slide appears, and to its left is the Thumbnails pane, containing a set of thumbnail images that represent the presentation's slides.

FIGURE 1.19

Normal view, the default, shows slide thumbnails at the left and an editing window at the right.

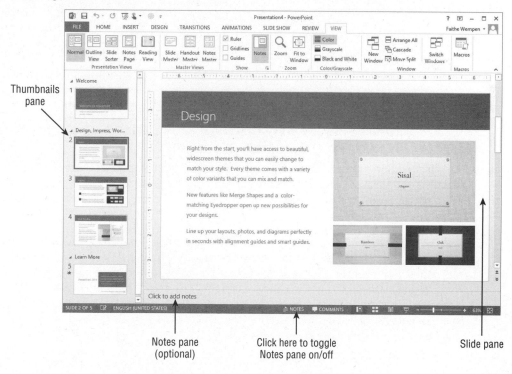

Thumbnails pane

Notes pane (optional)

Click here to toggle Notes pane on/off

Slide pane

Outline view (shown in Figure 1.20) is identical to Normal view except instead of the slide thumbnails on the left, you see a text outline.

FIGURE 1.20

Outline view shows a text outline at the left and an editing window at the right.

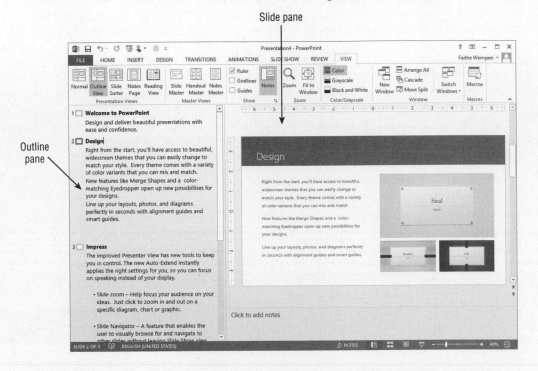

An optional Notes pane is available at the bottom of the window in Normal or Outline view; click Notes on the status bar to display or hide it. An optional Comments pane appears and disappears on the right when you click Comments on the status bar. (Normal view only, as shown in Figure 1.19).

Each of the panes in Normal view has its own scroll bar, so you can move in it independently of the other panes. You can resize the panes by dragging the dividers between the panes. For example, to give the notes area more room, point the mouse pointer at the divider line between it and the slide area so that the mouse pointer becomes a double-headed arrow, and then hold down the left mouse button as you drag the line up to a new spot. To get the Thumbnails (or Outline) pane out of the way, drag the divider between it and the slide editing pane as far as possible to the left.

The left pane is useful because it lets you jump quickly to a specific slide by clicking its thumbnail (Normal view) or some of its text content (Outline view).

Slide Sorter View

If you have ever worked with hard copies of slides, such as 35mm slides, you know that it can be helpful to lay the slides out on a big table and plan the order in which to show them. You rearrange them, moving this one here, that one there, until the order is perfect. You might even start a pile of backups that you will not show in the main presentation but will hold back in case someone asks a pertinent question. That's exactly what you can do with Slide Sorter view, as shown in Figure 1.21. It lays out the slides in miniature, so you can see the big picture. You can drag the slides around and place them in the perfect order. You can also return to Normal view to work on a slide by double-clicking the slide.

FIGURE 1.21

Use the Slide Sorter view for a bird's-eye view of the presentation.

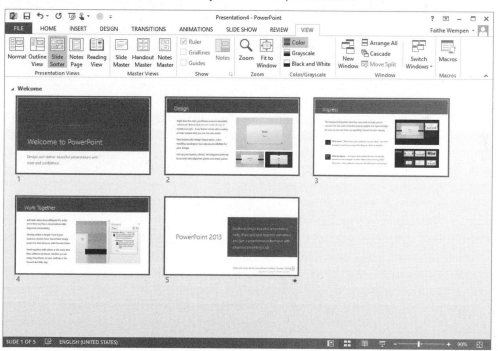

Slide Show View and Reading Views

When it's time to rehearse the presentation, nothing shows you the finished product quite as clearly as Slide Show view does. In Slide Show view, the slide fills the entire screen, as shown in Figure 1.22. You can move from slide to slide by pressing the Page Up and Page Down keys or by using one of the other movement methods available (covered in Chapter 19).

The default slide dimensions in PowerPoint 2013 are set for a wide-screen monitor (16:9 aspect ratio). If you are using a regular monitor (4:3) but showing wide-screen slides, black bars fill in the extra space at the top and bottom. You can correct this problem by changing the slide size on the Design tab. When you change the slide size, PowerPoint prompts you to specify how to adjust the existing content to fit the new format.

FIGURE 1.22

Slide Show view lets you practice the presentation in real life.

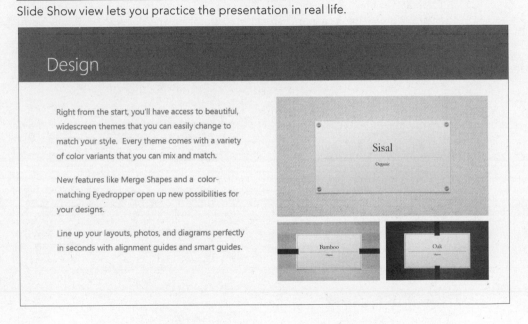

When you move your mouse in Slide Show view, buttons appear in the bottom-left corner for controlling the show without leaving it (These aren't shown in Figure 1.22.). To leave the slide show, choose End Show from the menu or just press the Esc key.

> **TIP**
>
> When entering Slide Show view, the method you use determines which slide you start on. If you use the Slide Show View button in the bottom-right corner of the screen, the presentation will start with whatever slide you have selected. (You can also press Shift+F5 to do this or choose Slide Show ⇨ From Current Slide.) If you use the Slide Show ⇨ From Beginning command, or press F5, the presentation will start at the beginning.

Reading view is like Slide Show view except it runs within the PowerPoint app window rather than full screen and it doesn't have the powerful slide show tools that you get with Slide Show view (covered in Chapter 18), such as the ability to draw on a slide or skip to a certain slide. You still see the PowerPoint app's title bar, and you still see the status bar at the bottom. You can move between slides by clicking with the mouse or by using the arrow keys on the keyboard. As with Slide Show view, you can exit from Reading view by pressing Esc to return to the previously accessed view.

Notes Page View

When you give a presentation, your props usually include more than just your brain and your slides. You typically have all kinds of notes and backup material for each slide — figures on last quarter's sales, sources to cite if someone questions your data, and so on. In the old days of framed overhead transparencies, people used to attach sticky notes to the slide frames for this purpose and hope that nobody asked any questions that required diving into the four-inch-thick stack of statistics they brought.

Today, you can type your notes and supporting facts directly in PowerPoint. As you saw earlier, you can type them directly into the Notes pane below the slide in Normal or Outline view. Just click the Notes button in the status bar to display the Notes pane, and start typing away. However, if you have a lot of notes to type, you might find it easier to work with Notes Page view instead.

Notes Page view is accessible only from the View tab. In this view, you see a single slide (uneditable) with an editable text area below it called the *notes placeholder*, which you can use to type your notes. See Figure 1.23. You can refer to these notes as you give an on-screen presentation, or you can print notes pages to stack neatly on the lectern next to you during the big event. If your notes pages run off the end of the page, PowerPoint even prints them as a separate page. If you have trouble seeing the text you're typing, zoom in on it, as described in the next section.

Zooming In and Out

If you need a closer look at your presentation, you can zoom the view in or out to accommodate almost any situation. For example, if you have trouble placing a graphic exactly at the same vertical level as some text in a box next to it, you can zoom in for more precision. (The new Smart Guides feature in PowerPoint 2013 helps with that situation too.) You can view your work at various magnifications on-screen without changing the size of the surrounding tools or the size of the print on the printout.

In Normal view, each of the panes has its own individual zoom. To set the zoom for the Thumbnails pane only, for example, select it first; then choose a zoom level. Or to zoom only in the Slide pane (the main editing pane), click it first. In a single-pane view such as Notes Page or Slide Sorter, a single zoom setting affects the entire work area.

FIGURE 1.23

Notes Page view offers a special text area for your notes, separate from the slides.

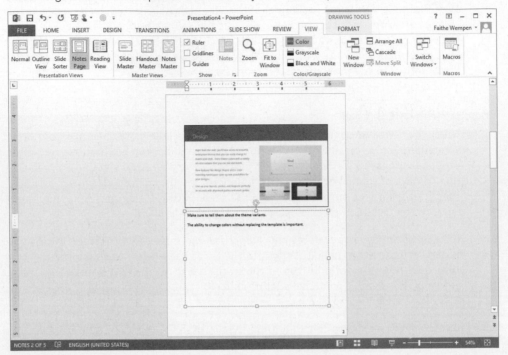

The larger the zoom number, the larger the details on the display. A zoom of 10% would make a slide so tiny that you couldn't read it. A zoom of 400% would make a few letters on a slide so big they would fill the entire pane.

An easy way to set the zoom level is to drag the Zoom slider in the status bar, or click its plus or minus buttons to change the zoom level in increments, as shown in Figure 1.24. You can also hold down the Ctrl key and roll the scroll wheel on your mouse, if it has one.

FIGURE 1.24

Zoom in or out to see more or less of the slide(s) at once.

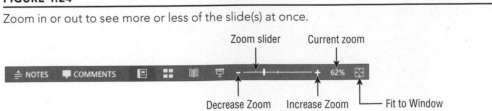

To resize the current slide so that it is as large as possible while still fitting completely in the Slides pane, click the Fit Slide to Current Window button, or Choose View ⇨ Fit to Window.

Another way to control the zoom is with the Zoom dialog box. Choose View ⇨ Zoom to open it. (You can also open that dialog box by clicking the % next to the Zoom slider in the lower-right corner of the screen.) Make your selection, as shown in Figure 1.25, by clicking the appropriate button, and then click OK. Notice that you can type a precise zoom percentage in the Percent text box. You can specify any percentage you like, up to 400%. (Some panes and views will not go higher than 100%.)

FIGURE 1.25

You can zoom with this Zoom dialog box rather than the slider if you prefer.

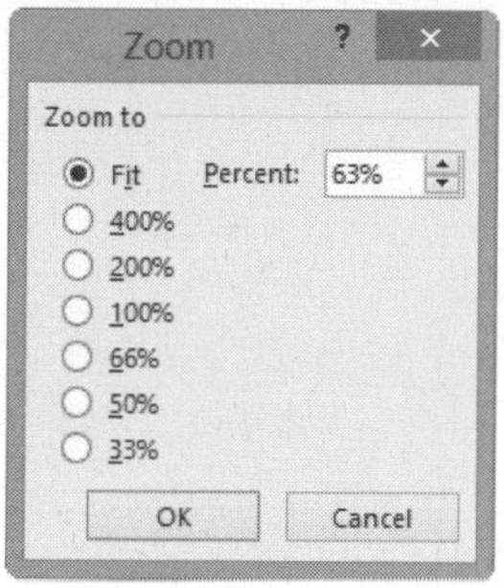

Enabling Optional Display Elements

PowerPoint has a lot of optional screen elements that you may (or may not) find useful, depending on what you're up to at the moment. The following sections describe them.

Ruler

Vertical and horizontal rulers around the Slide pane can help you place objects more precisely. To toggle them on or off, select or deselect the Ruler check box on the View tab, as shown in Figure 1.26. Rulers are available only in Normal, Outline, and Notes Page views.

The rulers help with positioning no matter what content type you are working with, but when you are editing text in a text frame they have an additional purpose. The horizontal ruler shows the frame's paragraph indents and any custom tab stops, and you can drag the indent markers on the ruler just as you can in Word.

FIGURE 1.26

Rulers and gridlines help position objects on a slide.

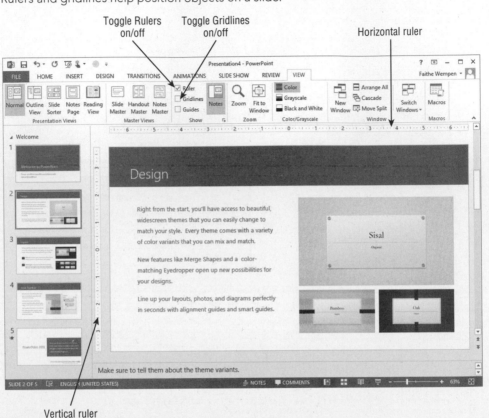

NOTE

The ruler's unit of measure is controlled from Regional Settings in Control Panel in Windows. Choose Clock and then Language and Region, and then click the Region heading in Windows 8 (or Region and Language in Windows 7) to open the Region (or Region and Language) dialog box. On the Formats tab, click Additional Settings and choose U.S. or Metric from the Measurement System drop-down list.

TIP

The display of the vertical ruler is optional. To disable it while retaining the horizontal ruler, choose File ➪ Options, click Advanced, and in the Display section, clear the Show Vertical Ruler check box.

Gridlines

Gridlines are nonprinting dotted lines at regularly spaced intervals that can help you line up objects on a slide. Figure 1.26 shows gridlines (and the ruler) enabled.

To turn gridlines on or off, use either of these methods:

- Press Shift+F9.
- On the View tab, in the Show group, select or deselect the Gridlines check box.

There are many options you can set for the gridlines, including whether objects snap to it, whether the grid is visible, and what the spacing should be between the gridlines. To set grid options, follow these steps:

1. **On the View tab, click the dialog box launcher in the Show group.** The Grid and Guides dialog box opens (see Figure 1.27).

   FIGURE 1.27

   Set grid options and spacing.

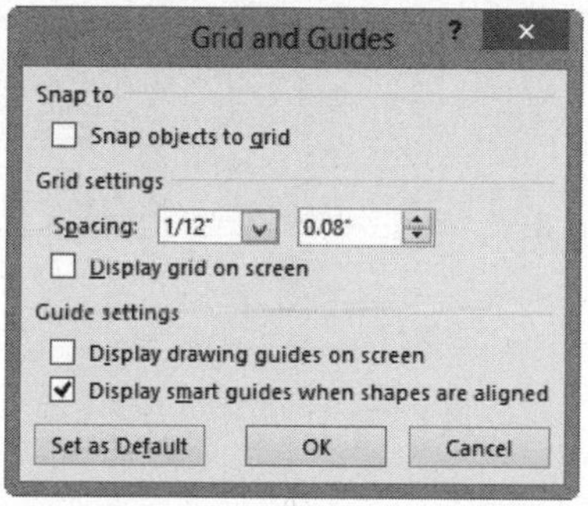

2. **In the Snap To section, select or deselect the Snap Objects to Grid check box.** This setting specifies whether or not objects will automatically align with the grid.

3. **In the Grid Settings section, enter the amount of space you want between gridlines.**

4. **Select or deselect the Display Grid On Screen check box to display or hide the grid.** (Note that you can make objects snap to the grid without the grid being displayed.)

5. **Click OK.**

Guides

Guides are like gridlines except they are individual lines, rather than a grid of lines, and you can drag them to different positions on the slide. As you drag a guide, a numeric indicator appears to let you know the ruler position, as shown in Figure 1.28. Use the Grid and Guides dialog box shown in Figure 1.27 to turn guides on/off, or press Alt+F9.

FIGURE 1.28

Guides are movable, nonprinting lines that help with alignment.

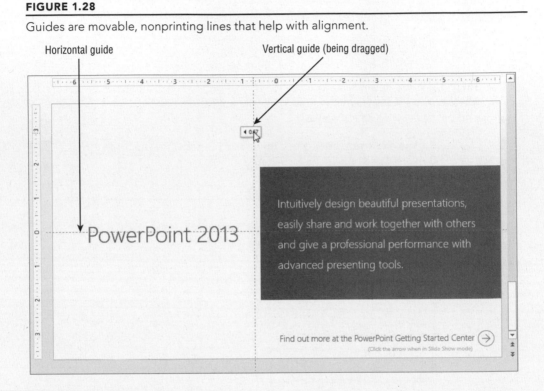

You can create additional sets of guide lines by holding down the Ctrl key while dragging a guide (to copy it). You can have as many horizontal and vertical guides as you like, all at positions you specify. You can also save your custom guides (new in PowerPoint 2013).

Ribbon

For a cleaner look to PowerPoint, as well as more screen space, you can choose to hide (or as Microsoft calls it, "un-pin") the Ribbon when it's not in use. To hide the Ribbon, click the Unpin the Ribbon icon (the up-pointing arrow button at the far right end of the Ribbon). From that point on, the Ribbon doesn't appear unless you click one of its tabs. To get it back to always-on status, view the Ribbon (by clicking one of the tabs) and then click the Pin the Ribbon icon (which is a pushpin icon in the same spot that the Unpin the Ribbon arrow icon appeared in before).

Color/Grayscale/Pure Black and White Views

Most of the time you will work with your presentation in color. However, if you plan to print the presentation in black and white or grayscale (for example, on black-and-white handouts), you should check to see what it will look like without color.

> **TIP**
>
> This Color/Grayscale/Pure Black and White option is especially useful when you are preparing slides that will eventually be faxed because a fax is pure black and white in most cases. Something that looks great on a color screen could look like a shapeless blob on a black-and-white fax. It doesn't hurt to check.

Click the Grayscale or the Pure Black and White button on the View tab to switch to one of those views. When you do so, a Grayscale or Black and White tab becomes available. The Grayscale tab is shown in Figure 1.29. From its Change Selected Object group, you can fine-tune the grayscale or black-and-white preview. Choose one that shows the object to best advantage; PowerPoint will remember that setting when printing or outputting the presentation to a grayscale or black-and-white source.

FIGURE 1.29

Select a grayscale or a black-and-white preview type.

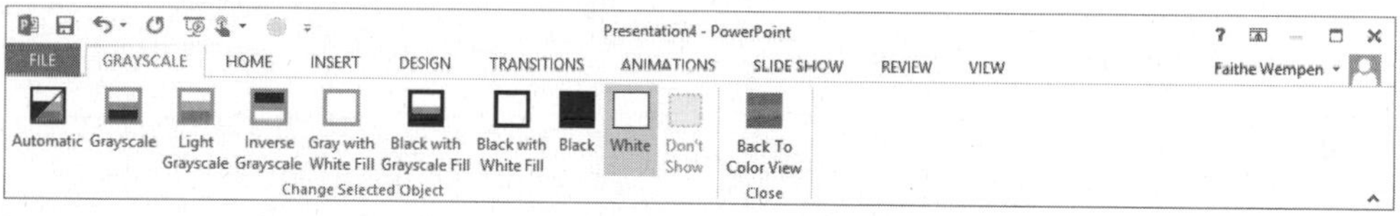

When you are finished, click the Back to Color View button on the Grayscale or Black and White tab. Changing the Black and White or Grayscale settings doesn't affect the colors on the slides; it only affects how the slides will look and print in black and white or grayscale.

Opening a New Display Window for the Same Presentation

Have you ever wished you could be in two places at once? Well, in PowerPoint, you actually can. PowerPoint provides a way to view two spots in the presentation at the same time by opening a new window.

To display a new window, display the View tab and click New Window in the Window group. Then use Arrange All or Cascade to view both windows at once.

You can use any view with any window, so you can have two slides in Normal view at once, or Slide Sorter and Notes Pages view, or any other combination. Both windows contain the same presentation, so any changes you make in one window are reflected in the other window.

Arranging Windows

When you have two or more windows open, whether they are for the same presentation or different ones, you need to arrange them for optimal viewing. You saw earlier in this chapter how to resize a window, but did you know that PowerPoint can do some of the arranging for you?

When you want to arrange the open windows, do one of the following:

- **Tile the windows.** On the View tab, click Arrange All to tile the open windows so there is no overlap.
- **Cascade the windows.** On the View tab, click Cascade to arrange the open windows so that the title bars cascade from upper left to lower right on the screen. Click a title bar to activate a window.

These commands do not apply to minimized windows. If you want to include a window in the arrangement, make sure you restore it from its minimized state first.

Switching among Windows

If you have more than one window open and can see at least a corner of the window you want, click it to bring it to the front. If you have one of the windows maximized, on the other hand, or if another window is obscuring the one you want, click Switch Windows (on the View tab) and select the window you want to view.

Using the Help System

The PowerPoint help system is like a huge instruction book in electronic format. You can look up almost any PowerPoint task you can imagine and get step-by-step instructions for performing it.

To open the PowerPoint Help window, press F1, or click the Help icon (the question mark) in the upper-right corner of the PowerPoint window, as shown in Figure 1.30.

There are two ways to look up information in the help system:

- Click one of the topics on the default PowerPoint Help window shown in Figure 1.30, and then keep clicking subtopics to narrow down the search until you arrive at what you want.

■ Type a keyword or phrase in the Search Help box, and then click the Search Help icon (the magnifying glass) or press Enter to find all help articles that contain it.

FIGURE 1.30

Get help with PowerPoint via the PowerPoint Help window.

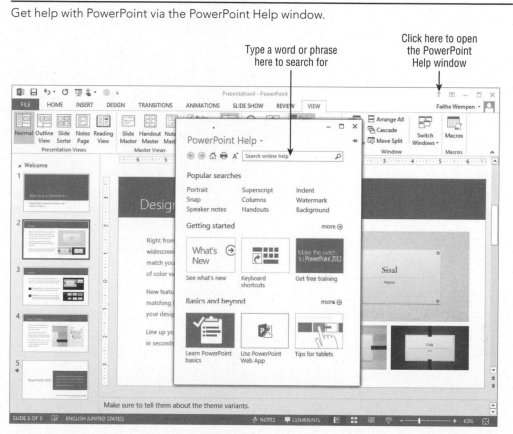

Type a word or phrase here to search for

Click here to open the PowerPoint Help window

When you browse or search the help system, a list of articles matching the topic or search term appears. Click an article to read it. Figure 1.31 shows an article on saving files, for example.

FIGURE 1.31

A typical article in the help system contains some background information and step-by-step instructions.

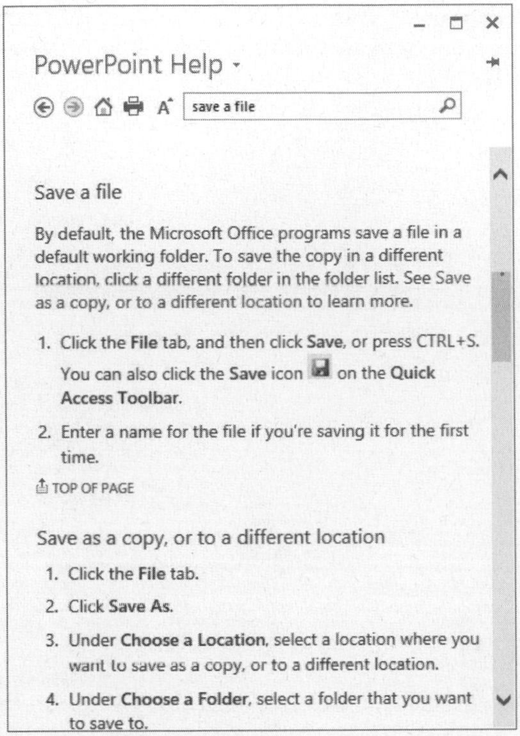

The PowerPoint Help window's toolbar contains the buttons shown in Table 1.1.

TABLE 1.1   Help Window Icons

Icon(s)	Name	Description
⬅ ➡	Back and Forward	These are the same as they are in Internet Explorer; Back goes back to a previously viewed topic and Forward goes forward again afterward.
⌂	Home	Returns to the default list of topics (Figure 1.30).
🖶	Print	Prints the currently displayed article.
A	Change Font Size	Toggles the text in the Help window between regular and large size.
📌	Pin Help	Keeps the Help window on top of all other windows.

Summary

This chapter provided an introduction to PowerPoint. You learned about PowerPoint 2013's new features, how to navigate the new user interface, how to control the view of the PowerPoint window, and how to get help and support. In the next chapter, you'll learn how to create and save presentation files. There are more options than you might think, so don't be too quick to dismiss that topic as something you already know!

1

Creating and Saving Presentation Files

IN THIS CHAPTER

Starting a new presentation

Saving your work

Setting passwords for file access

Closing and reopening presentations

Setting file properties

I f you're an experienced Windows and PowerPoint user, starting new presentations and saving files may be second nature to you. If so — great! You may not need this chapter. On the other hand, if you aren't entirely certain about some of the finer points, such as saving in different formats or locations, stick around.

Even people who consider themselves "advanced" users may benefit from this chapter because it looks at some of the unique advanced saving features of Office applications and explains how to secure files with passwords.

Starting a New Presentation

You can start a blank presentation, or you can base the new presentation on a template or on another presentation. Using a template or existing presentation can save you some time. However, if you have a specific vision you're going for, starting a presentation from scratch gives you a clean canvas to work from.

Starting a Blank Presentation

When you open PowerPoint, a Start screen appears. From here you can click Blank Presentation, as shown in Figure 2.1, or you can just press Esc at the Start screen to access a blank presentation.

FIGURE 2.1

Use the Blank Presentation tile on PowerPoint's Start screen to start a new presentation.

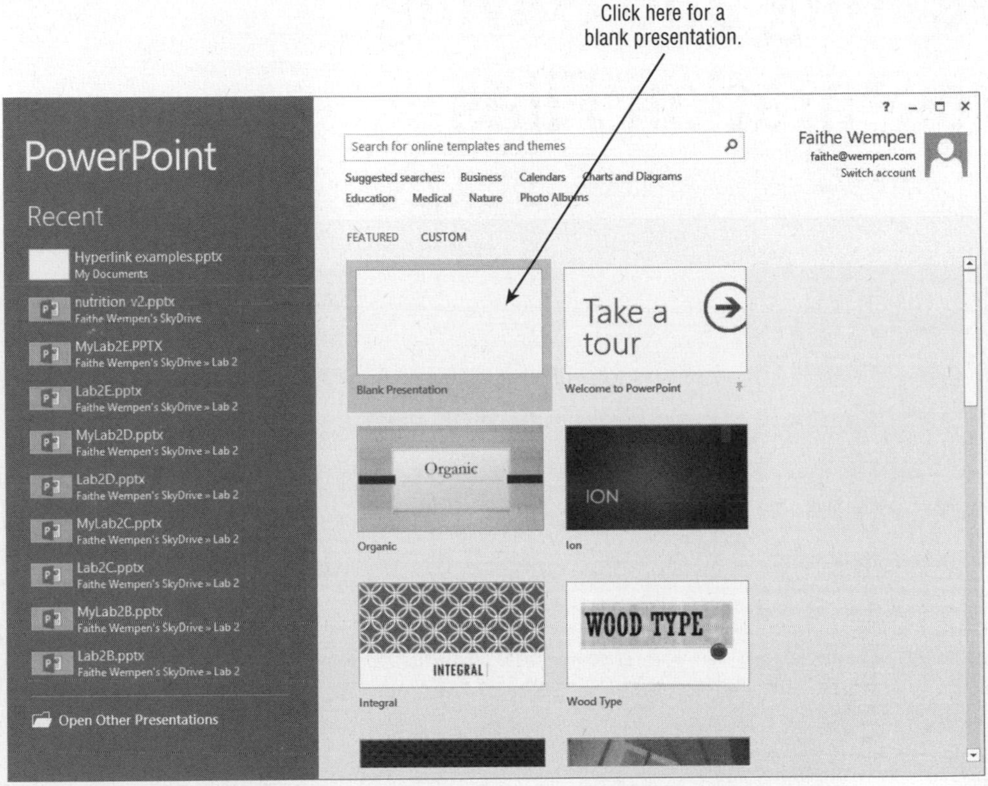

If you want to start a blank presentation at some time other than when you start up PowerPoint, you can do the following:

1. **Choose File ⇨ New.** The same selection of templates and themes appears as in Figure 2.1.

2. **Click Blank Presentation.**

> **TIP**
>
> Press the Ctrl+N shortcut key to start a new blank presentation.

A new blank presentation begins automatically with one slide. Just add your content to it, add more slides if needed, change the formatting (as you'll learn in upcoming chapters), and go for it.

Starting a Presentation from a Template

A *template* is a file that contains starter settings — and sometimes starter content — on which you can base new presentations. Templates vary in their exact offerings but can include sample slides, a background graphic, custom color and font themes, and custom positioning for object placeholders.

The sample templates stored on your computer appear as tiles on the Start screen (Figure 2.1) and on the New screen when you choose File ⇨ New, as in the preceding section. You can click whichever one you want to use.

Only a few sample templates are stored on your hard disk because Microsoft assumes that most people have an always-on Internet connection these days. When you are connected to the Internet, you can access the complete Microsoft library of template files. Use the Search box to search for templates in a particular category or with certain keywords associated with them.

Follow these steps to locate a template and use it to start a new presentation:

1. **Choose File ⇨ New.**
2. **In the Search box, type a keyword to search for and press Enter, or click one of the category links on the Suggested Searches line below the Search box.** See Figure 2.2. A list of templates appears that match your criteria.

FIGURE 2.2

Search for templates by keyword or click a category.

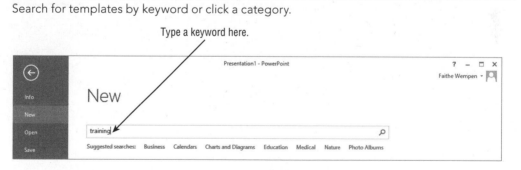

3. **Click a template to see a preview of it, as shown in Figure 2.3.**
4. **Click Create.** A new presentation is created based on that template.

FIGURE 2.3

Preview a template before selecting it.

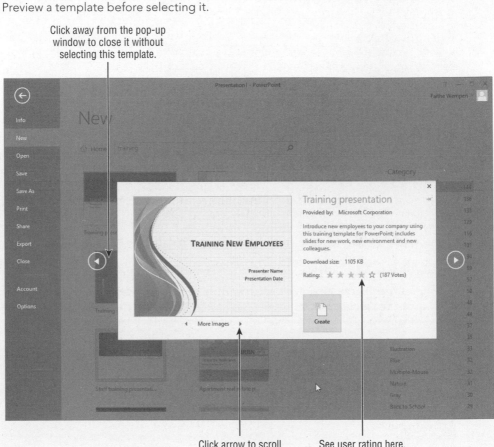

Click away from the pop-up window to close it without selecting this template.

Click arrow to scroll through the slides in the template.

See user rating here.

Using a Personal Template

In the section, "Saving as a Template," later in this chapter, you will learn how to save a presentation file in template format so you can use it as a basis for new presentations. These are called *personal templates* in PowerPoint 2013.

> **NOTE**
>
> For PowerPoint to find your personal templates, you must tell it where they are stored. To do so, choose File ➪ Options, click the Save category, and then enter the path to that location in the Default Personal Templates Location text box. Then click OK.

When you specify a default location for personal templates, the New screen has two categories below the suggested searches: Featured and Personal (or Custom). Personal appears if you have not specified a Workgroup Templates location (covered later in this chapter), and Custom appears instead of you have done so.

You can click Personal or Custom to see the locations that hold your own personal templates and themes. The Document Themes folder appears here (you'll learn more about it in Chapter 4, "Working with Layouts, Themes, and Masters") and also whatever folder you specified as the default personal templates location (see the preceding note). In addition, if you have specified a Workgroup Templates location, that folder appears here too.

To access your personal templates, follow these steps:

1. **Choose File ⇨ New.**
2. **Click Personal or click Custom.** An icon appears for the location you have defined as your personal template folder as well as an icon for Document Themes. There may also be a Workgroup Templates folder shown. See Figure 2.4.

FIGURE 2.4

Choose Personal or Custom to see your personal template location.

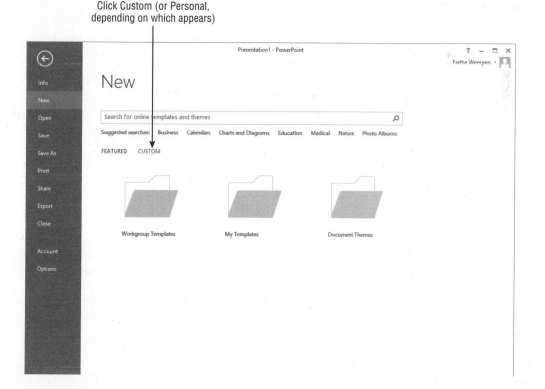

3. **Click the icon for your personal template folder (My Templates).** Thumbnails appear for your personal templates.

4. **Click the desired personal template.** A new presentation opens based on that template.

Basing a New Presentation on Existing Content

If you already have a presentation that's similar to the new one you need to create, you can base the new presentation on the existing one. To do so, open the existing presentation and then use Save As (covered in the next section, "Saving Your Work") to save it under a new name.

PowerPoint can open files in several formats other than its own, so you can start a new presentation based on some work you have done elsewhere. For example, you can open a Word outline in PowerPoint. The results might not be very attractive, but you can fix that later with some text editing, slide layouts, and design changes.

To open a file from another application, do the following:

1. **Choose File ⇨ Open.** The Open screen appears.

2. **Click Computer.**

3. **Click Browse.** The Open dialog box appears.

4. **Click the File Type button (currently set to All PowerPoint Presentations) and choose the file type.** For example, to open a text file, choose All Outlines, as shown in Figure 2.5.

5. **Navigate to the location containing the file you want to open.**

6. **Select the desired file, and then click Open.**

7. **Save your work as a PowerPoint file by choosing File ⇨ Save As.**

See the next section for more information about saving.

Saving Your Work

PowerPoint is typical of most Windows programs in the way that it saves and opens files. The entire PowerPoint presentation is saved in a single file, and any graphics, charts, or other elements are incorporated into that single file.

The first time you save a presentation, PowerPoint prompts you for a name and location. Thereafter, when you save that presentation, PowerPoint uses the same settings and does not prompt you for them again.

FIGURE 2.5

By changing the file type you can select a file of another supported type, such as a Word document.

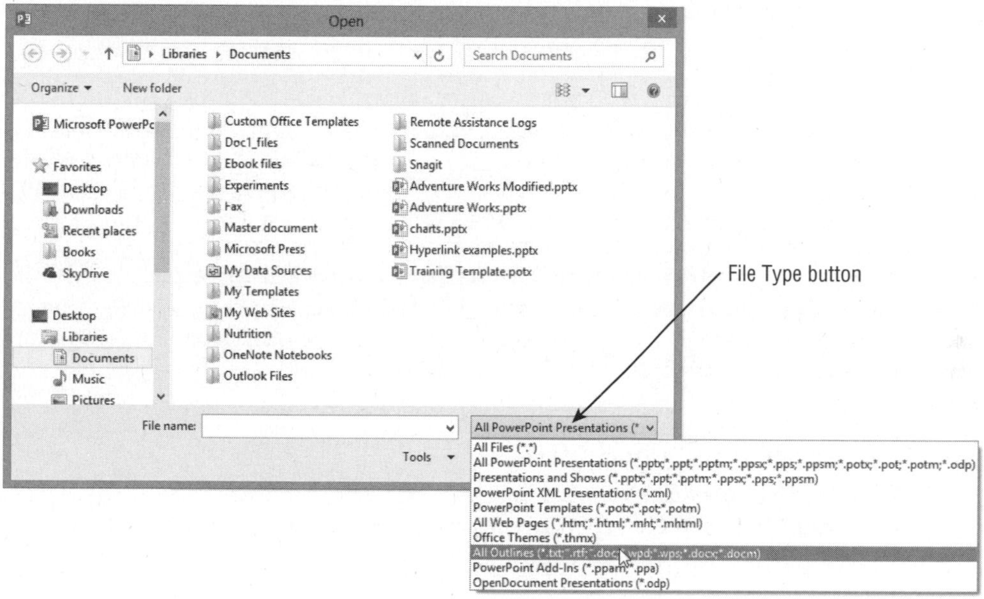

File Type button

Understanding Save Locations

Where can you save your files? You can save files in any location on your local hard disk, on a removable drive such as USB flash drive, to a network location, to your SkyDrive, or to a SharePoint server, just to name a few places. A more pertinent question is, where *should* you save your files? That depends on your situation.

In most Office 2013 apps, the default save location is your SkyDrive. Your SkyDrive is a free online storage location that Microsoft provides to anyone who wants it. (You don't even have to be a Windows or Office user.) Your SkyDrive is available no matter what computer you are logged into, as long as you have an Internet connection, so it's a good choice for people who have multiple PCs that they alternate between. See Appendix B for more information about SkyDrives.

> **NOTE**
>
> If you use SkyDrive as your primary storage system for your data files, you might consider installing the SkyDrive for Windows desktop app. Go to https://apps.live.com/skydrive and click Download the App. This creates a local folder app from which you can manage and sync your SkyDrive content, and it places a shortcut to that folder in the Favorites list in the File Explorer navigation pane. You can learn more about this app in Appendix B.

The main drawback to using your SkyDrive is that if your Internet connection isn't available, neither are your files. People with intermittent or inconsistent Internet service may want to store files on the local hard drive, where they are always available. Saving to your Documents library is a safe bet, but you can also create your own folders on your hard drive and save there.

If you have a local network in your home or office, you might have a central file storage location on that network. For example, all the people in your department might save their files to the same network share so that the files are available to everyone at all times. Some companies maintain SharePoint servers for file sharing; others just make network drives and folders available to all the users who need them.

If you want local portability, consider saving to a removable drive such as a USB flash drive or an external hard drive. You can then plug the storage device into some other computer whenever you need file transport, and you don't have to worry about a network or Internet connection being available.

Saving for the First Time

If you haven't previously saved the presentation you are working on, Save and Save As do the same thing: They open the Save As screen. From there, you can specify a name, file type, and file location. Follow these steps:

1. **Choose File ⇨ Save.** The Save As screen appears. Your SkyDrive is selected by default, as shown in Figure 2.6.

2. **(Optional) If you want to save to your Documents library, click Computer.**

> **TIP**
>
> Each user has a Documents library, which is a composite location that represents multiple actual folders. If you save to the Documents library, the file is actually saved in the default storage location for the library, which is `C:\Users\`*`username`*`\My Documents` where username is the Windows user name.

3. **Click the Browse button.** The Save As dialog box opens.

 To save in a different location than your SkyDrive or computer, see the section "Changing Drives and Folders" later in this chapter. To save in a different format, see the section "Saving in a Different Format."

4. **In the File name box, type the name you want to use for the presentation, replacing the placeholder name that appears there.** See Figure 2.7.

5. **Click Save.** The file is saved.

Filenames can be up to 255 characters. For practical purposes, however, keep the names short. You can include spaces in the filenames and most symbols except <, >, ?, *, /, and \. However, if you plan to post the file on a network or the Internet at some point, you should avoid using spaces; use the underscore character instead to simulate a space, if necessary. Filenames that include exclamation points also cause problems, so beware of that. Generally, it is best to avoid punctuation marks in filenames.

> **TIP**
>
> If you want to transfer your presentation file to a different computer and show it from there, and that other computer does not have the same fonts as yours, you should embed the fonts in your presentation so that the desired fonts are available on the other PC. To embed fonts from the Save As dialog box, click the Tools button, choose Save Options, select Embed Fonts in the File check box, and click OK. This option makes the saved file larger than normal, so choose it only when necessary. For more information on advanced saving features, see the section "Specifying Save Options."

FIGURE 2.6

The Save As screen

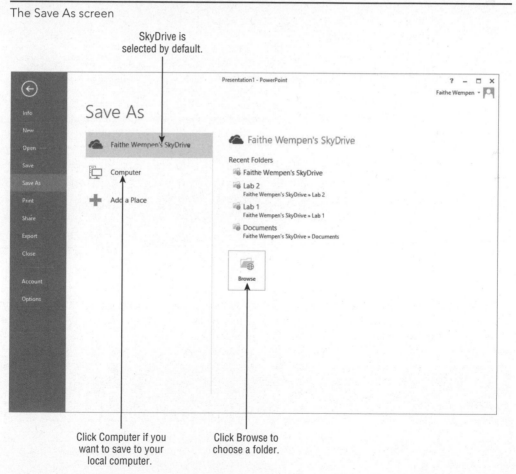

SkyDrive is selected by default.

Click Computer if you want to save to your local computer.

Click Browse to choose a folder.

FIGURE 2.7

The Save As dialog box

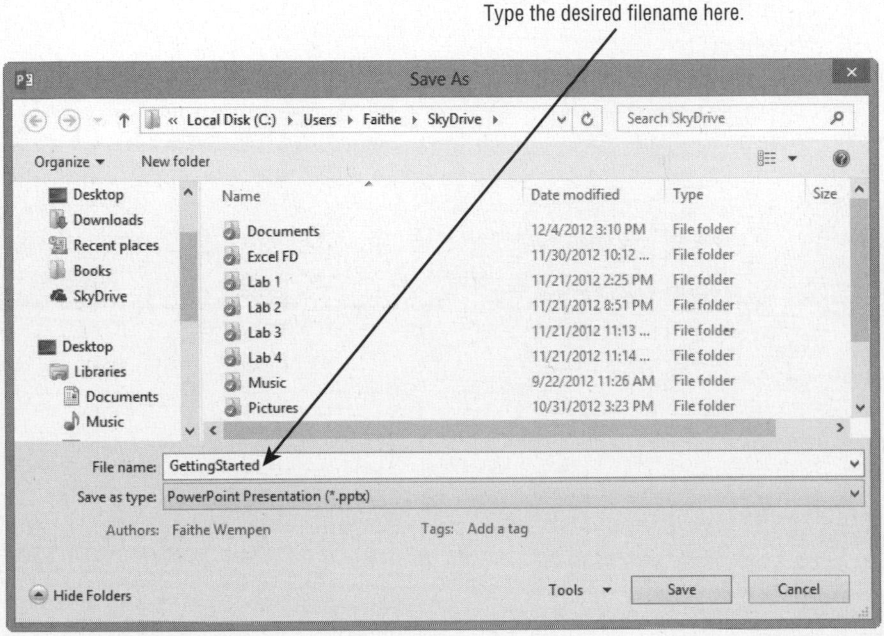

Type the desired filename here.

Saving Subsequent Times

After you have saved a presentation once, you can resave it with the same settings (same file type, name, and location) in any of the following ways:

- Choose File ⇨ Save.
- Press Ctrl+S.
- Click the Save button on the Quick Access Toolbar.

If you need to save your presentation under a different name, as a different file type, or in a different location, use the Save As command instead. This reopens the Save As screen, as in the preceding steps, so that you can save differently. The originally saved copy will remain under the original name, type, and location.

TIP

If you frequently use Save As, you may want to place a button for it on the Quick Access Toolbar. To do this, right-click the Save As command and choose Add to Quick Access Toolbar.

Changing Drives and Folders

By default, all files in PowerPoint (and all of the Office applications) are saved to your SkyDrive. Each user has their own personal storage area in SkyDrive so that each person's documents are kept separate. It's a convenient save location for beginners because they never have to worry about changing the drive or folder.

However, more advanced users will sometimes want to save files to other locations. These other locations can include local hard disk locations (both the Documents library, as you saw in the previous section, and other folders), flash drives, other hard disks in the same PC, hard disks on other PCs in a network, hard disks on web servers on the Internet, or writeable CDs.

The navigation pane on the left side of the Save As dialog box is home to several collapsible/expandable categories. Double-click a category to open it and then make selections from within it (see Figure 2.8). You can choose from the following categories:

- **Favorites.** Shortcuts for popular locations such as Downloads and Desktop appear in the Favorites list, and you can also add your own shortcuts here.

> **TIP**
> Add your own favorite locations to the Favorites list by dragging their icons into it.

- **Libraries.** Libraries are virtual folders that organize locations by the types of files they contain. Double-click Libraries and then click through a category such as Documents or Pictures.
- **Homegroup.** Windows 7 has a home networking feature called Homegroup; if you use it to set up your network, you can browse other network computers by clicking here.
- **Computer.** Browse the complete drive and folder listing for your local PC here.

You can also navigate via the Address bar. The Address bar shows the path to the currently displayed location. You can jump directly to any of those levels by clicking the name there. You can also click the right-pointing arrow to the right of any level to see a menu of other folders within that location and jump to any of them from the menu, as shown in Figure 2.9.

Saving in a Different Format

All PowerPoint 2007, 2010, and 2013 files save by default in an XML-based file format called PowerPoint Presentation (*.pptx). eXtensible Markup Language (XML) is a text-based coding system similar to HTML that describes formatting by using inline bracketed codes and style sheets. XML-based data files are smaller than the data files from earlier PowerPoint versions, and they support all of the latest PowerPoint features. For best results, use this format whenever you don't have a reason to use some other format.

There are also several variants of this format for specialty uses. For example, there's a macro-enabled version with a .pptm filename extension. There are also "show" variants (.ppsx and .ppsm) that open in Slide Show view by default and template variants (.potx and .potm) that function as templates.

Not everyone has PowerPoint 2007 or higher; you might sometimes need to share files with people who have some earlier version of PowerPoint. Users of PowerPoint 2003 can download a compatibility pack that will allow them to accept the new files, but you can't assume that everyone who has an earlier version of PowerPoint will download it. Therefore, you might need to save presentations in other file formats to share files with other people.

FIGURE 2.8

The Save As dialog box contains a number of shortcuts for navigation in the left pane.

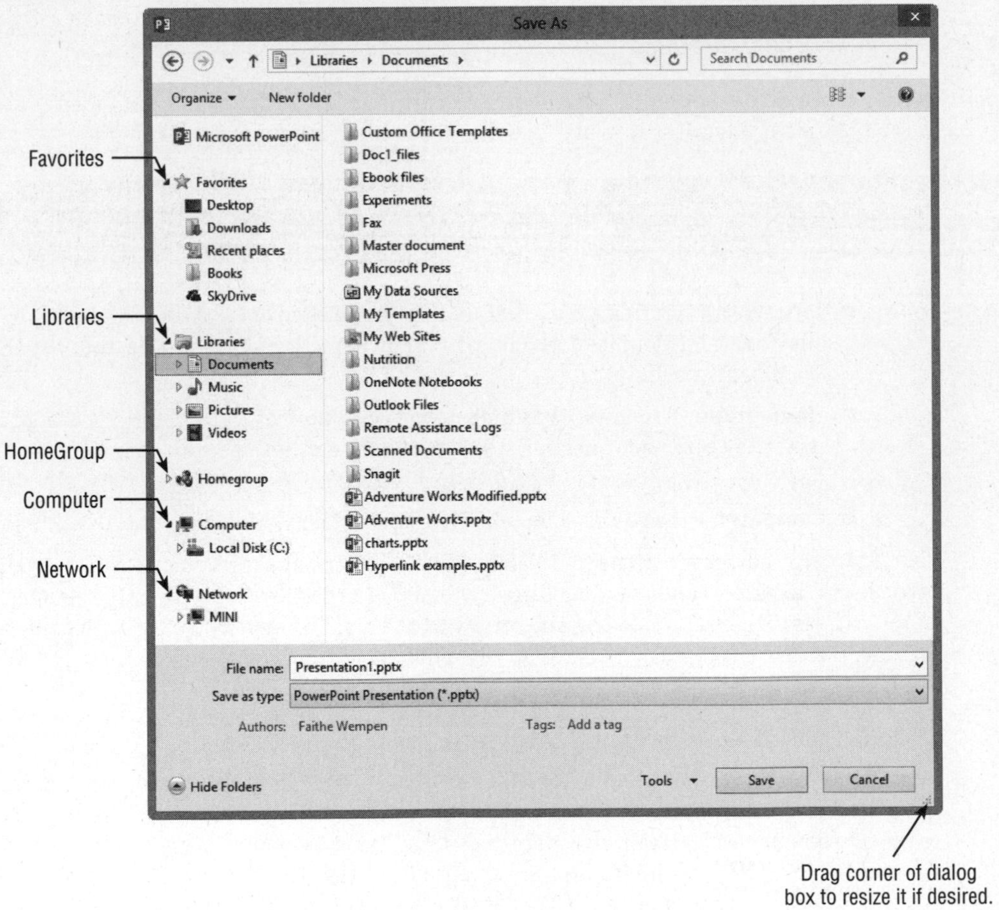

Drag corner of dialog box to resize it if desired.

FIGURE 2.9

Click an arrow on the Address bar to see a menu of locations at the chosen level within the current path.

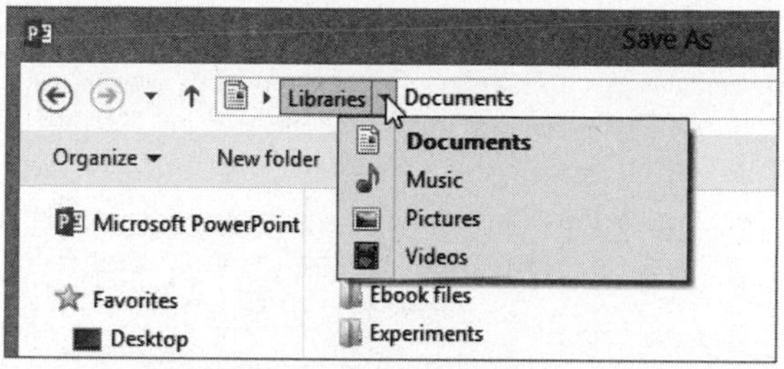

The available formats are shown in Table 2.1. In the Save As dialog box, open the Save As Type drop-down list and select the desired format, as shown in Figure 2.10.

FIGURE 2.10

Choose a different format, if necessary, from the Save As Type drop-down list.

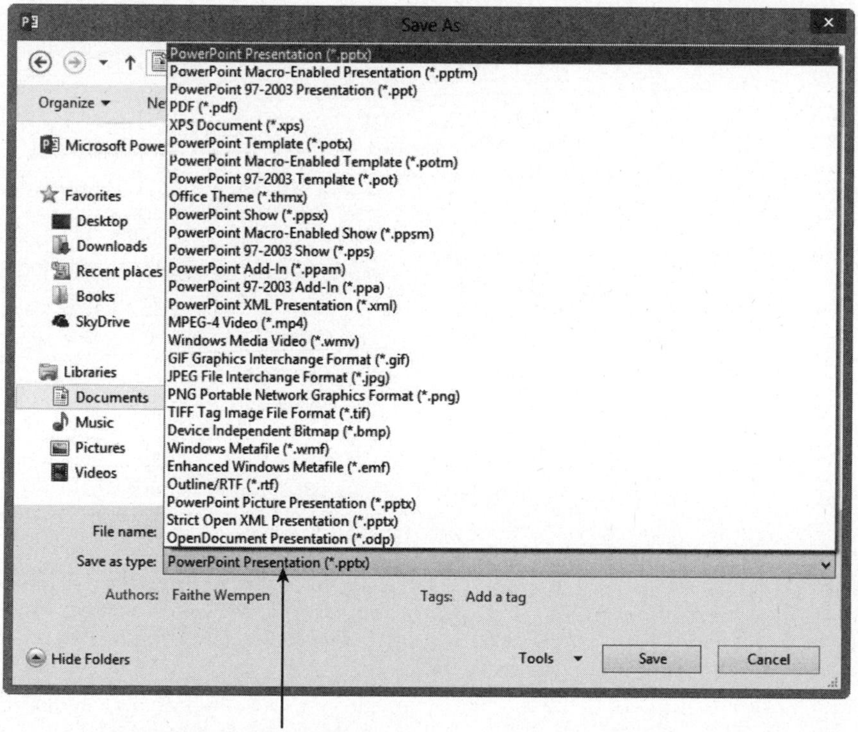

Click here to open list of file types.

TABLE 2.1 **PowerPoint Save As Formats**

Presentations		
Format	**Filename Extension**	**Usage Notes**
PowerPoint Presentation	`.pptx`	The default; use in most cases. Can open only in PowerPoint 2007 and higher (or on an earlier version with compatibility pack installed).
PowerPoint Macro-Enabled Presentation	`.pptm`	Same as `.pptx`, except it supports the storage of VBA or macro code.
PowerPoint 97–2003 Presentation	`.ppt`	A backward-compatible format for sharing files with users of PowerPoint 97, 2000, 2002 (XP), and 2003.
PDF	`.pdf`	Produces files in Adobe PDF format, which is a hybrid of a document and a graphic. It shows each page exactly as it will be printed and yet allows the user to mark up the pages with comments and to search the document text. You must have a PDF reader such as Adobe Acrobat to view PDF files.
XPS Document	`.xps`	Much the same as PDF except it's a Microsoft format. Windows Vista and higher comes with an XPS viewer application.
PowerPoint Template	`.potx`	A template file that is compatible with PowerPoint 2007 and higher.
PowerPoint Macro-Enabled Template	`.potm`	A template file that is compatible with PowerPoint 2007 and higher and that that supports the storage of VBA or macro code.
PowerPoint 97–2003 Template	`.pot`	A backward-compatible template file, also usable with PowerPoint 97, 2000, 2002 (XP), and 2003.
Office Theme	`.thmx`	Somewhat like a template, but it contains only theme settings (fonts, colors, and effects). Use this if you don't want to save any of the content. Theme files can be used to supply the colors, fonts, and effects to Word and Excel files too.
PowerPoint Show	`.ppsx`	Just like a regular PowerPoint file, except it opens in Slide Show view by default; useful for distributing presentations to the audience on disk.
PowerPoint Macro-Enabled Show	`.ppsm`	Same as PowerPoint Show (`.ppsx`), except it supports the storage of VBA or macro code.

PowerPoint 97–2003 Show	.pps	Same as a regular backward-compatible presentation file, except it opens in Slide Show view by default.
PowerPoint Add-In	.ppam	A file that contains executable code (usually VBA) that extends PowerPoint's capabilities.
PowerPoint 97–2003 Add-In	.ppa	Same as PowerPoint Add-In (.ppam), except the add-in is backward compatible.
PowerPoint XML Presentation	.xml	A presentation in XML format, suitable for integrating into an XML information storage system.
Graphics/Other		
MPEG-4 Video	.mp4	A video version of the presentation using MPEG-4 format.
Windows Media Video	.wmv	A video version of the presentation using WMV format.
GIF Graphics Interchange Format	.gif	Static graphic. GIFs are limited to 256 colors.
JPEG File Interchange Format	.jpg	Static graphic. JPG files can be very small, making them good for Web use. A lossy compression format, so picture quality may not be as good as with a lossless format.
PNG Portable Network Graphics Format	.png	Static graphic. Similar to GIF except without the color depth limitation. Uses lossless compression; takes advantage of the best features of both GIF and JPG.
TIFF Tagged Image File Format	.tif	Static graphic. TIF is a high-quality file format suitable for slides with high-resolution photos. A lossless compression format.
Device Independent Bitmap	.bmp	Static graphic. BMP is the native format for Windows graphics, including Windows background wallpaper.
Windows Metafile	.wmf	Static graphic. A vector-based format, so it can later be resized without distortion. Not Mac compatible.
Enhanced Windows Metafile	.emf	Enhanced version of WMF; not compatible with 16-bit applications. Also vector-based and not Mac compatible.
Outline/RTF	.rtf	Text and text formatting only; excludes all non-text elements. Only text in slide placeholders will be converted to the outline. Text in the Notes area is not included.
PowerPoint Picture Presentation	.pptx	Saves all the slides as pictures and puts them into a new blank presentation.

Continues

TABLE 2.1   *(continued)*

Strict Open XML Presentation	`.pptx`	A variant of XML that fully supports the Open XML standard.
OpenDocument Presentation	`.odp`	A presentation that conforms to the new OpenDocument standard for exchanging data between applications.

TIP

If you consistently want to save in a different format, choose File ⇨ Options and click Save. Then, choose a different format from the Save Files in This Format drop-down list. This makes your choice the default in the Save as Type drop-down list in the Save As dialog box. Not all of the formats are available here; your choices are PowerPoint Presentation (the default), PowerPoint Macro-Enabled Presentation, PowerPoint Presentation 97–2003, Strict Open XML Presentation, and OpenDocument Presentation.

Table 2.1 lists a lot of choices, but don't let that overwhelm you. You have three main decisions to make:

- **PowerPoint 2007–2013 format or backward compatible with PowerPoint 97–2003.** Unless compatibility is essential, go with the newer format because you get access to all of the new features. (See Table 2.2 to learn what you'll lose with backward compatibility.) If you use a backward-compatible format, some of the features described in this book work differently or aren't available at all.

- **Macro enabled or not.** If you plan to create and store macros, use a macro-enabled format; if not, use a file format that does not include macro support, for a slightly safer file (because a file cannot carry viruses if it can't carry macro code).

- **Regular presentation or PowerPoint Show.** The "show" variant starts the presentation in Slide Show view when it is loaded in PowerPoint; that's the only difference between it and a regular presentation. You can build your presentation in a regular format and then save in show format right before distribution. PowerPoint shows can be opened and edited in PowerPoint the same as any other file.

Most of the other choices from Table 2.1 are special-purpose formats and not suitable for everyday use. The following sections explain some of those special file types.

Saving Slides as Graphics

If you save your presentation in one of the graphic formats shown in the Graphics/Other section of Table 2.1, the file ceases to be a presentation and becomes a series of unrelated graphic files, one per slide. If you choose one of these formats, you're asked whether you want to export the current slide only or all slides. If you choose to export all slides, PowerPoint creates a new folder in the selected folder with the same name as the original presentation file and places the graphics files in it.

2

> **TIP**
>
> The Picture Presentation format does something unique: It converts each slide to an image and then places the images in a new presentation file. This is one way to make sure your slides are not edited by anyone who uses the presentation.

TABLE 2.2 PowerPoint 2013 Features Not Supported in the PowerPoint 97–2003 File Format

Feature	Issues
SmartArt graphics	Converted to uneditable pictures
Charts (except Microsoft Graph charts)	Converted to editable OLE objects, but the chart might appear different
Custom slide layouts	Converted to multiple masters
Drop shadows	Soft shadows converted to hard shadows
Equations	Converted to uneditable pictures
Heading and body fonts	Converted to non-theme formatting
Effects: ■ 2-D or 3-D WordArt text ■ Gradient outlines for shapes or text ■ Strikethrough and double-strikethrough ■ Gradient, picture, and texture fills on text ■ Soft edges, reflections, some types of shadows ■ Most 3-D effects	Converted to uneditable pictures
Themes	Converted to non-theme formatting
Theme colors	Converted to non-theme colors
Theme effects	Converted to non-theme effects
Theme fonts	Converted to non-theme fonts

Saving Slide Text Only

If you want to export the text of the slides to some other application, consider the Outline/RTF format, which creates an outline similar to what you see in the Outline pane in PowerPoint. This file can then be opened in Word or any other application that supports Rich Text format (RTF) text files. Only text in placeholders is exported, though, not text in manually inserted text boxes. If you aren't sure which text will be included, view the presentation in the Outline pane; any text that doesn't appear there will not be exported.

Specifying Save Options

The save options enable you to fine-tune the saving process for special needs. For example, you can employ save options to embed fonts, to change the interval at which PowerPoint saves AutoRecover information, and more.

There are two ways to access the Save options:

- Choose File ⇨ Options and click Save.
- From the Save As dialog box, click Tools ⇨ Save Options.

The PowerPoint Options dialog box appears (Figure 2.11). Set any of the options you want to set and click OK when you are finished.

FIGURE 2.11

Set save options to match the way you want PowerPoint to save your work.

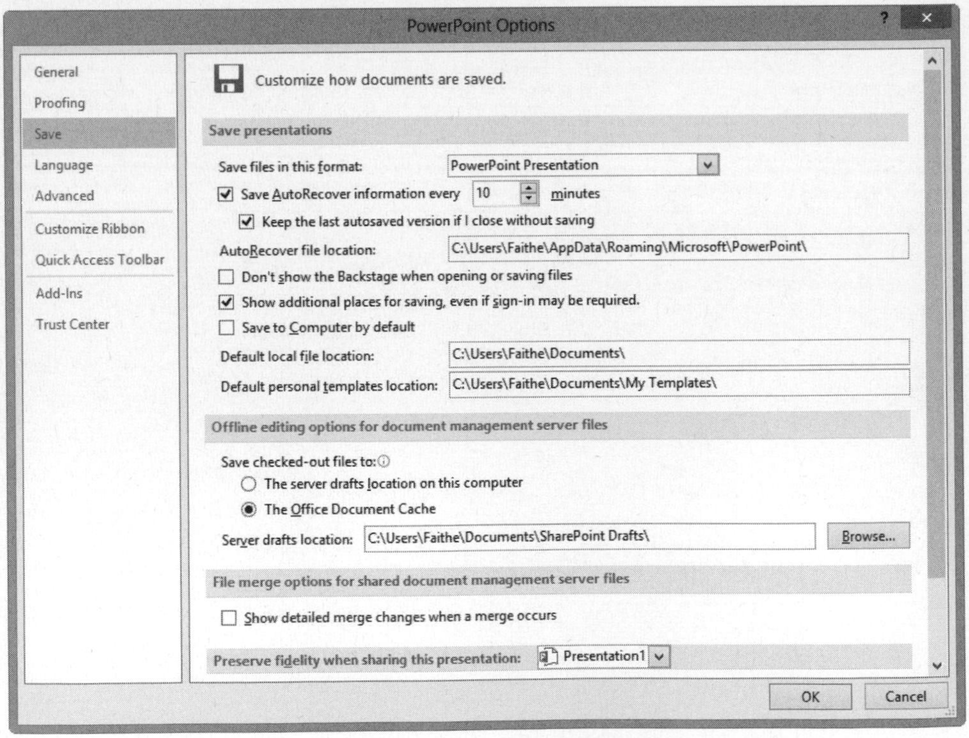

Table 2.3 summarizes the save options. One of the most important features described in Table 2.3 is AutoRecover, which is turned on by default. This means if a system error or a power outage causes PowerPoint to terminate unexpectedly, you do not lose all of your

work. The next time you start PowerPoint, it opens the recovered file and asks if you want to save it.

> **CAUTION**
>
> AutoRecover is *not* a substitute for saving your work the regular way. It does not save in the same sense that the Save command does; it only saves a backup version as PowerPoint is running. If you quit PowerPoint normally, that backup version is erased. The backup version is available for recovery only if PowerPoint terminates abnormally (because of a system lockup or a power outage, for example).

TABLE 2.3 Save Options

Feature	Purpose
Save files in this format	Sets the default file format to appear in the Save As dialog box. Your choices are a regular presentation, a macro-enabled presentation, or a 97–2003 backward-compatible presentation.
Save AutoRecover information every _____ minutes	PowerPoint saves your work every few minutes so that if the computer has problems and causes PowerPoint to terminate abnormally, you do not lose much work. Lower this number to save more often (for less potential data loss) or raise it to save less often (for less slowdown/delay related to repeated saving).
AutoRecover file location	Specify the location in which AutoRecover drafts should be saved. By default, it is `C:\Users\`*username*`\AppData\Roaming\Microsoft\PowerPoint`.
Don't show the Backstage when opening or saving files	When enabled, bypasses Backstage view (that is, the default File menu choices for opening and saving) and goes directly to the Open or Save dialog boxes, respectively.
Always show "Sign in to SkyDrive" location during Save	When disabled, hides the SkyDrive sign-in option; disable this if you never use SkyDrive to save your work.
Save to Computer by default	When enabled, saves to your default local file location (see the next option) by default.
Default local file location	Specify the location that you want to start from when saving with the Save As dialog box. By default, it is your Documents library.
Default personal templates location	Specify the location containing any templates you have created or acquired separately from the ones PowerPoint itself provides.
Save checked-out files to	Sets the location in which any drafts will be saved that you have checked out of a web server library such as SharePoint. If you choose "The server drafts location on this computer," then you must specify what that location will be in the Server drafts location box. If you choose to save to the Office document cache, it's not an issue because every save goes immediately back to the server.

Continues

TABLE 2.3   *(continued)*

Show detailed merge changes when a merge occurs	Shows full information about what was changed when you merge two PowerPoint files that are stored on a shared document management server.
Embed fonts in the file	Turn this on if you are saving a presentation for use on a different PC that might not have the fonts installed that the presentation requires. You can choose to embed the characters in use only (which minimizes the file size, but if someone tries to edit the presentation, they might not have all of the characters they need) or to embed all characters in the font set. Unlike the others, this setting applies only to the current presentation file.

Setting Passwords for File Access

If a presentation contains sensitive or confidential data, you can encrypt the file and protect it with a password. Encryption is a type of "scrambling" done to the file so that nobody can see it, either from within PowerPoint or with any other type of file-browsing utility.

You can enter two separate passwords for a file: the Open password and the Modify password. Use an Open password to prevent unauthorized people from viewing the file at all. Use a Modify password to prevent people from making changes to the file.

You can use one, both, or neither of the password types. For example, suppose you have a personnel presentation that contains salary information. You might use an Open password and distribute that password to a few key people in the human resources department who need access to it. But then you might use a Modify password to ensure that none of those people make any changes to the presentation as they are viewing it.

For the Open password, you can specify an encryption method and strength. Many encryption codes are available, and the differences between them are significant mostly to high-end technical users. However, if you do have a preference, you can choose it when you choose the Open password.

To manage a file's passwords and other security settings, follow these steps:

1. **Begin to save the file as you normally would from the Save As dialog box.**
2. **In the Save As dialog box, click Tools, and choose General Options.** The General Options dialog box opens (Figure 2.12).
3. **If you want an Open password, enter it in the Password to Open box.**
4. **If you want a Modify password, enter it in the Password to Modify box.** (You don't have to use both an Open and a Modify password; you can use just one or the other if you like.)

FIGURE 2.12

Set a password to prevent unauthorized access.

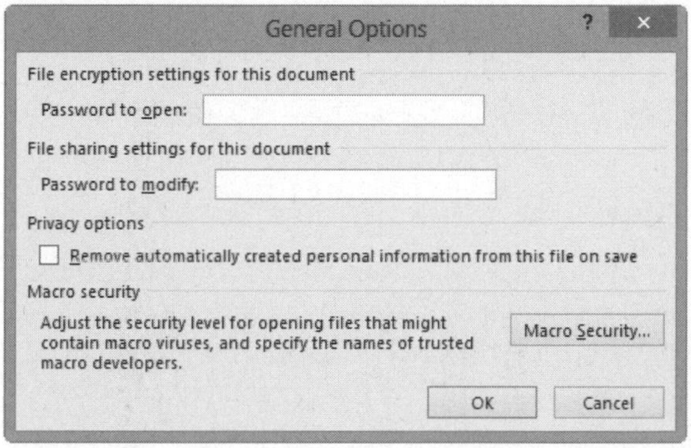

5. **(Optional) If you want your personal information stripped from the file, such as your name removed from the Author field of the Properties box, select the Remove Automatically Created Personal Information from This File on Save check box.**

6. **(Optional) If desired, adjust the macro security level for PowerPoint (all files, not just this one) by clicking the Macro Security button and making changes to the settings in the Trust Center; then click OK to return to the General Options dialog box.**

7. **Click OK.** If you specified a password in step 3, a confirmation box appears for it.

8. **If the confirmation box appears, retype the same password and click OK.** If you specified a password in step 4, a confirmation box appears for it.

9. **If the confirmation box appears, retype the same password and click OK.**

10. **Continue saving as you normally would.**

When you (or someone else) open the file, a Password prompt appears. The Open password must be entered to open the presentation file. The Modify password will *not* work. After that hurdle, if you have set a separate Modify password, a prompt for that appears. Your choices are to enter the Modify password, to cancel, or to click the Read-Only option to open the presentation in Read-Only mode.

> **CAUTION**
>
> Here's a security hole to be aware of: If you add a Modify password and then save it as a .pptx file, it can be opened *and* edited in PowerPoint 2003 or earlier if you installed the compatibility pack that allows opening of .pptx files, even if the user does not know the password. However, if you save the file in PowerPoint 2013 as a PowerPoint 97–2003 file (.ppt extension), it cannot be edited in earlier versions without the password.

Closing and Reopening Presentations

You can have several presentation files open at once and switch freely between them, but this can bog down your computer's performance somewhat. Unless you are doing some cut-and-paste work, it's best to have only one presentation file open — the one you are actively working on. It's easy to close and open presentations as needed.

Closing a Presentation

When you exit PowerPoint, the open presentation file automatically closes and you're prompted to save your changes if you have made any. If you want to close a presentation file without exiting PowerPoint, follow these steps:

1. **Choose File ⇨ Close.**

   If you have not made any changes to the presentation since the last time you saved, you're done. If you have made any changes to the presentation, you're prompted to save them.

2. **If you don't want to save your changes, click Don't Save, and you're done.**

3. **If you want to save your changes, click Save.** If the presentation has already been saved once, you're done. If the presentation has not been saved before, the Save As dialog box appears.

4. **Type a name in the File Name text box and click Save.**

Opening a Presentation

To open a recently used presentation, choose File ⇨ Open and click one of the presentations on the Recent Presentations list on the right. Up to 25 can appear by default (see Figure 2.13).

> **TIP**
> To pin a certain file to the File menu's list so that it never scrolls off, click the pushpin icon to the right of the file's name on the menu.

> **TIP**
> You can increase or decrease the number of recently used files that appear on the Recent Presentations list. Choose File ⇨ Options, click Advanced, and in the Display section, set the Show This Number of Recent Presentations box.

> **TIP**
> You can right-click an entry on the Recent Presentations list for additional options, such as Open a Copy, Copy Path to Clipboard, and Remove from List.

FIGURE 2.13

Recently opened presentations appear when you select Open from the File menu.

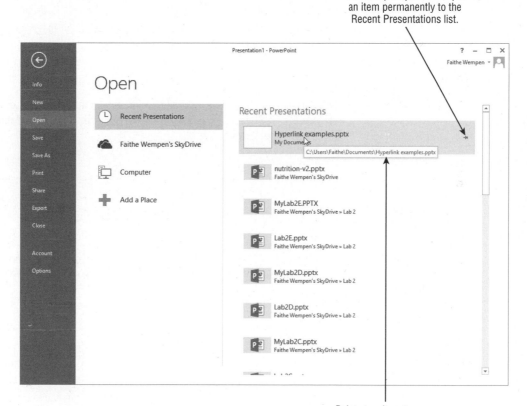

Click the pushpin icon to pin
an item permanently to the
Recent Presentations list.

Point at an item to see a
ScreenTip reporting its full path.

If the presentation you want to open does not appear on the Recent Presentations list, follow these steps to find and open it:

1. **If the Open screen does not already appear, choose File ⇨ Open.**
2. **Click the location from which you want to open a presentation, which may be your SkyDrive or computer (for locally stored files).**
3. **If a shortcut appears to the folder that contains the file you want, click it.** Otherwise, click Browse to browse for the location. The Open dialog box appears.
4. **Choose the file you want to open.** If necessary, change the location to find the file.

See the section "Changing Drives and Folders" earlier in this chapter if you need help.

5. **Click Open.** The presentation opens.

To open more than one presentation at once, hold down the Ctrl key as you click each file you want to open. When you click the Open button, they all open in their own windows. For more information, see the sidebar "Working with Multiple Presentations" later in this chapter.

The Open button in the Open dialog box has its own drop-down list from which you can select commands that open the file in different ways. See Figure 2.14, and refer to Table 2.4 for an explanation of the available options.

FIGURE 2.14

The Open button's menu contains several special options for opening a file.

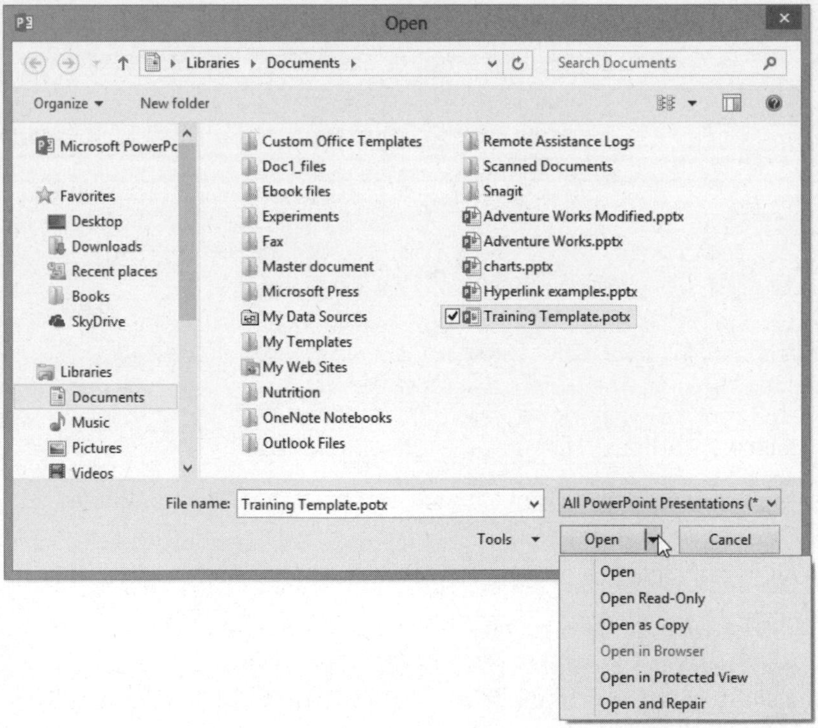

TABLE 2.4 **Open Options**

Open Button Setting	Purpose
Open	The default; simply opens the file for editing.
Open Read-Only	Allows changes but prevents those changes from being saved under the same name.
Open as Copy	Opens a copy of the file, leaving the original untouched.
Open in Browser	Applicable only for web-based presentations; opens it for viewing in a web browser. PowerPoint 2013 does not save in Web format, so it applies only to web-based presentations created in earlier versions of PowerPoint that supported that feature.
Open in Protected View	Opens the file in an uneditable view. This option not only prevents you from saving any changes to the file, it also prevents you from *making* changes.
Open and Repair	Opens the file, and identifies and repairs any errors it finds in it.
Show Previous Versions	Applicable only if the presentation file is stored on an NTFS volume under Windows 7, this feature enables you to access the Versions feature in Windows 7 that stores previous versions of files. It is not applicable to Windows 8, which does not store previous versions in the same way.

Opening a File from a Different Program

Just as you can save files in various program formats, you can open files from various programs. PowerPoint can detect the type of file and convert it automatically as you open it, so you do not have to know the exact file type. (For example, if you have an old PowerPoint file with a .ppt filename extension, you don't have to know what version it came from.) The only problem is with files that have filename extensions that PowerPoint doesn't automatically recognize. In that case, you must change the File Type setting in the Open dialog box to All Files so that the file to be opened becomes available on the file list, as shown in Figure 2.15. The change is valid for only this one use of the Open dialog box; the file type reverts to All PowerPoint Presentations, which is the default, the next time you open the dialog box.

> **CAUTION**
>
> PowerPoint opens only presentation files and text-based files such as Word outlines. If you want to include graphics from another program in a PowerPoint presentation, insert them using the Picture command on the Insert tab. Do not attempt to open them with the Open dialog box.

FIGURE 2.15

To open files from different programs, change the File Type setting to All Files

File Type button

Working with Multiple Presentations

You will usually work with only one presentation at a time. But occasionally you may need to have two or more presentations open at once — for example, to make it easier to copy text or slides from one presentation to another.

To open another presentation, choose File ➪ Open and select the one you want, the same as usual.

When more than one presentation is open, you can switch among them by selecting the one you want to see from the taskbar in Windows. Alternatively, you can click the Switch Windows button on the View tab and select any open presentation from there, as shown in the following screen shot.

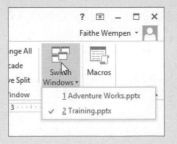

Switch between open windows of all applications — not just PowerPoint — by pressing Alt+Esc repeatedly to cycle through them or by holding down the Alt key and pressing Tab to browse through thumbnails of open windows.

Finding a Presentation File to Open

If you have forgotten where you saved a particular presentation file, you're not out of luck. The Open dialog box includes a Search box that can help you locate it, as shown in Figure 2.16.

FIGURE 2.16

Use the Search box in the Open dialog box to look for a file.

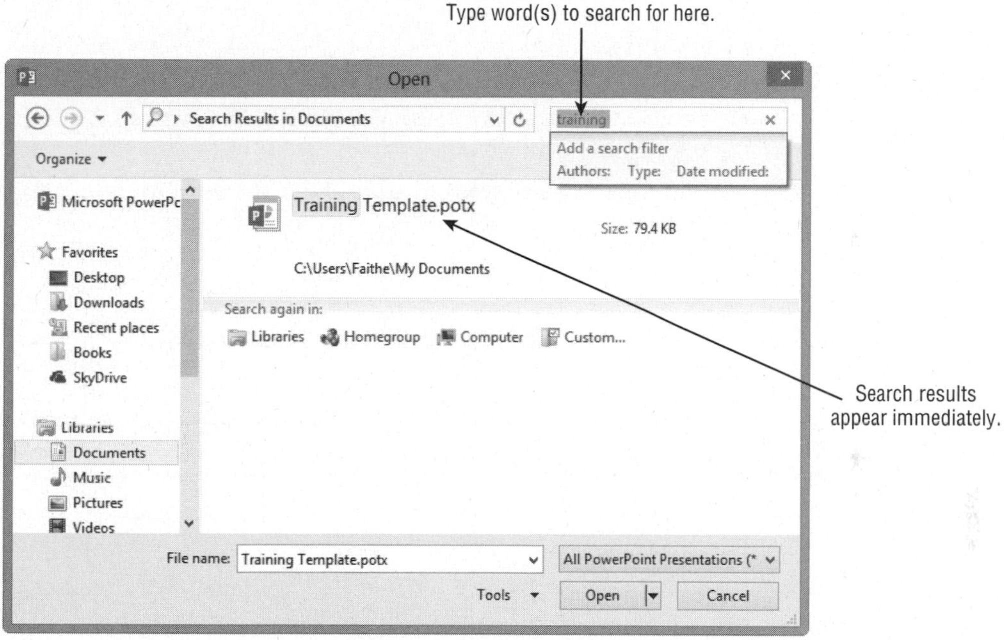

Type word(s) to search for here.

Search results appear immediately.

To search for a file, follow these steps:

1. **Choose File ➪ Open, click the location in which to search (SkyDrive or Computer), and then click Browse to display the Open dialog box.**
2. **Navigate to the general location of the file.** For example, if you know it is on the C: drive, display the top-level listing for the C: drive.
3. **Click in the Search box and type part of the filename (if you know it) or a word or phrase used in the file.**
4. **Press Enter.** A list of files that match that specification appears.
5. **Open the file as you normally would.**

Setting File Properties

File properties are facts about each file that can help you organize them. If you have a lot of PowerPoint files, using file properties can help you search intelligently for them using the Search feature you learned about in the preceding section. For example, you can specify an author, a manager, and a company for each file and then search based on those values.

You can set a file's properties by doing the following:

1. **Choose File ⇨ Info.**

2. **Click the Properties heading (on the right side of the Info screen), and on the menu that appears, click Show Document Panel.** A Properties Ribbon appears above the presentation window.

3. **Fill in any information you want to store about the presentation, as shown in Figure 2.17.**

FIGURE 2.17

Enter information to store in the file's properties.

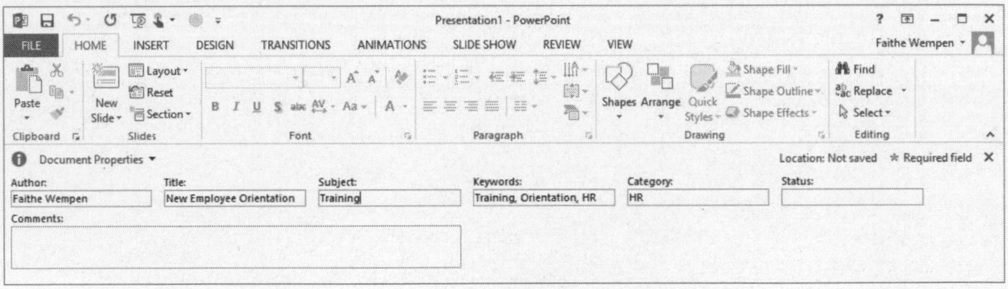

4. **Click the down arrow to the right of Document Properties in the Properties Ribbon, and choose Advanced Properties.** The Properties dialog box for the file appears.

5. **Click the Summary tab, and confirm or change any information there.** This is the same information that you entered in the Properties Ribbon, with the addition of a couple of other fields, as shown in Figure 2.18.

6. **Click the Custom tab, shown in Figure 2.19, choose any additional fields you need, and set values for them.** For example, click the Client field on the Name list, and type a value for it in the Value text box. Repeat this for any of the other custom fields.

FIGURE 2.18

The Summary tab has many of the same fields as the Properties panel on the Ribbon.

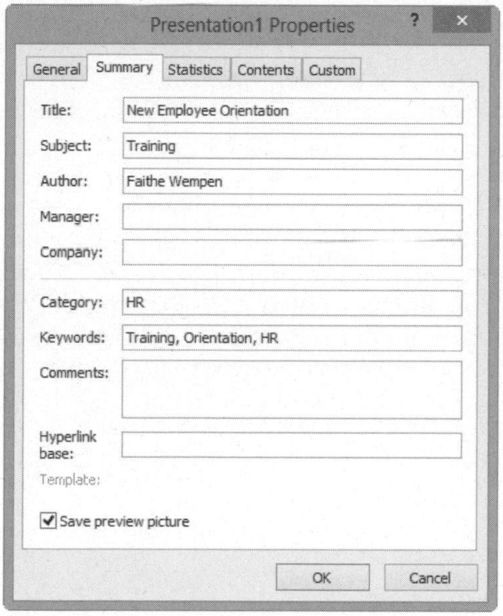

FIGURE 2.19

The Custom tab enables you to set custom properties based on your tracking needs.

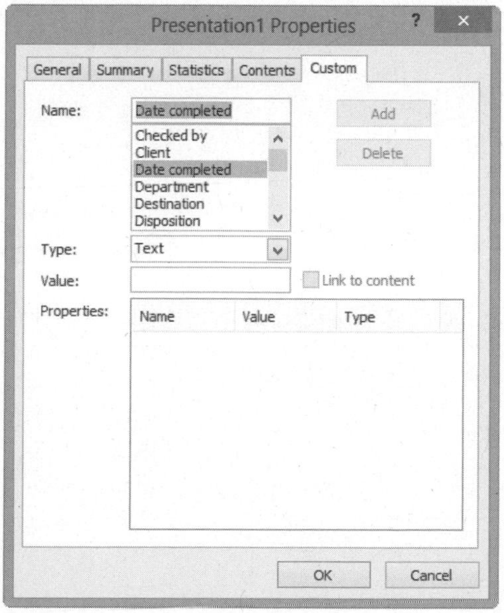

7. **Review the information on the Statistics and Contents tab if desired.** (You can't change that information.)

8. **Click OK.**

Now you can use the contents of the properties fields when performing a search.

Summary

This chapter made you a master of files. You can now confidently create new presentations, and save, open, close, and delete PowerPoint presentation files. You can also save files in different formats, search for missing presentations, and lots more. This is rather utilitarian knowledge and not very much fun to practice, but later you will be glad you took the time to learn it, when you have important files you need to keep safe.

In the next chapter, you learn about slide layouts and text-based presentations. You also learn how to create your own layouts, and how to create the text that will form the basis of your message.

Creating Slides and Text Boxes

IN THIS CHAPTER

Creating new slides

Inserting content from external sources

Managing slides

Using content placeholders

Creating text boxes manually

Working with text boxes

PowerPoint makes it easy to create consistent, attractive slides that use standard preset layouts. You just choose the layout that you want for a particular slide and then fill in its placeholders with text, graphics, or other content.

In this chapter, you'll learn how to build a simple text-based presentation by creating new slides and entering text on them. You'll learn how to import content from other programs, and how to create, size, and position text boxes to hold the text for your presentation.

Creating New Slides

Different templates start a presentation with different numbers and types of slides. A blank presentation has only a single slide, and you must create any others that you want.

There are several ways to create new slides. For example, you can type new text in the outline and then promote it to slide status, or you can add slides with the New Slide button that is on the Home tab. You can also copy existing slides, either within the same presentation or from other sources. The following sections outline these procedures in more detail.

Creating New Slides from Outline View

As discussed in Chapter 10utline view shows the text from the presentation's slides in a hierarchical tree, with the slide titles at the top level (the slide level) and the various levels of bulleted lists on the slides displaying as subordinate levels. Text that you type in the Outline pane appears on the slide, and vice versa, as shown in Figure 3.1.

FIGURE 3.1

When you type text into the Outline pane, it automatically appears on the current slide.

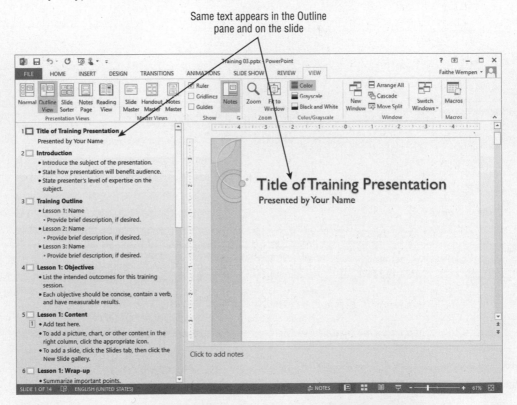

NOTE

Outline view doesn't show all of the text in all cases; see "Creating Text Boxes Manually" later in this chapter to find out why text in some text boxes does not appear in the outline.

Follow these steps to create a new slide from Outline view:

1. **Switch to Outline view (View ⇨ Presentation Views ⇨ Outline View).** As you learned in Chapter 1, Outline view is like Normal view except the left pane is an Outline pane, containing a text outline instead of slide thumbnail images.

2. **Click at the end of the existing line on the Outline pane that the new slide should follow.**

3. **Click Home ⇨ Slides ⇨ New Slide.** A new line appears in the Outline pane, with a slide symbol to its left.

4. **Type the title for the new slide.** The title appears both in the Outline pane and on the slide.

You can also create a new slide by starting a new line in the Outline pane and then promoting it to slide level by pressing Shift+Tab. Follow these steps to insert a new slide in this way:

1. **Position the insertion point at the end of the last line of the slide that the new slide should follow, and press Enter to start a new line.**

2. **Press Shift+Tab to promote the new line to the highest level (press it multiple times if needed), so that a slide icon appears to its left.**

3. **Type the title for the new slide.** The title appears both in the Outline pane and on the slide.

After creating the slide, you can continue creating its content directly in the Outline pane. Press Enter to start a new line, and then use Tab to demote, or Shift+Tab to promote, the line to the desired level. You can also right-click the text and choose Promote or Demote. Promoting a line all the way to the top level changes the line to a new slide title.

Creating a Slide from the Slides Pane

Here's a very quick method for creating a new slide, based on the default layout. It doesn't get much easier than this:

1. **Switch to Normal view if you're not already there (View ⇨ Presentation Views ⇨ Normal).**

2. **In the Slides pane, click the slide that the new slide should follow.**

3. **Press Enter.** A new slide appears. You can also right-click the slide that the new one should follow and choose New Slide.

The drawback to creating a slide in any of the ways you have learned about so far in this chapter is that you cannot specify the layout. You have to change the layout afterwards if you don't get the kind you want. To choose a layout other than the default one, see the next section.

> **NOTE**
>
> The layout you get when you create a new slide from the Slides pane depends on what layout the preceding slide has. If the preceding slide is Title Slide or Title and Content, you get a Title and Content slide. With any other type, you get the same type as the previous one. For example, if the previous slide was Title Only, that's what you get.

Creating a Slide from a Layout

A *slide layout* is a layout guide that tells PowerPoint what placeholder boxes to use on a particular slide and where to position them. Although slide layouts can contain placeholders for text, they also contain graphics, charts, tables, and other useful elements. After you create a new slide with placeholders, you can click a placeholder to open whatever controls you need to insert that type of object.

See the section, "Using Content Placeholders" for more information on inserting objects.

When you create new slides using one of the methods described in the preceding sections, the new slides use the Title and Content layout, which consists of a slide title and a single, large placeholder box for content. If you want to use another layout, such as a slide with two adjacent but separate frames of content, you must either switch the slide to a different layout after its creation (using the Layout button's menu on the Home tab), or you must specify a different layout when you initially create the slide.

To specify a certain layout as you are creating a slide, follow these steps:

1. **In Normal or Slide Sorter view, select or display the slide that the new one should follow.**

   You can select a slide by clicking its thumbnail image in Slide Sorter view or on the Slides pane in Normal view. You can also move the insertion point to the slide's text in the Outline pane.

2. **On the Home tab, do one of the following:**

   - To add a new slide using the default Title and Content layout, click the top (graphical) portion of the New Slide button.

   - To add a new slide using another layout, click the bottom (text) portion of the New Slide button and then select the desired layout from the menu, as shown in Figure 3.2.

> **TIP**
> The layouts that appear on the menu come from the slide master. To customize these layouts, click View ➪ MasterViews ➪ Slide Master. You will learn more about the slide master and about changing layouts in Chapter 4.

Copying Slides

Another way to create a new slide is to copy an existing one in the same presentation. This is especially useful when you are using multiple slides to create a progression because one slide is typically identical to the next slide in a sequence, except for a small change. (You can also build animation effects within a single slide using PowerPoint's animation effects, as you will learn in Chapter 17.)

FIGURE 3.2

Create a new slide, based on the layout of your choice.

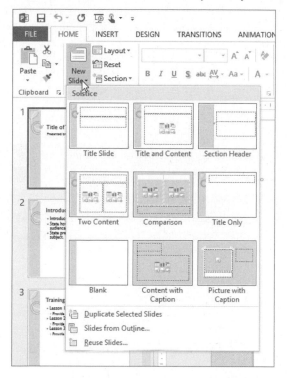

There are several ways to copy one or more slides. One way is to use the Windows Clipboard, as in the following steps:

1. **Select the slide or slides that you want to copy.** See "Selecting Slides" later in this chapter for more information about selecting slides.

CAUTION

If you select from the Outline pane in Outline view, make sure that you click the icon to the left of the slide's title so that the entire slide is selected; if you select only part of the text on the slide, then only the selected part is copied.

2. **Press Ctrl+C.** You can also click Home ➪ Clipboard ➪ Copy, or right-click the selection and click Copy.

3. **Select the slide that the pasted slide or slides should follow.** Or, if working in Outline view, click in the Outline pane to place the insertion point where you want the insertion.

4. **Press Ctrl+V.** You can also click Home ➪ Clipboard ➪ Paste, or right-click the destination and click Paste.

PowerPoint also has a Duplicate Selected Slides command that does the same thing as a copy-and-paste command. Although it may be a little faster, it gives you less control as to where the pasted copies will appear. PowerPoint pastes the slides immediately after the last slide in the selection. For example, if you selected slides 1, 3, and 6 and issued the Duplicate Selected Slides command, then the copies are placed after slide 6.

Follow these steps to try out the Duplicate Selected Slides command.

1. **Select the slide or slides to be duplicated.**
2. **On the Home tab, click the bottom part of the New Slide button to open its menu.**
3. **Click Duplicate Selected Slides.** As an alternative, you can right-click a slide (or a group of selected slides) in the Slides pane and choose Duplicate Slide.

> **TIP**
>
> To make duplication even faster, you can place the Duplicate Selected Slides command on the Quick Access toolbar. To do that, right-click the command on the menu and choose Add to Quick Access Toolbar.

Inserting Content from External Sources

Many people find that they can save a lot of time by copying text or slides from other programs or from other PowerPoint presentations to form the basis of a new presentation. There's no need to reinvent the wheel each time! The following sections look at various ways to bring in content from external sources.

Copying Slides from Other Presentations

There are several ways to copy slides from other presentations. You can:

- Open the presentation, save it under a different name, and then delete the slides that you *don't* want, leaving a new presentation with the desired slides ready for customization.
- Open two PowerPoint windows side-by-side and drag-and-drop slides between them.
- Open two PowerPoint presentations, copy slides from one of them to the Clipboard (Ctrl+C), and then paste them into the other presentation (Ctrl+V).
- Use the Reuse Slides feature in PowerPoint, as described next.

To reuse slides from other presentations with the Reuse Slides feature, follow these steps:

1. **On the Home tab, click the lower portion of the New Slide button to open its menu.**
2. **Click Reuse Slides.** The Reuse Slides pane appears at the right.

3. **Click the Open a PowerPoint File hyperlink.**Or, click the Browse button and then click Browse File.

4. **In the Browse dialog box, select the presentation from which you want to copy slides, and click Open.** Thumbnail images of the slides in the presentation appear in the Reuse Slides pane, as shown in Figure 3.3.

FIGURE 3.3

Choose individual slides to copy to the current presentation.

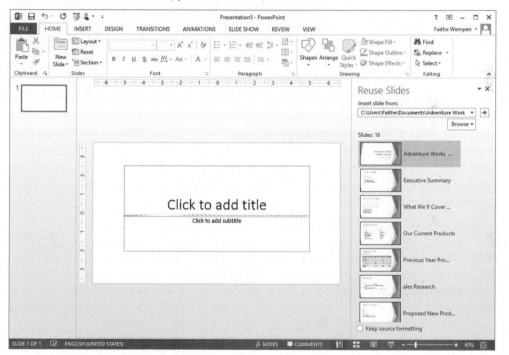

5. **(Optional) If you want to keep the source formatting when copying slides, select the Keep source formatting check box at the bottom of the task pane.**

6. **(Optional) To see an enlarged image of one of the slides, move the mouse pointer over it.**

7. **Do any of the following:**

   - To insert a single slide, click it.
   - To insert all slides at once, right-click any slide and choose Insert All Slides.
   - To copy only the theme (not the content), right-click any slide in the Reuse Slides pane and choose Apply Theme to All Slides, or Apply Theme to Selected Slides.

Inserting New Slides from an Outline

All of the Microsoft Office applications work well together, so it's easy to move content between them. For example, you can create an outline for a presentation in Microsoft Word and then import it into PowerPoint. PowerPoint uses the heading styles that you assigned in Word to decide which items are slide titles and which items are slide content. The top-level headings (Heading 1) form the slide titles.

To try this out, open Word, switch to Outline view (View ➪ Views ➪ Outline), and then type a short outline of a presentation. Press Tab to demote, or Shift+Tab to promote, a selected line. Then save your work, go back to PowerPoint, and follow these steps to import it:

1. **On the Home tab, click the lower portion of the New Slide button to open its menu.**
2. **Click Slides from Outline.** The Insert Outline dialog box opens.
3. **Select the file containing the outline text that you want to import.**
4. **Click Insert.** PowerPoint imports the outline.

If there were already existing slides in the presentation, they remain untouched. (This includes any blank slides, and so you might need to delete the blank slide at the beginning of the presentation after importing.) All of the Heading 1 lines from the outline become separate slide titles, and all of the subordinate headings become bullet points in the slides.

Tips for Better Outline Importing

Although PowerPoint can import any text from any Word document, you may not always get the results that you want or expect. For example, you may have a document that consists of a series of paragraphs with no heading styles applied. When you import this document into PowerPoint, it might look something like Figure 3.4.

Figure 3.4 is a prime example of what happens if you don't prepare a document before you import it into PowerPoint. PowerPoint makes each paragraph its own slide and puts all of the text for each one in the title placeholder. It can't tell which ones are actual headings and which ones aren't because there are no heading styles in use. The paragraphs are too long to fit on slides, and so they overrun their placeholders. Extra blank lines are interpreted as blank slides. Quite a train wreck, isn't it? Figure 3.4 also illustrates an important point to remember: Regular paragraph text does not work very well in PowerPoint. PowerPoint text is all about short, snappy bulleted lists and headings. The better that you prepare the outline before importing it, the less cleanup you will need to do after importing. Here are some tips:

■ Apply heading styles to the text that you want to import. Paragraphs formatted using non-heading styles in Word do not import into PowerPoint unless you use no heading styles at all in the document (as in Figure 3.4).

- Stick with basic styles only in the outline: for example, just Heading 1, Heading 2, and so on.

- Delete all blank lines above the first heading. If you don't, you will have blank slides at the beginning of your presentation.

- Strip off as much manual formatting as possible from the Word text, so that the text picks up its formatting from PowerPoint. To strip off formatting in Word, select the text and press Ctrl+spacebar.

- Do not leave blank lines between paragraphs. These will translate into blank slides or blank bulleted items in PowerPoint.

- Delete any graphic elements, such as clip art, pictures, charts, and so on. They will not transfer to PowerPoint anyway and may confuse the import utility.

FIGURE 3.4

A Word document consisting mainly of plain paragraphs makes for an unattractive presentation.

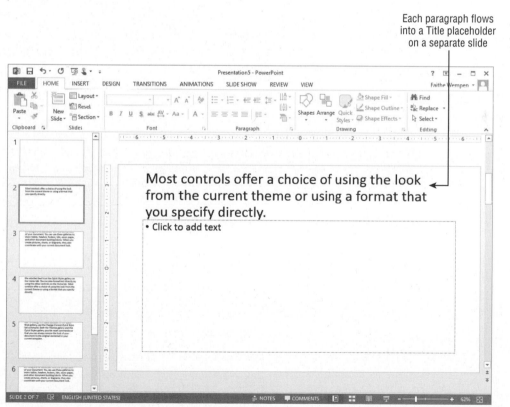

Each paragraph flows into a Title placeholder on a separate slide

Importing from Other Text-Based Formats

In addition to Word, PowerPoint also imports from plain-text files, from WordPerfect (5.x or 6.x), from Microsoft Works, from Rich Text Format, and from Web pages. The procedure is the same as in the preceding steps. By default, the file type in the Insert Outline dialog box is set to All Files, so you should see all usable files automatically, provided they have the correct extensions.

If you are setting up a plain-text file for import, you obviously won't have the outlining tools from Word at your disposal. Instead, you must rely on tabs. Each line that should be a title slide should start at the left margin; first-level bullet paragraphs should be preceded by a single tab; second-level bullets should be preceded by two tabs, and so on.

Post-Import Cleanup

After importing text from an outline, there will probably be a few minor corrections that you need to make. Run through this checklist:

- The first slide in the presentation might be blank. If it is, then delete it.
- The Title Slide layout may not be applied to the first slide; apply that layout, if necessary. (You can use the Layout list on the Home tab.)
- A theme may not be applied; choose one from the Design tab, if necessary, or format your slide masters and layouts as desired.

See Chapter 4 for more information on working with themes.

- Some of the text might contain manual formatting that interferes with the theme formatting and creates inconsistency. Remove any manual formatting that you notice. One way to do this is to switch to Outline view, select all of the text in the Outline pane by pressing Ctrl+A, and then stripping off the manual formatting by pressing Ctrl+spacebar or by clicking the Reset button in the Slides group on the Home tab.
- If some of the text is too long to fit comfortably on a slide, change to a different slide layout, such as a two-column list, if necessary. You might also need to split the content into two or more slides.
- There might be some blank bullet points on some slides (if you missed deleting all of the extra paragraph breaks before importing). Delete these bullet points.

Opening a Word Document as a New Presentation

Instead of importing slides from a Word document or other text-based document, as described in the preceding section, you can simply open the Word document in PowerPoint. PowerPoint starts a new presentation file to hold the imported text. This saves some time if you are starting a new presentation anyway, and you don't have any existing slides to merge with the incoming content.

To open a Word document in PowerPoint, follow these steps:

1. **Choose File ⇨ Open.** The Open screen appears.
2. **Select the location where the Word document is stored, such as your SkyDrive or Computer.**
3. **Click Browse, and then navigate to the folder containing the Word document.**
4. **Change the file type to All Outlines.**
5. **Select the document.**
6. **Click Open.** The document outline becomes a PowerPoint presentation, with all Heading 1 paragraphs becoming slide titles.

> **CAUTION**
>
> You can't open or insert a Word outline in PowerPoint if it is currently open in Word. This limitation is an issue only for Word files, not plain text or other formats.

Importing Text from Web Pages

PowerPoint accepts imported text from several Web-page formats, including HTML and MHTML (Single File Web Page). It is helpful if the data is in an orderly outline format, or if it was originally created from a PowerPoint file, because there will be less cleanup needed.

There are several ways to import from a Web page:

- Open a Web-page file as you would an outline (see the preceding section), but set the file type to All Web Pages.
- Insert the text from the Web page as you would a Word outline (in the Home tab, click Slides ⇨ New Slide ⇨ Slides from Outline).
- Reuse slides from a Web presentation as you would from any other presentation (in the Home tab, click Slides ⇨ New Slide ⇨ Reuse Slides).

> **CAUTION**
>
> You should use one of the above methods rather than pasting HTML text directly into PowerPoint. This is because when you paste HTML text, you might get additional HTML tags that you don't want, including cross-references that might cause your presentation to try to log onto a Web server every time you open it.

When importing from a Web page, don't expect the content to appear formatted the same way that it was on the Web page. We're talking strictly about text import here. The formatting on the Web page comes from HTML tags or from a style sheet, neither of which you can import. If you want an exact duplicate of the Web page's appearance, take a picture of the page with the Shift+PrintScreen command, and then paste it into PowerPoint (Ctrl+V) as a graphic.

If you are importing an outline from an MHTML-format Web page that contains pictures, the pictures are also imported into PowerPoint. If importing from a regular HTML file, you cannot import the pictures.

> **TIP**
>
> If you need to show a live Web page from within PowerPoint, try Shyam Pillai's free Live Web add-in, found at www.mvps.org/skp/liveweb.htm.

Managing Slides

After inserting a few slides into a presentation, and perhaps building some content on them, you might decide to make some changes, such as rearranging, deleting, and so on. The following sections explain how to manage and manipulate the slides in a presentation.

Selecting Slides

Before you can issue a command that acts upon a slide or a group of slides, you must select the slides that you want to affect. You can do this from either Normal or Slide Sorter view, but Slide Sorter view makes it easier because you can see more slides at once. From Slide Sorter view, or from the Slides pane in Normal view, you can use any of these techniques to select slides:

- To select a single slide, click it.
- To select multiple slides, hold down the Ctrl key as you click each one. Figure 3.5 shows slides 1, 3, and 6 selected, as indicated by the shaded border around the slides.
- To select a contiguous group of slides (for example, slides 1, 2, and 3), click the first slide, and then hold down the Shift key as you click the last one. All of the slides in between are selected as well.

To cancel the selection of multiple slides, click anywhere outside of the selected slides.

To select slides from Outline view, click the slide icon to the left of the slide's title; this selects the entire slide, as shown in Figure 3.6. It's important to select the entire slide and not just part of its content before issuing a command such as Delete, because otherwise, the command only affects the portion that you selected.

FIGURE 3.5

Select slides in Slide Sorter view by holding down the Ctrl key and clicking each slide.

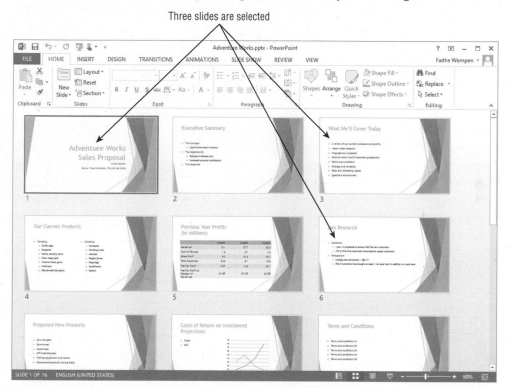

Deleting Slides

You may want to get rid of some of the slides, especially if you created your presentation using a template that contained a lot of sample content. For example, the sample presentation may be longer than you need, or you may have inserted your own slides instead.

Select the slide or slides that you want to delete, and then do either of the following:

- Right-click the selection and choose Delete Slide.
- Press the Delete key on the keyboard.

FIGURE 3.6

Select slides in the Outline pane by clicking the slide icon to the left of the slide title.

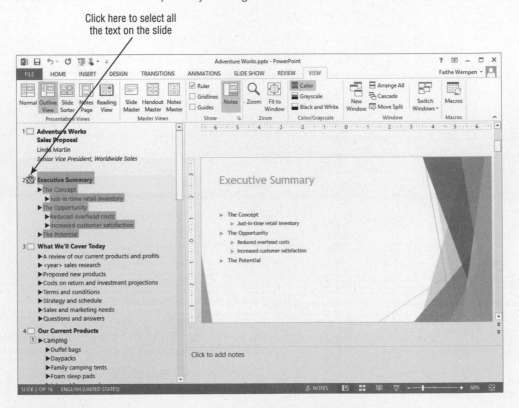

Undoing Mistakes

Here's a command that can help you in almost all of the other chapters in this book: undoing. The Undo command allows you to reverse past actions. For example, you can use it to reverse all of the deletions that you made to your presentation in the preceding section. The easiest way to undo a single action is to click the Undo button on the Quick Access toolbar or press Ctrl+Z. You can click it as many times as you like; each time you click it, you undo one action.

> **TIP**
>
> By default, the maximum number of Undo operations is 20, but you can change this. Choose File ⇨ Options, then click Advanced, and in the Editing Options section, change the Maximum Number of Undos setting. Keep in mind that if you set the number of undos too high, it can cause performance problems in PowerPoint.

You can undo multiple actions at once by opening the Undo button's drop-down list, as shown in Figure 3.7. Just drag the mouse across the actions that you want to undo (you don't need to hold down the mouse button). Click when the desired actions are selected, and presto, they are all reversed. You can select multiple actions to undo, but you can't skip around. For example, to undo the fourth item, you must undo the first, second, and third ones, as well.

FIGURE 3.7

Use the Undo button to undo your mistakes and the Redo button to reverse an Undo operation.

The Redo command is the opposite of Undo. If you make a mistake with the Undo button, you can fix the problem by clicking the Redo button. Like the Undo button, it has a drop-down list, and so you can redo multiple actions at once.

The Redo command is available only immediately after you use the Undo command. If Redo isn't available, a Repeat button appears in its place. The Repeat command enables you to repeat the last action that you performed (and it doesn't have to be an Undo operation). For example, you can repeat some typing, or some formatting. Figure 3.8 shows the Repeat button.

FIGURE 3.8

The Repeat button appears when Redo is not available, and enables you to repeat actions.

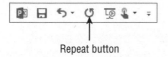

Rearranging Slides

The best way to rearrange slides is to do so in Slide Sorter view. In this view, the slides in your presentation appear in thumbnail view, and you can move them around on the screen to different positions, just as you would manually rearrange pasted-up artwork on a table. Although you can also do this from the Slides pane in Normal view, you are able to see fewer slides at once. As a result, it can be more challenging to move slides around, for example, from one end of the presentation to another. To rearrange slides, use the following steps:

1. **Switch to Slide Sorter view or Normal view.**
2. **Select the slide that you want to move.** You can move multiple slides at once if you like (which is a lot easier in Slide Sorter view than in Normal view).
3. **Drag the selected slide to the new location.** The slide moves as you drag, as shown in Figure 3.9.

FIGURE 3.9

Drag a slide to a different position in Slide Sorter view.

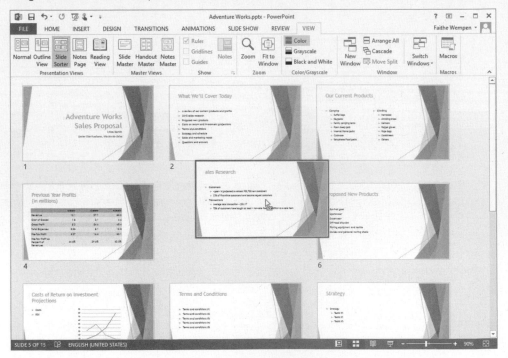

4. **Release the mouse button.** The slide moves to the new location.

You can also rearrange slides in Outline view. This is not quite as easy as using Slide Sorter view, but it's more versatile. Not only can you drag entire slides from place to place, but you can also move individual bullets from one slide to another.

Follow these steps to move content in Outline view:

1. **Switch to Outline view.**
2. **Position the mouse pointer over the slide's icon in the Outline pane.** The mouse pointer changes to a four-headed arrow.
3. **Click on the icon.** PowerPoint selects all of the text in that slide.
4. **Drag the slide's icon up or down to a new position in the outline and then release the mouse button.** All of the slide's text moves with it to the new location.

There are also keyboard shortcuts for moving a slide up or down in the Outline pane that may be faster than clicking the toolbar buttons. You can press the Alt+Shift+Up arrow keys to move a slide up, and the Alt+Shift+Down arrow keys to move a slide down.

These shortcuts work equally well with single bullets from a slide. Just click to the left of a single line to select it, instead of clicking the Slide icon in step 3.

Using Content Placeholders

Now that you know something about inserting and managing entire slides, let's take a closer look at the content within a slide. The default placeholder type is a multipurpose content placeholder, as shown in Figure 3.10.

FIGURE 3.10

A content placeholder can contain a variety of different elements.

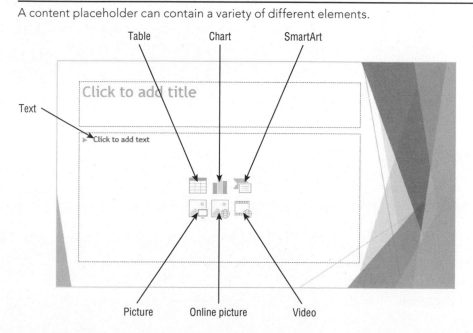

Inserting Content into a Placeholder

To type text into a content placeholder, click inside the placeholder box and start typing. You can enter and edit text as you would in any word-processing program. To insert any other type of content into a placeholder, click one of the icons shown in Figure 3.10. A dialog box opens to help you select and insert that content type.

 Chapters 5 and 6 cover the various formatting that you can apply to text on a slide. You will learn about these various content types later in the book:

Tables: Chapter 8

SmartArt: Chapter 10

Clip Art: Chapter 11

Pictures (from files): Chapter 11

Charts: Chapter 12

Video: Chapter 15

A content placeholder can hold only one type of content at a time. If you click in the placeholder and type some text, the icons for the other content types disappear. To access them again, you must delete all of the text from the placeholder.

Placeholders versus Manually Inserted Objects

You can insert content on a slide independently of a placeholder by using the Insert tab's buttons and menus. This technique allows you to insert an item in its own separate frame on any slide, to coexist with any placeholder content. You can learn how to insert each content type in the chapters in which they are covered (see the preceding list).

Creating Text Boxes Manually

The difference between a placeholder-inserted object and a manually inserted one is most significant with text boxes. Although you might think that text boxes are all alike, there are actually some significant differences between placeholder text boxes and manually inserted ones.

Here are some of the characteristics of a text placeholder:

- You cannot create new text placeholder boxes on your own, except in Slide Master view.

 You learn how to use Slide Master view to create your own layouts that contain custom text placeholders in Chapter 4.

- If you delete all of the text from a text placeholder, the placeholder instructions return (in Normal or Outline view).

- A text placeholder box has a fixed size on the slide, regardless of the amount or size of text that it contains. You can resize it manually, but if you reapply the layout, the placeholder box snaps back to the original size.

- AutoFit is turned on by default in a text placeholder, so that if you type more text than will fit, or resize the frame so that the existing text no longer fits, the text shrinks in size.

- The text that you type in a text placeholder box appears in the Outline pane in Outline view.

A manual text box, on the other hand, is one that you create yourself using the Text Box tool on the Insert tab. Here are some characteristics of a manual text box:

- You can create a manual text box anywhere, and you can create as many as you like, regardless of the layout.

- If you delete all of the text from a manual text box, the text box remains empty or disappears completely. No placeholder instructions appear.

- A manual text box starts out small vertically, and expands as you type more text into it.

- A manual text box does not use AutoFit by default; the text box simply becomes larger to make room for more text.

- You cannot resize a manual text box so that the text that it contains no longer fits; PowerPoint refuses to make the text box shorter vertically until you delete some text from it. (However, you can decrease its horizontal width.)

- Text typed in a manual text box does not appear in the Outline pane in Outline view.

Figure 3.11 shows two text placeholders (one empty) and a text box in Outline view. Notice that the empty placeholder contains filler text to help you remember that it is there. Notice also that only the text from the placeholder appears in the Outline pane; the text-box text does not. Empty text boxes and placeholders do not show up in Slide Show view, so you do not have to worry about deleting any unneeded ones.

When Should You Use a Manual Text Box?

Graphical content such as photos and charts can work well either in placeholders or as manually inserted objects. However, when it comes to text, you should stick with placeholders as often as possible. Placeholder text appears in the Outline pane in Outline view, whereas text in a manually inserted text box does not. When the bulk of a presentation's text is in manually created text boxes, Outline view becomes less useful because it doesn't contain the complete presentation text. In addition, when you change to a different formatting theme that includes different positioning for placeholders — for example, to accommodate a graphic on one side — the manual text boxes do not shift. As a result, they might end up overlapping the new background graphic with unattractive results. In a case such as this, you would need to manually go through each slide and adjust the positioning of each text box.

FIGURE 3.11

Two text placeholders and a text box.

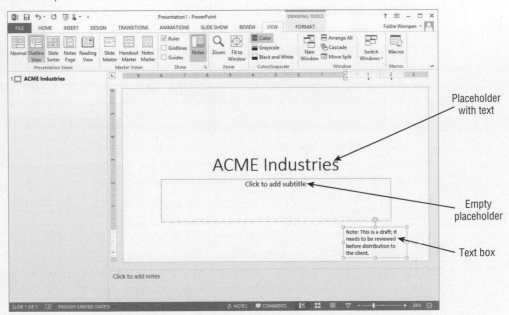

However, there are times when a manually created text box is preferable or even necessary. For example, suppose that you have a schematic diagram of a machine and you need to label some of the parts. Manually placed text boxes are perfect for these little snippets of text that are scattered over the surface of the picture. Manual text boxes are also useful for warnings, tips, and any other information that is tangential to the main discussion. Finally, if you want to vary the placement of the text on each slide (consciously circumventing the consistency provided by layouts), and you want to precisely position each box, then manual text boxes work well because they do not shift their position when you apply different themes or templates to the presentation.

TIP

If you insert text in a placeholder and then change the slide's layout so that the slide no longer contains that placeholder (for example, if you switch to Title Only or Blank layout), the text remains on the slide, but it becomes an *orphan*. If you delete the text box, then it simply disappears; a placeholder does not reappear. However, it does not become a manual text box, because its content still appears in the Outline pane, while a manual text box's content does not.

Creating a Manual Text Box

To manually place a text box on a slide, follow these steps:

1. **If necessary, reposition the existing placeholders or objects on the slide to make room for the new text box.**

2. **Click Insert ⇨ Text ⇨ Text Box.** The mouse pointer turns into a vertical line. You can alternately use the Text Box icon in any of the Shapes galleries, such as the one on the Insert tab.

3. **Do either of the following:**

   - To create a text box that automatically enlarges itself horizontally as you type more text, but does not automatically wrap text to the next line, click once where you want the text to start, and begin typing.

   - To create a text box with a width that you specify, and that automatically wraps text to the next line and grows in height as needed, click and drag to draw a box where you want the text box to be. Its height will initially snap back to a single line's height, regardless of the height that you initially draw; however, it will grow in height as you type text into it.

4. **Type the text that you want to appear in the text box.**

Working with Text Boxes

Text boxes (either placeholder or manual) form the basis of most presentations. Now that you know how to create them, and how to place text in them, let's take a look at how to manipulate the boxes themselves.

Are you looking for information about formatting text boxes — perhaps to apply a background color or a border to one? See the formatting text boxes discussion in Chapter 7.

Selecting Text Boxes

On the surface, this topic might seem like a no-brainer. Just click it, right? Well, almost. A text box has two possible "selected" states. One state is that the box itself is selected, and the other is that the insertion point is within the box. The difference is subtle, but it becomes clearer when you issue certain commands. For example, if the insertion point is in the text box and you press Delete, PowerPoint deletes the single character to the right of the insertion point. However, if you select the entire text box and press Delete, PowerPoint deletes the entire text box and everything in it.

To select the entire text box, click its border. You can tell that it is selected because the border appears as a solid line. To move the insertion point within the text box, click inside the text box. You can tell that the insertion point is there because you can see it flashing inside.

In the rest of this book, when you see the phrase "select the text box," it means the box itself should be selected, and the insertion point should *not* appear in it. For most of the upcoming sections it does not make any difference, although in a few cases it does.

TIP

When the insertion point is flashing in a text box, you can press Esc to select the text box itself.

You can select more than one text box at once by holding down the Shift key as you click additional text boxes. This technique is useful when you want to select more than one text box, for example, so that you can format them in the same way, or so that you can resize them by the same amount.

Sizing a Text Box

The basic techniques for sizing text boxes in PowerPoint are the same for every object type (for that matter, they are also the same as in other Office applications). To resize a text box, or any object, follow these steps:

1. **Position the mouse pointer over a selection handle for the object. The mouse pointer changes to a double-headed arrow.** If you want to resize proportionally, make sure that you use a corner selection handle, and hold down the Shift key as you drag.
2. **Click and drag the selection handle to resize the object's border.**

CAUTION

Allowing PowerPoint to manage placeholder size and position through layouts ensures consistency among your slides. When you start changing the sizes and positions of placeholders on individual slides, you can end up creating consistency problems, such as headings that aren't in the same spot from slide to slide, or company logos that shift between slides.

You can also set a text box's size from the Size group on the Drawing Tools Format tab. When the text box is selected, its current dimensions appear in the Height and Width boxes, as shown in Figure 3.12. You can change the dimensions within these boxes.

FIGURE 3.12

You can set an exact size for a text box from the Format tab's Size group.

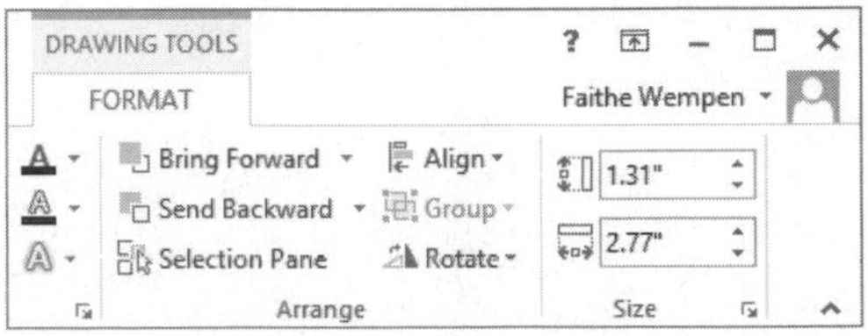

You can also set the size of a text box from the Size and Position task pane:

1. **Click the dialog box launcher in the Size group on the Drawing Tools Format tab, as shown in Figure 3.12.** The Format Shape task pane opens with the Size options displayed. See Figure 3.13.

FIGURE 3.13

You can adjust the size of the text box from the Size controls in the Format Shape task pane.

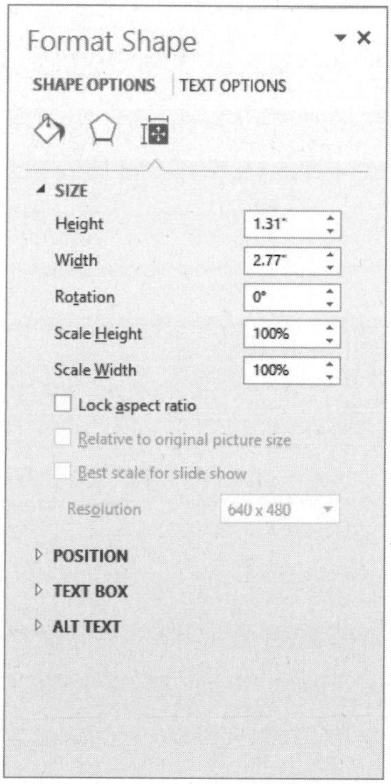

2. **Set the height and width for the text box in the Height and Width boxes, respectively..**

   To keep the size proportional, select the Lock Aspect Ratio check box in the Scale section before you start adjusting the height or width.

3. **(Optional) Click the Close (X) button in the upper right corner of the task pane to close it.**

TIP

Task panes are *non-modal*. This means that you can leave them open and continue to work on your presentation. It also means that any changes that you make are applied immediately; there is no OK button to accept your changes or Cancel button to reverse them. To reverse a change, you can use the Undo command (Ctrl+Z).

Positioning a Text Box

To move an object, drag it by any part of its border other than a selection handle. Select the object, and then position the mouse pointer over a border so that the pointer turns into a four-headed arrow. Then drag the object to a new position. With a text box, you must position the mouse pointer over a border and not over the inside of the frame; with all other object types, you don't have to be that precise; you can move an object by dragging anywhere within it.

You can also set an exact position by using the Format Shape task pane:

1. **Click the dialog box launcher in the Size group on the Drawing Tools Format tab, as shown in Figure 3.12.** The Format Shape dialog box opens with the Size controls displayed, as in Figure 3.13.

2. **Click the Size heading to collapse the Size section, and then click the Position heading to expand the Position section.** The Position controls appear, as shown in Figure 3.14.

FIGURE 3.14

You can adjust the position with the Position controls.

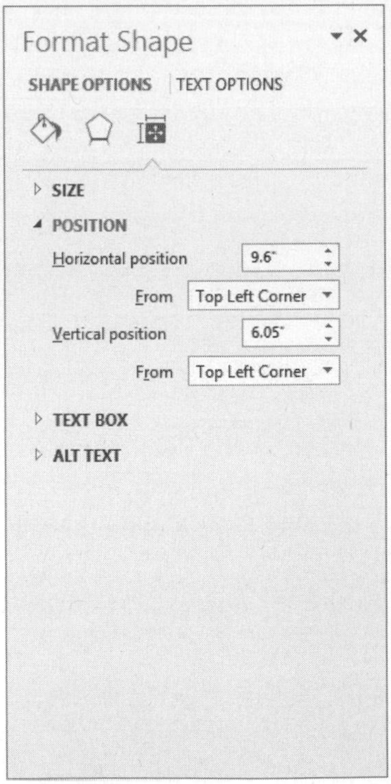

3. **Set the horizontal and vertical position, and the point from which it is measured.** By default, measurements are from the top-left corner of the slide.

4. **(Optional) Click the Close (X) button in the upper right corner of the task pane to close it.**

Changing a Text Box's AutoFit Behavior

When there is too much text to fit in a text box, there are three things that may happen:

- **Do not AutoFit.** The text and the box can continue at their default sizes, and the text can overflow out of the box or be truncated.

- **Shrink text on overflow.** The text can shrink its font size to fit in the text box. This is the default setting for placeholder text boxes.

- **Resize shape to fit text.** The text box can enlarge to the size needed to contain the text. This is the default setting for manual text boxes.

Whenever there is too much text in a placeholder box, the AutoFit icon appears in the bottom-left corner. Click that icon to display a menu, as shown in Figure 3.15. From that menu, you can turn AutoFit on or off. Depending on the text-box type, you might not have all the menu items shown in Figure 3.15.

FIGURE 3.15

You can use the AutoFit icon's menu to change the AutoFit setting for a text box.

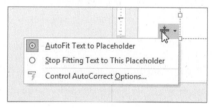

3

With a manual text box, the AutoFit icon does not appear, and so you must adjust the AutoFit behavior in the text box's properties. The following method works for both manual and placeholder boxes:

1. **Right-click the border of the text box and choose Format Shape.** The Format Shape task pane opens.

2. **Click Text Options.** Three icons appear: Text Fill & Outline, Text Effects, and Text Box.

   You can point at an icon to see a ScreenTip containing its name.

3. **Click the Text Box icon.** Controls appear that pertain to the text box itself. See Figure 3.16.

FIGURE 3.16

Click the Text Box icon to change text box options, including AutoFit behavior.

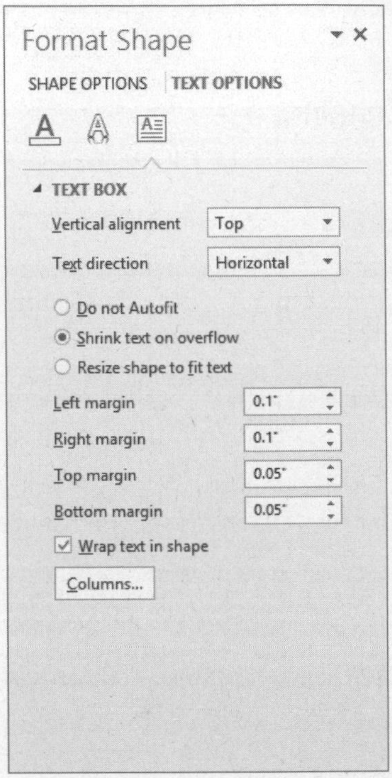

4. **Click one of the AutoFit options, as shown in Figure 3.16.**

5. **(Optional) Click the Close (X) button in the upper right corner of the task pane to close it.**

One other setting that also affects AutoFit behavior is the Wrap Text in Shape option. This on/off toggle, which appears as a check box in Figure 3.16, enables text to automatically wrap to the next line when it reaches the right edge of the text box. By default, this setting is On for placeholder text boxes and for manual text boxes that you create by dragging. However, it is Off by default for manual text boxes that you create by clicking.

Table 3.1 summarizes the various AutoFit behaviors and how they interact with one another.

TABLE 3.1 AutoFit and Resize Shape to Fit Text Behaviors

Setting	Default For	When Wrap Text in Shape Is On	When Wrap Text in Shape Is Off
Do Not Autofit	n/a	Text overflows at bottom of text box	Text overflows at right and text box only
Shrink Text on Overflow	Placeholders	Text shrinks to fit	Text shrinks to fit
Resize Shape to Fit Text	Manual text boxes	Text box expands vertically only (default for manual text that you create by dragging)	Text box expands vertically and horizontally (default for manual box that you create by text box clicking). However, if you clicked to create the text box initially, the width keeps expanding until you press Enter.

Summary

In this chapter, you learned how to create new slides, either from scratch or from outside sources. You learned how to select, rearrange, and delete slides, and how to place content on a slide. Along the way, you learned the difference between a content placeholder and a manually inserted object, and how to create your own text boxes, move and resize objects, and find or replace text. These are all very basic skills, and perhaps not as interesting as some of the more exciting topics to come, but mastering them will serve you well as you build your presentation.

In the next chapter, you'll learn about themes and layouts, two of the innovative features in PowerPoint 2013 that make it such an improvement over earlier versions. You'll find out how a theme differs from a template and how it applies font, color, and effect formatting to a presentation. You will then apply layouts and create your own custom layouts and themes.

3

Working with Layouts, Themes, and Masters

Most presentations consist of multiple slides, so you'll need a way of ensuring consistency among them. Not only will you want each slide (in most cases) to have the same background, fonts, and text positioning, but you will also want a way of ensuring that any changes you make to those settings later automatically populate across all your slides.

To accomplish these goals, PowerPoint offers layouts, themes, and masters. *Layouts* determine the positioning of placeholders; *themes* assign color, font, and background choices; and *masters* transfer theme settings to the slides and provide an opportunity for repeated content, such as a logo, on each slide. In this chapter you learn how to use layouts, themes, and masters to create a presentation that is attractive, consistent, and easy to manage.

Understanding Layouts and Themes

As you learned in Chapter 3, a *layout* is a positioning template. The layout used for a slide determines what content placeholders will appear and how they will be arranged. For example, the layout shown in Figure 4.1 is called Title Slide, and it contains a Title placeholder and a Subtitle placeholder.

FIGURE 4.1

This slide uses the Title Slide layout and the Facet theme.

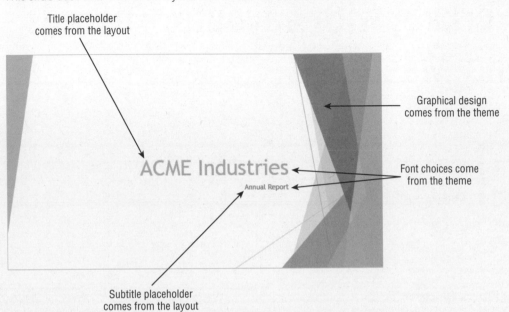

A *theme* is a group of design settings. It includes color settings, font choices, object effect settings, and in some cases also a background graphic. In Figure 4.1, the theme applied is called Facet, and it is responsible for the colored shapes and lines on the edges, the colors of those graphics, and the fonts used on the slide.

A theme is applied to a *slide master*, which is a sample slide and not part of the regular presentation, existing only behind-the-scenes to provide its settings to the real slides. It holds the formatting that you want to be consistent among all the slides in the presentation (or at least a group of them, because a presentation can have multiple slide masters). Technically, you do not apply a theme to a slide; you apply a theme to a slide master, and then you apply a slide master to a slide. That's because a slide master can actually contain some additional elements besides the formatting of the theme such as extra graphics, dates, footer text, and so on.

Themes versus Templates

As you learned in Chapter 1, a *template* is a file on which you can base new presentations. Templates typically have a `.potx` extension (or a `.potm` extension if macro-enabled). A template may contain one or more themes (that is, sets of design choices, like backgrounds, layouts, and font choices), plus one or more slides containing sample text.

A *theme* is both simpler than and more complex than a template. A theme can exist either inside of a template or as a separate file with a `.thmx` extension. A theme is simpler because it cannot hold some of the things a template can hold, such as sample content. A theme can provide only font, color, effect, and background settings to the presentation. (It can also provide slide layouts, but let's postpone that discussion for a bit.) On the other hand, a theme can also do *more* than a PowerPoint template, in that you can apply a theme saved as a separate file to other Office applications, so you can share its color, font, and effect settings with Word or Excel, for example.

Where Themes Are Stored

A theme is an XML file (or a snippet of XML code embedded in a presentation or template file). A theme can come from any of these sources:

- **Built-in:** Some themes are embedded in PowerPoint itself and are available from the Themes gallery on the Design tab regardless of the template in use.

- **Custom (automatically loaded):** The default storage location for user-created theme files is C:\Users*username*\AppData\Roaming\Microsoft\Templates\Document Themes. All themes (and templates containing themes) stored here are automatically displayed among the gallery of theme choices on the Design tab, in a Custom category.

> **TIP**
>
> If you don't want to delete a custom theme file, but you also don't want it showing up in the gallery all the time, move the file to a folder outside of the Document Themes folder hierarchy. For example, create an Unused Themes folder on your hard disk and move it there until you need it. When you want to use the custom color theme again, move the file back to its original location.

- **Inherited from starting template:** If you start a presentation using a template other than the default blank one, that template might have one or more themes included in it.

- **Stored in current presentation:** If you modify a theme in Slide Master view while you are working on a presentation, the modified code for the theme is embedded in that presentation file.

- **Stored in a separate file:** If you save a theme (using any of a variety of methods you'll learn later in this chapter), you create a separate theme file with a .thmx extension. These files can be shared among other Office applications, so you can standardize settings such as font and color choices across applications. (Some of the unique PowerPoint portions of the theme are ignored when you use the theme in other applications.)

Themes, Layouts, and Slide Master View

In PowerPoint 2013, the slide master has separate layout masters for each layout, and you can customize and create new layouts. Look at Figure 4.2, which shows Slide Master view. Notice along the left side that there is a different, separately customizable layout master

4

for each available layout, all grouped beneath the slide master. Any changes you make to the slide master trickle down to the individual layout masters, but you can also customize each of the individual layout masters to override a trickle-down setting. For example, on a particular layout you can choose to omit the background graphic to free up its space on the slide for extra content.

FIGURE 4.2

Slide Master view enables you to make design changes that affect the entire presentation.

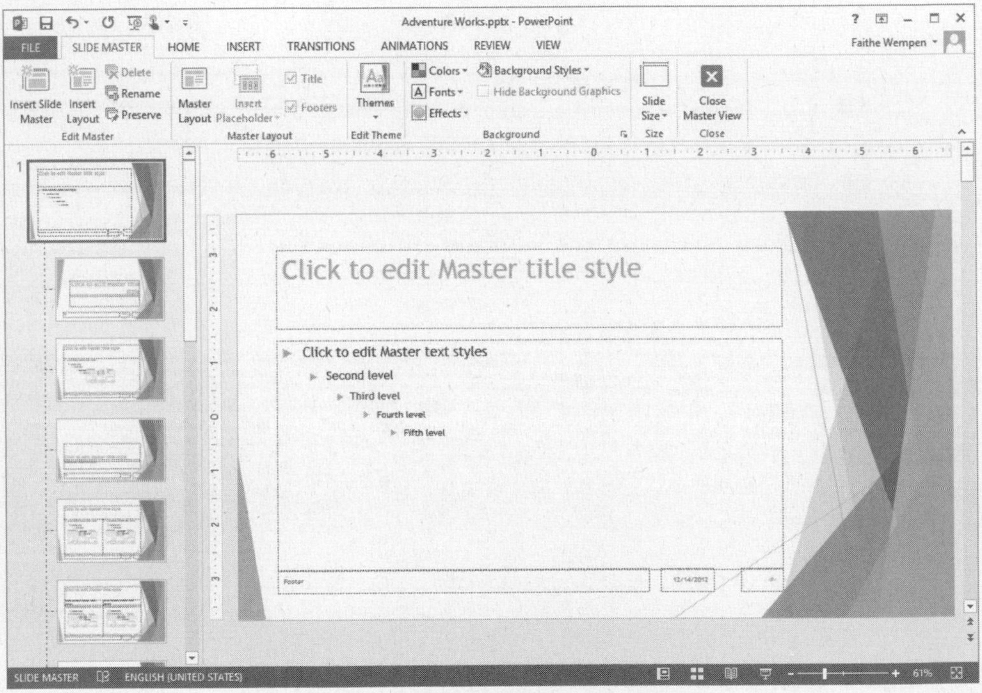

> **TIP**
>
> Figure 4.2 shows the left pane enlarged so that the slide master and layout masters appear larger than the default. If you would like your screen to look like that, drag the divider between the panes to the right until the thumbnails in the left pane are a readable size.

A *master* is a set of specifications that govern formatting and appearance. PowerPoint actually has three masters: the slide master (for slides), the handout master (for handouts), and the notes master (for speaker notes). This chapter deals only with the slide master.

For more on the handout and notes masters, see Chapter 17.

The *slide master* holds the settings from a theme and applies them to one or more slides in your presentation. A slide master is not exactly the same thing as a theme because the theme can also be external to PowerPoint and used in other programs, but there's a rough equivalency there. A slide master is the representation of a particular theme applied to a particular presentation.

NOTE

Which themes appear in Slide Master view? The ones you have applied to at least one slide in the presentation, plus any custom themes copied from another presentation (see the section "Copying a Theme from Another Presentation" for more details) and any themes inherited from the template used to create the presentation. The built-in themes do not show up here unless they are in use.

When you make changes to a slide master, those changes trickle down to the individual layout masters associated with it. When you make changes to an individual layout master, those changes are confined to that layout in that master only.

To enter Slide Master view, choose View ⇨ Master Views ⇨ Slide Master. A Slide Master tab appears. To exit from Slide Master view, choose Slide Master ⇨ Close ⇨ Close Master View or select a different view from the View tab.

Changing a Slide's Layout

As you construct your presentation, you may find it useful to change a slide's layout. For example, you might want to switch from a slide that contains one big content placeholder to one that has two side-by-side placeholders, to compare/contrast two lists, drawings, or diagrams.

Many of the layouts PowerPoint provides contain multipurpose placeholders that accept various types of content. For example, the default layout, called Title and Content, has placeholders for a slide title plus a single type of content—text, a table, a chart, a picture, a piece of clip art, a SmartArt diagram, or a video. You choose the layout you want based on the number and arrangement of the placeholders, and not the type of content that will go into them.

When you change to a different layout, you change the type and/or positioning of the placeholders on it. If the previous placeholders had content in them, that content shifts to a new location on the slide to reflect the different positioning for that placeholder type. If the new layout does not contain a placeholder appropriate for that content, the content remains on the slide but becomes *orphaned*. This means it is a free-floating object, outside of the layout. You need to manually position an orphaned object if it's not in the right spot. However, if you later apply a different layout that does contain a placeholder for the orphaned object, it snaps back into that placeholder.

4

To switch a slide to a different layout, follow these steps:

1. **Select the slide or slides to affect.**
2. **Click Home ⇨ Slides ⇨ Layout.** A menu of layouts appears, as shown in Figure 4.3.

FIGURE 4.3

Switch to a different layout for the selected slide(s).

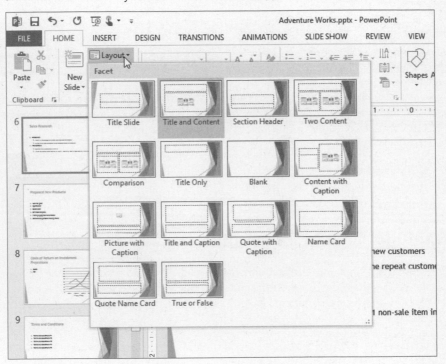

3. **Click the desired layout.**

> If you want to modify a built-in layout, or create your own layouts, see "Customizing and Creating Layouts" later in this chapter.

When a presentation has more than one slide master defined, separate layouts appear for each of the slide master themes. Figure 4.4 shows the Layout menu for a presentation that has two slide masters.

FIGURE 4.4

When there are multiple slide masters, each one's layout is separate.

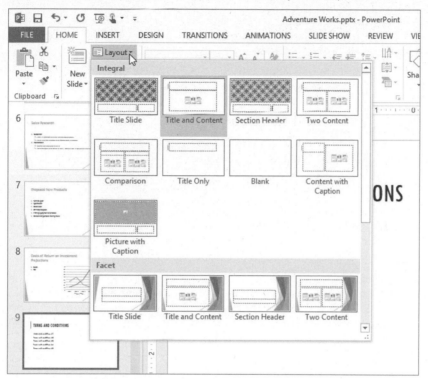

Applying a Theme

As you learned in "Understanding Layouts and Themes" at the beginning of this chapter, themes enable you to apply different designs to the presentation. A theme includes a background graphic (usually), color and font choices, and graphic effect settings. A theme can also include custom layouts.

The method for applying a theme depends on whether that theme is already available in the current presentation or not. Some themes are built into PowerPoint so that they are always available; other themes are available only when you use certain templates, or when you specifically apply them from an external file. The following sections explain each of those possibilities.

NOTE

Themes, also called *design themes*, contain a combination of colors, fonts, effects, backgrounds, and layouts. There are also more specialized themes: color themes, font themes, and effect themes. When this book uses the term "theme" alone, it's referring to a design theme. Where there is potential for confusion, the book calls it a design theme to help differentiate it from the more specific types of themes.

Applying a Theme from the Gallery

A *gallery* in PowerPoint is a menu of samples from which you can choose. You saw the Layout gallery in Figures 4.2 and 4.3, for example.

The Themes gallery is a menu of all of the built-in themes plus any additional themes available from the current template or presentation file.

To select a theme from the gallery, follow these steps:

1. **(Optional) If you want to affect only certain slides, select them.** (Slide Sorter view works well for this.)
2. **On the Design tab, in the Themes group, if the theme you want appears, click it, and skip the rest of these steps.** If the theme you want does not appear, you will need to open the gallery. To do so, click the down arrow with the line over it, as shown in Figure 4.5.

FIGURE 4.5

Open the Themes gallery by clicking the down arrow with the line above it.

Click here to open
the Themes gallery

The Themes gallery opens, as shown in Figure 4.6. The gallery is divided into sections based upon the source of the theme. Themes stored in the current presentation appear at the top, under the This Presentation heading; custom themes you have added (if any) appear next, under a Custom heading. Built-in themes appear at the bottom, under the Office heading.

FIGURE 4.6

Select the desired theme from the menu.

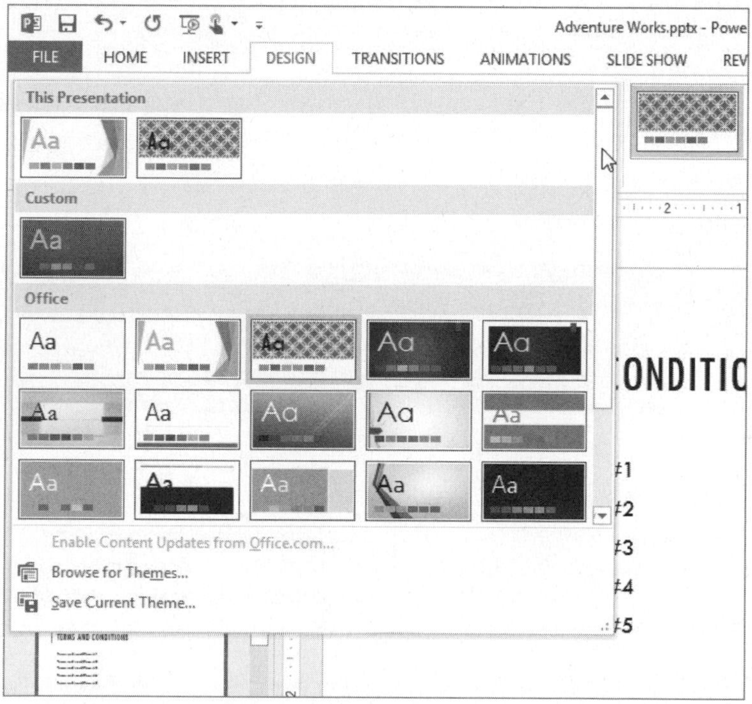

> **TIP**
>
> You can drag the bottom-right corner of the menu to resize the gallery.

3. **Click the theme you want to apply.**
   - If you selected multiple slides in step 1, the theme is applied only to them.
   - If you selected a single slide in step 1, the theme is applied to the entire presentation.

To override the default behavior in step 3, so that you can apply a different theme to a single slide, right-click instead of clicking in step 3 and choose Apply to Selected Slide(s) from the shortcut menu.

Applying a Theme from a Theme or Template File

You can open and use externally saved theme files in any Office application. This makes it possible to share color, font, and other settings between applications to create consistency between documents of various types. You can also save and load themes from templates.

To create your own theme files, see "Creating a New Theme" later in this chapter.

To apply a theme to the presentation from a theme or template file, follow these steps:

1. **On the Design tab, open the Themes gallery (see Figure 4.6) and click Browse for Themes.** The Choose Theme or Themed Document dialog box opens.

2. **Navigate to the folder containing the file and select it.**

3. **Click Apply.**

> **NOTE**
>
> Any custom themes you might have previously saved are located by default in C:\Users*username*\AppData\Roaming\Microsoft\Templates\Document Themes. However, you don't need to navigate to that location to open a theme file because all themes stored here are automatically included in the gallery already.

Applying a Theme Variant

Some themes come in several versions, called *variants*. These variants have the same basic slide layouts and background graphics as the original, but may have different color, font, and/or effect choices. For example, a theme that has a white background and black text might have a black-background variant with white text. Variants are new in PowerPoint 2013.

To apply a variant, first apply the desired theme, using any of the methods you learned about earlier in this chapter. Then, on the Design tab, click one of the variants in the Variants group. See Figure 4.7.

FIGURE 4.7

Select a variant for the chosen theme from the Design tab.

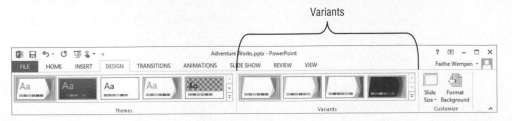

The Variants group, like the Themes group, has a down-pointing arrow button with a line over it that you can click to open up a full gallery of choices. However, most themes have only a few variants to choose from, so all the variants may already be visible without opening the gallery.

Managing Themes

Themes are applied to slide masters to specify the background, color, font, and effect formatting for all the slides that have that slide master assigned to them. (A single presentation file can have multiple slide masters, and therefore multiple themes.)

Some themes are built into PowerPoint, and you can also create and save your own themes as separate files and apply them to other presentations or even to other Office documents, such as in Word and Excel. In this section you learn how to create new themes, manage theme files, and apply themes across multiple presentations.

Creating a New Theme

To create a new theme, first format a slide master exactly the way you want, including any custom layouts, backgrounds, colors, and font themes. (You will learn how to make those changes later in this chapter.) Then save the slide master's formatting as a new theme by following these steps:

1. **Open Slide Master view if it is not already open (View ⇨ Master Views ⇨ Slide Master), and select the desired slide master in the left pane.**

   You should have already formatted this slide master the way you want the new theme to be. If you haven't yet, see the sections "Changing Colors, Fonts, and Effects" and "Changing the Background" later in this chapter to make the needed changes.

> **NOTE**
>
> As you learned in "Themes, Layouts, and Slide Master View" earlier in this chapter, the default slide master is the larger thumbnail at the top of the tree in the left pane. Notice that there are slightly smaller thumbnail images under it; those are its individual layout masters. There may be more than one slide master; scroll the left pane down to see if there's another Slide Master below the default one.

2. **Click Slide Master ⇨ Edit Theme ⇨ Themes ⇨ Save Current Theme.** The Save Current Theme dialog box opens.

   The default location shown in the Save Current Theme dialog box is C:\Users*username*\AppData\Roaming\Microsoft\Templates\Document Themes where *username* is the current Windows user.

3. **Type a name for the theme file in the File Name text box.** See Figure 4.8.

4. **Click Save.** The new theme is saved to your hard disk.

The new theme is now available from the Themes button's menu in all presentations you create, as long as you are signed into Windows as the same user on the same PC. All of the theme's formatting is available, including any custom color or font themes it includes.

4

You can use the saved theme in other programs too; in Word or Excel, choose Page Layout ⇨ Themes in one of those programs.

FIGURE 4.8

Save the current slide master's settings as a new theme.

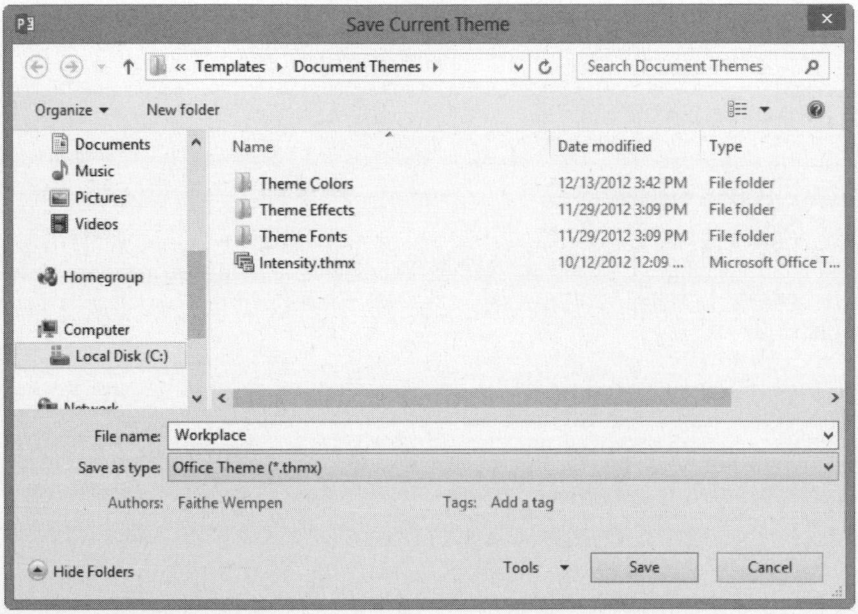

Renaming a Theme

You can rename a theme file by renaming the .thmx file from File Explorer (Windows Explorer), from outside of PowerPoint. By default, theme files are stored in: C:\Users\user-name\AppData\Roaming\Microsoft\Templates\Document Themes.

Don't want to leave PowerPoint to do this? You can also rename a theme file from inside PowerPoint by using any dialog box that saves or opens files. For example, to use the Choose Theme or Themed Document dialog box to rename a theme, follow these steps:

1. **From the Design or Slide Master tab, click Themes, and choose Save Current Theme.** The Choose Theme or Themed Document dialog box opens.
2. **If needed, navigate to C:\Users*username*\AppData\Roaming\Microsoft\ Templates\Document Themes.** (That location may appear automatically.)
3. **Right-click the theme file and choose Rename.** See Figure 4.9.
4. **Type the new name for the theme and press Enter.**
5. **Click Cancel to close the dialog box.**

FIGURE 4.9

Right-click the theme file and choose Rename.

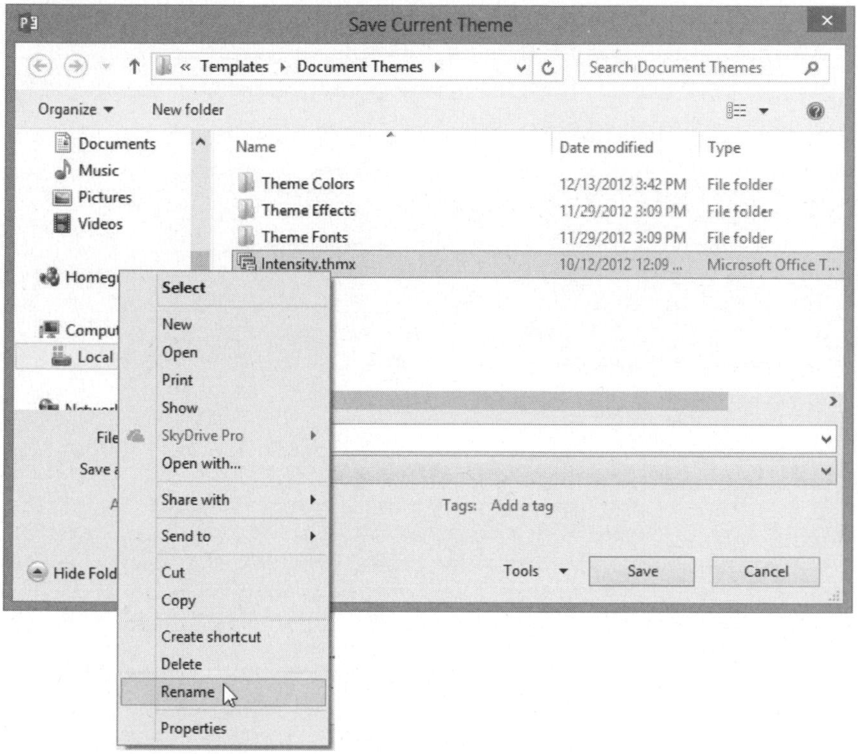

Deleting a Theme

A custom theme file continues appearing on the Themes gallery indefinitely. If you want to remove it from there, you must delete it. The easiest way to delete a theme is to right-click it in the Themes gallery and choose Delete.

You can also browse to the folder containing your saved custom themes and delete from there. See the previous section, "Renaming a Theme," to learn an easy way to get access to that folder without leaving PowerPoint.

Copying a Theme from Another Presentation

One easy way to copy a theme from one presentation to another is copy a slide master that has that theme applied to it. Follow these steps to learn how to do that:

1. **Open both presentations, and switch to Slide Master view in both presentations (View ⇨ Master Views ⇨ Slide Master).**

2. **Select the slide master that already uses the desired theme, and press Ctrl+C to copy it.**

3. **Switch to the other presentation (click View ⇨ Window ⇨ Switch Windows and click the other presentation's file name).**

4. **Press Ctrl+V to paste the slide master (and its associated theme and layouts) into Slide Master view in the other presentation.**

TIP

As you will learn in "Preserving a Slide Master" later in this chapter, you can preserve a slide master in Slide Master view so that it doesn't get deleted automatically when there are no slides based on it. By creating new slide masters, applying themes to them, and then preserving them, you can create a whole library of themes in a single presentation or template file. Then to make this library of themes available in another presentation, you simply base the new presentation on that existing presentation (or template).

Changing Colors, Fonts, and Effects

In addition to overall themes, which govern several types of formatting, PowerPoint also provides many built-in color, font, and effect themes that you can apply separately from your choice of design theme. So, for example, you can apply a design theme that contains a background design you like, as you learned to do earlier in this chapter, and then change the colors, fonts, and effects for it.

In the following sections, you'll learn how to apply some of these built-in color, font, and effect settings to a presentation without changing the theme. For example, you might choose to make changes in the colors, fonts, and/or effects to customize a theme, and then save it as a custom theme, as you learned in "Creating a New Theme" earlier in this chapter.

NOTE

You can change Color, Font, and Effect themes from Slide Master view, or you can choose them from the menu that appears when you open the Variants gallery on the Design tab. In this chapter we use the Slide Master method.

Understanding Color Placeholders

To understand how PowerPoint changes colors when you choose a different theme or variant, you must know something about how PowerPoint handles colors in general.

PowerPoint uses a set of color placeholders for the bulk of its color formatting. Because each item's color is defined by a placeholder, and not as a fixed color, you can easily change the colors by switching to a different color theme. This way if you decide, for example, that you want all the slide titles to be blue rather than green, you make the change once and it is applied to all slides automatically.

A group of colors assigned to preset placeholders is a *color theme*. PowerPoint contains 20+ built-in color themes that are available regardless of the overall theme applied to the presentation. Because design themes use placeholders to define their colors, you can apply the desired design theme to the presentation and then fine-tune the colors afterward by experimenting with the built-in color themes.

How many color placeholders are there in a color theme? There are actually 12, but sometimes not all of them are available to be applied to individual objects. When you choose a color theme, the gallery of themes from which you choose shows only the first eight colors of each color theme. It doesn't matter so much here because you can't apply individual colors from there anyway. When selecting colors from a color picker (used for applying fill and border color to specific objects), as in Figure 4.10, there are 10 theme swatches. And when you define a new custom color theme, there are 12 placeholders to set up. The final two are for visited and unvisited hyperlinks; these colors aren't included in a color picker.

FIGURE 4.10

PowerPoint uses color pickers such as this one to enable you to easily apply color placeholders to objects.

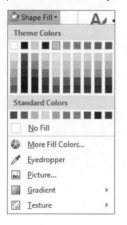

Changing the Color Theme

After applying the overall theme you want, you might want to apply different colors. One way to get different colors, as you saw earlier in this chapter, is to apply a variant. The variants are just the tip of the iceberg, though; many more color themes are available. To switch to a different color theme, follow these steps:

1. **Open Slide Master view (View ➪ Master Views ➪ Slide Master and click the desired slide master.**
2. **Click Slide Master ➪ Background ➪ Colors.** A gallery of color themes opens. See Figure 4.11.

FIGURE 4.11

Choose the desired color theme.

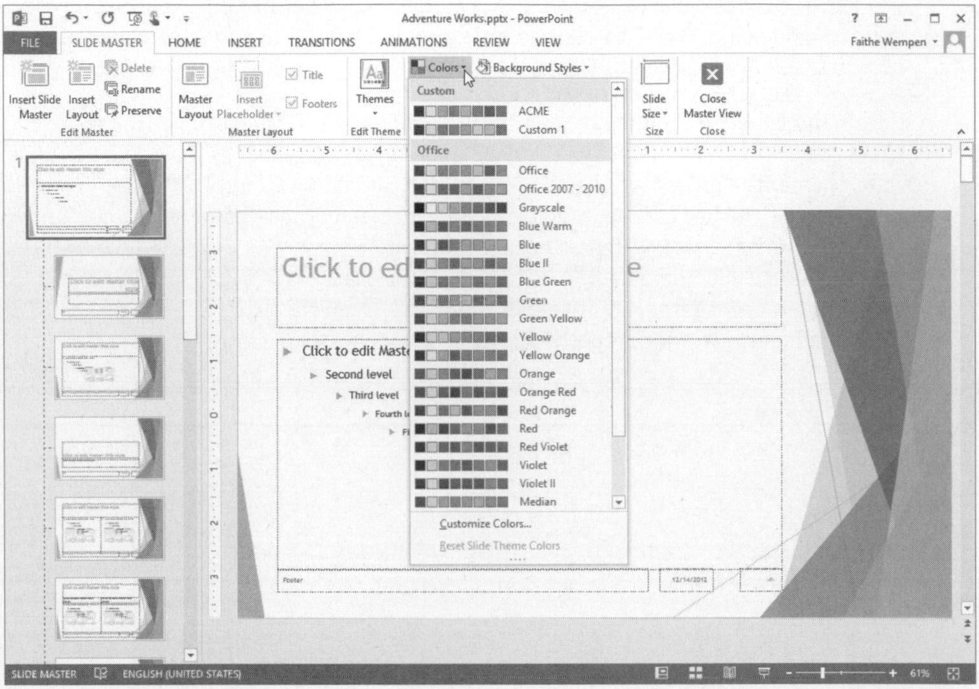

3. (Optional) Point to a color theme and observe the preview on the slide behind the list.

4. Click the desired color theme.

Understanding Font Placeholders

By default in most themes and templates, text box fonts are not set to a specific font, but to one of two designations: Heading or Body. Then a *font theme* defines what specific fonts to use. To change the fonts across the entire presentation, all you have to do is apply a different font theme.

A *font theme* is an XML-based specification that defines a pair of fonts: one for headings and one for body text. Then that font is applied to the text boxes in the presentation based on their statuses of Heading or Body. For example, all of the slide titles are usually set to Heading, and all of the content placeholders and manual text boxes are usually set to Body.

In a blank presentation (default blank template), when you click inside a slide title place-holder box, you see Calibri Light (Headings) in the Font group on the Home tab. Figure 4.12 shows that the current font is Calibri Light, and the (Headings) notation following the name indicates that it is being used only because the font theme specifies it. You could change the font theme to Verdana/Verdana, for example, and then the font designation for that box would appear as Verdana (Headings). The word (Headings) might be truncated, as it is in Figure 4.12, if your PowerPoint window is not wide enough to allow it to display in full.

FIGURE 4.12

When some text is using a font placeholder rather than a fixed font, (Headings) or (Body) appears after its name in the Font group on the Home tab.

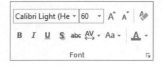

In some font themes, the same font is used for both headings and body. In many other font themes, though, the heading and body fonts are different. The default font theme for blank presentations is Calibri Light/Calibri—the same basic font, but with a thinner version for the headings.

Changing the Font Theme

After applying a design theme, you might decide you want to use different fonts in the presentation. To switch to a different font theme, follow these steps:

1. **Open Slide Master view (View ⇨ Master Views ⇨ Slide Master) and click the desired slide master.** See the note in the previous section about selecting slide masters vs. layout masters.

2. **Click Slide Master ⇨ Background ⇨ Fonts.** A gallery of font themes opens. See Figure 4.13.

3. **(Optional) Point to a font theme and observe the change on the slide behind the list.**

4. **Click the desired font theme.**

Changing the Effect Theme

Effect themes apply to several types of drawings that PowerPoint can construct, including SmartArt, charts, and drawn lines and shapes. They make the surfaces of objects formatted with 3-D attributes look like different textures (more or less shiny-looking, colors more or less deep, and so on).

4

FIGURE 4.13

Select the font theme you want for your slide.

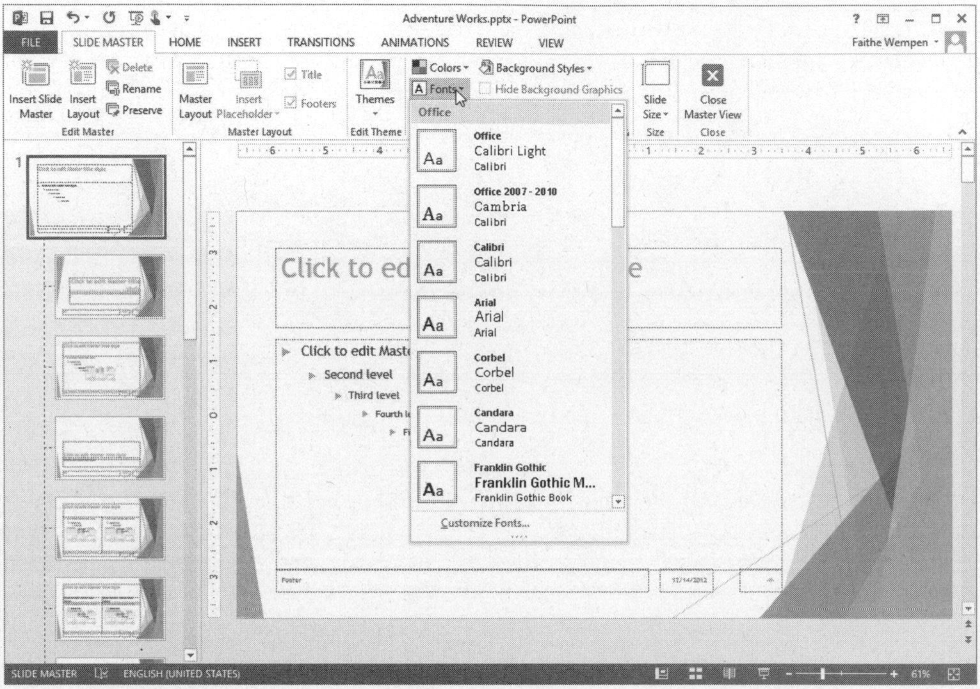

To change the effect theme, follow these steps:

1. **Open Slide Master view (View ⇨ Master Views ⇨ Slide Master) and click the desired slide master.** See the note in the previous section about selecting slide masters vs. layout masters.

2. **Click Slide Master ⇨ Background ⇨ Effects.** A menu of effect options appears. See Figure 4.14.

3. **(Optional) Point to a theme and observe the change on the slide master behind the list.** (This works only if you have an object on that slide that is affected by the effect theme; see the sidebar "Setting Up a Graphic on Which to Test Effect Themes" to set up such an object.)

4. **Click the desired effect theme.**

FIGURE 4.14

Select the desired effect theme.

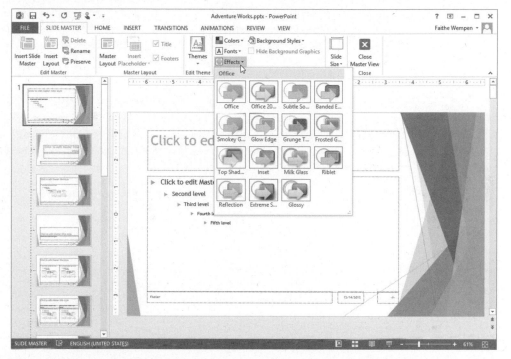

Setting Up a Graphic on Which to Test Effect Themes

Effect themes are most evident when you use colorful 3-D graphics, so do the following to construct a dummy diagram that you can use to try out effect themes:

1. **Switch to Slide Master view.**
2. **Click Insert ⇨ Illustrations ⇨ SmartArt.** The Choose a SmartArt Graphic dialog box opens.
3. **Click Cycle, click the top left diagram, and click OK.** A SmartArt diagram appears on the slide master.
4. **On the SmartArt Tools Design tab, click Change Colors, and click the first sample under Colorful.**
5. **On the SmartArt Tools Design tab, open the SmartArt Styles gallery and click the first sample under 3-D.**

Now you have a diagram on which you can see the effect themes applied. After using this diagram to help you choose the desired effect theme, delete the diagram from the slide master. To delete the diagram, select the diagram's outer frame and press the Delete key on the keyboard.

Creating a Custom Color Theme

You can define your own custom color themes, and save them for reuse in other presentations. By default these are saved in the personal folders for the logged-in user on the local PC, and they remain available to that user regardless of the theme or template in use. These custom color themes are also included if you save the design theme as a separate theme file (.thmx), so that you can take those settings to another PC or send them to some other user.

A custom color theme defines specific colors for each of the 12 color placeholders (including the two that you can't directly use—the ones for hyperlinks). To create a custom color theme, first apply a color theme to the current presentation that is as close as possible to the color theme you want. This makes it easier because you have to redefine fewer placeholders. Then follow these steps:

1. **Open Slide Master view if it is not already open (View ⇨ Master Views ⇨ Slide Master).**

2. **Click Slide Master ⇨ Background ⇨ Colors and choose Customize Colors.** The Create New Theme Colors dialog box opens.

3. **Type a name for the new color theme in the Name box, replacing the default name (Custom 1, or other number if there is already a Custom 1).**

4. **Click a color placeholder and open its menu.** See Figure 4.15.

FIGURE 4.15

Select the color for the chosen placeholder.

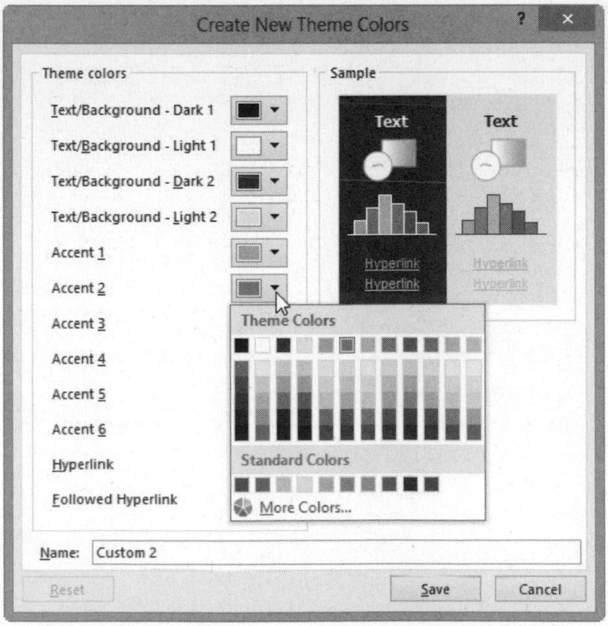

5. **Click a color in the Standard Colors section.** Or, if none of the colors there fit your needs, click More Colors, select a color from the Colors dialog box (see Figure 4.16), and click OK. The Colors dialog box has two tabs: The Standard tab has color swatches, and the Custom tab enables you to define a color numerically by its RGB (Red Green Blue) or HSL (Hue Saturation Lightness).

FIGURE 4.16

Choose a custom color if none of the standard colors is appropriate.

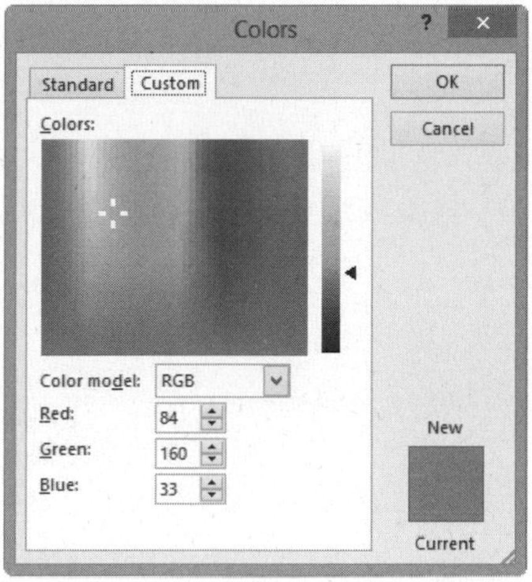

6. **Redefine any other colors as needed.**
7. **Click Save.** The color theme is saved, and now appears at the top of the Colors gallery, in the Custom area.

Creating a Custom Font Theme

You can create your own custom font themes, which are then available in all presentations. A custom font theme defines two fonts: one for headings and one for body text. To create a custom font theme, follow these steps:

1. **Open Slide Master view if it is not already open (View ⇨ Master Views ⇨ Slide Master).**
2. **Click Slide Master ⇨ Background ⇨ Fonts and choose Customize Fonts.** The Create New Theme Fonts dialog box opens. See Figure 4.17.
3. **Type a name for the new font theme in the Name box, replacing the default text there.**
4. **Open the Heading Font drop-down list and select the desired font for headings.**

FIGURE 4.17

Create a new custom font theme by specifying the fonts to use.

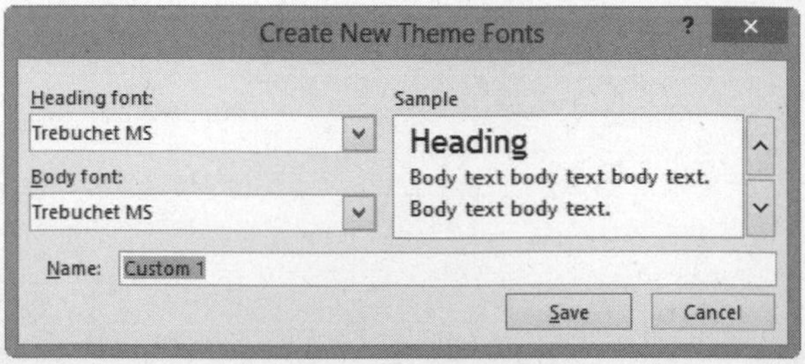

5. **Open the Body Font drop-down list and select the desired font for body text.**
6. **Click Save.** The font theme is saved, and now appears at the top of the Fonts list, in the Custom area.

> **NOTE**
> You cannot create custom effect themes.

Sharing a Custom Color or Font Theme with Others

A custom color theme or font theme is available only to the currently logged-in user on the PC on which it is created. If you want to share it with another user on the same PC, you can copy it into his or her user folder. In File Explorer (Windows Explorer), start out at C:\Users*username*\AppData\Roaming\Microsoft\Templates\Document Themes where *username* is your Windows sign-in name and then navigate to the appropriate subfolder there: Theme Colors or Theme Fonts.

The default color and font themes are located in C:\Program Files\Microsoft Office\Document Themes, in the Theme Colors or Theme Fonts folder, respectively.

Another way to share a custom color or font theme is to save the (design) theme to a theme file (.thmx). See "Creating a New Theme" earlier in this chapter. The resulting theme file will contain the custom colors and fonts.

Deleting a Custom Color or Font Theme

A custom color or font theme remains until you delete it. The easiest way to do so is to click the button for the appropriate type (Color or Font) on the Slide Master tab in Slide Master view, and then right-click the theme in the Gallery and click Delete.

You can also delete the color or font theme from outside of PowerPoint. To delete a theme color, use File Explorer (Windows Explorer) to navigate to this folder: C:\Users*username*\AppData\Roaming\Microsoft\Templates\Document Themes\Theme Colors where *username* is your Windows sign-in name, and you'll find an .xml file for each of your custom color themes. (You'll find the font themes in .xml files in the Theme Fonts folder.) Delete the files for the color or font themes that you want to delete.

Changing the Background

The *background* is the color, texture, pattern, or image that is applied to the entire slide (or slide master), on which everything else sits. By its very definition, it applies to the entire surface of the slide; you cannot have a partial background. However, you can have a *background graphic* overlaid on top of the background. A background graphic is a graphic image placed on the slide master that complements and works with the background.

It's important to understand the distinction between a background and a background graphic because even though most themes contain both, they are set up differently. Making the change you want to the overall appearance of your slides often involves changing both. For example, Figure 4.18 shows the Facet theme applied to a slide master. The slide background is pure white, and a green background graphic is overlaid on it. This background graphic is composed of several different shapes, colors with different shades of green, plus a few gray straight lines. Each of those graphic objects can be individually edited, moved, or even deleted from the slide master. The white background itself can be changed via the Format Background command.

FIGURE 4.18

A slide's background is separate from its background graphic(s) if any are present.

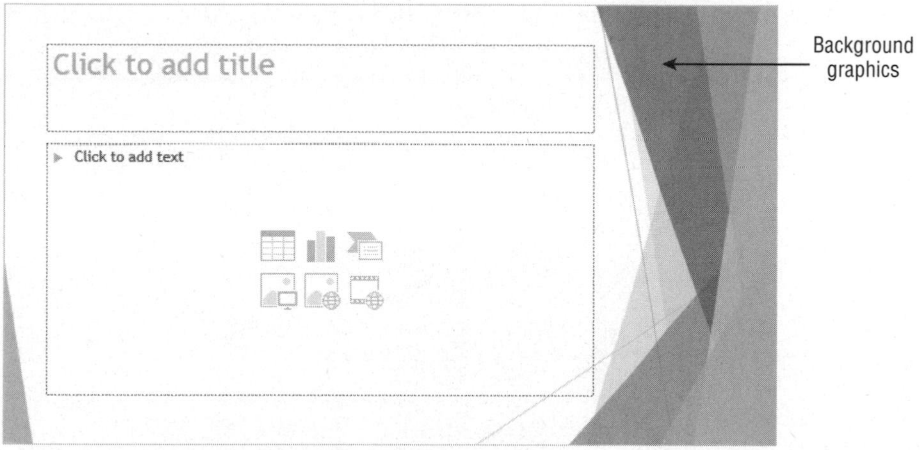

Background graphics

Most themes consist of both background formatting (even if it is just a solid color) and a background graphic. The background graphics included in the built-in themes in PowerPoint are unique to those themes, and not available as separate graphics outside of them. So, for example, if you want the colored shapes shown in Figure 4.18, the only way to get them is to apply the Facet theme. Because the decorative background graphics are unique to each theme, many people choose a theme based on the desired background graphics, and then customize the slide master's appearance to modify the theme as needed.

> **TIP**
>
> To use a background graphic from one template with the look-and-feel of another, apply the first theme to a slide, and then in Slide Master view copy the background graphic to the clipboard. Then apply the second theme and paste the graphic from the clipboard onto the second Slide Master.

Applying a Background Style

Background styles are preset background formats that come with the built-in themes in PowerPoint. Depending on the theme you apply, different background styles are available. These background styles use the color placeholders from the theme, so their color offerings change depending on the color theme applied.

To apply a background style, follow these steps:

1. **Switch to Slide Master view.**

2. **(Optional) To affect certain layouts, select the layout(s) to affect from the left pane.** To select more than one layout at once, hold down the Ctrl key as you click the layouts you want. Or, to affect all layouts, select the slide master itself.

3. **Click Slide Master ⇨ Background ⇨ Background Styles.**

   A gallery of styles appears, as shown in Figure 4.19.

FIGURE 4.19

Apply a preset background style.

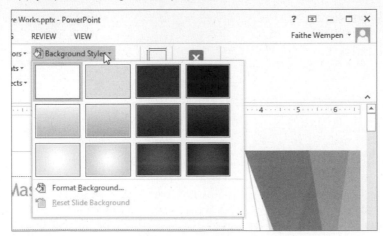

4. **Click the desired style to apply it to the selected layouts only (or to all layouts if you selected the Slide Master in step 2).** Alternatively, you can right-click the desired style and choose Apply to All Layouts to apply the change to all layouts even if you did not select the Slide Master in step 2.

You cannot customize background styles or add your own custom background styles; there are always 12 of them, and they are always determined by the theme. If you need a different background, you can apply a custom background fill, as described in the following sections, which lets you modify the background in a variety of ways.

Applying a Custom Background Fill

A custom background fill can include solid colors, gradients, textures, or graphics. Because Chapter 9 covers those fill types in more detail, this section covers how to specify your own background fill, which involves the following steps:

1. **(Optional) To affect only certain slides, select them.** You can do this in Normal, Outline, or Slide Sorter view. (Or, to affect certain layouts, go into Slide Master view and choose the layouts you want to customize, or select the slide master to customize all layouts at once.)

2. **Click Design ⇨ Customize ⇨ Format Background.** Or, if you are in Slide Master view, click Slide Master ⇨ Background ⇨ Background Styles ⇨ Format Background. The Format Background dialog box opens.

   Notice that there are three icons under the Format Background heading in the task pane: Fill, Effects, and Picture. Fill is selected by default, as shown in Figure 4.20. Each of these opens a separate set of options when clicked. However, the Effects and Picture controls are active only when certain picture or texture fills are in use, so we'll stick with the Fill settings in this procedure.

3. **Choose the option button that best describes the type of fill you want.** The controls change for the type you chose. Figure 4.20 shows the controls for a solid fill.

4. **Set the options for the fill type that you chose.** For example, in Figure 4.20, click the Color button and choose a color. The changes you make apply immediately.

⟫ See Chapter 9 for details about the fill types and how to configure their options.

5. **(Optional) To apply the change to all slides, click Apply to All.** Otherwise the change will apply only to the slides (or layouts) you selected in step 1.

6. **(Optional) To apply a different background to some other slides, select them and repeat steps 3 and 4.** The Format Background task pane can stay open as long as you need it. Its changes are applied immediately.

7. **When you are finished with the Format Background task pane, click its Close (X) button in its upper right corner to close it.**

FIGURE 4.20

With the Fill icon selected, choose the fill type that best fits your needs.

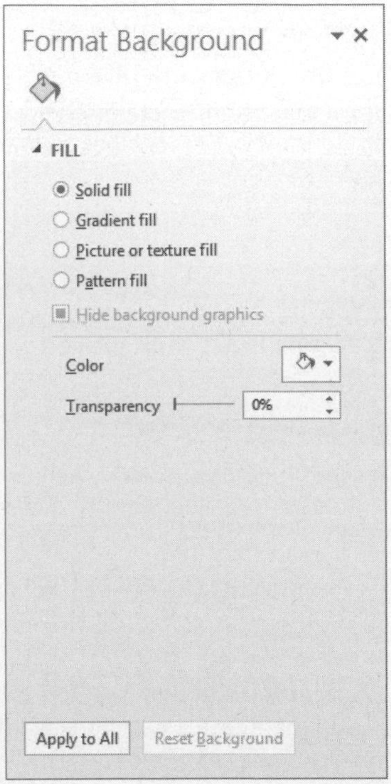

Working with Background Graphics

In Figure 4.20, one of the fill types you saw on the list was Picture or texture fill. This type of fill covers the entire background with the picture or texture that you specify.

That's not what we mean by a background graphic in this section, however. A *background graphic* in the context of the following discussion is an object or a picture overlaid on top of the background on the slide master, like those shapes I pointed out in Figure 4.18. The background graphics complement the background, and might or might not cover the entire background.

> **NOTE**
>
> Many of the theme-provided background graphics actually consist of multiple shapes, and in some cases they are grouped together. You can ungroup them, as shown in Chapter 9, so that you can modify or remove only a portion of the background graphic.

Displaying and Hiding Background Graphics

Sometimes a background graphic can get in the way of the slide's content. For example, on a slide that contains a large chart or diagram, a background graphic around the border of the slide can overlap the content. You don't have to delete the background graphic entirely to solve this problem; you can turn it off for individual slides. To hide the background graphics on one or more slides, follow these steps:

1. **Select the slide or slides to affect.**
2. **Click Design ⇨ Customize ⇨ Format Background.** The Format Background task pane opens with the Fill icon selected.
3. **Select the Hide background graphics check box.** The background graphic disappears from the slide. See Figure 4.21.

FIGURE 4.21

Mark the Hide background graphics check box to suppress the background graphics on the selected slide.

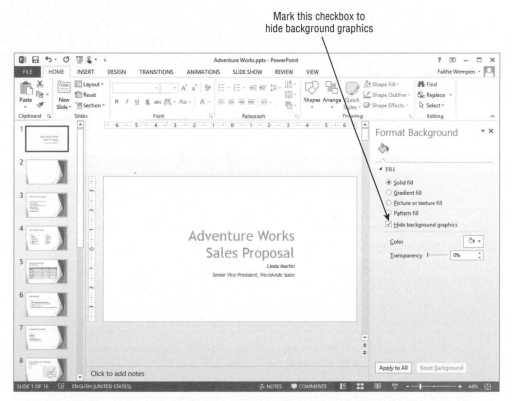

Mark this checkbox to hide background graphics

Deselect the check box to redisplay the background graphics later as needed.

If you want to hide the background graphics on all the slides that use a particular layout master or slide master, do the following:

1. **Click View ⇨ Master Views ⇨ Slide Master to enter Slide Master view.**

2. **In the left pane, select the slide master or layout master(s) to affect.**

3. **On the Slide Master tab, mark the Hide Background Graphics check box.**

Deleting Background Graphics

The background graphics reside on the slide master, so to remove one, you must use Slide Master view. Follow these steps:

1. **Click View ⇨ Master Views ⇨ Slide Master.** Slide Master view opens.

2. **Select the slide master or layout master that contains the graphic to delete.**

3. **Click the background graphic to select it.**

4. **Press the Delete key on the keyboard.**

> **TIP**
>
> Some background graphics are on the slide master itself, and others are on individual layout masters. The background graphics on the slide master trickle down to each of its layout masters, but can't be selected/deleted from the individual layout masters.
>
> To use a background graphic only on certain layouts, cut it from the slide master to the Clipboard (Ctrl+X), and then paste it individually onto each layout master desired (Ctrl+V). Alternatively, turn on the background graphic for the slide master and then use Hide Background Graphics on individual layout masters that should not contain it.

Adding Your Own Background Graphics

You can add your own background graphics, either to the slide master or to individual layout masters. This works just like adding any other graphic to a slide (see Chapter 11), except you add it to the master instead of to an individual slide.

Inserting pictures is covered in greater detail in Chapter 11, but here are the basic steps for adding a background graphic:

1. **Display the slide master or layout master on which you want to place the background graphic.**

2. **Do any of the following:**

   - Click Insert ⇨ Images ⇨ Pictures. Select a picture to insert and click Insert.
   - Click Insert ⇨ Images ⇨ Online Pictures. Search for a piece of clip art to use, or an image from another online source, and insert it on the master.
   - In any application (including PowerPoint), copy any graphic to the Clipboard by pressing Ctrl+C; then display the master and paste the graphic by pressing Ctrl+V.

> **TIP**
>
> Most of the background graphics that come with the built-in themes are either semi-transparent or use one of the placeholder colors for their fill. Therefore changing the color theme or theme variant also changes the color of the background graphic. Keep that in mind if you are creating your own background graphics; it's better to use theme colors or transparency than to use fixed colors that might clash with a color theme that you later apply.

Working with Placeholders

Recall from earlier in this chapter that when you enter Slide Master view, one or more slide masters appear in the left pane, each with its own subordinate layout masters. The slide master and each layout master has five preset placeholders that you can individually remove or move around. Figure 4.22 points them out on a slide master with the Facet theme applied, but they might be in different locations in other themes:

FIGURE 4.22

Each slide master contains these placeholders (or can contain them).

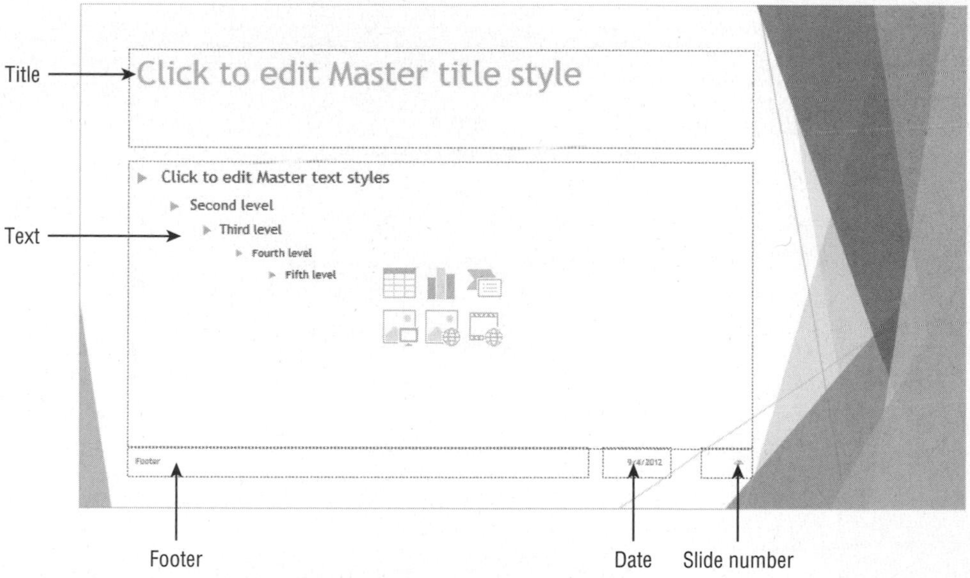

- **Title:** The placeholder for the title on each slide
- **Text:** The main content placeholder on each slide
- **Date:** The box that displays the current date on each slide

- **Slide number:** The box that displays the slide number on each slide
- **Footer:** A box that displays repeated text at the bottom of each

Each of these elements on the slide master trickles down to the layout masters beneath it, so formatting, moving, or deleting one of these elements from the slide master also changes it on each of the layouts.

Even though the placeholders are there on the slide master and/or layout master, the Date, Slide number, and Footer placeholders do not display on the slides unless you enable them. See "Displaying the Date, Number, and Footer on Slides" later in this chapter to learn how.

Formatting a Placeholder

You can format the text in each of the placeholders on the slide master just like any regular text, and that formatting carries over to all slides and layouts based on it. For example, if you format the code in the Slide Number box with a certain font and size, it will appear that way on every slide that uses that slide master. You can also format the placeholder boxes just like any other text boxes. For example, you can add a border around the page number's box, and/or fill its background with color.

TIP

If you want to make all of the text in a heading all-caps or small-caps, use the Font dialog box. To do so, from the Home tab, click the dialog box launcher in the Font group and select the Small Caps or All Caps check box there.

See Chapters 5 and 6 to learn how to format text. See Chapter 6 for more information about formatting text boxes.

Moving, Deleting, or Restoring Placeholders

You can move each of the placeholders on the slide master or an individual layout master. For example, you might decide you want the Footer box at the top of the slide rather than the bottom, or that you want to center the slide number at the bottom of the slide:

- To move a placeholder, click it to select it and then drag its border, just as you did with text boxes in Chapter 3.
- To delete one of the placeholders on the slide master, select its box and press the Delete key on the keyboard. Deleting it from the slide master deletes it from all of the associated layouts as well. It also deletes any special formatting they had, so if you add them back later, you have to reformat them.
- On an individual layout master, you can quickly delete and restore the Title and Footer placeholders by selecting or deselecting the Title and Footers check boxes on the Slide Master tab. The "footer" that this check box refers to is actually all three

of the bottom-of-the-slide elements: the actual footer, the date box, and the slide number box.

- You can also individually delete the placeholders from a layout master, the same as you can on a slide master. Just select a placeholder box and press the Delete key.

- To restore deleted Date, Footer, or Slide Number placeholders on an individual layout master, display the Slide Master tab and select the Footers check box. If any of the footer placeholders (Date, Footer, or Slide Number) were previously deleted, they reappear.

- To control the status for each of the placeholders on the slide master, select the slide master in the left pane and then click Slide Master ⇨ Master Layout ⇨ Master Layout to open the Master Layout dialog box. From there, mark the check boxes for the placeholders you want to display or hide and click OK. See Figure 4.23. This action is available only for the slide master, not for individual layout masters.

FIGURE 4.23

Set each placeholder's on/off status in the Master Layout dialog box.

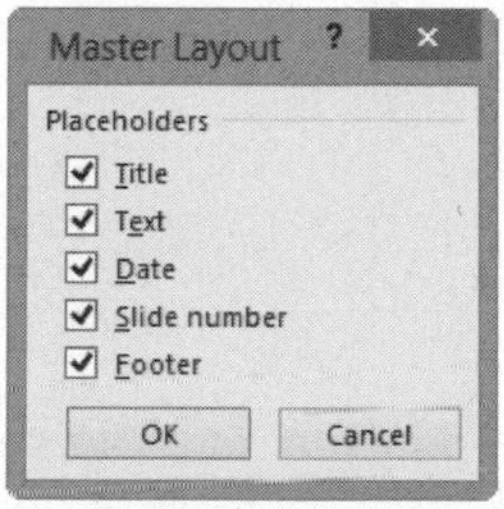

CAUTION

Restored placeholders might not appear in the same spots as they did originally; you might need to move them. To put the placeholders back to their original locations, reapply the theme from the Themes button on the Slide Master tab.

Displaying the Date, Number, and Footer on Slides

Even though the placeholders for Date, Number, and Footer might appear on the slide master, they do not appear on the actual slides in the presentation unless you enable them. This might seem counterintuitive at first, but it's actually a benefit. PowerPoint enables you to turn the date, number, and footer on and off without having to delete, recreate, or reformat their placeholders. You can decide at the last minute whether you want them to display or not, and you can choose differently for different audiences and situations.

You can control all three areas from the Header and Footer dialog box. To open it, click Insert ⇨ Text ⇨ Header and Footer. Then on the Slide tab, select the check boxes for each of the three elements that you want to use, as shown in Figure 4.24.

FIGURE 4.24

Choose which footer elements should appear on slides.

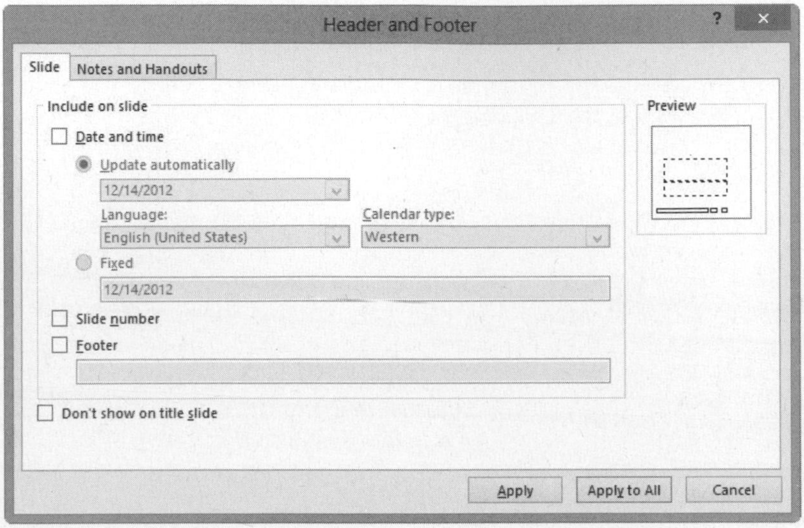

Date and Time

You can set Date and Time either to Update Automatically or to Fixed:

- **Update Automatically** pulls the current date from the computer's clock and formats it in whatever format you choose from the drop-down list. You can also select a language and a Calendar Type (although this is probably not an issue unless you are presenting in some other country than the one for which your version of PowerPoint was developed).

- **Fixed** prints whatever you enter in the Fixed text box. When Fixed is enabled, it defaults to today's date in the mm/dd/yyyy format.

> **TIP**
>
> In addition to (or instead of) placing the date on each slide, you can insert an individual instance of the current date or time on a slide, perhaps as part of a sentence. To do so, position the insertion point inside a text box or placeholder and then click Insert ➪ Text ➪ Date and Time. Select the format you want from the dialog box that appears and click OK. If the insertion point is not in an editable text area when you click Date and Time, the Header and Footer dialog box opens instead; click Cancel, reposition the insertion point, and try again.

Slide Number

This option shows the slide number on each slide, wherever the Number placeholder is positioned. You can format the Number placeholder on the slide master with the desired font, size, and other text attributes.

See Chapter 5 for more on formatting.

By default, slide numbering starts with 1. You can start with some other number if you like by following these steps:

1. **Close Slide Master view if it is open.** To do so, click Slide Master ⇨ Close ⇨ Close Master View.

2. **Click Design ⇨ Customize ⇨ Slide Size ⇨ Custom Slide Size.** The Slide Size dialog box opens.

3. **In the Number Slides From box, increase the number to the desired starting number.**

4. **Click OK.**

> **TIP**
>
> You can insert the slide number on an individual slide, either instead of or in addition to the numbering on the slide master. Position the insertion point, and then click Insert Text Insert Slide Number. If you are in Slide master view, this places a code on the slide master for the slide number that looks like this: <#>. If you are on an individual slide, it inserts the same code, but the code itself is hidden and the actual number appears. If the insertion point is not in an editable text area when you click Insert Slide Number, the Header and Footer dialog box opens instead; click Cancel, reposition the insertion point, and try again.

Footer

The footer is blank by default. Select the Footer check box, and then enter the desired text in the Footer box. You can then format the footer text from the slide master as you would any other text (see Chapter 5 for details about formatting). You can also enter the footer text in the Header and Footer dialog box's Footer text box.

Don't Show on Title Slide

This check box in the Header and Footer dialog box suppresses the date/time, page number, and footer on slides that use the Title Slide layout. Many people like to hide those elements on title slides for a cleaner look and to avoid repeated information (for example, if the current date appears in the subtitle box on the title slide).

Customizing and Creating Layouts

In addition to customizing the slide master (including working with its preset placeholder boxes, as you just learned), you can fully customize the individual layout masters.

A layout master takes some of its settings from the slide master with which it is associated. For example, by default it takes its background, fonts, theme colors, and preset placeholder positioning from the slide master. But the layout master also can be individually

4

customized; you can override the slide master's choices for background, colors, and fonts, and you can create, modify, and delete various types of content placeholders.

Understanding Content Placeholders

You can insert seven basic types of content on a PowerPoint slide: Text, Picture, Chart, Table, Diagram, Media (video or sound), and Clip Art. A placeholder on a slide master or layout master can specify one of these types of content that it will accept, or you can designate it as a Content placeholder, such that it will accept any of the seven types. Most of the layouts that PowerPoint generates automatically for its themes use the Content placeholder type because it offers the most flexibility. By making all placeholders Content placeholders rather than a specific type, PowerPoint can get by with fewer separate layout masters because users will choose the desired layout based on the positioning of the placeholders, not their types.

A Content placeholder appears as a text placeholder with a small palette of icons in the center, one for each of the content types. Each content placeholder can hold only one type of content at a time, so as soon as the user types some text into the content placeholder or clicks one of the icons in the palette and inserts some content, the placeholder becomes locked into that one type of content until the content is deleted from it.

> **NOTE**
>
> If a slide has a placeholder that contains some content (any type), selecting the placeholder and pressing Delete removes the content. To remove the placeholder itself from the layout, select the empty placeholder and press Delete. If you then want to restore the placeholder, reapply the slide layout to the slide.

You can move and resize a placeholder on a layout master as you would any other object. Drag a selection handle on the frame to resize it, or drag the border of the frame (not on a selection handle) to move it.

The Content placeholders are shown in Chapter 3 in Figure 3.10. You can also see Chapter 3 for more on moving and resizing an object.

Adding a Custom Placeholder

You can add a custom placeholder to an individual layout master. This makes it easy to build your own custom layouts.

To add a custom placeholder, follow these steps:

1. **In Slide Master view, select the layout master to affect.**

2. **On the Slide Master tab, click the bottom part of the Insert Placeholder button to open its menu.**

3. **Click Content to insert a generic placeholder, or click one of the specific content types.** See Figure 4.25. The mouse pointer becomes a cross-hair.

FIGURE 4.25

Create a new placeholder on a slide.

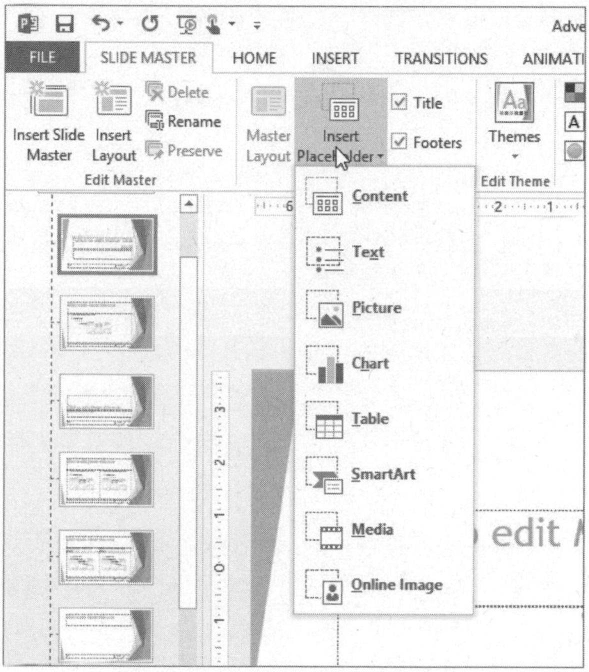

4. **Drag on the slide to draw the placeholder box of the size and position desired.**
   A rectangle appears showing where the placeholder box will go. When you release the mouse button, the new placeholder appears on the slide.

Deleting and Restoring a Custom Placeholder

To delete a custom placeholder, select it and press the Delete key, just as you learned to do earlier with the preset placeholders.

The difference between custom and preset placeholders is not in the deleting, but rather in the restoring. You can immediately undo a deletion with Ctrl+Z, but you cannot otherwise restore a deleted custom placeholder from a layout master. PowerPoint retains no memory of the content placeholders on individual layouts. Therefore, you must recreate any content placeholders that you have accidentally deleted.

> **TIP**
> To restore one of the built-in layouts, copy it from another slide master. See the sections "Duplicating and Deleting Layouts" and "Copying Layouts Between Slide Masters" later in this chapter.

Overriding the Slide Master Formatting for a Layout

You can apply formatting to a layout in almost exactly the same ways as you apply formatting to a regular slide or to a slide master. Only a few things are off-limits:

- You cannot apply a different theme to individual layouts under a common slide master. To use a different theme for some slides, you have to create a whole new slide master (covered later in this chapter).

- You cannot apply a different font, color, or effect theme, because these are related to the main theme and the slide master. If you need different fonts or colors on a certain layout, specify fixed font formatting for the text placeholders in that layout, or specify fixed color choices for objects.

For more on slide masters, see the section "Managing Slide Masters" earlier in this chapter. For more on formatting text placeholders, see Chapter 5. For more on specifying colors for objects, see Chapter 9.

- You cannot delete a background graphic that is inherited from the slide master; if you want it only on certain layouts, delete it from the slide master, and then paste it individually onto each layout desired, or select Hide Background Graphics from certain layouts.

- You cannot change the slide orientation (portrait or landscape) or the slide size.

So what *can* you do to an individual layout, then? Plenty. You can do the following:

- Apply a different background.

- Reposition, resize, or delete preset placeholders inherited from the slide master.

- Apply fixed formatting to text placeholders, including different fonts, sizes, colors, attributes, indents, and alignment.

- Apply formatting using theme colors and theme fonts.

- Apply fixed formatting to any placeholder box, including different fill and border styles and colors.

- Create manual text boxes and type any text you like into them. You might do this to include copyright notice on certain slide layouts, for example. However, keep in mind that such text boxes can't be edited on the individual slides.

- Insert pictures or clip art that should repeat on each slide that uses a certain layout.

Creating a New Layout

In addition to modifying the existing layouts, you can create your own brand-new layouts, defining the exact placeholders you want. To create a new layout, follow these steps:

1. **From Slide Master view, click the slide master with which to associate the new layout.**

2. **Click Slide Master ⇨ Edit Master ⇨ Insert Layout.** A new layout appears. Each new layout you create starts with preset placeholders inherited from the slide master for Title, Footer, Date, and Slide Number.

3. **(Optional) Hide or delete any of the preset placeholders that you don't want.**

4. **Insert new placeholders as needed.**

To insert a placeholder, see the section "Adding a Custom Placeholder" earlier in the chapter. To name the layout, see the next section "Renaming a Layout."

5. **(Optional) Name the layout.** See "Renaming a Layout" later in this chapter to do so.

NOTE

The new layout is part of the slide master, but not part of the theme. The theme is applied to the slide master, but at this point their relationship ends; and changes that you make to the slide master do not affect the existing theme. To save your custom layout(s), you have two choices: You can save the presentation as a template, or you can save the theme as a separate file. You learned about saving themes in "Managing Themes" earlier in this chapter.

Renaming a Layout

Layout names can help you determine the purpose of a layout if it is not obvious from viewing its thumbnail image.

To change the name of a layout, or to assign a name to a new layout you've created, follow these steps:

1. **In Slide Master view, right-click the layout and choose Rename Layout.** The Rename Layout dialog box opens.

2. **Type a new name for the layout, replacing the existing name.**

3. **Click Rename.**

Duplicating and Deleting Layouts

You might want to copy a layout to get a head start on creating a new one. To copy a layout, right-click the layout in Slide Master view and choose Duplicate Layout. A copy of the layout appears below the original.

If you are never going to use a certain layout, you might as well delete it; every layout you can delete makes the file a little bit smaller. To delete a layout, right-click the layout in Slide Master view and choose Delete Layout.

4

CAUTION

You might have a couple of layouts at the bottom of the list that employ vertical text. These are for users of Asian languages. They show up in the New Slide and Layout galleries on the home tab if you have certain Asian languages enabled on your system. Don't delete them if you will sometimes need to create Asian-language slides.

Copying Layouts Between Slide Masters

When you create additional slide masters in the presentation, any custom layouts you've created for the existing slide masters do not carry over. You must manually copy them to the new slide master.

To copy a layout from one slide master to another, follow these steps:

1. **In Slide Master view, select the layout to be copied.**
2. **Press Ctrl+C.**
3. **Select the slide master under which you want to place the copy.**
4. **Press Ctrl+V.**

You can also copy layouts between slide masters in different presentations. To do so, open both presentation files, and then perform the previous steps. The only difference is that after step 2, you must switch to the other presentation's Slide Master view.

Managing Slide Masters

Let's review the relationship one more time between slide masters and themes. A theme is a set of formatting specs (colors, fonts, and effects) that can be used in PowerPoint, Word, or Excel. Themes are not applied directly to slides—they are applied to slide masters, which govern the formatting of slides. The slide masters exist within the presentation file itself. You can change them by applying different themes, but they are essentially "built in" to the presentation file.

When you change to a different theme for all of the slides in the presentation, your slide master changes its appearance. You can tweak that appearance in Slide Master view. As long as all of the slides in the presentation use the same theme, you need only one slide master. However, if you apply a different theme to some of your slides, you need another slide master, because a slide master can have only one theme applied to it at a time. PowerPoint automatically creates the additional slide master(s) for you when you apply a different design to some slides but not to others.

If you later reapply a single theme to all of the slides in the presentation, you do not need multiple slide masters anymore, so the unused one is automatically deleted. In addition to all this automatic creation and deletion of slide masters, you can also manually create and delete slide masters on your own. Any slide masters that you create manually are automatically preserved, even if they aren't always in use. You must manually delete them if you don't want them anymore.

In the following sections, you learn how to create and delete slide masters manually, and how to rename them. You also learn how to lock one of the automatically created slide masters so that PowerPoint does not delete it if it falls out of use.

Creating and Deleting Slide Masters

To create another slide master, start out in Slide Master view (of course), and then click Slide Master ⇨ Edit Master ⇨ Insert Slide Master. The new slide master appears below the existing slide master(s) and all its individual layout masters in the left pane of Slide Master view. From there, just start customizing it. You can apply a theme to it, modify its layouts and placeholders, and all the usual things you can do to a slide master. Another way to create a new slide master is to duplicate an existing one. To do this, right-click the existing slide master and choose Duplicate Master.

To delete a slide master, select it in Slide Master view (make sure you select the slide master itself, not just one of its layouts) and press the Delete key. If any of that slide master's layouts were applied to any slides in the presentation, those slides automatically convert to the default slide master's equivalent layout. If no exact layout match is found, PowerPoint does its best: it uses its default Title and Content layout and includes any extra content as orphaned items.

Renaming a Slide Master

Slide master names appear as category headings on the Layout list as you are selecting layouts. For example, in Figure 4.26, the slide master names are Facet and Ion.

To rename a slide master, follow these steps:

1. **In Slide Master view, right-click the slide master and choose Rename Master.** The Rename Master dialog box opens.
2. **Type a new name for the master, replacing the existing name.**
3. **Click Rename.**

Preserving a Slide Master

Unless you have created the slide master yourself, it is temporary. Slide masters come and go as needed, as you format slides with various themes. To lock a slide master so that it doesn't disappear when no slides are using it, right-click the slide master and choose Preserve Master, or click Slide Master ⇨ Edit Master ⇨ Preserve. The Preserve button on the Slide Master tab appears selected, indicating the slide master is preserved. To unpreserve it, click the Preserve button again, or right-click the slide master again and choose Preserve Master. See Figure 4.27.

4

FIGURE 4.26

Slide master names form the category titles on the Layout list.

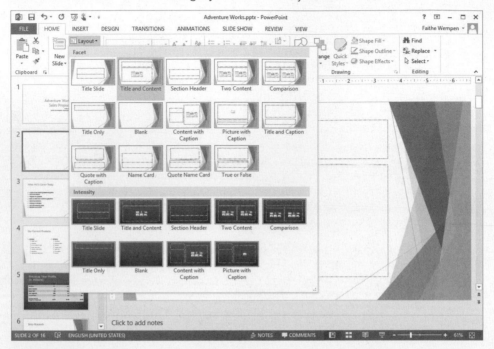

FIGURE 4.27

The Preserve Master command saves a slide master so that PowerPoint cannot automatically delete it.

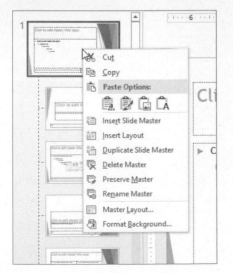

Summary

In this chapter you learned how themes and slide masters make it easy to apply consistent formatting in a presentation, and how layout masters are associated with slide masters and provide consistent layouts for the slides based on them. You learned how to create, edit, rename, and delete themes, masters and layouts, and how to copy themes between presentations.

Now that you know how to format entire presentations using themes, you're ready to start learning how to make exceptions to the formatting rules that the themes impose. In the next chapter you will learn how to format text in PowerPoint, and apply different fonts, sizes, attributes, and special effects. You can use this knowledge to make strategic changes to the text placeholders on slide masters to further customize your themes, or you can make changes to text on individual slides on a case-by-case basis to make certain slides stand out from the rest.

4

Formatting Text

IN THIS CHAPTER

Changing the font and font size

Adjusting character spacing

Changing font color/text fill

Applying text attributes and effects

Applying WordArt styles

Copying formatting with Format Painter

Inserting symbols

Inserting math equations

*T*ext formatting is formatting that you can apply to individual characters of text. It includes font (typeface), size, attributes such as bold and underline, fill color, and border color. (Formatting that affects entire paragraphs only, such as indentation or bullet style, is called *paragraph formatting*, not text formatting, and is covered in Chapter 6, "Formatting Paragraphs and Text Boxes.")

As you learned in Chapter 4,"Working with Layouts, Themes, and Masters," PowerPoint automates text formatting by applying themes to slide masters. The slide masters then dictate the default text size, font, color, and attributes that should be used on slides. By applying text formatting through the slide masters, rather than to individual slides, you ensure consistency and make it much easier to make global font and text formatting changes later on.

However, you may need to change the formatting of some text. For example, the font size for titles on the slide master may be a bit too large; in this case, you can decrease the font size for the Title placeholder, and this change will apply to all of the layouts for that master. You can even save the changes to a new theme file so that you can reuse the theme with the smaller title text later on.

In some cases, you might need to manually change the text formatting for an individual text box, or even an individual paragraph or word. For example, you may create text boxes manually that label the parts of a diagram; in this case, you would probably want to use a fixed font and size for those labels, so that they do not change if you switch themes later on.

Changing the Font

There are several ways to change the font that is used in a presentation. Whenever possible, in order to maintain consistency, you should use the method that affects an entire slide master. However, in some cases, you may need to change the font in an individual text box, or even individual characters within the text box. Office 2013 comes with a lot of different fonts, and you may also have acquired some additional fonts by installing other programs. A *font* is a typeface, or a style of lettering. To see an example of two different font styles, compare the lettering of the preceding heading to the lettering in this paragraph.

> **NOTE**
>
> In the past, when most fonts were not scalable, a distinction was sometimes drawn between the term "typeface" — referring to a certain style of lettering — and the term "font" — which referred to a specific typeface used at a certain size, with a certain combination of attributes, such as bold and italic. Nowadays, however, the terms font and typeface are synonymous for all practical purposes.

Windows fonts are generic — that is, they work with any program. For example, a font that came with a desktop publishing program such as Adobe InDesign also works with Microsoft Word and with PowerPoint. Within PowerPoint, you have access to all of the installed Windows fonts on your system.

The majority of the fonts that come with Windows and Office are *outline fonts*, which means that they consist of unfilled, mathematically created outlines of each character. When you assign a size, you are sizing the outline; each outline is then filled in with black (or whatever color you choose) to form each character. As a result, these fonts look good at any size.

In terms of appearance, there are two basic groups of fonts: *serif* (those with little tails on each letter, such as the small horizontal lines at the bases of the letters i and t) and *sans-serif* (those without the tails). The regular paragraph text in this book uses a serif font. The headings use a sans-serif font.

Choosing the Right Fonts

A font can make a tremendous difference in the readability and appeal of your presentation, so selecting the right ones is very important. But how do you choose from among all of the fonts that are installed on your system? Here are some general rules:

- Strive for consistency. (Yes, I keep harping on that, but it's important.) You should avoid changing the font on an individual slide, and instead, make font changes to the slide master, or, in some cases, to a master layout.
- Whenever possible, rather than choosing a fixed font, use the (Headings) or (Body) placeholders at the top of the Font menu (see Figure 5.1). You can then redefine

WEMPEN, FAITHE.

MICROSOFT POWERPOINT 2013 BIBLE.

                            Paper   804 P.
HOBOKEN: JOHN WILEY, 2013

GUIDEBOOK.

LCCN 2012-924233
  ISBN 1118488113   **Library PO#** FIRM ORDERS

	List	39.99	USD
8395 NATIONAL UNIVERSITY LIBRAR	**Disc**	5.0%	
App. Date 3/18/15 E-SETC-CS 8214-08	**Net**	37.99	USD

SUBJ: MICROSOFT POWERPOINT (COMPUTER FILE)

CLASS P93.53   DEWEY# 005.58   LEVEL GEN-AC

YBP Library Services

WEMPEN, FAITHE.

MICROSOFT POWERPOINT 2013 BIBLE.

                            Paper   804 P.
HOBOKEN: JOHN WILEY, 2013

GUIDEBOOK.

  LCCN 2012-924233
  ISBN 1118488113   **Library PO#** FIRM ORDERS

	List	39.99	USD
8395 NATIONAL UNIVERSITY LIBRAR	**Disc**	5.0%	
App. Date 3/18/15 E-SETC-CS 8214-08	**Net**	37.99	USD

SUBJ: MICROSOFT POWERPOINT (COMPUTER FILE)

CLASS P93.53   DEWEY# 005.58   LEVEL GEN-AC

those placeholders using a font theme. This makes it much easier to change the fonts for the entire presentation later on.

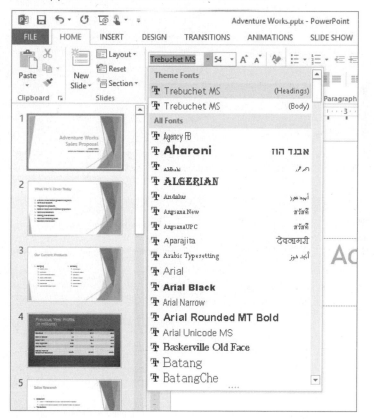

For more on font themes, see Chapter 4.

FIGURE 5.1

Fonts appear on the Fonts list on the Home tab.

- Try to use a sans-serif font for the "Headings" font, because sans-serif is easier to read at large sizes.
- Some people recommend using serif fonts for the body if the presentation is very text-heavy, because serif fonts are easier to read in long paragraphs (such as in this book) However, for on-screen presentations, sans-serif is more accessible. See this article for details about fonts and accessibility: http://webaim.org /techniques/fonts/#screenfonts.

- Avoid serif fonts for tiny text, because the serifs tend to break up on-screen at small sizes.

- Avoid script fonts in presentations, because they are hard to read.

- Avoid novelty fonts, because they take the focus away from your message.

Another consideration when choosing fonts is whether the PC on which you present the show is likely to have the same fonts installed. If you stick with Windows-supplied fonts such as Arial and Times New Roman, which are available in Windows XP and newer versions, this is a non-issue. However, if you use a font that came with Office 2007 and later only, such as Calibri or Cambria, but you plan to present on a PC that uses Office 2003 or earlier, then you might want to embed the fonts in the presentation when you are saving it. If you present or edit the show on a PC that does not have the right fonts, and the fonts are not embedded, then PowerPoint will use fonts that are as close as possible to a match. Although this is helpful, it can also cause strange and unexpected line breaks in your text.

TIP

When you install the free Compatibility Pack in PowerPoint 2003 or earlier, it not only enables you to open PowerPoint 2007 and later files, but it also installs the fonts introduced in PowerPoint 2007 such as Calibri.

TIP

To embed fonts when saving the presentation, choose Tools ⇨ Save Options in the Save As dialog box. Select the Embed Fonts in the File check box, and click OK.

If you end up on the other side of that equation and are stuck with a presentation that uses fonts that your system doesn't have, use Replace Fonts to replace all instances of the missing font with one that is available on your PC. See "Replacing Fonts" later in this chapter.

Changing the Font Theme

Choosing a different font theme is covered in Chapter 4 because of the connection between themes and fonts, but let's have another look at it here in the context of font formatting. A font theme is a specification that names two fonts: one for headings (titles) and one for body text (everything else). Font themes apply to all text that uses the font placeholders rather than a fixed font. To switch to a different font theme, follow these steps:

1. **Switch to Slide Master view (View ⇨ Slide Master).**

2. **If you have more than one slide master in this presentation, click the slide master you want to affect.**

NOTE

Any of that slide master's layout masters can be selected in the left pane; you do not have to select the slide master thumbnail itself in order to apply the font theme change to all layouts in that slide master.

3. **Click Slide Master ⇨ Background ⇨ Fonts.** The Fonts menu opens to display samples of the available font themes. These include both built-in font themes and any custom themes that you've created.

4. **Hover the mouse pointer over a theme to see it previewed on the master behind the open menu.**

5. **Click the font theme that you want to apply.**

6. **Click Slide Master ⇨ Close ⇨ Close Master View to exit from Slide Master view.**

To create your own custom font themes, see Chapter 4.

TIP

You have to be in Slide Master view to change the font theme because the Slide Master tab is the only place you can access the Font Theme button. However, if you add that button to the Quick Access toolbar, you can access it from Normal view too.

Applying a Fixed Font

If you apply a specific font to some text, that text will no longer use the font that is specified by the font theme. That font will not change when you change the presentation's overall font theme or when you change to a different overall theme.

If this is what you want, then you have two ways to apply a specific font: from the Home tab or from the mini toolbar.

To apply a font from the Home tab, follow these steps:

1. **Select the text to be formatted.** It can be on a slide master (most preferable for consistency's sake), on a layout master, or on an individual slide.

2. **On the Home tab, in the Font group, open the Font drop-down list (Figure 5.1).**

3. **Point to a font other than the ones designated (Headings) and (Body).** The selected text is previewed in that font.

4. **Click the font that you want.** PowerPoint applies the font to the text.

If you want to return to using the theme fonts, select the "Headings" or the "Body" font from the top of the menu.

The *mini toolbar* is just what it sounds like — a small toolbar. It appears above and to the right of selected text. When the mouse pointer is directly on top of the selected text, the mini toolbar appears dimmed, but if you move your mouse up to the mini toolbar, it becomes fully visible.

5

To apply a font from the mini toolbar, follow these steps:

1. **Select the text to be formatted.** It can be on a slide master (most preferable), on a layout master, or on an individual slide.

2. **Hover the mouse pointer over the selection so that the mini toolbar appears, as shown in Figure 5.2.** If it does not appear, right-click the selection.

FIGURE 5.2

Use the mini toolbar to apply a font.

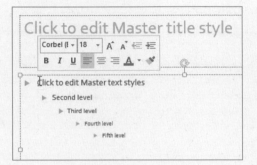

3. **On the mini toolbar, open the Font drop-down list.**

4. **Point to a font other than the ones marked (Headings) or (Body).** The selected text is previewed in that font.

5. **Click the font that you want.** PowerPoint applies the font to the text.

Using the Font Dialog Box

The Font dialog box (shown in Figure 5.3) provides a third way of changing the font. It also gives you access to the controls for setting font size, color, and attributes, all of which you will learn about later in this chapter.

To open the Font dialog box, click the dialog launcher in the Font group on the Home tab. Then make your selections in the dialog box, just as you would from the Home tab's Font group. Notice in Figure 5.3 that the Font drop-down list is labeled Latin Text Font. In this case, "Latin" just means regular text characters.

Replacing Fonts

If you restrain yourself from using a lot of manual text formatting, and rely on the theme to control the way the text appears, you should not have a problem with inconsistent font usage. Whenever you need to make a change, you can do it once on the slide master and be done with it.

FIGURE 5.3

The Font dialog box provides access to many different text-formatting controls, as well as the font list.

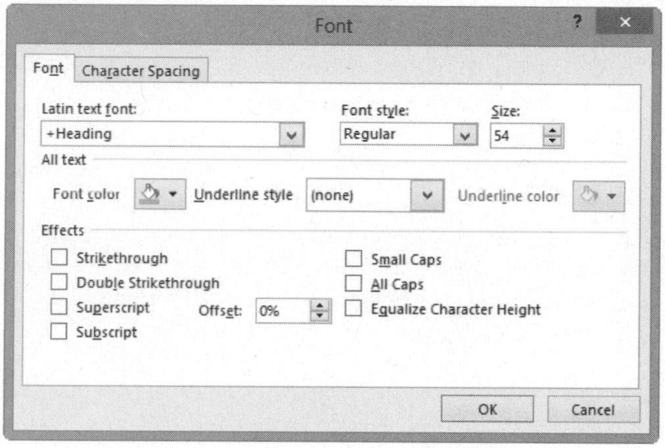

However, not everyone can be counted on to show such discipline and good design sense as you. Suppose your coworker created a long presentation in which he sporadically applied a certain font for some special elements. Now you need to work on that presentation, but you don't have that font. You will need to go through and hunt for all instances of that font and change them to some other font. Fortunately, PowerPoint has a Replace Fonts feature that can help you to find all of these instances. Follow these steps:

1. **On the Home tab, click the down arrow for the Replace button and choose Replace Fonts.** The Replace Font dialog box appears, as shown in Figure 5.4.

   FIGURE 5.4

   Replace all instances of one font with another.

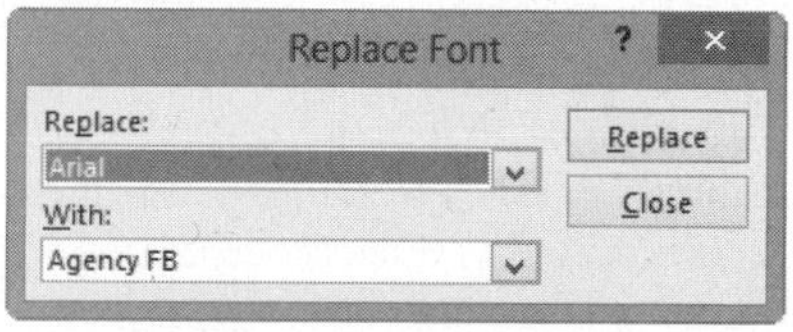

2. **In the Replace drop-down list, select the font that you want to replace.** Only the fonts that are currently in use in the presentation appear on this list, and so it's easy to navigate.

3. **In the With drop-down list, select the desired replacement font.** All of the available fonts on your system appear here.

4. **Click Replace.** All of the instances of that font are replaced.

5. **Repeat steps 2 to 4 to replace another font, or click Close when you're finished.**

5

CAUTION
Replacing the theme fonts makes the placeholders no longer respond to font theme changes. You have to reset the slide master by reapplying the Headings or Body fonts to the placeholders if you "un-theme" them using Replace Fonts.

Changing the Font Size

Each theme has a specified font size that it uses for titles and for body text, with different sizes typically used for different levels of bulleted lists. You can use the default settings, or you can edit the placeholders on the slide master to change them. In some cases, you might also need to change the size of an individual block of text on an individual slide.

NOTE
As you learned at the end of Chapter 3, PowerPoint has an AutoFit or Resize Shape feature that you can turn on or off for each text box. When enabled, AutoFit permits the text size to shrink so that the text fits into the text box, or Resize Shape to Fit Text permits the text box to grow so that the text fits at its current size. However, AutoFit does not change the text's font size as applied by the Font Size setting; if you enlarge the text box, the text goes back to its regular size.

Choosing the Right Sizes

The size of the text is just as important as the font. If the text is too large, it looks unattractive and amateurish, but if it's too small, the people in the back row won't be able to follow along.

Font size is measured in points, and each point measures 1/72 of an inch when printed. However, PowerPoint slides are usually shown on a screen rather than in print, and so the appropriate font size depends mainly upon the presentation medium. For example, a 72-point letter on a 15-inch monitor is very different than a 72-point letter on a 12-foot projection screen.

The default sizes that are specified in the built-in themes provide you with a good starting point. You can increase or decrease the sizes on the slide masters as necessary. Here are some things to consider when choosing font size:

- The farther away the audience will be sitting from the slides, and the smaller the display screen, the larger the text should be.
- Very thick and very thin letters are harder to read at small sizes. A font of moderate thickness is most readable.
- Very tight spacing can make thick letters difficult to read; on the other hand, very loose spacing can emphasize the individual letters to the point where the words

they comprise are not as obvious. See the section "Adjusting Character Spacing" later in this chapter.

■ If any of your slide titles are so long that they wrap to an additional line within the title placeholder box, consider slightly decreasing the font size for the title placeholder on the slide master so that the wrapping doesn't occur. Make your changes to the slide master — not the individual slide on which the problem occurs. This is because audiences find it jarring when the slide title is not in the same place or not the same size on every slide.

Specifying a Font Size

The Font Size drop-down list, shown in Figure 5.5, is on the Home tab and is actually also an input box. You can click it and type a font size directly into the text box, or you can open the drop-down list and select a value. Typing your own value is useful if the size that you want doesn't appear on the list. At the smaller sizes, the list increments by one point, but at the larger sizes, it makes bigger jumps, and so not all values are available.

FIGURE 5.5

Select a font size from the drop-down list, or click in the Font Size text box and type a value.

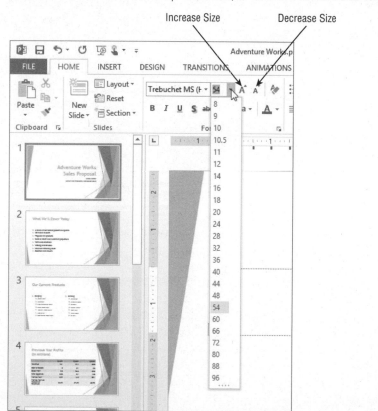

As a shortcut, you can also use the Increase Font and Decrease Font buttons, which are available both on the Home Ribbon and on the mini toolbar. They are shown in Figure 5.5, and they increase or decrease the font size by one position on the Font Size list. (As noted earlier, for the smaller sizes, the increment occurs at one point at a time, but for larger sizes there is more of a jump between sizes.) You can also use the following keyboard shortcuts:

- Increase Font: Ctrl+Shift+>
- Decrease Font: Ctrl+Shift+<

Adjusting Character Spacing

Character spacing is the amount of blank space between individual letters. You can adjust this spacing to make more or less text fill a text box. Character spacing can affect the appearance and readability of both titles and body text, and Figure 5.6 shows examples of the various character spacing presets that are available with examples of how it affects your text.

FIGURE 5.6

Character spacing, which you set from the Home tab, affects the appearance and readability of your text.

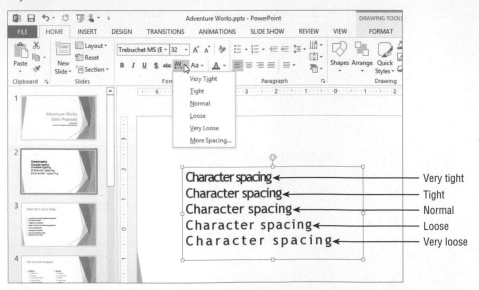

To adjust character spacing, select the text and then choose a setting from the Character Spacing drop-down menu on the Home tab.

To set custom spacing, choose More Spacing from the drop-down menu. This opens the Font dialog box to the Character Spacing tab, as shown in Figure 5.7.

FIGURE 5.7

Adjust character spacing and kerning using custom settings in the Font dialog box.

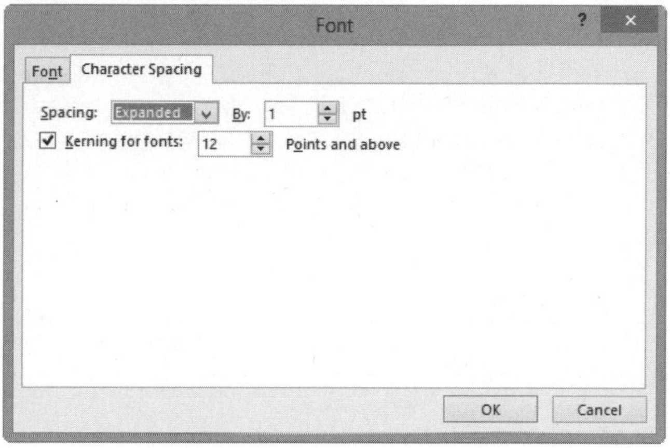

To set custom spacing, choose either Expanded or Condensed from the Spacing list, and then enter a number of points by which to expand or condense. As a point of reference, Table 5.1 lists the presets from Figure 5.6 and their expand/condense values; use these as a basis for fine-tuning.

TABLE 5.1 **Equivalent Expanded/Condensed Settings for Character Spacing Presets**

Preset	Custom Spacing Equivalent
Very Tight	Condense by 3 points
Tight	Condense by 1.5 points
Normal	Normal
Loose	Expand by 3 points
Very Loose	Expand by 6 points

You can also adjust kerning in the Font dialog box. *Kerning* decreases the amount of space between two letters, based upon their shapes. For example, when capital letters A and V appear next to each other, you can reduce the space between them without them overlapping because of their shapes. Kerning takes the shapes of the letters into account as it selectively tightens the spacing. Kerning looks best when you apply it to large text, and so the Kerning for Fonts setting enables you to specify a minimum font size below which text is not kerned, as shown in Figure 5.7.

Changing Font Color/Text Fill

To set the font color for individually selected text, use the Font Color button on the Home tab, or use the Text Fill button on the Drawing Tools Format tab in the WordArt Styles group. Why are there two buttons that do the same thing? Well, they don't do *exactly* the same thing. The Font Color button on the Home tab applies only simple, solid-color formatting, and is available even in legacy presentations (that is, presentations in PowerPoint 97-2003 format). The Text Fill button on the Drawing Tools Format tab has a wider array of fill options, including gradients, textures, and even picture fills. It is available only in a PowerPoint 2007 or later presentation. Figure 5.8 shows these two buttons and their menus.

FIGURE 5.8

The Font Color button (left) and the Text Fill button (right) can both apply solid-color formatting, but only the Text Fill button can apply special fill effects.

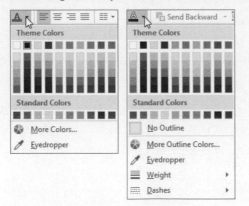

TIP

The Eyedropper command on the menus in Figure 5.8 enables you to pick up any color on any object in the presentation. When you choose it, the mouse pointer becomes an eyedropper graphic, with a square floating nearby it. Hover the eyedropper over an object so that the desired color appears in the square, and then click. You can use the Eyedropper tool for text, drawn objects, text box backgrounds, and just about anything else to which you can assign a color in PowerPoint.

For text color and fill, as with the colors of all objects, it is usually best to stick with the theme color placeholders rather than using fixed colors. This way, if you want to change the color theme or the overall theme later on, the colors will automatically update. This doesn't necessarily mean that you have to forego special fill effects; you just have to base them on theme colors. For example, if you're creating a gradient effect, you should use two theme colors for the gradient.

For more on color placeholders, see Chapter 4. For more on special fill effects, see Chapter 9.

Applying a Text Outline

PowerPoint 2013 can apply graphics-like formatting to any text. For example, you can apply outlines to text, just as you can apply borders to drawn shapes, text boxes, or other objects. Figure 5.9 shows some text with an outline.

FIGURE 5.9

You can apply borders to regular text.

By default, text has no outline. To apply an outline, select the text and then choose a color from the Text Outline button in the WordArt Styles group on the Drawing Tools Format tab. You can choose either a theme color or a standard (fixed) color. You can also choose an outline weight from the Weight submenu, as shown in Figure 5.10. Chapter 9 covers object outlines (borders) in more detail.

> **NOTE**
>
> You can also apply dashes to the text outline, although this is usually not a good idea for text. Dashes are more suitable for the borders of larger objects.

Applying Text Attributes

Text attributes are modifiers that you apply to the text, such as bold, italics, underline, strikethrough, shadow, and so on. PowerPoint offers several attributes, as shown in Figure 5.11.

5

FIGURE 5.10

You can apply a text outline color, as well as a different line thickness, or weight.

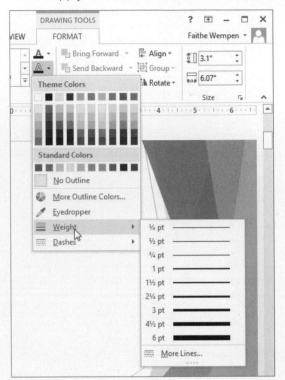

FIGURE 5.11

Text attributes that are available in PowerPoint 2013.

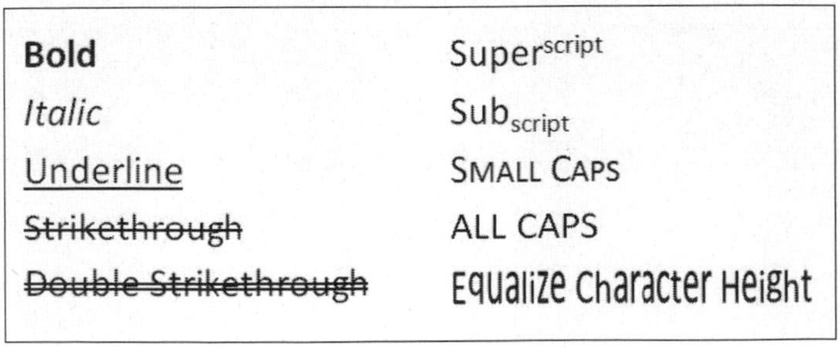

Bold   Super^script

Italic   Sub_script

<u>Underline</u>   SMALL CAPS

~~Strikethrough~~   ALL CAPS

~~Double Strikethrough~~   Equalize Character Height

There are actually several types of text attributes, and they can be divided into the following major groups:

- Bold and italic are actually considered *font styles*. You can apply one of these four styles to your text: Regular, Bold, Italic, or Bold Italic. In some fonts, each of these styles is formed with a separate character set that is embedded in the font file, and the letters are actually different shapes. However, in other fonts, bold is simulated by making each character a little thicker, and italics are simulated by tilting each character to the right. Figure 5.12 shows the difference between these font types.

FIGURE 5.12

Some fonts use different character sets for bold and italic, while others do not.

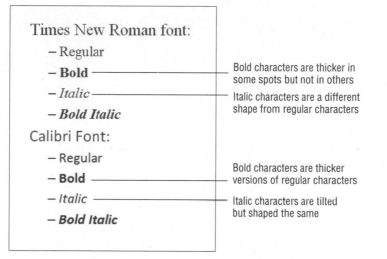

- Some attributes apply an effect on top of — or in addition to — the text. These include underlining, strikethrough, and double strikethrough.

- Superscript and Subscript attributes are used for setting off symbols and numbers for footnotes, chemical notations, exponents, and so on. They raise or lower the affected text and also shrink it by about 30 percent (this is the default setting, although you can also customize the percentage).

- Shadow formatting takes two forms. If you apply it with the button in the Font group, then it is available in all presentations, even legacy ones, and it simply places a slightly offset gray copy behind the characters. You can also apply shadow formatting from the WordArt Styles group to create different types of shadows.

- All Caps formatting appears to change lowercase letters to their uppercase equivalents. However, they are not really uppercase; they're just formatted this way. Removing the All Caps attribute returns the text to its normal appearance.

- Small Caps formatting is similar to All Caps except that letters that are normally lowercase appear slightly smaller than letters that were already uppercase to begin with.

5

NOTE

Small Caps formatting was not available in versions of PowerPoint prior to 2007, and if you save the presentation in PowerPoint 97-2003 format and open it in an earlier version, the Small Caps attribute is removed.

- Equalize Character Height formatting forces each letter to be the full height that is allotted for capital letters. This distorts the letters and is most useful when working with shaped WordArt text (which is covered later in this chapter).

As shown in Figure 5.13, the five most popular text attributes appear as toggle buttons in the Font group on the Home tab. They are Bold, Italic, Underline, Shadow, and Strikethrough.

FIGURE 5.13

Use the Font group's buttons for these five attributes.

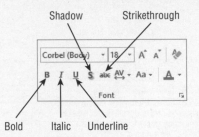

The other attributes are available in the Font dialog box. You can access them by following these steps:

1. **On the Home tab, click the dialog box launcher in the Font group.** The Font dialog box opens, as shown in Figure 5.14.

2. **In the Font Style drop-down list, choose the combination of bold and italic that you want: Regular, Bold, Italic, or Bold and Italic.**

3. **Choose a text color from the Font Color drop-down list.** (You learned about font color earlier in this chapter.)

4. **If you want underlined text, choose an Underline Style from the drop-down list.** The default color for an underline is the same as the color of the text; if you want a different color, you can choose it from the Underline Color drop-down list.

5. **In the Effects section, select or deselect the check boxes for any attributes that you want.** Some of these attributes are mutually exclusive, and so one is deselected when you select the other:

   - Strikethrough and Double-strikethrough
   - Superscript and Subscript
   - All Caps and Small Caps

6. **Click OK to apply your choices.**

FIGURE 5.14

Choose font attributes from the Font dialog box.

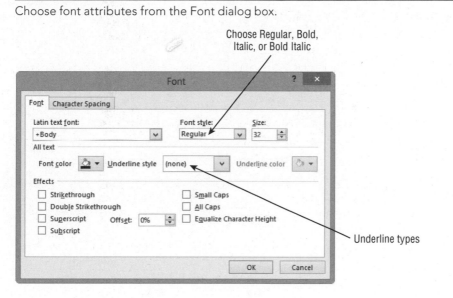

Changing Text Case

Each character has a numeric value stored in the presentation file, and uppercase character numbers are completely different from their lowercase counterparts. For example, a capital B is not just formatted differently from a lowercase b — it is a different character.

As you learned in the preceding section, you can apply the All Caps attribute to some text to force it to appear in all uppercase format, but this is just an illusion. The identifying numbers for the characters have not changed; they're just wearing a mask. When you remove the attribute, the characters go back to the way they normally look.

If you want to *really* change the case of some text, including changing the numeric identifiers for the characters behind the scenes, then you must either retype the text or use the Change Case feature. You can access the Change Case attribute in the Font group on the Home tab, as shown in Figure 5.15. Change Case enables you to set a block of text to any of the following settings:

- **Sentence case.** Capitalizes the first letter of the first word in the sentence, and the first letter of the first word after a sentence-ending punctuation mark such as a period.
- **Lowercase.** Converts all characters to lowercase that are not already so. (It does not do anything to numbers or symbols.)
- **Uppercase.** Converts all characters to uppercase that are not already so. (It does not do anything to numbers or symbols.)

5

FIGURE 5.15

Change the case of the selected text by selecting a Change Case option from the menu.

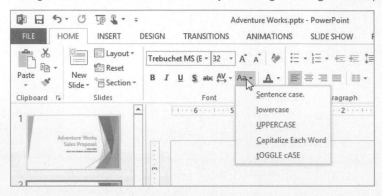

- **Capitalize each word.** Capitalizes the first letter of each word.
- **Toggle case.** Reverses the case of every letter. For example, it would change "Smith" to "sMITH."

When you use the Change Case attribute, the text retains no memory of its previous capitalization state. For example, if you used the Capitalize Each Word option on the word *PowerPoint*, it would convert to *Powerpoint*. If you wanted to re-capitalize the middle P, then you would have to manually retype it (or select only that P and choose Change Case ➪ Uppercase).

> **TIP**
>
> Most style guides dictate that you should capitalize all important words in titles, but not *every* word. For example, in the title "The Best of the Best," you do not capitalize the words "of" and "the." Unfortunately, the Capitalize Each Word option in PowerPoint cannot make that distinction for you, and so you must make those changes manually. However, Microsoft Word's grammar checker *does* identify and fix these capitalization errors. If you have a long, text-heavy presentation, you might find it worthwhile to export the text to Word, perform a grammar check, and then re-import it.

Applying WordArt Styles

WordArt enables you to apply formatting features to text that would normally be used only with graphics, such as special fills, outlines, glows, reflections, and other special effects. It's pretty amazing stuff, as you'll see in the following sections.

Up until PowerPoint 2007, WordArt had always been a rather compartmentalized specialty feature. However, in PowerPoint 2007 and later, you can apply WordArt Styles to *all* text.

There is no distinction between WordArt and regular text, and so you do not have to choose between cool special effects and including text in the outline and spell checks.

A *WordArt Style* is a preset combination of fill color, outline color, and text effects. WordArt Styles are built into PowerPoint — you can't customize them or add to them. However, you can apply one and then make changes to it.

 For more on text effects, see the section "Applying Text Effects."

To apply a WordArt Style, follow these steps:

1. **(Optional) To make the style apply to certain text, select that text.**
2. **In the WordArt Styles group on the Drawing Tools Format tab, click the More button to open the gallery.** A gallery of WordArt presets appears. See Figure 5.16.

FIGURE 5.16

Select a WordArt Style.

3. **Hover the mouse pointer over the styles to preview them on the text on the slide.**
4. **Click the desired style to apply it.**

To remove a previous WordArt effect, open the WordArt Styles gallery again and choose Clear WordArt.

If you choose a WordArt style that is supposed to apply only to the selected text, but you have not selected any text, then PowerPoint applies it to the word at the insertion point's location. The insertion point can be at the beginning of the word or anywhere within it, but not following the word. If the insertion point follows a word, PowerPoint tries to apply the style to text that is to the right of the word. If this is a blank space, the style applies to the blank space and the change is not apparent.

5

CAUTION

WordArt effects are not available when working in Compatibility mode (that is, on a PowerPoint 97-2003 format presentation). When you save a presentation in PowerPoint 97-2003 format, any text box that contains text with WordArt formatting applied is converted to a graphic that you cannot edit. If you need to edit the text in PowerPoint 2003 or earlier, make sure that you remove the WordArt effects before saving in that format.

Applying Text Effects

The text effects that you apply using the Text Effects button in the WordArt Styles group — Shadow, Reflection, Glow, Bevel, 3-D Rotation, and Transform — are similar to regular attributes such as bold, italic, and underline, in that they apply modifiers to the basic text to produce some special appearance. However, this chapter looks at these effects separately because they are part of the WordArt functionality.

NOTE

When working with text for presentations that need to be backward-compatible with PowerPoint 2003 and earlier, stick with the effects that you can access from the Font group.

All of these effects, except for Transform, are also available for formatting graphics objects such as drawn shapes, SmartArt, and charts.

To customize and fine-tune each of these text effects, see Chapter 9.

Shadow

There are two ways to apply a shadow — one is available in all PowerPoint presentation versions, and the other is available only in PowerPoint 2007 and later presentations.

The Shadow button on the Home tab (in the Font group) applies a default shadow to any text, and you can use it even in a backward-compatible presentation. Its shadow appears slightly below and to the right of the text, and the shadow color is automatically based on the background color.

For more flexibility, click Drawing Tools Format ➪ WordArt Styles ➪ Text Effects ➪ Shadow to open a gallery of shadow presets. These presets are divided into categories, including Outer (the default type), Inner, and Perspective, as shown in Figure 5.17. You can scroll down in the gallery to access more presets.

FIGURE 5.17

Select a shadow preset.

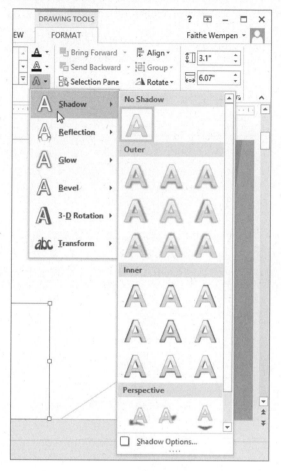

You can also customize the shadow by choosing Shadow Options, which opens the Format Shape task pane with the Text Effects options displayed and the Shadow category expanded. You can then fine-tune the shadow by changing its color, transparency, size, and so on.

Chapter 9 looks at each of the shadow settings available in the Format Shape task pane in detail.

5

Reflection

Reflection creates a partial mirror image of the text beneath the original, making it appear as if it were looking into a reflecting pool. Figure 5.18 illustrates the effect.

Choose a reflection preset from the Reflection submenu of the Text Effects menu, as shown in Figure 5.18.

To remove the reflection effect, choose No Reflection from the top of the gallery menu.

FIGURE 5.18

Select a reflection preset to apply a Reflection effect to text.

You can also choose Reflection Options to open the Reflection options in the Format Shape task pane, from which you can fine-tune any of the following (see Figure 5.19):

- **Transparency.** The extent to which anything behind the text shows through the reflection
- **Size.** The size of the reflection

- **Distance.** The distance between the reflection and the text or object being reflected
- **Blur.** The sharpness or blurriness of the reflection effect

FIGURE 5.19

Fine-tune a reflection effect in the Format Shape task pane.

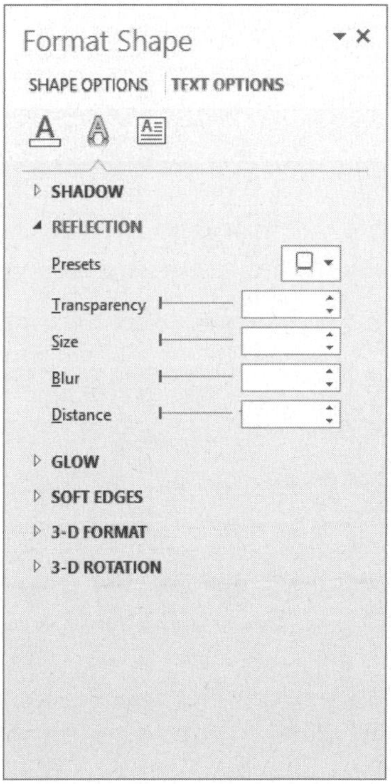

Glow

Glow appears as a soft halo effect around the text. You can choose from four levels of thickness for the glow, as well as any glow color. Figure 5.20 shows a glow effect.

You can choose a glow preset from the Glow submenu of the Text Effects menu. You must first select the level that you want by clicking one of the presets in the gallery, as shown in Figure 5.20. The presets use the colors in the current theme. Then, if you cannot find the desired color, you can reopen the submenu and choose More Glow Colors. You can then click the color that you want from the color picker. Keep in mind, though, that if you use one of the other colors, and then change the colors in the presentation, the object won't change color. To remove the glow, choose No Glow from the top of the gallery menu.

5

FIGURE 5.20

You can select a glow preset, as well as a different color.

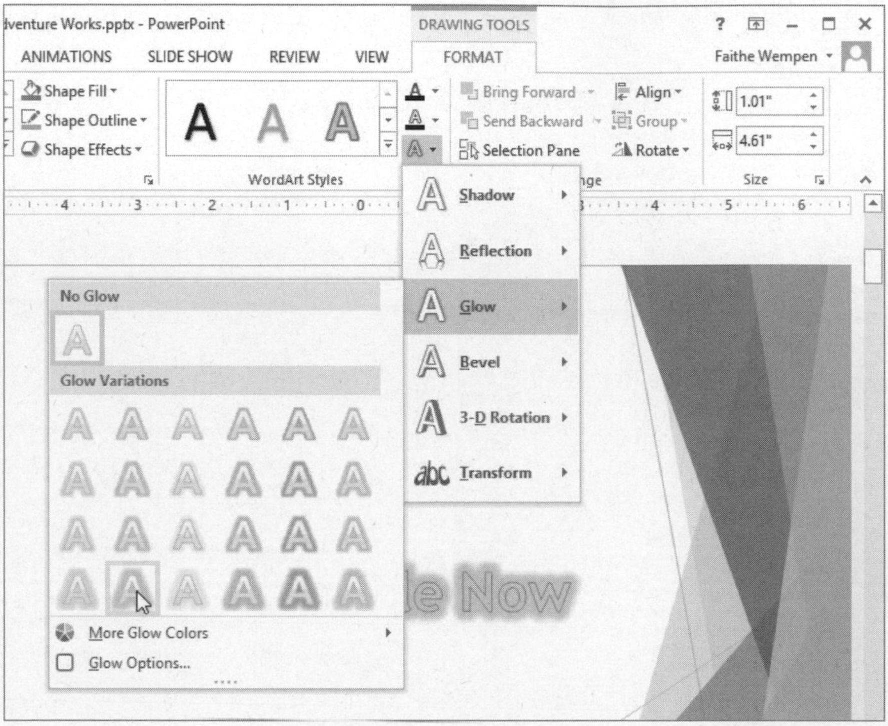

You can also choose Glow Options to open the Glow settings in the Format Shape task pane, from which you can specify the following (see Figure 5.21):

- **Presets.** Choosing a preset from this list is the same as choosing one from the Glow submenu in Figure 5.20.
- **Color.** Sets the color of the glow.
- **Size.** Sets the size of the glow around the text or object.
- **Transparency.** Determines the extent to which whatever is behind the glow shows through.

The Soft Edges option applies only to shapes, not to text, so those options are grayed out (unavailable) in the Format Shape task pane when text is selected.

Bevel (3-D format)

A *bevel* is a slanting, curving, or rounding off of the edges of an object. It is not a very obvious effect when applied to most text, and so it's mostly for larger, drawn objects and pieces of charts and diagrams. However, on large, thick letters in light colors, beveling is sometimes useful to create a raised or textured effect. For example, in Figure 5.22, a bevel effect adds a raised appearance to the letters.

FIGURE 5.21

Fine-tune the glow in the Format Shape task pane.

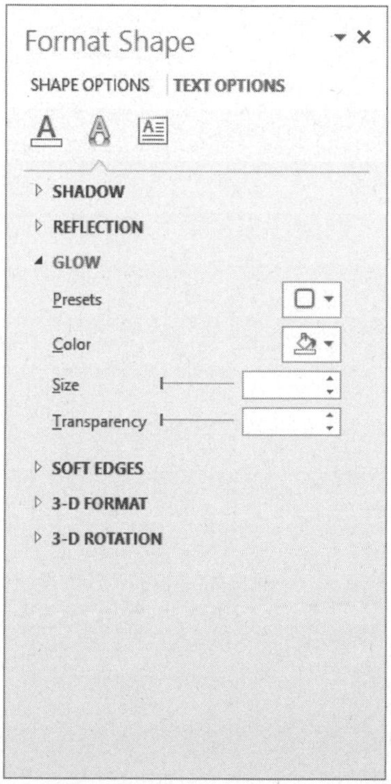

> **NOTE**
> Bevel effects are not easily visible at the default zoom in Normal view. To really see the bevel effect, zoom in on the letters to at least 300 percent. Bevels work well with light or bright-colored text; they are not usually visible with black text.

Choose a bevel preset from the Bevel submenu of the Text Effects menu, as shown in Figure 5.22.

Beveling is a subset of a larger category of formatting known as 3-D. With 3-D, you can apply not only bevels to the edges, but also depth, contours, and surface effects. The 3-D effects are not as effective with text as with other types of objects because text is relatively small and thin, and the effects are not readily visible.

5

For more on depth, contours, and surface effects, see Chapter 9.

FIGURE 5.22

You can select a bevel preset and add depth or texture to text.

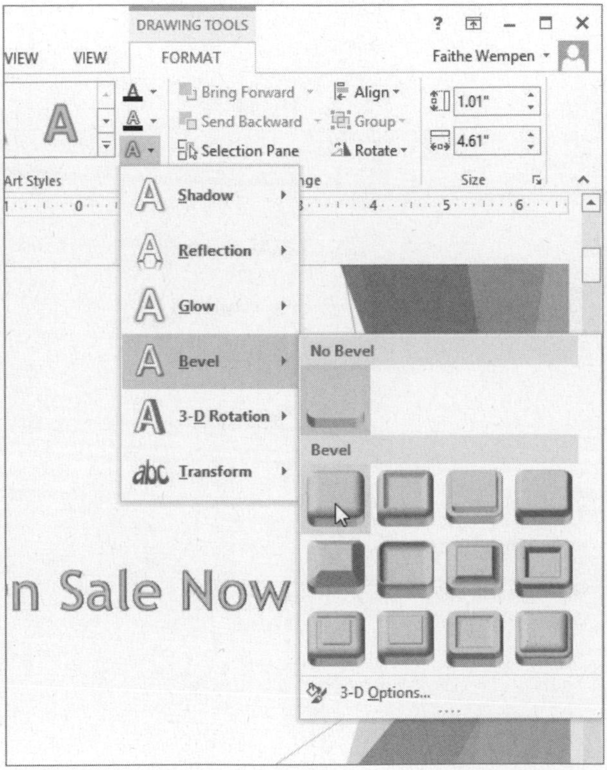

To fine-tune the bevel effect, select 3-D Options from the bottom of the Bevel submenu. The Format Shape task pane opens with the 3-D Format settings displayed, as shown in Figure 5.23. From here you can adjust the width and height of the top and bottom bevel effect (in points), and you can also experiment with the colors and sizes of the depth and contour settings, as well as the 3-D lighting and surface effects.

> **TIP**
>
> The Contour section governs the outline that appears around the text when you apply beveling. If you do not want the beveled text to have an outline, set the Size to 0 points in the Contour section, as shown in Figure 5.23.

FIGURE 5.23

Fine-tune the bevel settings in the Format Text Shape task pane.

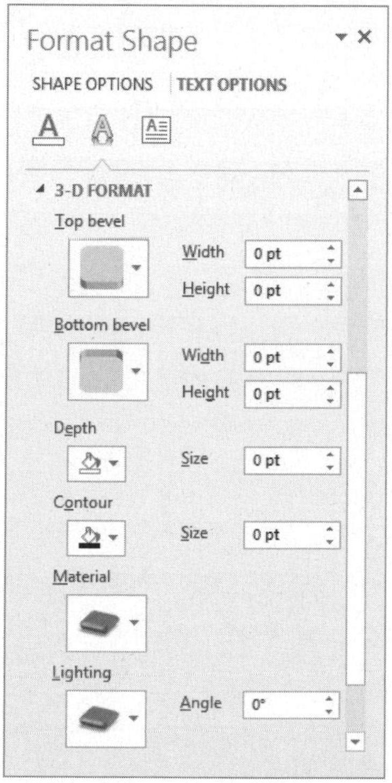

Format Shape

SHAPE OPTIONS | TEXT OPTIONS

4 **3-D FORMAT**

Top bevel

Width | 0 pt
Height | 0 pt

Bottom bevel

Width | 0 pt
Height | 0 pt

Depth

Size | 0 pt

Contour

Size | 0 pt

Material

Lighting

Angle | 0°

The Depth setting in the 3-D Format settings controls the length of the 3-D effect that is applied to the text. It doesn't do anything until you apply a Rotation setting, which is covered in the next section. However, when you rotate the text, it shows "sides" according to its depth setting. For example, in Figure 5.24, the text has a five-degree X rotation and a depth of 60 points.

FIGURE 5.24

The Depth setting sets the length of the sides of the text. These sides are visible only when you apply a rotation to the text.

5

3-D Rotation

The 3-D Rotation effect slants, tilts, or otherwise manipulates the text so that it looks as if it is being viewed at an angle. You can slant and tilt the letters themselves, as shown in Figure 5.25.

FIGURE 5.25

The 3-D rotation effect makes text appear to tilt, slant, and rotate.

There are four factors that make up a 3-D rotation setting:

- **X.** Left-to-right rotation
- **Y.** Top-to-bottom rotation
- **Z.** Rotation around a center point
- **Perspective.** The height at which you are viewing (above or below)

The 3-D rotation presets combine these factors to create commonly used effects. Select a rotation preset from the 3-D Rotation submenu of the Text Effects menu, as shown in Figure 5.26.

To adjust each of the four factors separately, choose 3-D Rotation Options from the bottom of the submenu and set the angles for each factor in the Format Text Effects dialog box. By combining them with the 3-D Format settings in that same dialog box, you can create almost any effect that you want.

For more on the various rotation settings, see Chapter 9.

FIGURE 5.26

Choose a 3-D rotation preset.

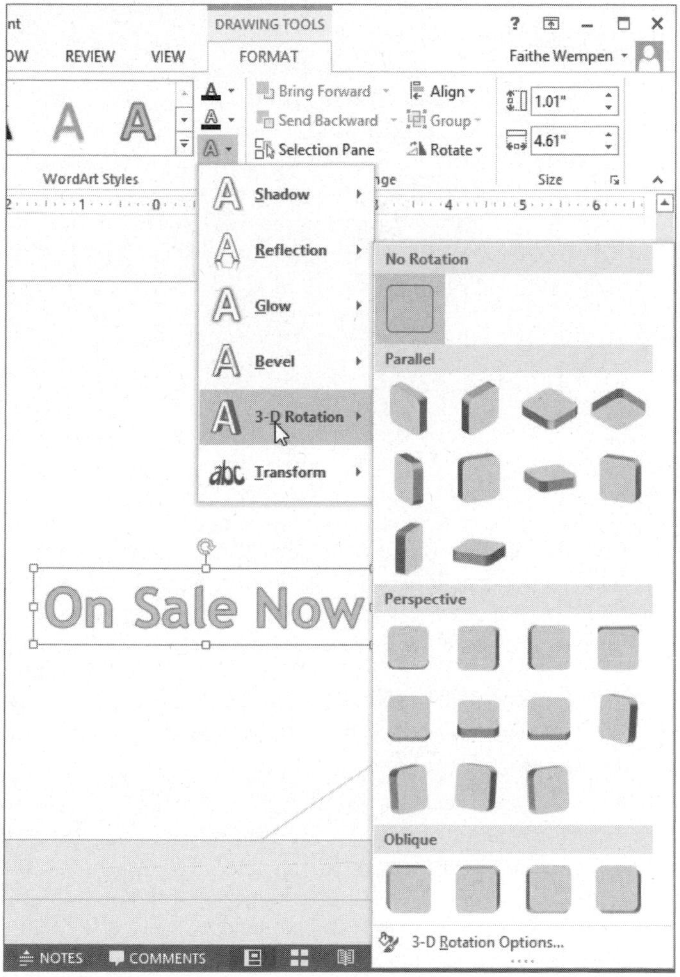

Transform

Transform settings are just for text and are not available for graphic objects such as drawn shapes. You can think of transformations — which were called WordArt Shapes in some earlier versions of PowerPoint — as "molds" into which you squeeze text in order to change its shape. Figure 5.27 shows some examples of various transformations that are not rotated. However, you can combine a transformation with 3-D rotation to create some even more unusual effects.

FIGURE 5.27

Some examples of transformation effects.

Applying a Transformation

There are two categories of transformation: Follow Path and Warp. Follow Path is the "traditional" type of WordArt transformation, squeezing the text into various shapes. Follow Path does not reshape the text itself, but makes the characters hug a curved path. The bottom-right example in Figure 5.27 is a Follow Path effect; the others are Warp effects.

To apply a transformation effect, select it from the Transform submenu of the Text Effects menu, as shown in Figure 5.28. To remove a transformation effect, choose No Transform.

Modifying a Transformation

After applying a transformation, you might be able to modify its shape somewhat, depending on the transformation that you have chosen. Once you select the Transform setting, look for a purple square in the WordArt text. Figure 5.29 shows an example. You can drag this square to reshape the effect, making it more or less dramatic. You can drag the purple square in the center of the WordArt to stretch or compress the center. Lines appear as you drag to show the new position.

> **NOTE**
>
> You can also rotate the WordArt by dragging the circular arrow graphic at the top. This works just like rotating any other object and is covered in Chapter 9.

Tips for Using the Follow Path Transformations

The Follow Path transformations are a bit different from the Warp transformations, and so it might not be obvious how to manipulate them. Here are some tips:

■ If the text seems to follow the path in a lopsided manner (especially common with short text phrases), set the text's horizontal alignment to Center. To do this, use the Center button in the Paragraph group on the Home tab.

For more on text alignment, see Chapter 6.

FIGURE 5.28

Choose a transformation effect.

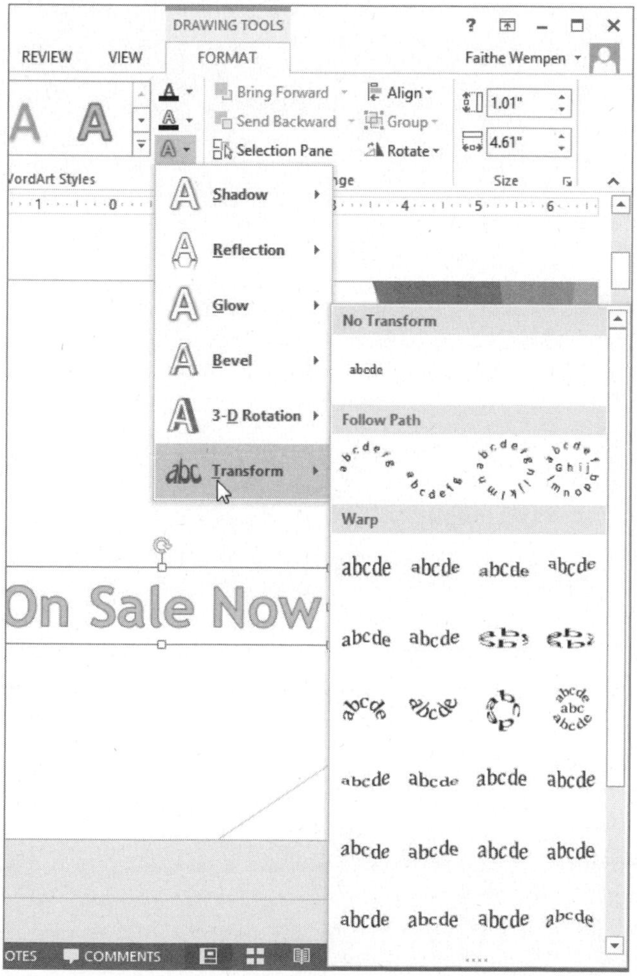

■ The third Follow Path transformation (Circle) makes text appear in a circle. Where it starts depends on the horizontal alignment setting for the text. You can set horizontal alignment using the buttons in the Paragraph group on the Home tab. If you set the text to be left-aligned, it starts at the left; if you center the text, the text bends around the right side as a center point. If you use right alignment, the text starts upside-down.

FIGURE 5.29

Modify the shape of the transformation effect by dragging a purple square.

Drag purple square

- The fourth Follow Path transformation (Button) makes text appear above a center line, on a center line, and then below a center line. To indicate what text should appear where, press Enter to insert paragraph breaks between the text segments.

Copying Formatting with Format Painter

Once you have formatted text exactly the way you want it, you might want to copy it to other blocks of text. To do this, you can use the Format Painter tool. Format Painter picks up the formatting of any object (including text) and "paints" it onto other objects.

To use Format Painter, follow these steps:

1. **Select the text or other object whose formatting you want to copy.**

2. **Click Home ⇨ Clipboard ⇨ Format Painter, as shown in Figure 5.30.** The mouse pointer changes to a paintbrush. If you want to copy the formatting onto more than one object or section of text, double-click the Format Painter icon instead of just clicking it.

3. **Click the object, or drag across the text, to which you want to apply the formatting.**

4. **(Optional) If you double-clicked the Format Painter icon in step 2, Format Painter is still enabled; click additional objects to apply the formatting.** Press Esc to cancel the Format Painter when you are finished.

> **NOTE**
> To clear the formatting from a block of text, click the Home ⇨ Font ⇨ Clear All Formatting.

FIGURE 5.30

Format Painter copies formatting, not only for text but also for other objects.

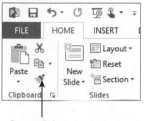

Format Painter

Inserting Symbols

Occasionally you might need to insert a character that doesn't appear on your keyboard, such as a copyright© or™ trademark symbol, or a letter with an accent mark over it. You can easily insert these symbols by using the Symbol dialog box.

Follow these steps to insert a symbol:

1. **Choose Insert ⇨ Symbols ⇨ Symbol.** The Symbol dialog box opens, as shown in Figure 5.31.

FIGURE 5.31

Use the Symbol dialog box to insert any character from any font.

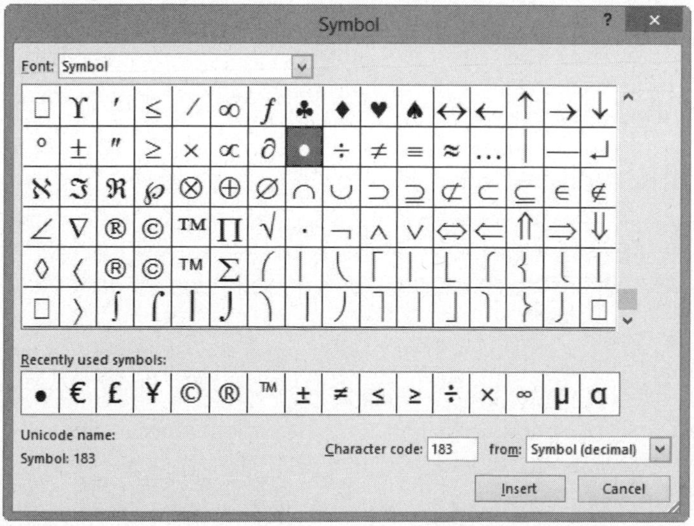

2. **If necessary, open the Font drop-down list and select the font from which the symbol should be selected.** The default is normal text, which displays the symbols from the font currently in use.

3. **Click the symbol you want to insert.**

4. **Click Insert.**

5. **Click Close.**

Inserting Math Equations

Math has its own language, complete with special symbols and syntax, and even special types of line breaks, dividers, and superscript/subscript requirements. It's no wonder, then, that most text-editing programs are inadequate for expressing complex mathematical equations.

PowerPoint 2013 includes the same robust Equation Editor utility that is in Microsoft Word; you can use it to construct and format any equation you need. This makes PowerPoint useful for math classes, for example, and for scientific and technical presentations.

Inserting a Preset Equation

In algebra and trigonometry, certain equations are used frequently, such as the Pythagorean Theorem and the quadratic formula. Instead of re-creating them each time you need them, you can insert them as a preset equation from Word.

Follow these steps to insert an equation preset:

1. **Click in a text box.**

2. **On the Insert tab, click the down arrow below the Equation button to open its gallery.**

3. **Click one of the presets.**

Creating a New Equation

If none of the presets match your needs, create a new, blank equation object instead by clicking the Equation button (click its face, not its down arrow). The Equation Tools Design tab appears, and *Type equation here* appears in the text box, showing where to begin typing your equation. See Figure 5.32.

To create a simple equation, just start typing it in the equation frame. You can use any number, letter, or symbol from the keyboard. You can also select from a wide variety of math symbols in the Symbols group on the Equation Tools Design tab.

Basic math symbols are shown by default in the Symbols group's gallery, as shown in Figure 5.32. Open the gallery and choose a different set of symbols if necessary, as shown in Figure 5.33.

FIGURE 5.32

Construct an equation using the Equation Tools Design tab.

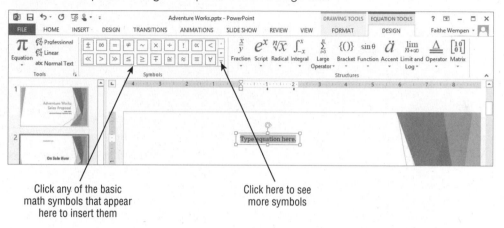

Click any of the basic
math symbols that appear
here to insert them

Click here to see
more symbols

FIGURE 5.33

Select from other symbol sets if needed.

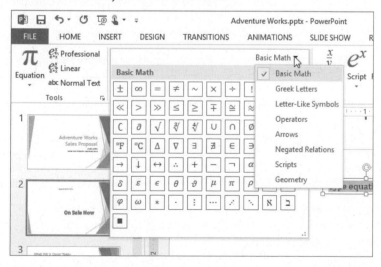

Depending on the equation, you may need one or more structures. *Structures* are symbols and/or combinations of text placeholder boxes that help you create math expressions that could not be easily expressed on a single line of text.

A stacked fraction is one of the simplest and most common examples. It consists of two placeholder boxes, one on top of the other, with a horizontal line between them (see Figure 5.34).

FIGURE 5.34

Structures contain one or more placeholder boxes.

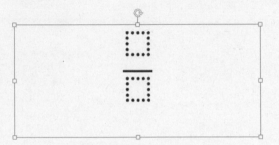

Follow these steps to insert and fill a structure:

1. **In the equation, position the insertion point where you want the structure to be inserted.**
2. **On the Equation Tools Design tab, click one of the buttons in the Structures group to open its menu.** For example, click the Fractions button.
3. **Click on the desired structure to insert it.**
4. **Click in a placeholder and type or insert the content.** Repeat this for each placeholder.

> **TIP**
> Structures can be nested. You can place one structure inside the placeholder box for another structure, creating complex nests of structures and equations.

Follow these steps to insert a simple subscript box into an equation:

1. **In the equation, position the insertion point where you want the structure to be inserted.**
2. **Click Equation Tools Design ⇨ Structures ⇨ Script.**
3. **In the Subscripts and Superscripts section of the menu, click Subscript.** Two placeholder boxes appear: one regular-sized and one smaller and slightly lowered.

4. Click in the first placeholder box and type or insert the content that should precede the characters in subscript.

5. Click in the second placeholder box and type or insert the content that should appear in subscript.

All the other structures work exactly the same way, although some of them might appear intimidating and complex. Just click in the placeholders and fill in the content.

Switching Between Professional and Linear Layout

The default type of equation layout is Professional, which shows structures spread out on multiple lines wherever appropriate. Professional layout makes math formulas that are easy to read and understand.

However, when space is an issue on a slide, you might be unwilling to give up two or more lines in order to show an equation. To save space, it's helpful to switch the equation's view to Linear. Using a Linear view runs the equation on a single line, changing the symbols where needed to alternatives that can be expressed in a linear fashion (see Figure 5.35).

FIGURE 5.35

Comparison of Professional (top) and Linear (bottom) views.

$$f(x) = a_0 + \sum_{n=1}^{\infty} \left(a_n \cos\frac{n\pi x}{L} + b_n \sin\frac{n\pi x}{L} \right)$$

$$f(x) = a_{\downarrow}0 + \sum_{\downarrow}(n1)^{\uparrow}\infty \text{▓}(a_{\downarrow}n \ \cos[\![n\pi x/L]\!])$$

To switch between Linear and Professional views, use the corresponding buttons in the Tools group on the Equation Tools Design tab.

Formatting an Equation

There are some differences in the formatting capabilities for equations versus regular text. Here's a quick summary:

- **Font.** Cambria Math is used for formulas by default. While you can change this (right-click the equation and choose Font, or select the font from the Home tab), font changes will not take effect unless the font you choose supports mathematical symbols. Because Cambria Math is the only font that ships with Office 2013 that fully supports all math symbols used in the Equation Editor, it is in effect your only choice.

5

- **Size.** By default, the baseline font for an equation is 18 point. Some characters can be larger or smaller than that depending on their context. You can select the equation's frame and then choose a different font size from the Home tab to adjust the overall size of the equation up or down proportionally from there.

- **Color.** Use the Font Color button on the Home tab to change the color of the text used for the equation if desired. Keep in mind, however, that equations are nearly always utilitarian objects, not decorative.

- **Bold.** You can apply boldface to individual characters or to the entire equation.

- **Strikethrough.** You can apply strikethrough to individual characters or to the entire equation.

- **Italics.** Letters in an equation are italicized by default, as are some symbols. It is usually best to leave these at their default, because people expect to see those items italicized, and the italics help them make sense of the equation.

- **Underline.** Underline cannot be applied to individual characters; it can be applied only to the equation as a whole.

Summary

In this chapter, you learned many techniques for formatting text. You learned how to apply different fonts, sizes, colors, and attributes, and how to bend and shape text with 3-D effects and WordArt transformations. In the next chapter, you'll continue to look at text formatting, focusing on paragraph-wide effects such as bulleted and numbered lists, indentation, and alignment.

CHAPTER 6

Formatting Paragraphs and Text Boxes

In the previous chapter you learned how to format text by applying fonts, sizes, colors, attributes, and WordArt special effects. Now that your text is looking its best, you can expand the focus to the next level: paragraphs.

What can you do to an entire paragraph, as opposed to an individual text character? Plenty. For example, you can define multiple levels of bulleted and numbered lists, and you can adjust the tab stops, indentations, line spacing, and horizontal alignment for each paragraph.

All of these things happen within the context of text boxes, of course, because PowerPoint places all text in text boxes. So this chapter also takes a look at text box formatting, including fills, borders, vertical alignment, and rotation.

Formatting Bulleted Lists

For better or for worse, most PowerPoint presentations contain a lot of bulleted lists. When you create a slide based on a layout that includes a bulleted list, or when you type a new slide in the outline pane, you get bullets automatically.

See Appendix A, "What Makes a Great Presentation?" for an analysis of why bulleted lists are sometimes not the best way to present information, and see Lab 1, "Presenting Content without Bulleted Lists," at the end of the book to learn about alternatives.

CAUTION

If you apply text formatting such as bold to a paragraph, the bullet character will also be affected. To avoid this, leave a blank space after the final character in the paragraph and then make sure you select only the text, not the entire paragraph, before applying text effects.

Bullets and the Slide Master

You can apply the bulleted list changes that you learn about in the following sections to individual paragraphs, but your best bet is to apply them to the slide master, or at least to individual layout masters. That way, you ensure consistency throughout the presentation. On the slide master, five levels of bullets are defined, as shown in Figure 6.1. (You can add additional levels by pressing Enter and then Tab after the last level.) You can customize any of these levels individually. Here's a high-level overview of the process:

FIGURE 6.1

To ensure consistency, make bullet format changes on the slide master.

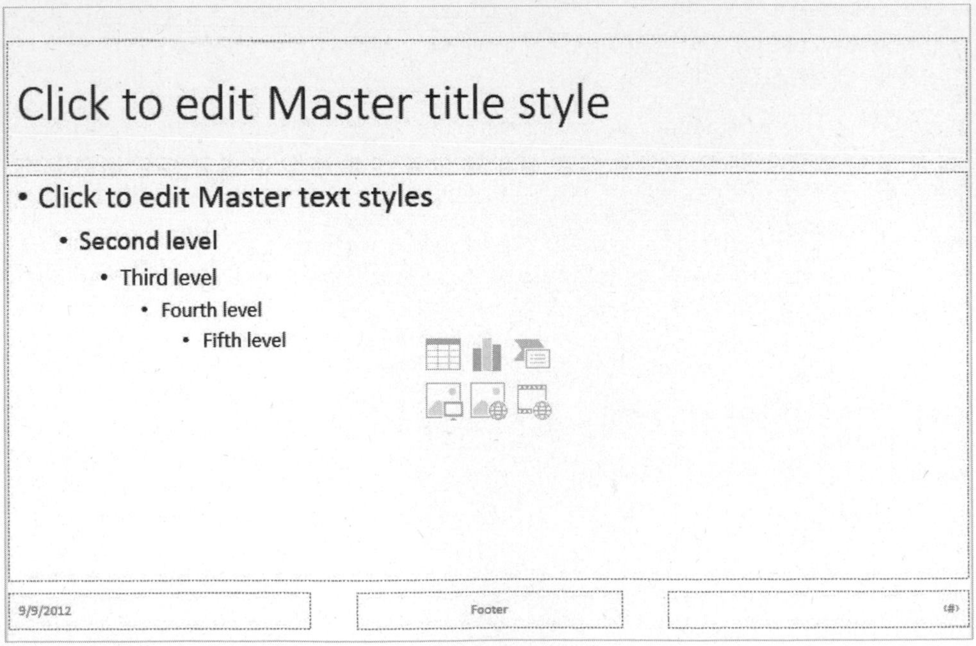

Click to edit Master title style

- Click to edit Master text styles
  - Second level
    - Third level
      - Fourth level
        - Fifth level

9/9/2012 | Footer | ⟨#⟩

1. **Click View ⇨ Master Views ⇨ Slide Master.**
2. **Click the top thumbnail in the left pane, selecting the slide master itself (not one of its subordinate layouts).**
3. **Click on the slide, in the "Click to edit Master text styles" line.**
4. **Customize the bullet character, as in the following sections.**
5. **Click in the "Second level" line, and customize it.**
6. **Repeat the preceding steps for other levels that you want to customize.** (If you do not plan to use all nine levels, you do not need to make changes to them.)
7. **Click Slide Master tab ⇨ Close ⇨ Close Master View.**

Using Bullet Presets

You can turn off the bullets for any paragraph(s) or text placeholders by selecting them and clicking the Bullets button on the Home tab to toggle the bullet(s) off. In that same way, you can apply bullets to paragraphs or text placeholders that don't currently have them.

The default bullet character depends on the theme but is usually one of the presets on the Bullets button's menu, shown in Figure 6.2. To switch among the presets, select the paragraph(s) to affect, open the button's menu, and click a different preset. The menu also has a None command, an alternative for toggling bullets off.

FIGURE 6.2

Click the Bullets button to toggle bullets on/off or open its drop-down list.

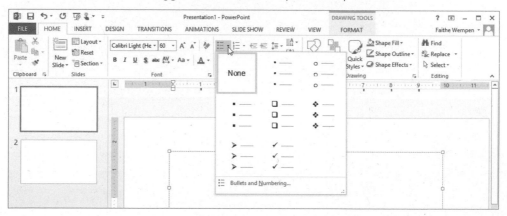

Each of the seven presets in the Bullets button's menu is a placeholder. By default, each placeholder is populated with a certain symbol, but you can modify any or all of the placeholders to be different sizes or colors, and you can even replace the characters with your own choices of symbols or graphics. In the following sections you learn how to select your own bullet characters.

Changing Bullet Size and Color

Each of the bullet presets (see Figure 6.2) is actually a character from a symbol font. It is text — and as such, you can format it like text. You can increase or decrease its size, and you can change its color. To change a bullet's size and color, follow these steps:

1. **Select the paragraph(s) to affect.** For best results, make the change on the slide master to ensure consistency.

2. **On the Home tab, open the Bullets button's menu and choose Bullets and Numbering.** The Bullets and Numbering dialog box appears with the Bulleted tab displayed.

3. **In the Size box, use the increment buttons to increase or decrease the size.** The size is in relation to the text size of the paragraph.

4. **Click the Color button, and select a color from the Color Picker.** See Figure 6.3.

FIGURE 6.3

Change bullet size and color.

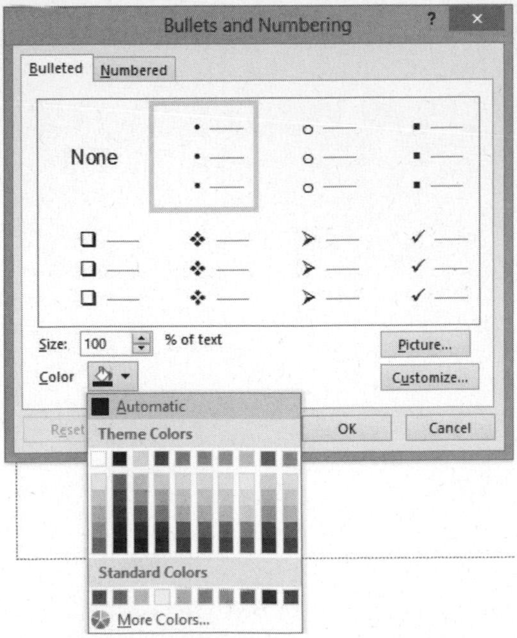

5. **Click OK to apply the changes.**

NOTE
The color and size changes you make in the Bullets and Numbering dialog box affect all presets.

Changing the Bullet Symbol

If you do not like any of the preset bullets, you can change to a different character. You can use any character from any font installed on your system, including any letter or number.

If you want a numbered list, see the section "Formatting Numbered Lists" later in this chapter.

To select a different bullet symbol, follow these steps:

1. **Select the paragraph(s) to affect.** For best results, make the change on the slide master to ensure consistency.
2. **Open the Bullets button's menu and choose Bullets and Numbering.** The Bullets and Numbering dialog box appears with the Bulleted tab displayed, as shown in Figure 6.3.
3. **Click the preset that you want to replace, and then click Customize.** The Symbol dialog box opens (Figure 6.4).

FIGURE 6.4

Select an alternative symbol to use as a bullet.

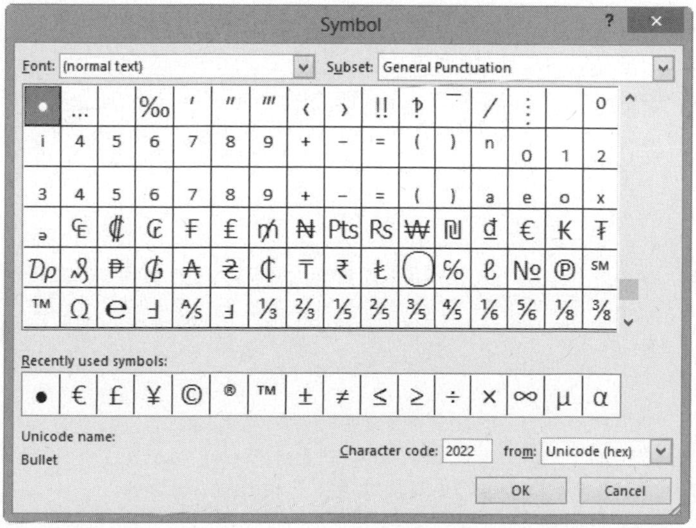

4. **Select the desired font from the Font list.** Although all fonts are available, most of the characters suitable for bullets are in the Wingdings fonts.

5. **Click the desired character.** Notice the scroll bar to the right of the characters; there are more characters than can be displayed at once.

6. **Click OK.** The new symbol appears on the Bulleted tab.

7. **(Optional) Change the new symbol's size and color if desired, as in the preceding section.**

8. **Click OK to apply the new symbol to the selected paragraph(s).**

Resetting a Bullet Preset

After you have customized a bullet preset, you might decide you want to go back to its original setting. To reset it, follow these steps:

1. **Open the Bullets button's menu and choose Bullets and Numbering.** The Bullets and Numbering dialog box appears with the Bulleted tab displayed, as shown in Figure 6.3.

2. **Click the preset that you want to reset.**

3. **Click the Reset button.** The position is reset.

4. **Click OK to apply the reset character.** Do not click Cancel or the reset will be canceled. If you don't actually want to apply the character, change it afterward.

> **TIP**
> If the Reset button is unavailable, try clicking another preset and then clicking back to the desired one again.

Using a Picture Bullet

Microsoft's clip art collection contains many small graphics that work well as bullets. Such graphics have a keyword of *bullet* assigned to them. The Insert Pictures dialog box, which you can access by clicking the Picture button in the Bullets and Numbering dialog box, enables you to locate and use bullet-suitable clip art.

To use a picture bullet, follow these steps:

1. **Select the paragraph(s) to which you want to apply the picture bullet.** For best results, make the change on the slide master to ensure consistency.

2. **Open the Bullets button's menu and choose Bullets and Numbering.** The Bullets and Numbering dialog box appears with the Bulleted tab displayed.

3. **Click Picture.** The Insert Pictures dialog box opens.

4. **In the Office.com Clip Art section of the dialog box, click in the Search Office. com box, type *bullet* (as in Figure 6.5), and press Enter.**

FIGURE 6.5

Search for clip art with the keyword *bullet*.

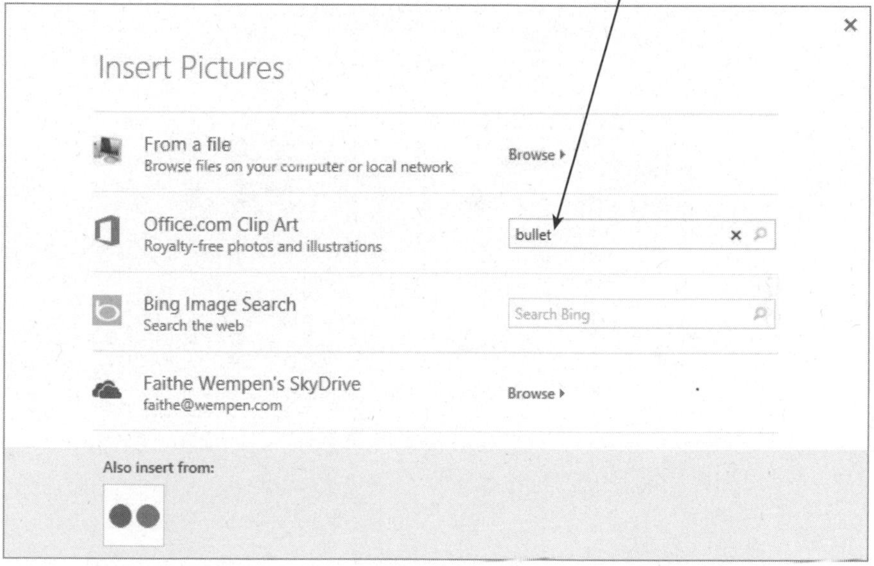

Type *bullet* here and press Enter

5. **Select the desired graphic in the search results that appear.** Most of the graphics that appear are suitable bullet characters; a few of them may be graphics of objects that contain the word *bullet* in their names, and you can ignore those. See Figure 6.6.

6. **Click Insert.** The graphic is immediately applied to the paragraphs you selected in step 1.

Most of the picture bullets are a fixed color (or combination of colors); they do not change color when you change the theme, and they are not affected by the Color setting in the Bullets and Numbering dialog box.

You can also add your own pictures as bullets. For best results, stick with very small, simple graphics. A detailed photo might look great as a full-screen image, but as a bullet it will probably look blurry and unrecognizable. To import your own picture, follow these steps:

1. **Select the paragraph(s) to which you want to apply the picture bullet.** For best results, make the change on the slide master to ensure consistency.

2. **Open the Bullets button's menu and choose Bullets and Numbering.** The Bullets and Numbering dialog box appears with the Bulleted tab displayed.

3. **Click Picture.** The Insert Pictures dialog box opens (Figure 6.5).

FIGURE 6.6

Select one of the small graphics in the search results.

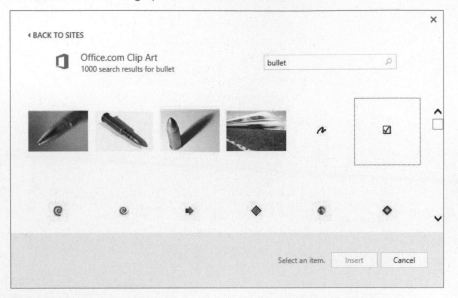

4. **Click From a File, and click Browse.** The Insert Picture dialog box opens.
5. **Select the graphic you want to use and click Open.** The picture appears as a bullet to the selected paragraph(s).

> **TIP**
> If the picture bullet is too small or too large, reopen the Bullets and Numbering dialog box and increase or decrease the Size setting.

Formatting Numbered Lists

Numbered lists are very similar to bulleted ones except instead of using the same character for each item, they use sequential numbers or letters. Use a numbered list whenever the order of the items is significant.

Using Numbering Presets

To switch from bullets to numbering, or to apply numbering to text that has neither bullets nor numbering applied already, click the Numbering button on the Home tab. This applies the default numbering style — the one in position #1 of the presets.

Like the Bullets button, the Numbering button also has a drop-down list with seven preset formats plus None, as shown in Figure 6.7. You can apply any of those presets from the menu.

FIGURE 6.7

Click the Numbering button to toggle numbering on/off or open its drop-down list and select a preset.

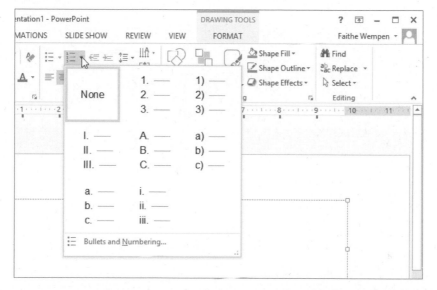

TIP

You usually don't want to apply numbering to the slide master because it's not the norm — bullets are. Also, the optimal amount of space between paragraphs is often different when numbered lists are used. Consider creating a special master layout for numbered lists and applying your number formatting to that layout in Slide Master view.

Changing Number Size and Color

Numbers can have different sizes and colors in relation to the rest of the paragraph text, just as bullets can. Using a different size and/or color can make the numbers stand out. To change a number's size and color, follow these steps:

1. **Select the paragraph(s) to affect.** If you want to create a layout master to store the numbering formatting, switch to Slide Master view and work on that layout master.

2. **On the Home tab, open the Numbering button's menu and choose Bullets and Numbering.** The Bullets and Numbering dialog box appears with the Numbered tab displayed.

3. **Click the numbering style preset to affect if it is not already selected.**

4. **In the Size box, use the increment buttons to increase or decrease the size.** The size is in relation to the text size of the paragraph. See Figure 6.8.

FIGURE 6.8

Change numbering size and color.

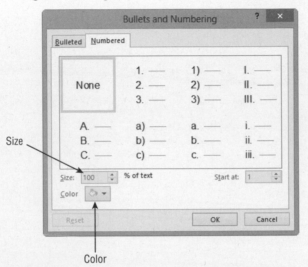

5. **Click the Color button, and select a color from the color picker.**

6. **Click OK to apply the changes.**

NOTE

The color and size changes you make in the Bullets and Numbering dialog box affect all seven presets.

Changing the Start Number

To start the numbered list at some number other than 1, change the Start At value in the Bullets and Numbering dialog box (see Figure 6.8). You might do this, for example, if a numbered list continues from one slide or one text box to the next.

Setting Indents and Tabs

In the following sections you will learn about indents and tabs and how to use them to control the horizontal positioning of paragraph text within a text box in PowerPoint.

Working with Indents

Each level of bullet (or numbering) on the Slide Master has a preset indent defined for it. There are two separate indents: one for the first line of the paragraph and another for subsequent lines. They are represented on the ruler by triangles:

- **First line indent.** This down-pointing triangle represents the positioning of the first line of the paragraph. Because bulleted lists are the default and the bullet character hangs to the left of the rest of the paragraph, by default, the first line indent is set to be farther to the left.

- **Hanging indent.** This up-pointing triangle represents the positioning of the second and subsequent lines in a multiline paragraph. If it is a single-line paragraph, this indent is ignored.

- **Left indent.** This rectangle controls both of the triangles as a single unit. If you want to move both triangles and maintain the spacing between them, you would drag this rectangle.

You can drag these symbols, shown in Figure 6.9, on the horizontal ruler to change their positions. (Hold down Ctrl as you drag if you want finer control over the positioning.) You can also click the Increase List Level or Decrease List Level buttons in the Paragraph group on the Home tab to change the overall left indent.

FIGURE 6.9

Adjust the indents by dragging their markers.

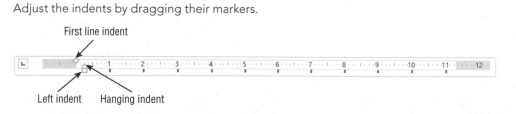

First line indent

Left indent   Hanging indent

You can also control indentation more precisely by using the Paragraph dialog box's Indentation controls. These controls let you specify indentation at intervals as small as $\frac{1}{10}$

of an inch, but they do not have an exact one-to-one relationship with the indent markers on the ruler, so you have to do a bit of mental translation.

There are three indentation settings in the Paragraph dialog box, as shown in Figure 6.10. Open this dialog box by clicking the dialog box launcher in the Paragraph group on the Home tab. The settings are as follows:

- **Before Text.** This is a general left indent setting. It sets both the hanging indent marker and the left indent marker.
- **Special.** This controls what happens to the first line. The choices are Hanging, First Line, or None. To indent the first line to the left of the others, choose Hanging. If you want the first line to the right of the others, choose First Line.
- **By.** If you chose Hanging or First Line, this sets the amount by which the first line will be offset from the Before Text setting.

FIGURE 6.10

You can set up indentation via the Paragraph dialog box.

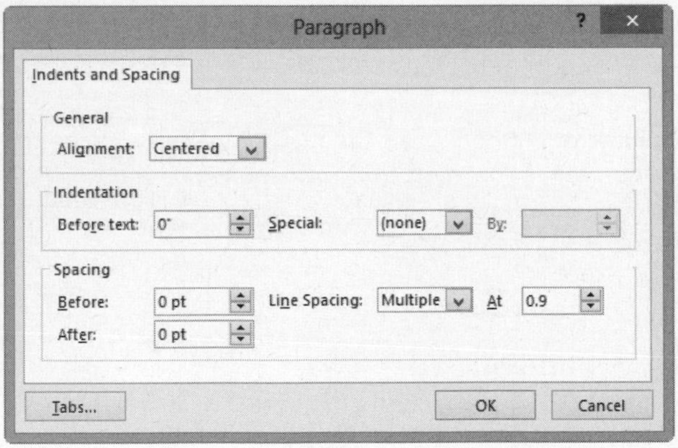

NOTE

Unlike in Word, there is no right indent marker for paragraphs in PowerPoint.

Working with Tabs

Preset tab stops occur every 1" on the ruler by default. Each time you press the Tab key (except at the beginning of a paragraph), the insertion point moves to the next tab stop. If you press Tab at the beginning of a paragraph, the paragraph is demoted one outline level. (Usually that demotion involves an indentation as well, but the indentation is defined on the slide master in that case.) The preset tab stops appear as gray squares at regular intervals below the ruler, as you saw in Figure 6.9. Drag one of those gray squares to the right or left to change the preset tab stop interval. Preset tab stops are always left-aligned stops.

Each paragraph can have its own separate custom tab stops set. If you set the tab stops for one of the outline level paragraphs on the slide master or a layout master, it affects all bullets of that outline level. To set tab stops, follow these steps:

1. **View the slide containing the text box in Normal, Outline, or Slide Master view and select the paragraphs to affect.**
2. **If the horizontal ruler does not appear, choose View ⇨ Show ⇨ Ruler.**
3. **Click the ruler where you want to set the tab.** A little *L* appears, showing that you've just placed a left tab stop.

You can also set centered, right-aligned, or decimal-aligned tab stops. To set one of these, click the Tab Type button at the far left of the ruler. Each time you click this button, it cycles through the available tab stop types, shown in Table 6.1.

TABLE 6.1 Tab Stop Types

Tab Appearance	Type
L	Left
⊥	Center
⌐	Right
⊥	Decimal

To get rid of a tab stop, drag and drop it off the ruler.

You can also set tab stops via a Tabs dialog box for more precision. To access the Tabs dialog box, follow these steps:

1. **Select the paragraph(s) to affect.** To affect all slides, select the placeholders on the slide master in Slide Master view.
2. **On the Home tab, click the dialog box launcher in the Paragraph group.** The Paragraph dialog box opens.

3. **Click the Tabs button.** The Tabs dialog box opens (Figure 6.11). From the Tabs dialog box, you can do any of the following:

- **Set a tab stop.** Type a number in the Tab Stop Position box to represent the number of inches from the left edge of the text box. Click the button in the Alignment section that represents the desired alignment, and then click Set.

- **Clear a tab stop.** To clear just one stop, select the stop to clear and then click the Clear button. To clear all custom tab stops, click Clear All.

- **Change the default tab stop interval.** The default interval is 1". To change that, use the increment buttons in the Default Tab Stops box to increase or decrease the value, or type a new value directly into the box.

FIGURE 6.11

Set or clear tab stops in the Tabs dialog box.

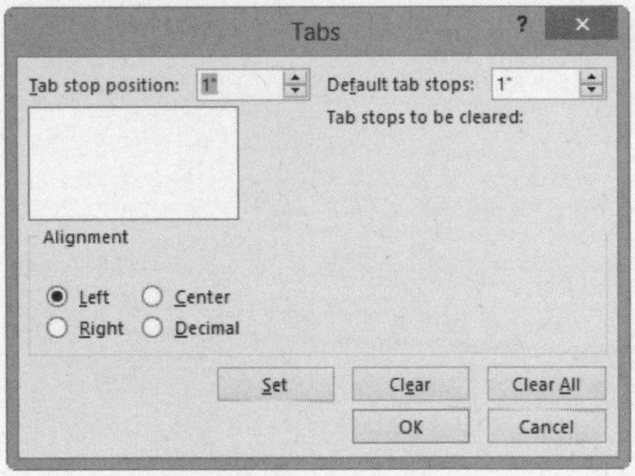

Adjusting Line Spacing

Depending on the theme, PowerPoint leaves varying amounts of space between lines and between paragraphs. The default blank theme leaves some extra space between each paragraph to make the divisions between them clearer; other themes tighten this up.

If the chosen theme doesn't provide the line spacing you want, open it up in Slide Master view and make changes to the text placeholders on the slide master(s). For example, you can make the following changes:

- If most of your bulleted lists are single line, you can eliminate any extra space between paragraphs to make them seem closer together.

- If most of your bulleted lists are multiline paragraphs, you can add space between paragraphs to help differentiate them.

- If you want to make a large paragraph easier to read, you can add extra space between the lines.

To set basic line spacing, click Home ⇨ Paragraph ⇨ Line Spacing and select one of the presets, as shown in Figure 6.12.

FIGURE 6.12

Choose a line spacing preset from the button's menu.

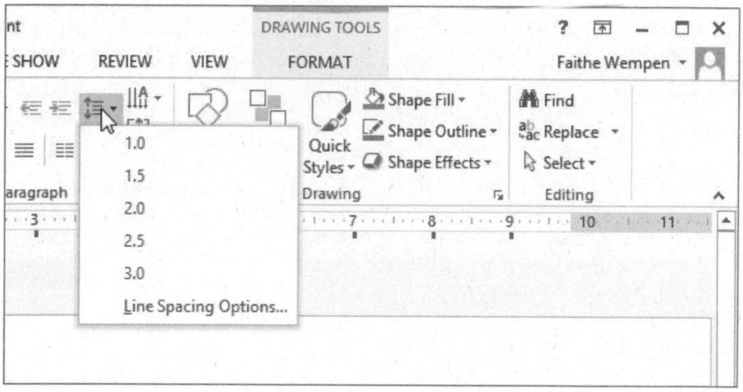

If you want more line spacing options, click the dialog box launcher for the Paragraph group on the Home tab or choose Line Spacing Options at the bottom of the Line Spacing button's menu. The Paragraph dialog box contains the line spacing controls, as shown in Figure 6.13. There are three line spacing settings you can adjust:

FIGURE 6.13

Adjust line spacing in the Paragraph dialog box.

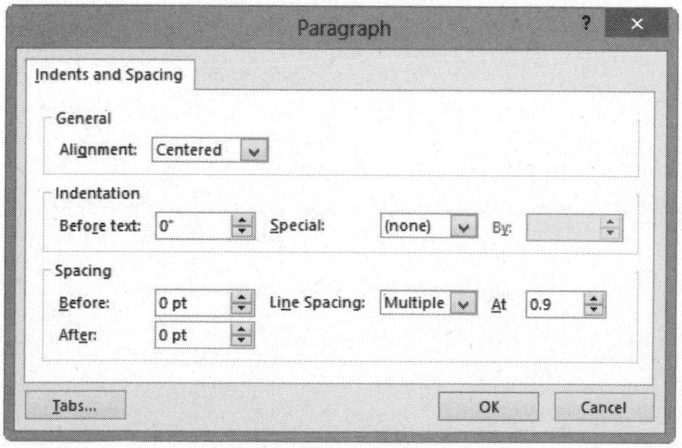

- **Before.** Space before the paragraph
- **After.** Space after the paragraph
- **Line Spacing.** Space between the lines within the paragraph

Before and After are pretty straightforward; you can set their values in points. (Remember, one point is $\frac{1}{72}$ of an inch on a printed page.) It may be helpful to think about the spacing in relation to the font size that you are using. For example, if you are using 24-point text, an After setting of 8 points would leave $\frac{1}{3}$ of a line between paragraphs.

You can set Line Spacing to a preset value of Single, 1.5 Lines, or Double. You can also set it to Multiple and then enter a custom value in the At box. For example, a Multiple value of 1 is single spacing; a Multiple value of 0.9, as shown in Figure 6.13, is slightly less than single spacing, for just a bit of extra tightness in the layout.

All of the previously mentioned line spacing values are based on the text size in the paragraph and not fixed amounts. As the text size changes, the line spacing will adjust automatically. If you need fixed line spacing that does not change when the font changes, choose Exactly from the Line Spacing list. Then you can enter an exact number of points for the spacing in the At box.

Changing Horizontal Alignment

You can set horizontal alignment on a paragraph-by-paragraph basis. The default alignment is Left, but you can also have Centered, Right, Justified, and Distributed:

- **Left, Centered, and Right.** These are fairly self-explanatory. They refer to the point at which each line of text aligns with the other lines of text. For example, the text in this book is left aligned; the left edge of the paragraph is uniform and the right edge is ragged.

- **Justified.** The text aligns with both the right and left margins of the text box. Space is added between words and letters to make that happen. The final line of the paragraph is not justified; it is left aligned. Many newspapers use this alignment. It works best for long lines of text where there is a lot of text in which to spread out the extra spacing. Although justify looks good with large paragraphs, it is of limited usefulness for the brief bullet points that are the hallmark of most slides because it does not affect the last line, and in brief bullets the first line *is* the last line.

- **Distributed.** This is just like Justified, except it includes the last line of the paragraph. You can use it to apply the Justified look to a single-line paragraph.

The Paragraph group on the Home tab contains buttons for Left, Centered, Right, and Justified. Click a button to change the alignment of the selected paragraph(s), as shown in Figure 6.14.

FIGURE 6.14

Click a button on the Paragraph group to set alignment.

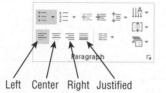

Left Center Right Justified

To use Distributed alignment, you must use the Paragraph dialog box. Click the dialog box launcher for the Paragraph group, and then choose the alignment from the Alignment drop-down list. Distributed appears on that list along with the other alignments.

> **TIP**
>
> *Alignment* refers to the text's position in its text box, not on the slide. If you want a text box centered on the slide but the text is left aligned within the box, simply move the text box where you want it. To align objects rather than individual text paragraphs, see "Aligning or Distributing Objects" in Chapter 9.

Formatting Text Boxes

In addition to formatting the paragraphs within a text box, you can format the text box itself. In Chapter 3, "Creating Slides and Text Boxes," you learned how to create, resize, and move text boxes; now it's time to find out how to change their appearances.

Applying Fills and Outlines

Text boxes are just like any other object in their fill and outline formatting. You get the full details of object formatting in Chapter 9, but here's a quick look.

The *fill* is the center of the text box, and the *outline* is the border. They can have separate formatting. For example, you can have a transparent fill with a solid border or vice versa. You can apply one of the Shape Styles presets from the Format tab to apply both at once, or you can adjust them separately with their respective menus on the Format tab. See Figure 6.15.

FIGURE 6.15

Format a text box using the Shape Styles group on the Drawing Tools Format tab.

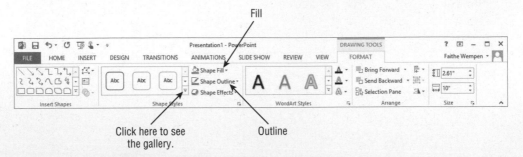

To apply one of the presets, click it, or open the gallery if the one you want doesn't appear. At the bottom of the gallery is Other Theme Fills, as shown in Figure 6.16. The fills on this submenu are the same as the background fills available from the Design tab, covered in Chapter 4. If you switch themes such that the background fill presets change, the background of the text box changes too, if it is formatted with one of these.

FIGURE 6.16

Choose Other Theme Fills to select one of the theme's backgrounds for the fill of the text box.

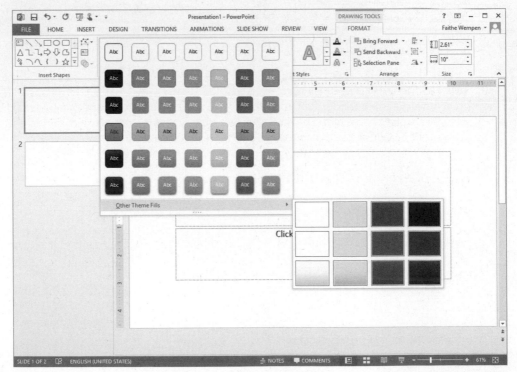

6

The Shape Fill and Shape Outline buttons, and their respective menus, will be familiar if you've reviewed Chapter 5, "Formatting Text," because they're very much the same as for text (WordArt). For the fill, you can choose a solid color, a gradient, a picture, or a texture. For the outline, you can select a color, thickness, and dash style. See Chapter 9 for the full details on fills and outlines.

> **TIP**
>
> Don't forget that you also have the Eyedropper tool available, which I mentioned in Chapter 5. It enables you to pick up any color on any object in the presentation, and you can use it from any color chooser in PowerPoint. For a text box, you can access it for the fill color by clicking Drawing Tools Format ⇨ Shape Styles ⇨ Shape Fill ⇨ Eyedropper. Then hover the mouse pointer over the color you want on any existing object and click to pick up and apply that color. To pick up a color for the shape outline, use Drawing Tools Format ⇨ Shape Styles ⇨ Shape Outline ⇨ Eyedropper.

Selecting one of the background fills in Figure 6.16 fills the text box separately with one of the background presets. It does not necessarily pick the *same* background preset as is applied to the slide master. If you want the text box to always have the same fill as the current background, you can either leave it set to No Fill (the default fill) or set its fill to match the background:

1. **Right-click the text box's border and choose Format Shape.** The Format Shape task pane opens.
2. **Click Fill to expand that category if it is not already expanded.**
3. **Click Slide Background Fill.**
4. **Close the task pane.**

There is only one minor difference between No Fill and a Slide Background Fill. If there are any objects stacked behind the text box, the text box obscures them when set to Background but shows them when set to No Fill. Figure 6.17 shows the difference for two text boxes placed on a wood grain background with a filled oval overlaid.

FIGURE 6.17

A slide background fill ignores any intervening objects.

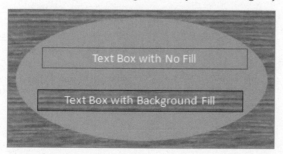

> **CAUTION**
>
> After you've set the text box's fill to Background, the Shape Styles presets no longer work on it until you go back into the Format Shape dialog box and set the fill to Solid Fill or one of the other fills.

Setting Fill Transparency

Fill transparency determines how much of the background (or whatever is layered behind the text box) shows through it. By default, it is set to 0, which means the text box is not transparent at all when it has a fill assigned to it. To set the fill transparency, follow these steps:

1. **Apply the desired fill (a solid, gradient, picture, or texture fill).**
2. **Right-click the text box and choose Format Shape.** The Format Shape task pane opens.
3. **Click Fill to expand the Fill controls if they are not already displayed.**
4. **Drag the Transparency slider or enter a percentage in its text box.** See Figure 6.18.

FIGURE 6.18

Set a text box's transparency in the Format Shape dialog box.

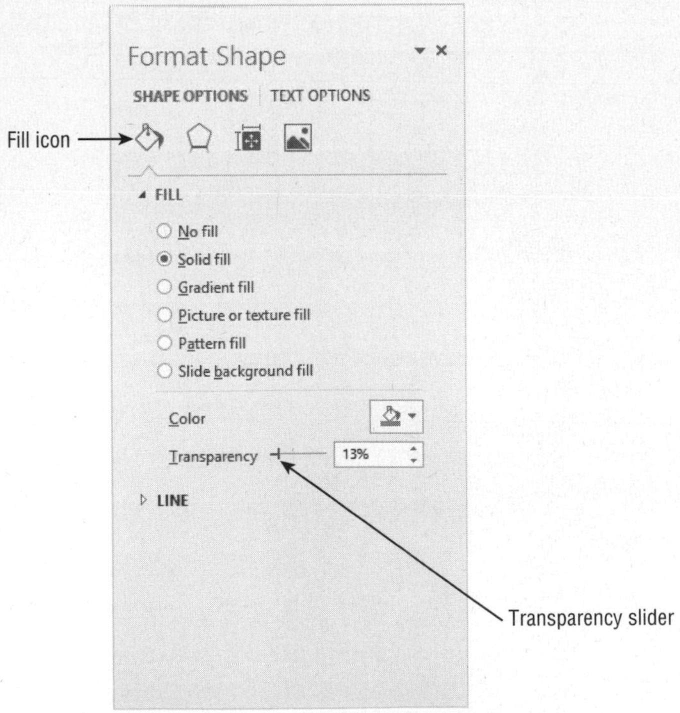

5. **Click Close.**

> **TIP**
>
> If the fill is a gradient, you must set the transparency separately for each of the gradient stops. (A *stop* is a color in the gradient.) Set the Gradient Stops drop-down list to Stop 1, adjust the transparency, set it to Stop 2, adjust the transparency, and so on. Chapter 9 explains gradients in more detail.

There is another way to set transparency, but it only works when you are applying solid fixed colors as follows:

1. **Select the text box.**
2. **Click Drawing Tools Format ⇨ Shape Styles ⇨ Shape Fill ⇨ More Fill Colors.**
3. **Select the desired color.**
4. **Drag the Transparency slider at the bottom of the dialog box to a new value, as shown in Figure 6.19.**

FIGURE 6.19

You can set fill transparency for solid-colored text boxes in the Color dialog box.

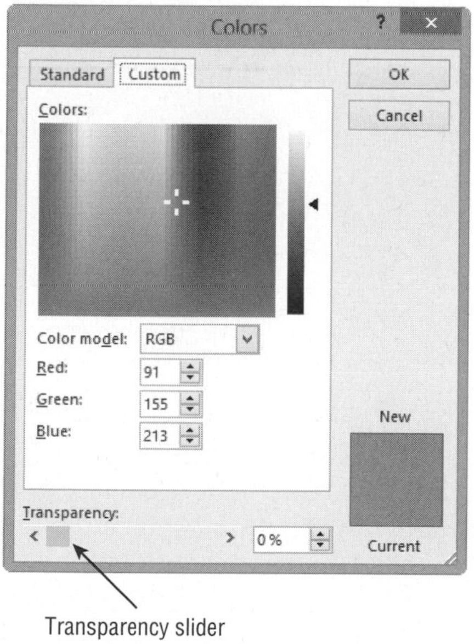

Transparency slider

5. **Click OK.**

Controlling Vertical Alignment

The vertical alignment is the positioning of the text vertically within the text box. The default vertical alignment is Top, which means that if there is extra space in the text box, it congregates at the bottom.

For the main text placeholders in a presentation, Top alignment is usually the best because it prevents the first line of text on each slide from looking like it is inconsistently placed. However, for a manual text box on an individual slide, Middle alignment often looks better, especially in a text box that has an outline or fill defined.

You can choose Top, Middle, or Bottom alignment, or centered versions of each (Top Centered, Middle Centered, or Bottom Centered). The centered versions center the text horizontally within the text box, but it's not the same thing as horizontal alignment on a paragraph level. The text remains left aligned with itself, but it scoots over to the center of the text box. Figure 6.20 shows the difference.

FIGURE 6.20

Vertical centering combinations with paragraph-level horizontal alignment.

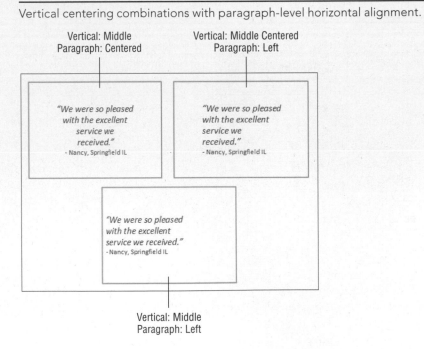

If you want one of the basic three alignments, click Align Text in the Paragraph group on the Home tab, as shown in Figure 6.21, and select Top, Middle, or Bottom.

FIGURE 6.21

Select a vertical alignment from the Align Text button's menu.

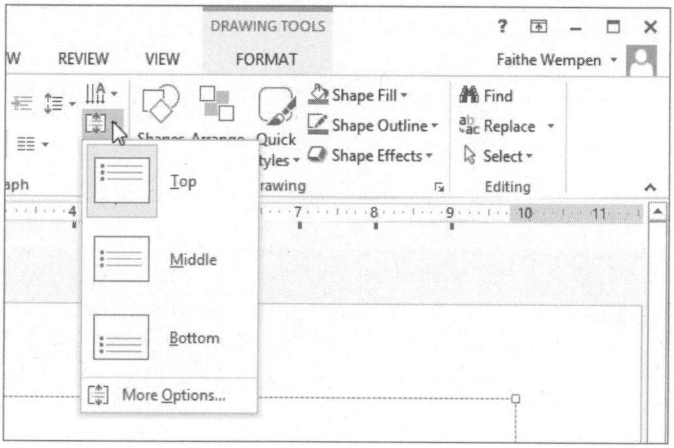

If you want one of the centered-type alignments, you must use the Paragraph dialog box. Follow these steps:

1. **Choose Home ⇨ Paragraph ⇨ Align Text ⇨ More Options, or right-click the text box and choose Format Shape, to open the Format Shape task pane.**

2. **Click Text Options.**

3. **Click the Text Box icon.**

4. **Choose a Vertical alignment setting.** See Figure 6.22.

5. **In the AutoFit section, choose Do Not AutoFit or Shrink Text on Overflow.**

   If Resize Shape to Fit Text is selected here, the text box can't be made any taller than is necessary to accommodate the text in it, so there will be no blank space to allocate vertically and no difference between the vertical alignment settings.

6. **Close the task pane.**

Changing Text Box Rotation

PowerPoint provides several types of rotation. You can spin things around a center point (the traditional 2-D type of rotation), or you can apply several 3-D rotation effects. However, the 3-D type is not well suited for text boxes because it tends to distort the text.

See Chapter 9 to learn more about the 3-D type and to experiment with a text box. See Chapter 5 for 3-D type as it pertains to WordArt.

FIGURE 6.22

Choose a vertical alignment option.

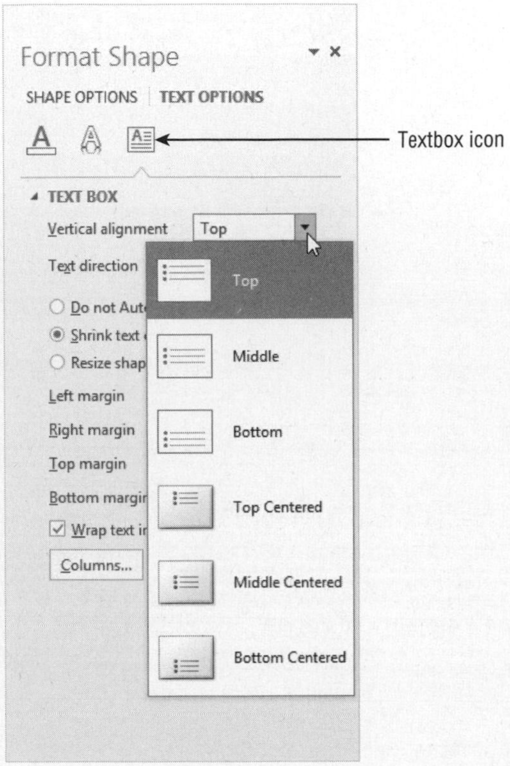

You can rotate a text box in 2-D by dragging its rotation handle, the green circle at the top of the text box. The text stays with it, so you can create upside-down text, sideways text, or text at whatever angle you like, as shown in Figure 6.23.

FIGURE 6.23

Rotate a text box by dragging its rotation handle.

If you want to rotate the text box only, but not the text within it, here's how to accomplish that:

1. **Apply a border or fill to the text box (of any type) so you can see the rotation results.**
2. **Right-click the text box and choose Format Shape.**
3. **Click Shape Options, and then click the Effects icon.**
4. **Click 3-D Rotation to expand that set of controls.**
5. **Select the Keep Text Flat check box.**
6. **Click the buttons on the Z Rotation: row to rotate the text box while leaving the text as is.**
7. **Close the task pane.**

Changing Text Direction

Instead of rotating the text box, you might prefer to just rotate the text within it. Text can run vertically on its side, facing either to the left or right, or the letters can be at normal orientation individually but stacked vertically. To set a text direction, use the Text Direction button in the Paragraph group on the Home tab. Figure 6.24 shows the menu and some examples of the text direction settings.

FIGURE 6.24

You can set text direction separately from text box rotation.

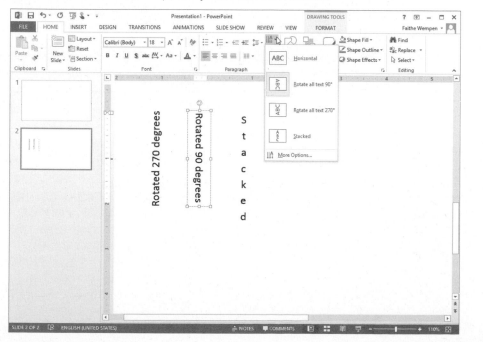

CAUTION

After changing the text direction, you might need to resize the text box so that the text flows in the new direction.

TIP

When text is rotated 90 or 270 degrees, it often looks better if you use the Character Spacing button in the Font group to set its spacing to Loose. Conversely, stacked text often looks better when set to Very Tight.

Setting Internal Margins

A text box's internal margins control the amount of blank space between the edge of the box and the text inside it, just like the margins in a word-processing document except that each text box has its own individual margin settings. To set a text box's internal margins, follow these steps:

1. **Right-click the text box's border and choose Format Shape.** The Format Shape task pane opens.
2. **Click Text Options, and then click the Textbox icon.** The Text Box settings appear (Figure 6.25).
3. **Change the Left Margin, Right Margin, Top Margin, and Bottom Margin settings as needed.**
4. **Close the task pane.**

Creating Multiple Columns

In PowerPoint 2013, you can set up a text box to create multiple linked columns within a single text frame. This provides an easy way to convert a single-column layout into a multi-column one. To adjust the number of columns used in a text box, follow these steps:

1. **Select the text box.**
2. **Click Home ⇨ Paragraph ⇨ Add or Remove Columns.**
3. **Select a number of columns from the menu, as shown in Figure 6.26.**

If you need a different number of columns, or you want to specify the spacing between them, choose More Columns from the menu. Then in the Columns dialog box (see Figure 6.27), enter a number to specify the number of columns and set an amount of spacing in inches.

FIGURE 6.25

Set the internal margins for a text box.

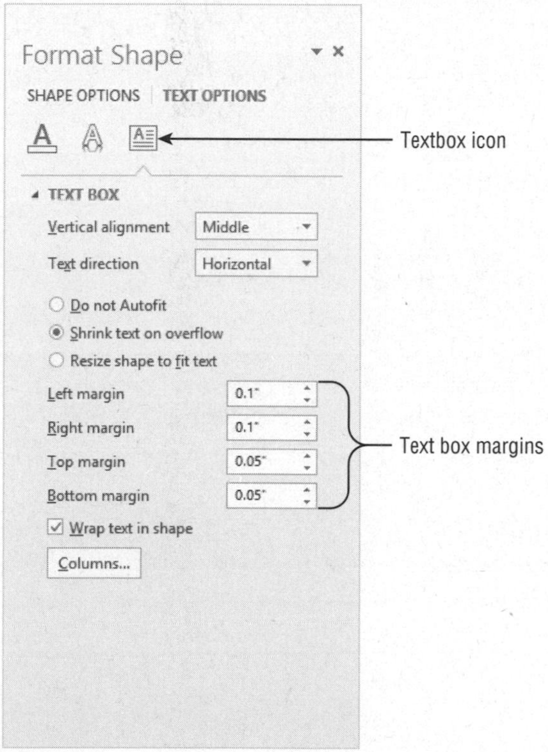

FIGURE 6.26

Choose a number of columns for the text box.

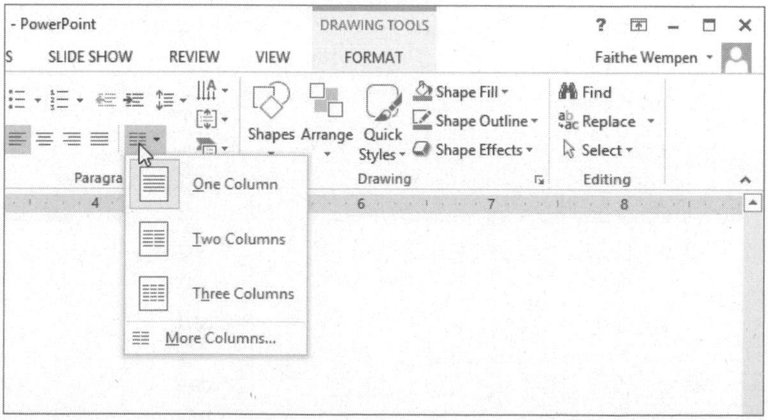

FIGURE 6.27

Use the Columns dialog box to enter a larger number of columns than 3 or to adjust spacing between columns.

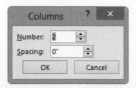

Summary

In this chapter, you learned how to format text boxes and the paragraphs within them. You learned about bulleted and numbered lists, tabs and indents, vertical and horizontal alignment, and more. Now you have the tools you need to set up a text-based presentation. (Don't worry, graphics are coming up in Part II of the book!)

But what good is nice-looking text if it's inaccurate or contains spelling errors? In the next chapter, you learn how to make corrections to text with the spelling checker and the research tools, and you learn how to automate certain types of corrections.

Correcting and Improving Text

IN THIS CHAPTER

Finding and replacing text

Correcting your spelling

Setting the editing language

Using AutoCorrect to fix common problems

Using AutoFormat as you type

Using smart tags

Using the research tools

PowerPoint contains many tools that can help you avoid embarrassing mistakes in your presentation's text, and this chapter takes a look at some of them. You'll learn how to replace one text string with another, perform a spelling check, set up PowerPoint to correct your most common errors automatically, and use the research tools in PowerPoint, including encyclopedias, translation guides, and thesauruses.

Finding and Replacing Text

Like all Microsoft applications, PowerPoint has a built-in Find tool, which lets you search for — and, optionally, replace — a string of text anywhere in your presentation. This feature works in all views except for Slide Show, in which it isn't applicable. However, in Slide Sorter view, it finds and replaces all instances only; you cannot interactively confirm each instance.

We will first take a look at the Find function. For example, let's say that Bob Smith was fired this morning. (Poor Bob.) Now you need to go through your presentation and see whether Bob's name is mentioned so that you can take out any lines that refer to him. Follow these steps to find a text string (such as *Bob Smith*):

1. **Click Home ⇨ Editing ⇨ Find, or press Ctrl+F.** The Find dialog box appears.
2. **Type what you want to find in the Find What text box, as shown in Figure 7.1.** If you want to find a text string that you have searched for before, open the Find What drop-down list and select it. This is sometimes faster than retyping.

FIGURE 7.1

Type what you want to find, and then click the Find Next button.

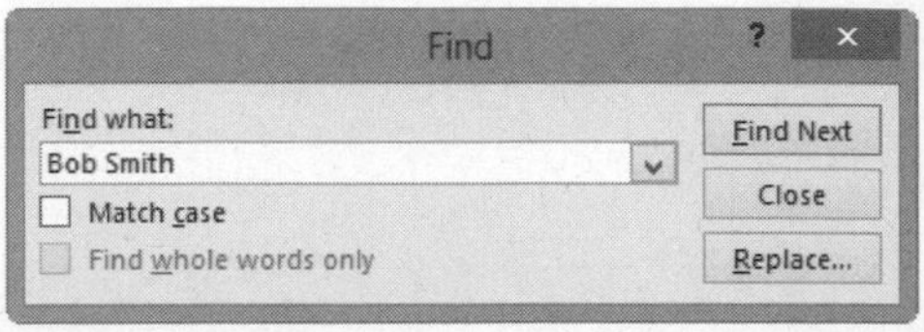

3. **If you want to find only whole words or to match the case, select the appropriate check box.**

4. **Click Find Next.** The display jumps to the first instance of the text in your presentation, starting from the insertion point, working downward through the presentation, and then looping back to the top.

5. **If the found instance was not the one that you were looking for, or if you want to see if there are other instances, click the Find Next button again.** You can continue clicking the Find Next button until you have seen all of the instances. When PowerPoint cannot find any more instances, the message "The search text was not found" appears and you must click OK to clear it.

6. **Click Close when you are finished.**

You can also perform a replace, which adds functionality to the Find feature. This action finds the specified text and then replaces it with other text that you specify. For example, suppose that you are preparing a presentation for the Acme Corporation's sales staff. Two days before the presentation, you find out that the Primo Corporation has purchased Acme. You now need to go through the entire presentation and change every instance of *Acme* to *Primo*.

TIP

While you are using the Find feature, as explained in the preceding steps, you can switch to the Replace dialog box by clicking the Replace button. When you do so, the Find string transfers over to the Replace dialog box, so that you don't have to retype it.

To find and replace a text string, follow these steps:

1. **Click Home ⇨ Editing ⇨ Replace, or press Ctrl+H.** The Replace dialog box appears.

NOTE

The Replace button on the Home tab has a drop-down list. From this list, you can tell Replace Fonts to do a find-and-replace for certain font usage. You learn more about this in Chapter 5, "Formatting Text."

2. **Type the text that you want to find in the Find What text box.** If you have previously used Find or Replace, the most recent text that you found appears in the text box.

3. **Type the new text in the Replace With text box.** For example, if you were replacing *layoffs* with *downsizing*, it would look like Figure 7.2.

FIGURE 7.2

Enter what you want to find and what you want to replace it with.

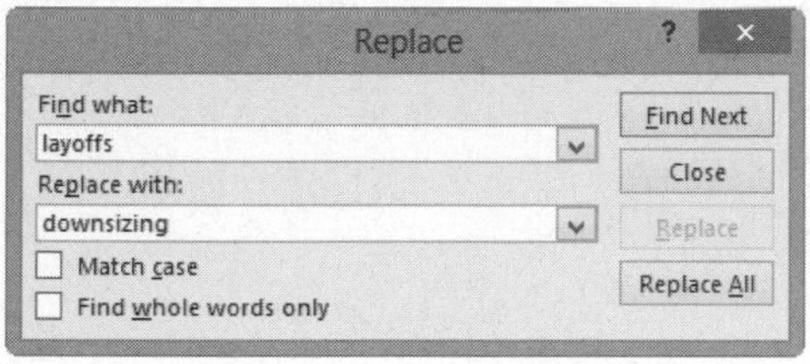

4. **If you want whole words only or a case-sensitive search, select the appropriate check box.**

5. **Click Find Next to find the first instance.**

6. **If you want to replace that instance, click the Replace button.** The next instance appears automatically. After this, click Find Next to go on.

7. **Repeat step 6 to check and selectively replace each instance, or click the Replace All button to change all instances at once.**

8. **When you are finished, click Close.** You may have to click OK first to clear a dialog box telling you that the specified text was not found.

Correcting Your Spelling and Grammar

If you think that a spelling and grammar check can't improve the look of your presentation, just think for a moment how ugly a blatant spelling error would look in huge type on a five-foot projection screen. Frightening, isn't it? If that image makes you nervous, it should. Spelling and grammar mistakes can creep past even the most literate people, and pop up where you least expect them, often at embarrassing moments.

Fortunately, like other Microsoft Office programs, PowerPoint comes with a powerful spelling and grammar program that can check your work for you at any time, minimizing the number of embarrassing mistakes. The Office programs all use the same spelling and grammar checker, and so if you are familiar with it in another Office application, you should be able to breeze through a spell check in PowerPoint with no problem.

Checking an Individual Word

As you work, PowerPoint underlines words that aren't in its dictionary, plus any potential grammar errors, with a red, wavy line. Whenever you see a red-underlined word, you can right-click it to see a list of spelling or grammar suggestions, as shown in Figure 7.3. Click the correction that you want, or click one of the other commands.

FIGURE 7.3

Right-click a red-underlined word for quick spelling advice.

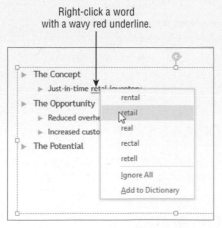

For a grammar error, an additional command is available at the bottom of the suggestion list: Ignore. It only ignores this instance of the potential grammar error.

For a spelling error, two other commands are available:

- **Ignore All.** Ignores this and all other instances of the word in this PowerPoint session. If you exit and restart PowerPoint, the list is wiped out.

■ **Add to Dictionary.** Adds this word to PowerPoint's custom dictionary. (You learn more about the custom dictionary later in this chapter.)

TIP

If you don't want to see the red wavy underlines on-screen, you can turn the feature off by selecting File ⇨ Options and then clicking Proofing. Click the Hide Spelling and Grammar Errors check box and click OK. This just turns the underlines off; it doesn't stop PowerPoint from checking spelling as you type. A separate Check Spelling As You Type check box, in the same location, does that. Turning off Check Spelling As You Type relieves PowerPoint of a small processing burden, making it run a bit faster.

Checking the Entire Presentation

If your presentation is long, it can become tiresome to individually right-click each wavy-underlined word or phrase. In such cases, it's easier to use the Spelling feature in PowerPoint to check all of the words in the presentation.

To begin the spell check, click Review ⇨ Proofing and then click the Spelling button, or press F7. If there are no misspelled words in your presentation, PowerPoint presents a dialog box telling you that your spell check is complete. Click OK to close this dialog box. If, on the other hand, PowerPoint finds a misspelled word, a Spelling task pane opens (or a Grammar task pane if it's a grammar error), and you can choose from several options. Figure 7.4 shows the Spelling task pane.

The following options are on the Spelling task pane:

■ **Suggestions list.** Lists words that are close to the spelling of the word that you actually typed. Choose the one you want by clicking it and then click the Change button.

■ **Change button.** Changes the selected instance of the word to the word selected in the Suggestions list.

■ **Change All button.** Changes all occurrences of the word in the entire presentation to the word selected in the Suggestions list.

■ **Ignore button.** Skips the selected instance of the word, removing the red underline that indicates it may be misspelled.

■ **Ignore All button.** Skips over all occurrences of the word in this PowerPoint session only.

■ **Add button.** Adds the word to PowerPoint's custom dictionary so that it is recognized in the future.

■ **Pronunciation button.** Pronounces the word pronounced that is currently selected in the Suggestions list.

■ **Language box.** Selects a different language (and thereby a different dictionary) with which to check spelling.

FIGURE 7.4

When PowerPoint finds a misspelled word with the spell checker, you can respond to it using these controls.

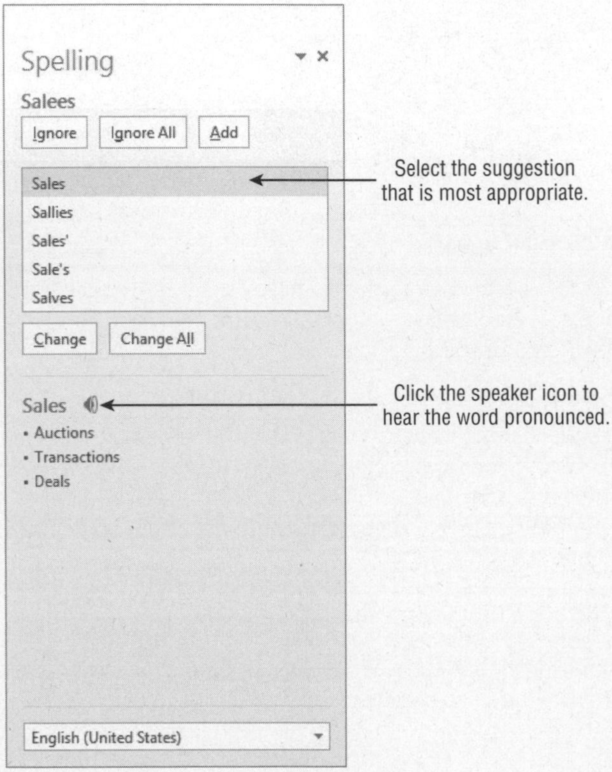

Spelling

Salees

Ignore   Ignore All   Add

Sales
Sallies
Sales'
Sale's
Salves

Change   Change All

Select the suggestion that is most appropriate.

Sales 🔊

• Auctions
• Transactions
• Deals

Click the speaker icon to hear the word pronounced.

English (United States)

When PowerPoint can't find any more misspelled words, it displays a dialog box to let you know this; click OK to close it.

TIP

If you have more than one language dictionary available (for example, if you use PowerPoint in a multilingual office and have purchased multiple language packs from Microsoft), then you can specify which language's dictionary to use for which text. To do so, select the text that is in a different language than the rest of the presentation, and then click Review ➪ Language ➪ Language ➪ Set Proofing Language. Select the appropriate language from the list and click OK.

If PowerPoint is configured to also check for grammar errors (see the next section, "Setting Spelling and Grammar Options"), a Grammar task pane appears when it detects one. Figure 7.5 shows an example. The options are much simpler; you can choose to ignore the grammar error or to change to one of the suggestions on the Suggestions list.

FIGURE 7.5

When PowerPoint finds a grammar error, you can respond to it using these controls.

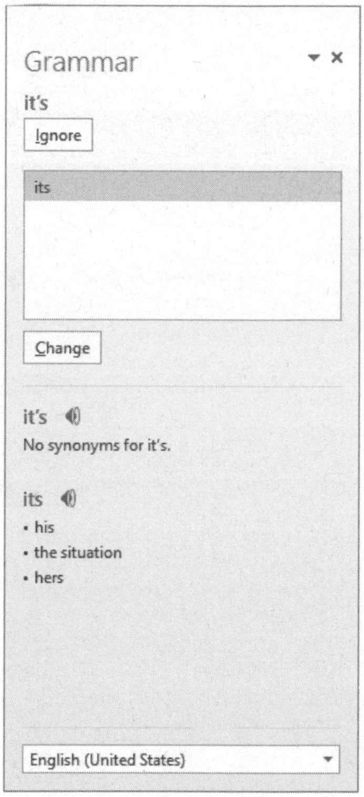

Setting Spelling and Grammar Options

There are many options available for controlling the spelling and grammar corrections in PowerPoint. On the Proofing tab, the options under the When Correcting Spelling in Microsoft Office Programs section carry over to other Office programs, so when you make a settings change in one Office app, it affects all of your other Office apps. The settings in the When Correcting Spelling in PowerPoint section apply only to PowerPoint.

To control how (and whether) the spelling and grammar checkers operate in PowerPoint, do the following:

1. **Choose File ⇨ Options, and click Proofing.** The Proofing options appear (Figure 7.6).

2. **Select or deselect any of the check boxes as desired in the When Correcting Spelling in Microsoft Office Programs section:**

   - **Ignore Words in UPPERCASE.** Prevents the spell checker from flagging acronyms.

   - **Ignore Words That Contain Numbers.** Prevents the spell checker from noticing words with digits in them, such as license plate numbers or model numbers.

- **Ignore Internet and File Addresses.** Prevents the spell checker from flagging Web or e-mail addresses, network paths, or file paths.

- **Flag Repeated Words.** Flags second and subsequent instances of the same word in a row, preventing you from making mistakes like writing "the the."

- **Enforce Accented Uppercase in French.** Suggests accents for uppercase letters as appropriate. Applicable only when the editing language is French.

- **Suggest from Main Dictionary Only.** Ignores any custom spelling dictionaries if any are present.

- **Foreign language modes.** Includes drop-down lists for each of the languages that appear so you can fine-tune the spell check for each language. In Figure 7.6, the choices are French modes and Spanish modes.

FIGURE 7.6

You can set spelling options here.

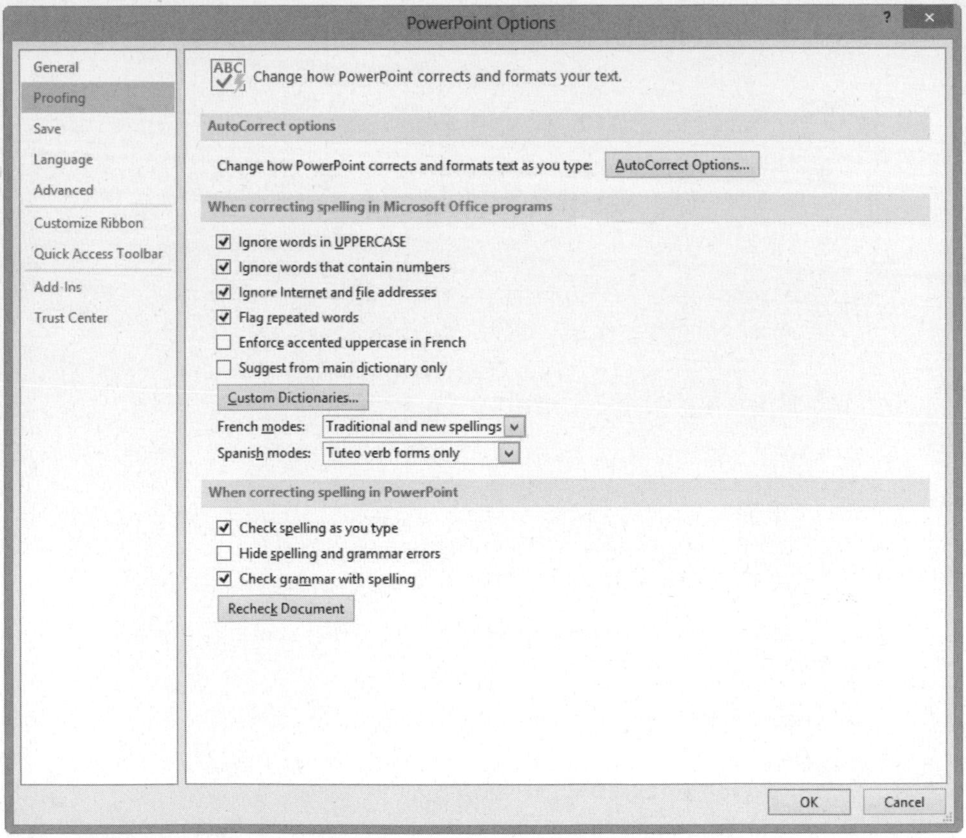

3. **Select or deselect any of the check boxes as desired in the When Correcting Spelling in PowerPoint section:**

   - **Check Spelling As You Type.** This option is on by default. Turning it off prevents the spell checker from noticing and underlining words in red that it can't find in its dictionary. This can cause a small improvement in performance on a slow computer; you will not notice the difference on a fast computer.

   - **Hide Spelling and Grammar Errors.** This option is off by default. Selecting this check box prevents the red, wavy underline from appearing beneath misspelled words. It does not prevent the spell checker from checking them; you can right-click a misspelled word to see suggestions for it, as you normally would.

   - **Check Grammar with Spelling.** This option is off by default; when you turn it on, grammar checking becomes available, both with red wavy underlines for individual instances and with the Spelling command on the Review tab.

4. **Click OK to accept the new settings.**

Working with Custom Dictionaries

The main spelling dictionary in PowerPoint is read-only, and so the words you add to the dictionary have to be stored somewhere else. This is where custom dictionaries come in. A custom dictionary contains a list of words that should not be flagged as misspellings. It can include proper names, acronyms, abbreviations, or any other codes or text strings that you frequently type.

> **NOTE**
> PowerPoint shares custom dictionaries with the other Office 2013 applications, so you can use them in PowerPoint or in one of the other applications.

Specifying the Default Custom Dictionary

As you are spell-checking, you can click Add (in the Spelling task pane) or Add to Dictionary (from the shortcut menu when you right-click a red wavy-underlined word) to add the word to the default custom dictionary.

In Office 2013, the default custom dictionary is `RoamingCustom.dic`, and it's stored in `C:\Users\`*username*`\AppData\Roaming\Microsoft\Office\15.0\89bd0643 \Proofing`. You should leave this dictionary as the default in most cases. This dictionary is shared via SkyDrive or Active Directory with other devices on which you run Office.

In Office 2007 and 2010, the default custom dictionary was `Custom.dic`, stored in `C:\Users\`*username*`\AppData\Roaming\Microsoft\UProof`, and this custom dictionary is still available in Office 2013. If you need to share a custom dictionary with Office 2007 or 2010 applications, you should continue to use this dictionary as your default.

To change which dictionary is the default to which new words will be saved, follow these steps:

1. **Choose File ➪ Options.**
2. **Click Proofing.**
3. **Click Custom Dictionaries.**
4. **Select the desired custom dictionary from the list.** See Figure 7.7.
5. **Click Change Default.** That dictionary becomes the default, and (Default) appears next to it.
6. **Click OK to close the Custom Dictionaries dialog box.**
7. **Click OK to close the PowerPoint Options dialog box.**

FIGURE 7.7

Choose which custom dictionary will be the default for new word storage.

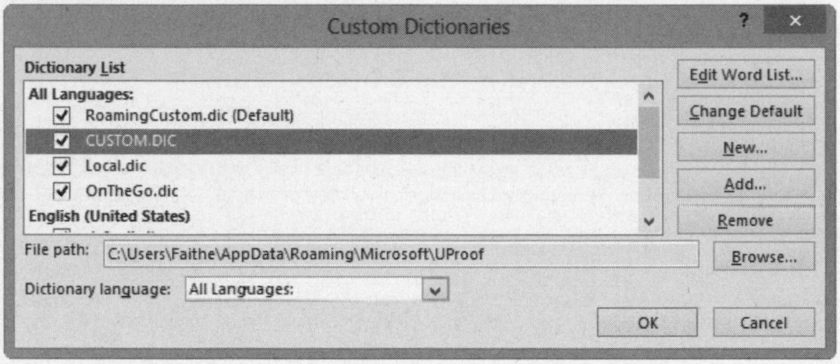

Editing a Custom Dictionary

One way to get words into the default custom dictionary is to type them in a presentation and then use the Spelling feature to add them. However, you can also add words to the custom dictionary without having to type them in the presentation and then spell-check them. Follow these steps to add words:

1. **Choose File ➪ Options.**
2. **Click Proofing.**
3. **Click Custom Dictionaries.** The Custom Dictionaries dialog box opens (Figure 7.7).
4. **Select the desired custom dictionary from the list.**
5. **Click Edit Word List.** A dialog box appears, listing all of the words that are currently in that dictionary. See Figure 7.8.
6. **To add a new word, type it in the Word(s) text box and click Add.** Words can be no longer than 64 characters.

FIGURE 7.8

Add a word to the custom dictionary.

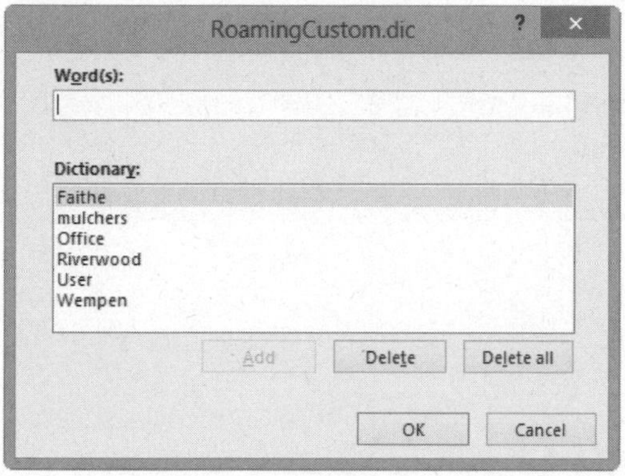

7. **(Optional) To delete a word, select it and click Delete.** To clear the entire custom dictionary, click Delete All.

8. **Click OK when you are finished editing the custom dictionary.**

> **CAUTION**
>
> The custom dictionary accepts multiword entries, but you should enter them as separate words in the list; it does not recognize spellings that consist of only part of the entered word. For example, you could enter *Shawna Browslawski*, but the spell checker would not recognize *Shawna* or *Browslawski* by itself. However, if you enter them as separate words, they are accepted either individually or together.

If you have a lot of words to add to the dictionary, you might prefer to edit the dictionary file manually. Dictionary files are plaintext files, so you can edit them in Notepad. You can even combine two or more separate dictionary files into a single file by copying and pasting lists of words between them. To edit a dictionary file, open it in a text editor such as Notepad. Remember, the paths for the Microsoft-supplied dictionary files are as follows:

- Users*username*\\AppData\\Roaming\\Microsoft\\Office\\15.0\\89bd0643
  \\Proofing\\RoamingCustom.dic

- Users*username*\\AppData\\Roaming\\Microsoft\\UProof\\custom.dic

Creating a New Custom Dictionary

A custom dictionary file can be as large as 64KB in size, or 5,000 words. If you need a larger custom dictionary than this, you must create another dictionary file. You might also want additional custom dictionaries to keep sets of words separate for different clients or projects. For example, when working for a client with many trademarked product names that consist of nontraditional spellings of common words, you might want to set those names as correctly spelled, but when working for another client who does not use those names, you might want those words to be flagged as possible misspellings. You can enable or disable each custom dictionary, so you can enable only the dictionaries that apply to the present project.

> **TIP**
>
> All spell checks use the main dictionary as well as all of the custom dictionaries that are selected in the Dictionary List section in the Custom Dictionaries dialog box. To disable a certain dictionary from being used, deselect its check box in the Custom Dictionaries dialog box.

To create a custom dictionary, follow these steps:

1. **Choose File ⇨ Options.**
2. **Click Proofing.**
3. **Click Custom Dictionaries.**
4. **Click New.** The Create Custom Dictionary dialog box appears.
5. **Navigate to the location in which you want to store the dictionary.** Where you store it depends on which users you want to be able to access it:

   - To make the dictionary accessible to all users of your PC, create a new folder on the C drive called Dictionaries (or anything else you want to call it) and store dictionaries there.

   - To make the dictionary accessible to only the current Windows user, store it in the default custom dictionary location, `Users\`*username*`\AppData\Roaming \Microsoft\UProof`, which is where `custom.dic` is stored.

6. **Type a name for the dictionary in the File Name text box.**
7. **Click Save.**

The new dictionary appears in the Dictionary List section in the Custom Dictionaries dialog box.

> **TIP**
>
> All enabled custom dictionaries are checked automatically during the spell-check process, but newly added words are placed only in the default custom dictionary. To set the default dictionary, select a custom dictionary in the Custom Dictionaries dialog box and then click the Change Default button, as you learned earlier in this chapter.

Setting the Editing Language

PowerPoint performs spell check using the native language for your copy of Office. For example, if you bought your copy in the United States, then English (U.S.) is the default language. It is important that you select the correct country as well as the correct language because some countries have different spellings than others for the same language. For example, in the United Kingdom, *s* substitutes for the American *z* in words like *realise/ realize*, so if you use the wrong editing language, words will be marked as misspelled when they really aren't. The Language setting is also used by some of the research tools, which are covered later in this chapter.

To mark a passage of text as a certain language (and country if applicable), follow these steps:

1. **Select the text that you want to mark.** To mark text on more than one slide, select the text from the Outline pane in Outline view.

2. **Click Review ⇨ Language ⇨ Language ⇨ Set Proofing Language.** The Language dialog box opens.

3. **Select the language and country from the list, as shown in Figure 7.9.**

FIGURE 7.9

Select a language for the text.

4. **(Optional) To set a certain language as the default, select it and click Default; then click Yes to confirm.**

5. **Click OK.**

Using AutoCorrect to Fix Common Problems

With AutoCorrect, PowerPoint can automatically correct certain common misspellings and formatting errors as you type. For example, one of the AutoCorrect actions that is already set up by default is to change *teh* to *the*. To access AutoCorrect and manage the automatic corrections it makes, follow these steps:

1. **Choose File ⇨ Options.**

2. **Click Proofing.**

3. **Click AutoCorrect Options.** The AutoCorrect dialog box opens.

4. **If it is not already displayed, click the AutoCorrect tab, shown in Figure 7.10.**

FIGURE 7.10

Set up the corrections that you want PowerPoint to handle automatically as you type.

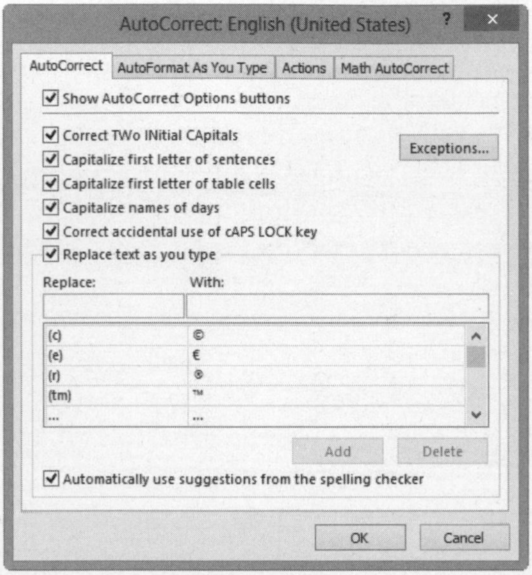

5. **Select the options that you want.** At the top of the dialog box is a series of check boxes that help you to fine-tune some other corrections that AutoCorrect makes in addition to spelling corrections:

   ■ **Show AutoCorrect Options Buttons.** This option controls whether a button is available to reverse an AutoCorrect action after the action occurs. (For more on how to use this button, see the end of this section.)

   ■ **Correct TWo INitial CApitals.** If you accidentally hold down the Shift key too long and type two capital letters in a row (such as MIcrosoft), PowerPoint corrects this error if you leave this option selected.

   ■ **Capitalize First Letter of Sentences.** Leave this option selected to have PowerPoint capitalize the first letter of the first word after a sentence-ending punctuation mark, such as a period, or to capitalize the first letter of the word that occurs at the beginning of a paragraph.

TIP

Click the Exceptions button to open an AutoCorrect Exceptions dialog box. Here, you can enter a list of capitalization exceptions, such as abbreviations that use periods but aren't at the end of a sentence (for example, *approx.* and *Ave.*). You can also set up a list of TWo INitial CApitals exceptions.

- **Capitalize First Letter of Table Cells.** Leave this option selected to capitalize the first letter of the first word within a table cell. Otherwise, PowerPoint does not treat text in a table as a sentence for capitalization purposes.

- **Capitalize Names of Days.** Leave this option selected to make sure that the names of days, such as *Sunday*, *Monday*, and so on, are capitalized.

- **Correct Accidental Use of cAPS LOCK key.** If you accidentally leave Caps Lock on, PowerPoint can sometimes detect it and fix this problem. For example, if you type the sentence, "hE WAS GLAD TO SEE US," PowerPoint may conclude that the Caps Lock is inappropriately on, and so it turns the Caps Lock off for you and fixes the sentence.

- **Replace Text as You Type.** This option activates the main portion of AutoCorrect, the word list. You must leave this option selected if you want AutoCorrect to correct spelling as you are typing. For example, if you type *yoiu*, PowerPoint automatically changes it to *you*.

6. **Add items that you commonly misspell to the Replace/With list at the bottom of the dialog box.** By default, this list already contains a number of word and symbol pairs. To the left is the common misspelling, and to the right is the word that PowerPoint substitutes in its place. Scroll through this list to see the types of corrections that PowerPoint makes. To add a word pair to the list, type the misspelling in the Replace text box and then type the replacement in the With text box. Then click the Add button. You can also add corrections through the Spelling dialog box.

> **TIP**
>
> You can use AutoCorrect to insert typographical symbols. The (C) entry is already set up to insert a copyright symbol, for example, and the (R) entry will insert a registered trademark symbol. If there is a symbol you use frequently yourself, feel free to set up an AutoCorrect entry to insert it more easily.

If PowerPoint insists on making a correction that you do not want, you can delete that correction from the list. Simply select it from the list and click Delete. For example, one of my clients likes me to code certain headings with (C) in front of them, and so the first thing that I do in any Office program is to remove the AutoCorrect entry that specifies that (C) must be converted to a copyright symbol ©.

7. **When you are finished, click OK to close the AutoCorrect dialog box.**
8. **Click OK to close the PowerPoint Options dialog box.**

> **CAUTION**
>
> Don't use AutoCorrect for misspellings that you may sometimes want to change to some other word or you may introduce embarrassing mistakes into your document. For example, if you often type *pian* instead of *pain*, and you also sometimes type *pian* instead of *piano*, don't tell PowerPoint to always AutoCorrect to *pain* or you may find that PowerPoint has corrected your attempt at typing *piano* and made it *pain*!

When an AutoCorrect action occurs, provided you have not turned off the icon, a short horizontal line appears when you point at the AutoCorrected word. Place your cursor over it to display an AutoCorrect Options icon, and then click the icon to see a menu, as shown in Figure 7.11. From here, you can reverse the action, disable that particular correction, or open the AutoCorrect Options dialog box.

FIGURE 7.11

You can reverse an action, disable a correction, or open the AutoCorrect Options dialog box.

Using AutoFormat As You Type

The AutoFormat As You Type feature enables PowerPoint to convert certain letter combinations to typographical characters that look nicer on a slide than plain text. For example, one of the AutoFormat As You Type actions is to convert two dashes (--) into a single long dash (—).

Other actions include automatic bulleted and numbered lists. For example, in a manual text box, you might type 1, press Tab, and type a paragraph, then type 2, press Tab, and type another paragraph. In this case, PowerPoint would guess that you want a numbered list and apply the Numbering format to those paragraphs (just as if you had clicked the Numbering button on the toolbar). Figure 7.12 shows all of the AutoFormat As You Type options.

To change the AutoFormat As You Type settings, follow these steps:

1. **Choose File ⇨ Options.**
2. **Click Proofing, and then click AutoCorrect Options.**
3. **Click the AutoFormat As You Type tab.**
4. **Select or deselect the options for the features that you want.** See Figure 7.12.
5. **Click OK.**

For more on the AutoFit Title Text to Placeholder and AutoFit Body Text to Placeholder features, as well as changing a text box's AutoFit behavior in general, see Chapter 3, "Creating Slides and Text Boxes."

FIGURE 7.12

You can select the AutoFormat As You Type options that you want in this dialog box.

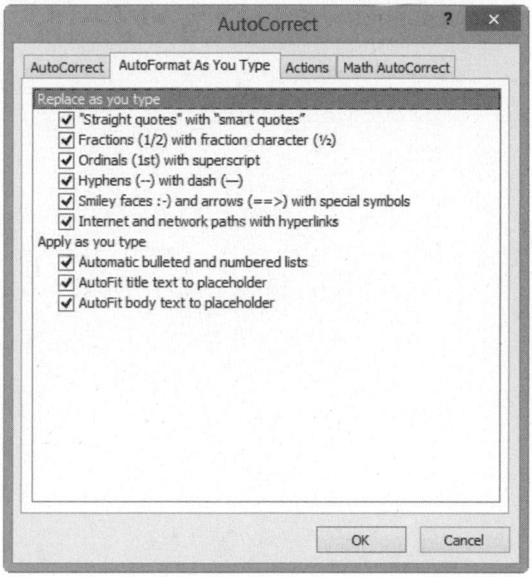

Using the Research Tools

The Research feature is available in most of the Office applications, including PowerPoint. It enables you to connect with various online and offline data stores to look up information. This may include online encyclopedias, dictionaries, and news services.

The available tools are divided into two broad categories of sites: *reference* and *research*. Reference sites include dictionaries, thesauruses, and translation utilities; research sites include encyclopedias and news services.

You can consult all of the reference sites as a group, or you can consult an individual tool. For example, you can look up a word in the dictionary, thesaurus, or translator all at once, or you can just use the thesaurus.

Looking Up a Word in a Dictionary

To get a simple, concise definition of a word, a dictionary is your best bet. Here's how to use the dictionary in PowerPoint:

1. **Click Review ⇨ Proofing ⇨ Research.** The Research task pane opens.
2. **Open the drop-down list of references at the top of the task pane and choose Encarta Dictionary: English (North America) or whatever language and country is appropriate.**

3. **In the Search For text box, type the word that you want to look up, and either press Enter or click the green arrow icon.** A definition of the word appears, as shown in Figure 7.13.
4. **Close the task pane when you are finished using the dictionary.**

FIGURE 7.13

Look up a word in the *Encarta Dictionary*.

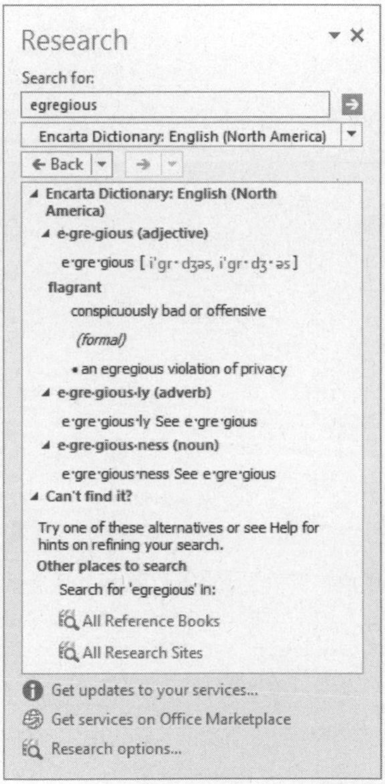

TIP

There are multiple dictionaries available; click the Research Options link at the bottom of the task pane to open a dialog box from which you can select other dictionaries. For example, the English version of Office comes with both North American and United Kingdom dictionaries, although only one is enabled by default (depending on the country in which you purchased Office).

Finding Synonyms and Antonyms with the Thesaurus

The Thesaurus feature works just like a hardbound thesaurus book. It lets you look up synonyms and antonyms for a word so that you can make your vocabulary more varied and colorful.

NOTE

Synonyms are words that have similar meanings. Antonyms have opposite meanings.

To look up a word in the thesaurus, follow these steps:

1. **Select a word that you want to look up.**

2. **Click Review ➪ Proofing ➪ Thesaurus.** The Thesaurus task pane opens with the word's synonyms and antonyms displayed.

   Synonyms are grouped by general meaning. Antonyms are followed by the word (*Antonym*).

NOTE

If the word that you want to look up does not already appear in the presentation, skip step 1, and then, after clicking the Thesaurus button, type the desired word in the Search For text box. Then press Enter or click the green arrow icon.

3. **To insert a word into the presentation, do the following:**

   a. Position the insertion point where you want to insert the found word, or select the word that you want to replace (if you did not select it already in step 1).

   b. Open the task pane menu for the word that you want to insert. (Move your cursor over the word to display a down arrow, and then click the down arrow.)

   c. Click Insert. As you can see in Figure 7.14, you can also click Copy (to copy it to the Clipboard for later insertion).

4. **Close the task pane when you are finished using the thesaurus.**

Translating Text into Another Language

Translation helps you to translate text into a variety of languages. It's not a perfect translation by any means, so don't embarrass yourself and try to translate your entire presentation for a foreign audience. However, for simple words and phrases, as well as rough approximations of meaning, it can serve you well.

To translate text in a presentation, follow these steps:

1. **Select the text to be translated.**

2. **On the Review tab, click Review ➪ Language ➪ Translate ➪ Translate Selected Text.** The Translation tools appear in the Research task pane.

3. **Select the desired languages in the From and To drop-down lists, as shown in Figure 7.15.** A translation appears for the selected text.

4. **Close the Research task pane when you are finished using the Translator.**

FIGURE 7.14

Select a word in the Thesaurus, and then insert it or copy it.

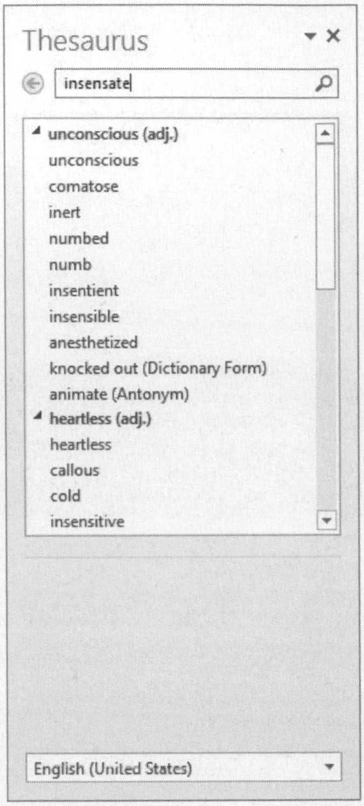

Office 2013 also includes a Mini Translator utility that can quickly help you translate text into a specified language. To enable it, choose Review ⇨ Language ⇨ Translate ⇨ Translate ⇨ Mini Translator. In the dialog box that appears, choose the language you want to translate into and click OK. After doing that, you can point to a word to pop up a Mini Translator, which provides a translation for the word if one is available. See Figure 7.16.

Using Research Sites

The research sites are sources that provide more in-depth information about a particular word or phrase, such as encyclopedias and news services. To use one of these services, follow these steps:

1. **Select the word or phrase that you want to look up.**
2. **Click Review ⇨ Proofing ⇨ Research.** The Research task pane opens. If it was already open, it closes; click the Research button again to reopen it.

3. **Open the list of services and choose All Research Sites (or a particular site, if desired).**

4. **In the results that appear, click a hyperlink to read the information it points to, as shown in Figure 7.17.** Depending on what you select, a separate web browser window may open.

FIGURE 7.15

Translate a word or phrase from your language to another language, or vice versa.

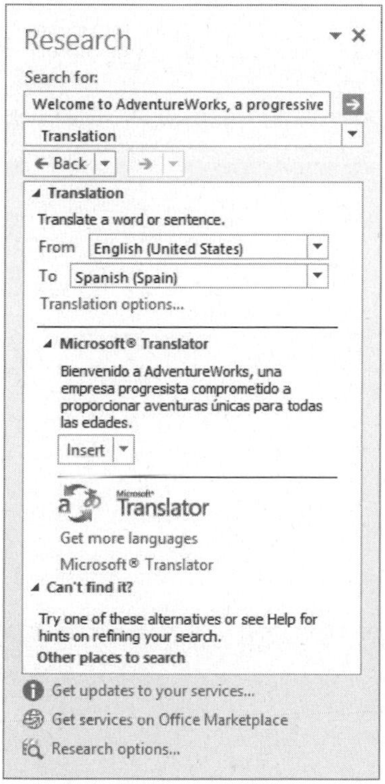

Research

Search for:

Welcome to AdventureWorks, a progressive

Translation

← Back

◢ Translation

Translate a word or sentence.

From   English (United States)

To   Spanish (Spain)

Translation options...

◢ Microsoft® Translator

Bienvenido a AdventureWorks, una empresa progresista comprometido a proporcionar aventuras únicas para todas las edades.

Insert

Translator

Get more languages

Microsoft® Translator

◢ Can't find it?

Try one of these alternatives or see Help for hints on refining your search.

Other places to search

ⓘ Get updates to your services...

  Get services on Office Marketplace

  Research options...

FIGURE 7.16

The Mini Translator pops up a quick definition of the selected word.

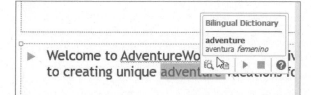

FIGURE 7.17

Find in-depth information about a term or phrase with the Research group of sources.

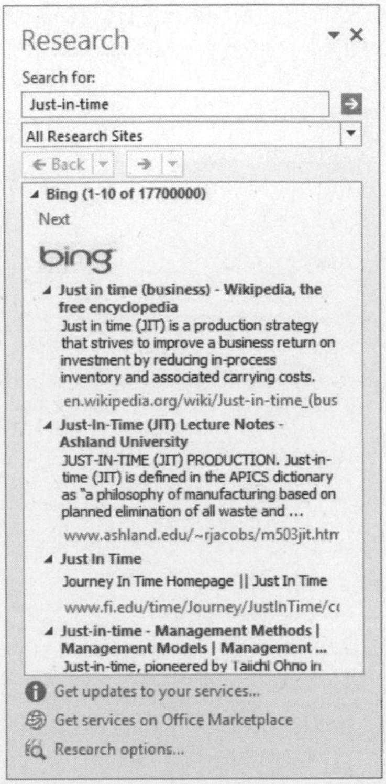

> **CAUTION**
>
> Keep in mind that proper attribution of sources is a must. If you copy information from an online source such as an encyclopedia or news service, you must cite your source. Also, depending on the source, you might need to get written permission to use the data. This is especially true with photographs. Very few news services permit you to reuse their photos without permission.

Summary

In this chapter, you learned how to use the spelling, proofing, and reference tools in PowerPoint to make a good impression on your audience. You learned how to find and replace text, how to look up reference information online without leaving PowerPoint, and even how to create custom dictionaries to use for different clients. Now you can present with confidence!

In the next chapter, you'll learn how to create and manage tables in PowerPoint.

Creating and Formatting Tables

IN THIS CHAPTER

Creating a new table

Moving around in a table

Selecting rows, columns, and cells

Editing a table's structure

Applying table styles

Formatting table cells

Copying tables from Word

Copying worksheet cells from Excel

You can type tabular data — in other words, data in a grid of rows and columns — directly into a table or import it from other applications. You can also apply much of the formatting that you learned about in Chapter 5, "Formatting Text," and Chapter 6, "Formatting Paragraphs and Text Boxes," but there are some special methods that you must consider when working with tabular data. In this chapter, you'll learn how to create and manage PowerPoint tables and how to insert tabular data from other sources.

Creating a New Table

A table is a great way to organize little bits of data into a meaningful picture. For example, you might use a table to show sales results for several salespeople or to contain a multicolumn list of team member names.

> **NOTE**
> Text from a table does not appear in the presentation's outline.

There are several ways to insert a table, and each method has its purpose. The following sections explain each of the table creation methods. (Methods that involve using other programs, such as

Word or Excel, are covered later in the chapter, in the sections "Using Tables from Word" and "Integrating Excel Cells into PowerPoint.")

A table can be part of a content placeholder, or it can be a separate, free-floating item. If the active slide has an available placeholder that can accommodate a table, and there is not already content in that placeholder, the table is placed in it. Otherwise the table is placed as an independent object on the slide and is not part of the layout.

> **TIP**
>
> Depending on what you want to do with the table, it could be advantageous in some cases to *not* have the table be part of the layout. For example, perhaps you want the table to be a certain size and to not change when you apply a different theme. To ensure that the table is not part of the layout, start with a slide that uses a layout that contains no table-compatible placeholder, such as Title Only.

Creating a Table with the Insert Table Dialog Box

To create a basic table with a specified number of rows and columns, you can use the Insert Table dialog box. You can open it in either of two ways (see Figure 8.1):

FIGURE 8.1

Open the Insert Table dialog box from either the Table button's menu or a content placeholder.

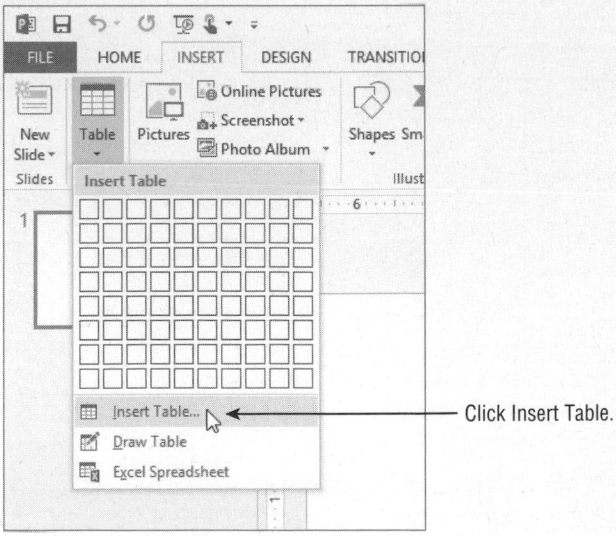

- In a content placeholder, click the Table icon.
- On the Insert tab, click Tables ➪ Table ➪ Insert Table.

In the Insert Table dialog box, shown in Figure 8.2, specify a number for rows and columns and click OK. The table then appears on the slide.

FIGURE 8.2

Enter the number of rows and columns to specify the size of the table that you want to create.

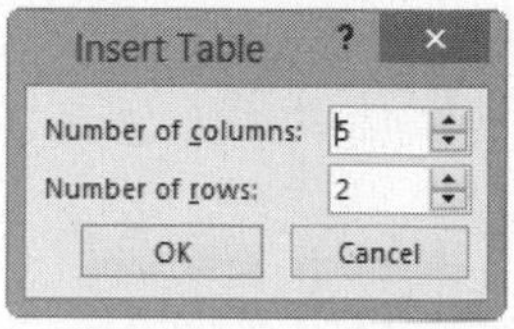

Creating a Table from the Table Button

When you opened the Table button's menu (see Figure 8.1) in the preceding section, you probably couldn't help but notice the grid of white squares. Another way to create a table is to drag across this grid until you select the desired number of rows and columns. The table appears immediately on the slide as you drag, so you can see how it will look, as shown in Figure 8.3.

FIGURE 8.3

Drag across the grid in the Table button's menu to specify the size of the table that you want to create.

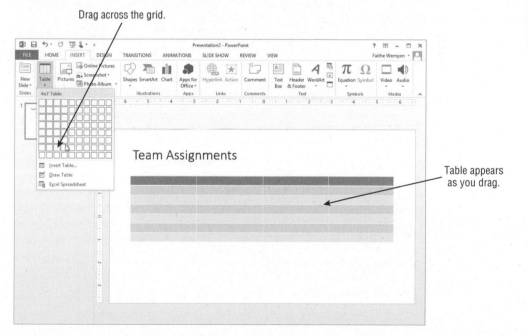

231

Other than the method of specifying rows and columns, this process is identical to creating a table via the Insert Table dialog box because the same issues apply regarding placeholders versus free-floating tables. If a placeholder is available, PowerPoint uses it.

> **NOTE**
> When you create a table from the Insert Table dialog or the Table button, the table is automatically formatted with one of the preset table styles. You learn how to change this later in the chapter.

Drawing a Table

I've saved the most fun method for last. Drawing a table enables you to use your mouse pointer like a pencil to create every row and column in the table in exactly the positions you want. You can even create unequal numbers of rows and columns. This method is a good one to use whenever you want a table that is nonstandard in some way — different row heights, different column widths, different numbers of columns in some rows, and so on. To draw a table, follow these steps:

1. **Start on a new slide, and click Home ➪ Slides ➪ Layout ➪ Title Only to switch to a layout that contains no content placeholders.** Add a title in the Title place-holder if you want one.

   Opening a new slide with a Title Only layout isn't a requirement for drawing a table, but it will make it easier your first time because it gives you a blank area in which to draw the table, without any placeholders in the way.

2. **Click Insert ➪ Tables ➪ Table ➪ Draw Table.** The mouse pointer turns into a pencil.

3. **Drag to draw a rectangle representing the outer frame of the table.** Then release the mouse button to create the outer frame and to display the Table Tools Design tab.

4. **On the Table Tools Design tab, click Draw Table to re-enable the Pencil tool if it is not already enabled.**

5. **Drag to draw the rows and columns you want.** You can draw a row or column that runs all the way across or down the table's frame, or you can stop at any point to make a partial row or column. See Figure 8.4. When you begin to drag vertically or horizontally, PowerPoint locks into that mode and keeps the line exactly vertical or horizontal and straight. (Exception: It allows you to draw a diagonal line between two corners of existing cells.)

6. **(Optional) To erase a line, click the Eraser button on the Table Tools Design tab, and then click the line to erase.** Then click the Draw Table button on the Table Tools Design tab to return the mouse pointer to its drawing (pencil) mode.

7. **When you finish drawing the table, press Esc or click Draw Table again to toggle the drawing mode off.**

FIGURE 8.4

You can create a unique table with the Draw Table tool.

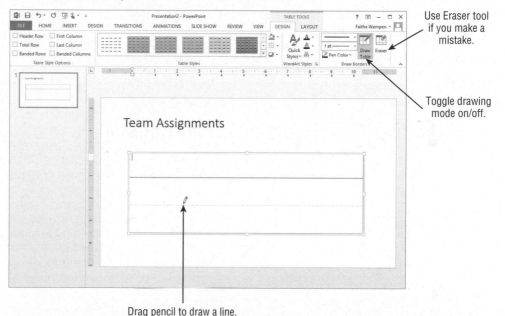

Use Eraser tool if you make a mistake.

Toggle drawing mode on/off.

Drag pencil to draw a line.

> **TIP**
>
> If you need a table that is mostly uniform but has a few anomalies, such as a few combined cells or a few extra divisions, create the table using the Insert Table dialog box or the grid on the Table button, and then use the Draw Table and/or Eraser buttons on the Table Tools Design tab to modify it.

Moving around in a Table

Each cell is like a little text box. To type in a cell, click in it and type. It's pretty simple! You can also move between cells with the keyboard. Table 8.1 lists the keyboard shortcuts for moving the insertion point in a table.

TABLE 8.1 **Moving the Insertion Point in a Table**

To Move To:	Press This:
Next cell	Tab
Previous cell	Shift+Tab
Next row	Down arrow
Previous row	Up arrow
Tab stop within a cell	Ctrl+Tab
New paragraph within the same cell	Enter

Selecting Rows, Columns, and Cells

If you want to apply formatting to one or more cells or issue a command that acts upon them, such as Copy or Delete, you must first select the cells to be affected, as shown in Figure 8.5:

FIGURE 8.5

Select a row or column with the Select button's menu, or click above or to the left of the column or row.

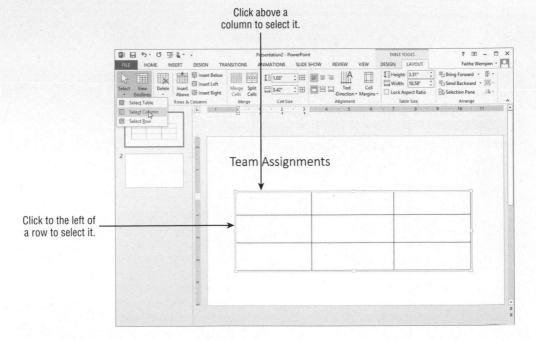

Click above a
column to select it.

Click to the left of
a row to select it.

Team Assignments

- **A single cell.** Move the insertion point by clicking inside the desired cell. At this point, any command acts on that individual cell and its contents, not the whole table, row, or column. Drag across multiple cells to select them.

- **An entire row or column.** Click any cell in that row or column and then click Table Tools Layout ⇨ Table ⇨ Select and choose Select Column or Select Row. Alternatively, position the mouse pointer above the column or to the left of the row, so that the mouse pointer turns into a black arrow, and then click to select the column or row. (You can drag to extend the selection to additional columns or rows when you see the black arrow.)

There are two ways to select the entire table — or rather, two senses in which the entire table can be "selected":

- **Select all table cells.** When you select all of the cells, they all appear with shaded backgrounds, and any text formatting command that you apply at that point affects all of the text in the table. To select all cells, do any of the following:

  - Drag across all of the cells in the entire table.

  - Click inside the table, and then press Ctrl+A.

- **Select the entire table.** When you do this, the table's frame is selected, but the insertion point is not anywhere within the table and cells do not appear with a shaded background. You do this kind of selection before moving or resizing the table, for example. To select the entire table, do any of the following:

  - Click Table Tools Layout ⇨ Table ⇨ Select ⇨ Select Table, shown in Figure 8.5.

  - Click the frame of the table.

  - Click inside the table, and then press Esc once.

  - Right-click the table and choose Select Table.

- **Drag a marquee around the table.** You can use the mouse to drag a marquee (a box) around the table. This is also called *lassoing*. When you release the mouse button, everything inside the area is selected.

Editing a Table's Structure

Now that you've created a table, let's look at some ways to modify the table's structure, including resizing the entire table, adding and deleting rows and columns, and merging and splitting cells.

Resizing the Overall Table

As with any other framed object in PowerPoint, dragging the table's outer frame resizes it. Position the mouse pointer over one of the selection handles (the white squares on the sides and corners) so that the mouse pointer becomes a double-headed arrow, and drag to resize the table. See Figure 8.6.

8

FIGURE 8.6

To resize a table, drag a selection handle on its frame.

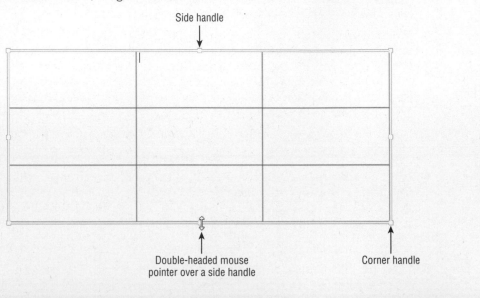

Side handle

Double-headed mouse
pointer over a side handle

Corner handle

> **NOTE**
>
> If you drag when the mouse pointer is over any other part of the frame, so that the mouse pointer becomes a four-headed arrow, you move the table rather than resize it.

To maintain the aspect ratio (height to width ratio) for the table as you resize it, hold down the Shift key as you drag a corner of the frame. If maintaining the aspect ratio is not critical, you can drag either a corner or a side.

All of the rows and columns maintain their spacing proportionally to one another as you resize them. However, when a table contains text that would no longer fit if its row and column were shrunken proportionally with the rest of the table, the row height does not shrink fully; it shrinks as much as it can while still displaying the text. The column width does shrink proportionally, regardless of cell content.

You can also specify an exact size for the overall table frame by using the Table Size group on the Table Tools Layout tab, as shown in Figure 8.7. From there you can enter Height and Width values. To maintain the aspect ratio, select the Lock Aspect Ratio check box *before* you change either the Height or Width setting.

Inserting or Deleting Rows and Columns

Here's an easy way to create a new row at the bottom of the table: Position the insertion point in the bottom-right cell and press Tab. Need something more complicated than that?

The Table Tools Layout tab contains buttons in the Rows & Columns group for inserting rows or columns above, below, to the left, or to the right of the selected cell(s), as shown in Figure 8.8. By default, each button inserts a single row or column at a time, but if you select multiple existing ones beforehand, these commands insert as many as you've selected. For example, to insert three new rows, select three existing rows and then click Insert Above or Insert Below.

FIGURE 8.7

Set a precise height and width for the table from the Table Size group.

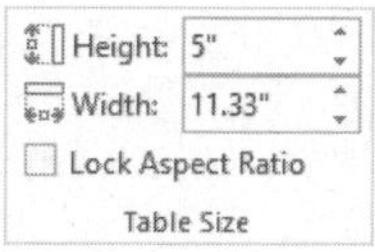

FIGURE 8.8

Insert rows or columns by using these buttons on the Layout tab.

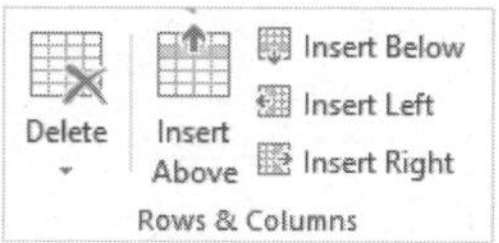

Alternatively, you can right-click any existing row or column, point to Insert, and choose one of the commands on the submenu. These commands are the same as the names of the buttons in Figure 8.8.

CAUTION

Adding new rows increases the overall vertical size of the table frame, even to the point where it runs off the bottom of the slide. You might need to adjust the overall frame size after adding rows. On the other hand, inserting columns does not change the overall frame size; it simply resizes the existing columns so that they all fit and are all a uniform size (unless you have manually adjusted any of them to be a custom size).

To delete a row or column (or more than one of each), select the row(s) or column(s) that you want to delete, and then open the Delete button's menu on the Table Tools Layout tab and choose Delete Rows or Delete Columns.

NOTE

You cannot insert or delete individual cells in a PowerPoint table. (This is unlike in Excel, where you can remove individual cells and then shift the remaining ones up or to the left.)

Merging and Splitting Cells

If you need more rows or columns in some spots than others, you can use the Merge Cells and Split Cells commands. Here are some ways to merge cells:

- Click Table Tools Design ⇨ Draw Borders ⇨ Eraser, and then click the line you want to erase. The cells on either side of the deleted line are merged.
- Select the cells that you want to merge and click Table Tools Layout ⇨ Merge ⇨ Merge Cells.
- Select the cells to merge, right-click them, and choose Merge Cells.

Here are some ways to split cells:

- Click Table Tools Design ⇨ Draw Borders ⇨ Draw Table, and then drag to draw a line in the middle of a cell to split it.
- Select the cell that you want to split, right-click it, and choose Split Cells. In the Split Cells dialog box (see Figure 8.9), select the number of pieces in which to split in each direction, and click OK.
- Select the cell to split, and then click Table Tools Layout ⇨ Merge ⇨ Split Cells. In the Split Cells dialog box (see Figure 8.9), select the number of pieces in which to split in each direction, and click OK.

FIGURE 8.9

Specify how the split should occur.

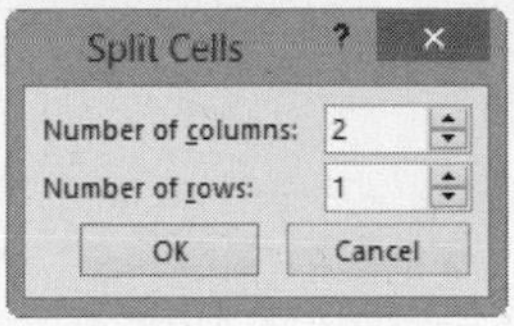

Applying Table Styles

The quickest way to format a table attractively is to apply a table style to it. When you insert a table using any method except drawing it, a table style is applied to it by default; you can change to some other style if desired, or you can remove all styles from the table, leaving it plain black and white.

When you hover the mouse pointer over a table style, a preview of it appears in the active table. The style is not actually applied to the table until you click the style to select it, however.

If the style you want appears in the Table Tools Design tab's Table Styles group, you can click it from there without opening the gallery. If not, you can scroll row by row through the gallery by clicking the up/down arrow buttons, or you can open the gallery's full menu, as shown in Figure 8.10.

FIGURE 8.10

Apply a table style from the gallery.

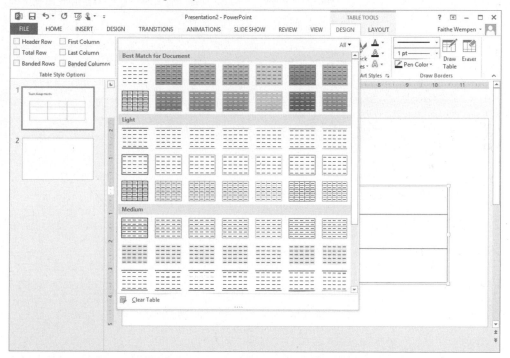

To remove all styles from the table, choose Clear Table from the bottom of the gallery menu. This reverts the table to default settings: no fill, and plain black 1-point borders on all sides of all cells.

The table styles use theme-based colors, so if you change to a different presentation theme or color theme, the table formatting might change. (Colors, in particular, are prone to shift.)

By default, the first row of the table (a.k.a. the *header row*) is formatted differently from the others, and every other row is shaded differently. (This is called *banding*.) You can control how different rows are treated differently (or not) from the Table Style Options group on the Table Tools Design tab. There is a check box for each of six settings:

- **Header Row.** The first row
- **Total Row.** The last row
- **First Column.** The leftmost column

- **Last Column.** The rightmost column
- **Banded Rows.** Every other row formatted differently
- **Banded Columns.** Every other column formatted differently

> **CAUTION**
>
> With some of the styles, there is not a whole lot of difference between some of the settings. For example, you might have to look very closely to see the difference between First Column being turned on or off; ditto with Last Column and Total Row.

> **TIP**
>
> You can right-click one of the thumbnails in the Table Style gallery and choose Set as Default to change the default table style.

Formatting Table Cells

Although table styles provide a rough cut on the formatting, you might want to fine-tune your table formatting as well. In the following sections you learn how to adjust various aspects of the table's appearance.

Changing Row Height and Column Width

You might want a row to be a different height or a column a different width than others in the table. To resize a row or column, follow these steps:

1. **Position the mouse pointer on the border below the row or to the right of the column that you want to resize.** The mouse pointer turns into a line with arrows on each side of it.

2. **Hold down the mouse button as you drag the row or column to a new height or width.** A dotted line appears showing where it will go.

3. **Release the mouse button.**

You can also specify an exact height or width measurement using the Height and Width boxes in the Cell Size group on the Table Tools Layout tab. Select the row(s) or column(s) to affect, and then enter sizes in inches or use the increment buttons, as shown in Figure 8.11.

The Distribute Rows Evenly and Distribute Columns Evenly buttons in the Cell Size group (see Figure 8.11) adjust each row or column in the selected range so that the available space is occupied evenly among them. This is handy especially if you have drawn the table yourself rather than allowed PowerPoint to create it initially. If PowerPoint creates the table, the rows and columns are already of equal height and width by default.

You can also double-click between two columns to size the column to the left so that the text fits exactly within the width.

Set a precise size for a row or column.

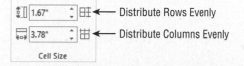

Table Margins and Alignment

Remember, PowerPoint slides do not have any margins per se; everything is in a frame. An individual cell does have *internal* margins, however.

You can specify the internal margins for cells using the Cell Margins button on the Table Tools Layout tab, as follows:

1. **Select the cells to which the setting should apply.** To apply settings to the entire table, select the entire table.
2. **Click Table Tools Layout ⇨ Alignment ⇨ Cell Margins.** A menu of margin presets opens.
3. **Click one of the presets or choose Custom Margins, and then follow these steps:**

   a. In the Cell Text Layout dialog box, set the Left, Right, Top, and Bottom margin settings, as shown in Figure 8.12.

   b. Click OK.

FIGURE 8.12

You can set the internal margins on an individual cell basis for each side of the cell.

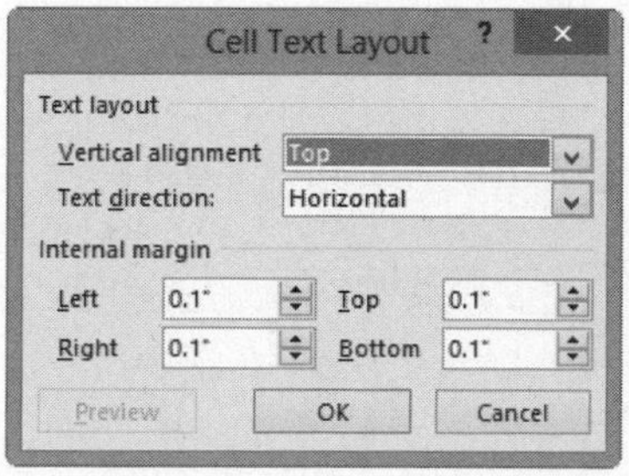

Applying Borders

The border lines around the cells are very important because they separate the data in each cell from the data in other cells. By default (without a table style), there's a 1-point border around each side of each cell, but you can make some or all borders thicker, a different line style (dashed, for example), or a different color, or remove them altogether to create your own effects. Here are some ideas:

- To make items appear to "float" in multiple columns on the slide (that is, to make it look as if they are not really in a table at all — just lined up extremely well), remove all table borders.

- To create a header row at the top without using the settings in the Table Style Options group, make the border beneath the first row of cells darker or thicker than the others.

- To make certain rows or columns appear as if they are outside of the table, turn off their borders on all sides except the side that faces the other cells.

- To make certain items appear as if they have been crossed off a list, format the cells they are in with diagonal borders. This creates the effect of an *X* running through each cell. These diagonal lines are not really borders in the sense that they don't go around the edge of the cell, but they're treated as borders in PowerPoint.

When you apply a top, bottom, left, or right border, those positions refer to the entire selected block of cells if you have more than one cell selected. For example, suppose you select two adjacent cells in a row and apply a left border. The border applies only to the leftmost of the two cells. If you want the same border applied to the line between the cells too, you must apply an inside vertical border.

To apply a border, follow these steps:

1. **Select the cell(s) that you want to affect.**

2. **In the Draw Borders group on the Table Tools Design tab, select a line style, width, and color from the Pen Style, Pen Weight, and Pen Color drop-down lists, shown in Figure 8.13.**

FIGURE 8.13

Use the Draw Borders group's lists to set the border's style, thickness, and color.

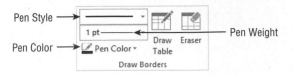

TIP
Try to use theme colors rather than fixed colors whenever possible so that if you change to a different color theme later, the colors you originally chose won't clash.

3. **Open the Borders button's menu in the Table Styles group and choose the sides of the selected area to which the new settings should apply.** See Figure 8.14. For example, to apply the border to the bottom of the selected area, click Bottom Border.

FIGURE 8.14

Select the side(s) to apply borders to for the chosen cells.

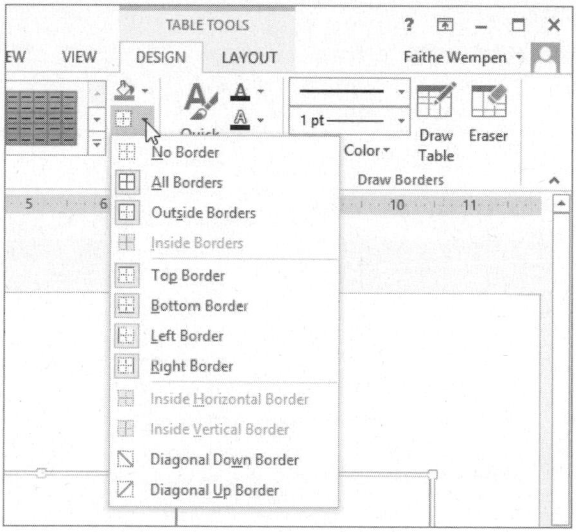

If you want to remove all borders from all sides, choose No Border from the menu.

4. **If necessary, repeat step 3 to apply the border to other sides of the selection.** Some of the choices on the Borders button's menu apply to only one side; others apply to two or more at once.

Applying Fills

By default, table cells have a transparent background so that the color of the slide beneath shows through. When you apply a table style, as you learned earlier in the chapter, the style specifies a background color — or in some cases, multiple background colors depending on the options you choose for special treatment of certain rows or columns.

8

You can also manually change the fill for a table to make it either a solid color or a special fill effect. You can apply this fill to individual cells, or you can apply a background fill for the entire table.

Filling Individual Cells

Each individual cell has its own fill setting; in this way a table is like a collection of individual object frames, rather than a single object. To set the fill color for one or more cells, follow these steps:

1. **Select the cell(s) to affect, or to apply the same fill color to all cells, select the table's outer frame.**
2. **On the Table Tools Design tab, click the down arrow next to the Shading button to open its palette.**
3. **Select the desired color or fill effect.** See Figure 8.15.

FIGURE 8.15

Apply a fill effect to the selected cell(s).

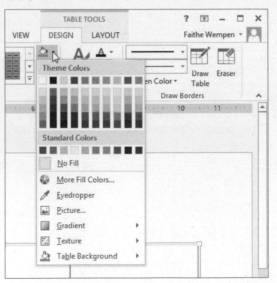

For more on the various effects, see Chapter 9, "Drawing and Formatting Objects." Also see "Filling a Table with a Picture" later in this chapter for some issues involving picture fills specific to tables.

TIP

For a semitransparent, solid-color fill, first apply the fill and then right-click the cell and choose Format Shape. In the Format Shape dialog box, drag the Transparency slider. For some types of fills, you can also set the transparency when you initially apply the fill.

Applying an Overall Table Fill

You can apply a solid color fill to the entire table that is different from the fill applied to the individual cells. The table's fill color is visible only in cells in which the individual fill is set to No Fill (or a semitransparent fill, in which case it blends).

To apply a fill to the entire table, open the Shading button's menu and point to Table Background, as shown in Figure 8.16, and then choose a color.

FIGURE 8.16

Apply a fill to the table's background.

To test the new background, select some cells and choose No Fill for their fill color. The background color appears in those cells. If you want to experiment further, try applying a semitransparent fill to some cells, and see how the color of the background blends with the color of the cell's fill.

Filling a Table with a Picture

When you fill one or more cells with a picture, each cell gets its own individual copy of it. For example, if you fill a table with a picture of a koala and the table has six cells, you get six koalas, as shown in Figure 8.17.

FIGURE 8.17

When you apply a picture fill to a table, each cell gets its own copy.

If you want a single copy of the picture to fill the entire area behind the table, do the following:

1. **Select the table's outer frame.**
2. **Click Table Tools Design ⇨ Table Styles ⇨ Shading (down arrow) ⇨ Table Background ⇨ Picture.**
3. **In the Insert Pictures dialog box, to use your own picture, click Browse and locate and select the picture.** Or, to find a picture online, type a keyword for the picture in the Office.com Clip Art box and press Enter, and then click the desired picture.

Applying a Shadow to a Table

You can apply a shadow effect to a table so that it appears "raised" off the slide background. You can make it any color you like, and adjust a variety of settings for it.

NOTE

If the cells have no fill, the shadow will apply to the gridlines, not to the table as a whole object.

FIGURE 8.18

Select a picture to use as the background of the table.

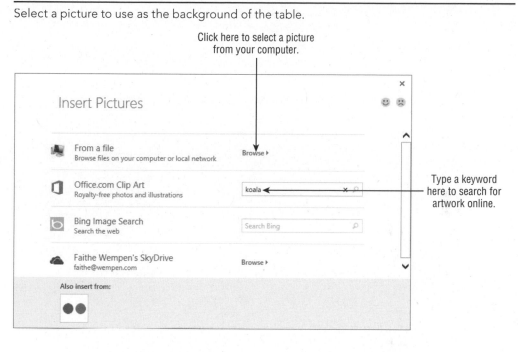

Click here to select a picture
from your computer.

Type a keyword
here to search for
artwork online.

Here's a very simple way to apply a shadow to a table:

1. **Select the table's outer frame.**
2. **Choose Table Tools Design ⇨ Table Styles ⇨ Effects ⇨ Shadow.**
3. **Click the shadow type you want.**

Here's an alternative method that gives you a bit more control:

1. **Select the table's outer frame, and then right-click the frame and choose Format Shape.** The Format Shape task pane appears.
2. **Click Shape Options, and then click the Effects icon.**
3. **Click Shadow to expand that category, as shown in Figure 8.19.**
4. **Click the Presets button, and click the desired preset.**
5. **Click the Color button, and click the desired color.**
6. **(Optional) If desired, drag any of the sliders to fine-tune the shadow.** These are covered in greater detail in Chapter 9.
7. **Click Close to close the Format Shape task pane when you are finished.**

FIGURE 8.19

Apply a shadow to a table.

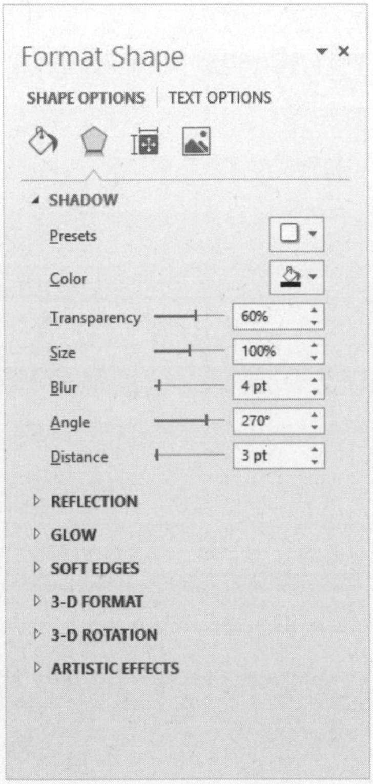

Applying a 3-D Effect to a Table

PowerPoint does not enable you to apply 3-D effects to tables, so you have to fudge that by creating the 3-D effect with rectangles and then overlaying a transparent table on top of the shapes. As you can see in Figure 8.20, it's a pretty convincing facsimile.

FIGURE 8.20

This 3-D table is actually a plain table with a 3-D rectangle behind it.

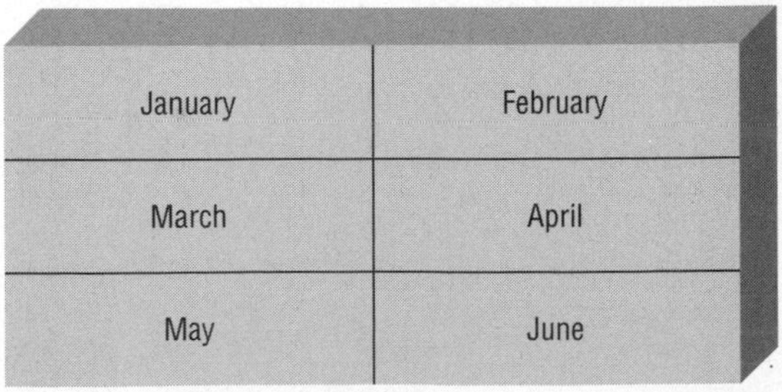

You might need to read Chapter 9 first to do some of these steps, but here's the basic procedure:

1. **Create a rectangle from the Shapes group on the Insert tab, and apply a 3-D effect to it (from Drawing Tools Format ➪ Shape Styles ➪ Shape Effects ➪ 3-D Rotation).** Use any effect you like. To create the traditional "box" appearance as in Figure 8.22, apply the second Oblique preset, and then in the 3-D Format options, increase the Depth setting to about 100 points.

2. **Size the rectangle so that its face is the same size as the table.**

3. **Click Drawing Tools Format ➪ Arrange ➪ Send Backward ➪ Send to Back to send the rectangle behind the table.**

4. **Set the table's fill to No Fill if it is not already transparent.**

5. **(Optional) Set the table's outer frame border to None to make its edges appear to blend with the edges of the rectangle.** To do that, open the Borders button's menu on the Table Tools Design tab and select Outside Borders to toggle that off.

Changing Text Alignment

If you followed the preceding steps to create the effect shown in Figure 8.20, you probably ran into a problem: Your text probably didn't center itself in the cells. That's because, by default, each cell's vertical alignment is set to Top and horizontal alignment is set to Left.

Although the vertical and horizontal alignments are both controlled from the Alignment group on the Table Tools Layout tab, they actually have two different scopes. Vertical alignment applies to the entire cell as a whole, whereas horizontal alignment can apply differently to individual paragraphs within the cell. To set vertical alignment for a cell, follow these steps:

1. **Select one or more cells to affect.** To affect only one cell, you do not have to select it; just click inside it.

2. **On the Table Tools Layout tab, in the Alignment group, click one of the vertical alignment buttons: Align Top, Center Vertically, or Align Bottom.** See Figure 8.21.

FIGURE 8.21

Set the vertical and horizontal alignment of text from the Alignment group.

Horizontal alignment

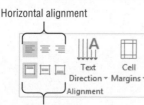

Vertical alignment

To set the horizontal alignment for a paragraph, follow these steps:

1. **Select one or more paragraphs to affect.** If you select multiple cells, all paragraphs within those cells are affected. If you click in a cell without selecting anything, the change affects only the paragraph in which you clicked.

2. **On the Table Tools Layout tab, in the Alignment group, click one of the horizontal alignment buttons: Align Left, Center, or Align Right.** See Figure 8.21. You can also use the paragraph alignment buttons on the Home tab for horizontal alignment or the buttons on the mini toolbar.

TIP

The horizontal alignments all have keyboard shortcuts: Ctrl+L for left, Ctrl+E for center, and Ctrl+R for right.

Changing Text Direction

The default text direction for table cells is Horizontal, which reads from left to right (at least in countries where that's how text is read). Figure 8.22 shows the alternatives.

FIGURE 8.22

You can set types of text direction.

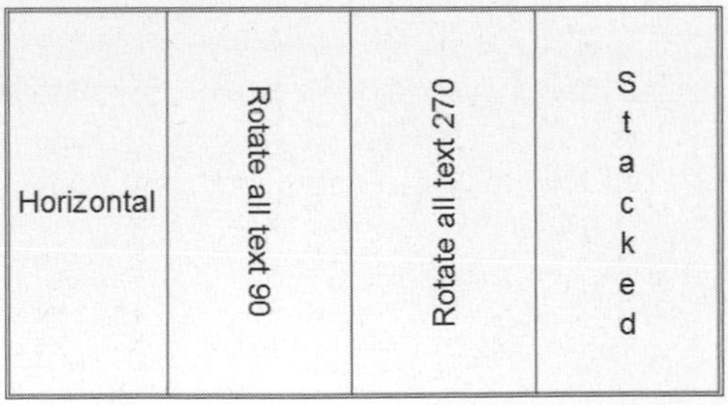

To change the text direction for a cell, follow these steps:

1. **Select the cell(s) to affect.** To affect only a single cell, move the insertion point into it.

2. **On the Table Tools Layout tab, click Text Direction.**

3. **Select a text direction from the menu that appears.**

NOTE

You cannot set text direction for individual paragraphs; the setting applies to the entire cell.

Using Tables from Word

If a table already exists in Word, you can copy it into PowerPoint. PowerPoint will convert the Word table to a PowerPoint table. From that point on, it is a part of the presentation, and maintains no relationship to Word. You can edit its text directly in PowerPoint.

To paste a table from Word to PowerPoint, copy it to the Clipboard (Ctrl+C) in Word, and then paste it onto a slide in PowerPoint (Ctrl+V). The resulting table appears in the center of the slide.

NOTE

When you copy a table from Word to PowerPoint, you might need to increase the font size; Word's default size for body text is great for printed documents but too small for most PowerPoint slides.

A pasted Word table is placed into a content placeholder on the slide if an appropriate one is available. Here are the basic rules for what goes on:

- If the slide has an appropriate content placeholder that is empty, the table is placed into it but retains its own size and shape.
- If the slide does not have an appropriate empty content placeholder, the table is inserted as a free-floating object, unrelated to any placeholders.

Word's table feature is somewhat more robust than PowerPoint's. If you want to maintain all the Word capabilities in the table, paste the table as a Word object instead of doing a regular paste. Follow these steps:

1. **Copy the table in Word (Ctrl+C).**
2. **In PowerPoint, display the slide on which the table should be pasted.**
3. **On the Home tab, open the Paste button's menu and click Paste Special.** The Paste Special dialog box opens.
4. **Click the Paste option button.**
5. **In the As list, choose Microsoft Office Word Document Object.** See Figure 8.23.
6. **Click OK.** The table appears as a free-floating object (not in any placeholder).

You can also use the Paste Options button that appears immediately after you paste the table. Click the third icon: Embed. See Figure 8.24.

The resulting table is an embedded object and cannot be edited directly using PowerPoint's table feature. To edit the object, you must double-click it to open it in Word.

8

TIP

To maintain a dynamic link between the Word file and the PowerPoint presentation, choose Paste Link instead of Paste in step 4. However, be aware that if you move the Word file, an error will appear in PowerPoint when it cannot find the file referenced in the link. See Chapter 13, "Incorporating Content from Other Programs," for more information about linking and embedding.

FIGURE 8.23

Paste the table as a Microsoft Word document object.

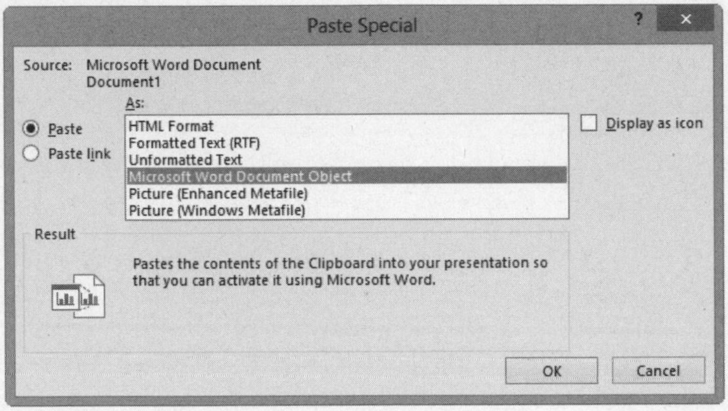

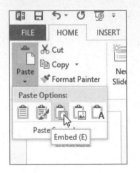

FIGURE 8.24

Click the Embed icon.

Integrating Excel Cells into PowerPoint

If you need the calculating capabilities in a table, consider embedding Excel cells into the slide instead of using a traditional PowerPoint table.

Object linking and embedding is covered in detail in Chapter 13, but here's a quick look at how to use Excel from within PowerPoint:

1. **Display the slide on which you want to place the Excel cells.**

2. **If desired, select a placeholder into which the table should be placed.**

3. **On the Insert tab, click the Table button, and on its menu, choose Excel Spreadsheet.** A small frame with a few cells of an Excel spreadsheet appears, and the Ribbon changes to the tabs and tools for Excel. See Figure 8.25.

FIGURE 8.25

An Excel object can substitute for a table grid and can provide Excel-specific capabilities.

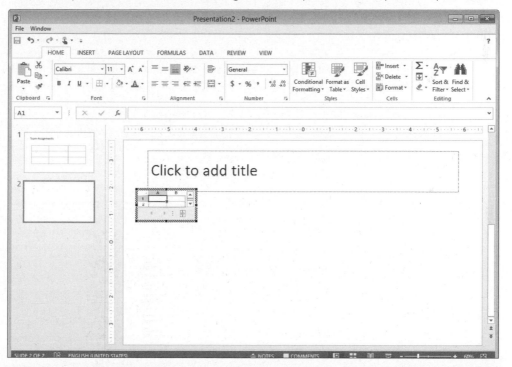

> **NOTE**
>
> Don't worry that an Excel object you insert does not seem to be correctly aligned at the top and left. The cell row and column labels appear as you edit, and they disappear when you click away from the object.

4. **If desired, enlarge the Excel object by doing the following:**
   a. Click once on the Excel object's border to select it. Black selection handles appear around it.
   b. Drag a corner selection handle to enlarge the area of the object.

5. **Create the table using Excel's tools and features.**

6. **(Optional) If there are unused cells, resize the object again (using its selection handles) so that they are not visible.**

7. **Click away from the object to deselect it and return to PowerPoint.**

You've just created an embedded Excel object. It does not exist outside of this PowerPoint file; it's a mini-Excel spreadsheet that you use just for this one presentation. If you want to embed content from an existing Excel file, copy and paste it as in the earlier section on Word tables, or see Chapter 13 for more information about your options for linking and embedding content.

Summary

In this chapter, you learned the ins and outs of creating and formatting tables in PowerPoint, including how to insert, draw, move, and resize the various cells of a table as well as how to add fills, styles, and effects. You also learned how to integrate Excel cells into your PowerPoint slides. In the next chapter, you learn how to draw and format objects.

Part II

Using Graphics and Multimedia Content

IN THIS PART

Drawing and Formatting Objects

IN THIS CHAPTER

Working with the drawing tools

Selecting and deleting objects

Moving and copying objects

Resizing and arranging objects

Merging shapes

Applying Shape or Picture Styles

Applying object borders and fills and effects

Everything on a slide is a separate object. An *object* is anything that is in its own rectangular frame and can be moved, sized, and formatted independently. For example, each drawn shape is an object, as is each text box and each chart, diagram, and clip art image. So far in this book, you've learned about several types of objects that you can format with borders, shading, and other special effects, including text boxes and tables. In upcoming chapters, you learn about even more types of objects that you can format, such as SmartArt, charts, and clip art.

Most of the manipulation that you can apply to an object is the same, regardless of the object type. Rather than repeat the details for formatting each object type in individual chapters, almost everything you need to know about object formatting can be found in this chapter. You will practice these techniques on drawn lines and shapes, and in the process you will learn about the drawing tools. You can then apply these same techniques to text boxes and to virtually every type of graphic object that PowerPoint supports.

Working with the Drawing Tools

PowerPoint comes with a set of drawing tools that allow you to create simple lines and shapes on your slides. The graphics that you create with these tools are called *shapes*. (Lines are also called shapes, which seems counterintuitive, but there it is.)

The drawing tools create simple, line-based vector graphics, each of which is a separate object on the slide. For example, if you make a drawing that consists of four rectangles, an oval, and several lines, you can move and resize each of these objects separately. You can stack them to create a more complex drawing, format each one individually, and even group and merge them to create a single object that you can format, move, and resize as a single unit.

> To learn how to group shapes, see "Working with Object Groups" later in this chapter. Merging shapes is new in PowerPoint 2013; to learn about it, see "Merging Shapes" later in this chapter.

A *vector graphic* is one that is based on a mathematical formula, such as one you would work with in geometry class. For example, if you draw a vector graphic line, PowerPoint stores the line start point, line endpoint, and line properties (width, color, and so on) as numeric values. When you move or resize the line, PowerPoint updates these numbers. Most clip-art images are also vector graphics. In contrast, a scanned image or a photo is a bitmap graphic, in which each individual colored pixel is represented by a separate numeric value. This is why bitmap files are so much larger than vector files — because there are more values to track.

Here are the most important advantages of using vector graphics:

- **Size.** Vector graphics files do not require much storage space because not every pixel of the image needs to be represented numerically.
- **Scalability.** When you resize a vector graphic, the math is recalculated and the shape is redrawn. This means that the picture is never distorted and its lines never become jagged the way bitmap graphics do.

The main drawback to vector graphics is their lack of realism. No matter how good an artist you are, a vector graphic will always have a flat, cartoonish quality to it.

> **NOTE**
>
> 3-D graphics programs such as AutoCAD are also based on vector graphics. They start out with a wireframe image of a 3-D object (such as a cube), combine it with other wireframe images to make an object, and then use a rendering tool to cover the wireframe with a color, pattern, or texture that makes it look more like a real object. Most computer games also use vector graphics.

Drawing Lines and Shapes

The drawing tools in PowerPoint are the same as in other Office applications. For example, Word and Excel both have identical toolsets. The Shapes button appears on the Insert tab, and you can click it to open a menu of the available shapes, as shown in Figure 9.1.

To draw a shape, follow these steps:

1. **Select the desired shape from the Shapes palette (Figure 9.1).**
2. **(Optional) To constrain the dimensions of the shape — for example, to force a rectangle to be a square — hold down the Shift key.**
3. **Drag to draw the shape.** A silhouette of the shape appears as you drag. Release the mouse button when you have the shape you want.

FIGURE 9.1

Select a shape from the Shapes list.

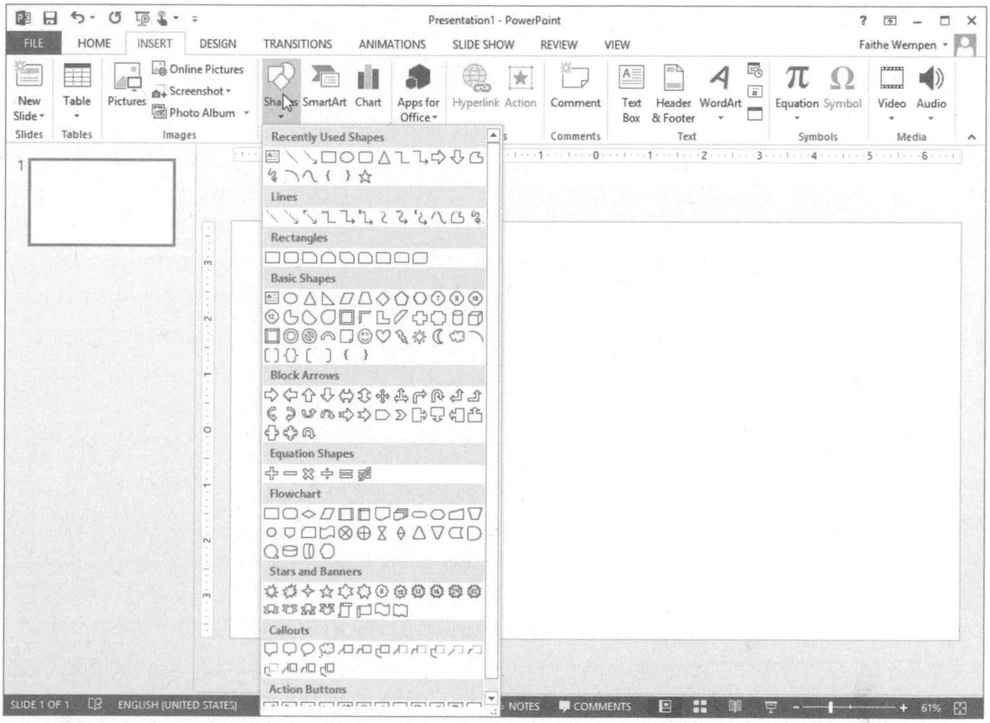

The preceding steps work well for most shapes, but there are a few special cases in which the drawing process works a little differently. The following sections explain these differences.

TIP

You can resize the Shapes menu by dragging its bottom-right corner.

TIP

More shapes are available through Microsoft's online clip art collection. When searching for clip-art images (see Chapter 11, "Working With Clip Art and Photos"), use *AutoShape* as the keyword; you will see many more shapes, including ones that look like various types of office furniture and computers (which are useful in office plans).

TIP

To draw multiple objects of the same shape, you can lock the drawing tool on. Instead of clicking the shape to select it in the Shapes palette, right-click it and choose Lock Drawing Mode. It then stays on until you press Esc to turn it off.

Straight or Curved Lines

The drawing tools include several types of lines, as shown in Figure 9.2. Here are some tips for using some of the line tools:

FIGURE 9.2

Line tools

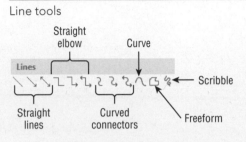

- **Straight line.** Click the start point and then click the endpoint. The line is now complete and the tool turns off. You can also draw lines with arrows at one or both ends.

- **Straight (elbow) connector.** Click and hold at the start point, and then drag to the endpoint. You can adjust the position of the elbow by dragging the yellow diamond in the center. If you click and release at the start point, a default size connector appears, which you can then move or resize. You can also draw lines with arrows at one or both ends.

- **Curved connector.** Click and hold at the start point, and then drag to the endpoint. Click a second time to complete the line. You can adjust the shape of the curve by dragging the yellow diamond in the center. If you click and release at the start point, a default size connector appears, which you can then move or resize. You can also draw lines with arrows at one or both ends.

- **Curve.** This is a freeform, multisegment curve. Click the start point, click again to create a second point, and then click again to create more points. Between points, drag the mouse pointer to adjust the curve. When you are finished, double-click the mouse.

- **Scribble.** This is a freeform line. Hold down the mouse button and drag to draw; release the mouse button to finish.

Freeform Shapes

The *Freeform* tool is in the Lines group (Figure 9.2), but it actually draws shapes consisting of multiple straight-line segments. It enables you to draw each line segment one by one, with the mouse pointer functioning as a pencil. To use this tool, follow these steps:

1. **Open the Shapes palette and click the Freeform button.**
2. **Click to place the start point, and then release the mouse button.**

3. **Click another location to place the next point.** A line appears between the two points. Repeat this step as needed to create more points.

4. **End the shape:**
   - For an open shape, double-click where you want to place the final point.
   - For a closed shape, click the start point again as the final point.

You can fine-tune a freeform shape by adjusting its points. You can also convert existing shapes to freeform ones that you can then adjust point by point.

See the section "Editing a Shape's Points" in this chapter for more information about shape editing.

Flow-Chart Connectors

Flow-chart shapes are just ordinary shapes that happen to correspond to those used in standard flow charts.

To experiment with flow-chart connectors, draw a couple of shapes (any closed shapes) and then draw a straight line or an elbow connector between them. As you move the mouse pointer over the edge of the first shape, certain points on the shape, like the corners, show small markers, indicating they are valid attachment points for the line. Click to anchor one end of the line there. Drag to draw the line to the other shape, and when the mouse pointer gets there, small gray squares on that shape's border appear to show its valid attachment points. Finish dragging the line to one of those points to complete the connection. When you move one of the shapes, the connector line moves as needed to keep the connection.

When there is a completed connection between two shapes, both ends of the line show green circles when the line is connected, as in Figure 9.3. When one end is disconnected from a shape, that end of the line appears with a plain white square on its endpoint, rather than a green circle.

FIGURE 9.3

Connectors have green circles on the ends when they are connected.

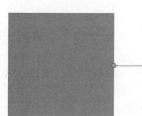

Connecting a line to a shape offers two advantages. One advantage is that you don't have to adjust the line exactly so that it touches the shape but does not overlap it. It lines up perfectly with the edge of the shape at all times. Another advantage is that if you move the shape, the line moves with it, changing its length and angle as needed so that the line remains anchored at both ends. All shapes can be connected, not just the ones from the Flow Chart group.

Callouts

A *callout* is a regular shape except it has a resizable point on it that can be dragged to point to other objects. Drag the yellow square selection handle on the callout shape to move its point.

Action Buttons

An *action button* is a type of drawing object that has an action associated with it. When users click the action button during the presentation, something happens. For example, perhaps a certain slide appears, an external program launches, or a sound plays.

The main difference between placing an action button and placing other types of drawing objects is that after you draw the action button, an Action Settings dialog box appears, prompting you for the action.

> You can learn how to use the Action Settings dialog box in Chapter 20, "Preparing a Presentation for Mass Distribution."

Choosing a Different Shape

If you chose the wrong shape to draw, it's easier to just delete the shape and start over if you have not applied any special formatting to it. However, if you have formatted the shape already, you might find it easier to change the shape rather than re-create it. To do so, follow these steps:

1. **Click the shape to select it.**
2. **Click Drawing Tools Format ⇨ Insert Shapes and then click the Edit Shape button and choose Change Shape from the menu.** The same palette of shapes appears as when you initially created the shape, as shown in Figure 9.4.
3. **Click the new shape that you want.**

> **NOTE**
> Lines cannot be changed using the Change Shape command. You must right-click them and choose Connector Types to change their type, and you can only change between a straight connector, elbow connector, and curved connector.

FIGURE 9.4

Use the Change Shape option in the Edit Shape drop-down menu to reselect a shape.

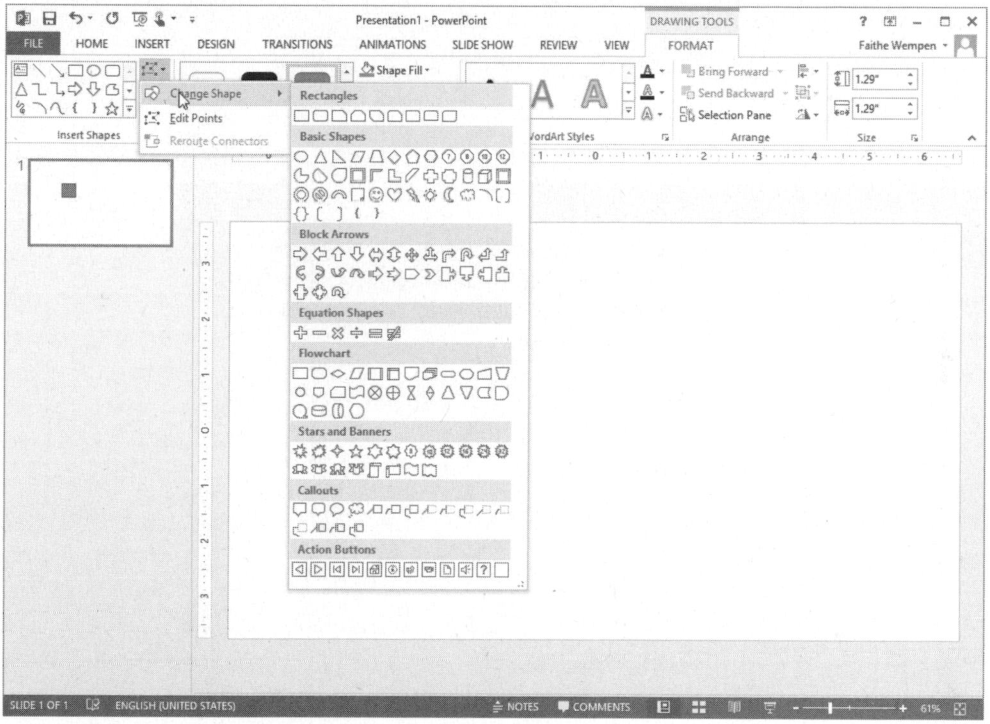

Editing a Shape's Points

Each shape consists of a series of points that are connected with straight or curved lines. You can adjust the positions of these points to change the shape of the object. Follow these steps:

1. **Select the shape.**
2. **On the Drawing Tools Format tab, open the Edit Shape drop-down menu (see Figure 9.4) and select Edit Points.** The selection handles on the shape turn black, indicating that they can be moved individually.

   You can also right-click the shape and choose Edit Points.

3. **Drag one or more of the selection handles (see Figure 9.5) to change the shape.**
4. **Click away from the shape or press Esc.**

FIGURE 9.5

Fine-tune a shape by adjusting its points.

Drag a black square
to change the shape.

PowerPoint 2013 enables you to merge multiple shapes together to create more complex shapes than you might feel comfortable drawing on your own or creating by dragging a shape's points. To learn about combining shapes, see "Merging Shapes" later in this chapter.

Adding Text to a Shape

You can use almost all of the closed shapes in PowerPoint as text boxes. PowerPoint recognizes a manually created text box as a variation on a rectangle with some text in it. As a result, you can just as easily place text in a shape of any other type. To add text to a shape, follow these steps:

1. **Right-click the shape and choose Edit Text.**
2. **Click inside the shape.** A flashing insertion point appears inside the shape.
3. **Type the desired text.**

TIP

You can also use the Text Box button to insert a new blank text box from the Drawing Tools Format tab, independent of any existing shape. Instead of clicking inside a shape in step 3, click a blank area of the slide and begin typing to create a new text box. A text box is just a rectangular shape with no border or fill. You can change it to a different shape by selecting from the Edit Shape ⇨ Change Shape menu, as shown in the section "Choosing a Different Shape" earlier in this chapter. You can then apply a shape style, as explained in the section "Applying Shape or Picture Styles" later in this chapter, or apply a custom border or fill to it.

Text wraps within a shape automatically, in a rectangular area. If the shape is irregular, PowerPoint finds the largest available rectangular area within its center and confines the text to that area. If you have adjusted the shape's points, the text wrapping inside the shape may not look right. For example, in Figure 9.6, the sides of the arrow have been pulled in a bit manually, but the original text area still applies, resulting in some overhang of the text. To correct this, you can manually insert line breaks where you want them by pressing Shift+Enter.

FIGURE 9.6

If the text overflows the shape (left), press Shift+Enter to insert line breaks where needed (right).

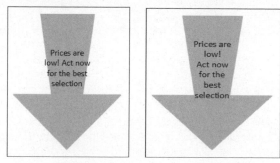

Selecting Objects

No matter what type of object you are dealing with, you can select it by clicking it with the mouse. Selection handles that look like white squares appear around the object, as shown in Figure 9.7.

FIGURE 9.7

Selection handles appear around a selected object.

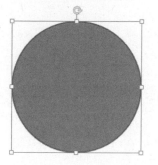

You have already learned that you can select a single object by clicking it. However, sometimes you might want to select multiple objects so that you can act upon them as a single unit. For example, suppose you have drawn several shapes and you want to select them as a group so that you can move them or apply the same formatting to them.

To select more than one object, click the first one to select it, and then hold down the Shift key as you click additional objects. They all become selected.

If you can't easily click each object (perhaps because they are overlapping one another), an easy way to select a whole group is to drag the cursor around them. For example, if you wanted to select several stacked shapes, you would drag the cursor over them to select them all, as follows: Simply click and hold down the mouse button above and to the left of the objects, and drag down and to the right until you create a box around them. This is called lassoing, as you learned in Chapter 8. The box adds a light-blue shading over the top of the area, as shown in Figure 9.8. Then, release the mouse button. All objects that were entirely inside the boundary that you drew are selected, as shown in Figure 9.9.

FIGURE 9.8

Hold down the mouse button and drag a box that includes all of the shapes that you want to select.

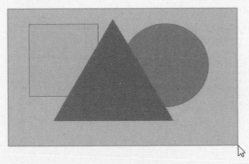

FIGURE 9.9

Each selected object displays its own selection handles.

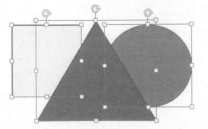

Another way to select objects is with the Selection pane. To display this pane, click Home ➪ Editing ➪ Selection Pane. In the Selection pane, you can click any object's name to select it or hold down the Ctrl key and click multiple objects to select them. Figure 9.10 shows three selected objects.

FIGURE 9.10

The Selection pane assists you in selecting objects.

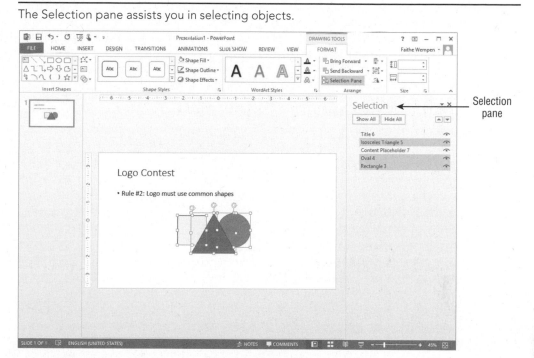

The Selection pane does more than just select objects. For example, you can use the Bring Forward and Send Backward arrow buttons at the top of the pane to change the stacking of objects, which is also covered later in this chapter in the section "Layering Objects." You can also click the eye icon next to an object to toggle its display on or off in the slide. This provides a way of temporarily hiding an object without affecting its presence or position on the slide.

TIP

If you have more than one of a certain type of object, PowerPoint names them generically in the Selection pane — for example, Oval 22, Isosceles Triangle 23, and so on. It is easier to keep track of which shape is which if you change their names to something more meaningful. To change the name of an object, click its name in the Selection pane, and then click it again. The insertion point appears inside the name, and you can edit it. Having recognizable names for objects also helps when you are sequencing their animation (covered in Chapter 16, "Creating Animation Effects and Transitions").

Deleting Objects

To delete an object, the easiest way is to select it and then press the Delete key on the keyboard. To delete more than one object at once, you can select multiple objects before pressing the Delete key.

You can also right-click the selected object or objects and choose Cut. When you cut an object, it is not the same as deleting it; the Cut command moves the object to the Clipboard, so that you can use the Paste command to place it somewhere else. However, if you cut something and then never paste it, this is actually the same as deleting it.

Moving and Copying Objects

You can move or copy objects anywhere you like: within a single slide, from one slide to another, or from one presentation to another. You can even copy or move an object to a completely different program, such as Word or Excel.

Within a Slide

To move an object on a slide, you can simply drag it with the mouse. Just position the mouse pointer over any part of the object except for a handle. When the mouse pointer changes to a four-headed arrow, drag the object to a new location. To copy by dragging, hold down the Ctrl key as you drag the object.

> **TIP**
>
> Holding down the Shift key as you drag constrains the movement of the object, making it possible to drag it *only* horizontally or *only* vertically.

To copy an object on a slide using the Clipboard, use the Copy command. Select the object and press Ctrl+C to copy it, or click the Copy button on the Home tab. Then, press Ctrl+V to paste the object, or click the Paste button on the Home tab. You can then drag the copy to wherever you want it on the slide.

> **NOTE**
>
> Whenever you need to cut, copy, or paste, you have a variety of methods to choose from. There are the Cut, Copy, and Paste buttons on the Home tab; the Cut, Copy, and Paste commands on the right-click menu; and the shortcut key combinations, Cut (Ctrl+X), Copy (Ctrl+C), and Paste (Ctrl+V).

> **TIP**
>
> Ctrl+D works as a combination Copy-and-Paste command by duplicating the object or objects that you have selected.

From One Slide to Another

To move an object to a different slide, cutting and pasting works best. Select the object and press Ctrl+X, or click Cut on the Home tab. Then display the slide on which you want the object to appear, and press Ctrl+V, or click Paste on the Home tab.

To copy an object to a different slide without removing it from the original slide, you can do the same thing except that you need to use the Copy command (Ctrl+C or Copy button) instead of the Cut command.

NOTE

If you want an object to appear in the same spot on every slide in the presentation, add the object to the slide master rather than trying to copy it onto every slide. See Chapter 4, "Working with Layouts, Themes, and Masters," for more information.

TIP

When you copy and paste an object onto the same slide, the copy is offset from the original to allow for easy selection. When you copy and paste an object onto a different slide, the copy appears in the same position as the original.

From One Presentation to Another

To move or copy from one presentation to another, use the Cut, Copy, and Paste commands. First, select the object, and then cut or copy it. Display the destination slide (in normal view) in the other presentation, and then paste.

TIP

An object that you move or copy to a different presentation might change its color because the destination file is using a different color theme. This is because objects with colors from a color theme rather than colors defined by a fixed color will change colors when you apply a different theme or template.

9

To Another Program

You can also move and copy objects from PowerPoint into other programs. For example, suppose that you have created a table on a slide and you want to include it in a report in Word. You can move or copy it to a Word document by cutting and pasting. For more information on tables, see Chapter 8, "Creating and Formatting Tables."

TIP

Depending on the object and the destination application, copying and pasting usually results in smaller file sizes than dragging and dropping.

Using the Office Clipboard

The Microsoft Office Clipboard lets you store more than one object at a time. You can copy or cut multiple objects to the Clipboard and then paste them all into the same or different locations afterward. To use the Clipboard in multi-clip mode, click the dialog box launcher for the Clipboard group on the Home tab. The Clipboard pane appears.

As you copy or cut items, they appear on a list in the Clipboard pane. When you want to paste an item, display the slide on which you want to paste it — position the insertion point at the desired location if the item is text — and then click the item in the Clipboard pane. The Clipboard can hold up to 24 items. To remove an item, click the drop-down arrow next to it and choose Delete, as shown in Figure 9.11.

FIGURE 9.11

Move or copy multiple items using the Clipboard pane.

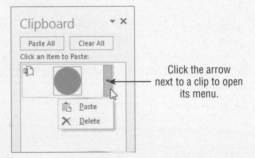

Click the arrow next to a clip to open its menu.

> **TIP**
>
> Click the Options button at the bottom of the Clipboard pane to display a list of on/off toggles that you can set for Clipboard operation. For example, you can specify that the Clipboard pane appears automatically when you press Ctrl+C twice in a row and whether it displays an icon on the taskbar when it is active.

Understanding Object Formatting

Up until this point, we've considered all objects to be equal, but there are actually two major classes of objects that PowerPoint supports: those that you create from within PowerPoint and those that you import from other sources. Each object type causes a different version of the Format tab to display when you select it.

For drawn shapes, charts, SmartArt, and text boxes, the Drawing Tools Format tab in Figure 9.12 appears. From here you can apply shape styles, as well as WordArt formatting, to the text within the object.

FIGURE 9.12

For drawn objects, charts, and text boxes, these formatting options are available.

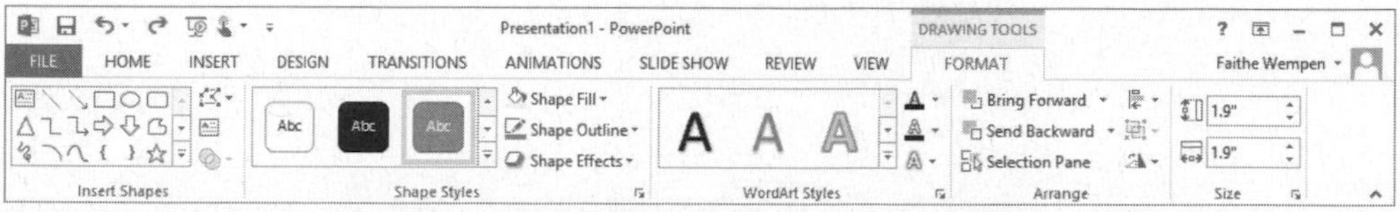

> **NOTE**
>
> SmartArt has some formatting features in common with drawn shapes and charts, but it also has some special features and quirks of its own. For more information, see Chapter 10, "Creating SmartArt Graphics."

For photos and clip art, the Picture Tools Format tab in Figure 9.13 appears. It focuses on applying filters through which you view the image (such as brightness and contrast) and applying Picture Styles that affect the shape and border of the frame.

FIGURE 9.13

For photos and clip art, these formatting options are available.

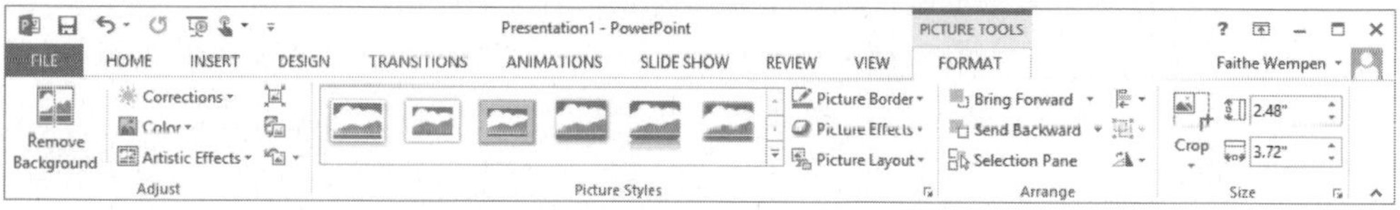

Both of these versions of the Format tab (Drawing Tools and Picture Tools) have Size and Arrange groups that work the same way.

The following sections explain how to apply formatting to the two types of objects, by using the Drawing Tools Format tab or the Picture Tools Format tab. Some features are unique to one object type or the other; other features can be used for both types, although some features that do basically the same thing have different names, depending on the object type.

Resizing Objects

Let's start with something that all objects have in common: resizing. You can resize any object on a slide, either by dragging a selection handle on its border or by using the Size group in the Format tab.

In Chapter 3, "Creating Slides and Text Boxes," you learned how to resize a text box; you can resize any object in this same way, simply by dragging a corner or side selection handle to change the object's size and shape. The mouse pointer changes to a double-headed arrow when you move it over a selection handle.

> **TIP**
>
> Some objects, such as photos, maintain their aspect ratio by default when you resize them using a corner selection handle. In other words, the ratio of height to width does not change when you resize using the corner selection handles. If you want to distort the object by changing its aspect ratio, drag one of the side selection handles instead of a corner one. Other objects, such as drawn shapes, do not maintain the aspect ratio unless you hold down the Shift key as you drag a corner selection handle.

You can also size an object by using the increment buttons to change the values in the Size group on the Format tab or by typing numbers directly into these text boxes.

Alternatively, you can click the dialog box launcher for the Size group to open a Format Shape (or Format Picture) task pane with the Size tab settings, from which you can enter a height and width, the same as you would in the Size group on the Ribbon (see Figure 9.14). This same dialog box is available for all object types, although more of the options are available for photos than for drawn objects. Figure 9.14 shows the dialog box for a photo. For a drawn object, some of the Scale options are unavailable, as well as the Crop From and Original Size sections.

FIGURE 9.14

Adjust an object's size from the Size settings in the Format Shape (or Format Picture) task pane or from the Size controls on the Format tab.

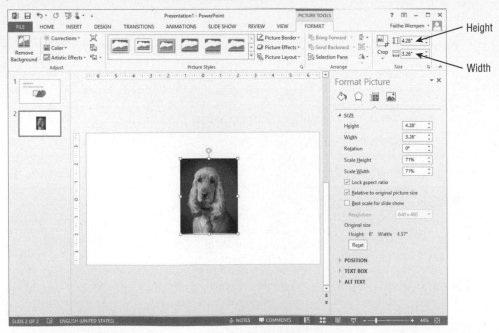

An advantage of using the task pane is that you can adjust the scale of the object by a percentage. For example, you can shrink the object to 45 percent of its original size by changing its Scale Height and Scale Width values to 45 percent each. This feature is more useful for photos than for drawn objects, but it works for all object types.

For imported objects only — such as photos, clip art, and so on — you can also set these scale options:

- **Relative to Original Picture Size.** The measurements in the Scale Height and Scale Width boxes refer to the original picture size if you select this option; otherwise, they refer to the previous size of the picture.

- **Best Scale for Slide Show.** When you select this option, PowerPoint adjusts the picture size to match the resolution at which you show the presentation, as you have specified in the Resolution drop-down list.

The Original Size section is also available only for imported objects. You can click the Reset button in this section to reset the object back to the size that it was when you initially placed it on the slide.

Arranging Objects

Arranging is another action that you can perform with all object types. For example, you can specify an object's position in relation to the slide or to other objects, change the stacking order, rotate the object, group or merge it with other objects, and much more.

Rotating and Flipping Objects

Most objects display a circle at the top when you select them; this is called the *rotation handle*. See Figure 9.15. You can drag it to rotate the object. This action is called *free rotation* because there is no precise numeric measurement that is related to the amount of rotation, although by holding down the Shift key while rotating, you can rotate the object by 15-degree increments.

You can also rotate an object by exactly 90 degrees. To do so, click the Rotate button on the Format tab and select Rotate Right 90° or Rotate Left 90°, as shown in Figure 9.16.

On this same menu, you can also flip an object either vertically or horizontally. Flipping is different from rotating in that it creates a mirror image of the object, not just a rotated version.

To set a precise amount of rotation for an object, use the Rotation text box in the Format Shape (or Format Picture) task pane, shown in Figure 9.14. Use the increment buttons to increase or decrease the rotation amount, or enter a precise number of degrees.

9

FIGURE 9.15

Rotate an object by dragging its rotation handle.

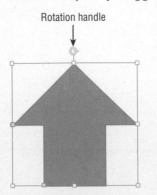

FIGURE 9.16

Rotate an object 90 degrees or flip an object from the Rotate menu.

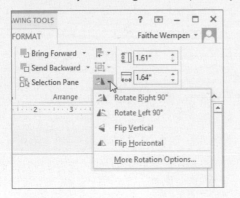

Aligning or Distributing Objects

PowerPoint provides many different ways to precisely position objects in relation to one another. There are grids, guides, Smart Guides, and several commands for alignment and distribution.

Here are some examples of what you can do:

- You can align an object to the top, bottom, left, right, or center of a slide.

- You can align two or more objects in relation to one another so that they are at the same vertical or horizontal position.

- You can distribute three or more objects so that the spacing between them is even.

Snapping Objects to a Grid

There is an invisible grid on every slide to which all objects snap. If you move an object and position it so that it doesn't quite align with the gridlines, when you release the object, it moves slightly to snap into alignment with the nearest gridlines. If PowerPoint doesn't seem to be doing that, the Snap feature may be turned off.

To turn snapping on or off, follow these steps:

1. **On the View tab, click the dialog box launcher for the Show group.** The Grid and Guides dialog box opens.

2. **Mark or clear the Snap Objects to Grid option, shown in Figure 9.17.**

FIGURE 9.17

Choose whether or not to snap objects to the grid.

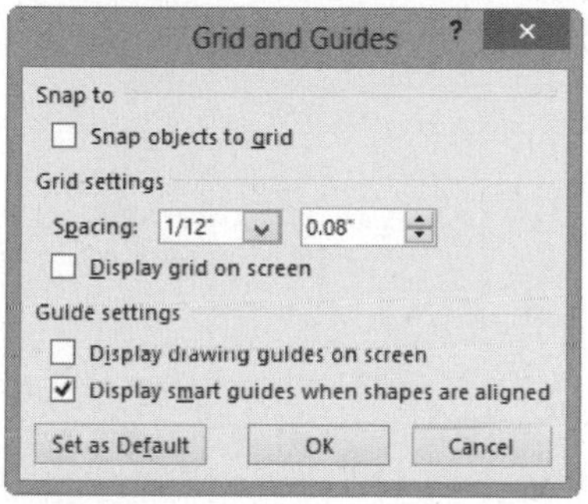

3. **Click OK.**

TIP

If snapping to the grid is turned on but you want to bypass it for a specific operation, hold down the Alt key as you drag the object. The object moves smoothly, unencumbered by the grid.

To display or hide the alignment grid on the screen, select or deselect the Display Grid on Screen option in the Grid and Guides dialog box (Figure 9.17), or mark or clear the Guides check box on the View tab. To change the grid spacing, enter the desired amount in the Spacing text box.

Using Guides

Guides are nonprinting vertical or horizontal lines that you can move around on the slide to help you gauge where an object should be positioned. To turn the display of guides off or on, mark or clear the Guides check box on the View tab, or right-click the slide, point to Grid and Guides, and click Guides. By default there is one vertical and one horizontal guide-line when guides are displayed; to add more, right-click the slide, point to Grid and Guides, and click Add Vertical Guide or Add Horizontal Guide. You can drag guides to reposition them on the slide as you work. An object will also snap to the guide if you drop the object near the guide. New in PowerPoint 2013, you can add permanent custom guides to the Slide Masters too. See Chapter 4 for details.

Using Smart Guides

PowerPoint also has a *Smart Guides* feature, which pops up temporary guidelines to help you to align objects with one another as you are dragging. Smart Guides give you the benefit of guide without having to have the regular guides displayed all the time.

When one object's top, bottom, or middle starts to be nearly aligned with an adjacent object, a dotted line appears showing where the alignment point would be, so you can find it easily. The object also snaps into alignment with that dotted line when you drop it anywhere near the dotted line. See Figure 9.18.

FIGURE 9.18

Smart Guides are dotted lines that help you align one object with another.

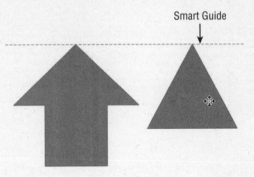

To turn the Smart Guides feature on or off, right-click the slide, point to Grid and Guides so that a submenu appears, and click Smart Guides.

Nudging Objects

If you are one of those people who have a hard time positioning objects precisely when you drag them, you'll appreciate the Nudge command. It moves an object slightly in the direction that you want without altering it in the other plane. For example, suppose you have positioned a text box in exactly the spot you want vertically but a little bit too far to the right. If you drag it manually, you might accidentally change the vertical position. Instead, you can press an arrow key to move it. Hold down Ctrl to override snapping to the grid.

Nudging moves the object one space on the grid when you have enabled the Snap Objects to Grid option. (See the section, "Snapping Objects to a Grid" earlier in this chapter.) When the Snap Objects to Grid option is turned off, you can nudge the object one pixel at a time.

> **TIP**
>
> Certain objects, such as SmartArt, will sometimes refuse to be moved (including by nudging) after you have applied a 3-D Quick Style with a perspective view. To move such an object, click Edit in 2-D on the SmartArt Tools Format tab. You can then move the object. Afterward, you can click Edit in 2-D again to toggle it back to its regular 3-D appearance. Charts are quirky that way too; before you can nudge a chart, you have to Ctrl+click it to select it.

> **TIP**
>
> Nudge buttons are not available on the Ribbon. However, if you would like, you can add them to the Quick Access Toolbar, or you can customize the Ribbon to include them. See Chapter 22, "Customizing PowerPoint," for more details.

Aligning an Object in Relation to the Slide

You can align objects in relation to the slide itself. For example, you might want an object to be centered vertically and horizontally on the slide. To align a single object in relation to the slide, follow these steps:

1. **Select the object.**
2. **Click Format ⇨ Arrange ⇨ Align Objects, and make sure the Align to Slide command has a check mark next to it.** If it doesn't, click the command to place one there.
3. **Click Align Objects again if the menu is not already open and choose one of the horizontal alignment commands: Align Left, Align Center, or Align Right, as shown in Figure 9.19.**

FIGURE 9.19

Choose an alignment for the object in relation to the slide.

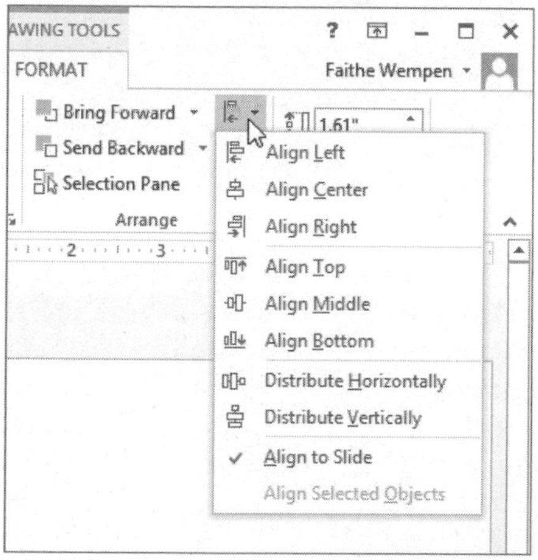

4. **Click Align again and choose one of the vertical alignment commands: Align Top, Align Middle, or Align Bottom.**

Aligning Two or More Objects with One Another

You can align two objects in relation to one another by assigning the same setting to both objects. For example, in the left illustration in Figure 9.20, the objects are in their starting positions. The right illustration shows what happens when you use the Align Top command to move the lower object to the same vertical position as the higher one. If you use Align Bottom, the higher object moves to match the lower one. If you use Align Center, both objects move to split the difference between their two positions.

FIGURE 9.20

The original positioning (left) and the positioning after you apply the Align Top command (right)

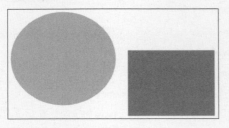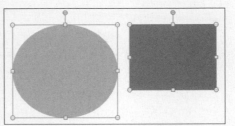

To align two or more objects with one another, follow these steps:

1. **Select the objects.**

2. **Click Format ⇨ Arrange ⇨ Align Objects, and make sure Align Selected Objects is selected.** If it's not, click it to select it.

3. **Click the Align button again to reopen the menu if needed, and choose the desired alignment, either vertical or horizontal.**

> **NOTE**
> If you use the Align Top command and the objects move to the very top of the slide, you probably have selected the Align to Slide option. Undo (Ctrl+Z) the action and try again.

Distributing Objects

Distribution works only in relation to the slide or with three or more objects selected. When you distribute objects, you spread them evenly over a given space. For example, suppose you align three boxes vertically and now you want to even out the space between each box, as shown in Figure 9.21. You can apply the Distribute Horizontally command to create the uniform spacing. To distribute objects, follow these steps:

1. **Select the objects.** To do so, hold down the Shift key while you click each one, or drag an outline that encircles all of the objects.

2. **Click Format ⇨ Arrange ⇨ Align Objects, and then click either Distribute Vertically or Distribute Horizontally.**

FIGURE 9.21

The original positioning (left) and the positioning after applying the Distribute Horizontally command (right)

If you have only two objects selected, you cannot distribute them unless you have already selected Align to Slide.

Layering Objects

You can stack objects on top of each other to create special effects. For example, you might create a logo by stacking a text box on top of an oval or a rectangle, as shown in Figure 9.22.

FIGURE 9.22

You can create all kinds of logos, artwork, and other special effects by layering objects.

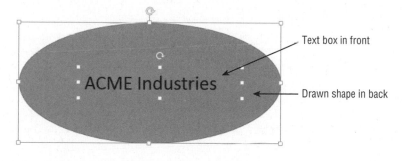

ACME Industries

Text box in front

Drawn shape in back

To create a text box, see Chapter 3.

> **TIP**
> You can also type text directly into a drawn shape without using layering; simply right-click the shape and choose Edit Text. You can also just begin typing while the shape is selected.

By default, objects stack in the order in which you create them. For example, in Figure 9.22, the text box appears over the shape because the shape was created first, and so it is on the bottom of the stack. You can move the shape, but it will continue to be on the layer under the text box.

If you need to reorder the objects in a stack, follow these steps:

1. **Click an object in the stack.**
2. **Use one of the buttons in the Arrange group on the Format tab:**
   - Click Bring Forward to bring the object forward one position in the stack.
   - Open the Bring Forward drop-down menu and choose Bring to Front to bring the object to the top of the stack.
   - Click Send Backward to send the object backward one position in the stack.
   - Open the Send Backward drop-down menu and choose Send to Back to send the object to the bottom of the stack.
3. **Repeat the steps to change the position of other objects in the stack as needed.**

Another way to reorder object stacking is to use the Selection pane:

1. **Click Home ⇨ Editing ⇨ Select ⇨ Selection Pane to display the Selection pane.**
2. **Click an object's name on the list.**
3. **Click the Bring Forward (up arrow) or Send Backward (down arrow) button to move the object up or down in the stacking order.**

Working with Object Groups

You have already learned how to select multiple objects and work with them as a single unit. For example, you might select several shapes together that collectively form a picture that you have drawn. If you intend to treat these objects as a single unit, you can save yourself some time by grouping them. When you group two or more objects, they become a single object for the purposes of moving and resizing. They also lose their animation, if any was applied to them. You can always ungroup them later if you need to work with the objects separately. Dissimilar objects can be grouped, so, for example, you could group a photo, a drawn shape, and a text box into a single unit.

WARNING
You can't group placeholders with other objects.

To group two or more objects together, follow these steps:

1. **Select all of the objects that you want to group.**
2. **Click Format ⇨ Arrange ⇨ Group Objects ⇨ Group.** (Alternatively, you can press Ctrl+G.) The objects now form a group.

To ungroup a collection of objects, select the object group, open the Group drop-down menu again, and choose Ungroup, or press Ctrl+Shift+G. After ungrouping them, you can make changes to the objects separately. Then, if you want to regroup the same objects again, open the Group drop-down menu and choose Regroup.

> **TIP**
>
> You can make some changes to objects even when they are part of a group, so it is not as necessary to ungroup before editing or formatting an object. Try editing it first as part of the group, and if that doesn't work, resort to ungrouping.

> **CAUTION**
>
> If you are moving a group, make sure you have selected the whole group and not an object within it. If a single object is selected in the group, it will move individually when you drag it.

Merging Shapes

One of the most welcome new features in PowerPoint 2013 (and in all of Microsoft Office 2013, for that matter) is the ability to combine multiple drawn lines and shapes into more complex shapes. This feature makes the drawing tools in Office applications much more useful and flexible.

To apply one of the merge operations, select two or more shapes in a stack (that is, where they overlap one another at least partially). Then click Drawing Tools Format ⇨ Insert Shapes ⇨ Merge Shapes and then one of the merge operations. There are five basic merge operations you can perform, and each of them creates a new shape out of these two pieces in a different way.

Suppose, for example, you have two shapes, as shown in Figure 9.23: a blue oval and a yellow triangle on top of it. Table 9.1 summarizes the operations and compares the results.

FIGURE 9.23

The original two shapes used for the merge examples in Table 9.1

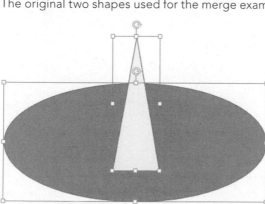

9

TABLE 9.1 Merge Operation Examples

Operation	Description	Example
Union	Combines the areas of both shapes, and takes on the formatting of the top shape	
Combine	Includes areas where one of the two shapes appears, but excludes areas where both shapes overlap	
Fragment	Combines the areas of both shapes, but breaks the shapes into multiple pieces where overlap begins and ends	
Intersect	Includes only the areas where the top shape overlaps the bottom shape	
Subtract	Includes only the areas where the top shape did not overlap the bottom shape	

Applying Shape or Picture Styles

Both the Drawing Tools Format tab and the Picture Tools Format tab (shown in Figures 9.12 and 9.13 respectively) have a style group from which you can apply preset formatting. For drawn objects and charts, it is called Shape Styles; for photos and clip art, it is called Picture Styles.

Using Shape Styles

Shape Styles are formatting presets that you can apply to drawn shapes, text boxes, and charts. Shape Styles make it easy to apply common border and fill combinations that use colors from the current theme. A Shape Style is a combination of three things:

- **Shape Fill.** The color and style of the inside.
- **Shape Outline.** The color and style of the outer border.
- **Shape Effects.** Special effects that are applied to the object, such as shadows, reflection, or beveled edges.

Each of these can be separately applied, as you will learn later in this chapter. To apply a Shape Style, follow these steps:

1. **Select the shape or shapes that you want to affect.**
2. **On the Drawing Tools Format tab, open the Shape Styles gallery and click a style, as shown in Figure 9.24.**

The styles that appear on the gallery menu are built into PowerPoint, and you cannot change them. Their colors change according to the color theme that is currently applied to the presentation.

> **TIP**
>
> The Other Theme Fills option at the bottom of the gallery menu opens an extra palette that contains several light and dark background fills that match the styles that display when you click Background Styles on the Design tab. See Chapter 4 for more about applying background styles. Filling a shape with the same color as the background makes it blend in with the background.

9

Applying Picture Styles

Picture Styles are like Shape Styles, except that they apply to photos, clip art, and media clips. A Picture Style applies different formatting than a Shape Style applies because pictures have different needs. For example, a picture does not need a fill color because the picture is the fill. A Picture Style applies these things:

- **Picture Shape.** The shape of the frame in which the picture is placed.
- **Picture Border.** The color and style of the outside of the picture frame.
- **Picture Effects.** Special effects such as beveled edges and shadows.

FIGURE 9.24

Apply a Shape Style as a shortcut to formatting a drawn object or a chart element.

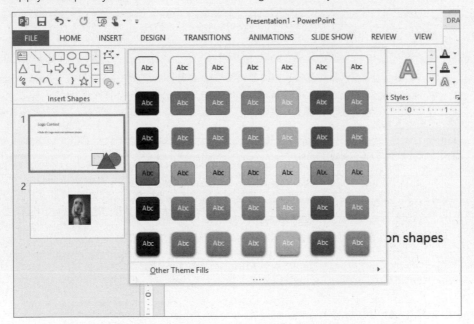

To apply a Picture Style, follow these steps:

1. **Select the picture that you want to affect.**
2. **On the Picture Tools Format tab, open the Picture Styles gallery (Figure 9.25) and click a style.**

The styles that appear on the gallery menu are built into PowerPoint, and you cannot change them.

FIGURE 9.25

Apply a Picture Style to quickly format an imported graphic such as a photo.

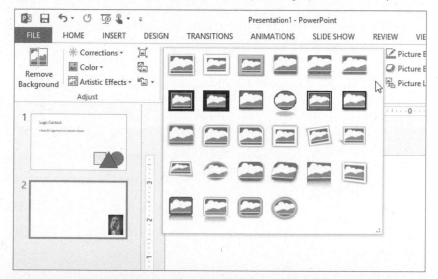

> **TIP**
>
> The formatting that you apply through Picture Styles is not dependent on the color theme, but some of the border formatting is partially dependent on the background that you have chosen. For the Picture Styles that include a border, the border color is either black or white, and it changes depending on whether you are using a light or dark background. (You can choose a background from the Background Styles button on the Design tab.) If you want a different color border than the Picture Style provides, you can modify the border color after applying the style.

Understanding Color Selection

To apply a custom border or fill color to an object, you must know something about how PowerPoint uses and applies colors. Although this is covered in Chapter 4, here is a quick review.

PowerPoint uses a set of color placeholders for the bulk of its color formatting. Because each item's color is defined by a placeholder, and not as a fixed color, you can easily change the colors by switching to a different color theme. For example, if you decide that you want all of the slide titles to be blue rather than green, you can make the change once and PowerPoint applies it to all of the slides automatically.

9

A set of colors that is assigned to the preset positions is a *color theme*. You can apply both border (outline) and fill colors using *color pickers*. A color picker is a menu that shows the colors from the currently chosen color theme, along with tints (light versions) and shades (dark versions) of each of the theme colors. To stick with theme colors, which I recommend in most cases, choose one of the theme colors or one of its tints or shades (Figure 9.26).

FIGURE 9.26

A color picker offers the current color theme's colors and also some standard (fixed) colors.

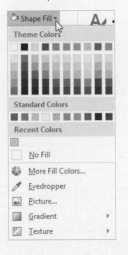

You also have the following options:

- To use a color that has already been used in this presentation, choose it from the Recent Colors section. In Figure 9.26 there is one color in that section.
- If you need a color that does not change when you switch color themes, you can instead click one of the swatches in the Standard Colors section on the color picker.
- If you need a color that is not represented in the Standard Colors section, you can choose More Colors. (The command name varies, depending on what you are coloring; in Figure 9.26, it is More Fill Colors.) This opens the Colors dialog box. The Standard tab in the Colors dialog box contains swatches for many common colors. Most people can find the color that they want on the Standard tab. Click the color that you want and click OK.

If you need a color that does not appear in the swatches, you may need to use the Custom tab, shown in Figure 9.27. There are a number of things you can do on this tab:

- You can enter the precise numbers for a color; for example, you can match the exact color for a company logo.

FIGURE 9.27

Use the Custom tab of the Colors dialog box to precisely define a color that you want to use.

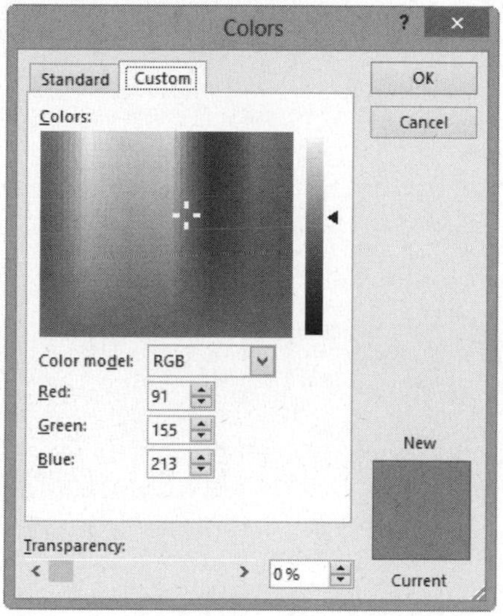

- You can define colors numerically using either the *HSL* (hue, saturation, and luminosity) or *RGB* (red, green, blue) color models. Choose the color model that you want from the Color Model drop-down list.

- If you are using the HSL model, you can type the numbers into the Hue, Sat, and Lum fields on the Custom tab. The hue is the tint (that is, green versus blue versus red). A low number is a color at the red end of the spectrum, while a high number is a color at the violet end. Saturation refers to the vividness of the color, and luminosity is the lightness or darkness. A high luminosity mixes the color with white, while a low luminosity mixes the color with black.

- An alternative way to define colors is by specifying numbers for red, green, and blue. Using this measurement, 0, 0, 0 is pure black and 255, 255, 255 is pure white. All other colors are some combination of the three colors. For example, pure blue is 0, 0, 255. A very pale blue would be 200, 200, 255. You can play around with the numbers in the fields on the Custom tab. The new color appears in the New area near the bottom of the dialog box. Click OK to accept your choice.

TIP

You can create an interesting see-through effect with a color by using the transparency slider. When this slider is used for a color, it creates an effect like a watercolor paint wash over an item so that whatever is beneath it can partially show through. For photos, you can get a similar tint effect for the whole picture using the Color drop-down list on the Picture Tools Format tab.

Applying an Object Border

A border (outline) around an object can draw attention to it as well as separate it from surrounding items.

When describing the buttons that create borders around an object, PowerPoint uses inconsistent terminology between the two versions of the Format tab. For drawn objects, the button that applies borders is called the *Shape Outline* button; for pictures it is called the *Picture Border* button. Both buttons open essentially the same menu — a standard color picker like the one shown in Figure 9.26.

NOTE

The only difference between the Picture Border and the Shape Outline color pickers is that the latter has an Arrows command. This command is available only when the selected object is a line (not a closed shape); it applies arrowheads to one or both ends of the line.

Border Attributes

A border has three basic attributes: its color, its width (thickness), and its dash style (solid, dashed, dotted, etc.). You can set each of these basic attributes using the color picker, which contains fly-out menus at the bottom for weight and dashes. Each fly-out menu has presets that you can select.

To control the more advanced attributes of the line, or to make a selection other than a preset, choose More Lines from one of the fly-out submenus. This opens the Format Shape task pane with Line controls expanded, as shown in Figure 9.28.

TIP

You can also right-click and choose Format Picture to apply borders from the Format Picture dialog box.

In the Line controls of the Format Shape task pane, you can set the following:

- **Width.** The thickness of the line in points.
- **Compound Type.** The number of parallel lines the overall line comprises and their relative thicknesses.
- **Dash Type.** The style of line (solid, dashed, dotted).
- **Cap Type.** The style for the ends of the line (applicable to lines only).
- **Join Type.** The style for the corners of the shape.
- **Arrow settings.** The types and sizes of the arrow heads (applicable to lines only).

FIGURE 9.28

Use the Format Shape task pane to fine-tune the border (line) style.

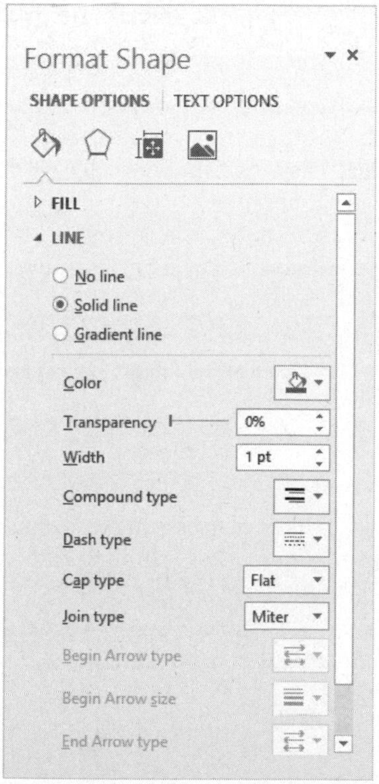

> **NOTE**
>
> For a gradient line, click Gradient Line in the Format Shape task pane. From there, you can choose a preset gradient or define your own. For more information about gradients, see the section "Gradient Fills" later in this chapter.

Creating a Semitransparent Border

By default, a line is not transparent at all. To specify a level of transparency for it, you can drag the Transparency slider to the right, or enter a transparency percentage in the text box provided, in the Format Shape task pane (Figure 9.28).

> **NOTE**
>
> Some of the picture or shape effects also affect the border of the object. These are covered later in this chapter, in the section "Applying Object Effects."

Applying an Object Fill

An object can have no fill (that is, it can be transparent), or it can be filled with a solid color, a gradient, a texture, a pattern, or a picture. Fills mostly apply to objects that you draw yourself, such as shapes, charts, and SmartArt. Although Fill commands are available for imported art such as pictures and clip art, these commands are not commonly applied to them. Because a picture takes up the entire frame that it is in, any fill that you might apply would not be visible anyway (unless the picture has a transparent color set for it). With clip art, you might occasionally want to apply a fill because most clip art has a transparent background. By applying a fill to it, you make the clip art's background visible so that it appears to be in a rectangular box rather than floating on the background.

PowerPoint 2013 contains some interesting features for working with pictures, including one that helps you remove the background from a photo. See Chapter 11, "Working with Clip Art and Photos," for details.

Solid Fills

To apply a solid fill for a shape, or other type of object that uses the Drawing Tools Format tab, you can choose a fill type from the color picker that you access through the Shape Fill button. See Figure 9.29.

FIGURE 9.29

Use the Shape Fill button's palette to choose a solid color.

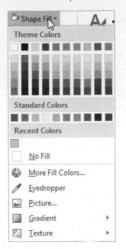

To apply a solid fill for an object that uses the Picture Tools Format tab, you must open the Format Picture task pane, and then click Fill. Follow these steps:

1. **Right-click the object and choose Format Picture.** The Format Picture task pane opens.

2. **Click the Fill & Line icon, and then click Fill to expand the fill options.**
3. **Click Solid Fill.**
4. **Click the Color button in the task pane to open a color picker.**
5. **Select the desired color.** See Figure 9.30.

See the section "Understanding Color Selection" earlier in this chapter for more on selecting color.

FIGURE 9.30

Set a color fill for a picture type of object via the Format Picture task pane.

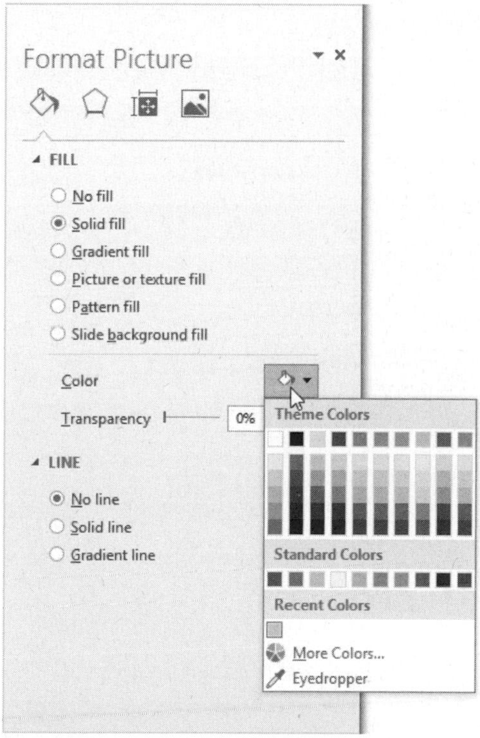

6. **(Optional) Drag the Transparency slider to set transparency.**
7. **Click Close.**

Copying a Fill Color with the Eyedropper Tool

Matching exact colors can be tricky, especially when you don't know the numeric value of a color you are trying to duplicate. A new feature in PowerPoint 2013 is the Eyedropper tool. You can pick up a color from any object in your presentation and use that as a fill color for other objects. So, for example, you could pick up the exact shade of green in the leaves on a tree in a photo you have and use it as the text color for an adjacent note or as the border around the photo.

To copy a color, follow these steps:

1. **Select the object, choose the attribute you want to format (for example, Picture Border, Shape Fill, or Shape Outline), and open the color picker.**

2. **Click the Eyedropper command.** The mouse pointer turns into an eyedropper graphic, and a square appears above the pointer. Wherever you hover the eyedropper, the square magnifies the color of that spot. See Figure 9.31.

FIGURE 9.31

Pick up a color with the Eyedropper tool.

Eyedropper
hovers over a
pixel in the image.

Square magnifies
the pixel so you
can see its color.

3. **When the square shows the desired color, click to accept it.** The item you are coloring receives the chosen color.

After you pick up a color with the Eyedropper tool, you can easily reapply that same color in the same presentation by choosing it from the Recent Colors section of any color picker.

Gradient Fills

Whenever one color turns gradually into another color, the transition is called a *gradient*. For example, when you watch a sunset, you can see how the red of the sun slowly fades into the blue-black of the evening sky, and the sky's color is a gradient. In graphic design, gradients are often used on large shapes, on logos, and on backgrounds to add more inter-est than a single flat color can provide.

PowerPoint 2013 has powerful gradient capabilities. For example, you can create gradients that consist of many different colors, and you can specify the spot at which one color shifts to another.

Applying a One-Color Gradient Preset

For drawn shapes (and other objects that use the Drawing Tools Format tab), you can use the Shape Fill button to access preset gradients that blend one color with either black or white. These presets apply only to drawn objects, not to picture objects. Follow these steps to apply a one-color preset:

1. **Apply a solid color fill to the object; use the color that you want to combine with black or white.**

2. **Select the object and display the Drawing Tools Format tab.**

3. **Open the Shape Fill drop-down menu, point to Gradient, and click the desired gradient style, as shown in Figure 9.32.**

FIGURE 9.32

Apply a preset gradient from the Gradient submenu for a shape.

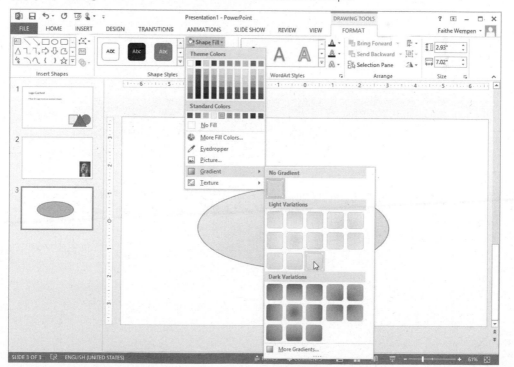

9

Applying a Custom Gradient

For more gradient options, use the Format Shape (or Format Picture) task pane. This method works for most types of objects, generally speaking, but not all pictures can take a gradient. (A .wmf file with a transparent background can, for example.)

When setting up a custom gradient, you define stops. A *stop* is a position along the gradient that specifies a certain color. Each stop has three properties: color, stop position, and transparency. A gradient typically has as many stops as it has colors; however, you can use the same color for multiple stops. For a default, evenly spaced gradient, the stops are spaced out evenly, measured in percentages. For example, if you defined three stops, they would be set at 0 percent, 50 percent, and 100 percent. You can also achieve different effects by spacing out the stops differently. Figure 9.33 shows some examples of various numbers and positions of stops.

FIGURE 9.33

Gradient stops define when and how the color will change.

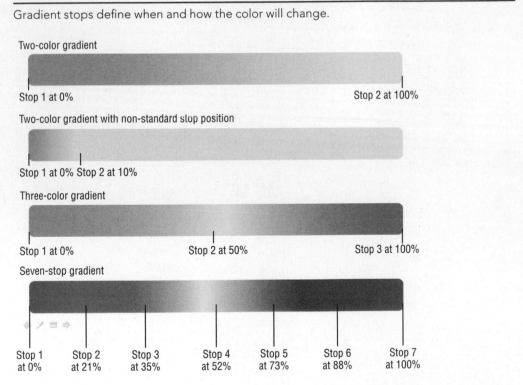

You can use the Fill controls in the Format Shape (or Format Picture) task pane to define a gradient, as shown in Figure 9.34.

FIGURE 9.34

You can define gradient stops and settings in the Format Shape (or Format Picture) task pane.

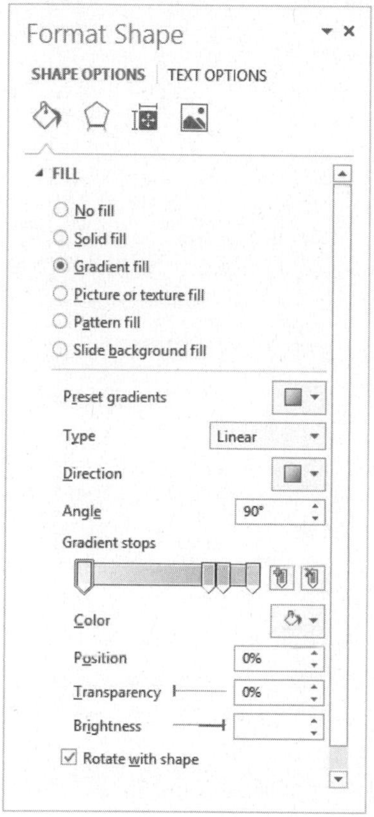

You can set gradients to the following types:

- **Linear.** A linear gradient, like the ones in Figure 9.33, travels from one point to another. You can set it to travel horizontally — as shown in Figure 9.33 — vertically, or diagonally, or you can set a specific angle.

- **Radial.** A radial gradient radiates out from a point. You can set it to radiate from the center of the object or from any of its corners.

- **Rectangular.** This gradient is similar to Radial except that it radiates as a rectangle rather than as a curve.

- **Path.** This gradient follows the shape of the object. Try applying it to a starburst, for example; the color radiates out from the center of the star.

You can also define your own colors and stops for a gradient, or you can start with one of the Preset Colors settings. These are different from the single-color presets in the Drawing Tools Format tab because they are color combinations with predefined stops. You can also start with one of these sets of combinations as a shortcut.

The Gradient Stops slider contains one or more markers, which you can drag to change its position. To add another stop, click the Add Gradient Stop button; to remove a stop, select it and click the Remove Gradient Stop button.

The Transparency setting adjusts the amount of transparency that is associated with a specified stop position in the gradient. You can use this setting to make certain areas of an object more transparent than others. For example, you could define the same color for all of the gradient stops but set different levels of transparency for each stop to make an object seem like it is fading away.

The Rotate with Shape option determines if the gradient rotates when you rotate a shape.

To create a custom gradient, follow these steps:

1. **Right-click the object to be filled and choose Format Shape or Format Picture, depending on the object type.** The Format Shape or Format Picture task pane opens.
2. **Click the Fill & Line icon, and then expand the Fill section if it is not already expanded.**
3. **Click Gradient Fill.** Controls for creating a custom gradient appear (Figure 9.34).
4. **(Optional) Select a preset from the Preset Gradients drop-down list.** If you select a preset, PowerPoint predefines two or more stops for you in the Gradient Stops section.
5. **Open the Type drop-down list and select the type of gradient you want: Linear, Radial, Rectangular, or Path.**
6. **If you chose Linear, Radial, or Rectangular, open the Direction drop-down list and choose a direction swatch.** If you chose Linear, change the incremental value in the Angle text box as needed to adjust the angle.
7. **Mark or clear the Rotate with Shape check box.**
8. **On the Gradient Stops slider, select the first marker.** (You can do them in any order; I usually start with the leftmost one and work to the right.)
9. **Do the following to modify the stop:**
   a. Open the Color palette and select the color for that position.
   b. (Optional) Use the increment buttons to adjust the Position value, or drag the marker to a different position on the slider.
   c. (Optional) Use the increment buttons to adjust the Transparency setting, or drag its slider. Zero percent is no transparency, while 100 percent is complete transparency.

    d. (Optional) Use the increment buttons to adjust the Brightness setting, or drag its slider.

10. **Select the next stop on the Gradient Stops slider bar, and repeat step 9.**

11. **(Optional) Add or remove stops:**

  - If you need to create more stops, click the Add Gradient Stop button and then repeat step 8 for each new stop.

  - If you need to delete a stop, select it and then click the Remove Gradient Stop button.

12. **Close the task pane.**

Texture and Picture Fills

A texture fill is actually a picture fill, but it is a special type of picture that, when tiled, looks like a surface texture such as wood, marble, or cloth. To apply a texture fill, select the object and then click Drawing Tools Format ➪ Shape Styles ➪ Shape Fill ➪ Texture and choose one of the textures on the gallery that appears. See Figure 9.35.

If you are filling an object that doesn't have a Shape Fill button on the Drawing Tools Format tab, such as a piece of clip art, you can use the task pane instead. Follow these steps:

1. **Right-click the object and choose Format Picture (or Format Shape, depending on the object type).** The task pane opens.

2. **Click the Fill & Line icon, and expand the Fill section if it is not already expanded.**

3. **Click the Picture or Texture Fill option button.**

4. **Click the Texture button and select a texture.** The textures are the same ones shown in Figure 9.35.

5. **Close the task pane.**

> **TIP**
>
> You can use your own pictures as textures. To do so, use the procedure for picture fills, and make sure you select the Tile Picture as Texture check box in the task pane. (This check box does not appear unless you have already applied a picture fill.)

You can also use a picture as an object fill. You can specify a picture from a file stored on your hard disk, from the contents of the Clipboard, or from artwork available online (such as clip art from Microsoft). Picture fills were discussed briefly at the end of Chapter 8 as they pertain to table cells, but you can fill almost any object with a picture, not just a text box or table cell.

9

TIP

You can fill a clip-art image that has a transparent background with another picture, creating a picture-on-picture effect.

FIGURE 9.35

Select one of the preset textures from the Texture gallery.

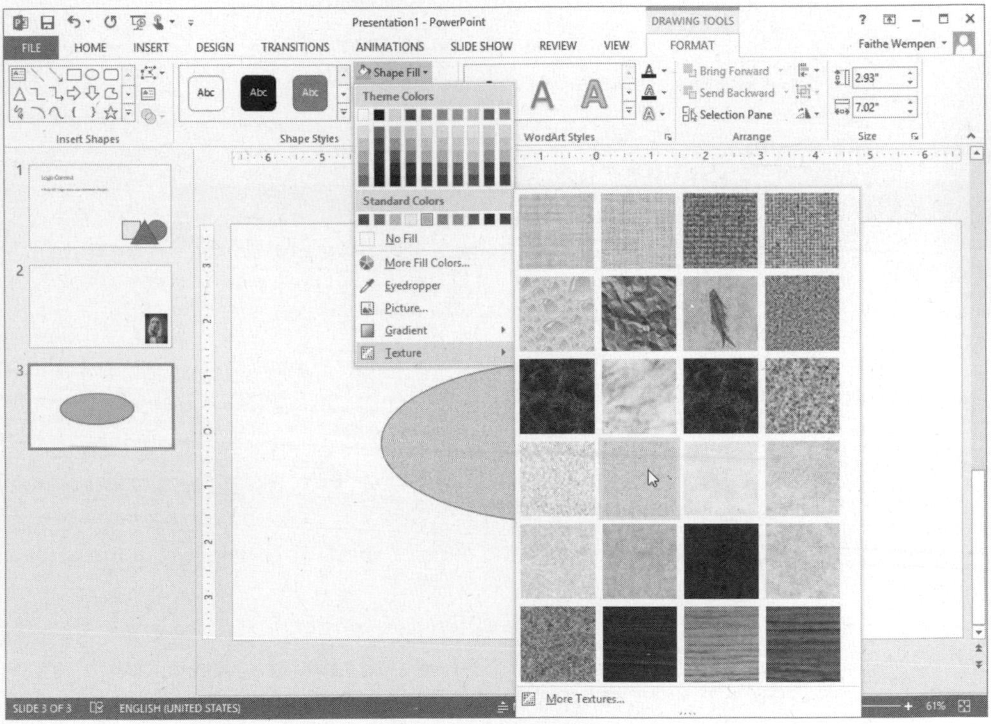

In the Format Shape or Format Picture task pane, when you select the Picture or Texture fill option, three buttons appear:

- **File.** Click this button to open an Insert Picture dialog box, and then select the picture that you want to use.

- **Clipboard.** Click this button to insert the contents of the Clipboard as the graphic to use. This technique works only with the last item that you placed on the Clipboard, not the full 24-item Office Clipboard.

- **Online.** Click this button to open an Insert Pictures dialog box. In the Office.com Clip Art box, type a keyword to search for a clip-art image, and then select and insert the clip art. Or, use the Bing Image Search box to search for a photo to use, or browse files from your own SkyDrive.

After you select the picture that you want to use, you can set any of the following options to control how it appears:

- **Tile Picture as Texture.** When you enable this option, the picture appears at its actual size as a background fill for the object. If the picture is smaller than the object that it is filling, then it tiles like a texture (where multiple copies are used). If the picture is larger than the object that it is filling, then a truncated copy appears.

- **Offset and Scale options.** These options control how the picture fill adjusts within the object. An offset moves it in the specified direction, and a scale value adjusts the size. See Figure 9.36.

FIGURE 9.36

Adjust tiling options.

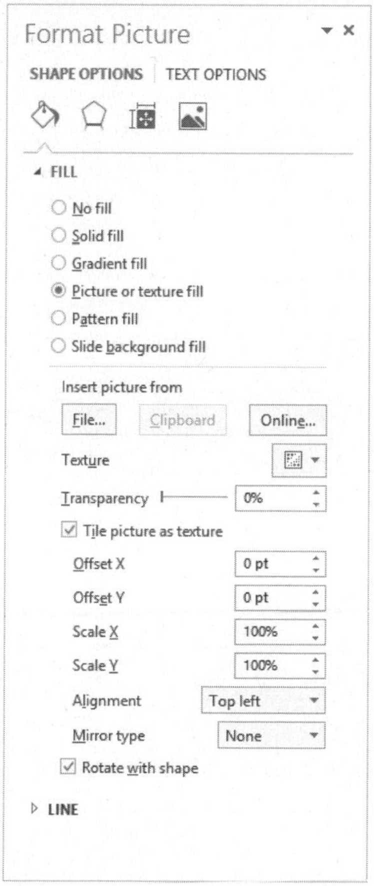

- **Transparency.** Drag the slider or enter a percentage if you want the picture fill to be semitransparent; this works just the same as with colors and gradients.

- **Rotate with shape.** Select or deselect this option to indicate whether the picture should rotate when the object is rotated. This is just the same as with gradients.

Background Fills

You can also apply the background as a fill for shapes and drawn objects. This is somewhat like setting the background fill to No Fill so that the background shows through, except that it hides any objects that are between the affected object and the background. In the example in Figure 9.37, the oval has the background as its fill, and it is sitting on top of a text box. This is better than filling the oval with the same pattern, gradient, or texture as the background because no matter where you move it on the slide, its background will continue to "match" with the slide's background. To apply a background fill, choose the Slide background fill option from the Fill settings in the Format Shape or Format Picture task pane.

FIGURE 9.37

A background fill allows the background to show through but hides any intervening objects.

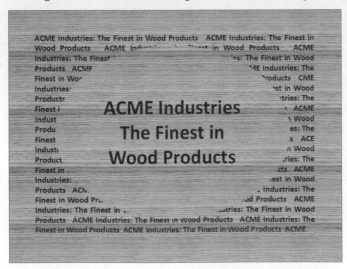

Applying Object Effects

Object effects are special transformations such as reflections, glows, and bevels. You can apply object effects from the Shape Effects or Picture Effects button on the Format tab, depending on the object type. The available effects are nearly identical for all types of objects, except for the different names of the buttons from which you select them. The following sections explain each effect.

Preset

Presets (in the context of object effects) are 3-D effects. They include combinations of gradient fills and edge formatting (such as bevels) that make an object appear to have some depth. You can start with one of these presets as a shortcut to a more complex effect, or you can just use them as they are. Figure 9.38 shows some of the presets applied to a circle.

FIGURE 9.38

You can use presets to apply 3-D object effects.

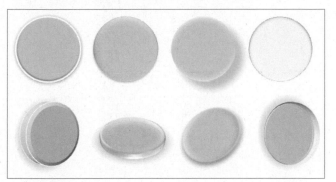

Shadow

You can create outer, inner, or perspective shadows, as shown in Figure 9.39. At first glance, an inner shadow might look the same as an outer one, but if you increase an inner shadow's size, you will notice that the increased size of the shadow decreases the size of the object — that is, the shadow cuts into the object rather than appearing behind it as a separate element.

From the drop-down menu of the Shape Effects or Picture Effects button, select Shadow and then click one of the shadow presets, or click More Shadows to open Shadow controls in the task pane, shown in Figure 9.40. To fine-tune a shadow, you can start with one of the presets from the Presets drop-down menu, customize it by choosing a color, and then drag the sliders for each of the shadow attributes: Transparency, Size, Blur, Angle, and Distance.

9

FIGURE 9.39

Outer (left), inner (center), and perspective (right) shadows.

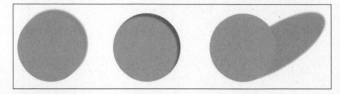

FIGURE 9.40

If none of the presets meets your needs, you can customize a shadow using the Format Picture or Format Shape task pane.

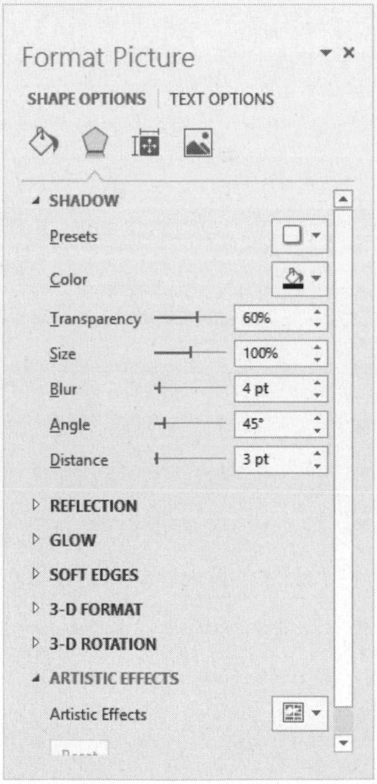

The shadow applies to either the object or its frame, depending on the object type and whether or not it has a transparent background. The following conditions create different results:

- **Text and drawn shapes.** A shadow applied to text, or to a drawn object, clings directly to the object regardless of the background fill.

NOTE

If text is typed in a shape, the shadow applies only to the shape. If you want text typed in a shape to have a shadow, you must use Text Effects in the WordArt Styles options.

CAUTION

If a shape containing text has no fill, the shadow you apply to the shape will apply to the text too. This can cause problems when animating, though; the shadow won't animate with the text. Therefore, it is not recommended to add a shape shadow to such a shape if you plan on assigning an animation event to it.

- **Inserted pictures (such as scanned photos).** The shadow applies to the rectangular frame around the picture; if the picture is inserted in a shape, the shadow applies to the shape.
- **Clip art, text boxes, and charts.** If the background is set to No Fill, the shadow applies to the object inside the frame; if you have an applied fill, the shadow applies to the frame.

CAUTION

If you change the shadow color, you should generally use a color that is darker than the object. Lighter-colored shadows do not look realistic. However, for black text, you should use a gray shadow.

Reflection

Reflection creates a mirror image of the object, below the original. A reflection is affected by two factors: the amount of reflection — partial or full — and the offset, or distance between it and the original. The presets on the Shape Effects (or Picture Effects) ⇨ Reflection submenu use various combinations of these two factors.

You can also customize the reflection by choosing Reflection Options, or by displaying the Reflection tab in the Format Shape or Format Picture task pane, as shown in Figure 9.41. Choose a preset to start with, and then drag the sliders to adjust it as needed. The factors you can change are Transparency, Size, Blur, and Distance.

Glow and Soft Edges

Glow creates a colored "halo" around the object. You can choose the color either from the theme colors or from a fixed color that you specify. To select a different color, choose More Glow Colors and then choose a color from the Colors dialog box. Choose Glow Options to open the Format Shape (or Format Picture) task pane, where you can adjust Color, Size, and Transparency for the effect.

9

Soft Edges is similar to the Glow effect. Whereas Glow creates a fuzzy halo around the outside of an object, Soft Edges uses the same color as the object to create a fuzzy effect by cutting into the edges of the object. The difference between these two effects is similar to the difference between an outer and an inner shadow. A shape can have either or both.

FIGURE 9.41

Customize a reflection effect on the Reflection tab of the Format Shape (or Format Picture) task pane.

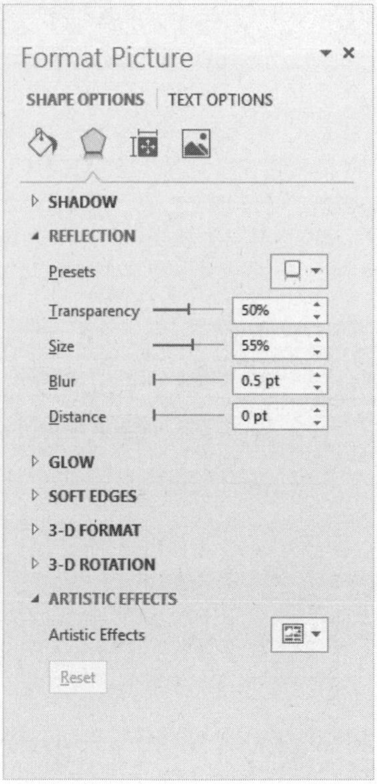

Bevels

A *bevel* is an effect that you apply to the edge of an object to make it look raised, sunken, or textured. You can apply beveling to flat shapes and other objects to give them a thick, three-dimensional appearance, or you can combine them with a real 3-D rotation effect, as described in the following section. Figure 9.42 shows some examples of bevels that you can create using presets. You can access these presets through the Bevel submenu in either the Shape Effects or Picture Effects drop-down menu.

FIGURE 9.42

Beveled edges give a shape a three-dimensional appearance without tilting or rotating the object.

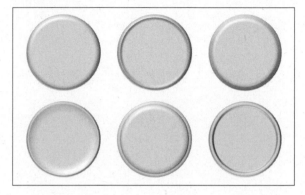

For more beveling choices, click 3-D Options at the bottom of the Bevel submenu. This opens the Format Shape (or Format Picture) task pane with the 3-D Format controls displayed, as shown in Figure 9.43. You can also access this task pane by right-clicking the object and choosing Format Shape (or Format Picture).

The Bottom Bevel setting has no apparent effect unless you apply a 3-D rotation to the object because you can't see the effect at zero rotation. As a result, we will only concern ourselves with the width and height settings for a top bevel:

- **Width.** Specifies how far the effect extends into the object.
- **Height.** Specifies how dramatic the effect is vertically.

You won't notice much height difference for a bevel unless you have applied a 3-D rotation to the object, but the width setting is immediately apparent for all objects.

3-D Rotation and 3-D Formatting

The 3-D rotation effect makes a two-dimensional object look three-dimensional by applying perspective to it. The 3-D rotation effect uses angle measurements for three dimensions: X, Y, and Z:

- **X rotation.** Rotation from side to side.
- **Y rotation.** Rotation from top to bottom.
- **Z rotation.** Pivoting around a center point.

X and Y rotation actually change the shape of the object on the slide to simulate perspective; Z rotation simply spins the object, just as you would with a rotation handle.

FIGURE 9.43

You can set bevels and other 3-D formatting effects in the 3-D Format section of the task pane.

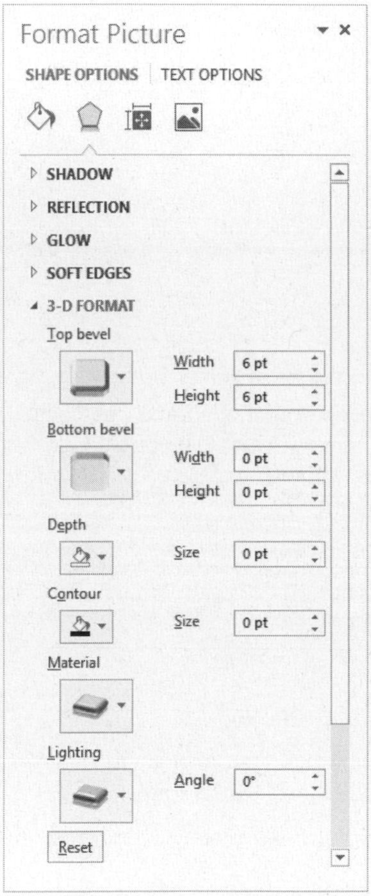

You can combine 3-D rotation with 3-D formatting to create interesting effects, such as adding "sides" to a flat object and coloring these sides in a certain way. For example, you could combine these effects to turn a square into a cube. The 3-D formatting effect is formatting (colors, lengths, and textures) that affects an object's 3-D appearance. The 3-D formatting effect consists of the following aspects:

- **Bevel.** As discussed in the preceding section, this effect alters the edges of the object. You can set top and bottom bevels separately.

- **Depth.** This allows you to specify the size and color of the sides of the object. However, the sides are not visible unless the object is three-dimensionally rotated.

- **Contour.** This allows you to specify the color and size of outlines that mark the edges of the 3-D effect.
- **Surface.** This allows you to specify the material and lighting that the object should simulate.

Figure 9.44 shows several types of 3-D rotation and formatting. Beveling is also a type of 3-D formatting, and so some examples of it are included.

FIGURE 9.44

Some examples of 3-D rotation and formatting.

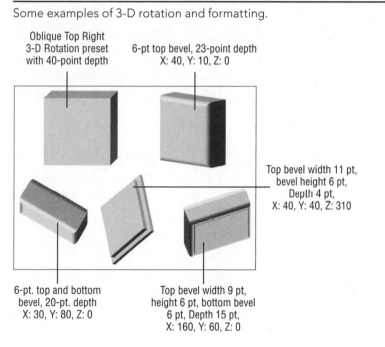

Oblique Top Right
3-D Rotation preset
with 40-point depth

6-pt top bevel, 23-point depth
X: 40, Y: 10, Z: 0

Top bevel width 11 pt,
bevel height 6 pt,
Depth 4 pt,
X: 40, Y: 40, Z: 310

6-pt. top and bottom
bevel, 20-pt. depth
X: 30, Y: 80, Z: 0

Top bevel width 9 pt,
height 6 pt, bottom bevel
6 pt, Depth 15 pt,
X: 160, Y: 60, Z: 0

Although you can use 3-D rotation and 3-D formatting together to create the effects shown in Figure 9.44, they are actually controlled separately in PowerPoint. Therefore, creating these effects is a two-step process.

Applying 3-D Rotation

To apply 3-D rotation, either you can use one of the 3-D Rotation presets or you can enter rotation amounts directly into the Format Shape (or Format Picture) task pane. To use a preset, click the Shape Effects (or Picture Effects) button on the Format tab, select 3-D Rotation, and click a preset. The Oblique presets at the bottom of the menu are the most similar to the older 3-D effects from PowerPoint 2003 and earlier.

CAUTION

If you have not yet added depth to the shape by using its 3-D Format settings, you won't see any effect from the Oblique presets because there are not yet any "sides" to the shape.

To rotate a precise amount, choose 3-D Rotation Options from the bottom of the presets menu, or right-click the object and choose Format Shape (or Format Picture) to open the Format Shape (or Format Picture) task pane. Then expand the 3-D Rotation settings, as shown in Figure 9.45. You can start with one of the presets by selecting it from the Presets drop-down menu.

FIGURE 9.45

Set X, Y, and Z rotation for the object in the Format Shape (or Format Picture) task pane.

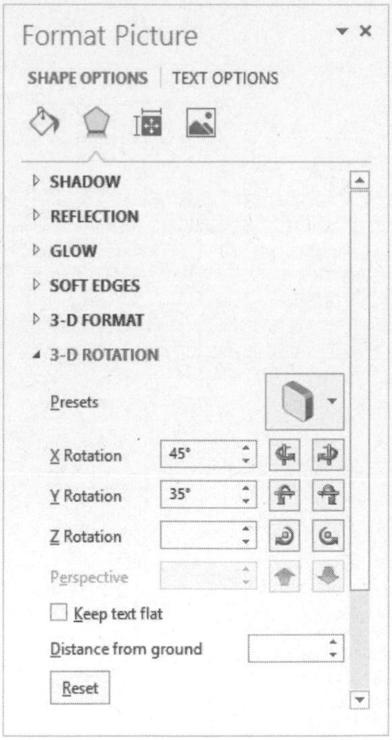

The other settings for rotation are as follows:

- **Keep Text Flat.** This option prevents any text in the shape from rotating on the X- or Y-axis.

- **Distance from Ground.** This setting adds space between the object and the background. To see this effect more clearly, rotate the object.

- **Reset.** You can press this button to remove all 3-D settings so that you can start fresh.

Applying 3-D Formatting

You can use 3-D formatting to control the colors and the amount of depth of the surfaces and sides of a 3-D rotated object. You control these settings from the 3-D Format section of the Format Shape (or Format Picture) task pane, as shown in Figure 9.46:

FIGURE 9.46

Apply formatting to the 3-D effects from the 3-D Format section of the task pane.

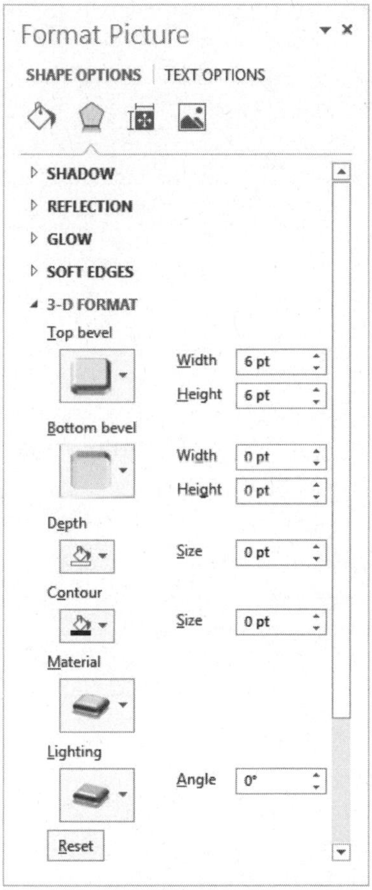

- **Depth**. The depth of an object determines the length and color of its sides. In most cases, you want to keep the sides set to the default color setting, Match Shape Fill. This enables the sides to change colors when the shape changes colors. Although the sides are a darker shade of the object's color in order to create the illusion of depth, you can adjust their color through the application of surface material and lighting.

- **Contour**. Contours are similar to outlines, or borders, except that contours go around each side of a 3-D object. For example, if you have a square with sides (a cube), the color and size that you set for Contours creates a border around the front face as well as around each visible side surface.

- **Material**. The surface material determines how shiny the surface appears and how bright its color is on the front face compared to the sides. The Material button opens a palette that displays various materials such as matte, plastic, and metal.

- **Lighting**. The Lighting button opens a palette that displays various types of lighting that you can apply to the object, such as Harsh, Soft, Bright Room, and so on. To adjust the direction from which the light hits the object, you can change the Angle setting.

Tips for Creating Common 3-D Objects

The 3-D formatting and rotation settings in PowerPoint 2013 are very powerful and can seem a little overwhelming at first because of the variety of available options. Take your time in exploring them, and I think you'll be pleasantly surprised at what you can accomplish. Here are some things you can try.

To create a perfectly round sphere, which stays round no matter how you rotate it, follow these steps:

1. **Draw an oval.**

2. **Select the oval and use the Size boxes on the Drawing Tools Format tab to set its height and width to the same value, thus making it a perfect circle.** For this experiment, use a whole number such as 1" or 2".

3. **Right-click the circle and choose Format Shape.**

4. **In the 3-D Format settings, set the top and bottom bevel, both Height and Width, to 36 points for every 1" of diameter.** For example, if your circle is 2" in diameter, use 72 points for each.

To create a four-sided pyramid, follow these steps:

1. **Draw a rectangle.**

2. **Select the rectangle and use the Size boxes on the Drawing Tools Format tab to set its height and width to the same value, making it a perfect square.** For this experiment, use 1".

3. **Right-click the square and choose Format Shape.**

4. **In the 3-D Format settings, for both the Top and Bottom bevel styles, choose Angle (the first preset on the second row).**

5. **Set the bevel settings as follows:**
   a. Top Width: 36 points for every 1" of the square's size, plus 1 point. For example, for a 1" square, use 37 points; for a 2" square, use 73 points.
   b. Top Height: 72 points for every 1" of the square's size.
   c. Bottom (height and width): 0 points.

6. **In the 3-D Rotation tab, rotate the object so that you can see it more clearly:**

   - X: 30
   - Y: 300
   - Z: 325

TIP

To create pyramids with different numbers of sides, use shapes other than squares. For example, to create a three-sided pyramid, start with a triangle. To create a cone, use a circle.

Summary

In this chapter, you learned how to draw lines and shapes, and how to format almost any type of object. You'll use these skills as you go forward in the rest of the book, learning about specific types of objects, including SmartArt, clip art, and so on. No matter what type of graphic you encounter, you'll be able to format it using these same techniques.

In the next chapter, you'll learn how to create and format SmartArt diagrams, which combine the best of a bulleted list with the best of drawn objects to present text data in an interesting way.

9

Creating SmartArt Graphics

IN THIS CHAPTER

Understanding SmartArt types and their uses

Inserting a SmartArt graphic

Editing SmartArt text

Modifying SmartArt structure

Modifying an organization chart structure

Resizing a SmartArt graphic

Manually restructuring a SmartArt graphic

Formatting a SmartArt graphic

Just as charts and graphs can enliven a boring table of numbers, a SmartArt graphic can enliven a conceptual discussion. SmartArt helps the audience understand the interdependencies of objects or processes in a visual way, so they don't have to juggle that information mentally as you speak. Some potential uses include organizational charts, hierarchy diagrams, and flow charts.

Understanding SmartArt Types and Their Uses

SmartArt is a special class of vector graphic object that combines shapes, lines, and text placeholders. SmartArt is most often used to illustrate relationships between bits of text.

The SmartArt interface is similar regardless of the type of graphic you are creating. You can type directly into the placeholders on the SmartArt graphic, or you can display a Text pane to the side of the graphic and type into that, much as you would type into an Outline pane, to have text appear in a slide's text placeholder boxes. See Figure 10.1. You can also select some text, right-click it, and choose Convert to SmartArt.

There are eight types of SmartArt graphics in PowerPoint 2013, and each is uniquely suited for a certain type of data delivery.

FIGURE 10.1

A typical SmartArt graphic being constructed.

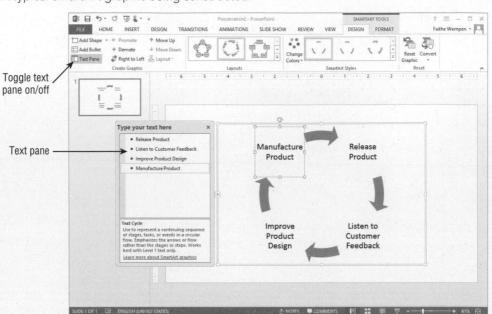

List

A List graphic presents information in a fairly straightforward, text-based way, somewhat like a fancy outline. List graphics are useful when information is not in any particular order or when the process or progression between items is not important. The list can have multiple levels, and you can enclose each level in a shape or not. Figure 10.2 shows an example.

Process

A Process graphic is similar to a list, but it has directional arrows or other connectors that represent the flow of one item to another. This adds an extra aspect of meaning to the graphic. For example, in Figure 10.3, the way the boxes are staggered and connected with arrows implies that the next step begins before the previous one ends.

Cycle

A Cycle graphic also illustrates a process, but a repeating or recursive one — usually a process in which there is no fixed beginning point or endpoint. You can jump into the cycle at any point. In Figure 10.4, for example, the ongoing process of product development and improvement is illustrated.

FIGURE 10.2

A List graphic de-emphasizes any progression between items.

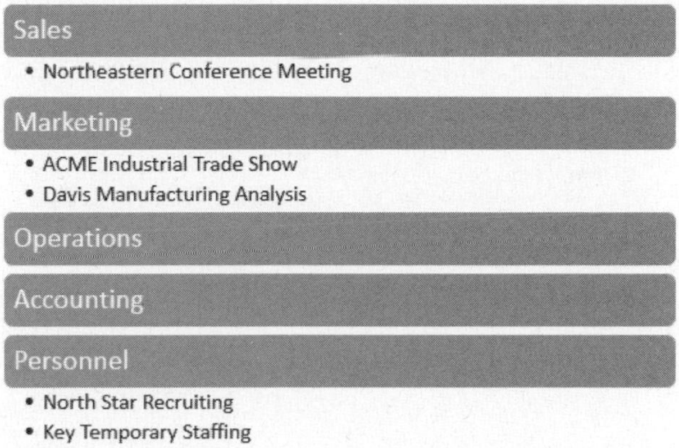

Sales
• Northeastern Conference Meeting
Marketing
• ACME Industrial Trade Show
• Davis Manufacturing Analysis
Operations
Accounting
Personnel
• North Star Recruiting
• Key Temporary Staffing

FIGURE 10.3

A Process graphic shows a flow from point A to point B.

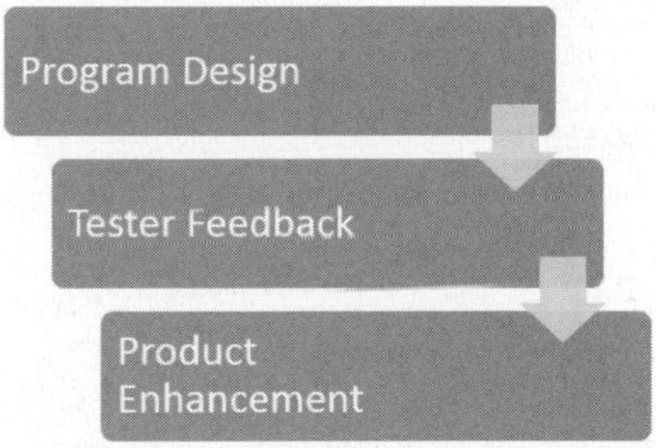

Program Design
Tester Feedback
Product Enhancement

FIGURE 10.4

A Cycle graphic traces the steps of a repeating process.

Plan
Design
Develop
Test
Evaluate

10

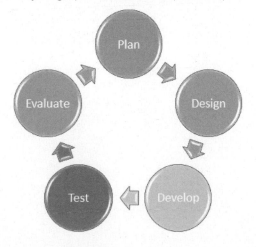

Hierarchy

A Hierarchy chart is an organization chart. It shows structure and relationships between people or things in standardized levels. For example, it can show who reports to whom in a company's employment system. It is useful when describing how the organization functions and who is responsible for what. In Figure 10.5, for example, three organization levels are represented, with lines of reporting drawn between each level. Hierarchy graphics can also run horizontally, for use in tournament rosters.

FIGURE 10.5

A Hierarchy graphic, also called an organization chart, explains the structure of an organization.

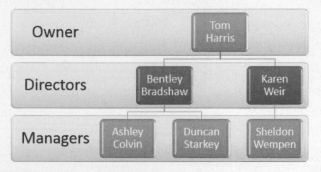

> **NOTE**
>
> Should you include your company's organization chart in your presentation? That's a question that depends on your main message. If your speech is about the organization, you should. If not, show the organization structure only if it serves a purpose to advance your speech. Many presenters have found that an organization chart makes an excellent backup slide. You can prepare it and have it ready in case a question arises about the organization. Another useful strategy is to include a printed organization chart as part of the handouts you distribute to the audience, without including the slide in your main presentation.

Relationship

Relationship graphics graphically illustrate how parts relate to a whole. One common type of Relationship graphic is a Venn diagram, as in Figure 10.6, showing how categories of people or things overlap. Relationship graphics can also break things into categories or show how parts contribute to a whole, as with a pie chart.

FIGURE 10.6

A Relationship graphic shows how parts relate to a whole.

Matrix

A Matrix also shows the relationship of parts to a whole, but it does so with the parts in orderly looking quadrants. You can use Matrix graphics when you do not need to show any particular relationship between items but you want to make it clear that they make up a single unit. See Figure 10.7.

FIGURE 10.7

A Matrix graphic uses a grid to represent the contributions of parts to a whole.

Pyramid

A Pyramid graphic is just what the name sounds like — it's a striated triangle with text at various levels, representing not only the relationship between the items but also that the items at the smaller part of the triangle are less numerous or more important. For example, the graphic in Figure 10.8 shows that there are many more workers than there are executives.

10

FIGURE 10.8

A Pyramid graphic represents the progression between less and more of something.

> **TIP**
>
> In Pyramid graphics and some other cases, labels do not confine themselves to within the associated shape. If this is a problem, you might be able to make the labels fit with a combination of line breaks (Shift+Enter) and font changes.

Picture

The Picture category is a collection of SmartArt graphic types from the other categories that include picture placeholders in them. You'll find List, Process, and other types of graphics here; the Picture category simply summarizes them.

> **TIP**
>
> The Office.com category shows additional SmartArt layouts that are available online from Office.com. If you are connected to the Internet, you can access these additional layouts for more choices.

Inserting a SmartArt Graphic

All SmartArt graphics start out the same way — you insert them on the slide as you can any other slide object. That means you can either use a SmartArt placeholder on a slide layout or insert the SmartArt graphic manually.

To use a placeholder, start with a slide that contains a layout with a SmartArt placeholder in it, or change the current slide's layout to one that does. Then click the Insert a SmartArt Graphic icon in the placeholder, as shown in Figure 10.9. To insert from scratch, click the SmartArt button on the Insert tab.

Another way to start a new SmartArt graphic is to select some text and then right-click the selection and choose Convert to SmartArt.

Any way you start it, the Choose a SmartArt Graphic dialog box opens (Figure 10.10). Select one of the SmartArt categories, click the desired SmartArt object, and click OK, and the graphic appears. From there it's just a matter of customizing.

FIGURE 10.9

Click the SmartArt icon in the placeholder on a slide.

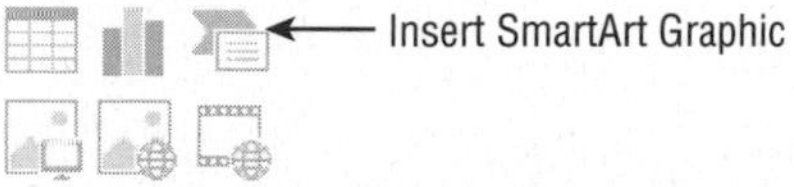

◄─────── Insert SmartArt Graphic

FIGURE 10.10

Select the graphic type you want to insert.

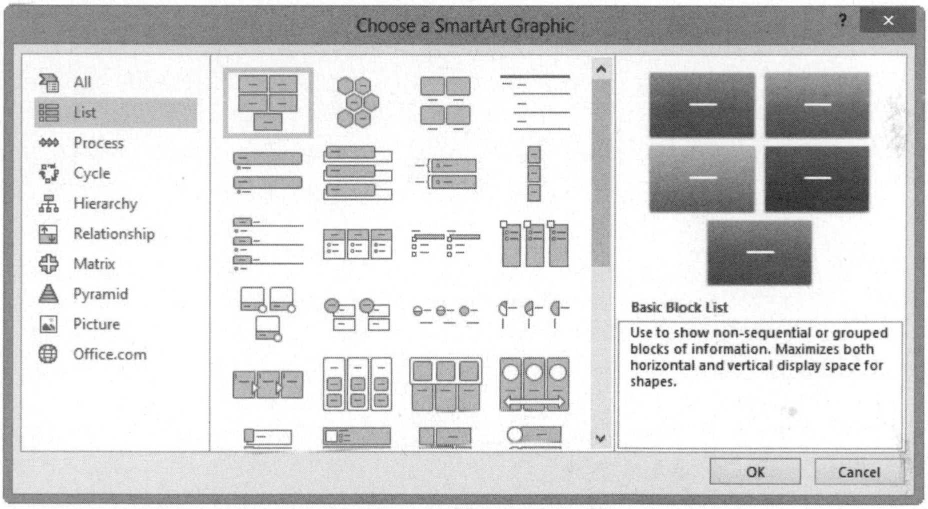

> **NOTE**
>
> Some graphics appear in more than one category. To browse all of the categories at once, select the All category. You can access additional graphics by choosing the Office.com category.

When you select a graphic, SmartArt Tools tabs become available (Design and Format). You will learn what each of the buttons on them does as this chapter progresses. The buttons change depending on the type of graphic.

Editing SmartArt Text

All SmartArt has text placeholders, which are basically text boxes. You simply click in one of them and type. Then use the normal text-formatting controls (Font, Font Size, Bold, Italic, and so on) on the Home tab to change the appearance of the text, or use the WordArt Styles group on the Format tab to apply WordArt formatting.

10

You can also display a Text pane, as shown in Figure 10.1, and type or edit the graphic's text there. The Text pane serves the same purpose for a graphic that the Outline pane in Outline view serves for the slide as a whole.

> **WARNING**
>
> The text in the Outline pane is not always in the order you would expect it to be for the graphic because it forces text to appear in linear form from a graphic that is not necessarily linear. It does not matter how the text appears in the Text pane because only you see that. What matters is how it looks in the actual graphic.

Here are some tips for working with SmartArt text:

- To leave a text box empty, just don't type anything in it. The *[Text]* placeholders do not show up in a printout or in Slide Show view.
- To promote a line of text, press Shift+Tab; to demote it, press Tab in the Text pane.
- Text wraps automatically, but you can press Shift+Enter to insert a line break if necessary.
- In most cases, the text size shrinks to fit the graphic in which it is located. There are some exceptions to that, though; for example, at the top of a pyramid, the text can overflow the tip of the pyramid.
- All of the text is the same size, so if you enter a really long string of text in one box, the text size in all of the related boxes shrinks too. You can manually format parts of the SmartArt graphic to change this behavior, as you will learn later in the chapter.
- If you resize the SmartArt graphic, its text resizes automatically.

Modifying SmartArt Structure

The structure of the SmartArt graphic includes how many boxes it has and where they are placed. Even though the graphic types are all very different, the way you add, remove, and reposition shapes in them is surprisingly similar across all types.

> **NOTE**
>
> When you add a shape, you add both a graphical element (a circle, a bar, or other) and an associated text placeholder. The same applies to deletion; removing a shape also removes its associated text placeholder from the SmartArt graphic.

Inserting and Deleting Shapes

To insert a shape in a SmartArt graphic, follow these steps:

1. **Click a shape that is adjacent to where you want the new shape to appear.**
2. **Click SmartArt Tools Design ⇨ Create Graphic ⇨ Add Shape.**

You can click the top part of the Add Shape button to add a shape of the same level and type as the selected one, or you can click the bottom part of the button to open a menu from which you can choose other variants. The choices on the menu depend on the graphic type and the type of shape selected. For example, in Figure 10.11, you can insert a shape into a SmartArt graphic either before or after the current one (same outline level), or you can insert a shape that is subordinate (below) or superior to (above) the current one.

FIGURE 10.11

Add a shape to the SmartArt graphic.

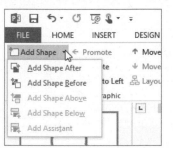

To delete a shape, click it to select it in the SmartArt graphic, and then press the Delete key on the keyboard. You might need to delete subordinate shapes before you can delete the main shape.

> **NOTE**
>
> Not all SmartArt graphic types can accept different numbers of shapes. For example, the four-square matrix graphic is fixed at four squares.

Adding Bullets

In addition to adding shapes to the SmartArt graphic, you can add bullets — that is, subordinate text to a shape. To do so, click the Add Bullet button. Bullets appear indented under the shape's text in the Text pane, as shown in Figure 10.12.

FIGURE 10.12

Create subordinate bullet points under a shape.

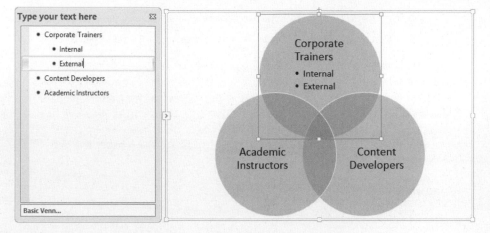

Promoting and Demoting Text

The difference between a shape and a bullet is primarily a matter of promotion and demotion in the Text pane's outline. The Text pane works just as the regular Outline pane does in this regard; you can promote with Shift+Tab or demote with Tab. You can also use the Promote and Demote buttons on the SmartArt Tools Design tab.

Changing the Flow Direction

Each SmartArt graphic flows in a certain direction. A Cycle graphic flows either clockwise or counterclockwise. A Pyramid flows either up or down.

If you realize after typing all of the text that you should have made the SmartArt graphic flow in the other direction, you can change it by clicking the Right to Left button on the SmartArt Tools Design tab. It is a toggle; you can switch back and forth freely.

Reordering Shapes

Not only can you reverse the overall flow of the SmartArt graphic, you can also move around individual shapes. For example, suppose you have a graphic that illustrates five steps in a process and you realize that steps 3 and 4 are out of order. You can move one of them without having to retype all of the labels.

The easiest way to reorder the shapes is to select one and then click the Reorder Down or Reorder Up button on the SmartArt Tools Design tab.

If you have more complex reordering to do, you might prefer to work in the Text pane instead, cutting and pasting text like this:

1. **Display the Text pane if it does not already appear.** You can either click the arrow button to the left of the graphic or click the Text Pane button on the SmartArt Tools Design tab.
2. **Select some text to be moved in the Text pane.**
3. **Press Ctrl+X to cut it to the Clipboard.**
4. **Click in the Text pane at the beginning of the line above which it should appear.**
5. **Press Ctrl+V to paste.**

Repositioning Shapes

You can individually select and drag each shape to reposition it on the SmartArt graphic. Any connectors between it and the other shapes are automatically resized and extended as needed. For example, in Figure 10.13, notice how the arrows that connect the circles in the Cycle graphic have elongated as one of the circles has moved out.

FIGURE 10.13

When you move pieces of a SmartArt graphic, connectors move and stretch as needed.

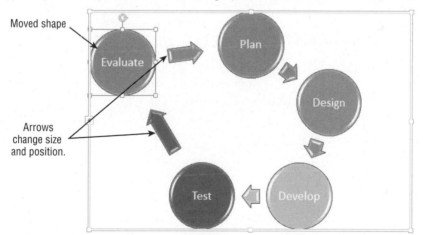

Resetting a SmartArt Graphic

After making changes to a SmartArt graphic, you can return it to its default settings with the Reset Graphic button on the SmartArt Tools Design tab. This strips off everything, including any SmartArt styles and manual positioning, and makes it exactly as it was when you inserted it except it keeps the text that you've typed.

Changing to a Different SmartArt Layout

The layouts are the graphic types. When you insert a SmartArt graphic you choose a type, and you can change that type at any time later.

To change the layout type, use the Layouts gallery on the Design tab, as shown in Figure 10.14. You can open the gallery and click the desired type, or click More Layouts at the bottom of its menu to redisplay the same dialog box as in Figure 10.10, the Choose a SmartArt Graphic dialog box, from which you can choose any layout.

FIGURE 10.14

Switch to a different graphic layout.

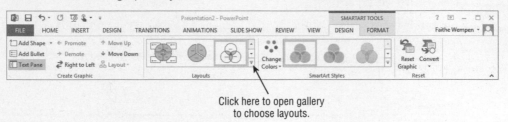

Click here to open gallery
to choose layouts.

Modifying a Hierarchy Graphic Structure

Hierarchy graphics (organization charts) show the structure of an organization. They have some different controls for changing their structure compared to other graphics, so the following sections look at them separately.

Inserting and Deleting Shapes

The main difference when inserting an organization chart shape (that is, a box into which you will type a name) is that you must specify which existing box the new one is related to and how it is related.

For example, suppose you have a supervisor already in the chart and you want to add some people to the chart who report to him. You would first select his box on the chart and then insert the new shapes with the Add Shape button. For a box of the same level, or of the previously inserted level, click the top part of the button; for a subordinate or other relationship, open the button's menu. See Figure 10.15. The chart can have only one box at the top level, however, just as a company can have only one CEO.

When you insert a new shape in a Hierarchy graphic, four of the options are the same as with any other SmartArt graphic, and one is new: Add Shape After and Add Shape Before insert shapes of the same level as the selected one, and Add Shape Above and Add Shape Below insert a superior and subordinate level respectively. The new option, Add Assistant, adds a box that is neither subordinate nor superior but a separate line of reporting, as shown in Figure 10.16.

FIGURE 10.15

Add more shapes to a Hierarchy graphic.

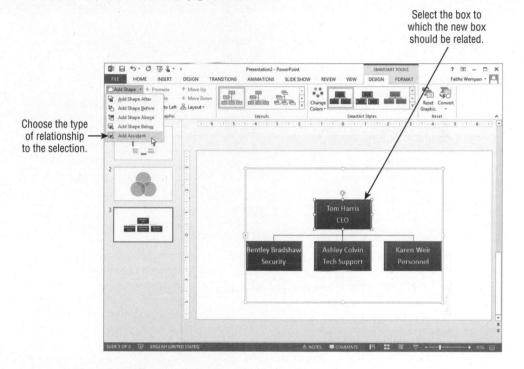

FIGURE 10.16

An Assistant box in a Hierarchy chart.

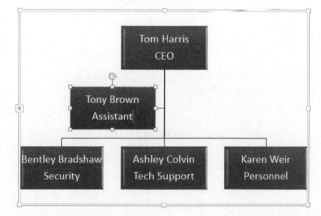

> **NOTE**
>
> An *assistant* is a person whose job is to provide support to a certain person or office. An executive secretary is one example. In contrast, a *subordinate* is an employee who may report to a manager but whose job does not consist entirely of supporting that manager. Confused? Don't worry about it. You don't have to make a distinction in your organization chart. Everyone can be a subordinate (except the person at the top of the heap, of course).

To delete a shape, select it and press the Delete key, as with all of the other graphic types.

Changing a Person's Level in the Organization

As the organization changes, you might need to change your chart to show that people report to different supervisors. The easiest way to do that is to move the text in the Text pane, the same way as you learned in the section "Reordering Shapes" earlier in this chapter. To promote someone, select their box and press Shift+Tab.

To change who someone reports to, select their box and press Ctrl+X to cut it to the Clipboard. Then select the box of the person they now report to, and press Ctrl+V to paste.

Controlling Subordinate Layout Options

When subordinates report to a supervisor, you can list the subordinates beneath that supervisor in a variety of ways. In Standard layout, each subordinate appears horizontally beneath the supervisor, as shown in Figure 10.17.

FIGURE 10.17

This is the standard layout for a branch of an organization chart.

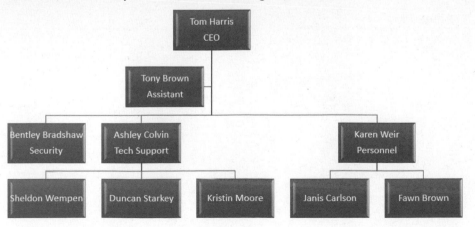

However, in a large or complex organization chart, the graphic can quickly become too wide with the Standard layout. Therefore, there are "hanging" alternatives that make the chart more vertically oriented. The alternatives are Both, Left Hanging, and Right Hanging. They are just what their names sound like. Figure 10.18 shows examples of Right Hanging.

FIGURE 10.18

Hanging layouts make the chart more vertically oriented.

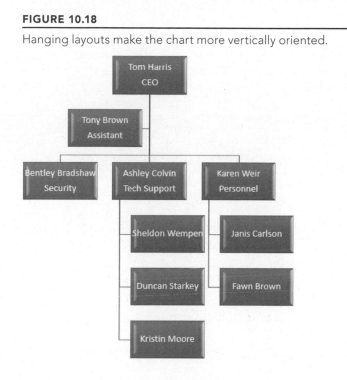

The layout is chosen for individual branches of the organization chart, so before selecting an alternative layout, you must click on the supervisor box whose subordinates you want to change. To change a layout, follow these steps:

1. **Click the box for the supervisor whose layout you want to change.**
2. **Choose SmartArt Tools Design ➪ Create Graphic ➪ Layouts on the Create Graphic section.** A menu of layout options appears.
3. **Choose one of the layouts (Standard, Both, Left Hanging, or Right Hanging).**

NOTE

If the Layouts button's menu is grayed out, you do not have a box selected in a Hierarchy graphic.

10

Formatting a SmartArt Graphic

You can format a SmartArt graphic either automatically or manually. Automatic formatting is the default, and many PowerPoint users don't even realize that manual formatting is a possibility. The following sections cover both.

Applying a SmartArt Style

SmartArt Styles are preset formatting specs (border, fill, effects, shadows, and so on) that you can apply to an entire SmartArt graphic. They make it easy to apply surface texture effects that make the shapes look reflective or appear to have 3-D depth or perspective.

> **NOTE**
> SmartArt Styles do not include color changes. Those are separately controlled with the Change Colors button on the SmartArt Tools Design tab.

To apply a SmartArt style, follow these steps:

1. **Select the SmartArt graphic so that the SmartArt Tools Design tab becomes available.**
2. **On the SmartArt Tools Design tab, click one of the SmartArt Styles samples (see Figure 10.19), or open the gallery and select from a larger list (see Figure 10.20).**

FIGURE 10.19

Select a SmartArt Style.

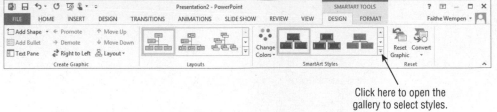

Click here to open the
gallery to select styles.

Changing SmartArt Colors

After you apply a SmartArt style, as in the preceding section, you might want to change the colors used in the graphic.

The easiest way to apply colors is to use the Change Colors button's menu on the Design tab. You can select from a gallery of color schemes. As shown in Figure 10.21, you can choose a Colorful scheme (one in which each shape has its own color, or the shapes at each level have their own colors), or you can choose a monochrome color scheme based on any of the current presentation color theme's color swatches.

FIGURE 10.20

Open the SmartArt Style gallery for more choices.

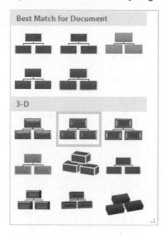

Notice the command at the bottom of the menu in Figure 10.21: Recolor Pictures in SmartArt Graphic. You can toggle this button on or off. When the button is toggled on, it applies a color tint to any pictures that are part of the graphic.

FIGURE 10.21

Select a color scheme from the Change Colors button's menu.

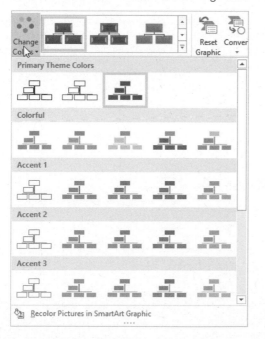

Manually Applying Colors and Effects to Individual Shapes

In addition to formatting the entire graphic with a SmartArt Style, you can format individual shapes using Shape Styles, just as you did in Chapter 9, "Drawing and Formatting Objects," with drawn objects. Here's a quick review:

1. **Select a shape in a SmartArt graphic.**
2. **On the SmartArt Tools Format tab, select a shape style from the Shape Styles gallery.**
3. **(Optional) Fine-tune the style by using the Shape Fill, Shape Outline, and/or Shape Effects buttons and their associated menus.**

Manually Formatting SmartArt Text

WordArt formatting works the same in a SmartArt graphic as it does everywhere else in PowerPoint. Use the WordArt Styles gallery and controls on the SmartArt Tools Format tab to apply text formatting to individual shapes, or select the entire graphic to apply the changes to all shapes at once.

Making a Shape Larger or Smaller

In some SmartArt types, it is advantageous to make certain shapes larger or smaller than the others. For example, if you want to emphasize a certain step in a process, you can create a SmartArt graphic where that step's shape is larger. Then you can repeat that same graphic on a series of slides, but with a different step in the process enlarged on each copy, to step through the process. There are several options for this:

- You can manually resize a shape by dragging its selection handles, the same as with any other object. However, this is imprecise, and can be a problem if you want multiple shapes to be enlarged because they won't be consistently so.
- You can set a precise size for the entire SmartArt graphic by adjusting the height and width measurements in the Size group on the SmartArt Tools Format tab, as shown in Figure 10.22. However, if different shapes are already different sizes and you want to resize them in proportion, this won't help.
- You can use the Larger or Smaller buttons on the Format tab to bump the sizes of one or more shapes up or down slightly with each successive click.

Resizing the Entire SmartArt Graphic Object

When you resize the entire SmartArt object as a whole, everything within its frame changes size proportionally. There are several ways to do this:

- Drag and drop a corner selection handle on the SmartArt graphic's outer frame.
- Use the Size controls on the SmartArt Tools Format tab to enter a precise height and width.
- Right-click the outer frame of the SmartArt object and choose Size and Position. The Format Shape task pane opens (Figure 10.23). Under the Size heading, enter a

height and width in inches, or scale it by a percentage in the Scale Height and Scale Width boxes. Select the Lock Aspect Ratio check box if you want to maintain the proportions.

FIGURE 10.22

Change the size of the entire SmartArt graphic or an individual shape.

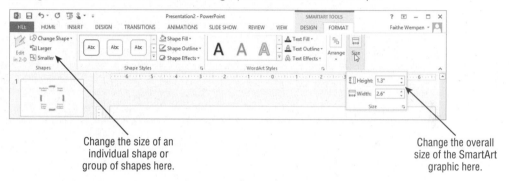

Change the size of an individual shape or group of shapes here.

Change the overall size of the SmartArt graphic here.

FIGURE 10.23

Right-click the graphic and choose Size and Position to open this task pane.

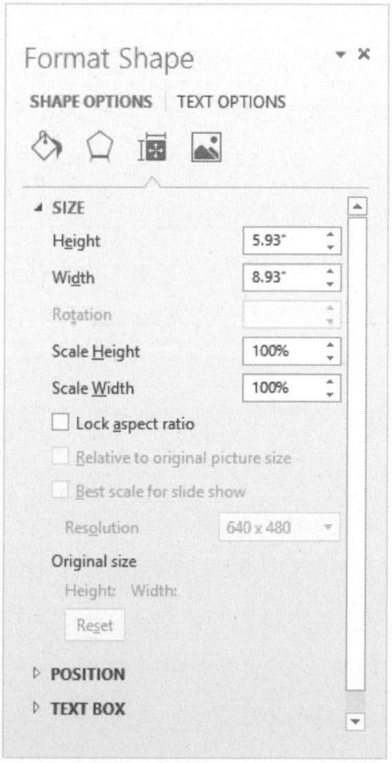

Editing in 2-D

If you choose one of the 3-D selections from the SmartArt Style gallery, the text might become a bit hard to read and edit when you are working with the graphic at a small zoom percentage. There are a couple of ways around this:

- Right-click a shape and choose Edit Text. The face of the shape appears in 2-D temporarily, making it easier to edit the text.
- Click the Edit in 2-D button on the SmartArt Tools Format tab. The entire graphic appears in 2-D temporarily.

> **WARNING**
> Even though the face of the shape appears in 2-D, which you think would make it easier to read, in some SmartArt types and styles the text might still be fuzzy and hard to read. You might be better off editing it in the Text pane.

Changing the Shapes Used

Each SmartArt layout has its own defaults that it uses for the shapes, but you can change these manually. On the SmartArt Tools Format tab, click Change Shape to open a palette of shapes just like the ones you learned to work with in Chapter 9. Then click the desired shape to apply to the selected shape. You can also access this from the right-click menu.

Each shape is individually configurable. If you simply select the entire graphic, the Change Shape button is not available; you must select each shape you want to change. Hold down the Shift key as you click on each one to be selected. Figure 10.24 shows a SmartArt graphic that uses some different shapes.

FIGURE 10.24

You can apply different shapes within a SmartArt graphic.

Saving a SmartArt Graphic as a Picture

SmartArt graphics work only within Office applications, but you can easily export one for use in any other application. It is exported as a picture (by default a PNG file), which you can then import into any application that accepts pictures. To save a SmartArt graphic as a picture, follow these steps:

1. **Select the outer frame of the SmartArt object.**
2. **Right-click the frame and choose Save as Picture.** The Save As Picture dialog box opens.
3. **(Optional) Open the Save as Type list and select a different file type if desired.**
4. **Click the Save button to complete the save.**

> **TIP**
>
> PowerPoint can save pictures in GIF, JPEG, TIFF, PNG, BMP, WMF, and EMF formats. Different formats have different qualities and advantages. EMF and WMF can be ungrouped, but not the other formats. EMF does not result in a quality loss when resized, but most of the others do. JPG doesn't use a transparent background, but PNG does.

Summary

In this chapter, you learned how to create SmartArt graphics. You learned how to select a SmartArt graphic type, how to rearrange shapes, how to apply formatting, and how to export SmartArt as pictures you can use in other programs. You will probably find lots of creative uses for SmartArt now that you know it's available!

In the next chapter, you'll learn how to incorporate online artwork, both from Microsoft and from other sources. This can include clip art from Office.com, photos from Bing, and more.

10

Working with Clip Art and Photos

IN THIS CHAPTER

Inserting clip art

Modifying clip art

Inserting photos into PowerPoint

Sizing and cropping photos

Adjusting and correcting photos

Compressing images

Exporting a photo from PowerPoint into a separate file

Creating a photo album layout

Whether you're putting together a slide show to display your vacation photos or adding photos of industrial products to a business presentation, PowerPoint has the tools and capabilities you need. In this chapter you'll learn the ins and outs of using clip art and photographs in a PowerPoint presentation. You'll find out how to locate, insert, and modify clip art and how to prepare and insert photos. You'll find out how to compress pictures so they take up less disk space and how to export pictures out of PowerPoint so you can save them separately.

Choosing Appropriate Artwork

Before we get started with the "how" of images in PowerPoint, take a moment to think about the "why." Don't just use any old image! You must never use artwork simply because you can; it must be a well-thought-out decision. Here are some tips for using artwork appropriately:

- **Use for fun.** Use cartoonish images only if you specifically want to impart a lighthearted, fun feel to your presentation.
- **Use one style.** The clip art available from Office.com includes many styles of drawings, ranging from simple black-and-white shapes to very complex, shaded color drawings and photographs. Try to stick with one type of image rather than bouncing among several drawing styles.

- **Use only one piece per slide.** Also, do not use artwork on every slide, or it becomes overpowering.

- **Avoid repetition.** Don't repeat the same artwork on more than one slide in the presentation unless you have a specific reason to do so.

- **Avoid graphics with bad news.** If your message is very serious, or you are conveying bad news, don't use artwork. It looks insensitive in these situations.

- **Better none than bad.** If you can't find artwork that is exactly right for the slide, then don't use any. It is better to have none than to have an inappropriate image.

- **Buy appropriate art.** If artwork is important, and Office.com doesn't have what you want, you can buy more. Don't try to struggle along with the clips and images that come with Office if they aren't meeting your needs; impressive artwork collections are available at reasonable prices at your local computer store as well as online.

Inserting Clip Art

Clip art is pre-drawn art that comes with PowerPoint or that is available from other sources (such as through the Internet). There are thousands of images that you can use royalty free in your work, without having to draw your own. For example, suppose you are creating a presentation about snow skiing equipment. Rather than hiring an artist to draw a picture of a skier, you can use one of PowerPoint's stock drawings of skiers and save yourself a bundle.

Being an owner of a Microsoft Office product entitles you to the use the huge clip-art collection that Microsoft maintains at Office.com, and if you are connected to the Internet while you are using PowerPoint, PowerPoint can automatically pull clips from that collection as easily as it can from your own hard drive.

Earlier versions of PowerPoint included robust search and management capabilities for clip art and an application called the Clip Organizer. In contrast, PowerPoint 2013 provides only a very basic search box for searching for clip art by keyword at Office.com.

You can insert clip art on a slide either with or without a content placeholder. If you use a content placeholder, PowerPoint inserts the clip art wherever the placeholder is; if you don't, PowerPoint inserts the clip art at the center of the slide. (You can move it afterward, of course.) To insert clip art into a content placeholder, click the Online Pictures icon on the placeholder (see Figure 11.1). To insert clip art without a content placeholder, choose Insert ➪ Images ➪ Online Pictures.

FIGURE 11.1

Click the Online Pictures icon in a content placeholder to insert clip art into the placeholder.

Online Pictures

Whichever method you use, the Insert Pictures dialog box opens (see Figure 11.2). In it are three options:

- **Office.com Clip Art:** You can use the Search box on this line to search Microsoft's clip-art collection by keyword.

- **Bing Image Search:** You can use the Search box on this line to use the Bing search engine to look for pictures on the Internet by keyword. These are mostly photographic images, which you'll learn more about later in this chapter.

- **(*Your Name*) SkyDrive:** You can click Browse to browse the content of your own SkyDrive and insert pictures from there. (See Appendix B, "Essential SkyDrive Skills," for more information about using your SkyDrive.)

FIGURE 11.2

Type a keyword in the Office.com Clip Art search box.

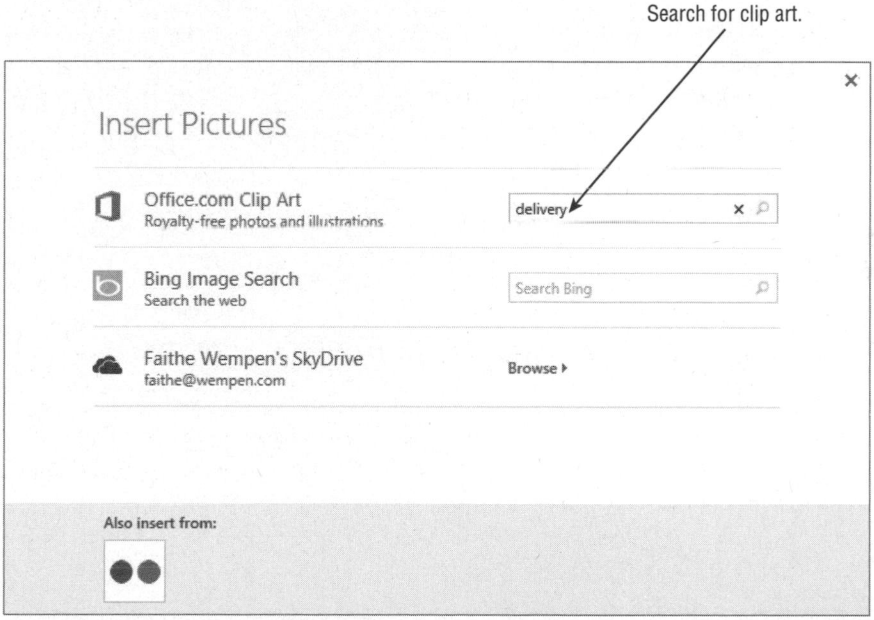

Search for clip art.

Type a keyword into the Search box next to Office.com Clip Art and then press Enter to perform the search. Search results appear in that same dialog box, as shown in Figure 11.3.

Click the image you want to insert (or click multiple images to insert several at once) and then click the Insert button. If the Insert button doesn't appear, make sure an image is selected; Insert doesn't appear until you do that.

FIGURE 11.3

Search results appear showing thumbnails of available images.

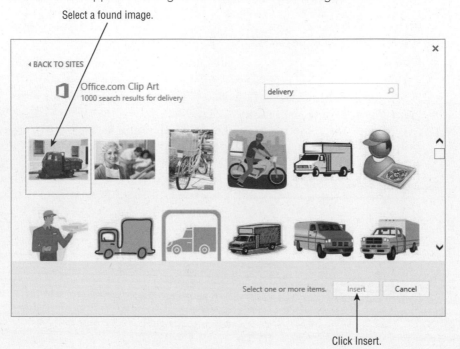

Browsing Clips At Office.com

When you search for clip art while connected to the Internet, as you learned to do in the preceding section, the Office.com clip art automatically appears. However, you can also visit the Office.com website to browse the clip art directly. There are some advantages to browsing clip art this way. For example, you can narrow down your search to only certain media types (such as only line-art illustrations or only photos), and you can filter the search results by image size.

To browse the Office.com clip art on the Web, open a web browser window, navigate to `http://office.microsoft.com` and click the Images link. From there, type a keyword in the Search All Images box at the top of the page and press Enter to initiate a search. See Figure 11.4. This page is constantly changing, so it may look different when you visit it.

In the search results window, a bar appears along the left side with filters for media types and image size. To limit the results to a certain category, click one of these filters. For example, in Figure 11.5, the list has been filtered to show only illustrations.

FIGURE 11.4

Visit the Office.com clip art web page for more information and more clip art.

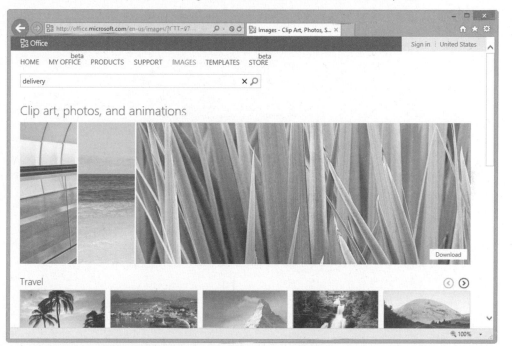

> **NOTE**
>
> What's the difference between an illustration and a photo? An illustration is a line art drawing, which some would call "true clip art." It is a drawing, rather than a photo. Clip-art images are vector graphics, which means they are created with mathematical formulas that draw each line and fill each shape with color. Vector graphics take up less disk space than photos, and they look good at any size. In contrast, photos are raster graphics; they are composed of a grid of tiny colored dots. See "Understanding Raster Graphics" later in this chapter for more details.

Another advantage of using the web interface for clip art is that you can copy the clip art to your hard disk for later use.

In the list of clips that the site finds, point to a clip that you want. A pop-up for it appears, as shown in Figure 11.6.

> **NOTE**
>
> The first time you attempt to select one of the options from a clip's pop-up, you may be prompted to download the Office.com ActiveX control. You must do so in order to access clip art via the Office.com website. If a User Account Control window appears asking if you want the program to make changes to this computer, click Yes. You may need to restart your computer and come back to the Office.com web page after the restart.

FIGURE 11.5

Search results from Office.com are filtered to show only illustrations.

FIGURE 11.6

Point at a found clip to display a pop-up.

The following options are available in the pop-up:

- **View Details.** Opens a web page specifically for this clip, where you can see information about the clip including its dimensions, resolution, and file size.
- **Copy.** Copies the clip to your Windows Clipboard, from which you can paste it into PowerPoint or any other application that accepts input from the Clipboard. After clicking Copy, switch to PowerPoint or whatever program you like, position the

insertion point or select the placeholder, and press Ctrl+V or choose Home ⇨ Clipboard ⇨ Paste.

- **Download.** Downloads the clip-art image's file to your hard drive so you can use it later when you don't have an Internet connection. An information bar appears at the bottom of the browser window asking whether you want to save or open the file. See Figure 11.7. Click Save, and the file is saved to the Downloads folder for your user account (`C:\Users\`*username*`\Downloads`). You can then insert it in PowerPoint using the procedure outlined in "Inserting Photos" later in this chapter. If you instead choose Open, the file is opened in Paint (or your default editor for the file type), where you can modify it if you like before inserting it into PowerPoint. However, the next section of this chapter covers modifying clip art from within PowerPoint, so you may want to investigate that method instead if you want to make some changes to the clip.

FIGURE 11.7

Respond to the information bar message by choosing to open or save the file.

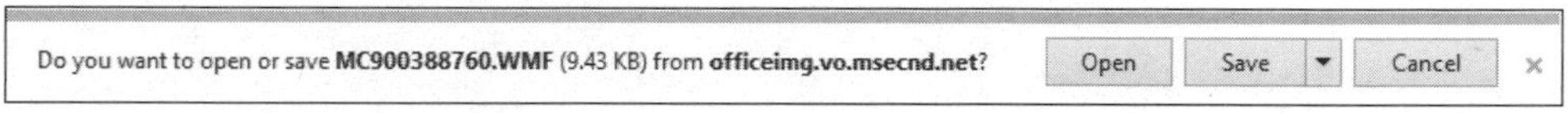

Do you want to open or save **MC900388760.WMF** (9.43 KB) from **officeimg.vo.msecnd.net**? | Open | Save ▼ | Cancel | ✕

Modifying Clip Art

Most of the modifications that you will learn about later in this chapter apply to both photographs and clip art. For example, you can increase or decrease brightness and contrast, apply color washes, crop, rotate, and so on. However, there are also some special modifications that apply only to clip art and other vector images. They are covered in the following sections.

Recoloring a Clip

One of the top complaints about clip art is that the colors are wrong. For example, you may have the perfect drawing, but its colors clash with your presentation design. You can recolor individual parts of a clip by changing it to a Microsoft drawing object and then selecting and coloring individual lines or shapes. For more information, see the section "Deconstructing and Editing a Clip" later in this chapter.

On a more basic level, PowerPoint 2013 provides a Recolor option that enables you to apply a single-color wash to an image based on any of the theme's colors or any fixed color. To apply a color wash to a clip, follow these steps:

1. **Insert the clip on a slide in PowerPoint, and then select the clip.** The Picture Tools Format tab becomes available.

2. **On the Picture Tools Format tab, click Color to open the menu shown in Figure 11.8.**

FIGURE 11.8

Select a color wash to apply to the clip.

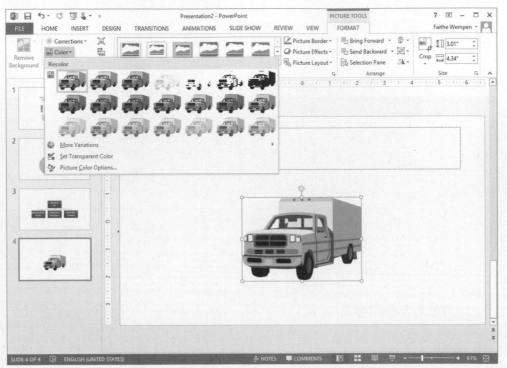

3. **Click the color wash that you want to apply, or click More Variations to choose another color.**

> **NOTE**
> More Variations opens a palette from which you can select light and dark tints of the theme colors or standard (fixed) colors. You can also choose More Colors to open a Color dialog box for more fixed colors.

Setting a Transparent Color

Some clips enable you to redefine one of the colors as see-through so that anything behind it shows through. This doesn't work on all clips because most clips already have a color defined as transparent: the background. This is why a clip-art image appears to float directly on a colored background rather than being locked into a rectangle. However, for clips that do not have a transparent color already defined, you can define one.

CAUTION

Setting a transparent color works best on clip art; in a photograph, an area that looks at first glance like a single color is often actually dozens of different shades of the same overall tint, and setting the transparent color sets only one of those many shades to be transparent.

To set a transparent color, open the Color menu, as in the preceding section (Figure 11.8). Then choose Set Transparent Color, and click a color in the image.

Deconstructing and Editing a Clip

Have you ever wished that you could open a clip-art image in an image-editing program and make some small change to it? Well, you can. And what's more, you can do it without leaving PowerPoint.

Because clip art is composed of vector-graphic lines and fills, you can literally take it apart piece by piece. Not only can you apply certain colors (as in the preceding section), but you can also choose individual lines and shapes from it to recolor, move, and otherwise modify.

Not all items that you find during a clip art search are vector graphic images that can be deconstructed and edited. Photos cannot be, for example. To deconstruct a piece of clip art, follow these steps:

1. **After placing the clip on a slide, right-click the clip and choose Edit Picture.** A message appears telling you that it is an imported picture and asking whether you want to convert it to a Microsoft Office drawing object.

CAUTION

Converting a clip resets previous color adjustments you may have made.

2. **Click Yes.** Each individual shape and line in the clip is now a separate object that you can select individually.

To recolor an individual line or shape, follow these steps:

1. **Select the line or shape to be modified within the image.** Selection handles appear around it.
2. **Click Drawing Tools Format ⇨ Shape Styles ⇨ Shape Fill and select a fill color.** See Figure 11.9.
3. **Click Drawing Tools Format ⇨ Shape Styles ⇨ Shape Outline and select an outline color.**

To move the pieces of the clip around, just drag the selected piece where you want it. If a particular piece doesn't move separately from the rest, right-click the image and choose

Group ➪ Ungroup to break up the image into individual shapes, and then the shape you want to move will be individually movable.

FIGURE 11.9

Change the fill color of an individual shape within the clip.

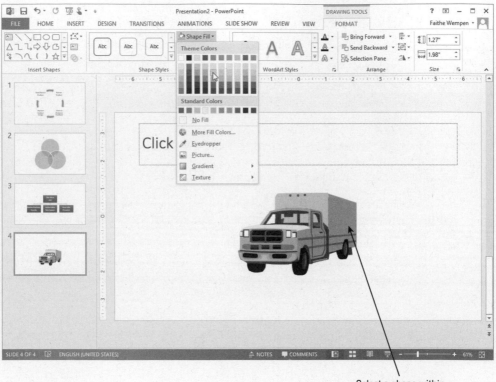

Select a shape within the clip to recolor it.

Understanding Raster Graphics

As I explained in Chapter 9 and also earlier in this chapter, there are two kinds of graphics in the computer world: *vector* and *raster*. Vector graphics (clip art, drawn lines and shapes, and so on) are created with mathematical formulas. Some of the advantages of vector graphics are their small file size and the fact that they can be resized without losing any quality. The main disadvantage of a vector graphic is that it doesn't look "real." Even when an expert artist draws a vector graphic, you can still tell that it's a drawing, not a photograph. For example, perhaps you've seen the game *The Sims*. Those characters and objects are 3-D vector graphics. They look pretty good but there's no way you would mistake them for real people and objects.

In the rest of this chapter, we'll be working mostly with raster graphics — in other words, digital photos, like the ones you might take with your own digital camera or phone. A raster graphic is made up of a very fine grid of individual colored *pixels* (dots). The grid is sometimes called a *bitmap*. Each pixel has a unique numeric value representing its color. Figure 11.10 shows a close-up of a raster image. You can create raster graphics from scratch with a "paint" program on a computer, but a more common way to acquire a raster graphic is by using a scanner or digital camera as an input device.

FIGURE 11.10

A raster graphic, normal size (right) and zoomed in to show individual pixels (left)

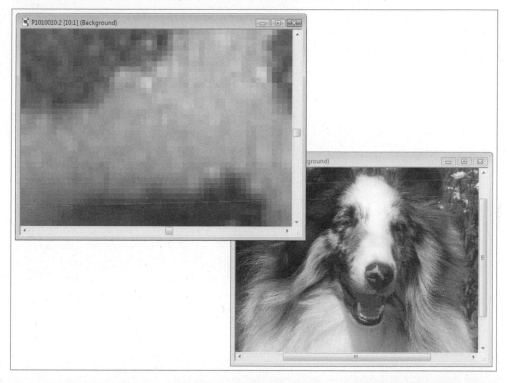

NOTE

The term *bitmap* is sometimes used to refer generically to any raster graphic, but it is also a specific file format for raster graphics, with a `.bmp` filename extension.

Because there are so many individual pixels and each one must be represented numerically, raster graphics are much larger than vector graphics. They take longer to load into the PC's memory, take up more space when you store them as separate files on disk, and make your PowerPoint presentation file much larger. You can compress a raster graphic so that it takes up less space on disk, but the quality may suffer. Therefore, it's best to use vector graphics when you want simple lines, shapes, or cartoons and reserve raster graphics for situations where you need photographic quality.

The following sections explain some of the technical specifications behind raster graphics; you'll need this information to make the right decisions about the way you capture the images with your scanner or digital camera and the way you use them in PowerPoint.

Resolution

The term *resolution* has two subtly different meanings. One is the size of an image, expressed in the number of pixels of width and height, such as 800 × 600. The other meaning is the number of pixels per inch when the image is printed, such as 100 dots per inch (dpi). The former meaning is used mostly when referring to images of fixed physical size, such as the display resolution of a monitor. In this book, the latter meaning is mostly used.

If you know the resolution of the picture (that is, the number of pixels in it) and the resolution of the printer on which you will print it (for example, 300 dpi), you can figure out how large the picture will be in inches when you print it at its native size. Suppose you have a picture that is 900 pixels square and you print it on a 300 dpi printer. This makes it 3" square on the printout.

Resolution on Preexisting Graphics Files

When you acquire an image file from an outside source, such as downloading it from a website or getting it from a CD of artwork, its resolution has already been determined. Whoever created the file originally made that decision. For example, if the image was originally scanned on a scanner, whoever scanned it chose the scan resolution — that is, the dpi setting. That determined how many individual pixels each inch of the original picture would be divided into. At a 100 dpi scan, each inch of the picture is represented by 100 pixels vertically and horizontally. At 300 dpi, each inch of the picture is broken down into three times that many.

If you want to make a graphic take up less disk space, you can use an image-editing program to change the image size, and/or you can crop off one or more sides of the image.

CAUTION

If you crop or decrease the size of an image in an image-editing program, save the changes under a different filename. Maintain the original image in case you ever need it for some other purpose. Decreasing the image resolution decreases its dpi setting, which decreases its quality. You might not notice any quality degradation on-screen, but you will probably notice a difference when you are printing the image at a large size. That's because the average monitor displays only 96 dpi but the average printer prints at 600 dpi or higher.

PowerPoint slides do not usually need to be printed at a professional-quality resolution, so image quality on a PowerPoint printout is not usually an issue. However, if you use the picture for something else later, such as printing it as a full-page color image on photo paper, then a high dpi file can make a difference.

Resolution on Graphics You Scan Yourself

When you create an image file yourself by using a scanner, *you* choose the resolution, expressed in dpi, through the scanner software. For example, suppose you scan a 4" × 6" photo at 100 dpi. The scanner will break down each 1" section of the photo horizontally and vertically into 100 separate pieces and decide on a numeric value that best represents the color of each piece. The result is a total number of pixels of 4 × 100 × 6 × 100, or 240,000 pixels. Assuming each pixel requires 3 bytes of storage, the fill becomes approximately 720KB in size. The actual size varies slightly depending on the file format.

Now, suppose you scan the same photo at 200 dpi. The scanner breaks down each 1" section of the photo into 200 pieces so that the result is 4 × 200 × 6 × 200, or 960,000 pixels. Assuming again that 1 pixel requires 3 bytes for storage (24 bits), the file will be approximately 2.9MB in size. That's a big difference.

The higher the resolution in which you scan, the larger the file becomes, but the details of the scan also become finer. However, unless you are zooming in on the photo, you cannot tell a difference between 100 dpi and a higher resolution. That's because most computer monitors display at 96 dpi, so any resolution higher than that does not improve the output.

Let's look at an example. In Figure 11.11 you can see two copies of an image open in a graphics program. The same photo was scanned at 75 dpi (left) and 150 dpi (right). However, the difference between them is not significant when the two images are placed on a PowerPoint slide, as shown in Figure 11.12. The lower-resolution image is at the top left, but there is no observable difference in the size at which they are being used.

FIGURE 11.11

At high magnification, the difference in dpi for a scan is apparent.

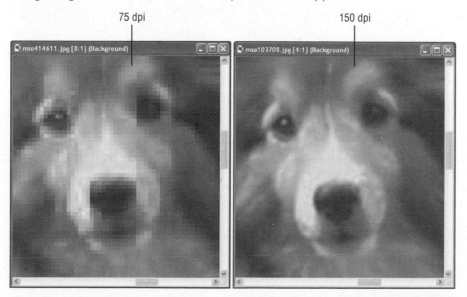

FIGURE 11.12

When the image is used at a normal size, there is virtually no difference between a high-dpi and low-dpi scan.

75 dpi

150 dpi

Scanners and Color Depth

If you are shopping for a scanner, you will probably notice that they're advertised with higher numbers of bits than the graphics formats support. This is for error correction. If there are extra bits, it can throw out the bad bits to account for "noise" and still end up with a full set of good bits. Error correction in a scan is a rather complicated process, but fortunately your scanner driver software takes care of it for you.

Resolution on Digital Camera Photos

Top-quality digital cameras today take very high-resolution pictures, much higher than you will need for an on-screen PowerPoint presentation. At a typical size and magnification, a high-resolution graphic file is overkill; it wastes disk space needlessly. Therefore, you may want to adjust the camera's image size so that it takes lower-resolution pictures for your PowerPoint show.

However, if you think you might want to use those same pictures for some other purpose in the future, such as printing them in a magazine or newsletter, then go ahead and take them with the camera's highest setting, but then compress them in PowerPoint or resize copies of them in a third-party image-editing program. See the section "Compressing Images" later in this chapter to learn how.

Color Depth

Color depth is the number of bits required to describe the color of a single pixel in the image. For example, in 1-bit color, a single binary digit represents each pixel. Each pixel is either black (1) or white (0). In 4-bit color, there are 16 possible colors because there are 16 combinations of 1s and 0s in a four-digit binary number. In 8-bit color there are 256 combinations.

For most file formats, the highest number of colors you can have in an image is 16.7 million colors, which is 24-bit color (also called *true color*). It uses 8 bits each for red, green, and blue.

There is also 32-bit color, which has the same number of colors as 24-bit but adds 8 more bits for an alpha channel. The alpha channel describes the amount of transparency for each pixel. This is not so much an issue for single-layer graphics, but in multilayer graphics, such as the ones you can create in high-end graphics programs like Photoshop, the extent to which a lower layer shows through an upper one is important.

> **TIP**
>
> For a great article on alpha channel usage in PowerPoint by Geetesh Bajaj, go to `www.indezine.com/products/powerpoint/ppalpha.html`.

A color depth of 48-bit is fairly new, and it's just like 24-bit color except it uses 16 rather than 8 bits to define each of the three channels: red, green, and blue. It does not have an alpha channel bit. Because the human eye cannot detect the small differences it introduces, 48-bit color depth is not really necessary. Of the graphics formats that PowerPoint supports, only PNG and TIFF support 48-bit color depth.

Normally, you should not decrease the color depth of a photo to less than 24-bit unless there is a major issue with lack of disk space that you cannot resolve any other way. To decrease the color depth, you would need to open the graphic file in a third-party image-editing program and use the command in that program for decreasing the number of colors. Before going through that, try compressing the images in the presentation (see the section "Compressing Images" later in the chapter) to see if that solves the problem.

File Format

Many scanners scan in JPEG format by default, but most also support TIF, and some also support other formats. Images you acquire from a digital camera are almost always JPEG.

Images from other sources may be any of dozens of graphics formats, including PCX, BMP, GIF, or PNG.

Different graphic formats can vary tremendously in the size and quality of the image they produce. The main differentiators between formats are the color depth they support and the type of compression they use (which determines the file size).

Remember earlier how I explained that each pixel in a 24-bit image requires 3 bytes? (That's derived by dividing 24 by 8 because there are 8 bits in a byte.) Then you multiply that by the height and then by the width to determine the image size. Well, that formula was not completely accurate because it does not include compression. *Compression* is an algorithm (basically a math formula) that decreases the amount of space that the file takes up on the disk by storing the data about the pixels more compactly. A file format will have one of these three states in regard to compression:

- **No compression.** The image is not compressed.
- **Lossless compression.** The image is compressed, but the algorithm for doing so does not throw out any pixels so there is no loss of image quality when you resize the image.
- **Lossy compression.** The image is compressed by recording less data about the pixels, so when you resize the image, there may be a loss of image quality.

Table 11.1 provides a brief guide to some of the most common graphic formats. Generally speaking, for most on-screen presentations JPEG should be your preferred choice for graphics because it is compact and Web-accessible (although PNG is also a good choice and uses lossless compression).

TABLE 11.1 Popular Graphics Formats

Extension	Pronunciation	Compression	Maintains Transparency	Notes
JPEG or JPG	"Jay-peg"	Yes	No	Stands for Joint Photographic Experts Group. Very small image size. Uses lossy compression. Common on the Web. Up to 24-bit.
GIF	"gif" or "jif"	Yes	No	Stands for Graphic Interchange Format. Limited to 8-bit (256 color). Uses proprietary compression algorithm. Allows animated graphics, which are useful on the Web. Color depth limitation makes this format unsuitable for photos.

PNG	"ping"	Yes	Yes	Stands for Portable Network Graphic. An improvement on GIF. Up to 48-bit color depth. Lossless compression, but smaller file sizes than TIF. Public domain format.
BMP	"B-M-P" or "bump" or "bitmap"	No	No	Default image type for Windows XP. Up to 24-bit color. Used for some Windows wallpaper and other Windows graphics.
PCX	"P-C-X"	Yes	No	There are three versions: 0, 2, and 5. Use version 5 for 24-bit support. Originally introduced by a company called ZSoft; sometimes called ZSoft Paintbrush format.
TIF or TIFF	"tiff"	Optional	Yes	Stands for Tagged Image File Format. Supported by most scanners and some digital cameras. Up to 48-bit color. Uses lossless compression. Large file size but high quality.

> **TIP**
> If you are not sure what format you will eventually use for an image, scan it in TIF format and keep the TIF copy on your hard disk. You can always save a copy in JPEG or other formats when you need them for specific projects. The TIF format's compression is lossless, so it results in a high-quality image.

Inserting Photos

Now that you know all about the factors that go into creating and selecting raster images, it's time to get down to the business of inserting the images on your PowerPoint slides. In the following sections you will learn to do just that. You'll find out how to acquire photos via a Bing search for situations in which you don't already have what you need and how to insert images from your own computer that you have already acquired.

Searching for Photos with Bing

Bing is Microsoft's search engine on the Web, and PowerPoint has a built-in interface for using Bing's image search capabilities to find photos you can use in your presentations. It's something like the clip-art search you learned about earlier in this chapter, but the search results are not confined to just Microsoft's own servers, and only photos (raster-based images) are shown.

To search for a photo with Bing and place it in your presentation, follow these steps:

1. **Display the slide on which you want to place the image.**

2. **Click the Online Pictures icon in the content placeholder, or choose Insert ⇨ Images ⇨ Online Pictures.** The Insert Pictures dialog box opens. It's the same dialog box as in Figure 11.2 earlier in the chapter.

3. **Click in the Search Bing text box and type the keyword to search for.** Then press Enter to perform the search. Search results appear in that same dialog box, as shown in Figure 11.13.

FIGURE 11.13

Search results appear showing thumbnails of available images.

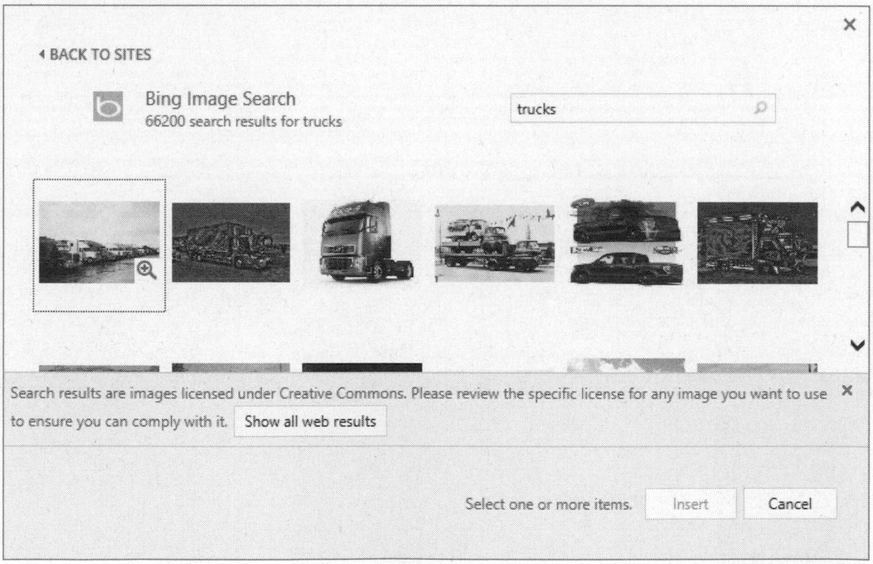

> **NOTE**
>
> By default, the Bing image search results contain only images that are licensed under Creative Commons. That means that you can use the images in your work without having to pay a fee or royalty to the owner. When the search results appear, a message explains that the search results are filtered as such. If you want to see all images, even the ones that you aren't necessarily entitled to legally use. Click the Show All Web Results button in the message bar to rerun the search with that filter off.

4. **Click the image you want to insert, and click the Insert button.** The image is downloaded to your PC and inserted on the slide. From here you can work with it just as if it was any other photo.

Inserting Pictures from Files

If you already have the picture(s) you want to use, you can insert them from your own computer's drive using the Pictures button on the Insert tab. Assuming you have already acquired the images you need, use the following steps to insert one into PowerPoint:

1. **Display the slide on which you want to place the image.**

2. **If the slide has a content placeholder for pictures, as in Figure 11.14, click it.** Otherwise, choose Insert ⇨ Images ⇨ Pictures. The Insert Picture dialog box opens. The default location shown is the Pictures library on your local hard disk.

FIGURE 11.14

You can insert a picture by using the Pictures content placeholder icon.

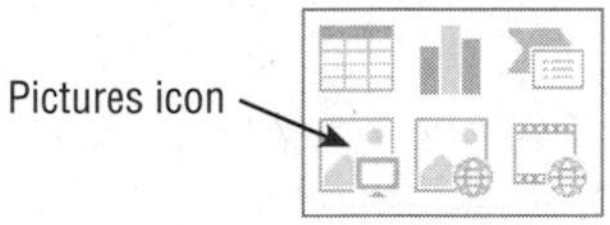

Pictures icon

3. **Select the picture to import.** See Figure 11.15. You can switch the view by using the View (or Views) button in the dialog box to see thumbnails or details if either is effective in helping you determine which file is which.

FIGURE 11.15

Select the picture to be inserted.

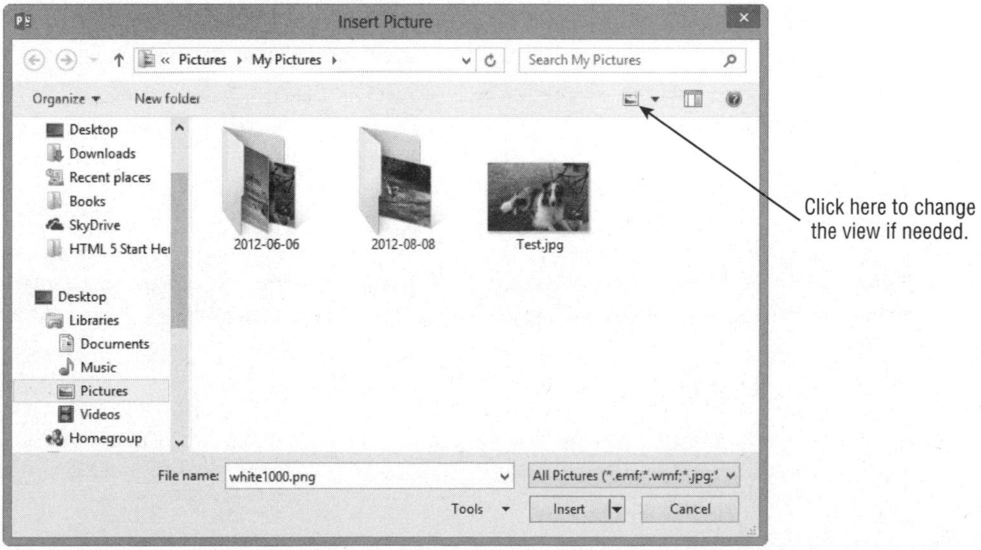

Click here to change the view if needed.

353

4. **Click Insert.** The picture is inserted.

> **TIP**
> If you have a lot of graphics in different formats, consider narrowing down the list that appears by selecting a specific file type from the file type list. By default it is set to All Pictures.

Linking to a Graphic File

If you have a sharp eye, you may have noticed that the Insert button in Figure 11.15 has a drop-down list associated with it. That list has these choices:

- **Insert.** The default, inserts the graphic but maintains no connection.
- **Link to File.** Creates a link to the file, but does not maintain a local copy of it in PowerPoint.
- **Insert and Link.** Creates a link to the file, and also inserts a local copy of its current state, so if the linked copy is not available in the future, the local copy will still appear.

Use Link to File whenever you want to insert a pointer rather than the original. When the presentation opens, it pulls in the graphic from the disk. If the graphic is not available, it displays an empty frame with a red X in the corner in the graphic's place. Using Link to File keeps the size of the original PowerPoint file very small because it doesn't actually contain the graphic — it only links to it. However, if you move or delete the graphic, PowerPoint won't be able to find it anymore.

The important thing to know about this link in the Link to File feature is that it is not the same thing as an OLE link. This is not a dynamic link that you can manage. It is a much simpler link and much less flexible. You can't change the file location to which it is linked, for example; if the location of the graphic changes, you must delete it from PowerPoint and reinsert it.

> **TIP**
> If you are building a graphic-heavy presentation on an older computer, you might find that it takes a long time to move between slides and for each graphic to appear. You can take some of the hassle away by using Link to File instead of inserting the graphics. Then temporarily move the graphic files to a subfolder so PowerPoint can't find them. It displays the placeholders for the graphics on the appropriate slides, and the presentation file is much faster to page through and edit. Then when you are ready to finish up, close PowerPoint and move the graphic files back to their original locations so PowerPoint can find them again when you reopen the presentation file.

Capturing and Inserting Screenshots

A *screenshot* is a picture that you take of your computer screen using Windows itself (or a screen capture utility). Most of the images in this book are screenshots. You might want to take screenshots to illustrate the steps in a computer-based procedure and then create a

PowerPoint presentation that teaches others to perform that procedure. You can also take screen shots on some mobile devices.

Windows has always had a basic screenshot capability built into it: the Print Screen key. You can press Print Screen at any time to copy an image of the screen to the Clipboard. Then you can paste directly onto your slide, or you can open a graphics-editing program such as Paint and paste from the Clipboard to save the file.

In PowerPoint 2013, you can also capture and insert screenshots directly, bypassing the Clipboard and an outside graphics program. The Screenshot command in PowerPoint also enables you to capture individual windows rather than the entire screen.

To capture a screenshot of an open window, follow these steps:

1. **Open the window for which you want to capture the screenshot.** Do not minimize it.

2. **Switch to PowerPoint, and display the slide on which you want to place the screenshot.**

3. **Choose Insert ⇨ Screenshot.** A menu appears showing thumbnails of the available windows. See Figure 11.16.

FIGURE 11.16

Capture a window using the Screenshot command.

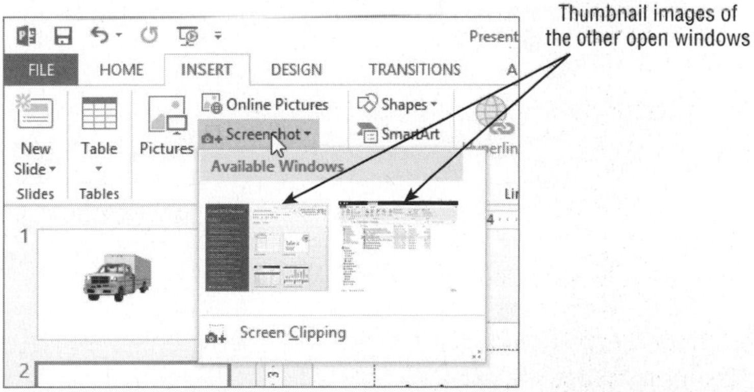

4. **Click the thumbnail image of the window you want to capture.** The image is immediately inserted as a new picture on the active slide.

NOTE

The Screenshot command does not show every open window as a thumbnail; it shows each tab of Internet Explorer and each open Office application window except for PowerPoint itself. If you want to capture a window other than the ones shown in the thumbnails, you must use the Screen Clipping command.

If the window you want does not appear on the thumbnails list, or if you want different cropping, use the Screen Clipping command instead. Follow these steps:

1. **Display the window that you want to capture.**

2. **Using the taskbar, switch to PowerPoint.**

3. **Choose Insert ⇨ Screenshot ⇨ Screen Clipping.** The PowerPoint window is mini-mized, and the window immediately beneath it appears, with a whitewash overlay on it.

4. **Click and drag to define the rectangular area you want to crop.** When you release the mouse button, the defined area appears in PowerPoint as a new image.

> **TIP**
> If you need better cropping than you can get with the Screenshot command, use the cropping techniques in the fol-lowing section to fine-tune the crop after insertion into PowerPoint. If you need more robust screen capture capabili-ties, consider an application that is specifically designed for screen captures such as SnagIt (`snagit.com`).

Sizing and Cropping Photos

After placing a picture on a slide, you will probably need to adjust its size, and/or crop it, to make it fit in the allotted space the way you want it. The following sections explain these techniques.

Sizing a Photo

Sizing a photo is just like sizing any other object. Drag its selection handles. Drag a corner to maintain the aspect ratio, or drag a side to distort it. (Distorting a photo is seldom a good idea, though, unless you're after some weird funhouse effect.)

You can also specify an exact size for a photo the same as for drawn objects. Right-click the photo and choose Size and Position to set a size in the Format Picture task pane (see Figure 11.17). Alternatively, you can display the Picture Tools Format tab and then use the Height and Width boxes in the Size group, also shown in Figure 11.17.

The most straightforward way to specify the size is in inches in the Height and Width boxes, either in the dialog box or on the tab. These measurements correspond to the mark-ers on the on-screen ruler in Normal view. The size of a slide varies depending on how you have it set up (by using the Page Setup tab), but an average slide size is 10 inches wide by 7.5 inches tall. You can also size the photo using the Scale controls in the Size and Position dialog box, in which you adjust the size based on a percentage of the original size.

Note that the scale is based on the original size, not the current size. So, for example, if you set Height and Width to 50%, close the dialog box, and then reopen it and set them each to

75%, the net result will be 75% of the original, not 75% of the 50%. However, you can override this by deselecting the Relative to Original Picture Size check box (see Figure 11.17).

FIGURE 11.17

Size a photo via either the dialog box or the Format tab.

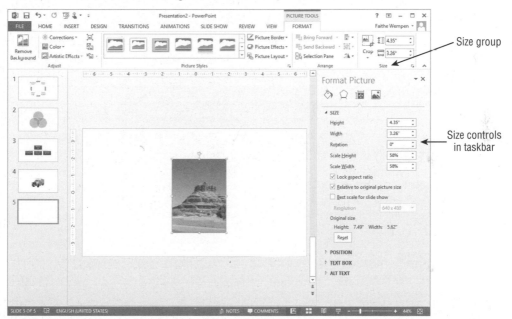

If you are setting up a presentation for the primary purpose of showing full-screen graphics, you can use the Best Scale for Slide Show check box (see Figure 11.17). This enables you to choose a screen resolution, such as 640 × 480 or 800 × 600, and size the pictures so that they will show to the best advantage in that resolution. Choose the resolution that corresponds to the display setting on the PC on which you will show the presentation. To determine what the resolution is on the PC, right-click the Windows Desktop and choose Screen Resolution.

> **TIP**
>
> When possible, develop your presentation at the same Windows screen resolution as the PC on which you present the show. Many digital projectors display at 1024 × 768.

Cropping a Photo

Cropping is for those times you want only a part of the image. For example, you might have a great photo of a person or animal, but there is extraneous detail around it, as shown in Figure 11.18. You can crop away all but the important object in the image with a cropping tool.

FIGURE 11.18

This picture can benefit from cropping.

Crop button

Crop handles appear in corners and on sides of image.

You can crop two sides at once by cropping at the corner of the image, or you can crop each side individually by cropping at the sides. To crop an image, do the following:

1. **Select the image so the Picture Tools Format tab becomes available.**
2. **Click Picture Tools Format ⇨ Size.** Your mouse pointer changes to a cropping tool (see Figure 11.18).
3. **Position the pointer over one of the selection handles on the image frame, and drag toward the center until the image is cropped the way you want.**

4. **Repeat step 3 for each side.** Then click the Crop button again, or press Esc, to turn cropping off.

5. **Resize the cropped image if needed.**

Figure 11.19 shows the result of cropping and resizing the image from Figure 11.18.

FIGURE 11.19

The picture has been improved by cropping and resizing it.

To undo a crop, reenter cropping mode by clicking the Crop button again, and then drag the side(s) back outward again. Or you can simply reset the photo, as described in the following section.

You can also crop to a shape or crop to a particular aspect ratio (that is, ratio of height to width).

Cropping to a shape crops the picture so that it fits inside one of the drawing shapes that PowerPoint provides, such as a star, triangle, or arrow.

To crop to a shape, follow these steps:

1. **Select the picture.**

2. **On the Picture Tools Format tab, click the down arrow under the Crop button, and point to Crop to Shape.** A palette of shapes appears, as shown in Figure 11.20.

3. **Click the shape to which you want the picture cropped.**

After cropping to a shape, you'll notice the central part of the image might not be exactly centered within the shape. To adjust the centering of the picture within the crop area, right-click the picture and choose Format Picture to open the Format Picture task pane.

Click the Picture icon (rightmost icon), and then adjust the values in the Crop section, as shown in Figure 11.21.

FIGURE 11.20

You can crop a picture to a shape.

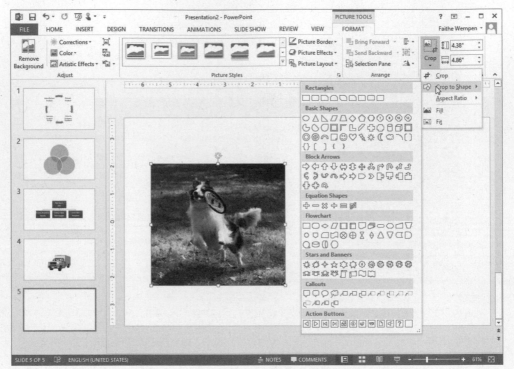

You can also crop to an aspect ratio. PowerPoint offers several preset ratios to choose from that correspond to common picture sizes, such as 2:3, 3:4, and 3:5. Here's how to apply an aspect ratio crop:

1. **Select the picture.**
2. **On the Picture Tools Format tab, click the down arrow under the Crop button, and point to Aspect Ratio.** A list of ratios appears.
3. **Click the ratio you want to use.** Crop marks appear on the image, and the portion of the image that will be excluded appears in gray.
4. **Drag the crop markers to adjust the crop as desired, and then click the Crop button or press Esc on your keyboard to finalize the cropping operation.**

FIGURE 11.21

Set a precise amount of cropping in the Format Picture task pane.

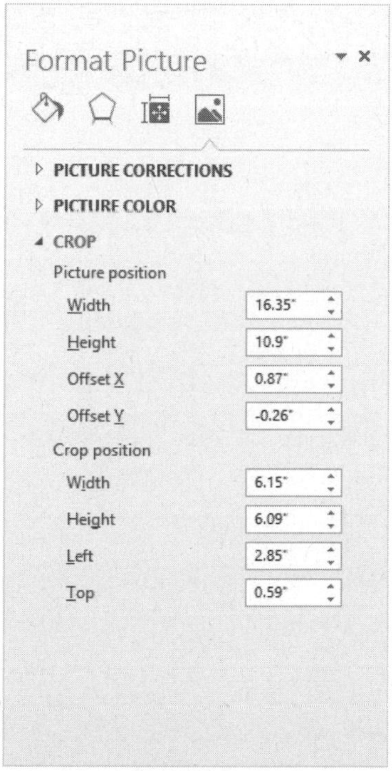

You can also crop "by the numbers" with the Crop settings in the Format Picture dialog box. Here's how to do that:

1. **Select the picture.**
2. **Right-click the picture and choose Format Picture to display the Format Picture task pane.**
3. **Click the Picture icon (rightmost icon) and then click Crop if needed to expand the Crop section.**
4. **Use the controls under Picture Position (see Figure 11.21) to manually enter cropping amounts for each side.**

NOTE

To crop from the bottom, decrease the Height setting; to crop from the right, decrease the Width setting. The Left and Top settings crop from those sides, respectively.

Resetting a Photo

Once the picture is in PowerPoint, any manipulations you do to it are strictly on the surface. It changes how the picture appears on the slide, but it doesn't change how the picture is stored in PowerPoint. Consequently, you can reset the picture back to its original settings at any time (provided you have not compressed the picture). This resetting also clears any changes you make to the image's size, contrast, and brightness (contrast and brightness changes are discussed in the next section).

To reset the picture, right-click it and choose Format Picture to display the Format Picture task pane. Click the Size & Properties icon (third from left), and in the Size section, click the Reset button.

Adjusting and Correcting Photos

PowerPoint has some powerful features for adjusting, correcting, and applying artistic effects to photos. Not only can you adjust the brightness and contrast, but you can sharpen or soften an image, tint it, make it black and white, and apply several types of artistic effects to it that make it look like it was created in some other medium, such as charcoal pencil or collage.

Applying Brightness and Contrast Corrections

You can adjust the brightness and contrast for any photo in PowerPoint, and you can adjust the sharpness or softness of the image.

Brightness refers to the overall level of light in a picture. The brighter the setting, the lighter each pixel of the image is. Brightness does not affect the color hues. You might increase the brightness on a photo that was taken in a dimly lit room, for example.

Contrast refers to the difference between the lighter areas and the darker areas of the photo. Adjusting contrast makes the lights lighter and the darks darker. Increasing the contrast of a picture makes its image more distinct; this can be good for an older, washed-out picture, for example.

Sharpness/softness is controlled with a slider, with the default being right in the middle between them. When you sharpen an image, the edges of the objects in the picture appear more distinct; when you soften an image, the edges are blurred. PowerPoint finds the edges of objects by looking for areas where the color changes dramatically from one spot to the adjacent one.

The easiest way to access those controls is through the Corrections button on the Picture Tools Format tab. Click the button and then click one of the preset thumbnails, as shown in Figure 11.22. Brightness and contrast are two separately adjustable settings, but the presets on the menu shown in Figure 11.22 combine them. In the Brightness/Contrast section, the sample in the upper-left corner decreases both, and the sample in the lower right increases both. In between, the samples combine settings in various ways. Point at a sample to see a pop-up ScreenTip listing its specifics.

FIGURE 11.22

Choose sharpen/soften, brightness, and contrast presets.

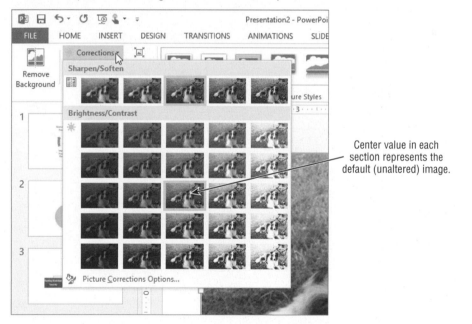

Center value in each section represents the default (unaltered) image.

To choose a value other than the ones listed, click Picture Corrections Options to open the Format Picture task pane to the Picture Corrections controls. From here you can choose presets, or you can drag sliders or enter exact percentages for each setting individually. See Figure 11.23.

Recoloring a Picture

Several color options are available from the Color button's drop-down list on the Picture Tools Format tab. You can apply color washes to the image, make it black and white or grayscale, make it look washed out, and more. You can point at a sample to see a preview of it on the selected image.

FIGURE 11.23

Drag sliders to adjust brightness, contrast, and sharpen or soften settings individually.

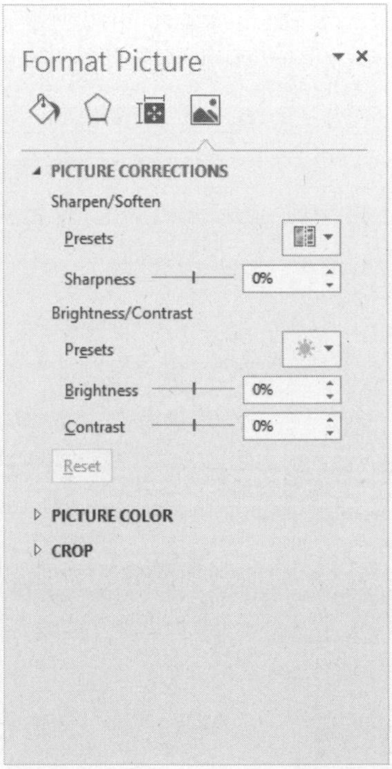

The Color menu has three sections (see Figure 11.24):

- **Color Saturation.** This refers to the vibrancy of the colors. At the low end is grayscale — no colors at all, or 0% saturation. The center point is 100% saturation, the default. At the high end is a very vividly colored version of the image at 400% saturation.

- **Color Tone.** The presets in this section enable you to adjust the "temperature" of the image, from very cool (increased blue and green) to very warm (increased red and yellow). Color tones are measured numerically; the higher the number, the warmer the tone. 4700 Kelvin (K) is very cool; 11200 K is very warm.

> **NOTE**
>
> Color temperature is measured by something called the Kruithof curve. It is named after Dutch physicist Arie Andries Kruithof, and it describes and assigns numeric values to colors like blue and green as cooler than colors like red and yellow. The temperatures are expressed on the Kelvin temperature scale (K).

■ **Recolor.** These presets enable you to radically adjust the colors of the image by choosing a grayscale, sepia, black-and-white, washout, or other preset or by applying a colored wash over the picture. Here's where you'll find the equivalent settings to the Recolor presets from earlier versions of PowerPoint, but also many more options. For more colors to choose from, point to More Variations and choose from the fly-out palette of colors. The last two rows of colors (darks and lights) are based on the theme colors.

FIGURE 11.24

Choose color presets to apply to the image.

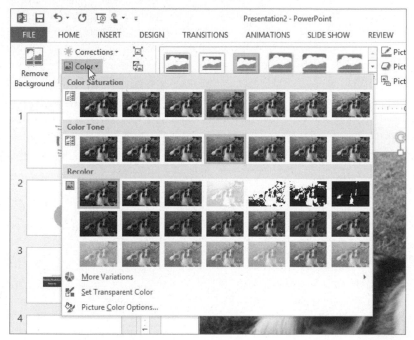

You can also choose Picture Color Options from the menu in Figure 11.24 to open the Format Picture task pane and display the Picture Color settings. Here you'll find buttons that open menus with the same presets as on the menu and also sliders for fine-tuning the Saturation and Temperature.

NOTE

In most areas of PowerPoint, the task pane method provides more flexibility than the menu method. One exception is when recoloring an image. On the Color button's menu you have more presets to choose from as well as a More Variations command that provides access to even more colors. In contrast, in the Format Picture task pane, fewer presets are available, and there is no way to choose an alternative color from a palette from there.

Setting a Transparent Color and Removing a Background

The Transparent Color feature, which you also learned about earlier in this chapter, can be used to remove one of the colors from the photo, making the areas transparent that were previously occupied by that color. For example, suppose you have a scanned photo of your CEO and you want to make the background transparent so it looks like his head is sitting right on the slide. This feature could help you out with that.

To set a transparent color, select the image and then choose Picture Tools Format ⇨ Color ⇨ Set Transparent Color. Then, on the image, click an area that contains the color you want to make transparent.

Setting a transparent color sounds like a great idea, but in reality it does not work as well with photos as it does with clip art. For one thing, it replaces all instances of that color, not just in the background. So, for example, if you have a picture of a man with a white shirt on a white background and choose to make white the transparent color (because you want to drop out the background), the man's shirt becomes transparent too.

Another reason it doesn't work that well on photos is that what looks like one color in a photo is not usually just one color. Think of a blue sky, for example. It probably consists of at least two dozen different shades of blue. If you try to make one of those shades of blue transparent using PowerPoint's transparency tool, you'll probably just end up with splotches of transparent areas.

So what's the solution? One workaround is to use alpha channels in a third-party image-editing program to create true transparency and save the image as TIF or PNG. (JPEG format does not support alpha channels.) An easier way, however, is to use PowerPoint's Remove Background command. It can do the trick in many cases and is easier to use than most photo-editing programs.

To remove the background, select the picture and then choose Picture Tools Format ⇨ Remove Background. The Background Removal tab becomes available, and the areas of the image that PowerPoint plans to remove appear with a purple wash over them (shown in Figure 11.25).

If PowerPoint has correctly guessed at the edges of the image subject, click Keep Changes to accept the background removal as is.

If it has not gotten it quite right, do any of the following to make corrections:

- **PowerPoint-generated border.** A dotted border appears around what PowerPoint thinks is the central part of the image. Drag the selection handles along this border to expand it to allow additional parts of the image to be preserved if needed.
- **To include more image sections.** Click Mark Areas to Keep and then drag on the image, in the purple shaded areas, to delineate additional parts of the image that should not be removed.

- **To exclude image sections.** Click Mark Areas to Remove and then drag on the image, in the areas that are *not* purple shaded, to mark additional parts of the image that *should* be removed.

- **For mistakes.** If you make a mistake and mark an area you shouldn't have, click Delete Mark and then click on that mark.

FIGURE 11.25

The Background Removal tab provides tools for helping you separate a picture's subject from its background.

Use these tools to mark areas to include or exclude.

Drag selection handles to change area.

Applying Artistic Effects

Artistic effects are special types of transformations you can apply to images to make them appear as if they were created in some medium other than photography. For example, you can make a photo look like a pencil sketch or a painting.

To apply artistic effects, select the picture and then choose Picture Tools Format ➪ Artistic Effects and choose from the menu that appears, as shown in Figure 11.26. Each effect is mutually exclusive with the others; when you select a different effect, the previously applied effect is removed.

FIGURE 11.26

Apply artistic effects from the Format tab.

Pencil sketch effect
has been applied.

For more control over the artistic effects, choose Artistic Effects Options. This opens the Format Picture task pane with the Artistic Effects settings displayed. From here, after selecting one of the effects, you can make fine adjustments with the sliders and other controls that appear. There are different controls for different effects; Figure 11.26 shows the ones for the Pencil Sketch effect.

Applying Picture Styles and Effects

You can format pictures using the same effects you learned for drawn objects in Chapter 9. Click the Picture Effects button on the Format tab, and then choose one of the categories there, such as Shadow, Reflection, Glow, or Bevel. Refer to Chapter 9 for the details of each effect type.

You can also choose a preset Picture Style from the Picture Styles group on the Picture Tools Format tab. Click one of the samples displayed in that group, or open the gallery of picture styles for even more choices. See Figure 11.27.

FIGURE 11.27

Choose a picture style as a shortcut to applying combinations of effects.

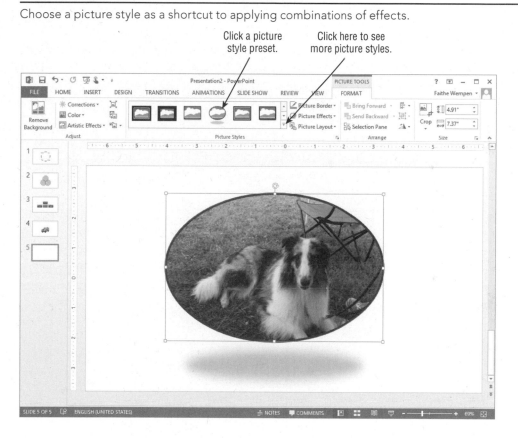

Compressing Images

Having an image that is too large (that is, too high a dpi) is not a problem quality wise. You can resize it in PowerPoint to make it as small as you like; just drag its selection handles. There will be no loss of quality as it gets smaller.

However, as mentioned earlier in the chapter, inserting a picture file that is much larger than necessary can increase the overall size of the PowerPoint file, which can become problematic if you plan to distribute the presentation in a form where space or bandwidth is an issue.

To avoid problems with overly large graphic files, you can compress the images to reduce their resolution and remove any cropped portions. You can do this from within PowerPoint or with a third-party utility.

Reducing Resolution and Compressing Images in PowerPoint

PowerPoint offers an image compression utility that compresses all of the pictures in the presentation in a single step and reduces their resolution to the amount needed for the type of output you specify (e-mail, Screen, or Print).

Picture resolution is measured in PowerPoint in pixels per inch, or ppi. This roughly translates to dots per inch (dpi) on a printout. A computer screen shows 96 pixels per inch, so you do not need higher resolution than that if you are only showing your presentation on-screen. However, if you are distributing the presentation in other forms, a higher resolution might be appropriate.

To reduce resolution and compress images, do the following:

1. **Click a picture so that the Picture Tools Format tab appears.**
2. **Choose Picture Tools Format ➪ Adjust ➪ Compress Pictures.** The Compress Pictures dialog box appears, as shown in Figure 11.28.

FIGURE 11.28

Click OK to compress with the default settings.

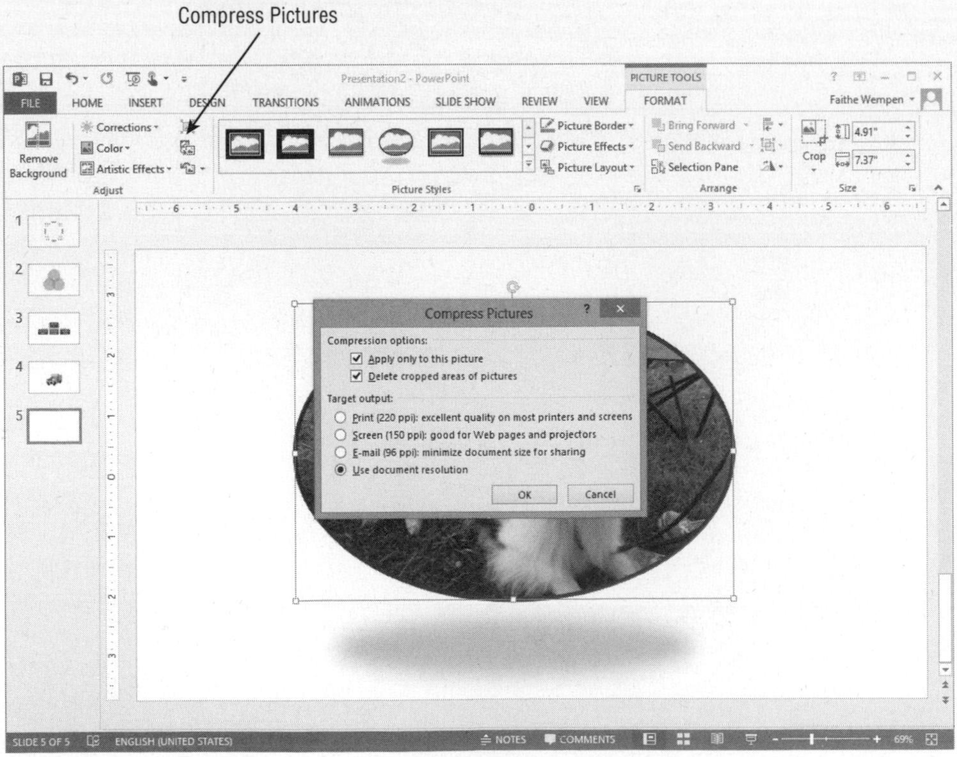

3. **(Optional) If you do not want to compress all of the pictures, make sure the Apply Only to This Picture check box is marked.**

4. **(Optional) If you wish to save additional space by deleting the cropped-out areas of pictures, select the Delete Cropped Areas of Pictures check box.**

5. **Select the desired amount of compression:**

   - **Print (220 ppi).** Choose this if you are printing the presentation on paper; it keeps the photos at a resolution where they will look crisp on a printout.

   - **Screen (150 ppi).** Choose this if you are displaying the presentation using a projector or distributing via the Internet. Some projectors have a higher resolution than a monitor.

   - **E-mail (96 ppi).** Choose this if you are e-mailing the presentation to others because this lower setting results in a smaller file that will transmit more easily via e-mail.

   - **Use Document Resolution.** Use this to match the resolution of the pictures to the resolution defined in PowerPoint Options (File ➪ Options ➪ Advanced).

6. **Click OK to perform the compression.**

CAUTION

Some e-mail servers have limits on the file sizes they will accept, so keeping the PowerPoint file as small as possible when distributing via e-mail is a good idea. If you send someone an e-mail with a large file attached to it, the server may reject the message, but you might not get an error message back from the server at all, or you might not get one for several days.

Reducing Resolution with a Third-Party Utility

Working with resolution reduction from an image-editing program is somewhat of a trial-and-error process, and you must do each image separately.

You can approximate the correct resolution by simply "doing the math." For example, suppose you have a 10" × 7.5" slide. Your desktop display is set to 800 × 600. So your image needs to be 800 pixels wide to fill the slide. Your image is a 5" × 3" image, so if you set it to 200 dpi, that gives you 1,000 pixels, which is a little larger than you need but in the ballpark.

Exporting a Photo from PowerPoint to a Separate File

What goes in must come out, right? Suppose you have a picture that exists only in PowerPoint, for whatever reason. Perhaps it was scanned directly into PowerPoint in an earlier version, for example, and you no longer have access to the original file.

There are two ways to get a graphic out of PowerPoint and make it a separate file again: You can use the Save As Picture feature in PowerPoint, or you can simply use the Windows Clipboard to copy and paste a graphic into an image-editing program.

Exporting a Graphic with Save As Picture

To save a picture separately from PowerPoint, do the following:

1. **Right-click the picture in PowerPoint and choose Save as Picture.**
2. **In the Save as Picture dialog box, display the location where you want to save the file.**
3. **Open the Save as Type list and choose the graphic format you want.** You can choose TIF, JPEG, or a variety of others. See the discussion of file formats earlier in this chapter for guidance.
4. **Enter a name in the File Name box.**
5. **Click Save.**

Exporting a Graphic with the Clipboard

Copy-and-paste is a fast and simple way of transferring a graphic from PowerPoint into an image-editing program, and from there you can save it in any supported format. Select a graphic in PowerPoint, copy it (Ctrl+C), open the graphics program, and paste it (Ctrl+V).

Exporting Entire PowerPoint Slides as Graphics

You can save entire slides — or all slides in the whole presentation — as images. Here's how:

1. **Choose File ⇨ Export ⇨ Change File Type.**
2. **Under Image File Types, click the type of graphic you want to create: PNG or JPEG.** See Figure 11.29. PNG results in a higher-quality, larger image file than JPEG.
3. **Click Save As.** The Save As dialog box opens.
4. **In the Save As dialog box, change the file location and name if desired.**
5. **Click Save.** A dialog box appears asking which slides you want to export.
6. **Click All Slides or Just This One, depending on your preference.**
7. **If you choose All Slides, a message appears that a folder has been created for the slide files.** Click OK. (Each slide is a separate graphic.)

FIGURE 11.29

Save slides as image files via the File ➪ Export ➪ Change File Type command.

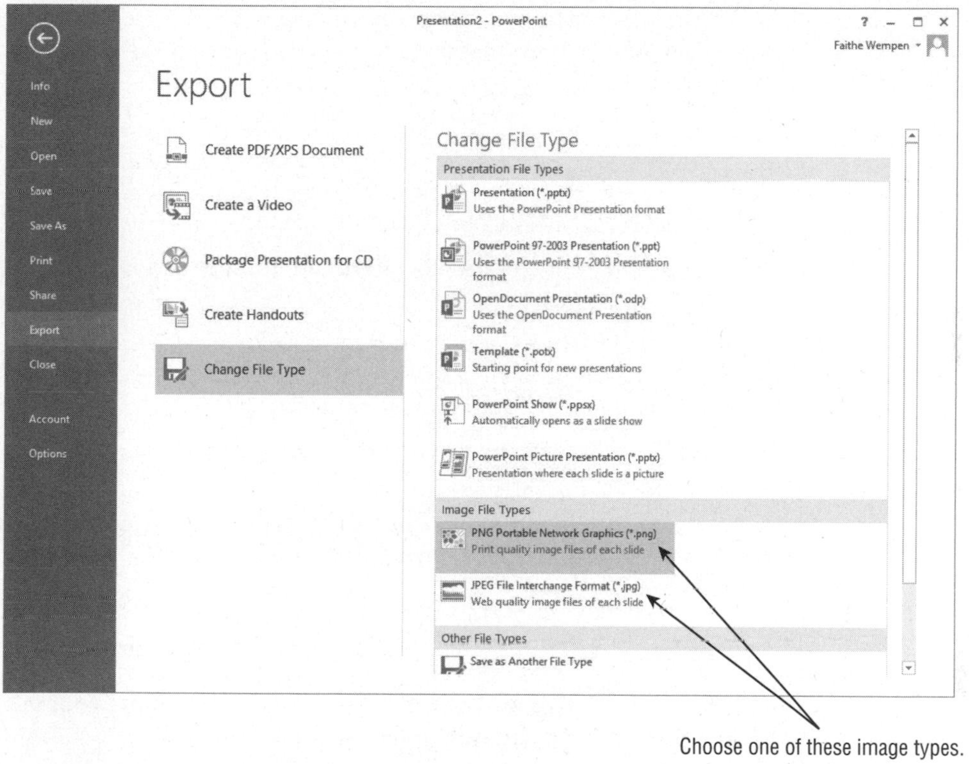

Choose one of these image types.

Creating a Photo Album Layout

Most presentations in PowerPoint are text based, with accompanying photographs. The default Blank Presentation template is biased in favor of text. Graphics, as you have seen in this chapter, require some extra effort.

The *Photo Albums* feature in PowerPoint creates a new presentation that is specifically designed as a carrier of pictures. It is useful when you need to create a presentation that is very heavy on graphics, with little or no text except picture captions.

Creating a New Photo Album

When you create a new photo album, it starts a new presentation for you. Any other presentations that you may have open are not disturbed, and you can switch back to them at any time with the View tab. The new presentation has a title slide as well as slides for the photos you place in the album.

To start a new photo album, follow these steps:

1. **On the Insert tab, click Photo Album.** (Click the main face of the button, not the arrow.) The Photo Album dialog box opens.

2. **To add a photo from a file, click the File/Disk button.** The Insert New Pictures dialog box opens.

3. **Select one or more pictures, and then click Insert.** (To select multiple pictures, hold down Ctrl or Shift as you click on the ones you want.) The photos appear in the Photo Album dialog box as shown in Figure 11.30.

4. **Repeat steps 2 and 3 as needed to insert all the photos from disk that you want.**

5. **For each image on the Pictures in Album list, select the picture and then apply any correction needed with the buttons beneath the Preview pane.** You can rotate right or left, increase or decrease the contrast, and increase or decrease the brightness.

6. **Use the arrows to move an image up or down in the order.**

7. **In the Album Layout section, open the Picture Layout box and choose the layout for the presentation slides.** For example, in Figure 11.30, Fit to Slide has been chosen.

8. **If available, choose a frame shape from the Frame Shape list.** Some choices from step 7 do not permit a frame shape to be chosen.

> **TIP**
>
> You can create themes specifically for photo albums and then use them here by clicking the Browse button to browse for a theme. You might also want to experiment with the photo album themes in the dialog box when you create the photo album initially.

9. **(Optional) To add caption boxes for each picture, select the Captions Below ALL Pictures check box.**

10. **(Optional) To show the pictures in black and white, select the ALL Pictures Black and White check box.**

11. **Click Create.** PowerPoint creates the new presentation containing the photos and the layout you specified.

12. **Save the photo album (File ➪ Save) as a presentation.**

FIGURE 11.30

Specify graphics to appear in the photo album, a page layout, and a style of photo frame.

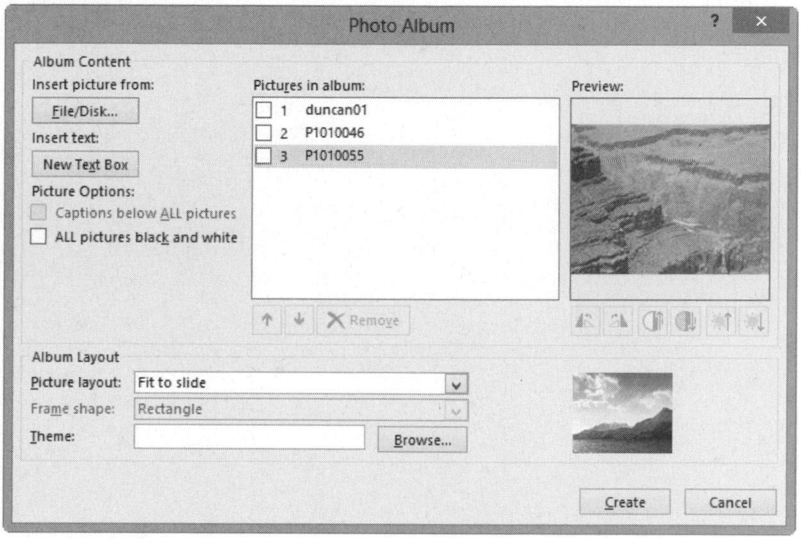

11

Modifying a Photo Album

You can reopen the dialog box from Figure 11.30 by clicking the down arrow beneath the Photo Album button on the Insert tab and choosing Edit Photo Album.

You can also modify the slides in the presentation individually. These are just regular, editable slides, and you can add anything to them that you like, including text boxes, clip art, and so on. Think of it as an on-screen scrapbook! You can crop the photos inserted via the photo album as well.

Summary

In this chapter, you learned how to insert and manage clip art and how to modify it in PowerPoint. You learned about the technical specs for graphics that determine their file size, quality, and flexibility, and you learned how to insert them into your presentations. You can format a photo and color, crop, and manipulate photos to create special effects.

In the next chapter, you'll learn how to work with charts. You'll find out how to take advantage of PowerPoint's graphics-like capabilities for structuring and formatting numeric data in chart format.

Working with Charts

IN THIS CHAPTER

Understanding the parts of a chart

Starting a new chart

Working with chart data

Chart types and chart layout presets

Working with labels

Controlling the axes

Formatting a chart

Rotating a 3-D chart

Working with chart templates

Many times when you include a chart in PowerPoint, it already exists in some other application. For example, you might have an Excel workbook that contains some charts that you want to use in PowerPoint. If this is the case, you can simply copy and paste them into PowerPoint or link or embed them, as you will learn in Chapter 13, "Incorporating Content from Other Programs."

However, when you need to create a quick chart that has no external source, PowerPoint's charting tool is perfect for this purpose. The PowerPoint charting interface is based upon the one in Excel, and so you don't have to leave PowerPoint to create, modify, and format professional-looking charts.

> **NOTE**
>
> What's the difference between a chart and a graph? Some purists will tell you that a chart is either a table or a pie chart, whereas a graph is a chart that plots data points on two axes, such as a bar chart. However, Microsoft does not make this distinction, and neither do I in this book. I use the term *chart* in this book for either kind.

Understanding the Parts of a Chart

PowerPoint's charting feature is based upon the same Escher 2.0 graphics engine that is used for drawn objects. Consequently, most of what you have learned about formatting objects in earlier chapters (especially Chapters 9, 10, and 11) also applies to charts. For example, you can apply shape styles to the individual elements of a chart and apply WordArt styles to chart text. However, there are also many chart-specific formatting and layout options, as you will see throughout this chapter.

The charting feature's controls in Office 2013 are different from those in earlier versions, so even if you have used charting in earlier versions of PowerPoint, you may still want to refer to this chapter to find out where the features are that you want to use.

The sample chart shown in Figure 12.1 contains these elements:

FIGURE 12.1

Parts of a chart

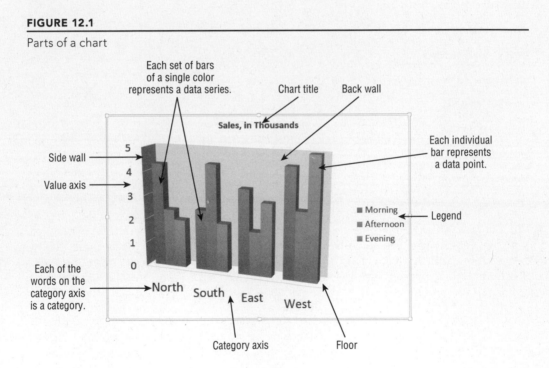

- **Data series.** Each different bar color represents a different series: Morning, Afternoon, and Evening.
- **Legend.** Colored squares in the Legend box describe the correlation of each color to a data series.
- **Categories.** The North, South, East, and West labels along the bottom of the chart are the categories.
- **Category axis.** The horizontal line running across the bottom of the chart is the category axis, also called the horizontal axis.
- **Value axis.** The vertical line running up the left side of the chart, with the numbers on it, is the value axis, also called the vertical axis.

- **Data points.** Each individual bar is a data point. The numeric value for that data point corresponds to the height of the bar, measured against the value axis.

- **Walls.** The walls are the areas behind the data points. On a 3-D chart, as shown in Figure 12.1, there are both back and side walls. On a 2-D chart, there is only the plot area behind the chart.

- **Floor.** The floor is the area on which the data points sit. A floor appears only in a 3-D chart.

Starting a New Chart

The main difficulty with creating a chart in a non-spreadsheet application such as PowerPoint is that there is no data table from which to pull the numbers. Therefore, PowerPoint creates charts using data that you have entered in an Excel window. By default, it contains sample data, which you can replace with your own data.

You can place a new chart on a slide in two ways: You can either use a chart placeholder from a layout or place one manually. Follow these steps to place a chart:

1. **On the Insert tab, click Chart. Or, click the Insert Chart icon on the content placeholder.** The Insert Chart dialog box opens (Figure 12.2).

FIGURE 12.2

Select the desired chart type.

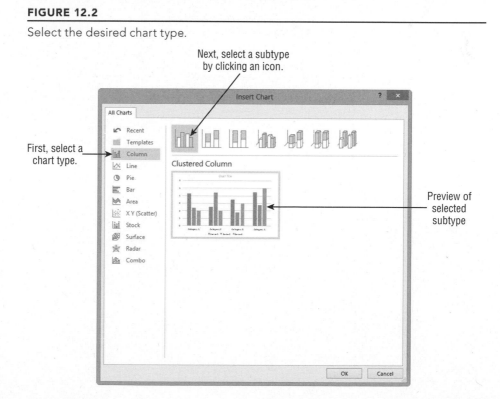

379

2. **In the list at the left, select the desired chart type.** Column is selected by default (and in Figure 12.2), but you can pick any type you like.

3. **From the icons along the top of the dialog box, click the icon that best represents the subtype of chart you want.** In Figure 12.2, the Clustered Column type is selected. A sample of the selected chart subtype appears below the icons.

   See Table 12.1 for an explanation of the chart types. Figure 12.3 and Figure 12.4 show examples of some of the chart types.

4. **Click OK.** The chart appears on the slide, and an Excel datasheet opens with sample data.

5. **Modify the sample data as needed.** To change the range of cells that appear in the chart, see the section "Redefining the Data Range" later in this chapter. If you want, you can then close the Excel window to move it out of the way.

> **NOTE**
> A chart inserted into PowerPoint is an embedded object; it exists only within PowerPoint, even though it is an Excel chart.

> **NOTE**
> After you have closed the Excel window, you can open it again by clicking Edit Data on the Chart Tools Design tab.

FIGURE 12.3

Examples of chart types, from top left, clockwise: column, line, bar, and pie.

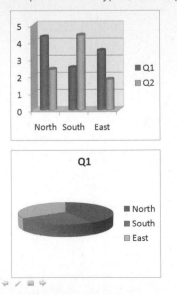
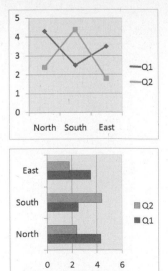

FIGURE 12.4

Examples of chart types, from top left, clockwise: area, scatter, donut, and surface..

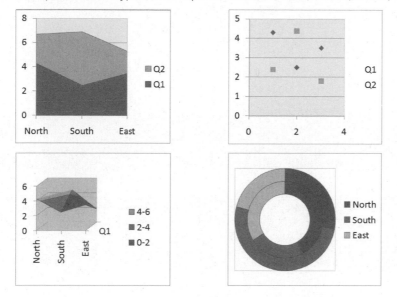

TABLE 12.1   Chart Types in PowerPoint's Charting Tool

Type	Description
Column	Vertical bars, optionally with multiple data series. Bars can be clustered, stacked, or based on a percentage and either 2-D or 3-D.
Line	Shows values as points, and connects the points with a line. Different series use different colors and/or line styles.
Pie	A circle broken into wedges to show how parts contribute to a whole. This de-emphasizes the actual numeric values. In most cases, this type is a single-series only. The donut variant is similar to a pie but with multiple concentric rings so that multiple series can be illustrated.
Bar	Just like a column chart, but horizontal.
Area	Just like a column chart, but with the spaces filled in between the bars.
XY (Scatter)	Shows values as points on both axes, but does not connect them with a line. However, you can add trend lines. The bubble variant uses bubbles of varying sizes to represent a third data variable rather than each data point being a fixed size.

Continues

TABLE 12.1 *(continued)*

Stock	A special type of chart that is used to show stock prices.
Surface	A 3-D sheet that is used to illustrate the highest and lowest points of the data set.
Radar	Shows changes of data frequency in relation to a center point.

> **NOTE**
>
> At any point, you can return to your PowerPoint presentation by clicking anywhere outside of the chart on the slide. To edit the chart again, you can click the chart to redisplay the chart-specific tabs.

> **TIP**
>
> If you delete a column or row by selecting individual cells and pressing Delete to clear them, the empty space that these cells occupied remains in the chart. To completely remove a row or column from the data range, select the row or column by clicking its header (letter for column; number for row) and click Delete on the Home tab in Excel.

Working with Chart Data

After you create a chart, you might want to change the data range on which it is based or how this data is plotted. The following sections explain how you can do this.

Plotting by Rows versus by Columns

By default, the columns of the datasheet form the data series. However, if you want, you can switch the data around so that the rows form the series. Figure 12.5 and Figure 12.6 show the same chart plotted both ways so that you can see the difference. (The data for this chart appears in the next section of the chapter, in Figure 12.7, in case you want to reference it.)

What does the term *data series* mean? Take a look at Figure 12.5 and Figure 12.6. Notice that there is a legend next to each chart that shows what each color (or shade of gray) represents. Each of these colors, and the label associated with it, is a series. The other variable (the one that is not the series) is plotted on the chart's horizontal axis.

FIGURE 12.5

A chart with quarters as the series

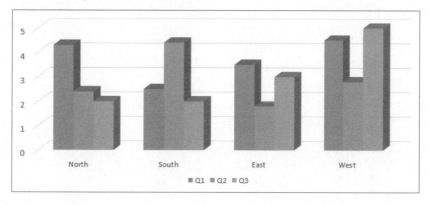

FIGURE 12.6

A chart with regions as the series

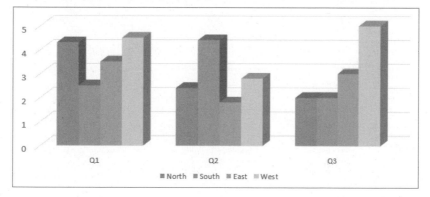

To switch back and forth between plotting by rows and by columns in the data sheet, click the Switch Row/Column button on the Chart Tools Design tab. If the button is not available, open the data sheet by choosing Chart Tools Design ⇨ Data ⇨ Edit Data, and then the button will become available.

A chart can carry a very different message when you arrange it by rows versus by columns. For example, in Figure 12.5, the chart compares the quarters. The message here is about improvement — or lack thereof — over time. Contrast this to Figure 12.6, where the series data is the regions. Here, you can compare one region to another. The overriding message here is about competition — which division performed the best in each quarter? It's easy to see how the same data can convey very different messages; make sure that you pick the arrangement that tells the story that you want to tell in your presentation.

Redefining the Data Range

After you have created your chart, you may decide that you need to use more or less data. Perhaps you want to exclude a month or quarter of data or to add another region or salesperson. To add or remove a data series, you can simply edit the datasheet. To do so, follow these steps:

1. **On the Chart Tools Design tab, click Edit Data.** The Excel datasheet appears. A blue outline appears around the range that is to be plotted, and other colors of outlines appear around the ranges containing the labels. The colors of those ranges vary depending on the chart type.

2. **(Optional) To change the data range to be plotted, drag the bottom-right corner of the blue outline.** For example, in Figure 12.7, the West division is being excluded.

   You can also enlarge the data range by expanding the blue outline. For example, you could enter another series in column E in Figure 12.7 and then extend the outline to encompass column E.

FIGURE 12.7

You can redefine the range for the chart by dragging the blue outline on the datasheet.

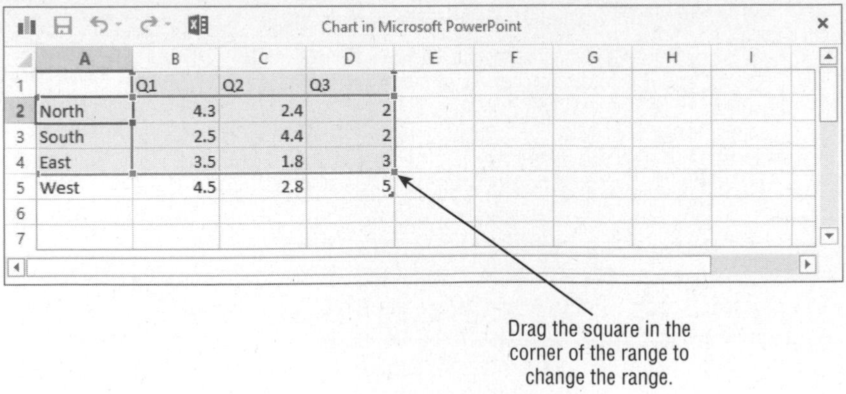

	A	B	C	D	E	F	G	H	I
1		Q1	Q2	Q3					
2	North	4.3	2.4	2					
3	South	2.5	4.4	2					
4	East	3.5	1.8	3					
5	West	4.5	2.8	5					
6									
7									

Chart in Microsoft PowerPoint

Drag the square in the corner of the range to change the range.

The preceding steps work well if the range that you want to include is contiguous, but what if you wanted to exclude a row or column that is in the middle of the range? To define the range more precisely, follow these steps:

1. **On the Chart Tools Design tab, click Select Data.** The Select Data Source dialog box opens, shown in Figure 12.8, along with the Excel datasheet if it was not already displayed.

FIGURE 12.8

To fine-tune the data ranges, you can use the Select Data Source dialog box.

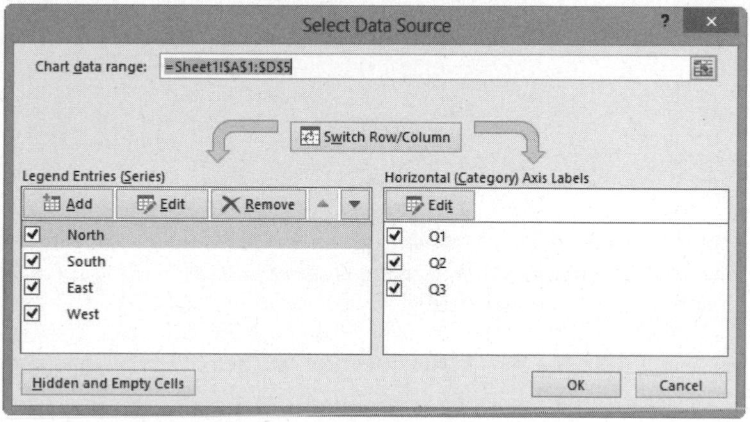

2. **Do any of the following:**
   - To remove a series, select it from the Legend Entries (Series) list and click Remove.
   - To add a series, click Add, and then drag across the range on the datasheet to enter it into the Edit Series dialog box; then click OK to accept it.
   - To edit a series, select it in the Legend Entries (Series) list and click Edit. Then drag across the range or make a change in the Edit Series dialog box, and click OK.

3. **(Optional) To redefine the range from which to pull the horizontal axis labels, click the Edit button in the Horizontal (Category) Axis Labels section.** A dotted outline appears around the current range; drag to redefine that range and click OK.

4. **(Optional) To redefine how empty or hidden cells should be treated, click the Hidden and Empty Cells button.** In the Hidden and Empty Cell Settings dialog box that appears, choose whether to show data in hidden rows and columns and whether to define empty cells as gaps in the chart or as zero values. Then click OK. The Hidden and Empty Cells Settings dialog box is shown in Figure 12.9.

FIGURE 12.9

Specify what should happen when the data range contains blank or hidden cells.

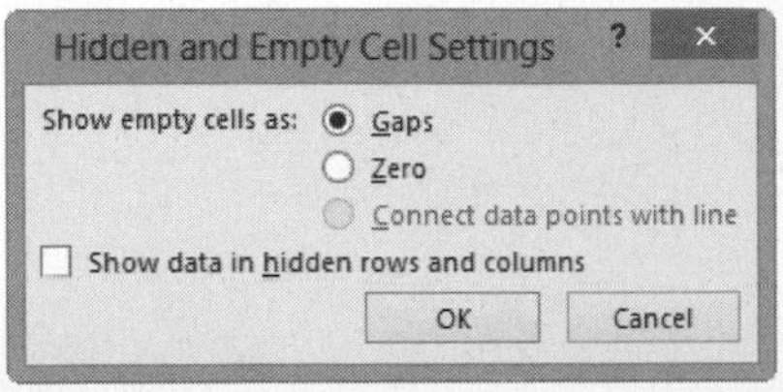

5. **When you are finished editing the settings for the data ranges, click OK to close the Select Data Source dialog box.**

6. **(Optional) Close the Excel datasheet window, or leave it open for later reference.**

Filtering the Chart Data

New in PowerPoint 2013, you can use the Chart Filters feature to quickly exclude certain rows or columns from the chart. When the chart is selected on the slide, a set of three icons appears to its right: Chart Elements, Chart Styles, and Chart Filters. If you click Chart Filters, a pop-up panel appears with check boxes for each of the series and categories, as shown in Figure 12.10. Clear the check box for anything you don't want to see on the chart, and then click Apply. The Select Data hyperlink at the bottom of the panel opens the Select Data Source dialog box, the same as in the previous section.

FIGURE 12.10

Turn off certain series or categories from this panel if desired.

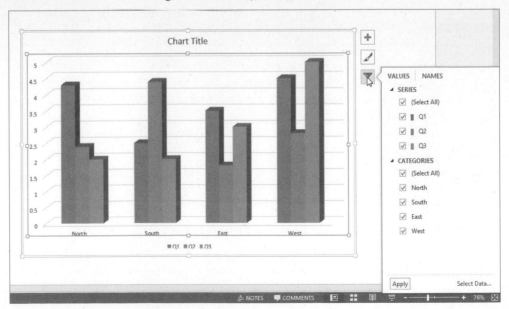

Chart Types and Chart Layout Presets

The default chart is a 2-D clustered column chart. However, there are a lot of alternative chart types to choose from. Not all of them will be appropriate for your data, of course, but you may be surprised at the different spin on the message that a different chart type presents.

> **CAUTION**
>
> Many chart types come in both 2-D and 3-D models, and you can choose which chart type looks most appropriate for your presentation. However, try to be consistent. For example, it looks nicer to stay with all 2-D or all 3-D charts rather than mixing the types in a presentation.

You can revisit your choice of chart type at any time by following these steps:

1. **Select the chart, if needed, so that the Chart Tools Design tab becomes available.**
2. **Click Chart Tools Design ⇨ Type ⇨ Change Chart Type.** The Change Chart Type dialog box opens. It looks just like the Insert Chart dialog box you saw in Figure 12.2.
3. **Select the desired type, just as you did when you originally created the chart.**
4. **Click OK.**

This is the basic procedure for the overall chart type selection, but there are also many options for fine-tuning the layout. The following sections explain these options.

> **TIP**
>
> To change the default chart type, right-click the icon for the desired subtype in the Change Chart Type dialog box and choose Set as Default Chart.

PowerPoint provides a limited number of preset Quick Layouts for each chart type. A layout is a combination of optional chart elements (such as legend, data table, data labels, and so on) in a particular arrangement. Quick Layouts are good starting points for creating your own layouts, which you will learn about in this chapter. To choose a Quick Layout, click Chart Tools Design ⇨ Chart Layouts ⇨ Quick Layouts and select a layout from the gallery, as shown in Figure 12.11. Although you cannot add your own layouts to these presets, you can create chart templates, which are basically the same thing with additional formatting settings. See "Working with Chart Templates" later in this chapter.

Working with Chart Elements

Charts are effective only if the audience understands what the data points represent. Labels and other descriptive elements on a chart can make all the difference in its usability. Figure 12.12 points out some of the various *chart elements* that you can use.

12

FIGURE 12.11

You can choose one of the preset Quick Layouts that fits your needs.

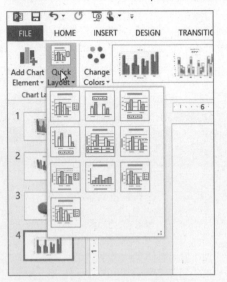

FIGURE 12.12

Chart elements such as labels help to make it clear to the audience what the chart represents.

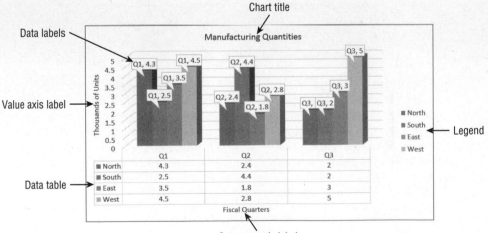

To change the setting for a particular element, choose Chart Tools Design ⇨ Chart Layouts ⇨ Add Chart Element to open a menu of elements. Then point at a particular element to see a fly-out menu with additional options on it. If none of the choices on the fly-out menu meet your needs, click More Options to open a task pane with a more extensive set of options. The exact name of the More Options command varies depending on the chart element; for example, for Chart Title, it is More Title Options. Figure 12.13 shows the fly-out menu for Chart Title.

FIGURE 12.13

Control individual chart elements from the Add Chart Element button's menu.

TIP

When working with a chart element such as data labels that could potentially affect the whole chart, a single data series, or a single data point, make sure you select the part of the chart you want to affect before issuing the command. For example, to apply data labels to all data points on the whole chart, select the outer frame of the chart first, or to add them only to a specific data series, select that data series first.

You can also quickly control chart elements with the Chart Elements button that appears to the right of the chart when the chart is selected. Mark or clear the check boxes in the Chart Elements panel to toggle a particular element on or off. For some elements, if you hover the mouse pointer over the option in the panel, a right-pointing triangle appears to its right. You can click that triangle for a submenu, as shown in Figure 12.14.

FIGURE 12.14

Click the Chart Elements icon to the right of a chart for quick access to chart elements.

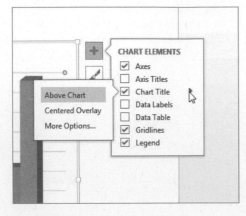

You can format the text in any of the chart elements just as you format any other text. To do this, select the text and then use the controls in the Font group on the Home tab. This allows you to choose a font, size, color, alignment, and so on. To format more than one chart element at a time, select one, and then hold down Ctrl as you click on other chart elements to select them also.

TIP

To quickly increase the size of all text in the chart, select the chart's outer frame, and then on the Home tab, in the Font group, click the Increase Font Size button repeatedly until all text is the desired size.

You can also format a chart element by right-clicking it and choosing Format *Name*, where *Name* is the type of element. For example, you could right-click the vertical axis title on the chart and then choose Format Axis Title. This opens a task pane with controls appropriate for the selected chart element. As with other task panes, there are section names in all caps at the top, and under the chosen selection name are icons that represent pages of options. Within a page of options are smaller uppercase headings indicating collapsible/expandable sections. Figure 12.15 shows an example.

NOTE

PowerPoint uses Format task panes that are related to the various parts of the chart. These task panes are *nonmodal*, which means that they can stay open indefinitely, that their changes are applied immediately, and that you don't have to close the task pane to continue working on the presentation.

FIGURE 12.15

Task pane options are organized as shown here.

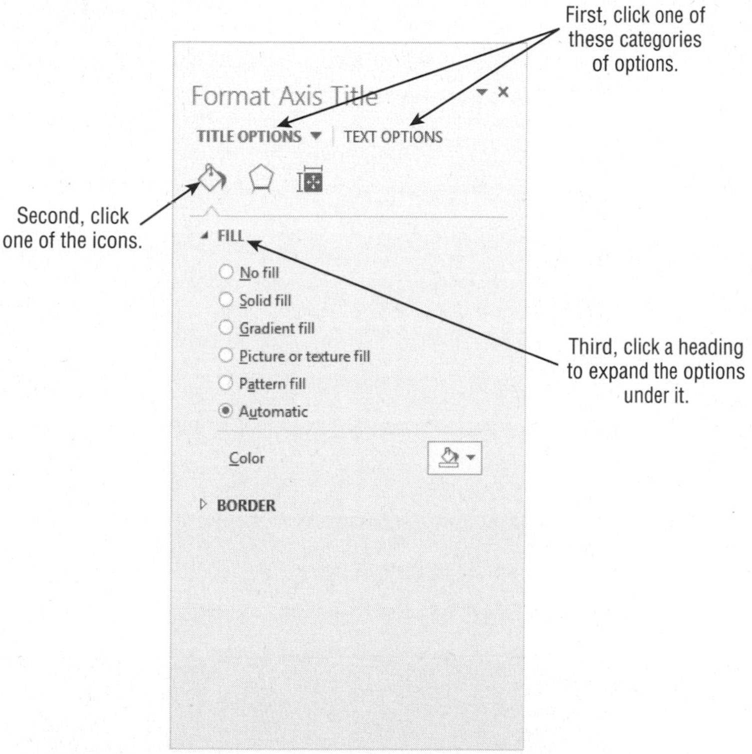

First, click one of these categories of options.

Second, click one of the icons.

Third, click a heading to expand the options under it.

Format Axis Title

TITLE OPTIONS ▾ | TEXT OPTIONS

◢ FILL
○ No fill
○ Solid fill
○ Gradient fill
○ Picture or texture fill
○ Pattern fill
◉ Automatic

Color

▷ BORDER

In some cases, the task pane contains only standard formatting controls that you would find for any object, such as Border, Fill, Shadow, Glow, Alignment, and so on. These controls should already be very familiar to you from Chapter 9, "Drawing and Formatting Objects." In other cases, in addition to the standard formatting types, there is also a unique section that contains extra options that are specific to the content type. For example, there is a Legend Options section in which you can set the position of a legend.

The following sections look at each of the chart elements more closely. These sections will not dwell on the basic formatting that you can apply to them (fonts, sizes, borders, fills, and so on) because this formatting is the same for all of them, as it is with any other object. Instead, they concentrate on the options that make each chart element different.

Working with Chart Titles

A *chart title* is text that typically appears above the chart — and sometimes overlapping it — and indicates what the chart represents. Although you would usually want either a chart title *or* a slide title, but not both, this could vary if you have multiple charts or different content on the same slide.

You can select a basic chart title, either above the chart or overlapping it, from the Chart Title submenu from the Add Chart Element button's menu, as shown in Figure 12.13. You can also drag the chart title around after placing it. For more options, you can choose More Title Options from the bottom of the submenu to open the Format Chart Title task pane. However, in this dialog box there is nothing that specifically relates to chart titles; the available options are for formatting (Fill, Border, and so on), as for any text box.

Working with Axis Titles

An *axis title* is text that defines the category or the unit of measurement on an axis. For example, in Figure 12.12, the vertical axis title is Thousands of Units.

Axis titles are defined separately for the vertical and the horizontal axes. Click Chart Tools Design ➪ Chart Layouts ➪ Add Chart Element ➪ Axis Titles and then select either Primary Horizontal or Primary Vertical to toggle one or the other on or off. Alternatively, you can click the Chart Elements button to the right of the chart frame and mark the Axis Titles check box to turn both of them on at once or point to the right-pointing arrow and then mark or clear the Primary Horizontal and Primary Vertical check boxes individually, as shown in Figure 12.16. When you turn on an axis title, a text box appears containing default place-holder text, "Axis Title." Click in this text box and type your own label to replace it.

> **CAUTION**
> If you turn off an axis title and then turn it back on again, you will need to retype the axis title; it returns to the generic placeholder text.

If you've plotted any data on a secondary axis, you'll see Secondary Horizontal and Secondary Vertical Axis Title options as well on the submenu.

FIGURE 12.16

Turn axis titles on or off from the Axis Titles submenu.

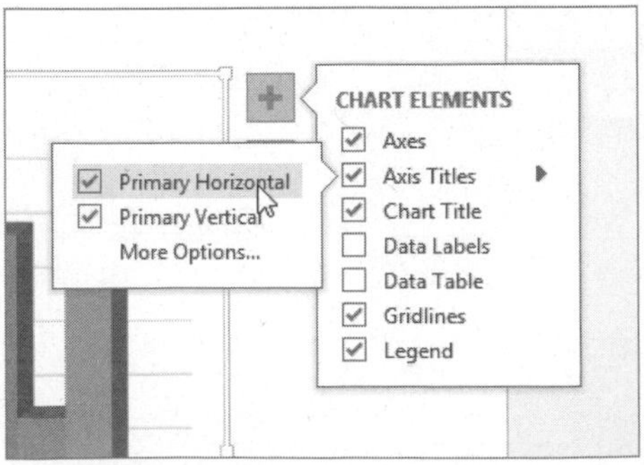

TIP
You can easily select all of the placeholder text by clicking in the text box and pressing Ctrl+A.

For more control, choose More Options from the submenu, or right-click the axis title and choose Format Axis Title, to open the Format Axis Title task pane.

Look back at Figure 12.12 and notice that the vertical axis title runs sideways from top to bottom. You can change the text's orientation for an axis by doing the following:

1. **Right-click the vertical axis title and choose Format Axis Title.** The Format Axis Title task pane opens.

2. **Click Title Options, and then click the Size & Properties icon.** The Alignment controls appear. See Figure 12.17.

FIGURE 12.17

Select a text direction from the task pane.

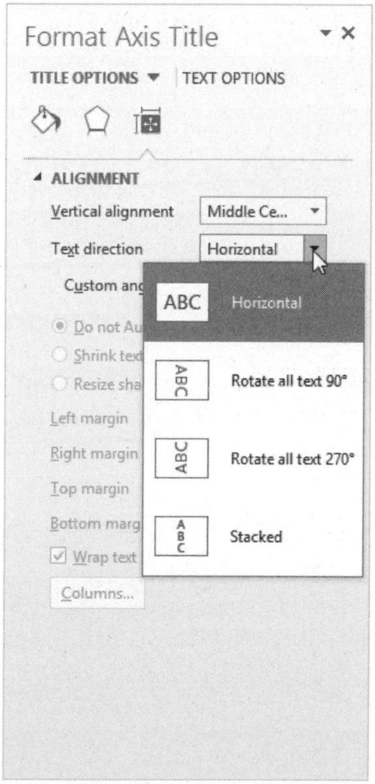

3. **Open the Text Direction drop-down list and choose the desired text direction.**

- **Horizontal.** The title appears horizontally, like regular text, to the left of the vertical axis.

- **Rotate All Text 90°.** The title appears vertically along the vertical axis, with the letters rotated 90 degrees (so that their bases run along the axis from top to bottom).

- **Rotate All Text 270°.** The title appears vertically along the vertical axis, with the letters rotated 270 degrees (so that their bases run along the axis from bottom to top).

- **Stacked.** The title appears vertically along the vertical axis, but each letter remains unrotated, so that the letters are stacked one on top of the other.

Figure 12.18 shows some examples.

FIGURE 12.18

Text direction examples. From left to right: Rotate All Text 270°, Stacked, and Horizontal.

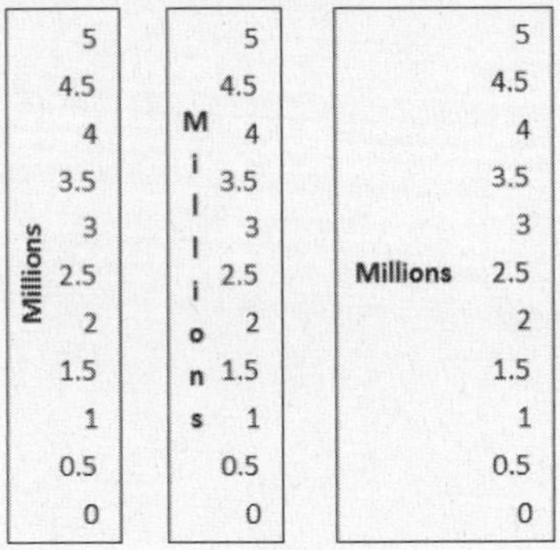

Each type of vertical axis shrinks the chart somewhat when you activate it, but the Horizontal option shrinks the chart more than the others because it requires more space to the left of the chart.

Working with Legends

The *legend* is the little box that appears next to the chart (or sometimes above or below it). It provides the key that describes what the different colors or patterns mean. For some chart types and labels, you may not find the legend to be useful. If it is not useful for the chart that you are working on, you can turn it off. To turn off the legend, you can do any of the following:

- Click the legend box to select it and press the Delete key on the keyboard.
- Click Chart Tools Design ➪ Chart Layouts ➪ Add Chart Element ➪ Legend ➪ None.

■ Click the Chart Elements button to the right of the chart, and in the Chart Elements panel, clear the Legend check box.

To turn the legend back on, click the Chart Elements button again and mark the Legend check box; this places the legend in the default position for that chart type. If you want to choose a different legend location, click Chart Tools Design ⇨ Chart Layouts ⇨ Add Chart Element ⇨ Legend and select the position that you want for it, as shown in Figure 12.19.

FIGURE 12.19

You can select a legend position, or turn the legend off altogether, from the Legend submenu.

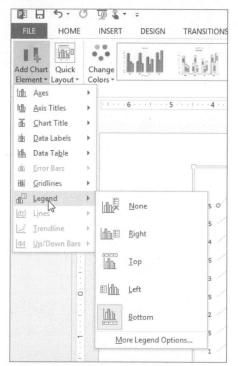

To resize a legend box, you can drag one of its selection handles. The text and keys inside the box do not change in size, although they may shift in position.

When you right-click the legend and choose Format Legend, or when you choose More Legend Options from the Legend submenu (see Figure 12.19), the Format Legend task pane opens with the Legend Options controls displayed, as shown in Figure 12.20. From here, you can choose the legend's position in relation to the chart and whether or not it should over-lap the chart. If it does not overlap the chart, the plot area will be automatically reduced to accommodate the legend.

FIGURE 12.20

You can set legend options in the Format Legend task pane.

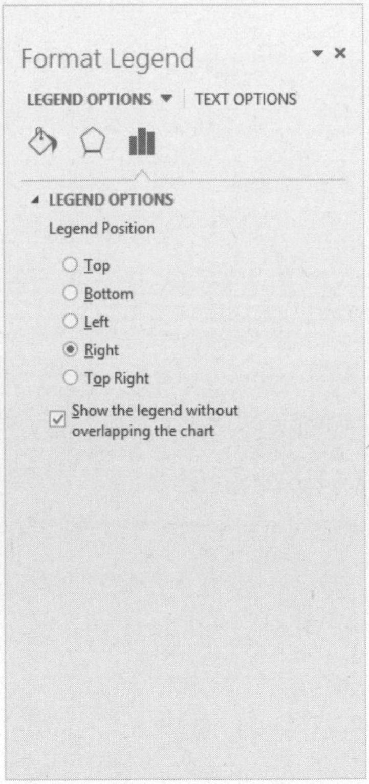

NOTE

The controls in the Legend Options section refer to the legend's position in relation to the chart, not to the orienta-tion or alignment of the legend text within the legend box.

Adding Data Labels

Data labels show the numeric values (or other information) that are represented by each bar or other shape on the chart. These labels are useful when the exact numbers are important or where the chart is so small that it is not clear from the axes what the data points represent.

To turn on data labels for the chart, do one of the following:

- Click the Chart Elements icon to the right of the chart, and in the panel that appears, mark the Data Labels check box. This method places plain black numeric labels on each data point, with a transparent background on the data label box and no border.
- Click Chart Tools Design ➪ Chart Layouts ➪ Add Chart Element ➪ Data Labels ➪ Data Callout. This method places white callout boxes for each data point, showing both the numeric value and the category name.

If you want additional options besides those two data label types, follow these steps:

1. **Select the data series or data point you want to affect.** To select a data series, click one of the bars (or other shapes) in the desired data series. To select a single data point, click again on the same bar (or shape).

> **NOTE**
>
> In a multiseries chart, only one series' data labels change at once when you make data label changes with the Format Data Label task pane. Make the changes you want to make to the first series, and then select the next data series in the chart (for example, the next color of bars on a column chart) and repeat the process.

2. **Choose Chart Tools Design ➪ Chart Layouts ➪ Add Chart Element ➪ Data Labels ➪ More Data Label Options to open the Format Data Labels task pane.**

   Make sure the Label Options heading is selected, and make sure the Label Options icon is selected. If needed, expand the Label Options controls under the icon, as shown in Figure 12.21. The options available depend on whether it's a 2-D or 3-D chart and on what type of chart it is. Figure 12.21 shows the options for a 3-D column chart.

3. **Mark or clear the check boxes for the types of label content under the Label Contains heading.** For example, you can show the series and/or category name, the value, and the legend key (the colored square that represents the series name).

4. **If you are working with a 2-D chart, choose a label position from the Label Options controls in the task pane.** A label can be on the center of the bar (or other shape), inside it, or outside it. This option does not appear when you're working with a 3-D chart.

FIGURE 12.21

Control data label options from the Format Data Labels task pane.

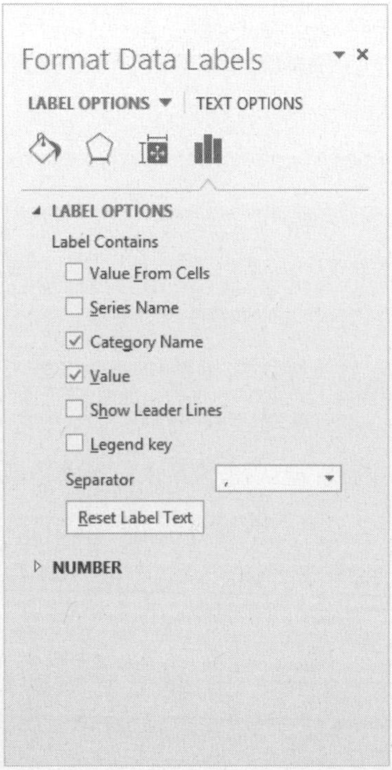

5. **To change the shape of the data label text box, right-click any of the data labels in the series and choose Change Data Label Shapes, and then click the desired shape.** See Figure 12.22.

6. **To change the fill of the data label text box, in the Format Data Labels task pane, click Label Options, and then click the Fill & Line icon and expand the Fill category to display the fill options.** To make the data label text boxes transparent, choose No Fill, or to apply some other fill color, select it as you would for any text box or drawn shape. See Figure 12.23.

Adding a Data Table

Sometimes the chart tells the full story that you want to tell, but other times the audience may benefit from seeing the actual numbers on which you have built the chart. In these cases, it is a good idea to include the data table with the chart. A data table contains the same information that appears on the datasheet.

To display the data table with a chart, click Chart Tools Design ➪ Chart Layouts ➪ Add Chart Element ➪ Data Table and choose to include a data table either with or without a legend key. See Figure 12.24.

FIGURE 12.22

Change the shape of the data label box if desired.

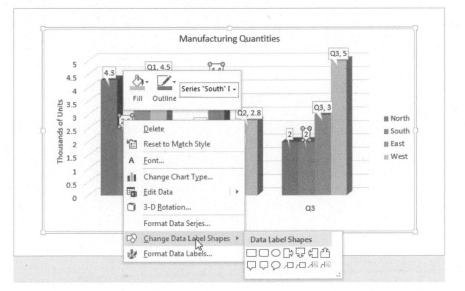

FIGURE 12.23

Change the background fill for the data label box if desired.

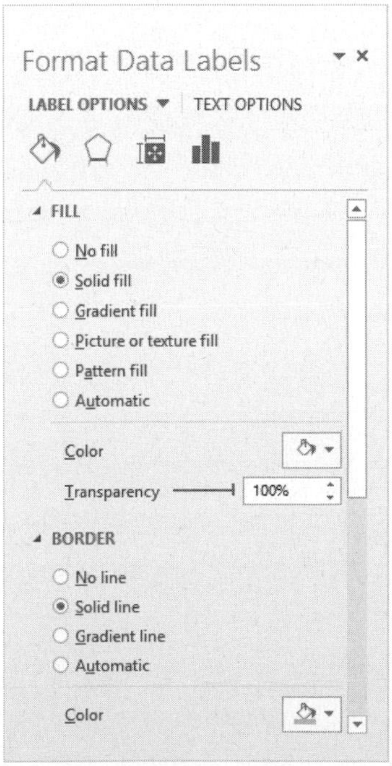

FIGURE 12.24

Use a data table to show the audience the numbers on which the chart is based.

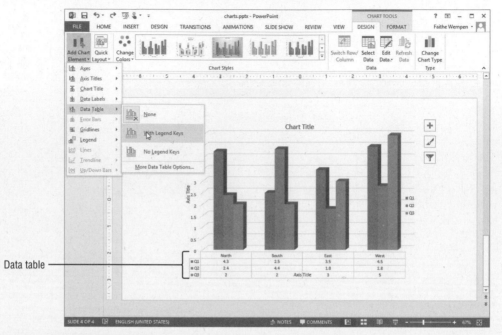

Data table

To format the data table, choose More Data Table Options from the Data Table submenu in Figure 12.24. In the Format Data Table task pane that appears, you can set data table border options, as shown in Figure 12.25. For example, you can display or hide the horizontal, vertical, and outline borders for the table from here.

Controlling the Axes

No, axes are not the tools that chop down trees. *Axes* is the plural of *axis*, and an axis is the side of the chart containing the measurements against which your data is plotted.

You can change the various axes in a chart in several ways. For example, you can make an axis run in a different direction (such as from top to bottom instead of bottom to top for a vertical axis), and you can turn the text on or off for the axis and change the axis scale.

Displaying or Hiding an Axis

Most of the time you will want to display all axes for a chart. However, in some special cases it may be appropriate to turn off an axis. To do so, click Chart Tools Design ⇨ Chart Layouts ⇨ Add Chart Element ⇨ Axes and then click Primary Horizontal or Primary Vertical to toggle either of those off (or back on again). See Figure 12.26.

FIGURE 12.25

Use the Data Table Options controls to specify which borders should appear in the data table.

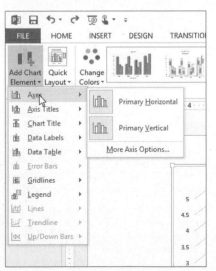

FIGURE 12.26

Turn axes off or on here.

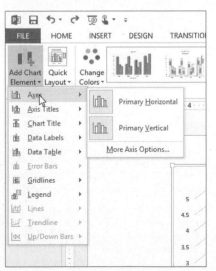

To control how an axis appears (other than just whether or not it appears at all), choose More Axis Options from the submenu. The options for axes are covered in the following sections.

Setting Axis Scale Options

The *scale* determines which numbers will form the start point and endpoint of the axis line. PowerPoint 2013 calls the scale the *bounds* of the axis because the minimum and maximum values on the scale define lower and upper boundaries for the axis.

Changing the axis scale can make a big difference in how an audience perceives the same data. For example, take a look at the chart in Figure 12.27. The bars are so close to one another in value that it is difficult to see the difference between them. Compare this chart to one showing the same data in Figure 12.28, but with an adjusted scale. Because the scale is smaller, the differences now appear more dramatic.

FIGURE 12.27

This chart does not show the differences between the values very well.

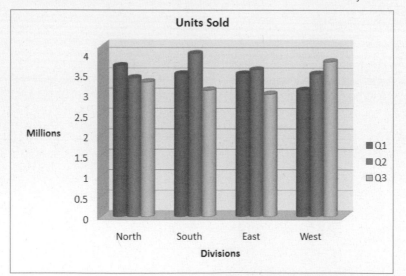

FIGURE 12.28

A change to the values of the axis scale makes it easier to see the differences between values.

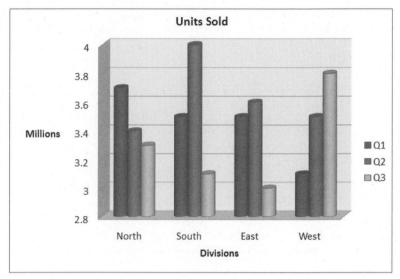

To set the scale (bounds) for an axis, follow these steps:

1. **Right-click the axis on the chart that contains the values you are plotting, and click Format Axis.** (This is typically the vertical axis on a column chart.)

   The Format Axis task pane appears, displaying the Axis Options, as shown in Figure 12.29.

2. **If you do not want the automatic value for one of the measurements, enter a different number in its text box under Bounds.** To change your mind and go back to automatic settings for these, click Auto next to the text box.

   - **Minimum** is the starting number. The usual setting is 0, as shown in Figure 12.27, although in Figure 12.28, it is set to 2.8.
   - **Maximum** is the top number. This number is 4 in both Figure 12.27 and Figure 12.28.

3. **If you want the units on the axis to display differently, change the values in their boxes under Units.** To change your mind and go back to automatic settings for these, click Auto next to the box.

   - **Major** determines the axis text. It is also the unit by which gridlines stretch out across the back wall of the chart. In Figure 12.27, gridlines appear at increments of 0.5 million units; in Figure 12.28, they appear by 0.2 million units.
   - **Minor** is the interval of smaller gridlines between the major ones. Most charts look better without minor units because they can make a chart look cluttered.

In most cases, you should leave this setting at Auto. You can also use this feature to place tick marks on the axes between the labels of the major units.

FIGURE 12.29

You can set axis options in the Format Axis task pane, including the axis scale (bounds).

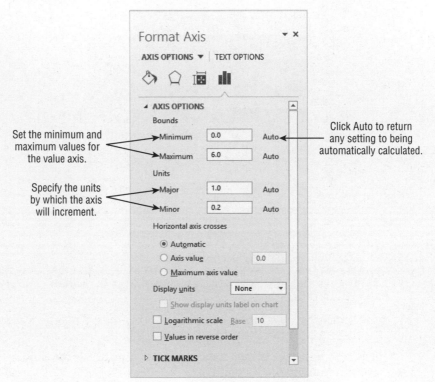

Set the minimum and maximum values for the value axis.

Specify the units by which the axis will increment.

Click Auto to return any setting to being automatically calculated.

4. **(Optional) If you want to change where the axes cross, select Axis Value in the Horizontal Axis Crosses section, and then enter a numeric value in its box.** Changing this value recalculates the numbers in the Bounds and Units sections that are set to Auto.

5. **(Optional) If you want to activate any of these special features, select their check boxes.**

   ■ **Logarithmic Scale.** Rarely used by ordinary folks, this check box recalculates the Minimum, Maximum, Major, and Minor values according to a power of 10 for the value axis, based on the range of data. (If this explanation doesn't make any sense to you, then you're not the target audience for this feature.)

   ■ **Values in Reverse Order.** This check box turns the scale backward so that the greater values appear at the bottom or left.

6. **(Optional) Choose a display unit from the Display Units drop-down list.** This option can help simplify large numbers. For example, if you set display units to Thousands, then the number 1000 appears as 1 on the chart. If you then select the Show Display Units Label on Chart check box, an axis label will appear as Thousands.

7. **(Optional) Expand the Tick Marks section below the axis options, and set tick-mark types for major and minor marks (see Figure 12.30).** These marks appear as little lines on the axis to indicate the units. You can use tick marks either with or without gridlines.

FIGURE 12.30

You can choose what tick marks to use, if any.

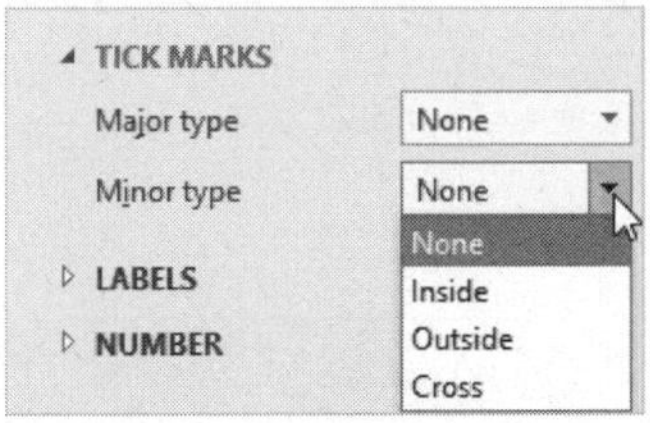

8. **Close the task pane when finished.**

Setting a Number Format

You can apply a number format to axes and data labels that show numeric data. This is similar to the number format that is used for Excel cells; you can choose a category, such as Currency or Percentage, and then fine-tune this format by choosing a number of decimal places, a method of handling negative numbers, and so on.

To set a number format, follow these steps:

1. **Right-click the axis containing the numbers you want to format, and choose Format Axis.**

2. **In the Format Axis task pane that appears, click the Axis Options text at the top, and then click the Axis Options icon.**

3. **Expand the Number section if it is not already expanded.** (Collapse any previously open sections for easier reading.)

4. **Choose a number format.** You can select the number format in either of two ways:

   ■ Select the Linked to Source check box if you want the number format to be taken from the number format that is applied to the datasheet in Excel. If you use this method, you don't have to complete the rest of the steps here.

   ■ Click the desired number format in the Category list. Options appear that are specific to the format that you selected. For example, Figure 12.31 shows the options for the Number type of format, which is a generic format.

FIGURE 12.31

Select a number format in the Format Axis task pane.

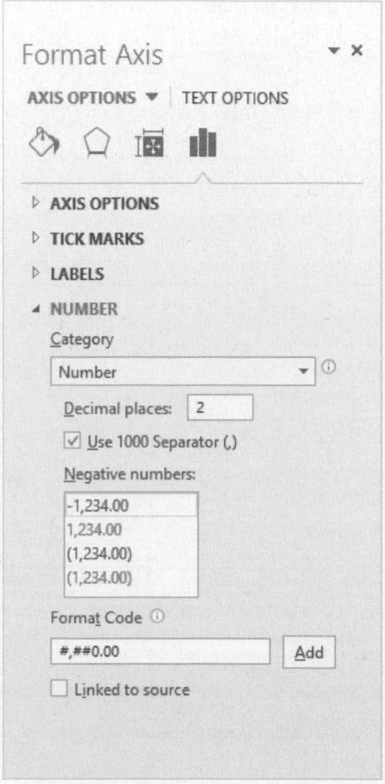

5. **(Optional) Fine-tune the numbering format by changing the code in the Format Code text box.** The number signs (#) represent optional digits, while the zeroes represent required digits.

6. **Close the task pane.**

> **NOTE**
> To see some examples of custom number formats that you might use in the Format Code text box, choose Custom as the number format category.

Formatting a Chart

In the following sections, you learn about chart formatting. There is so much that you can do to a chart that this subject could easily take up its own chapter! For example, just as with any other object, you can resize a chart. You can also change the fonts; change the colors and shading of bars, lines, or pie slices; use different background colors; change the 3-D angle; and much more.

> **NOTE**
>
> To clear the formatting that is applied to a chart element, select it and then click Chart Tools Format ⇨ Current Selection ⇨ Reset to Match Style. This strips off the manually applied formatting from that element, returning it to whatever appearance is specified by the chart style that you have applied. (See "Applying Chart Styles" later in this chapter for details about styles.)

There are several ways of formatting a chart's elements. For text elements, you can use the Font group's tools on the Home tab. The text elements on a chart use the exact same text formatting controls as any other text on a slide. You can change the font, the size, the text attributes (like bold and italic), and so on. PowerPoint treats the individual text boxes within the chart as it would treat any other text boxes.

For simple formatting of a graphical element, like changing its outline or fill color, your best bet is the Chart Tools Format tab's controls. You can select any chart element and then choose its border and fill color from here. For example, in Figure 12.32, Vertical (Value) Axis Major Gridlines is selected, which you can see in the selection box at the far left end of the Ribbon. You could use the Shape Outline drop-down list at this point to choose a different color or thickness for the gridlines.

FIGURE 12.32

Format a chart element's outline and fill quickly and easily from the Chart Tools Format tab.

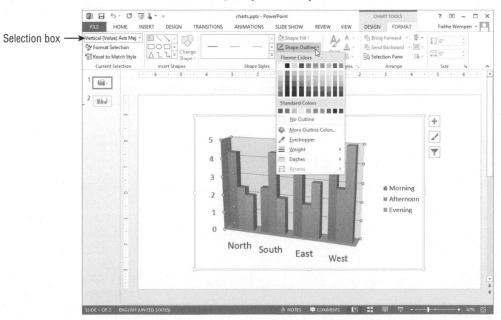

For more extensive or uncommon formatting, use the task pane instead. You can open the task pane for the selected chart element by right-clicking it and choosing Format *Element Name* from the submenu, or by choosing Chart Tools Format ➪ Current Selection ➪ Format Selection.

> **TIP**
>
> Sometimes it can be difficult to position the mouse accurately to right-click on a particular chart element. If you have trouble selecting the chart element you want to work with, open the drop-down list in the Current Selection group of the Chart Tools Format tab and choose the desired chart element. Then to open its task pane, click Format Selection, also in the Current Selection group.

The sections in the task pane vary, depending on the type of chart element you are formatting. There are generally two main sections, indicated by words at the top of the task pane. For example, in the Format Chart Title task pane, the two main sections are Title Options and Text Options. Beneath these main section headings are a series of icons. The icons are different depending on the main section that's active. For example, in Figure 12.33, with Title Options selected, the three icons that appear are Fill & Line, Effects, and Size & Properties. In Figure 12.34, with Text Options selected, the icons that appear are Text Fill & Outline, Text Effects, and Textbox. This is an example of just one task pane; each chart element type has its own unique combination of options in its task pane.

FIGURE 12.33

When Title Options is selected for a chart title, these are the icons available.

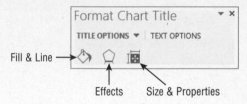

FIGURE 12.34

When Text Options is selected for a chart title, these are the icons available.

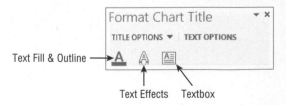

For most chart elements, the following sections are available from the Fill & Line icon:

- **Fill.** You can choose No Fill, Solid Fill, Gradient Fill, Picture or Texture Fill, Pattern Fill, or Automatic. When you select Automatic, the color changes to contrast with the background color specified by the theme.

- **Border.** You can choose No Line, Solid Line, Gradient Line, or Automatic. When you select Automatic, the color changes to contrast with the background color specified by the theme. You can also set a width, a compound type (that is, a line made up of multiple lines), and a dash type.

Most chart elements include these choices with the Effects icon:

- **Shadow.** You can apply a preset shadow in any color you want, or you can fine-tune the shadow in terms of transparency, size, angle, and so on. You might need to apply a fill to the box in order for the shadow to appear. This shadow is for the text box, not for the text within it; use the Font group on the Home tab to apply the text shadow, or use the shadows available for WordArt.

- **Glow.** These options add a colored halo effect around the element. You can choose a preset or select a color, size, and amount of transparency yourself.

- **Soft Edges.** These options blur the edges of the element. You can choose a preset or specify a precise size of the soft edge.

- **3-D Format.** You can define 3-D settings for the text box, such as Bevel, Depth, Contour, and Surface.

Depending on the chart element selected, the third icon may be Size & Properties, as in Figure 12.33, or something else. For example, for legends, it is Legend Options. Some elements may even have a fourth icon. For example, for data labels, there is both a Size & Position icon and a Label Options icon. If the selected element has a Size & Position icon, you can use its controls to set vertical and horizontal alignment, angle, and text direction as well as control AutoFit settings for some types of text.

> **NOTE**
> Alignment is usually not relevant in a short label or title text box. The text box is usually exactly the right size to hold the text, and so there is no other way for the text to be aligned. Therefore, no matter what alignment you choose, the text looks very much the same.

From the Home tab or the mini toolbar, you can also choose all of the text effects that you learned about earlier in this book, such as font, size, font style, underline, color, alignment, and so on.

Applying Chart Styles

Chart styles are presets that you can apply to charts in order to add colors, backgrounds, and fill styles. The Chart Styles gallery, shown in Figure 12.35, is located on the Chart Tools

Design tab, which appears when you select a chart. Point to a sample in the gallery to see its style previewed on the chart.

FIGURE 12.35

You can apply a chart style using the Chart Styles gallery.

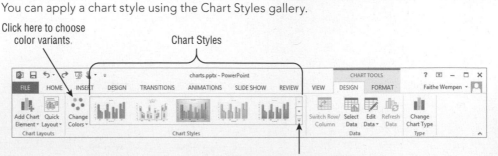

Click here to choose color variants.

Chart Styles

Click here to open the full gallery.

If you used PowerPoint 2010, it might seem at first glance that there are fewer chart styles in PowerPoint 2013. However, this is an illusion because in PowerPoint 2010, the different color variations were included in the Chart Style gallery as separate entities. By separating the color choices from the style choices, PowerPoint 2013 actually provides more choices and more flexibility.

Each of the chart styles uses whatever colors are assigned to the placeholders in your current color theme for the presentation. You can change the colors for the chart only, without having to change the colors for the whole presentation, by clicking the Change Colors button to the left of the Chart Styles gallery. However, the colors on the Change Colors button's menu are indirectly related to the color theme in use for the whole presentation; they are various tints and shades of the theme colors, in various combinations. To change colors completely, you must change the whole presentation's colors, as you learned to do in Chapter 4, "Working with Layouts, Themes, and Masters."

> **NOTE**
> You cannot add to the presets in the Chart Styles gallery, but you can save a group of settings as a template. To do this, right-click the chart's outer frame and choose Save as Template.

New in PowerPoint 2013, you can also apply chart styles via the Chart Styles icon that appears to the right of the chart when it is selected on the slide. Click the Chart Styles icon, as shown in Figure 12.36, and then click the desired style. You can click Color at the top of the panel to select colors from there also, as you would from the Change Colors button on the Chart Tools Design tab.

FIGURE 12.36

Click the Chart Styles icon to the right of the chart to quickly apply a different style or color.

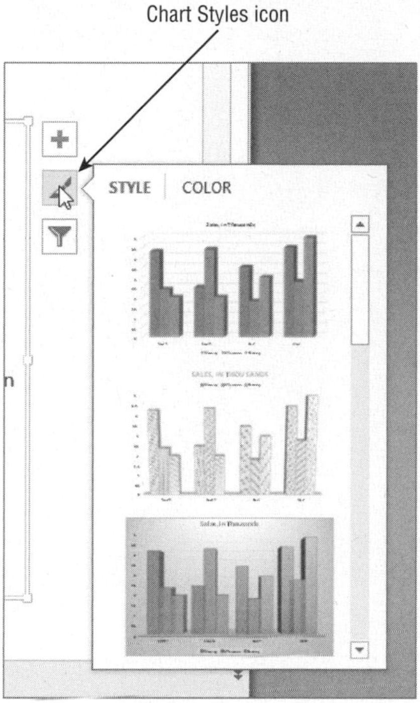

Chart Styles icon

Formatting the Chart Area and Plot Area

The *chart area* is the entire chart, everything within the big frame that contains the plotted data and all the associated elements: the legend, the data series, the data table, the titles, and so on. Right-click anywhere within the chart area (not on any specific element) and choose Format Chart Area to open the Format Chart Area task pane.

The Format Chart Area task pane has many of the same sections the task pane for text boxes has. Under Chart Options you'll find Fill & Line, Effects, and Size & Properties. Under Text Options are Text Fill & Outline, Text Effects, and Textbox. Any settings you apply to the chart area will apply to all the text and objects within the chart area unless a specific chart element is formatted differently to override that.

The *plot area* is the part of the chart where the data is plotted. It includes the data series and axes as well as any data labels, but it excludes the axis titles, the chart title, and the legend. You can choose to format the plot area differently from the chart area if you like, although it's not common to do so. For example, you could apply a different background fill color to the plot area, as in Figure 12.37. By default the plot area's background is transparent, so the background of the chart area shows through. If, in turn, the chart area is also transparent, then the background of the slide behind them both shows through.

FIGURE 12.37

The plot area has a different fill color than the chart area in this example.

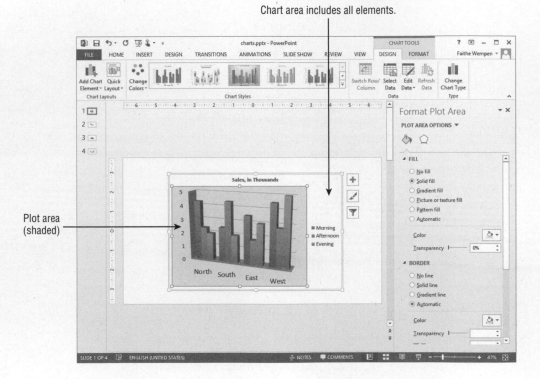

Chart area includes all elements.

Plot area (shaded)

Formatting the Legend

When you use a multiseries chart, the value of the legend is obvious — it tells you which colors represent which series. Without the legend, your audience will not know what the various bars or lines mean. You can do all of the same formatting for a legend that you can for other chart elements. Just right-click the legend, choose Format Legend from the shortcut menu, and then use the Format Legend task pane to make your modifications. For example, you could apply a background fill to the legend box, place a border around it, and so on. You could also change the font and size used for the legend text from the Fonts group on the Home tab.

Formatting Gridlines and Walls

Gridlines help the reader's eyes move across the chart. Gridlines are related to the axes, which you learned about earlier in this chapter. Although both vertical and horizontal gridlines are available, most people use only horizontal ones. To turn gridlines on or off, click Chart Tools Design ⇨ Chart Layouts ⇨ Add Chart Element ⇨ Gridlines. See Figure 12.38.

FIGURE 12.38

Turn gridlines on and off from the Add Chart Element button's menu.

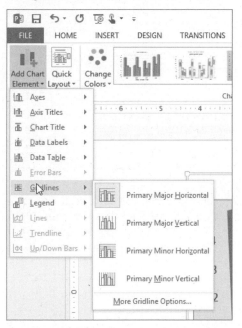

In most cases, the default gridlines that PowerPoint adds work well. However, you may want to make the lines thicker or a different color. Apply those changes by selecting the gridlines and then using the Chart Tools Format tab's commands. You can select one of the Shape Styles from there, or use the Shape Outline and/or Shape Effects drop-down lists to apply formatting.

Walls are nothing more than the space between the gridlines, formatted in a different color than the plot area. You can set the walls' fill to None to hide them. To set the wall color, right-click the wall and choose Format Wall, and then choose a fill color in the Format Wall task pane.

Formatting the Data Series

To format a data series, just right-click the bar, slice, or chart element, and choose Format Data Series from the shortcut menu. Then, depending on your chart type, different series options appear that you can use to modify the series appearance. Here are the icons available for bar and column charts, for example:

- **Fill & Line.** These options enable you to choose a fill and a border for the series, with choices for fill including solid, gradient, or picture/texture. Under Border you can choose a border color, style, and thickness. This is just like filling drawn shapes, as you learned in Chapter 9.

- **Effects.** These options include the same standard options available for any drawn object, including Shadow, Glow, Soft Edges, and 3-D Format.

- **Series Options.** This section contains options that are specific to the selected chart type. For example, when you're working with a 3-D bar or column chart, the series options include Gap Depth and Gap Width, which determine the thickness and depth of the bars. For a pie chart, you can set the rotation angle for the first slice as well as whether a slice is "exploded" or not. For charts involving bars and columns, you can choose a shape option such as Box, Full Pyramid, Partial Pyramid, Cylinder, Full Cone, or Partial Cone. The partial options truncate the top part of the shape when it is less than the largest value in the chart.

Other chart types have very different series options available. For example, a line chart has Marker Options, Marker Fill, Line Color, Line Style, Marker Line Color, and Marker Line Style.

Rotating a 3-D Chart

3-D charts can be rotated in one or more directions: X (side to side), Y (top to bottom), and Perspective (the angle from which you view it). There is also a Z rotation (pivoting around a center point), but it is inactive for most chart types.

The Right Angle Axes check box (in the Format Plot Area task pane) is very important when setting chart rotation for most chart types. If the Right Angle Axes option is enabled, the chart axes do not rotate — only the data bars (or other shapes) rotate. If Right Angle Axes is disabled, the entire content of the plot area rotates together as a whole, including the axes. Figure 12.39 shows a rotated chart where Right Angle Axes is turned off, and Figure 12.40 shows a rotated chart where it is turned on.

FIGURE 12.39

Right Angle Axes is disabled, and both X Rotation and Y Rotation are set to 30°.

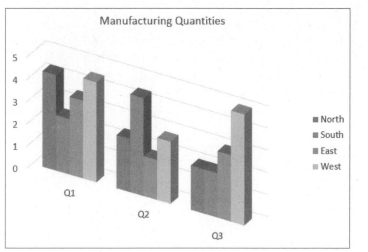

FIGURE 12.40

Right Angle Axes is enabled, and both X Rotation and Y Rotation are set to 30°.

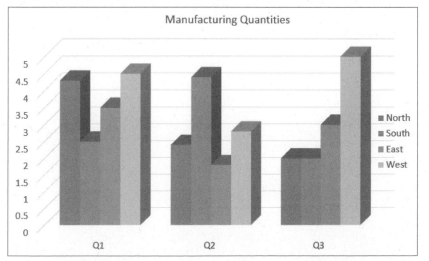

415

To set a chart's rotation, follow these steps:

1. **Select the chart's plot area.** You can do this by clicking it, or by displaying the Chart Tools Format tab and selecting Plot Area from the drop-down list in the Current Selection group.

2. **Display the Format Plot Area task pane.** You can do this by right-clicking the plot area and choosing Format Plot Area, or by clicking Chart Tools Format ⇨ Current Selection ⇨ Format Selection.

3. **In the Format Plot Area task pane, click the Effects icon, and then expand the 3-D Rotation controls.**

4. **Mark or clear the Right Angle Axes check box as desired, depending on how you want the chart to appear.** If the feature is off, the whole plot area rotates, including the axes; if the feature is on, only the data series rotate.

5. **Click the increment buttons to increase or decrease the X Rotation, Y Rotation, and/or Perspective settings as desired.** You may need to experiment with these to find the settings that show your chart the way you want it. See Figure 12.41.

FIGURE 12.41

Set the 3-D Rotation options for the chart in its Format Plot Area task pane.

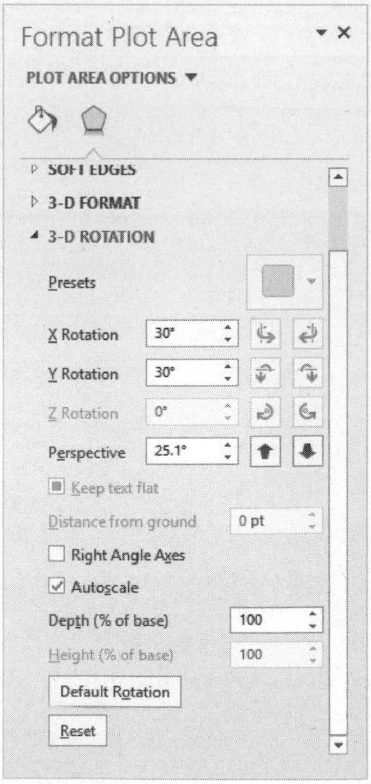

6. **Close the task pane when you are finished working with the chart's rotation.**

Working with Chart Templates

After you have formatted a chart the way you want it, you can save it as a template. You can then apply these same formatting options to other charts at a later time.

Creating a Chart Template

To create a chart template, follow these steps:

1. **Select a chart that is formatted exactly the way you want the template to be.** If you want the template to use theme colors, use them in the chart; if you want the template to use fixed colors, apply them instead.

2. **Right-click the chart and click Save as Template.** The Save Chart Template dialog box opens.

3. **Type a name for the template.**

4. **Click Save.**

> **NOTE**
> By default, chart templates are stored in `C:\Users\`*`username`*`\AppData\Roaming\Microsoft\Template\Charts`, with a `.crtx` (Chart Template) filename extension. You can copy templates from another PC and store them in that location and they will show up on your list of chart templates on the current PC.

Applying a Chart Template

To apply a chart template to an existing chart, follow these steps:

1. **Select the chart, and on the Chart Tools Design tab, click Change Chart Type.**

   You can also right-click the chart and choose Change Chart Type.

2. **At the top of the list of categories, click Templates.** PowerPoint displays all of the custom templates that you have created.

3. **Click the template that you want to use.**

4. **Click OK.**

To apply a chart template to a new chart as you are creating it, after choosing Insert ⇨ Chart, choose Templates as the chart type, and select the desired template.

Managing Template Files

Chart template files remain on your hard disk until you delete them. If you want to get rid of a chart template, or rename it, you can do so by opening the folder location that contains the templates. Although you can manually browse to the location (`C:\Users\`*username*`\AppData\Roaming\Microsoft\Template\Charts`), this is an easier way:

1. **On the Insert tab, click Chart.**
2. **In the Insert Chart dialog box, click Templates, and then click Manage Templates.** The folder location opens in a File Explorer window. From here, you can rename or delete files.

Summary

In this chapter, you learned how to create and format charts using PowerPoint. You learned how to create charts, change their type and their data range, and use optional text elements on them such as titles, data labels, and so on. You also learned how to format charts and how to save formatting in chart templates. In the next chapter, you learn how to incorporate data from other sources, including programs that do not necessarily have anything to do with PowerPoint or Office.

Incorporating Content from Other Programs

IN THIS CHAPTER

Working with external content: An overview

Copying content from other programs

Introducing OLE

Working with linked and embedded objects

Exporting PowerPoint objects to other programs

A s you have already seen, PowerPoint contains an assortment of tools for creating various types of objects: charts, WordArt, SmartArt diagrams, clip art, and so on. You have also learned how to place graphics into PowerPoint from a saved file, how to embed Excel charts on slides, and how to borrow slides from other PowerPoint presentations and outlines from Word or other text editors.

However, PowerPoint doesn't have a special command for bringing in a lot of other objects that don't fall exactly into any of these categories. Examples include a flow chart from a program like Microsoft Visio, a slide from a different presentation application, some records from a database, and a map from a mapping program.

This chapter looks at the various ways to import and create content from other applications in PowerPoint as well as how to export PowerPoint objects for use in other programs.

Working with External Content: An Overview

There are several ways to bring content from other programs into your presentation. The method you choose depends on how you want the content to behave once it arrives. You can make the inserted content a full citizen of the presentation — that is, with no ties to its native application or data file — or you can help it retain a connection to its original application (called *embedding*) or to its original data file (called *linking*).

The simplest way to import content into PowerPoint is to use the Copy and Paste commands. For text-type data from most applications, this results in the incoming data integrating itself with PowerPoint without retaining any connection to the source. For example, you can select some cells from an Excel worksheet and then click Copy on the Home tab to copy them to the Clipboard. Then in PowerPoint, you can paste them by clicking Paste and the Excel cells become a PowerPoint table. You can also do the same thing by dragging and dropping from one application to the other.

> **CAUTION**
>
> Not all data types exhibit the behavior described here. With some source data types, especially types that are more graphical than text based, copying and pasting results in an embedded object that will open its native application for editing. For example, when you copy and paste a chart from Excel, it is by default linked.

Another choice is to *embed* the data. You can do this for existing or new data. Embedding it maintains the relationship between the data and its native application, so that you can double-click it to edit it with that native application later. To embed existing data, you copy the data to the Clipboard, use the Paste button's menu to select Paste Special, and then choose the appropriate data type from the list. For example, suppose you want to be able to edit the pasted cells in Excel later. You can use Paste Special and choose Microsoft Excel Worksheet Object as the type. (More on this shortly.)

To embed new data, you use the Object button on the Insert tab and then choose to create a new embedded object of the desired type. (More on this shortly, too.) For example, suppose you have a favorite program for creating organization charts. You can start a new embedded organization chart on a PowerPoint slide instead of using PowerPoint's own SmartArt hierarchy chart. That organization chart is then stored only within your PowerPoint file, not separately.

Yet another choice is to link the data from its original source file. When you do this, PowerPoint maintains information about the name and location of the original, and each time you open the presentation file it rechecks the original data file to see if any changes have been made to it. If so, PowerPoint updates its copy of the object to the latest version. For example, suppose you want to include data from an Excel workbook that a coworker is creating. Your coworker warns you that the data is not final yet, but you want to create the presentation anyway. By creating a link to the data, rather than pasting a static copy of it, you ensure that you will always have the latest data no matter how many times your coworker changes it.

You can create a link to an entire file or to a specific part of a file. For example, you can link to the entire Excel workbook or just to a certain range of cells on a certain sheet. The procedures are different — for the entire file you use Object (Insert tab), but for a portion of the file you use Paste Special (Home tab). Both methods create a link to the entire Excel workbook, but Object automatically displays the entire first sheet of the workbook in your PowerPoint file, whereas Paste Special displays only the cells that you've selected.

Copying Content from Other Programs

Let's assume for the moment that you don't need any special linking or embedding. You just want the content from some other program to be placed on a PowerPoint slide. You have two choices: Use the Clipboard, or drag and drop the content from the other program to PowerPoint.

Using the Clipboard

The easiest way to place something into PowerPoint is to use the Windows Clipboard. Because almost all Windows-based programs employ the Clipboard, you can move data from any program to almost any other with a minimum of fuss. Follow these steps:

1. **Create the data in its native program or open a file that contains it.**
2. **Select the data you want, and click Copy on the Home tab, or if it is not an Office program, choose Edit ⇨ Copy.**
3. **Switch to PowerPoint, and display the slide on which you want to place the content.**
4. **Click Paste on the Home tab.** The content appears on the slide. PowerPoint makes its best guess as to the correct formatting. For example, if you paste Excel worksheet cells, it attempts to convert them to a table because that's the closest match among the native PowerPoint layouts.
5. **Move or resize the new content as necessary on the slide.**

> **NOTE**
> Don't forget that there are many alternative methods for using the Copy and Paste commands. The shortcut keys are among the fastest: Ctrl+C for copy and Ctrl+V for paste.

PowerPoint, like all Office 2013 applications, has an enhanced version of the Clipboard that is available when both the source and destination locations are Microsoft Office applications. It enables you to copy more than one item at a time to the Clipboard and then choose among them when pasting. When pasting to a non-Office application, however, only the last item copied to the Clipboard is available.

When you copy twice in a row without pasting while in an Office application, the Clipboard task pane appears, with each copied clip separately listed. You can also open this Clipboard task pane by clicking the dialog box launcher in the Clipboard group on the Home tab.

> **TIP**
> If pressing Ctrl+C twice doesn't open the Clipboard, open the task pane the other way (by clicking the dialog box launcher in the Clipboard group on the Home tab), and then click the Options button and click Show Office Clipboard When Ctrl+C Is Pressed Twice.

13

You can then open the destination and click the clip you want to paste. Or you can click the down arrow next to a clip and choose Delete to delete it. See Figure 13.1.

FIGURE 13.1

Using the Office 2013 Clipboard task pane enables you to copy more than one clip to the Clipboard.

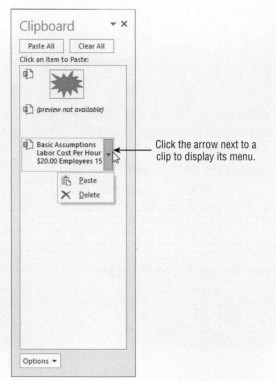

Click the arrow next to a clip to display its menu.

You can fine-tune the way the Clipboard works in Office 2013 applications by clicking the Options button at the bottom of the Clipboard task pane. This opens a menu from which you can specify when and how the Clipboard task pane appears. For example, you can set it to show a Clipboard icon in the taskbar. See Figure 13.2.

As mentioned earlier, when you are copying and pasting some types of content, especially graphical types, PowerPoint embeds the content by default rather than simply pasting it.

Embedding the content tends to increase the size of the PowerPoint presentation file, so avoid doing it unless you think you will need that capability. (More on embedding later in the chapter.) You can tell whether content has been embedded by double-clicking it. If it's embedded, its native application will open within PowerPoint (or in a separate window). If it's not embedded, a PowerPoint dialog box will open for the content. To avoid embedding content that PowerPoint wants to embed by default, follow these steps:

1. **Copy the data to the Clipboard in its native application.**
2. **In PowerPoint, on the Home tab, open the Paste button's menu and click Paste Special.**
3. **Choose a different format for the paste, such as Bitmap.** Do not choose the format that ends with the word *Object* or you will get an embedded copy.
4. **Click OK.**

FIGURE 13.2

Click Options to configure the Clipboard's behavior.

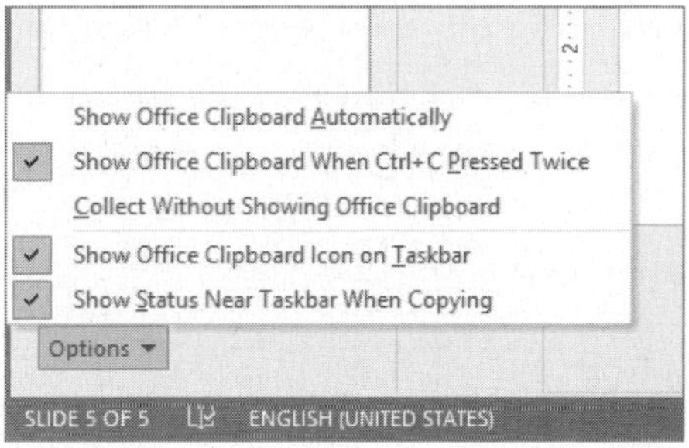

Alternatively, you can use one of the icons at the bottom of the Paste Special menu to quickly choose a specific type of paste operation. See Figure 13.3. For example, you can choose to keep the source formatting, use the destination theme, paste as a picture, or paste as plain text.

FIGURE 13.3

Use the buttons on the Paste Special menu to choose how a paste should occur.

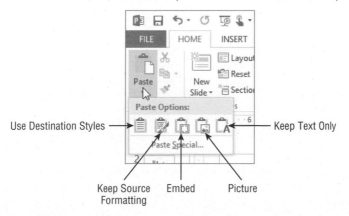

423

Using the Drag-and-Drop Feature

In some cases, you can also use the drag-and-drop feature to move an object from some other application (or from a file management window) to PowerPoint. Not all Windows programs support this feature though. If you're not sure whether a program supports it, try it and see. Here's how to drag and drop something:

1. **Create the object in its native program or open the file that contains it.** The object can be a single unit such as an entire graphic, or it can be a small piece of a larger document or image such as a few cells selected from a large worksheet.

2. **Open PowerPoint and display the slide on which you want to place the data.**

3. **Resize both applications' windows so that both the data and its destination are visible on-screen.**

4. **Select the data in its native program.**

5. **If you want to copy, rather than move, hold down the Ctrl key.**

6. **Drag the content to the PowerPoint slide.** An outline appears on the PowerPoint slide showing where the data will go.

7. **Release the mouse button.** The data is moved or copied.

> **CAUTION**
>
> When you're dragging and dropping data from Excel, it arrives in PowerPoint in a plain text box, with columns and rows separated by spaces. If you want to retain the original tabular format from Excel, use the copy-and-paste feature, not the drag-and-drop feature.

As with copying and pasting, not all content gets the "plain paste" treatment when you drag and drop. Generally speaking, text-based data will drag without embedding, but graphical-based data will usually embed. (There are exceptions.) Use the Paste Special method described earlier rather than dragging and dropping if you run into this situation.

Inserting Graphics from a File

When you copy and paste or drag and drop to insert content from a graphical-based application, as mentioned in the preceding section, PowerPoint embeds by default. This makes the file size larger than necessary for the PowerPoint presentation, however, so it's better to use the Pictures button (Insert tab) when you insert graphics. This inserts a plain old copy of the picture, without embedding, and keeps the PowerPoint file size more manageable.

Introducing OLE

The abbreviation *OLE* stands for *Object Linking and Embedding*. It enables Windows-based applications that support it to share information dynamically. That means that the object remembers where it came from and has special abilities based on that memory. Even though the term *OLE* is a little scary (it ranks right up there with SQL in my book!), the concept is very elementary, and anyone can understand and use it.

You already understand the term *object* in the PowerPoint sense, and the term is similar to that in the case of OLE. An object is any bit of data (or a whole file) that you want to use in another program. You can paste it in with no connection to its source, or you can link or embed it.

Two actions are involved in OLE: linking and embedding. Here are quick definitions of each:

- **Linking** creates a connection between the original file and the copy in your presentation, so the copy is always updated.
- **Embedding** creates a connection between the object in the presentation and the application that originally created it, so you can edit the object in that original application at any time from within PowerPoint.

The key difference is that linking connects to the source data file whereas embedding connects to the source *application*.

For a link to be updatable, linked objects must already exist independently of the PowerPoint presentation. For example, if you want to link an Excel chart, you must first create that chart in Excel and save your work in an Excel file. That way, PowerPoint has a filename to refer to when updating the link.

CAUTION

Links can slow down your presentation's loading and editing performance. Therefore, you should create links last, after you have finished adding content and polishing the formatting.

Linking and embedding are not appropriate for every insertion. If you want to use content (such as cells from an Excel worksheet or a picture from a graphics program) that will not change, it's best to copy it normally. For the Excel data cells or text from a Word document, use regular Copy/Paste; for the graphic image, use Picture (on the Insert tab). Reserve linking for objects that will change and will be used in a presentation that must always have the most current data. Reserve embedding for objects that you plan to edit later and require the native application's editing tools to do so.

Here are some ideas of when linking or embedding might be useful:

- If you have to give the same presentation every month that shows the monthly sales statistics, link to the Excel worksheet where you track them during the month. Your presentation will always contain the most current data.
- If you want to draw a picture in Paint (a program that comes with Windows) or some other graphics program, embed the picture in PowerPoint. That way, you don't have to open Paint (or the other program) separately every time you want to work on the picture while you're fine-tuning your presentation. You can just double-click

13

the picture in PowerPoint. You can always break the link when you finalize the presentation if you want to cut down on the file size.

■ If you know that a coworker is still finalizing a chart or drawing, link to their working file on the network. Then whenever changes are made to it, your copy will also be updated. (Beware, however, that once you take your presentation away from the computer that has network access, you can no longer update the link.)

Linking and/or Embedding Part of a File

As I mentioned earlier, you can link or embed either a part of an existing file or the whole file. If you need only a part of an existing file, such as a few cells from a worksheet, an individual chart, or a few paragraphs of text, you use the following procedure:

1. **In its native application, create or open the file containing the data you want to copy.**
2. **If you have just created the file, save it.** The file should have a name before you go any further if you are linking; this is not necessary for embedding, but it won't hurt anything.
3. **Select the data you want.**
4. **On the Home tab, click Copy, or press Ctrl+C.**
5. **Switch to PowerPoint and display the slide on which you want to paste the data.**
6. **On the Home tab, open the Paste button's menu and click Paste Special.** The Paste Special dialog box opens.
7. **If you want to embed, leave Paste selected.** If you want to link, click Paste Link. See Figure 13.4.

FIGURE 13.4

Use the Paste Special dialog box to link or embed a piece of a data file from another program.

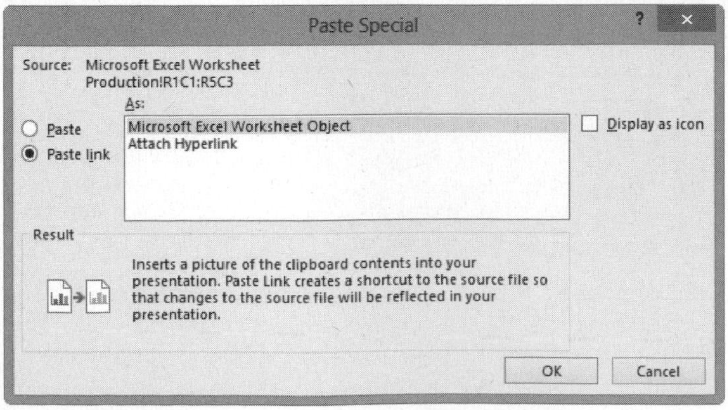

8. **Choose the format from the As list.** Because you want to link or embed, choose a type that ends with the word *object*.

9. **If you want the pasted object to appear as an icon instead of as itself, mark the Display as Icon check box.** This check box might be unavailable if the object type you chose in step 8 does not support it.

10. **Click OK.** The object is placed in your presentation.

If you link the object, each time you open your PowerPoint presentation, PowerPoint checks the source file for an updated version. If you embed the object, you can double-click it at any time to open it in its native application for editing.

Perhaps you are wondering about the other data types. If you chose Paste in step 7 (rather than Paste Link), you will see other formats on the list besides formats with *object* in their names. All of these are non-linkable, non-embeddable formats. The choices depend on the type of data but include some of the following:

- **Formatted Text (RTF).** This data type formats text as it is formatted in the original file. For example, if the text is formatted as underlined in the original file, it is pasted as underlined text in PowerPoint.

- **HTML Format.** This option formats the content as it would be formatted on a web page.

- **Unformatted Text.** This option ignores the formatting from the native file and formats the text as the default PowerPoint font you've specified.

- **Picture (Windows Metafile).** The object appears as a 16-bit WMF-format graphic.

- **Picture (Enhanced Metafile).** The object appears as a 32-bit EMF-format graphic.

- **Device Independent Bitmap.** The object comes in as a bitmap picture, like a Windows Paint image.

> **NOTE**
>
> Enhanced Metafile is, as the name implies, an updated and improved file format from Windows Metafile. It is a 32-bit format, whereas Windows Metafile is a 16-bit format. Enhanced metafile graphics cannot be used in MS-DOS or 16-bit Windows applications.

Embedding an Entire File

Sometimes you might want to place an entire file on a PowerPoint slide — for example, if the file is small and contains only the object that you want to display, like a picture. To create this connection, you use the Object button (on the Insert tab), which is handier than the procedure you just learned because you do not have to open the other application. Here's how:

1. **In PowerPoint, display the slide on which you want to place the file.**

2. **Choose Insert ⇨ Text ⇨ Object.** The Insert Object dialog box opens.

3. **Click the Create from File button.** The controls change to those shown in Figure 13.5.

FIGURE 13.5

Enter the filename or browse for it with the Browse button.

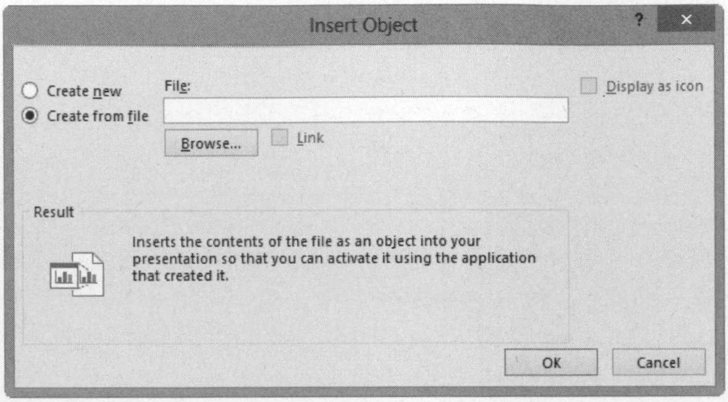

4. **Click Browse, and use the Browse dialog box to locate the file you want.** Then click OK to accept the filename.

5. **(Optional) If you want to link instead of embed the file, mark the Link check box.**

> **CAUTION**
>
> Do not link to a file housed on a disk that might not always be available during your presentation. For example, don't link to a removable drive unless you are also storing the presentation file on the same drive. And don't link to a network drive unless you know the network will be available at show time from the computer on which you will present.

6. **Click OK. The file is inserted on your PowerPoint slide.**

You can tell that the file is embedded, rather than simply copied, because when you double-click it, it opens in its native application. In contrast, when you double-click an item that is copied without embedding, its Properties box or some other PowerPoint-specific dialog box opens in PowerPoint. If you choose to link the object, you need to edit it in the native application.

Embedding a New File

If you want to embed a foreign object, but you haven't created that object yet, a really easy way to do so is to embed it on the fly. When you do this, the controls for the program open within PowerPoint (or in a separate application window, depending on the application) and you can create your object. Then, your work is saved within PowerPoint rather than as a separate file. To embed a new file, follow these steps:

1. **Open PowerPoint and display the slide on which you want to put the new object.**

2. **Choose Insert ⇨ Text ⇨ Object.** The Insert Object dialog box appears.

3. **Click Create New.** A list of available object types appears. See Figure 13.6.

FIGURE 13.6

Choose the object type you want to create. The object types listed come from the OLE-compliant programs installed on your PC.

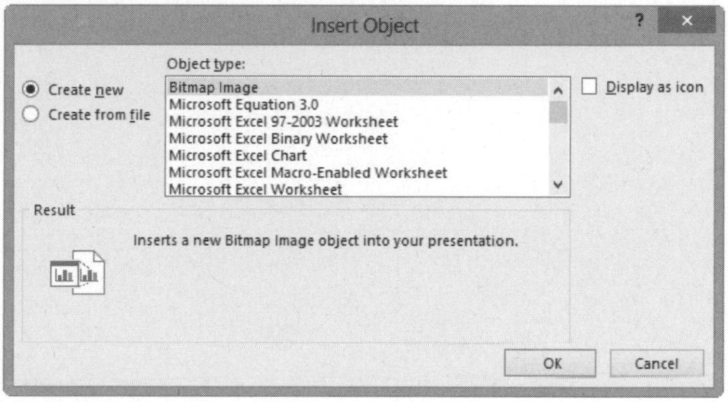

4. **Click the object type you want and then click OK.** The application opens.

5. **Depending on the application, additional dialog boxes might appear.** For example, if you are creating a new graphic object, a box might appear asking you about the size and color depth. Respond to any dialog boxes that appear for creating the new object.

6. **Create the object using the program's controls.** The program might be in a separate window from PowerPoint, or it might be contained within the PowerPoint window as in Figure 13.7.

7. **When you are finished, if the program was opened within PowerPoint, click anywhere on the slide outside of that object's frame.** Or, if the application was in a separate window, choose File ⇨ Exit and Return to *Document*. If you are prompted to save the file, choose No.

TIP

If you are prompted to save the object in a file and you choose Yes, the application creates a copy of the object that exists outside of PowerPoint. The copy is not linked to or embedded in PowerPoint.

If you are asked whether you want to update the object in the PowerPoint document before proceeding, you should choose Yes. This prompt occurs in many of the applications that open in separate windows.

8. **Resize and move the object on the slide as necessary.**

Because you are creating a file that doesn't have a name or saved location separate from the PowerPoint presentation, there is no need to link it to anything. Embedding is the only option.

FIGURE 13.7

The embedded program's controls appear, with PowerPoint in the background.

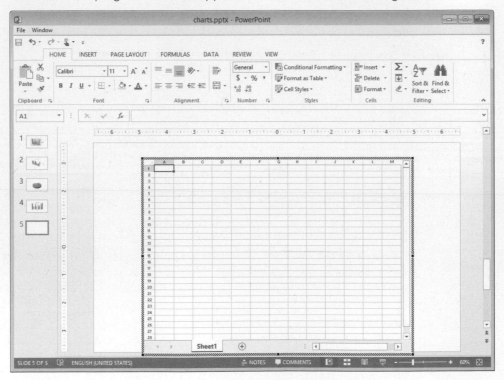

Working with Linked and Embedded Objects

Now that you have a linked or embedded object, what can you do with it? Many things. You can edit an embedded object by double-clicking it, of course. And you can update, change, and even break the links associated with a linked object. The following sections provide some details.

Opening and Converting Embedded Objects

When you select an embedded object in PowerPoint and then right-click the object, you can choose *Data Type* Object, where *Data Type* is the object type. (Its exact name depends on the object type, for example, Worksheet Object.) From the submenu you can choose the following:

- **Edit.** Opens the object for editing within PowerPoint (if possible). Some applications can work from within PowerPoint, such as the Excel example in Figure 13.7. If the object is related to an application that can't do this, the object opens for editing in a separate window for that application.

- **Open.** Opens the object for editing in a separate window for the application with which it is associated.

- **Convert.** Opens a dialog box that enables you to convert the object to some other type (if possible). This sounds great in theory, but in practice there are usually very few alternatives to choose from.

> **TIP**
>
> Although Convert options also appear for linked objects, you cannot convert them; you must break the link first. That's because a linked object must have a certain object type to maintain its link. Even after breaking a link, there might not be any viable choices for converting it to other formats.

Editing a Linked or Embedded Object

To edit a linked or embedded object, follow these steps:

1. **Display the slide containing the linked or embedded object.**

2. **Double-click the object.** The object's program controls appear. They might be integrated into the PowerPoint window, such as the ones for Excel that you saw in Figure 13.7, or they might appear in a separate window.

3. **Edit the object as needed.**

4. **Return to PowerPoint by doing one of the following:**
   - If the object is embedded (not linked), click the slide behind the object to return to PowerPoint.
   - If the object is linked, close the application window in which the object appears. When you are asked to save your changes, click Yes.

You can also edit a linked object directly in its original application, independently from PowerPoint. Close your PowerPoint presentation and open the original application. Do your editing, and save your work. Then, reopen your PowerPoint presentation and the object will reflect the changes to the linked objects.

13

Changing How Links Update

OLE links are automatically updated each time you open your PowerPoint file. However, updating these links slows down file opening considerably, so if you open and close the file frequently, you might want to set the link updating to Manual. That way, the links are updated only when you issue a command to update them. To set a link to update manually, follow these steps:

1. **Open the PowerPoint presentation that contains the linked object(s).** The presentation must have been previously saved.

2. **Choose File ⇨ Info and then click the Edit Links to Files hyperlink in the lower-right corner.** The Links dialog box appears (see Figure 13.8).

FIGURE 13.8

You can change the update setting for the links in your presentation here.

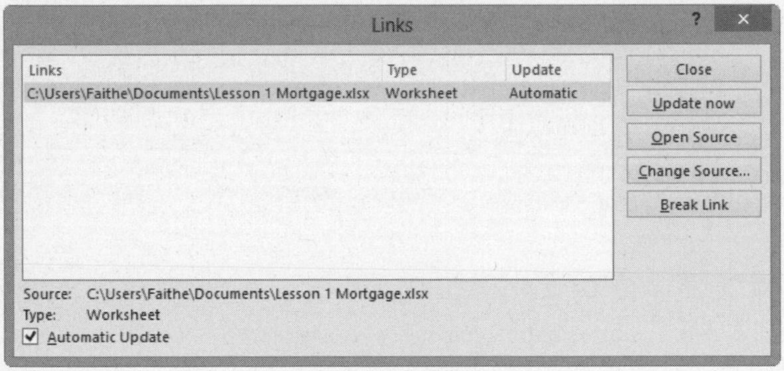

3. **Click the link that you want to change.**

4. **Uncheck the Automatic Update check box.**

5. **If you want to change any other links to manually update, repeat steps 3 and 4.** You can also use the Shift and Ctrl keys to select more than one link at once.

6. **If you want to update a link now, select it and click the Update Now button.**

7. **Click Close to close the Links dialog box.** Backstage view still appears.

8. **Choose Save to save the presentation changes (including the changes to the link settings).**

When you set a link to manually update, you have to open the Links dialog box and click Update Now, as in step 6, each time you want to update it. Or, you can right-click the object and choose Update Link from its shortcut menu.

Breaking a Link

When you break a link, the object remains in the presentation, but it becomes an ordinary object, just like any other picture or object you might have placed there. You can't double-click it to edit it anymore, and it doesn't update when the source changes. To break a link, reopen the Links dialog box shown in Figure 13.8 (File ➪ Info ➪ Edit Links to Files), click the link to break, and then click Break Link. If a warning box appears, click OK.

When you break a link, embedding information disappears too. For example, if you have a linked Excel chart and you break the link, the result is a simple pasted image of the chart with no ties to the Excel application. To reestablish a link, simply re-create it using the process you used when you created it originally.

Changing the Referenced Location of a Link

If you move files around on your hard disk, or move them to other storage locations, you might need to change the link location reference. For example, perhaps you are moving the presentation file to a flash drive and you want to place all of the linked files needed for the presentation in a separate folder on the flash drive. To change a link reference, do the following:

1. **Copy or move the files where you want them.** For example, if you want to transfer the presentation and linked files to a CD, do that first.
2. **Open the PowerPoint presentation that contains the linked object(s) to change.** If you copied the presentation to some new location, make sure you open the copy that you want to change.
3. **Choose File ➪ Info ➪ Edit Links to Files.** The Links dialog box opens (Figure 13.8).
4. **Click the link you want to change.**
5. **Click Change Source.** A Change Source dialog box opens. It is just like the normal Open dialog boxes you have worked with many times.
6. **Select the file to be linked from its new location, and click Open.** The link is updated.
7. **In the Links dialog box, click Close.**

> **CAUTION**
>
> If you change the location of a link to a different file, depending on the object type, the link may change to refer to the entire file, as if you had inserted it with Insert ➪ Text ➪ Object. If you used Edit ➪ Paste Special and then select Paste Link to insert only a part of the original file, that aspect might be lost and the entire file might appear as the object in the presentation. In such situations, it is better to delete the object and re-create the link from scratch.

13

Exporting PowerPoint Objects to Other Programs

You can copy any object in your PowerPoint presentation to another program, either linked or unlinked. For example, perhaps you created a chart using the PowerPoint charting tools for one of your PowerPoint slides and now you want to use that chart in a Microsoft Word document. To use a PowerPoint object in another program, you do the same basic things that you've learned in this chapter, but you start with PowerPoint. Here are some examples:

- To copy an object from PowerPoint, select it in PowerPoint and copy it to the Clipboard (Ctrl+C). Then switch to the other program and paste (Ctrl+V).

- To embed (or optionally link) an object from a PowerPoint presentation into another program's document, choose it in PowerPoint and copy it (Ctrl+C). Then, switch to the other program and use Paste Special. (In programs that use a menu bar rather than a Ribbon, the command is usually Edit ⇨ Paste Special.)

- To embed or link an entire PowerPoint presentation in another program's document, use the Object command in the other program (probably on an Insert tab or menu), and choose your PowerPoint file as the source.

You can also save individual slides as various types of graphics with the File ⇨ Save As command, as you learned to do in Chapter 2, "Creating and Saving Presentation Files."

Summary

In this chapter, you learned the mysteries of OLE, a term you have probably heard bandied about but were never quite sure what it meant. You can now use objects freely between PowerPoint and other programs and link or embed them whenever appropriate.

In the next chapter, you learn how to add sound effects, music, and soundtracks to a presentation.

CHAPTER 14

Adding Sound Effects, Music, and Soundtracks

IN THIS CHAPTER

How PowerPoint uses audio

When to use sounds and when not to

Inserting an audio clip as an icon

Assigning a sound to an object

Adding a digital music soundtrack

Adding a CD audio soundtrack

Configuring sound playback

Using the advanced timeline to fine-tune sound events

Whether it's a simple sound effect or a complete musical soundtrack, sounds in a PowerPoint presentation can make a big difference in the audience's perception of your message. In this chapter, you will learn when and how to use sounds, how to place them in the presentation, and how to manage their playback.

How PowerPoint Uses Audio

There are several ways that you can include audio in a presentation:

- **Insert an audio file as an icon.** The audio plays during the presentation whenever anyone points to or clicks its icon, or it plays automatically, depending on the settings that you specify. This is useful in an interactive presentation because it gives the audience a choice of whether to play the sound.

- **Associate a sound with an object** (such as a graphic) so that the sound plays when anyone points to or clicks that object. This is another good technique for interactive presentations.

- **Associate a sound with an animation effect** (such as a series appearing in a graph) so that the sound plays when the animation effect occurs. For example, you might have some text "drive in" onto a slide and associate the sound of an engine revving with that action.

- **Associate a sound with a slide transition** (a move from one slide to the next) so that the sound plays when the next slide appears. For example, you may assign a shutter-click sound, such as the sound that a slide projector makes when it changes slides, to the transitions between slides.

- **Insert a musical soundtrack that plays automatically in the background.** This is useful for unattended (kiosk-style) presentations.

- **Link to online audio.** You can create a link in your presentation to an online audio source. When it is triggered for playback in the presentation, PowerPoint accesses the clip via the Internet.

- **Record and embed a new audio clip.** You a can use the sound recorder that is built into PowerPoint to record your own new sounds with your computer's microphone and embed them in your presentation file.

CAUTION

If you download sounds from the Internet or acquire them from other sources, you must be careful not to violate any copyright laws. Sounds recorded from television, radio, or compact discs are protected by copyright law, and you or your company might face serious legal action if you use them in a presentation without the permission of the copyright holder.

When to Use Sounds — and When Not To

Sounds should serve the purpose of the presentation; you should never use them simply because you can. If you add a lot of sounds purely for the fun of it, then your audience may lose respect for the seriousness of your message. That being said, there are many legitimate reasons to use sounds in a presentation. Just make sure that you are clear on what your reasons are before you start working with them. Here are some ideas:

- **For new slides.** You can assign a recognizable sound, such as a beep or a bell, to each slide so that when your audience hears the sound, they know to look up and read the new slide.

- **For voice-overs.** You can record a short voice-over message from a CEO or some other important person who could not be there in person.

- **For emphasis or humor.** You can punctuate important points with sounds or use sounds to add occasional humorous touches.

However, if you are trying to pack a lot of information into a short presentation, you might want to avoid sounds that take up presentation time when they play, such as elaborate sound effects. You should also avoid sounds and other whimsical touches if you are delivering very serious news. You may also want to avoid sounds if you intend to present on a very old and slow computer because any kind of media clip — whether sound or video — will slow the system down even more, both when you load the presentation and when you present it.

Now that you know how to make intelligent decisions about using sounds, let's start using them in your presentations.

Inserting an Audio Clip as an Icon on a Slide

The most elementary way to use an audio clip in a presentation is to place the clip directly on a slide as an object. An icon appears on the slide, and you can click the icon during the presentation to play the clip. This method works well if you want to play the sound at exactly the right moment in the presentation.

> **TIP**
>
> You can also assign the sound to an existing object on the slide, as explained in the section "Assigning a Sound to an Object" later in this chapter. When you do this, the object to which you attach the sound serves the same function as an icon; you click the object to play the sound.

Inserting an Audio Clip from a File

You might already have the audio file you need on your own PC. If you do, the process of inserting it is simple. Follow these steps to insert an audio clip from a file on your PC:

1. **Click Insert ⇨ Audio ⇨ Audio on My PC.** The Insert Audio dialog box opens.
2. **Navigate to the drive and folder that contain the audio clip that you want.** If you have any audio clips, look in the `Windows\Media` folder on the hard disk where Windows is installed for some small, simple sound effect files you can practice with. You can also use music clips from your music library.
3. **Click the file that you want to use, as shown in Figure 14.1, and then click Insert.** A speaker icon appears on the slide, as shown in Figure 14.2. Playback controls appear beneath it when it's selected. You can test the clip by clicking the Play button (the big right-pointing triangle).

> **TIP**
>
> To hide the icon, drag it off the edge of the slide. The sound still works, but the audience cannot see the icon. You can also mark the Hide During Show check box on the Audio Tools Playback tab to prevent the icon from appearing.

14

FIGURE 14.1

Choose a file from your hard disk or other location (such as your company's network).

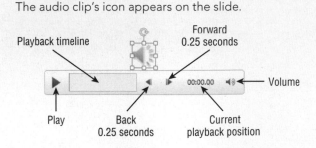

FIGURE 14.2

The audio clip's icon appears on the slide.

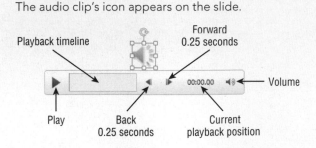

Notice the arrow next to the Insert button in the Insert Audio dialog box (Figure 14.1). It opens a menu from which you can choose to link the file instead of embedding it. Normally PowerPoint embeds almost all content, but linking may be appropriate in special situations, such as when large audio or video files are available on your network and you don't want to duplicate them in your PowerPoint file in every presentation in which you reference them.

Inserting an Online Audio Clip

You can insert audio clips from the Office.com clip art collection directly from within PowerPoint. Even though the collection is called "clip art," it contains more than just the typical line art that most people think of as clip art. It also contains photos, audio clips, and even some video clips.

The process for inserting online audio clips is very similar to that for inserting clip art, covered in Chapter 11, "Working With Clip Art and Photos." The main difference is the type of results that appear in the search (sounds rather than images).

Follow these steps to find and insert an audio clip from Office.com:

1. **Click Insert ⇨ Audio ⇨ Online Audio.** The Insert Audio dialog box opens. Notice that there is only one source available here, whereas in the Insert Pictures dialog box (shown in Figure 11.2 in Chapter 11), there were several sources.

2. **Type a keyword in the Office.com Clip Art text box and press Enter.** Figure 14.3 shows some example results.

FIGURE 14.3

Results from an Office.com search for online audio.

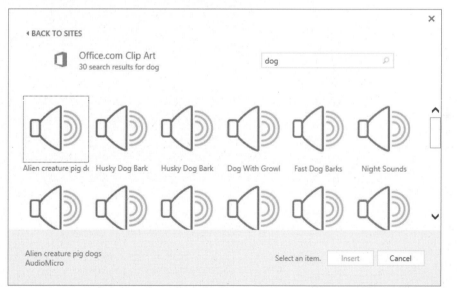

3. **Click a clip to hear it.** (Make sure the sound in Windows is not muted.)

4. **Click the desired clip to insert and click the Insert button.** The sound's icon appears on the slide, the same as in Figure 14.2.

Recording Your Own Sounds

Most PCs have a microphone jack on the sound card where you can plug in a small microphone. You can then record your own sounds to include in the presentation. In this case,

I am referring to simple, short sounds. If you want to record a full-blown voice-over narration, see Chapter 19, "Designing User-Interactive or Self-Running Presentations."

To record a sound, follow these steps:

1. **Display the slide on which you want to place the sound clip.**

2. **Click Insert ➪ Audio ➪ Record Audio.** The Record Sound dialog box appears. See Figure 14.4.

   FIGURE 14.4

   You can record your own sounds using your PC's microphone.

   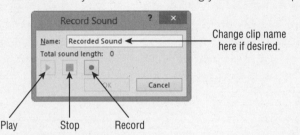

3. **(Optional) Type a name for the sound, replacing the generic name (Recorded Sound) in the Name box.**

4. **Click the Start Recording button (the red circle).**

5. **Record the sound.** When you are finished, click the Stop Recording button (the black square).

6. **(Optional) To play back the sound, click the Play button (the black triangle).**

7. **Click OK to place the sound on the slide.** A sound icon appears on the slide.

Assigning a Sound to an Object

Many presenters prefer to assign sounds to an existing object on a slide rather than inserting an audio clip as its own separate icon. This way, they still have precise control over when the clip plays (for example, when they click a clip-art image with which the audio is associated), but the control mechanism is hidden.

Although you can assign an audio clip to any object, many people assign audio clips to graphics. For example, you might attach an audio file of a greeting from your CEO to the CEO's picture. The picture would be set up as the trigger, and clicking it would play the audio clip.

The drawback to this method is that only WAV files can be used (the actual WAV file format, with a .wav filename extension, not just waveform-type audio files), so you must convert your existing audio clip to the WAV format using a third-party sound-editing program before you add it to your PowerPoint presentation. A workaround for other file formats is to put them under Run Program so that the clip plays in the external program associated with it.

Follow these steps to assign a sound to an object:

1. **Insert the object that you want to associate with the sound.** For example, the object can be a graphic, chart, or text box.

2. **Select the object, and click Insert ⇨ Links ⇨ Action.** The Action Settings dialog box appears.

3. **Click either the Mouse Click tab or the Mouse Over tab, depending on which action you want.** Mouse Click plays the sound when you click the object, while Mouse Over plays the sound when you move your mouse pointer over the object.

4. **Mark the Play Sound check box.** Then open the drop-down list and click one of the sample sounds (from `C:\Windows\Media`) or click Other Sound to open the Add Sound dialog box and pick a sound from any location. You can use only WAV sounds for this, though.

FIGURE 14.5

You can choose the sound that you want to assign to the object.

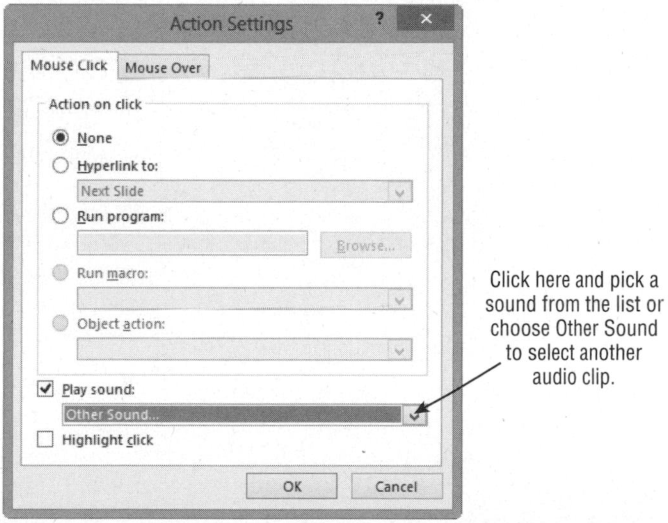

Click here and pick a sound from the list or choose Other Sound to select another audio clip.

5. **Click OK.** The object now has the sound associated with it so that when you click it or move the mouse over it during the presentation, the sound plays.

NOTE

Chapter 16 is devoted entirely to transitions and animation effects, and so this chapter does not describe them in detail. In Chapter 16, you learn how to assign sounds to the transition between slides or to the movement (animation) of any object on any slide.

Adding a Digital Music Soundtrack

Digital music clips, such as MP3 and WMA files, work just like other audio clips. You insert them using the Insert ➪ Audio ➪ Audio on My PC command, as described earlier in this chapter in "Inserting an Audio Clip from a File."

In most cases, you will want the music to continue through multiple slides; see "Setting a Clip to Continue across Multiple Slides" later in this chapter to learn how to do that. (The easiest way is to display the Audio Tools Playback tab and mark the Play Across Slides check box.) In addition, you will probably want to hide the icon for the audio track so that it doesn't get in the way. To do this, select the icon on the slide and then choose Audio Tools Playback ➪ Audio Options ➪ Hide During Show.

By default, MP3 and WMA music tracks are embedded in the file rather than linked. If you want to link them, click the arrow next to the Insert button in the dialog box where you select the clip and choose to link to the file. This works the same as with any other audio clip. (Note that embedding was not the default in PowerPoint 2007 and earlier, so if you are working with a file created in an earlier version that already has a music soundtrack, the file may be linked; the easiest way to change that is to remove it and reinsert it.)

Adding a CD Audio Soundtrack

If you want to use music from a CD as the background music for your presentation, you might want to rip the track(s) you want to your hard disk first. To *rip* means to make a copy of the track in a digital audio format such as MP3 or WMA and save it on your computer. You can then play the track without having to have the CD in the computer. Nearly any music player software will rip tracks for you; Audacity is one such program that works well, for example. (Avoid using Windows Media Player because it adds digital rights management restrictions.) After ripping the tracks, insert them into the presentation as you would any other audio file. See the previous section for an outline of the process.

In some instances you may prefer to use audio tracks directly from the CD. This method keeps the size of the presentation file small because the music clip is not embedded in it, but it requires you to have the CD in the PC as you show the presentation. You cannot use CD audio tracks in presentations that you plan to distribute as self-running presentations on a data CD or over the Internet because the computers on which it will run will not have access to the CD.

Adding the Insert CD Audio Command to the Quick Access Toolbar

Microsoft recommends that you use digital audio tracks such as MP3 and WMA files for the music in your presentation, so it has de-emphasized the command for inserting CD audio in PowerPoint 2013. The command does not appear on the Ribbon by default. Therefore, if you want to use this feature, you must add the command to the Quick Access Toolbar or to the Ribbon. I'll review the procedure for adding it to the Quick Access Toolbar here because it is simpler; if you want to add it elsewhere on the Ribbon, see Chapter 22, "Customizing PowerPoint."

To add the Play CD Audio Track command to the Quick Access Toolbar, follow these steps:

1. **Choose File ⇨ Options.** The PowerPoint Options dialog box opens.
2. **Click Quick Access Toolbar.**
3. **Open the Choose Commands From drop-down list (above the left column) and select Commands Not in the Ribbon.**
4. **Scroll through the list of commands.** Select Play CD Audio Track, and then click the Add >> button to move it to the list on the right. See Figure 14.6.

FIGURE 14.6

Add the Play CD Audio Track button to the Quick Access Toolbar.

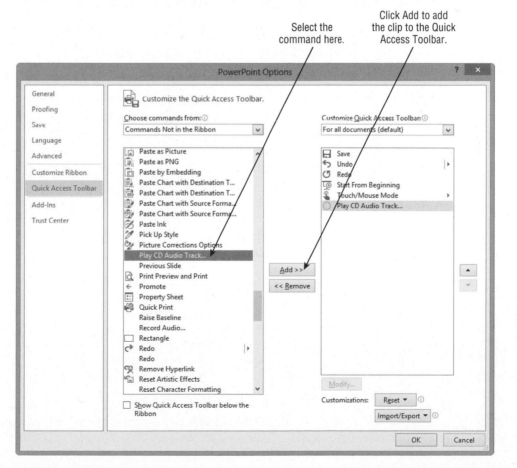

5. **Click OK.** The command now appears on the Quick Access Toolbar (the row of buttons above the File and Home tabs).

Placing a CD Soundtrack Icon on a Slide

To play a CD track for a slide, you must place an icon for it on the slide. You can place a range of tracks, such as multiple tracks from a CD, using a single icon. To do so, follow these steps:

1. **Insert the CD in your PC.**

2. **Click the Play CD Audio Track icon on the Quick Access Toolbar.** (You learned how to place it there in the previous section.) The Insert CD Audio dialog box appears.

3. **Specify the starting track number in the Start at Track text box in the Clip selection section.**

4. **Specify the ending track number in the End at Track text box.** If you want to play only a single track, the Start at Track and End at Track numbers should be the same. The start or end time changes only after you click one of the up or down arrows next to the time. For example, if you want to play tracks 1, 2, and 3, you should select track 1 as the start track and track 3 as the end track (as opposed to track 4).

5. **If you want to begin the starting track at a particular spot (other than the beginning), enter this start time in the Time text box for that track.** For example, to start the track 50 seconds into the song, you would type **00:50**.

6. **If you want to stop the ending track at a particular spot, enter this end time in the Time text box for that track.** By default, PowerPoint plays an entire track. You can see the total playing time at the bottom of the dialog box.

7. **(Optional) If desired, adjust the volume with the Sound Volume button.** Click the button and then drag its slider.

8. **Click OK.** The CD icon appears in the center of the slide. You can drag it off the edge of the slide if it interferes with your slide content. You can also resize it if you want, just as you can any other object.

9. **Click the CD Audio Tools Options tab.**

10. **Open the Play Track list and choose Play Across Slides.**

TIP

You can play any number of tracks from a single CD using a single icon as long as they are contiguous and you play them in their default order. If you need noncontiguous tracks from the CD, or you want to play them in a different order, or you just want certain segments of some of the clips, then you must place each clip individually on the slide and then control their order in the Animation pane. See Chapter 16, "Creating Animation Effects and Transitions," for details. If you do not want the icons to appear on the slide, then drag them off the slide's edge.

The CD track is now an animated object on your slide. By *animated*, I mean that it is an object that has some action associated with it.

Controlling When a CD Track Plays

You can set many of the same properties for a CD track on a slide that you can for a digital audio file icon. You can also use the Animation controls to specify precisely when and how a track will play. To do this, follow these steps:

1. **Choose Animations ⇨ Advanced Animation ⇨ Animation Pane to turn on the Animation Pane if it is not already displayed.**

2. **Select the CD icon on the slide.** A gray box appears around its name in the Custom Animation pane.

3. **Open the drop-down menu for the selected clip and choose Effect Options.** This opens the Play CD Audio dialog box.

From this point, the options are exactly the same as those for regular sound files that you will learn about in the next section, "Configuring Sound Playback." All of the same tabs are available, including Effect, Timing, and Sound Settings.

Configuring Sound Playback

Now let's look at some ways to control when the sound plays. You can adjust some basic settings on the Audio Tools Playback tab or fine-tune playback settings with the Animation pane.

Adjusting Basic Playback Settings

Using the Audio Tools Playback tab, you can configure a variety of basic options that define how the sound clip will play. For example, you can set whether it plays automatically or not, how loudly it will play in relation to the other sounds in the presentation, and whether or not it should repeat continuously.

To configure the sound's basic playback properties, do the following:

1. **Click the audio clip icon to select it.** Play controls appear beneath it and selection handles appear around the icon.

2. **On the Audio Tools Playback tab, open the Start drop-down list and choose an option: On Click or Automatically.** See Figure 14.7.

3. **(Optional) Mark one or more of the check boxes in the Audio Options section of the Ribbon:**

14

- The Play Across Slides check box enables the sound to continue to play even if the presentation advances to the next slide (or more). The default is to play across 999 slides; you will learn how to specify a different number of slides in the next section.

- The Loop Until Stopped check box makes the sound play continuously until you move to another slide on which it does not play. By default the sound plays only once.

- The Hide During Show check box hides the sound icon in Slide Show view.

- The Rewind After Playing check box is available for sounds, but it doesn't do much. Rewinding leaves the clip at its start point, rather than its end point, after playback. For a video, this makes a difference because it controls which frame of the video remains on-screen after playback; for audio that's not an issue.

FIGURE 14.7

Configure basic playback options on the Audio Tools Playback tab.

The most popular reason for adjusting these settings is to make a music clip play in the background across multiple slides. To do this, you adjust four settings: set Start to Automatically, turn on Play Across Slides, turn on Loop Until Stopped, and turn on Hide During Show. As a shortcut, PowerPoint provides a Play in Background button on the Audio Tools Playback tab. Click that button to automatically apply all four of those settings at once. This Audio Styles feature is new in PowerPoint 2013; there is only the one audio style, but it's a useful one. (Unfortunately, you can't create your own audio styles.)

Setting a Clip to Play on Mouse Click or Mouse Over

Even if you set up a clip to play automatically, it still will play (or replay) if you click it. That's because, by default, it has an *action setting* applied to it that plays it on-click.

Action settings are a form of trigger animation. They set up the clip to be triggered (to play) when something happens — for example, when they are clicked or touched with the mouse. (Chapter 16 covers trigger animations in more detail.)

The Action Settings dialog box for a clip is accessed via the Insert ⇨ Action command. The dialog box has two tabs: Mouse Click and Mouse Over. Each tab is identical in its controls. With them, you can define what happens when someone clicks the icon and when someone rolls the mouse over the icon (without clicking).

You may remember the Action Settings dialog box from "Assigning a Sound to an Object" earlier in the chapter. However, at that point we were looking at assigning a sound to an existing object to avoid having a separate audio icon, whereas here the audio clip icon itself is the object.

As you can see in Figure 14.8, the selected sound clip will play when clicked. (Object Action is set to Play on the Mouse Click tab.) On the Mouse Over tab, by default, no action is selected.

FIGURE 14.8

An audio clip's icon has Play set as its object action on the Mouse Click tab by default.

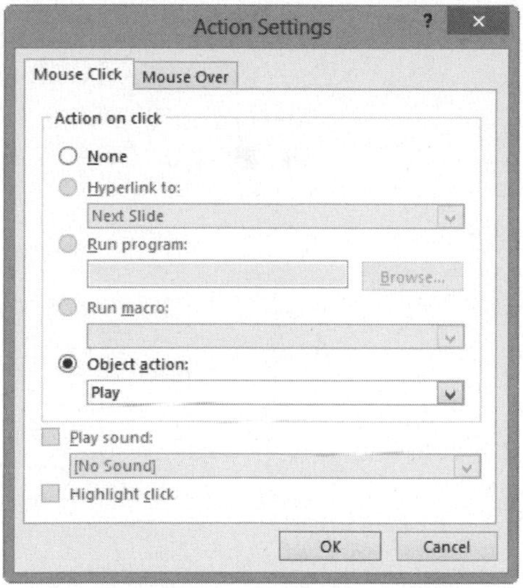

To set up a sound clip so that it plays when you roll the mouse over it (without clicking), follow these steps:

1. **Select the clip on the slide.**
2. **Choose Insert ⇨ Links ⇨ Action.** The Action Settings dialog box opens.
3. **Click the Mouse Over tab.**
4. **Click the Object Action option button.**
5. **Open the Object Action drop-down list and choose Play.**
6. **Click OK.**

Fine-Tuning Playback Settings in the Animation Pane

The Start setting for the clip (On Click or Automatically) that you select on the Audio Tools Playback tab sets up an animation event for the sound clip. You can view and change this animation event from the Animation pane. You will learn a lot more about the Animation pane in Chapter 16, but I'll give you a quick rundown here on the parts that pertain specifically to audio clips.

To access an audio clip's animation settings, choose Animations ⇨ Advanced Animation ⇨ Animation Pane. The Animation pane appears, and any audio or video clips you have inserted on the active slide appear on the list there, along with any animations you have set up (see Chapter 16). In Figure 14.9, there is only one animation: the one for the Tin Man audio clip.

FIGURE 14.9

The inserted clip appears in the Animation pane.

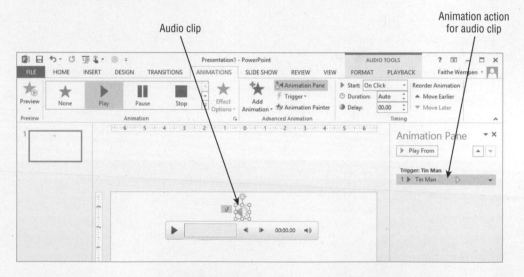

Audio clip

Animation action
for audio clip

> **TIP**
>
> Clips that you insert from Office.com using the Insert ⇨ Audio ⇨ Online Audio command have names that may be difficult to remember and distinguish; for example, an audio clip might have a mostly numeric name like MS900388197. You can rename a clip by choosing Home ⇨ Editing ⇨ Select ⇨ Selection Pane, and in the Selection task pane, clicking the clip, clicking it again (to rename), and typing a new name for it. That new name will also be used in the Animation pane to refer to the clip.

Controlling When a Clip Will Play

On the Animations tab's Start drop-down list (shown in Figure 14.7), you can choose from three settings for a clip to play:

- **On Click.** Sets up a trigger animation so that the sound plays when you click its icon.

- **With Previous.** Plays the sound simultaneously with the previous animation (if any) or with the transition if it is the first animation. For this to work, Automatically must be set for the start value on the Audio Tools Playback tab.

- **After Previous.** Plays the sound automatically after the previous animation (if any). For this to work, Automatically must be set for the start value on the Audio Tools Playback tab.

These same options are available by right-clicking the clip's name on the Animation pane. A menu opens; click the desired setting, as shown in Figure 14.10.

FIGURE 14.10

An audio clip can be set to play on click, after the previous animation event, or simultaneously with the previous animation event.

If there are no other animated events on the slide, the "previous event" is the slide itself appearing, and the effect is identical to Start After Previous. The difference is apparent only if you have multiple animation events on the slide; this setting enables you to synchronize multiple events to occur simultaneously. Chapter 16 covers this in more detail.

When specifying a start point on the Audio Tools Playback tab, choosing On Click starts the sound file when you click the mouse *anywhere* on the slide, even if you do not click the sound icon itself. If you want the sound to play only when the sound icon is clicked (the default when you insert a sound), make sure a trigger is set up for it. To check this out, right-click the sound's entry in the Animation pane and choose Timing. Then in the Play Audio dialog box, click Triggers if needed to expand the Triggers options, select the Start Effect on Click Of option button, and make sure the sound clip's name is chosen from the drop-down list. See Figure 14.11.

14

FIGURE 14.11

Set the sound to play only when the sound icon is clicked by changing the Timing setting.

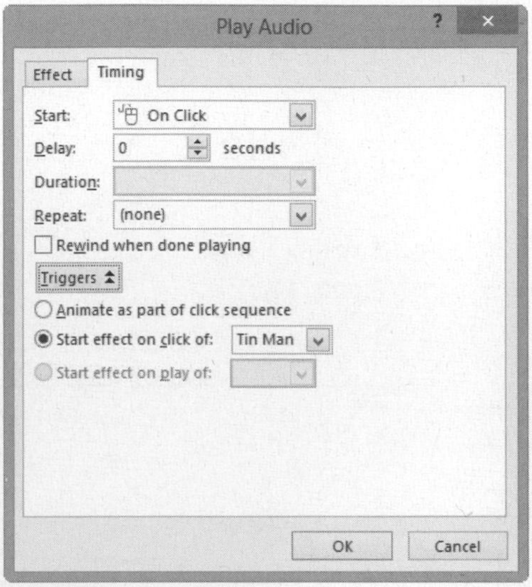

> **TIP**
>
> In Slide Show view, a set of playback controls appears along with the sound icon, so you can pause and play the clip using those controls during the show. This makes it less critical to have pause and play triggers set up for the icon itself.

Delaying or Repeating a Sound

Depending on the situation, it may be useful to have a sound play after a short delay or to repeat the sound more than once. In Chapter 16, you can learn more about setting animation options. However, here are some quick instructions for customizing a sound:

1. **On the Animations tab, click Animation Pane to open the Animation pane if it does not already appear.**
2. **On the slide, select the icon for the audio clip.** The clip becomes selected in the Animation pane.
3. **Open the menu for the clip in the Animation pane and choose Timing.** The Play Audio dialog box opens with the Timing tab displayed.
4. **Enter a number of seconds in the Delay text box.** The delay occurs between when the previous event happens and when the sound begins.
5. **Open the Repeat drop-down list and choose the number of times that the sound should repeat.** You can choose 2, 3, 4, 5, or 10 times as well as Until Next

Click and Until End of Slide. You can also type in your own number of times to repeat (up to 9999). See Figure 14.12.

FIGURE 14.12

You can use the Timing controls to delay the sound and to make it repeat.

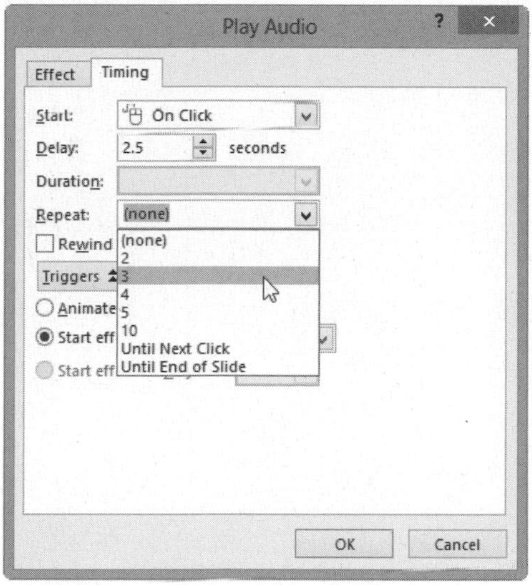

6. **Click OK.**

Choosing the Starting and Ending Point for a Sound Clip

There might be times when you want to start the clip from some point other than the beginning. For example, you may have a really good sound clip, except that the first five seconds are garbled or it may contain content that you do not want to use, or you may want to play just the first 15 seconds of the clip.

PowerPoint supports two methods of controlling a clip's starting point. The older method involves using the Effect Options command and works in all presentations. The newer method uses the Trim feature, which is available only in PowerPoint 2010 and higher. The Trim feature allows you to set both a starting and an ending point for the clip; Effect Options can only alter the starting point. I recommend that you use the Trim feature whenever possible, falling back to the older method only when working with older existing presentations that already use that feature.

Setting the Starting Point with Effect Options

The Effect Options method enables you to set a starting point for the clip that is a certain number of seconds into it. It also enables you to specify whether the clip should start from the beginning if you temporarily stop it and then restart or whether it should start from the point at which you left off.

To control the point at which a clip starts, do the following:

1. **Open the Animation pane if it does not already appear (Animations ➪ Animation Pane).**

2. **Open the menu for the sound clip in the Animation pane and choose Effect Options.** The Play Audio dialog box opens with the Effect tab displayed, as shown in Figure 14.13.

FIGURE 14.13

You can specify that a clip plays at a different time than the beginning or set it to restart playing from wherever it left off if you stop it.

3. **In the Start Playing area, choose one of these options:**

   ▪ **From the Beginning**, which is the default play mode.

   ▪ **From the Last Position**, if you want it to pick up where it left off when you stopped it.

   ▪ **From Time**, and then enter the number of seconds into the clip that it should begin playing.

4. **Click OK.**

Setting the Starting and Ending Point by Trimming

Trimming works with both audio and video clips, and in many cases it can help you avoid having to use a third-party video- or audio-editing program to make simple cuts to a clip.

To trim an audio clip, follow these steps:

1. **Select the clip's icon on the slide.**

2. **On the Audio Tools Playback tab, click Trim Audio.** The Trim Audio dialog box opens.

3. **Drag the green marker to the right to trim a portion of the beginning of the clip.** See Figure 14.14. Alternatively, enter a number of seconds to trim in the Start Time box.

FIGURE 14.14

Trim from the beginning and/or end of the clip.

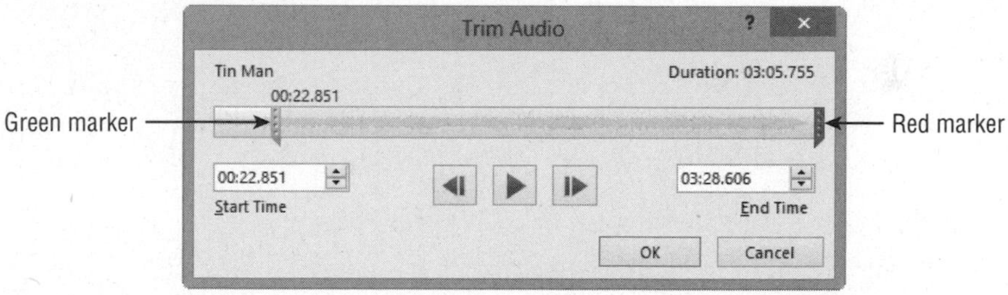

4. **Drag the red marker to the left to trim a portion of the end of the clip.** Alternatively, enter a number of seconds to trim in the End Time box.

5. **Preview the trimming by clicking the Play button.** Then adjust the trimming as needed.

6. **When you are satisfied with the trim points, click OK to accept the trim.**

NOTE

Trimmed parts of the clip will be deleted if you use the File ⇨ Info ⇨ Compress Media command to decrease the size of your presentation file.

NOTE

If you use both methods to specify a clip's starting point — Effect Options and trimming — the effects are not cumulative, but the longer of the two delays takes effect. So, for example, if you specified 10 seconds using the Effect Options command and 20 seconds in the Start Time box in the Trim Audio dialog box, the clip would be trimmed by 20 seconds at the beginning. Confusing? Yes. Stick with one method or the other when possible.

Adjusting the Fade Duration

The *fade duration* is the amount of time at the beginning and/or end of the clip when the volume will gradually increase (at the beginning) or decrease (at the end).

To set a fade duration, follow these steps:

1. **Select the clip's icon on the slide.**
2. **On the Audio Tools Playback tab, enter a number of seconds in the Fade In box.**
3. **Enter a number of seconds in the Fade Out box.**

Setting a Clip to Continue across Multiple Slides

Normally a clip will stop playing after it has played once (or however many times you have set it up to play) or when you click the mouse or advance to the next slide. However, if you are using a music track such as an MP3 file, you might want it to continue playing across multiple slides.

Earlier in the chapter, you learned how on the Audio Tools Playback tab you can mark the Play Across Slides check box or click the Play in Background button. When you do either of those things, PowerPoint sets up that sound to continue playing through 999 slides (or as many slides as you have, if fewer than that).

If you would like the clip to stop after fewer slides than that, you must adjust the Stop Playing setting in the Play Audio dialog box. Follow these steps:

1. **In the Animation pane, right-click the clip and choose Effect Options.** The Play Audio dialog box opens with the Effect tab displayed.
2. **In the Stop Playing area, choose one of these options:**
   - **On Click** to go back to the default play mode (same as choosing Start on Click elsewhere).
   - **After Current Slide** to stop the audio when you move to the next slide or when the clip has finished playing, whichever comes first. This setting allows the clip to continue playing through mouse clicks, as long as the slide does not advance.
   - **After _____ Slides**, and then enter a number of slides; the audio will continue until the specified number of additional slides have passed. Use 999 for the entire presentation, or use a smaller number, as in Figure 14.15.
3. **Click OK.**

TIP

What if you want to jump around in an audio clip? For example, suppose you want to play the first 20 seconds of the clip and then skip to the 75-second point. You can do that by inserting two separate copies of the clip. Set each one with the start time desired for it, and then in the Animation pane, set one of them to After Previous and make the other copy the previous animation event. Alternately, you can set bookmarks on the audio control and then add triggers to the bookmarks. (That latter method has the advantage of keeping the file size smaller because you have only one copy of the clip in the presentation.) Those instructions will make more sense to you after you have read Chapter 16, which covers custom animation effects in detail.

FIGURE 14.15

Set the number of slides through which the audio track should play.

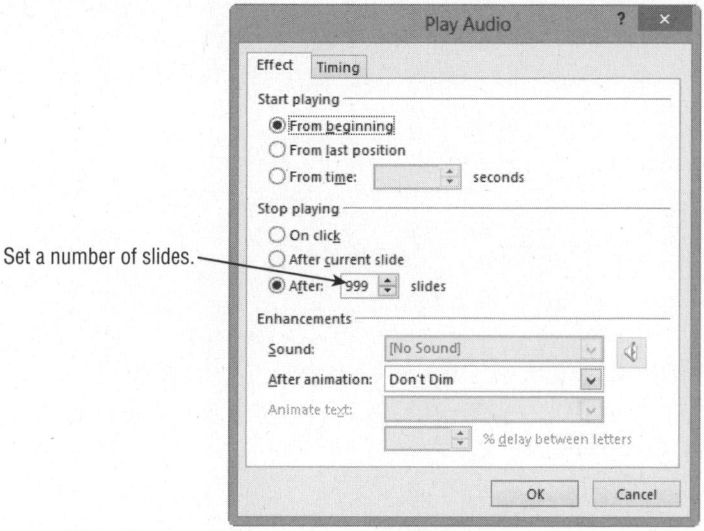

Set a number of slides.

Specifying the Sound Volume

When you give your presentation, you can specify an overall volume using the computer's volume controls in Windows. However, sometimes you might want the volume of one sound to be different from others. To set the volume for a specific sound, follow these steps:

1. **Select the clip on the slide.**
2. **On the Audio Tools Playback tab, click the Volume button.** A menu appears.
3. **Choose the volume level you want (Low, Medium, High, or Mute).**

You can also use a volume slider to adjust the volume more precisely than is possible with the presets available in the preceding steps. Here's how:

1. **Click the clip on the slide.** Play controls appear under its icon.
2. **Click the speaker icon on the play controls.** A Volume slider pops up. See Figure 14.16.
3. **Drag the slider up or down to adjust the clip's volume.**

14

TIP

The sound will play at a consistent volume throughout the duration of the clip. If you need the volume to change partway through, you can use a sound-editing program to change the clip volume before inserting it.

FIGURE 14.16

Adjust the volume via the speaker icon on the clip's playback controls.

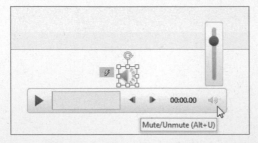

Changing the Appearance of the Sound Icon

The sound icon on the slide can be formatted like any other drawn object. You can resize it by dragging its selection handles, or set a specific height and width from the Audio Tools Format tab.

You can also right-click the sound icon and choose Format Picture to open the Format Picture task pane, and from there you can apply any effects that you like (shadow, reflection, and so on). All the controls in the Format Picture task pane are strictly appearance based and focused on the icon; there is nothing there that controls the way the sound plays.

Using the Advanced Timeline to Fine-Tune Sound Events

The Advanced Timeline option is turned on by default. A timeline appears at the bottom of the Animation pane, and indicators appear next to each clip to show how long it will take to play and at what point it starts. This is useful when you are trying to coordinate several sound and/or video clips to play sequentially with a certain amount of space between them. It also saves you from having to calculate their starting and ending times in relation to the initial appearance of the slide.

To turn the Advanced Timeline option on or off, do the following:

1. **If the Animation pane does not already appear, click Animation Pane on the Animations tab.**

2. **Open the drop-down menu for any of the items in the pane and choose Show Advanced Timeline.** (If the command Hide Advanced Timeline appears instead,

the advanced timeline is already displayed; close the menu without selecting anything.)

3. **(Optional) Widen the Animation pane by dragging its left border toward the center of the slide so that you have more working room.**

4. **(Optional) Click the word *Seconds* at the bottom of the pane.** This opens a menu where you can choose Zoom In or Zoom Out to change the zoom on the timeline.

5. **Click a clip to select it on the Animation pane.** A right-pointing arrow appears next to the clip. The arrow position corresponds to the place on the timeline where the clip is currently set to begin.

6. **Open the clip's drop-down menu and choose either With Previous or After Previous, depending on how you want it to relate to the clip that precedes it.**

CAUTION

If there is more than one sound clip set to After Previous, a vertical line appears where the first clip will finish. If a clip is set to After Previous, it cannot start before the clip that precedes it. Therefore, any delay that you set up for a subsequent clip will be in relation to the end of the preceding clip. If the clip is set to With Previous, the two can overlap.

---

7. **(Optional) To reorder the clips on the list, click a clip and then click the up or down Re-Order arrow at the top of the pane.**

8. **To change the amount of delay that is assigned to a clip, drag the arrow next to the clip to the right or left.** This is the same as changing the number in the Delay text box in the clip's properties. A ScreenTip appears as you drag telling how much delay you are adding. See Figure 14.17.

FIGURE 14.17

You can use a timeline to graphically set the timing between clips on a slide.

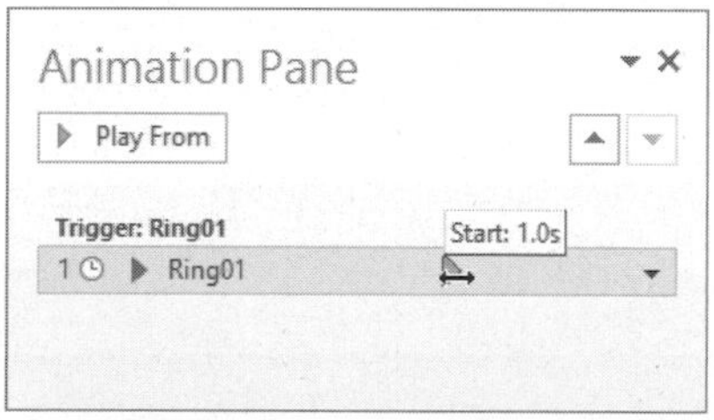

TIP

You can use custom animation to create complex systems of sounds that play, pause, and stop in relation to other animated objects on the slide. Chapter 16 contains full details.

Summary

In this chapter, you learned about the many ways that you can use sound in your presentation. You learned how to place a sound object on a slide from your own PC or from Office.com, how to record your own sounds, how to associate sounds with other objects, how to use a CD soundtrack, and how to fine-tune the playback settings for a sound. The next chapter continues to discuss multimedia by looking at how you can place video clips on slides.

Incorporating Motion Video

IN THIS CHAPTER

Understanding video types

Placing a video on a slide

Managing clip files and links

Changing the video's formatting

Specifying playback options

Troubleshooting video problems

PowerPoint 2013 has great support for motion video. It not only supports many video types (including Flash, which was difficult to integrate with PowerPoint in some earlier versions), but it allows you to trim the clip, bookmark a point in it, and add a wide variety of formatting to it. In this chapter, you'll learn how to insert and configure motion video.

Understanding Video Types

Three cheers for Microsoft for increasing the number of video file types that PowerPoint supports! Presentation developers have long been frustrated by PowerPoint's inability to accept certain file formats, but that problem is largely in the past now. PowerPoint 2013 supports the formats listed in Table 15.1.

> **NOTE**
> What's the difference between a movie and a video? There really isn't any. PowerPoint uses the terms interchangeably.

PowerPoint treats most video types similarly, in terms of how much control you have over their appearance and playback, except for the final two in Table 15.1: Adobe Flash Media and animated GIFs. Both of these deserve a bit of special discussion.

TABLE 15.1 **Supported Video Formats**

Format	Most Common Filename Extension	Other Filename Extensions
Windows Media file	`.asf`	`.asx, .dvr-ms, .wpl, .win, .wmx, .wmd, .wmz`
Windows video file	`.avi`	
QuickTime Movie file	`.mov`	`.qt, .dv, .mp4`
MP4 video	`.mp4`	`.m4v, .mp4v, .3gp, .3gpp, .3gz, .3gp2`
Movie file	`.mpeg`	`.mpeg, .mpg, .mpe, .m1v, .m2v, .mod, .mpv2, .mp2v, .mpa`
MPEG-2 TS video	`.m2ts`	`.m2t, .mts, .ts, .tts`
Windows Media Video	`.wmv`	`.mvx`
Adobe Flash media	`.swf`	
Animated GIF	`.gif`	

Adobe Flash Media

Flash media (`.swf`) is a very versatile format for creating animated, and sometimes interactive, demos and games. Other names for this format are Shockwave and Macromedia Flash. (Macromedia was the company that developed Flash; it was acquired by Adobe.)

Flash media is commonly used in education because of its interactivity. Not only can a Flash clip show movement through a process, it can accept mouse clicks from a viewer. So, for example, after illustrating a process, the clip can offer a multiple-choice quiz for review, with the viewer clicking the answers.

Flash is unique in PowerPoint in that it is not embedded in the file like other video formats; by default it is linked.

PowerPoint does not offer a full set of controls for a Flash clip; you can't trim it, for example, and you can't set it to fade in or out. However, you can place a Flash clip on a slide, resize it, and control many appearance aspects of it, such as frame color.

Animated GIF

Animated GIFs are not really videos in the traditional sense. An animated GIF is a special type of graphic that stores multiple versions of itself in a single file and flips through them in sequence, like an animation created by flipping the corners of a book. When the file is displayed — on a presentation slide, a web page, or some other place — it cycles through the still graphics at a certain speed, making a very rudimentary animation. You cannot control the animation of an animated GIF through PowerPoint, nor can you set it up to repeat a certain number of times. That information is contained within the GIF file itself. PowerPoint simply reads that information and plays the GIF accordingly. They are more like animated clip art than real videos, but they do add an active element to an otherwise static slide.

> **TIP**
>
> It is possible to convert an animated GIF to a "true" video format such as AVI. However, you can't do it using PowerPoint alone; you need a conversion utility. Corel Animation Shop will do this (`http://www.corel.com`), as will many GIF-editing programs.

Choosing a File Format for Your Video Recordings

You may not have a choice in the settings used for the recording of live video or the file format. If you do have a choice, AVI is among the best formats for use in PowerPoint because of its near-universal compatibility. There may be compatibility issues with video in some MPEG variants, such as MPEG-2 and MPEG-4, because you might need to install a separate DVD-playing utility or a specific codec to handle those formats.

See the section "Troubleshooting Videos That Won't Play" later in this chapter for more information on MPEG variants.

On the theory that Microsoft-to-Microsoft always works, the Windows Media Video format (`.wmv`) is also a good choice. Because Windows Movie Maker creates its videos in this format by default, it's a good bet that they will work well in PowerPoint.

Balancing Video Impact with File Size and Performance

Clip quality is usually measured either in frames per second (fps), which is anywhere from 15 (low) to 30 (high), or in kilobits and megabits per second, which is anywhere from 38 Kbps to 2.1 Mbps. You might experiment with different settings to find one with acceptable quality for the task at hand with the minimum file size. For example, with Windows Movie Maker, a wide variety of quality settings are available for creating video output.

When you are recording your own video clips with a video camera or other device, it is easy to overshoot. Video clips take up a huge amount of disk space, and inserting large video clips into a PowerPoint file can make that file very large. Even if you choose to link the clips instead of embedding them, the clips still take up space on your hard disk.

Depending on the amount of space available on your computer's hard disk, and whether you need to transfer your PowerPoint file to another PC, you may want to keep the number of seconds of recorded video to a minimum to ensure that the file size stays manageable. On the other hand, if you have a powerful computer with plenty of disk space and a lot of cool video clips to show, go for it!

15

TIP

After you have completed the bulk of the editing work on your presentation, you may wish to use the File ⇨ Info ⇨ Compress Media command to decrease the resolution and/or increase the compression ratio on the media clips in your presentation. Doing so may result in a minor loss of playback quality, but it may make the difference between a presentation fitting or not fitting on a particular disc.

Locating Video Clips

Not sure where to find video clips? Here are some places to start:

- **Your own video camera.** You can connect a digital video camera directly to your PC or connect an analog video camera to an adapter that digitizes its input. Then you use a video-editing program to clean them up and transfer them to your hard disk. Most video cameras come with such software; you can also use Windows Movie Maker.

TIP

Windows Movie Maker is not included with Windows 7 or 8. However, you can download it for free from this link: http://download.live.com/moviemaker.

- **Bing Video Search.** When you're connected to the Internet, you can use the Online Videos command to find and insert video clips from a Bing search.
- **YouTube.** PowerPoint 2013 includes a search box for YouTube in its Insert Video dialog box, so you can search YouTube archives without leaving PowerPoint.
- **The Internet in general.** There are millions of interesting video clips on every imaginable subject. Use the search term "video clips" plus a few keywords that describe the type of clips you are looking for. Google Images is a good place to start looking (http://images.google.com). Some clips are copyrighted or have usage limitations, but others can be used freely; check the usage information provided with the clip.
- **Your SkyDrive.** If you have stored videos on your SkyDrive, you can access them from within PowerPoint.

CAUTION

Whenever you get a video clip from the Internet, make sure you carefully read any restrictions or usage agreements to avoid copyright violations. If you create a presentation using copyrighted material in an unauthorized way, you or your company could potentially get sued.

- **Commercial collections of video clips and animated GIFs.** Many of these companies advertise on the Internet and provide free samples for downloading. Several such companies have included samples in the online content for this book at www.wiley.com/go/powerpoint2013bible.

- **The Internet Archive** (http://archive.org). This site contains links to huge repositories of public domain footage on all subjects, mostly pre-1960s material on which the copyright has expired. Warning — you can easily get sucked in here and waste several days browsing!

Placing a Video on a Slide

Your first step is to place the video on the slide. After that, you can worry about position, size, and playing options.

Just as with audio clips, you can place a video clip on a slide by inserting from a file or pasting from another application or by browsing for clips online.

Inserting a Video from a File

A video clip file inserted in PowerPoint 2013 can be either embedded or linked. (This is a change from PowerPoint 2007 and earlier, in which all clips were linked.)

- **Embedded.** The default. The clip is inserted into the presentation file, so if you copy or distribute the presentation file, the clip goes along with it automatically. Because the presentation file serves as a container for the clip, the presentation file's size grows by the size of the video clip file (plus a little extra for overhead).

- **Linked.** A link to the clip is placed on the slide, so the clip does not take up space in the presentation file. When you play back the presentation, the video clip must be in the expected location for it to work.

> **CAUTION**
>
> If you plan on moving the presentation to another location later, and you want to use links, place the video clip in the same folder as the presentation itself before you insert the video clip into the presentation. That way the path to it stored in the presentation file will be relative, and the link will still work after you move the presentation and video clip. Alternatively, you can use the Package Presentation for CD feature to transfer a presentation and all of its support files, including videos, to a new location. See "Giving a Presentation on a Different Computer" in Chapter 18, "Preparing for a Live Presentation."

Before inserting a clip, decide which method is best for your situation. Then follow these steps (for all video types except animated GIF):

1. **Display the slide on which the video should appear.**

2. **If there is a content placeholder on the slide that will accommodate a video clip, click that and then click the Browse button next to From a File.** Otherwise, choose Insert ➪ Media ➪ Video ➪ Video on My PC.

3. **In the Insert Video dialog box, locate and select the clip you want.** You might need to change the file type setting in the dialog box.

15

4. **If you want the clip to be embedded, click Insert.**

5. **Alternatively, if you want the clip to be linked, click the down arrow to the right of the Insert button and choose Link to File.** See Figure 15.1. The video clip appears on the slide.

FIGURE 15.1

To link, rather than embed, open the Insert button's menu and choose Link to File.

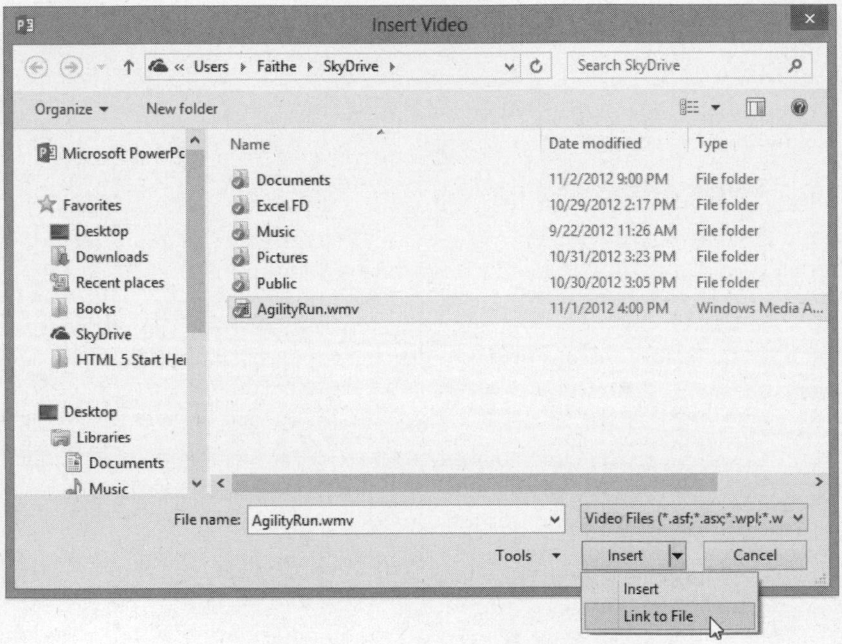

Inserting Video from Your SkyDrive

If you store videos on your SkyDrive, you can easily insert them into your presentations by browsing the SkyDrive contents. To do so, choose Insert ➪ Media ➪ Video ➪ Online Video and then click the Browse button next to your SkyDrive. Select the desired clip and click Insert.

If you have the SkyDrive for Windows app installed in Windows, you can also directly browse your SkyDrive just as if it were a local drive. Choose Insert ➪ Media ➪ Video ➪ Video on My PC, and then under Favorites, click SkyDrive. (Figure 15.1 shows the SkyDrive, rather than a local disk, being accessed.) If you don't have a SkyDrive shortcut under Favorites, you can get it for free. Go to http://www.skydrive.com and click the Get SkyDrive Apps hyperlink.

Inserting a Video from a Bing Search

Just as you searched for online pictures in Chapter 11, "Working With Clip Art and Photos," and online audio clips in Chapter 14, "Adding Sound Effects, Music, and Soundtracks," you can search Bing for online video clips. The process is mostly the same as in those other chapters.

Follow these steps to locate and insert a video clip using Bing:

1. **Choose Insert ⇨ Media ⇨ Video ⇨ Online Video.** The Insert Video dialog box opens.

2. **In the Bing Video Search text box, type the keyword(s) to search for, as shown in Figure 15.2, and press Enter.** The search results appear.

3. **Click the desired clip and click Insert.** The clip is downloaded and inserted into your presentation. (It is embedded, not linked.)

FIGURE 15.2

Use the Insert Video dialog box to insert from a Bing video search.

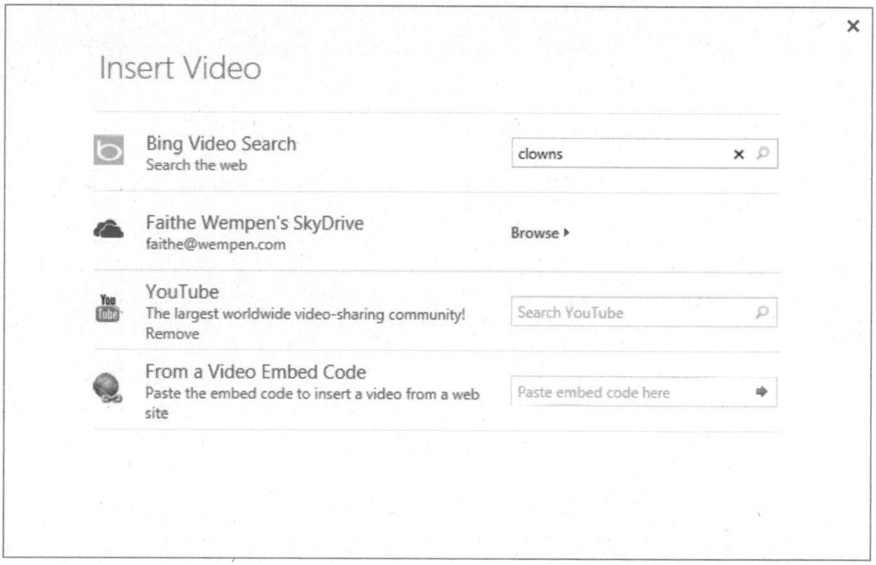

Linking to a YouTube Video

YouTube is a huge repository of video clips on the Internet. You can search it much as you can search Bing (see the previous section), but with one important difference: YouTube videos are not downloaded and embedded into your presentation; instead, a link is created in the presentation file that refers to a streaming copy of the video on http://www.youtube.com. When you play back the video during a presentation, you must have an active Internet connection in order for it to work.

The form of link used for a YouTube clip is not the traditional type of link whose properties you can edit in PowerPoint (as covered in "Managing Video Links" later in this chapter). It doesn't show up on a list of the links in the presentation, either. You can't break the link without removing the clip entirely from your presentation. Follow these steps to locate and link to a YouTube video:

1. **Choose Insert ⇨ Media ⇨ Video ⇨ Online Video.** The Insert Video dialog box opens.

2. **In the YouTube text box, type the keyword(s) to search for, and press Enter.**

The chosen clip appears on the active slide. You can resize it, and you can control its appearance in most of the same ways as other video clips (from the Video Tools Format tab), but most of the commands on the Video Tools Playback tab are unavailable for YouTube clips.

> **TIP**
>
> Not all YouTube clips can be placed on a slide because of the differences in licensing restrictions; if you see an error when trying to place a YouTube clip, you may have to try a different clip.

Embedding Code That Links to an Online Video

Some sites on the Internet encourage people to share links to their videos by providing embed codes for each video. An embed code is a URL that contains all the information needed to not only link to the clip but to present it at the destination in a certain way, such as with or without playback controls, at a certain size or resolution, and so on. For example, notice that the dialog box in Figure 15.3 contains a button you can click to get the embed code, which can easily be selected and copied to the Windows Clipboard and then pasted into an application.

As with YouTube clips, clips inserted by embed code are also not editable in PowerPoint, and you must have an Internet connection active when you show the presentation in order for them to play back successfully.

To use an embed code, follow these steps:

1. **Copy the embed code from the website where you found it to the Clipboard.**

2. **Choose Insert ⇨ Media ⇨ Video ⇨ Online Video.** The Insert Video dialog box opens.

3. **Click in the From a Video Embed Code box.**

4. **Press Ctrl+V to paste the embed code from the Clipboard and press Enter.**

Don't panic if the clip appears as a plain black box with no playback controls on the slide in Normal view. Switch to Slide Show view and you'll see the clip as it will appear to your audience.

FIGURE 15.3

Some websites provide embed codes to make video linkage easy.

Click here to get
the embed code.

Managing Clip Files and Links

In the following sections, you'll learn some ways to manage the compatibility, file size and performance, and linkage of video clips in a presentation.

Optimizing Media Compatibility

Versions of PowerPoint prior to 2010 did not allow videos to be embedded and supported a smaller number of file formats, so you may run into problems when you move a PowerPoint 2013 presentation to a PC that uses PowerPoint 2007 or earlier. This may come as a surprise to PowerPoint 2007 users because in most ways PowerPoint 2007 is very similar to 2010 and 2013. Videos are the one area in which they differ greatly.

To minimize the impact of such problems, there are two things you can do. One is to link all videos rather than embedding them. Delete the embedded versions and reinsert them, choosing Link to File from the Insert button's drop-down menu in the Insert Video dialog box.

The other is to run the Optimize Media Compatibility utility by following these steps:

1. **Choose File ➪ Info ➪ Optimize Media Compatibility.** If there are any videos that could be converted to another format to improve their compatibility, they are automatically processed, as shown in Figure 15.4.

2. **When the optimization process is complete, click the Close button to close the Optimize Media Compatibility dialog box.**

15

FIGURE 15.4

The AgilityRun video is being converted into a more compatible format.

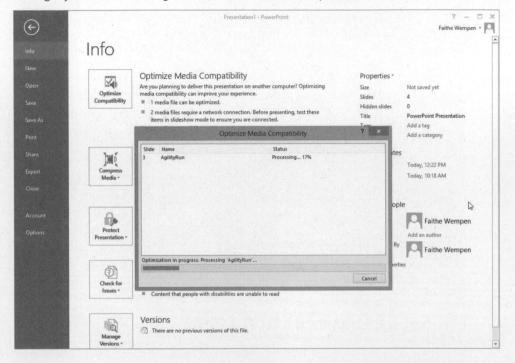

Some clip types may show as Unsupported in the results that appear after optimization. This means that the clip's format may not be playable in an earlier PowerPoint version; you might need to convert that clip to some other format using a third-party video editor and then reinsert it into PowerPoint.

> **CAUTION**
> If you back-save (that is, save in PowerPoint 97–2003 format) a presentation file that contains videos, any videos that are in formats unsupported by that version will be saved as static graphics (of the first frame of the video).

Optimizing Media Size and Performance

Video files can take up a lot of space and can result in a large PowerPoint presentation file. If the quality of the video playback is not of critical importance, you may want to sacrifice a certain amount of quality to get a smaller file that opens and closes more quickly, starts the video playback more quickly, and takes up less space.

CAUTION

Save a copy of your presentation with another name before you compress the media clips. That way, if the playback quality suffers too much, you can revert to the higher-quality version. This also gives you the high-quality version to play back locally.

To find out how much disk space the media files in your presentation (both video and audio) are currently occupying, choose File ⇨ Info and look under the Media Size and Performance heading. For example, in Figure 15.5, you can see that the media files take up 26MB of space. Then, if you want to make a change, click the Compress Media button, and from the menu that appears, click a quality setting that best describes the trade-off you want to make between quality and performance. The compression begins immediately. When it's finished, examine the results reported in the Compress Media dialog box, and then click the Close button.

FIGURE 15.5

Choose a compression amount to save disk space if desired.

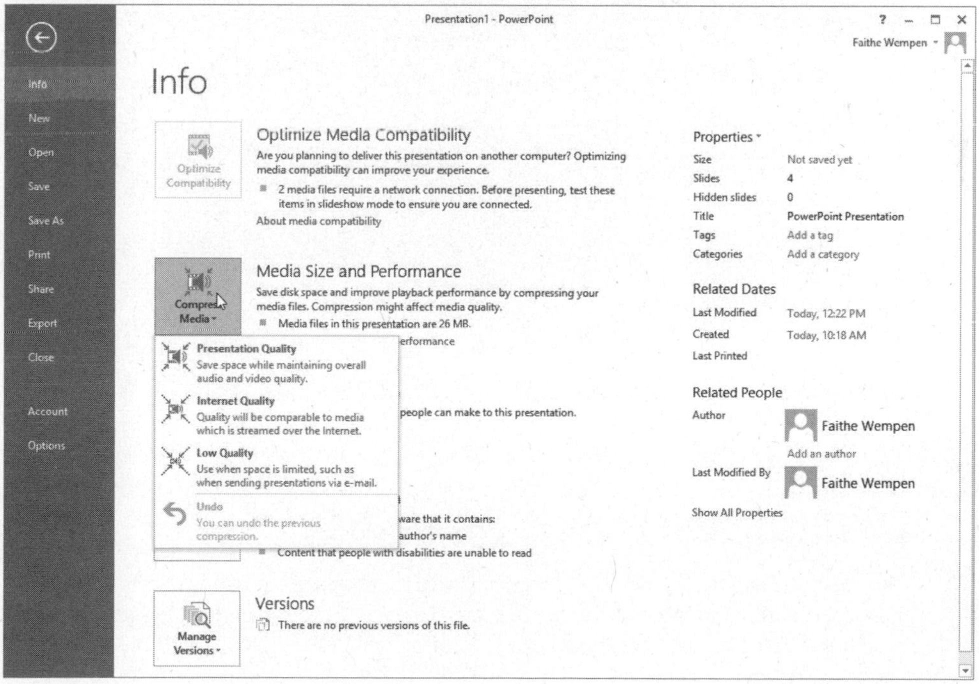

Managing Video Links

In Chapter 13, in the section "Working with Linked and Embedded Objects," you learned how to update and break links to outside content. Those same techniques work for linked video clips if you choose to link them rather than embed them. (An exception is if you have links to online video content like YouTube or an embedded link code; these can't be managed in PowerPoint.)

Choose File ⇨ Info ⇨ View Links. The View Links command is located under the Optimize Media Compatibility heading. If you don't see it there, your presentation has no links you can manage.

In the Links dialog box, you see all the links in your presentation, including those to external online sources like YouTube. However, when you select one of those links, you find that there is only one option available for it: Open Source (which plays the clip in a web browser at the original source page). For clips that are linked from other sources, such as your own LAN, all of the buttons are available, as in Figure 15.6.

FIGURE 15.6

Linked videos appear in the Links dialog box.

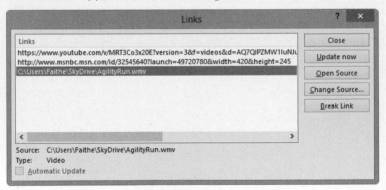

Changing the Video's Formatting

The *formatting* for a video clip refers to the size, shape, position, and effects of the frame in which the video appears. It doesn't have anything to do with the playback of the video itself. (See "Specifying Playback Options" later in this chapter for playback customization.)

The following sections explain how to affect the formatting of a video clip in various ways.

Choosing the Size of the Video Clip Window

You can resize a video clip's window just as you can any other object. Simply drag its selection handles. Be careful, however, that you do not distort the image by resizing in only one dimension. Make sure you drag a corner selection handle, not one on a single side of the object. To set an exact size, enter the dimensions in the Height and Width boxes on the Video Tools Format tab.

Also be aware that when you enlarge a video clip's window, the quality of the clip suffers.

If you make the clip large and are unhappy with its quality, you can reset it to its original size by following these steps:

1. **Right-click the clip and choose Size and Position, or click the dialog box launcher for the Size group on the Video Tools Format tab.** The Format Video task pane opens with the Size controls displayed.

2. **Click Reset.**

3. **Close the task pane.**

Setting the Initial Image (Poster Frame)

The *poster frame* is the image that appears when the clip is not playing. By default it is the first frame of the video clip. However, if the first frame of the video is a blank screen, you may want to use something else instead.

You can choose an external image file for the poster frame, or you select a frame from the video itself.

Choosing an External Poster Frame

To use an external still image as the poster frame, follow these steps:

1. **In Normal view, select the video.**

2. **Choose Video Tools Format ⇨ Adjust ⇨ Poster Frame ⇨ Image from File.** The Insert Pictures dialog box appears.

3. **Select the picture you want to use.** You can select from your own PC by clicking Browse next to From a File, or you can search Office.com or Bing or choose a file from your SkyDrive. See Chapter 11 for details about choosing the various types of pictures.

CAUTION

If the picture you choose is a different size than the video clip, the poster frame may stretch the image so that it loses its aspect ratio and becomes distorted-looking. Crop the picture ahead of time to match the aspect ratio of the video clip to avoid this problem.

15

Choosing a Video Frame as the Poster Frame

To use a frame from the video itself as the poster frame, do the following:

1. **In Normal view, select the video clip.**
2. **Verify that playback controls appear below the clip in Normal view.** (They do for most file types, but not for Flash, animated GIFs, or linked files from websites.) If there are no playback controls, you cannot proceed with these steps.
3. **Click the Play button (right-pointing triangle) on the controls below the clip.**
4. **When the video displays the frame you want to use, click the Pause button (two vertical bars) on the controls below the clip.**
5. **Choose Video Tools Format ➪ Adjust ➪ Poster Frame ➪ Current Frame.**

Resetting the Poster Frame

To return to the default poster frame (the first frame of the video clip), select the clip and then choose Video Tools Format ➪ Adjust ➪ Poster Frame ➪ Reset.

Applying Corrections and Color Washes

You can apply brightness and contrast corrections to a video clip in the same way you do to photographic images. This was covered in detail in Chapter 11. Choose Video Tools Format ➪ Adjust ➪ Corrections and then choose one of the sample images that reflects the changes to be made. See Figure 15.7.

FIGURE 15.7

Adjust the brightness and/or contrast of the clip if desired.

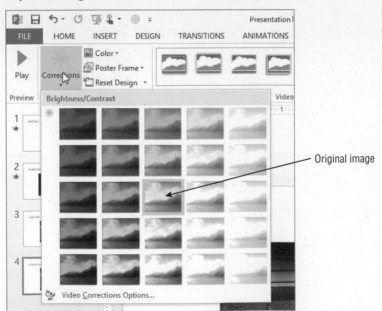

The same color washes that you learned about in Chapter 11 for photos also apply to most video clips. Click the Color button and choose a color wash, or choose More Variations for more color choices. Choosing a color from the Color button's menu (see Figure 15.8) will set the video to play as a monochrome (single-color) clip, using the color you chose.

FIGURE 15.8

Choose a color wash or other color setting.

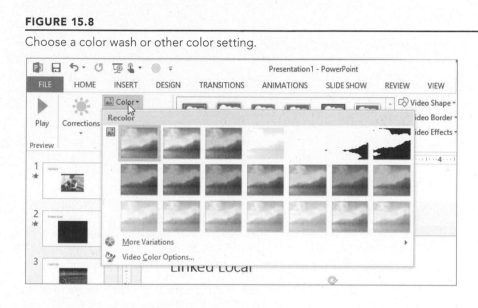

Applying Video Styles and Effects

On the Video Tools Format tab, you'll find the same style and effect options as for photos.

Here's a sampling of what you can do; refer to Chapter 11 for more details on each of these options.

- **Styles.** Open the Styles palette and pick one of the presets there to apply a combination of frame shape and image effects. You can also right-click the clip on the slide and then click the Style icon to select from a smaller pop-up list of styles.

- **Video Effects.** Click this button for access to the same formatting options as for images: Shadow, Reflection, Glow, Soft Edges, Bevel, and 3-D.

- **Video Border.** Click this button to choose a border color and thickness for the video clip's outer frame.

- **Video Shape.** Click this button and then choose one of the built-in shapes to alter the shape of the video clip's frame. You might choose to make it a rounded rectangle, for example, or an oval.

- **Crop.** You can crop the window of the clip so that part of the clip does not appear (uncommon).

15

- **Send Backward.** You can send the clip behind other objects on the slide. This makes it possible to use overlapping lines, shapes, and text boxes to annotate the video clip window. You can also Bring Forward to move a clip in front of other objects.

> **NOTE**
> The Reset Design button on the Video Tools Format tab resets everything you have done to a clip's formatting except the setting of the poster frame. To reset the poster frame, choose Format ⇨ Adjust ⇨ Poster Frame ⇨ Reset.

Specifying Playback Options

Playback options are the options that control when and how the clip plays. Unlike the formatting options you learned about in the previous sections, these controls affect the *action* of the clip, the unique qualities it has as a motion video object rather than a static image.

Displaying or Hiding Playback Controls

By default, when a video clip plays in Slide Show view, playback controls appear below it. They make it easy to start and stop the clip and to skip to a different section of it (by clicking on the timeline below the clip).

You may sometimes want to hide those controls, however. To hide them, on the Slide Show tab, clear the Show Media Controls check box. Note that this setting applies to the entire presentation; you unfortunately cannot disable or enable playback controls separately for individual clips.

Choosing a Start Trigger

There are a number of ways to specify when a clip starts playing. Let's take a look at some of these.

Making a Clip Play Automatically or On Click

A video clip's default playback setting is On Click, meaning that it plays during Slide Show view only when the clip itself is clicked. You can change this behavior, so that it plays automatically when it appears, by changing the Start setting on the Video Tools Playback tab, as shown in Figure 15.9. (You can also set this on the Animations tab, or you can right-click the video clip, click the Start icon, and choose a setting from its menu.)

> **NOTE**
> If you set the clip to start automatically, you can optionally specify a number of seconds that should pass before that occurs. On the Animations tab, enter a number of seconds in the Delay box to build in this delay. You'll learn more about delaying the start of an animation event in Chapter 16, "Creating Animation Effects and Transitions."

FIGURE 15.9

Set a clip to play back either automatically or on click.

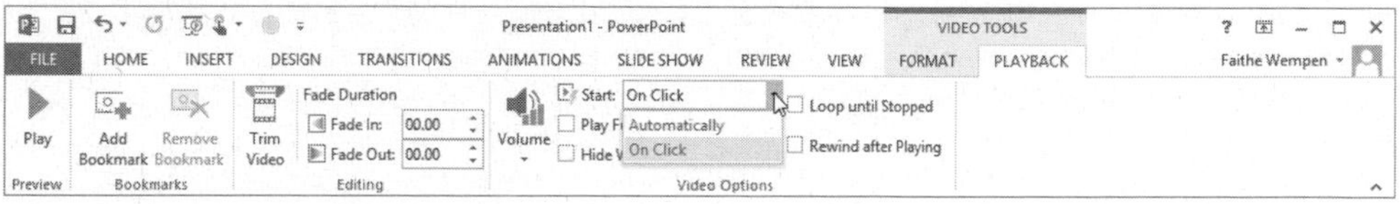

Playing the Clip on Mouseover

By default, an inserted clip is already set up to play on click, but not when the mouse pointer passes over it. To play the clip when the mouse pointer passes over it (mouseover), use the Action command, like this:

1. **Select the clip in Normal view.**
2. **Choose Insert ⇨ Links ⇨ Action.** The Action Settings dialog box opens.
3. **Click the Mouse Over tab.**
4. **Select the Object Action button.** The default action is Play, as shown in Figure 15.10. Leave it set that way.

FIGURE 15.10

Action settings on the Mouse Over tab control whether the clip plays when the mouse passes over it.

5. **Click OK.**

Triggering Play by Clicking Another Object

Triggers specify when the action should occur. They enable you to trigger an event as a result of clicking the event object or something other than the event object. For example, you could put a piece of clip art on the slide next to a video and have the video playback begin when you click the clip art.

Trigger animation is set automatically for the clip itself when you insert it so that the clip starts and pauses when you click it. To set up a trigger for an object other than the clip itself, follow these steps:

1. **Place both the video and the trigger object (such as a button or a piece of clip art) on the same slide.**

2. **Choose Animations ➪ Advanced Animation ➪ Animation Pane.** The Animation pane appears. There may already be an animation listed there that plays and pauses the video clip.

3. **Select the video clip and choose Animations ➪ Advanced Animation ➪ Add Animation ➪ Play.** If the clip begins playing immediately, click the Stop button in the Animation pane.

    A new Play animation event appears at the top of the Animation pane. See Figure 15.11.

FIGURE 15.11

Add a new Play animation for the video clip.

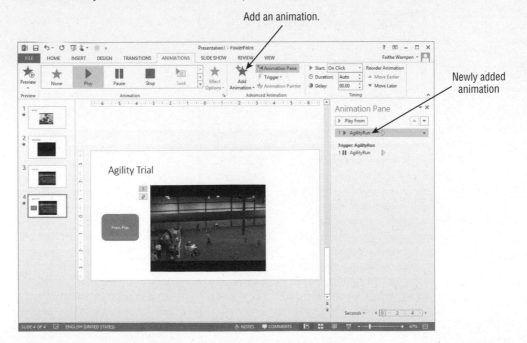

4. **Right-click this new event and choose Timing.** The Play Animation dialog box opens.

5. **Click the Triggers button to expand the Triggers controls if they are not already displayed.**

6. **Click Start Effect on Click Of.**

7. **Open the drop-down list and choose the object that will serve as the trigger.** For example, in Figure 15.12, the object is a rounded rectangle that has the words *Press Play* in it.

FIGURE 15.12

Set up optional triggers that make the clip play when you click something other than the clip.

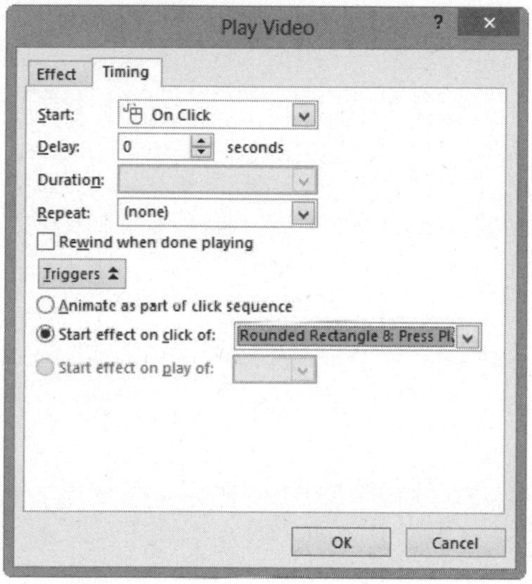

8. **Click OK.** If the clip begins playing again, click the Stop button in the Animation pane.

9. **Test the trigger in Slide Show view.**

Choosing Clip Playback Options

On the Video Tools Playback tab, the Video Options group contains a series of check boxes that govern various small details about the clip playback. Mark or clear any of these as desired:

- **Play Full Screen.** Switches the clip to full-screen size when it is playing in Slide Show view.

- **Hide While Not Playing.** Hides the still image (the poster frame) of the clip.

- **Loop Until Stopped.** Plays the clip over and over until you move to the next slide or stop it using its playback controls.
- **Rewind After Playing.** When the clip finishes, normally the final frame remains on-screen; marking this check box makes the first frame appear again instead.

> **CAUTION**
>
> If you are using an animated GIF, it plays the number of times specified in its header. That could be infinite looping (0), or it could be a specified number of times. You can't set it to do otherwise. (You can, however, delay its initial appearance with custom animation. See Chapter 16 for details.) Other videos, such as your own recorded video clips, have more settings you can control.

Controlling the Volume

The clip can have a different volume setting than the rest of the presentation's audio. That way you can compensate for a clip that is louder or quieter than the other audio in the presentation.

To change the clip's volume level, click the Volume button on the Video Tools Playback tab and then choose Low, Medium, High, or Mute from the menu.

Trimming the Clip

You can trim footage off the beginning or end of a video clip from within PowerPoint 2013. This makes it possible for you to do some rudimentary editing without having to use a separate video-editing program.

> **CAUTION**
>
> Not all types of clips can be trimmed. If the Trim Video button is unavailable on the Playback tab, the clip you have selected can be trimmed only by using a third-party program.

To trim a clip, follow these steps:

1. **Select the clip on the slide.**
2. **Choose Video Tools Playback ⇨ Editing ⇨ Trim Video.** The Trim Video dialog box opens.
3. **To trim off the beginning of the clip, do the following:**
   a. Click the Play button (right-pointing triangle) and wait until the part of the clip plays where you want to begin.
   b. Click the Pause button (the two vertical lines). A thin blue vertical line on the timeline shows where the clip has stopped.

If you didn't pause it at exactly the right place, use the Next Frame or Previous Frame button to move back or forward one frame per click until the marker is in the right spot.

You can also drag the thin vertical line to the left or right on the timeline to move it manually.

c. Note the number above the timeline; this tells you exactly how many seconds into the clip the marked position represents.

d. Drag the green marker on the left end of the timeline to the position you marked, using the number that appears above the timeline as a reference. Or, alternatively, enter the value you noted in step 3c in the Start Time box. See Figure 15.13.

FIGURE 15.13

You can trim footage off the beginning and/or end of the clip.

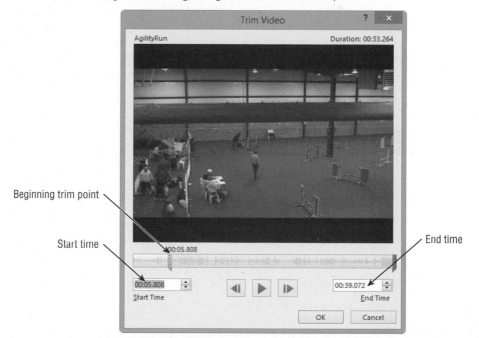

4. **To trim off the end of the clip, do the following:**

   a. Click the Play button (right-pointing triangle) and wait until the part of the clip plays where you want to stop. Then click the Pause button. Or, alternatively, click on the timeline to jump to a certain position and pause there.

   b. Note the number above the timeline; this tells you exactly how many seconds into the clip the marked position represents.

    c. Drag the red marker on the right end of the timeline to the position you marked, using the number that appears above the timeline as a reference. Or, alternatively, enter the value you noted in step 4b in the Start Time box.

5. **Click OK to accept the trimming.**

> **CAUTION**
> Compressing the media in the presentation (File ⇨ Compress Media) deletes the trimmed parts from the embedded copy of the clip.

Setting Fade In and Fade Out Durations

Some clips already begin and/or end with a "fade to black" effect. If one of your clips doesn't and you want such an effect, you can apply it manually from within PowerPoint.

Select the clip, and on the Video Tools Playback tab, enter values (in seconds) in the Fade In and/or Fade Out boxes. Seconds are expressed as whole numbers, so 1.25 would be 1.25 seconds. The larger the number you enter, the longer the effect will take and the more obvious it will seem. See Figure 15.14.

FIGURE 15.14

Set a clip to fade in and/or fade out if desired.

Fade controls

Setting a Bookmark

You can set bookmarks (in other words, markers) wherever you want within the video and then jump among those marked locations during a presentation. To jump ahead to the next bookmark in a video clip, you can press Alt+End; to jump backward to the previous bookmark, use Alt+Home.

To set a video bookmark, follow these steps:

1. **Select the video clip on the slide.**
2. **In Normal view, use the Play button (right-pointing triangle) below the video clip to begin a preview of it.**

3. **When the video playback gets to the point where you want the bookmark, click Pause to stop playback at that spot, and then choose Video Tools Playback ⇨ Bookmarks ⇨ Add Bookmark.**

A bookmark is inserted at that spot. A bookmark symbol (tiny white or gold circle) appears on the playback timeline under the clip. See Figure 15.15.

FIGURE 15.15

Set bookmarks within a clip's playback if desired.

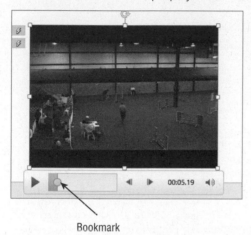

Bookmark

To remove a bookmark, click the bookmark symbol and then choose Video Tools Playback ⇨ Bookmarks ⇨ Remove Bookmark.

You can then set up a trigger to a bookmark so that something happens when the video playback reaches a certain point. For example, you could have some text appear over the top of the video at a certain point and then disappear. (Use Video Tools Format ⇨ Arrange ⇨ Send Backward to move the video behind the text box as needed.)

Here's how to set a trigger to a bookmark.

1. **Add the object to the slide that should appear at a certain point in the video playback.** For example, add a text box and type the needed text in it.

2. **Select the object that should appear, and add an entrance animation effect to it.** For example, for a simple "appear" effect, choose Animations ⇨ Animation ⇨ Appear. (You can choose an effect other than Appear if you like.).

3. **With the object still selected, choose Animations ⇨ Advanced Animation ⇨ Trigger ⇨ On Bookmark and click the desired bookmark.**

   The bookmarks are consecutively numbered, from left to right on the clip timeline.

15

If you want the object to exit at a certain point in the video, continue with these steps.

4. **(Optional) Set another bookmark at the point where the object should exit.**

5. **Add an exit effect to the object.** For example, for a simple "disappear" effect, choose Animations ⇨ Advanced Animation ⇨ Add Animation ⇨ Disappear. (It's in the Exit section of the menu.)

6. **Choose Animations ⇨ Trigger ⇨ On Bookmark and choose the bookmark that represents the position at which it should exit.**

You can repeat that process for multiple objects so that different text or graphics appear over the top of the video at different points.

Troubleshooting Video Problems

Here are some workarounds available for most of the common problems with PowerPoint video clips.

Working with Older Presentations in PowerPoint 2013

When you open a presentation created in PowerPoint 2007 or earlier, the video clips continue to play. However, you will probably want to update the file to the latest PowerPoint format so you can enjoy the additional capabilities.

After opening the file, choose File ⇨ Info ⇨ Convert to update it to PowerPoint 2013 format. In the Save As dialog box that appears, specify a name for the new converted version (the original remains intact) and click Save.

After you save the presentation in the new format, all PowerPoint 2013 video-editing features are available, just as if you had started this presentation in version 2013 from scratch.

Troubleshooting Videos That Won't Insert

If you are inserting a QuickTime clip, you will need to have a QuickTime player installed, and you need to have the 32-bit version of Office. The 64-bit version of PowerPoint cannot accept inserted QuickTime movie files because the 64-bit Windows operating system does not have the needed 64-bit codecs for that format. See http://support.microsoft .com/kb/982689 for more information.

To work around this issue, you can convert the clips to Windows Media Video (.wmv) format using a third-party file converter.

Troubleshooting Videos That Won't Play

For problems with videos that won't play, explore one or more of these possible fixes:

- **Update your players.** Make sure you have the latest versions of the following programs:
  - Windows Media Player (should be version 10 or higher)
  - Flash Player (should be version 9 or higher)
  - QuickTime
  - DirectX

- **Play it in an external player.** If your video won't play in PowerPoint but it will play outside of PowerPoint using one of your media players you have installed, insert the clip as an object with the Insert ⇨ Object command. That way it will play using an external player during the presentation.

- **Convert to WMV format.** PowerPoint easily handles Windows Media Video (WMV) format clips. You can import a video clip into Windows Movie Maker (free with Windows XP and Windows Vista and available for free download if you have Windows 7 or 8) and then export it to WMV format from there.

> **TIP**
>
> If you record video with your own video camera and it won't play in PowerPoint, it's probably because your camera uses a proprietary codec. Use the software that comes with the camera to re-render your video using a more common codec. A utility called GSpot, available at `http://www.headbands.com/gspot`, can identify what codecs are being used in your video files.

> **TIP**
>
> This may seem hard to believe, but it works. If you get an error message when you try to drag and drop an AVI video clip into your presentation or if you try to insert it and PowerPoint simply ignores you, try changing the filename extension from `.avi` to `.mpg`. This often will fix it.

Troubleshooting Poor Playback Quality

Be aware that slower, older computers, especially those with a meager amount of RAM, may not present your video clip to its best advantage. The sound may not match the video, the video may be jerky, and a host of other little annoying performance glitches may occur. On such PCs, it is best to limit the live-action video that you use and rely more on animated GIFs, simple WMV animations, and other less system-taxing video clips.

When you are constructing a presentation, keep in mind that you may be showing it on a lesser computer than the one on which you are creating it and therefore performance

15

problems may crop up during the presentation that you did not anticipate. Here are some ideas for at least partially fixing the problem:

- Make sure you test the presentation on the actual computer on which you are going to show it, especially if you need a nonstandard codec.

- Copy the entire presentation and all of its support files to the fastest hard disk on the system instead of running it from a CD. Hard disks have much faster access time. Use File ⇨ Export ⇨ Package Presentation for CD to collect the needed files, instead of manually copying them through Windows, to ensure that you get all of the files and properly resolve their links.

- Run the entire presentation on the playback PC from start to finish beforehand. If there are delays, jerks, and lack of synchronization, just let it play itself out. Then try the whole presentation again, and it will usually be much better the second time. This happens because the system caches some of the data, and it's faster to read it from the cache than from the disk.

- Make sure the playback PC is in the best shape it can be in. If feasible, upgrade its RAM. Run Disk Defragmenter and Disk Cleanup on it, and make sure its video driver is up to date.

- Work with the original media clips to decrease their complexity, and then reimport them into PowerPoint. For example, use video-editing software to lower the frames-per-second of video clips, and use image-editing software to lower the dots-per-inch of any large graphics.

- If possible, spread out the more complex slides in the presentation so that they are not adjacent to one another. Have an intervening slide that is just simple text.

- If all else fails, convert the presentation into a video, or transfer the presentation to DVD or videotape from the original PC (where presumably it plays correctly).

Summary

In this chapter, you learned how to place video clips on your slides and how to set them up to play when you want them to. You learned about the differences between various video formats and how to set up clips to play when you display the slide and/or when you click them. You can set a clip's volume and appearance and make it play at different starting points and stop at different ending points.

In the next chapter, you'll learn about transitions and object animation. With a transition, you can create special effects for the movement from one slide to another. With object animation, you can control the entry and exit of individual objects on a slide. You can make them fly in with special effects or build them dramatically one paragraph, bar, or shape at a time.

CHAPTER 16

Creating Animation Effects and Transitions

IN THIS CHAPTER

Assigning transitions to slides

Animating slide content

Layering animated objects

So far in this book, you have learned about several types of moving objects on a slide. One object type is a movie, or video clip, that has been created in an animation program or recorded with a video camera. Another type is an animated GIF, which is essentially a graphic that has some special properties that enable it to play a short animation sequence over and over.

However, neither of these types is what PowerPoint means by animation. In PowerPoint, *animation* is the way that individual objects enter or exit a slide. All of the objects on a slide with no animation simply appear at the same time when you display it. (Boring, eh?) However, you can apply animation to a slide so that the bullet points fly in from the left, one at a time, and the graphic drops down from the top afterward.

A *transition* is another kind of animation. A transition refers to the entry or exit of the entire slide rather than of an individual object on the slide.

Here are some ideas for using animation effectively in your presentations:

- Animate parts of a chart so that the data appears one series at a time. This technique works well if you want to talk about each series separately.

- Set up questions and answers on a slide so that the question appears first, and then, when you click the question, the answer appears.

- Dim each bullet point when the next one comes into view so that you are, in effect, highlighting the current one.

- Make an object appear and then disappear. For example, you might have an image of a lightning bolt that flashes on the slide for one second and then disappears or a picture of a race car that drives onto the slide from the left and then immediately drives out of sight to the right.

■ Rearrange the order in which objects appear on the slide. For example, you could make numbered points appear from the bottom up for a top ten list.

Assigning Transitions to Slides

Transitions determine how you get from slide A to slide B. Back in the old slide projector days, there was only one transition: the old slide was pushed out, and the new slide dropped into place. However, with a computerized presentation, you can choose from all kinds of fun transitions, including wipes, blinds, fly-ins, and much more. These transitions are almost exactly like the animations, except that they apply to the whole slide (or at least the background — the base part of the slide — if the slide's objects are separately animated).

> **NOTE**
>
> The transition effect for a slide refers to how the slide *enters* and not how it exits. As a result, if you want to assign a particular transition while moving from slide 1 to slide 2, you would assign the transition effect to slide 2.

The individual transitions are hard to describe in words; it is best if you just view them on-screen to understand what each one does. You should try out several transitions before making your final selection.

Setting Transition Effects and Timings

The default transition effect is None. One slide replaces another with no special effect. If you want something flashier than that, you must choose it from the Transitions tab.

As you are setting up the transition effect, you have a choice of allowing it to occur manually (that is, On Mouse Click) or automatically. Generally speaking, if there is a live person controlling and presenting the show, transitions should be manual. With manual transitions, the presenter must click the mouse to move to the next slide. This might sound like a lot of work, but it helps the speaker to maintain control of the show. If someone in the audience asks a question or wants to make a comment, the show does not continue on blindly but pauses to accommodate the delay. However, if you are preparing a self-running presentation, such as for a kiosk, automatic transitions are a virtual necessity.

Later you will learn how to set the timing between slides. Timings also are in effect when you record narration, as described in Chapter 19, "Designing User-Interactive or Self-Running Presentations."

To assign a transition effect and control its timing, follow these steps:

1. **View or select the slide in Normal or Slide Sorter view.** If you use Slide Sorter view, you can more easily select multiple slides to which you can apply the transition.

2. **(Optional) On the Transitions tab, in the Transition to This Slide group, click the transition you want to use.** Open the gallery to see additional transitions if needed.

   If you do not want a transition effect, do not choose a transition; instead leave the default transition (None) selected.

3. **Click Effect Options and select any options for the chosen effect transition as desired.** The effects listed will be different depending on the transition you chose. Figure 16.1 shows the options available for the Push transition.

FIGURE 16.1

Select a transition.

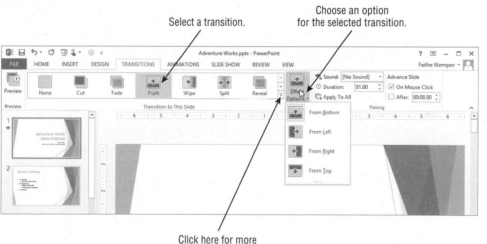

Select a transition.

Choose an option
for the selected transition.

Click here for more
transitions.

4. **In the Timing group, mark or clear the following check boxes:**

   ■ **On Mouse Click.** Transitions when you click the mouse.

   ■ **After.** Transitions after a specified amount of time has passed. (Enter the time, in seconds, in the associated text box.)

NOTE

It is perfectly okay to leave the On Mouse Click check box selected, even if you choose automatic transitions — in fact, this is a good idea. There may be times when you want to manually advance to the next slide before the automatic transition time has elapsed, and leaving this option selected allows you to do so.

> **CAUTION**
>
> You will probably want to assign automatic transitions to either all or none of the slides in the presentation, but not a mixture of the two. This is because mixed transition times can cause confusion when some of the slides automatically advance and others do not. However, there may be situations in which you need to assign different timings and effects to the various slides' transitions.

5. **(Optional) Adjust the Duration setting to specify how quickly the transition effect will occur.**

   This is not the timing between slides but rather the timing from the beginning to the end of the transition effect itself. For example, for a Fade transition, it determines how fast the fade occurs.

6. **(Optional) If you want a sound associated with the transition, select it from the Sound drop-down list.** See the next section for details.

7. **(Optional) If you want these same transition settings to apply to all slides in the presentation, click Apply to All.** Otherwise they apply only to the current slide.

Any automatically advancing transitions that you have set appear with the timings beneath each slide in Slide Sorter view, as shown in Figure 16.2.

FIGURE 16.2

You can view slide timings in Slide Sorter view.

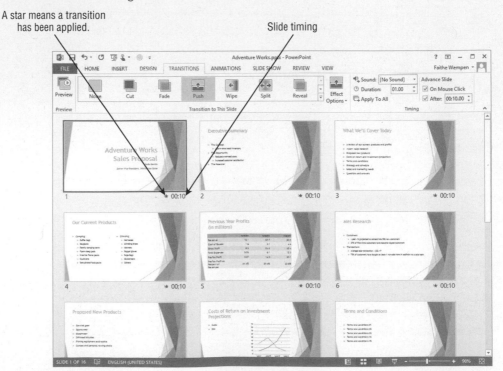

More about Transition Sounds

Transition sounds have different controls than the sounds described in Chapter 14, "Adding Sound Effects, Music, and Soundtracks." In the Transitions tab's Sound menu, shown in Figure 16.3, you can choose from among PowerPoint's default sound collection, or you can choose any of the following:

FIGURE 16.3

Select a transition sound.

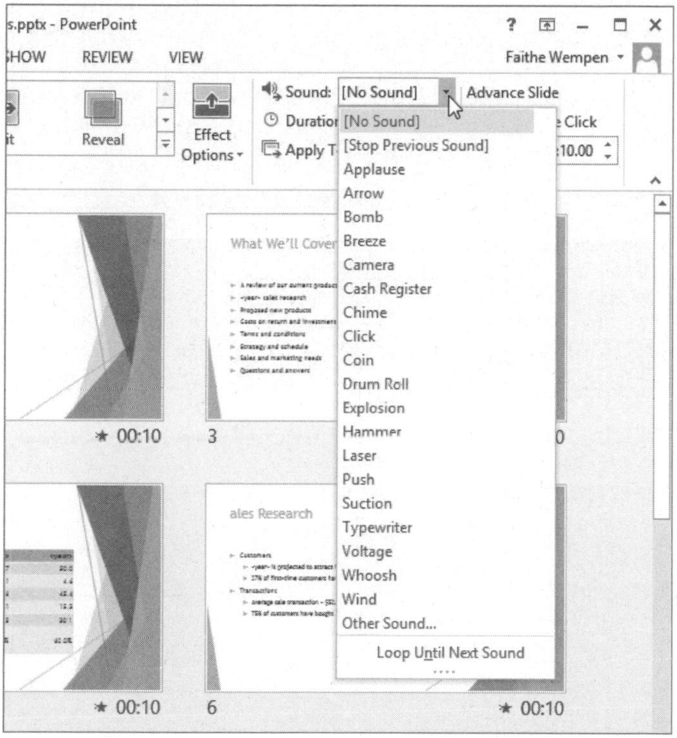

- **No Sound.** Does not assign a sound to the transition.
- **Stop Previous Sound.** Stops any sound that is already playing. This usually applies where the previous sound was very long and was not finished when you moved on to the next slide or in cases where you used the Loop Until Next Sound transition (see the last item on this list).
- **Other Sound.** Opens a dialog box from which you can select another WAV sound file stored on your system.
- **Loop Until Next Sound.** An on/off toggle that sets whatever sound you select to loop continuously either until another sound is triggered or until a slide transition or animated object appears that has Stop Previous Sound set.

Rehearsing and Recording Transition Timings

The trouble with setting the same automatic timings for all slides is that not all slides deserve or need equal time on-screen. For example, some slides may have more text than others or more complex concepts to grasp. To allow for the differences, you can manually set the timings for each slide, as described in the preceding section. However, another way is to use the Rehearse Timings feature to run through your presentation in real time and allow PowerPoint to set the timings for you, based on that rehearsal. This is especially important if you have complex animations on the slide, because the transition timing will force all animations to run within that timeframe despite the timing set on the individual animations. Therefore you want to make sure that the transition timing is adequate to incorporate all animations.

To set transition timings with the Rehearse Timings feature, follow these steps:

1. **On the Slide Show tab, click Rehearse Timings.** The slide show starts with the Recording toolbar, shown in Figure 16.4, in the upper-left corner.

FIGURE 16.4

Use the Recording toolbar to set timings for automatic transitions.

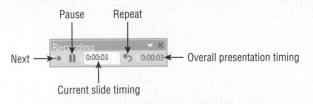

2. **Click through the presentation, displaying each slide for as long as you want it to appear in the actual show.** To move to the next slide, you can click the slide, click the Next button in the Recording toolbar (right-pointing arrow), or press Page Down.

When setting timings, it may help to read the text on the slide, slowly and out loud, to simulate how an audience member who reads slowly would proceed. When you have read all of the text on the slide, pause for one or two more seconds and then advance. If you need to pause the rehearsal at any time, click the Pause button. When you are ready to resume, click the Pause button again.

If you make a mistake on the timing for a slide, click the Repeat button to begin timing this slide again from 00:00.

When you reach the final slide, a dialog box appears, asking whether you want to keep the new slide timings.

TIP

If you want a slide to display for a fairly long time, such as 30 seconds or more, you might find it faster to enter the desired time in the Current Slide Timing text box on the Recording toolbar rather than waiting the full amount of time before advancing. To do this, click in the text box, type the desired time, and press Tab. You must press the Tab key after entering the time (do not click the Next button) or PowerPoint will not apply your change.

3. **Click Yes to accept the new slide timings.**

TIP

If you want to temporarily discard the rehearsed timings, deselect the Use Timings check box on the Slide Show tab. This turns off all automatic timings and allows the show to advance through mouse-clicks only. To clear timings altogether, choose Slide Show ⇨ Record Slide Show ⇨ Clear ⇨ Clear Timings on All Slides.

Animating Slide Content

Whereas transitions determine how a slide (as a whole) enters the screen, animations determine what happens to the slide's content after that point. You might animate a bulleted list by having each bullet point fade in one by one, for example, or you might make a picture gradually grow or shrink to emphasize it. The effects that you can create are limited only by your imagination.

Animation gives you full control over how the objects on your slides appear, move, and disappear. You can not only choose from the full range of animation effects for each object, but you can also specify in what order the objects appear and what sound is associated with their appearance.

Animation: A First Look

The Animations tab provides many settings and shortcuts for creating animation events. An *event* is an animation occurrence, such as an object entering or exiting the slide. An event can also consist of an object on the slide moving around in some way (spinning, growing, changing color, and so on).

Each animation event appears as a separate entry in the Animation pane. You can display or hide the Animation pane by choosing Animations ⇨ Advanced Animation ⇨ Animation Pane at any time.

When you animate bulleted lists and certain other types of text groupings, the associated events may be collapsed or expanded in the Animation pane. For example, in Figure 16.5, an animated bulleted list's events are collapsed.

Notice the following in Figure 16.5:

- The text box containing the bulleted list is named Rectangle 3. PowerPoint considers a text box a shape, and by default text boxes are rectangular.

- It has a green star on it. Green means entrance; this is an entrance effect. (Yellow means emphasis, and red means an exit effect.) A line instead of a star means it is a motion path (covered later in this chapter).

- It has a double down-pointing arrow below it. That indicates that there are collapsed animation events beneath it.

FIGURE 16.5

The animation events for a bulleted list are collapsed.

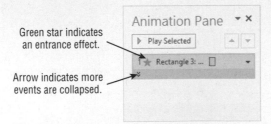

Green star indicates
an entrance effect.

Arrow indicates more
events are collapsed.

> **TIP**
>
> To assign meaningful names to slide objects so it's easier to tell what you are working with when animating, choose Home ⇨ Editing ⇨ Select ⇨ Selection Pane. Then in that pane, you can edit each object's name.

In Figure 16.6, the events are expanded. To expand or collapse a group of events, click the double up-pointing or down-pointing arrow. Notice that each bulleted list item on the slide has a number next to it that corresponds to one of the numbered animation events in the Animation pane.

FIGURE 16.6

The events are expanded.

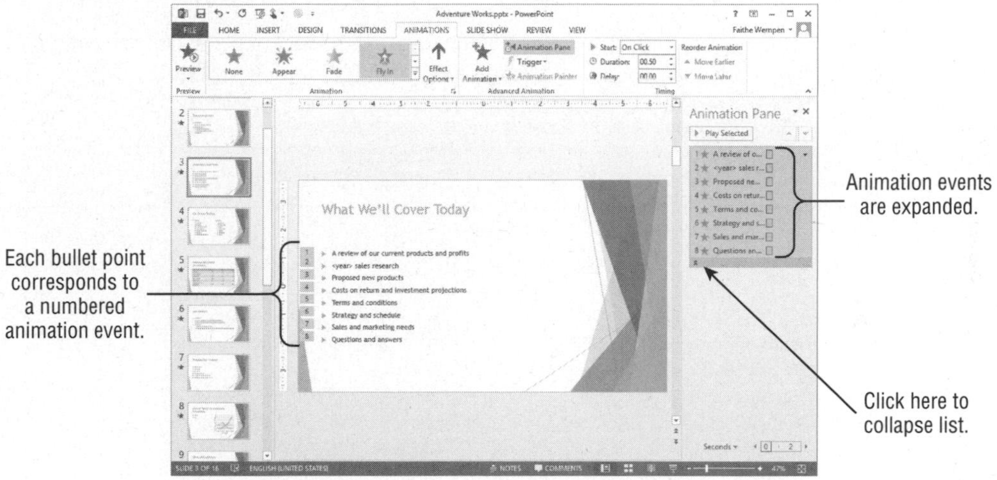

Each bullet point corresponds to a numbered animation event.

Animation events are expanded.

Click here to collapse list.

Choosing an Animation Effect

There are four categories of custom animation effects. Each effect has a specific purpose as well as a different icon color:

- **Entrance (green).** The item's appearance on the slide is animated. It does not appear right away when the rest of the slide appears, or it appears in some unusual way (such as flying or fading), or both.

- **Emphasis (yellow).** The item is already on the slide and is modified in some way. For example, it may shrink, grow, wiggle, or change color.

- **Exit (red).** The item disappears from the slide before the slide itself disappears, and you can specify that it does so in some unusual way.

- **Motion Paths (gray).** The item moves on the slide according to a preset path. Motion paths are discussed later in the chapter.

Within each of these broad categories are a multitude of animations. Although the appearance of the icons may vary, the colors (on the menus from which you choose them and on the effects listed in the Animation pane) always match the category.

Different effect categories have different choices. For example, the Emphasis category, in addition to providing movement-based effects, also has effects that change the color, background, or other attributes of the object.

You can choose animation effects in any of these ways (all from the Animations tab) after selecting the object to be animated:

- Click one of the animation samples in the Animation group.

- Click the Add Animation button, and choose an effect from the menu that appears. See Figure 16.7.

- Click the down arrow to open the gallery in the Animation group, and choose an effect from the gallery that appears. (This gallery is identical to the one provided by the Add Animation button.)

FIGURE 16.7

Choose an animation effect to apply.

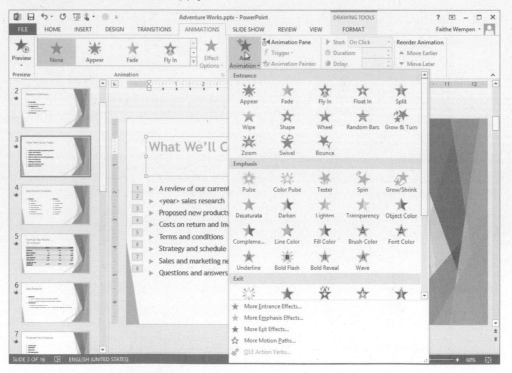

- Click the Add Animation button and then choose one of the "More" commands at the bottom, depending on the type of animation you want. For example, you might want to choose More Entrance Effects. This opens a dialog box with a full listing of the effects of that type, shown in Figure 16.8.

FIGURE 16.8

The More command opens a dialog box of effects for the chosen type.

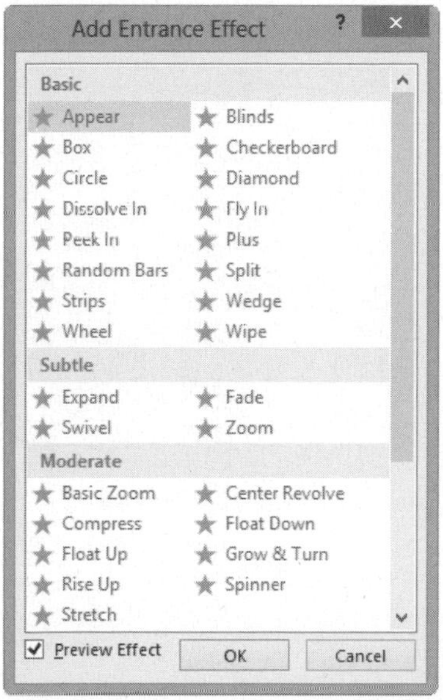

> **NOTE**
>
> Why are there two seemingly identical menus on the Animations tab — one in the Animation gallery and one from the Add Animation button? If an object does not currently have any animation assigned to it, there is no difference; either one will work equally well. However, if the object already has an animation, you can use the Animation gallery to change an existing animation. Add Animation can be used to add additional animation to an object that is already animated.

Changing an Effect's Options

After applying an animation, you can control its options with the Effect Options button on the Animations tab. The options that appear there depend on the effect you have chosen. Some effects have a direction for entrance or exit, for example.

For access to a full range of effect options, do the following:

1. **In the Animation pane, right-click the desired animation event and choose Effect Options.** An Effect Options dialog box opens for the chosen event. The controls that appear may be different depending on the event.

2. **On the Effect tab, use the controls provided to fine-tune the effect.** For example, as Figure 16.9 shows, you can smooth out the start and end of the

animation by a certain amount, set a bounce for the end, and dim the object after animation.

3. **Click OK to apply the effect settings.**

FIGURE 16.9

Fine-tune an effect's options from the Effect tab of the Effect Options dialog box.

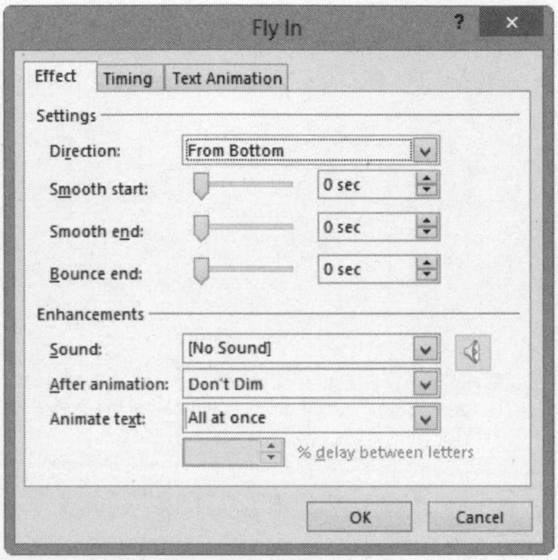

Setting Animation Timing

The timing controls for animations are located in the Timing group on the Animations tab, as shown in Figure 16.10.

FIGURE 16.10

Control the timing of an animation from the Timing group.

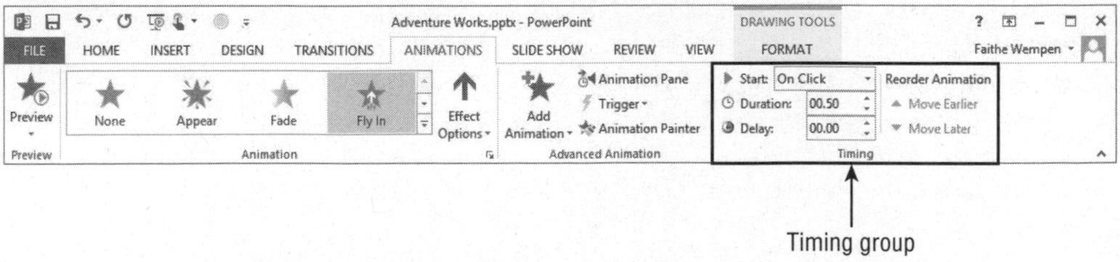

By default, animations are set to On Click. You can instead set them to occur automatically by choosing one of these settings from the Start drop-down list on the Animations tab:

■ **With Previous.** The animation occurs simultaneously with the start of the previous event in the Animation pane. If there is no previous event, the animation occurs simultaneously with the appearance of the slide itself.

- **After Previous.** The animation occurs after the previous animation event has finished occurring. If there is no previous event, the animation occurs after the appearance of the slide itself.

The difference between those two settings is subtle because most animation events are very short in duration. However, if an event is set to After Previous and the previous event takes a long time to execute, the difference may be more noticeable.

You can also set a delay for the animation (Animations ➪ Timing ➪ Delay). This delays the animation's start for a specified number of seconds after the previous event.

The Duration setting (Animations ➪ Timing ➪ Duration) controls the speed at which the animation occurs. The higher the duration setting, the slower it will execute.

For even more control over the timing, right-click the animation event in the Animation pane and choose Timing. Then set timing options in the dialog box that appears. All the same options are available as on the Animations task pane, plus a Repeat option is available that repeats the animation a certain number of times. There is also a Triggers set of options, which you'll learn about in the section "Setting Animation Event Triggers" later in this chapter.

Another minor difference between the dialog box and the Animations tab methods is that for Duration, the dialog box uses a drop-down list of presets, ranging from 0.5 seconds (Very Fast) to 5 seconds (Very Slow). You have to select one of the presets; you can't enter a precise amount. In contrast, the Duration setting on the Animations tab is a numeric text box in which you can enter any value you want.

Copying Animation

The Animation Painter is a very handy feature that enables you to copy an animation effect from one object to another. To use it, follow these steps:

1. **Select the object that is already animated the way you want.**
2. **Choose Animations ➪ Advanced Animation ➪ Animation Painter.**
3. **Click the object on which to paint the animation.** (You can navigate to a different slide before doing this.) That object's animation changes to match that of the object you selected in Step 1.

Special Options for Text Animation

When you are animating the text in a text box, some extra options become available, described in the following sections.

Changing the Grouping Level

You can choose the grouping that you want to animate. The *grouping level* is the detail level at which separate animations occur. Suppose, for example, that you have three levels of bullets in the text box, and you want them to be animated with each second-level bullet appearing separately. You can specify the second level as the animation grouping so that all third-level bullets appear as a group along with their associated second-level bullet.

You can change the grouping level by choosing Animations ➪ Animation ➪ Effect Options and then choosing one of these options:

- **As One Object.** Makes the entire content placeholder a single animation event.

- **All At Once.** Makes each paragraph a separate event, but assigns On Click to only the first one; the others are set to animate with the previous paragraph (With Previous), which means they occur simultaneously with the first one.

- **By Paragraph.** Animates each paragraph separately and assigns On Click to each event. This is the default.

If you have more than one level of bullets, the subordinate-level bullet points are animated along with their first-level parent when you use Animations ➪ Effect Options ➪ By Paragraph. If you want bullets that are other than first-level bullets to be separately animated, you must set that up in the Effect Options dialog box. Follow these steps:

1. **In the Animation pane, collapse the group (by clicking the double up arrow).** Then right-click the collapsed group and choose Effect Options.

2. **In the Effect Options dialog box, click the Text Animation tab.**

3. **Open the Group Text drop-down list and choose the level at which you want to group bullet points.** For example, in Figure 16.11, I am grouping by second-level paragraphs.

FIGURE 16.11

Group by a certain level of paragraphs (bullets).

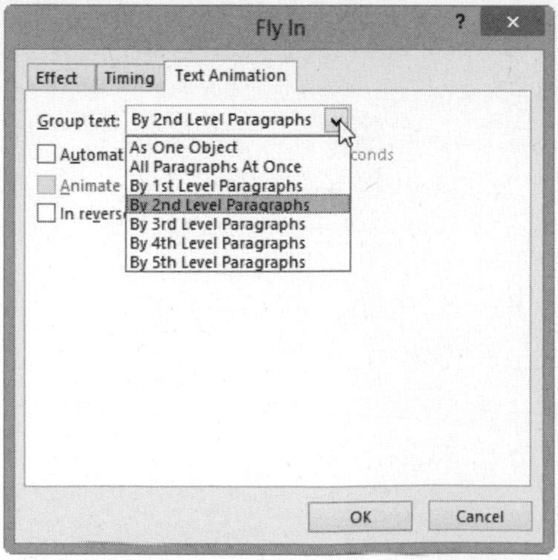

4. **Click OK to accept the new grouping setting.**

To animate the list in reverse order (that is, from the bottom up), mark the In Reverse Order check box.

Animating Each Individual Word or Letter

By default, when a paragraph animates, it does so all at once. You can optionally instead set it to animate one word at a time or even one letter at a time. (Be careful with this, though; it gets annoying quickly!)

To set this up, do the following:

1. **Right-click the animation event in the Animation pane and choose Effect Options.** The Effect Options dialog box for the chosen animation type opens.
2. **On the Effect tab, open the Animate Text drop-down list and choose a setting:**
   - All at once
   - By word
   - By letter
3. **Click OK.**

Removing an Animation Effect

You can remove the animation for a specific object or remove all of the animation for the entire slide. When an object is not animated, it simply appears when the slide appears, with no delay. For example, if the title is not animated, the slide background and the title appear first, after which any animation executes for the remaining objects. To remove animation from a specific object, do the following:

1. **Display the Animation pane (Animations ⇨ Advanced Animation ⇨ Animation Pane).**
2. **If the object is part of a group, such as a bulleted list, then expand or collapse the list, depending on the effect that you want to remove.** For example, to remove an animation effect from an entire text box, you must first collapse the list. To remove an animation effect from only a single paragraph, such as a bulleted item, you must first expand the list.
3. **Select the animation effect from the pane, and then press the Delete key on the keyboard, or right-click and choose Remove, or choose None from the Animation Gallery.** PowerPoint removes the animation and then renumbers any remaining animation effects.

Assigning Multiple Animation Effects to a Single Object

Some objects might need more than one animation effect. For example, you may want an object to have an Entrance and an Exit effect, or you may want a bulleted list to enter one way and then emphasize each point in a different way.

To assign a new animation effect to an object that is already animated, just select it and apply another animation event to it with Animations ⇨ Add Animation. You don't have to do anything special to it just because it already has an animation event. (You can't use the Animation Gallery to add an animation to an object that already has an animation because it will just change the existing event, not create a new event.)

After assigning another event to it, you may want to rearrange the order of the events; see the next section, "Reordering Animation Effects," for details.

> **NOTE**
>
> Keep in mind that the numbers that appear next to the objects on the slides when the Animations tab is displayed do not refer to the objects themselves — they refer to the animation events. If an object does not have any animation assigned to it, then it does not have a number. Conversely, if an object has more than one animation effect assigned to it, then it has two or more numbers.

Reordering Animation Effects

By default, animation effects are numbered in the order that you created them. To change this order, do the following:

1. **On the In the Animation pane, click the effect whose position you want to change.**
2. **Click the Move Earlier or Move Later buttons at the top of the pane, or on the Animations tab, to move the position of the animation in the list.** See Figure 16.12.

You can also drag and drop items in the animations list to rearrange them. Position the mouse pointer over an object so that the pointer turns into a double-headed up or down arrow, and then drag the object up or down in the list.

Setting Animation Event Triggers

Animation event triggers tell PowerPoint when to execute an animation. By default, an animation occurs as part of the normal animation sequence, using whatever settings you have assigned to it, such as On Click, With Previous, or After Previous.

When you set an animation to On Click, the click being referred to is *any* click. The mouse does not need to be pointing at anything in particular. In fact, pressing a key on the keyboard can serve the same purpose.

If you want an animation effect to occur only when you click something in particular, you can use a trigger to specify this condition. For example, you may have three bullet points on a list and three photos. If you want each bullet point to appear when you click its corresponding photo, you can animate each bullet point with the graphic object as its trigger.

FIGURE 16.12

Reorder animation effects from the task pane or the Animations tab.

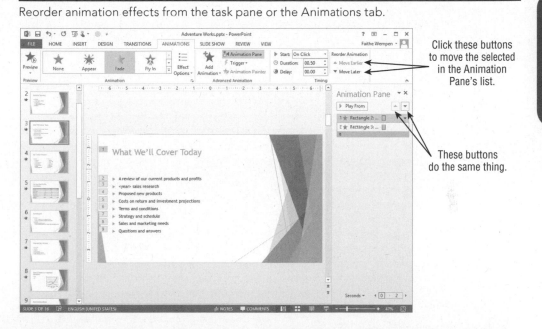

Click these buttons to move the selected in the Animation Pane's list.

These buttons do the same thing.

16

CAUTION

You can have only one trigger for each object, and in this case, *object* means the entire text placeholder. Therefore, if you want to animate bullet points separately with separate triggers, then you need to place each of them in a separate text box.

To set up a trigger, do the following:

1. **On the Animation pane, click the effect whose timing trigger you want to set.**

2. **Choose Animations ➪ Advanced Animation ➪ Trigger ➪ On Click Of and then click the object that should be used as the trigger for that event.** See Figure 16.13.

FIGURE 16.13

Choose a trigger object for the selected animation event.

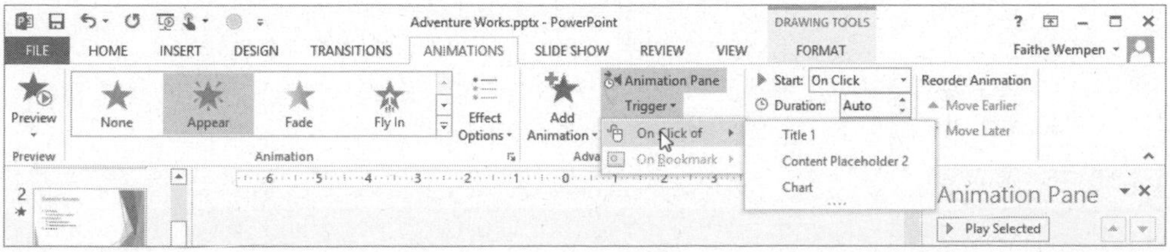

501

Here's an alternative method:

1. **On the Animation pane, right-click the effect whose timing you want to set and choose Timing.** The Animation dialog window appears with the timing tab selected.

2. **If the Triggers controls do not already appear, Click the Triggers button.** The controls for setting up a trigger appear on the Timing tab, as shown in Figure 16.14.

FIGURE 16.14

You can also set up a trigger via the Timing tab.

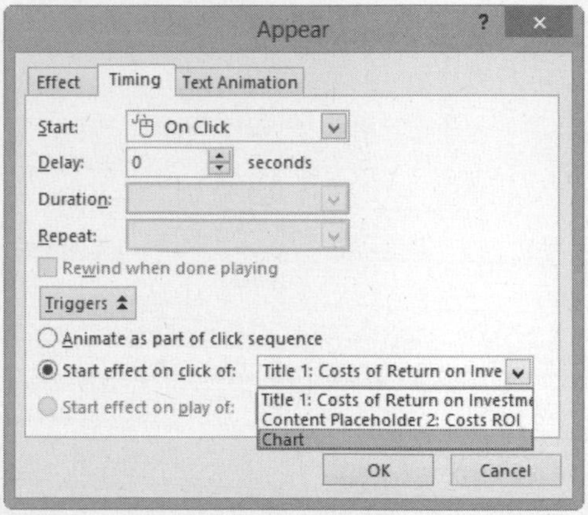

3. **Select the Start Effect on Click Of option, and then open the drop-down list and select an object.** All of the objects on the slide appear in this list.

4. **Click OK.**

> **CAUTION**
> Do not trigger the entrance of an object on click of itself or there will be no way to make it appear.

Associating Sounds with Animations

You learned about sounds in Chapter 14, "Adding Sound Effects, Music, and Soundtracks," including how to associate a sound with an object. However, associating a sound with an animation effect is different because the sound plays when the animation occurs, not necessarily when the object appears or is clicked. By default, animation effects do not have sounds assigned, but you can assign a sound by doing the following:

1. **In the Animation pane, select the animation effect to which you want to assign a sound.** Then open the drop-down list for the effect, and choose Effect Options.

2. **On the Effect tab (see Figure 16.15), open the Sound drop-down list and choose a sound.** You can choose any of the sounds in the list, or you can choose Other Sound to select a sound file from another location. (Only WAV files can be used for this.)

FIGURE 16.15

Choose a sound to be associated with the animation.

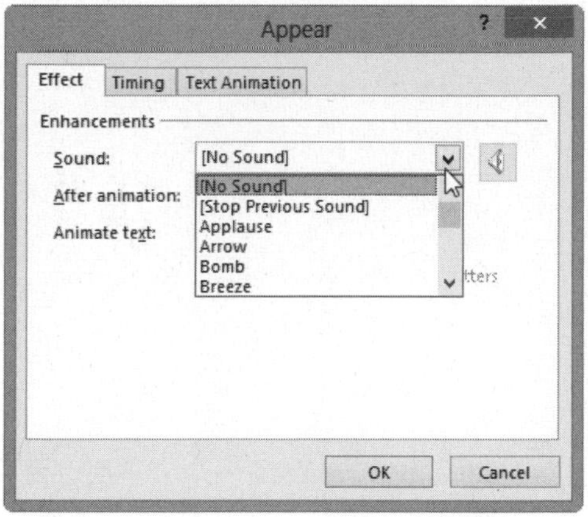

OR

To make a previously playing sound stop when this animation occurs, choose Stop Previous Sound from the Sound drop-down list.

3. **Click OK.**

Making an Object Appear Differently after Animation

After an object has been animated, you might want to have it appear differently on the slide. For example, after some text animates, you might want it to be dimmed. To set this up, follow these steps:

1. **In the Animation pane, select the animation effect.** Then open the drop-down list for the effect, and choose Effect Options.

2. **Open the After Animation drop-down list and choose one of the following options, as shown in Figure 16.16:**

   - **A theme color.** You can choose one of the colored squares, which represent each of the current theme colors.

   - **Don't Dim.** This is the default setting; it specifies that PowerPoint should do nothing to the object after animation.

   - **Hide After Animation.** This setting makes the object disappear immediately after the animation finishes.

■ **Hide on Next Mouse Click.** This setting makes the object disappear when you click the mouse after the animation has completed. For example, this is useful for showing and then hiding individual bullet points.

FIGURE 16.16

You can choose a color for the object after animation or specify that it should be hidden afterward.

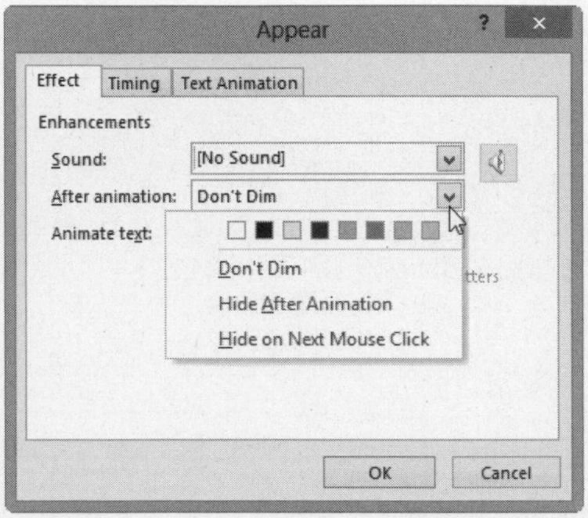

3. **Click OK.**

Working with Motion Paths

Motion paths enable you to make an object fly onto or off of the slide and also make it fly around on the slide in a particular motion path! For example, suppose you are showing a map on a slide and you want to graphically illustrate the route that you took when traveling in the area represented on the map. You could create a little square, circle, or other AutoShape to represent yourself and then set up a custom motion path for the shape that traces your route on the map.

Using a Preset Motion Path

PowerPoint comes with dozens of motion paths, in every shape that you can imagine. To choose one of them for an object, follow these steps:

1. **On the slide, click the object that you want to animate, and then choose Animations ⇨ Advanced Animation ⇨ Add Animation and then either scroll down to the bottom and click one of the paths on the list or choose More Motion Paths.**

2. **If you choose More Motion Paths, the Add Motion Path dialog box appears (Figure 16.17).** Click the path that you want.

FIGURE 16.17

You can select a motion path.

Add Motion Path

Basic

4 Point Star	5 Point Star
6 Point Star	8 Point Star
Circle	Crescent Moon
Diamond	Equal Triangle
Football	Heart
Hexagon	Octagon
Parallelogram	Pentagon
Right Triangle	Square
Teardrop	Trapezoid

Lines_Curves

Arc Down	Arc Left
Arc Right	Arc Up
Bounce Left	Bounce Right
Curvy Left	Curvy Right
Decaying Wave	Diagonal Down Right
Diagonal Up Right	Down
Funnel	Heartbeat

☑ Preview Effect   OK   Cancel

If you select the Preview Effect check box, the effect previews on the slide behind the dialog box; you can drag the dialog box to the side to see the preview more clearly.

3. **Click OK.** The motion path appears on the slide, adjacent to the object. A green circle or arrow shows where the object will begin, and a dotted line shows the path that it will take, as shown in Figure 16.18. A red circle or arrow shows where the path ends. If it's a closed path, you will only see the green circle or arrow.

FIGURE 16.18

The motion path appears on the slide.

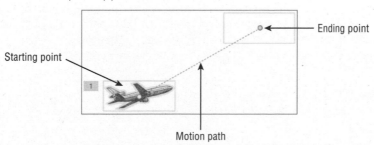

Starting point

Ending point

Motion path

At this point, you have a wide variety of options you can change:

- To change the starting point for the motion path, drag the green circle or arrow.
- To change the ending point, drag the red circle or arrow.
- You can change any of the settings for the motion path, just as you would for any other custom animation:
  - Change the Duration setting. The default is 2 seconds.
  - Change the Start setting. The default is On Click.
  - Change the path's timing or effects.

4. **Choose Animations ⇨ Animation ⇨ Effect Options and select any of the following options: Unlocked/Locked.** If the path is unlocked and you move the animated object on the slide, the path repositions itself with the object; if the path is locked, then it stays in the same place, even when you move the object on the slide. You can toggle these two options.

   - **Edit Points.** This option enables you to change the motion path and is discussed in the next section, "Editing a Motion Path."
   - **Reverse Path Direction.** This option does just what it says: It makes the animation run in the opposite direction.

5. **Click OK.**

If the Effect Options button on the Animations tab is not available, make sure the motion path is selected (not the animated object).

There are even more effect options available. To see them, right-click the animation in the Animation pane and choose Effect Options to open a dialog box for the effect. On the Effect tab (Figure 16.19), do any of the following:

- Set the Path to Locked or Unlocked. (This is the same as described in step 4.)
- Assign a number of seconds to Smooth Start, Smooth End, and/or Bounce End to fine-tune how the animation begins and ends.
- Mark the Auto-Reverse check box to make the animation reverse itself after executing so the shape ends up back where it started. (This is *not* the same thing as Reverse Path Direction in step 4. Reverse Path Direction makes the path run backward; Auto-Reverse makes it run forward and *then* backward.)
- Associate a sound with the animation.

Editing a Motion Path

You can move the motion path by dragging it or by nudging it with the arrow keys, as you would any object.

You can resize or reshape the motion path by dragging its selection handles (the circles around its frame); this is just like resizing any other object. To rotate the motion path, drag the rotation handle at the top of the path; this is just like rotating any other object.

FIGURE 16.19

Set motion path options.

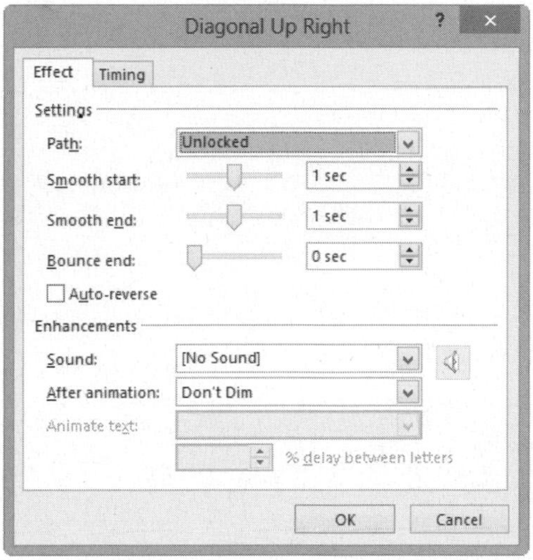

You can also modify the motion path manually by editing its points. A motion path consists of anchor points with straight lines or curves between them. These points are normally invisible, but you can also display them and change them.

To edit a motion path, follow these steps:

1. **Select the motion path on the slide (not the object itself).**

2. **Choose Animations ➪ Animation ➪ Effect Options ➪ Edit Points.** (You can also right-click the path and choose Edit Points.) Small black squares appear around the path.

> **NOTE**
>
> You can't edit the points on a straight line motion path because it doesn't have any points other than the starting and ending points.

3. **Click one of the black squares; a slightly larger white square appears near it.** A line with white squares on either end of the segment is a curve. These white squares are handles that you can drag to modify the point. You can also drag the black square itself; either way will work, although each method affects the path differently. For example, dragging the black square moves the point itself, whereas dragging the handle repositions the curve and leaves the point in place.

4. **Drag a square to change the path, as in Figure 16.20.**

FIGURE 16.20

You can edit a motion path by dragging the black or white squares that represent its anchor points.

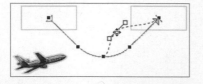

5. **When you are finished editing the path, choose Animations ⇨ Animation ⇨ Effect Options ⇨ Edit Points again, or press Esc, or click away from the path, to turn the editing feature off.**

Drawing a Custom Motion Path

If none of the motion paths suit your needs, or if you cannot easily edit them to the way you want, you can create your own motion path.

> **CAUTION**
>
> A custom motion path works best for paths that consist of one or more straight line segments; if you want a curved motion path, you are better off starting with one of the motion path presets and then editing its points to customize it.

To draw a custom motion path for an object, follow these steps:

1. **Select the object that you want to animate on the slide.**

2. **Choose Animations ⇨ Advanced Animation ⇨ Add Animation and then click Custom Path from the bottom of the menu.**

3. **Drag to draw the path on the slide.** Here are some hints:

   - **For a line**, click at the starting point and then click again at the ending point. The starting point will have a green arrow, and the ending point will have a red one.

   - **For a series of straight line segments**, click for each anchor point that you want; straight lines will appear between the anchor points. You can also click and drag to create non-straight lines. Double-click when you are finished.

   - **For a scribble**, draw on the slide with the mouse button held down. Double-click when you are finished.

4. **After drawing the path, edit and fine-tune it as you would any other motion path.**

Animating Parts of a Chart

If you create a chart using PowerPoint's charting tool, then you can display the chart all at once or apply a custom animation effect to it. For example, you can make the chart appear by series (divided by legend entries), by category (divided by X-axis points), or by individual element in a series or category. Figure 16.21 and Figure 16.22 show progressions based on series and category.

FIGURE 16.21

In this progression, the chart is appearing by series.

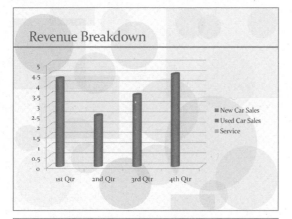

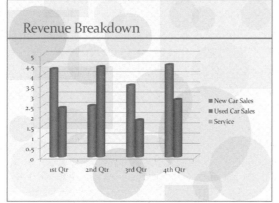

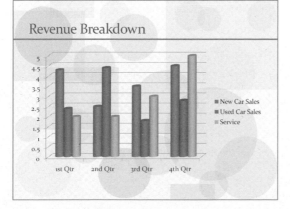

FIGURE 16.22

Here, the chart is appearing by category.

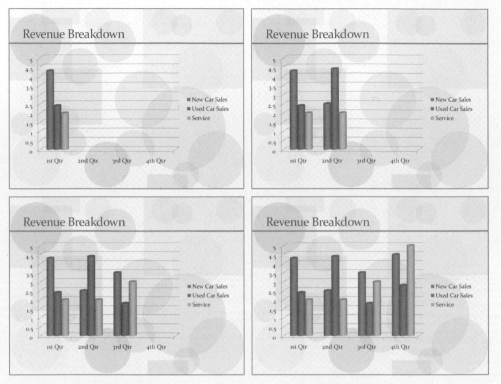

Along with making various parts of the chart appear at different times, you can also make them appear using any of the animated techniques that you have already learned, such as flying in, dropping in, fading in, and so on. You can also associate sounds with the parts and dim them or change them to various colors when the animation is finished.

To animate a chart, you must first set up the entire chart to be animated, just as you would any other object on a slide.

Then, to set up the chart so that different parts of it are animated separately, do the following:

1. **Choose Animations ➪ Animation ➪ Effect Options and then choose any of the following options from the Sequence section of the menu (see Figure 16.23):**

   - **As One Object.** The entire chart is animated as a single object.

   - **By Series.** In a multiseries chart, all of series 1 enters at once (all the bars of one color), then all of series 2 enters at once, and so on. This option doesn't appear for a single-series chart.

- **By Category.** All the bars for the first category appear at once (an entire grouping of multicolored bars), then the second category's bars, and so on.

- **By Element in Series.** Each data point is animated separately, in this order: each point (from bottom to top or left to right) in series 1, then each point in series 2, and so on. This option does not appear unless you have more than one category and series.

- **By Element in Category.** Each data point is animated separately, in this order: each point (from bottom to top or left to right) in category 1, then each point in category 2, and so on. This option does not appear unless you have more than one category and series.

FIGURE 16.23

You can animate the chart by series, by category, or by individual data points.

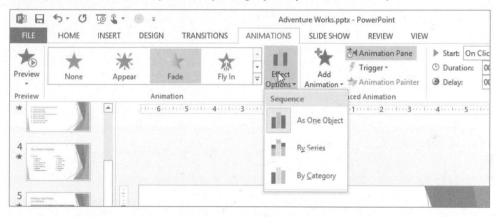

You can also set up chart animation from the Effect Options dialog box. Collapse the chart's animation in the Animation pane (if needed), and then right-click it and choose Effect Options. In the dialog box that appears, click the Chart Animation tab, and make your selection there. The choices are exactly the same as on the menu (Figure 16.23), plus there is one additional check box: Start Animation by Drawing the Chart Background, which is on by default. It animates the grid and legend. If you deselect this option, these items appear immediately on the slide, and the data bars, slices, or other chart elements appear separately from them.

You do not have to use the same animation effect for each category or each series of the chart. After you set up the chart to animate each piece individually, individual entries appear for each piece on the list in the Animation pane. You can expand this list and then apply individual settings to each piece. For example, you could have some data bars on a chart fly in from one direction, and other data bars fly in from another direction. You can also reorder the pieces so that the data points build in a different order from the default order.

Controlling Animation Timing with the Advanced Timeline

The animation timeline is a graphical representation of how animated content will appear on the slide. The timeline is also covered in Chapter 14, in the discussion about sounds and soundtracks. It is on by default. If you don't see it, right-click any animation event in the Animation pane and choose Show Advanced Timeline.

The timeline is useful because it can tell you the total time involved in all of the animations that you have set up, including any delays that you have built in. Figure 16.24 shows a timeline for a chart that is animated by category, in which each event is set to occur to occur after the previous one (After Previous).

FIGURE 16.24

The advanced timeline shows how much time is allotted to each animated element on the slide.

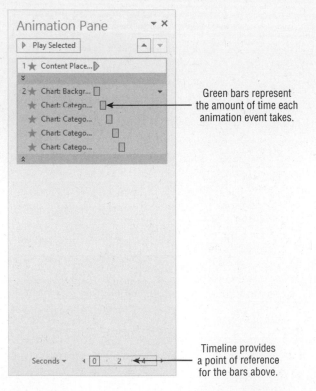

Green bars represent the amount of time each animation event takes.

Timeline provides a point of reference for the bars above.

For events that are set to On Click, the advanced timeline shows them to be occurring simultaneously, but this is not really true; they are just not time-sequenced with one another in the same way that events set to With Previous or After Previous are.

Notice also the Seconds button at the bottom in Figure 16.24. It opens a menu from which you can zoom in and zoom out on the timeline.

You can also use the timeline to create delays between animations and to increase the duration of individual animations. To increase the duration of an item, you can drag the right side of the bar representing its length in the Animation pane. Drag the left side of the bar to create a delay between animations. When you drag the bar for an item that is set to After Previous, the other bars also move. However, when you drag the bar for an item that is set to With Previous, PowerPoint allows an overlap.

Animation Tips

Here are some tips for using animation in your own work:

- Try to use the same animation effect for each slide in a related series of slides. If you want to differentiate one section of the presentation from another, use a different animation effect for the text in each different section.

- If you want to discuss only one bullet point at a time on a slide, set the others to dim or change to a lighter color after animation.

- If you want to obscure an element but you cannot make the animation settings do it the way you want, consider using a shape that is set to the same color fill as your background color and that has no outside border. This shape will appear "invisible" but will obscure whatever is behind it.

- Animate a chart based on the way you want to lead your audience through the data. For example, if each series on your chart shows the sales for a different division and you want to compare one division to another, you can animate by series. If you want to talk about the results of that chart over time rather than by division, you can animate by category instead.

- If you want to create your own moving graphic but you do not have access to a program that creates animated GIFs, you can build a very simple animation on a slide. Simply create the frames of the animation — three or more drawings that you want to progress through in quick succession. Then, lay them one on top of another on the slide and set the timings so that they play in order. You can adjust the delays and repeats as needed.

Layering Animated Objects

Part of the challenge of animation is in deciding which objects should appear and disappear and in what order. Theoretically, you could layer all of the objects for every slide in the entire presentation on a single slide and use animation to make them appear and disappear on cue.

CAUTION

If you are thinking about creating complex layers of animation where some objects disappear and are replaced by other objects on the same slide, step back and consider whether it would be easier to simply use two or more separate slides. When there is no delay or animation defined in the transition between two slides (if their content is identical or very similar), the effect is virtually identical to that of layered, animated objects — with much less time and effort required to set them up.

You can use layering when you want part of a slide to change while the rest of it remains static. For example, you could create your own animated series of illustrations by stacking several photos and then animating them so that the bottom one appears, then the next one on top of it, and so on. This can provide a rough simulation of motion video from stills, much like flipping through illustrations in the corners of a stack of pages. You can set the animation speeds and delays between clips as needed to achieve the effect you want.

When you stack objects, the new object that is placed on top of the old object obscures it, so it is not necessary to include an exit action for the old object. However, if the item being placed on top is smaller than the one beneath, then you need to set up an exit effect for the object beneath and have it occur concurrently (that is, With Previous) with the entrance of the new one. For example, suppose that you want to place a photo on the right side of a slide and some explanatory text for it on the left, and then you want to replace these elements with a different photo and different text, as shown in Figure 16.25. At the back of this book in Lab 2, "Adding Sound and Movement to a Presentation," you'll learn step-by-step how to set up this type of animation sequence.

FIGURE 16.25

Although these figures look like two separate slides, they are actually a single slide at two different points in the animation sequence.

To set up this animation to occur on the same slide, you would place the content that should appear first and then apply exit effects to it. For example, set the initial photo to

On Click for its exit trigger, which will make it disappear when you click the mouse. Set its associated text box to With Previous and have it animate immediately after this photo so that the text box disappears at the same time as the photo.

Next, place the other text box and other picture over the top of the first items. In Normal view, it looks like each spot has both a picture and a text box. You must now animate the new text box and the new picture with entrance effects that are set to With Previous so that both will appear at the same time the other two items are exiting. They all have the same animation number because they all occur simultaneously.

To preview animation effects while remaining in Normal view, click the Preview button on the Animations tab. To preview an animation sequence on a slide from a certain animation effect forward, select that animation effect in the Animation Pane and then click the Play From button on the Animation Pane.

It is always a good idea to preview animation effects in Slide Show view after creating them. To do this, choose Slide Show ⇨ Start Slide Show ⇨ From Current Slide. When you have finished checking the effects, press Esc to return to PowerPoint.

Summary

In this chapter, you learned how to animate the objects on your slides to create some great special effects and how to create animated transitions from slide to slide. You can specify sounds, speeds, and timing for effects and layer effects to occur sequentially or simultaneously. Use this newfound knowledge for good, not evil! In other words, do not apply so many animations that your audience focuses more on the effects than on your message. If you would like more practice with these effects, work through Lab 2 at the end of this book.

In the next chapter, you'll learn how to create support materials such as handouts and speaker notes for a presentation and how to format and fine-tune their formatting.

Part III

Interfacing with Your Audience

IN THIS PART

Creating Support Materials

IN THIS CHAPTER

Creating handouts

Creating speaker notes

Printing an outline

Exporting handouts or notes pages to Word

If you are presenting a live show, the centerpiece of your presentation is your slides. Whether you show them using a computer screen, a slide projector, or an overhead projector, the slides—combined with your own dazzling personality—make the biggest impact. But if you rely on your audience to remember everything you say, you may be disappointed. With handouts, the audience members can follow along with you during the show and even take their own notes. They can then take the handouts home with them to review the information later.

You probably want a different set of support materials for yourself than you want for the audience. Support materials designed for the speaker's use are called speaker notes. In addition to small printouts of the slides, the speaker notes contain any extra notes or background information that you think you may need to jog your memory as you speak. Some people get very nervous when they speak in front of a crowd; speaker notes can remind you of the joke you wanted to open with or the exact figures behind a particular pie chart.

The When and How of Handouts

Presentation professionals are divided about how and when to use handouts most effectively. Here are some of the many conflicting viewpoints. I can't say who is right or wrong, but each of these statements brings up issues that you should consider. The bottom line is that each of them is an opinion on how much power and credit to give to the audience; your answer may vary depending on the audience you are addressing.

- **You should give handouts at the beginning of the presentation. The audience can absorb the information better if they can follow along on paper.**

   This approach makes a lot of sense. Research has proven that people absorb more facts if presented with them in more than one medium. This approach also gives your audience free will; they can listen to you or not, and they still have the information. It's their choice, and this can be extremely scary for less-confident speakers. It's not just a speaker confidence issue in some cases, however. If you plan to give a lot of extra information in your speech that's not on the handouts, people might miss it if you distribute the handouts at the beginning because they're reading ahead.

- **You shouldn't give the audience handouts because they won't pay as close attention to your speech if they know that the information is already written down for them.**

This philosophy falls at the other end of the spectrum. It gives the audience the least power and shows the least confidence in their ability to pay attention to you in the presence of a distraction (handouts). If you truly don't trust your audience to be professional and listen, this approach may be your best option. However, don't let insecurity as a speaker drive you prematurely to this conclusion. The fact is that people won't take away as much knowledge about the topic without handouts as they would if you provide handouts. So, ask yourself if your ultimate goal is to fill the audience with knowledge or to make them pay attention to you.

- **You should give handouts at the end of the presentation so that people will have the information to take home but not be distracted during the speech.**

This approach attempts to solve the dilemma with compromise. The trouble with it, as with all compromises, is that it does an incomplete job from both angles. Because audience members can't follow along on the handouts during the presentation, they miss the opportunity to jot notes on the handouts. And because the audience knows that handouts are coming, they might nod off and miss something important. The other problem is that if you don't clearly tell people that handouts are coming later, some people spend the entire presentation frantically copying down each slide on their own notepaper.

Creating Handouts

To create handouts, you simply decide on a layout (a number of slides per page) and then choose that layout from the Print dialog box as you print. No muss, no fuss! If you want to get more involved, you can edit the layout in Handout Master view before printing.

Choosing a Layout

Assuming you have decided that handouts are appropriate for your speech, you must decide on the format for them. You have a choice of one, two, three, four, six, or nine slides per page.

- **1 Slide.** Places a single slide vertically and horizontally "centered" on the page.
- **2 Slides.** Prints two big slides on each page. This layout is good for slides that have a lot of fine print and small details or for situations in which you are not confident

that the reproduction quality will be good. There is nothing more frustrating for an audience than not being able to read the handouts!

- **3 Slides.** Makes the slides much smaller—less than one-half the size of the ones in the two-slide layout. But you get a nice bonus with this layout: lines to the side of each slide for note-taking. This layout works well for presentations with slides that are big and simple and the speaker is providing a lot of extra information that isn't on the slides. The audience members can write the extra information in the note-taking space provided.

- **4 Slides.** Uses the same size slides as the three-slide layout, but they are spaced out two-by-two without note-taking lines. However, there is still plenty of room above and below each slide, so the audience members still have lots of room to take notes.

NOTE

The four-, six-, and nine-slide handout layouts come in two varieties: vertical and horizontal. This does not refer to the orientation of the slides or the paper but rather to the order in which the slides appear. A vertical layout runs the first slide in the top-left corner, the second slide below that, and so on so that slides are ordered in vertical columns. A horizontal layout, in contrast, places the first slide in the top-left corner and the second slide to its right, running the slides in horizontal rows. Horizontal ordering is more common in the United States and Europe; vertical ordering is more common in Asia.

- **6 Slides.** Uses slides the same size as the three-slide and four-slide layouts, but crams more slides on the page at the expense of note-taking space. This layout is good for presentations with big, simple slides where the audience does not need to take notes. If you are not sure if the audience will benefit at all from handouts being distributed, consider whether this layout would be a good compromise. This format also saves paper, which might be an issue if you need to make hundreds of copies.

- **9 Slides.** Makes the slides very tiny, almost like a Slide Sorter view, so that you can see nine at a time. This layout makes them very hard to read unless the slide text is extremely simple. I don't recommend this layout in most cases because the audience really won't get much out of such handouts.

TIP

One good use for the nine-slide model is as an index or table of contents for a large presentation. You can include a nine-slides-per-page version of the handouts at the beginning of the packet that you give to the audience members and then follow it up with a two-slides-per-page version that they can refer to if they want a closer look at one of the slides.

Finally, there is an Outline handout layout, which prints an outline of all of the text in your presentation—that is, all of the text that is part of placeholders in slide layouts; any text in extra text boxes you have added manually is excluded. It is not considered a handout when you are printing, but it is included with the handout layouts in the handout master. More on this type of handout later in the chapter.

Printing Handouts

When you have decided which layout is appropriate for your needs, print your handouts as follows:

1. **(Optional) If you want to print only one particular slide or a group of slides, select the slide or slides you want in either Slide Sorter view or in the slide thumbnails task pane on the left.**

2. **Select File ⇨ Print.** The Print options appear.

3. **Enter a number of copies in the Copies text box.** The default is 1. If you want the copies collated (applicable to multipage printouts only), make sure you mark the Collate check box.

4. **Set options for your printer or choose a different printer.** See the section "Setting Printer-Specific Options" later in this chapter for help with this.

5. **If you do not want to print all the slides, type the slide numbers that you want into the Slides box.** Indicate a contiguous range with a dash. For example, to print slides 1 through 9, type **1-9.** Indicate noncontiguous slides with commas. For example, to print slides 2, 4, and 6, type **2, 4, 6.** Or to print slides 2 plus 6 through 10, type **2, 6-10.** To print them in reverse order, type them in reverse order, such as **10-6, 2.**

   Alternatively, you can click Print All Slides to open a menu of range choices and choose one of these from its list:

   - **Print Selection** to print multiple slides you selected before you issued the Print command. It is not available if you did not select any slides beforehand.

   - **Print Current Slide** to print whatever slide you selected before you issued the Print command.

   - **Custom Range** to print the slides whose numbers you type in the Slides text box. When you enter slide numbers in the Slides text box, this option gets selected automatically, so usually you don't have to select this option manually.

   - **Custom Show** to print a certain custom show you have set up. Each custom show you have created appears on the list. You won't see this option if you haven't created any.

6. **(Optional) Hidden slides are printed by default.** If you don't want to print hidden slides, click the same button again to reopen the menu and click Print Hidden Slides to toggle the check mark off next to that command.

7. **Click Full Page Slides to open a menu of views you can print.**

8. **On the menu that appears, click the number and layout of handouts you want.** See Figure 17.1.

> **NOTE**
> You can choose in step 8 to print an outline if you prefer. An outline can be a useful handout for an audience in certain situations.

FIGURE 17.1

Choose which handout layout you want.

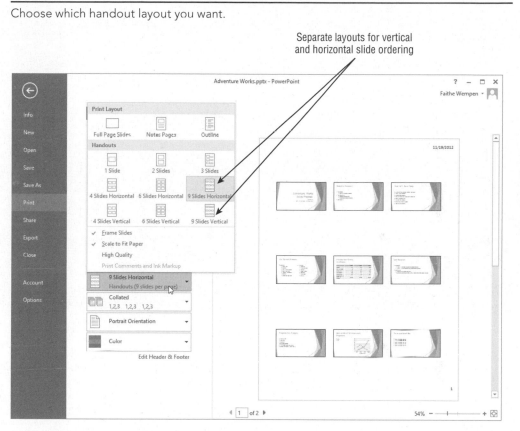

9. **(Optional) Click the Color button and select the color setting for the printouts:**

   ■ **Color.** This is the default. It sends the data to the printer assuming that color will be used. When you use this setting with a black-and-white printer, it results in slides with grayscale or black backgrounds. Use this setting if you want the handouts to look as much as possible like the on-screen slides.

   ■ **Grayscale.** Sends the data to the printer assuming that color will not be used. Colored backgrounds are removed, and if text is normally a light color on a dark background, that is reversed. Use this setting if you want PowerPoint to opti-mize the printout for viewing on white paper.

   ■ **Pure Black and White.** This format hides most shadows and patterns, as described in Table 17.1. It's good for faxes and overhead transparencies.

TABLE 17.1 **Differences Between Grayscale and Pure Black and White**

Object	Grayscale	Pure Black and White
Text	Black	Black
Text shadows	Grayscale	Black
Fill	Grayscale	Grayscale
Lines	Black	Black
Object shadows	Grayscale	Black
Bitmaps	Grayscale	Grayscale
Clip Art	Grayscale	Grayscale
Slide backgrounds	White	White
Charts	Grayscale	White

TIP

To see what your presentation will look like when printed to a black-and-white printer, on the View tab click Grayscale or Pure Black and White. If you see an object that is not displaying the way you want, right-click it and choose Grayscale or Black and White. One of the options there may help you achieve the look you're after.

10. **(Optional) If desired, open the drop-down list from which you chose the handout layout and select any of these additional options:**

- **Frame Slides.** Draws a black border around each slide image. Useful for slides being printed with white backgrounds.

- **Scale to Fit Paper.** Enlarges the slides to the maximum size they can be and still fit on the layout (as defined in the handout master, covered later in this chapter).

- **High Quality.** Optimizes the appearance of the printout in small ways, such as allowing text shadows to print.

- **Print Comments and Ink Markup.** Prints any comments that you have inserted with the Comments feature in PowerPoint (covered in Chapter 21, "Sharing and Collaborating").

11. **Check the preview of your handouts, which appears at the right.** Make any necessary changes.

12. **Click Print.** The handouts print, and you're ready to roll!

CAUTION

Be aware of the cost of printer supplies. If you are planning to distribute copies of the presentation to a lot of people, it may be tempting to print all of the copies on your printer. But the cost per page of printing is fairly high, especially if you have an inkjet printer. You will quickly run out of ink in your ink cartridge and have to spend $20 or more for a replacement. Consider whether it might be cheaper to print one original and take it to a copy shop.

Setting Printer-Specific Options

In addition to the Print settings in PowerPoint that you learned about in the preceding section, there are controls you can set that affect the printer you have chosen.

A printer's name appears under the Printer heading on the Print screen in Backstage view. Click that printer's name to open a menu of additional printers you can select instead. These are the printers installed on your PC (either local or network).

> **NOTE**
>
> Some of the "printers" listed are not really physical printers but drivers that create other types of files. For example, Fax saves a copy of the file in a format that is compatible with the fax driver included in Windows. It doesn't produce a hard copy printout.

After selecting the desired printer, click the Printer Properties hyperlink beneath the name. A Properties dialog box opens that is specific to that printer. Figure 17.2 shows the box for my Brother MFC-9320CW printer, an all-in-one laser. Notice that there are two tabs: Layout and Paper/Quality. The tabs may be different for your printer. For some printers, more settings are available if you click an Advanced button; when you click the Advanced button shown in Figure 17.2, for example, the Advanced Options dialog box in Figure 17.3 appears.

FIGURE 17.2

Each printer's options are slightly different, but the same types of settings are available for most printers.

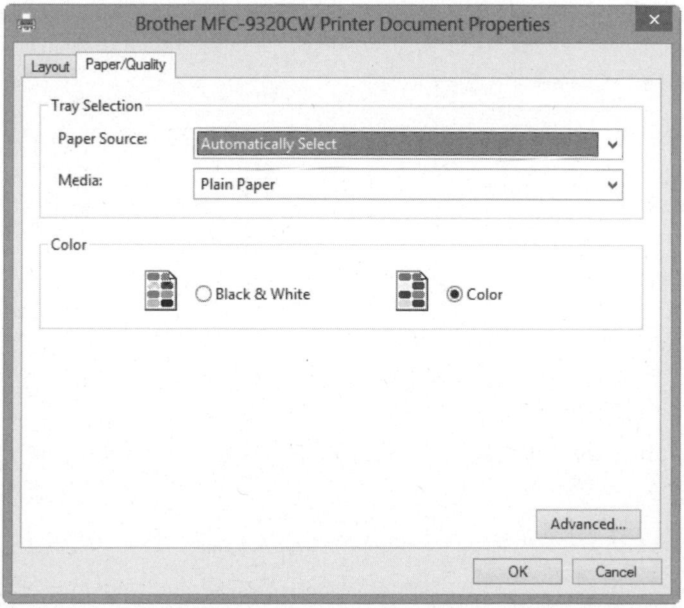

FIGURE 17.3

Some printers show more options in an Advanced Options dialog box (or similar).

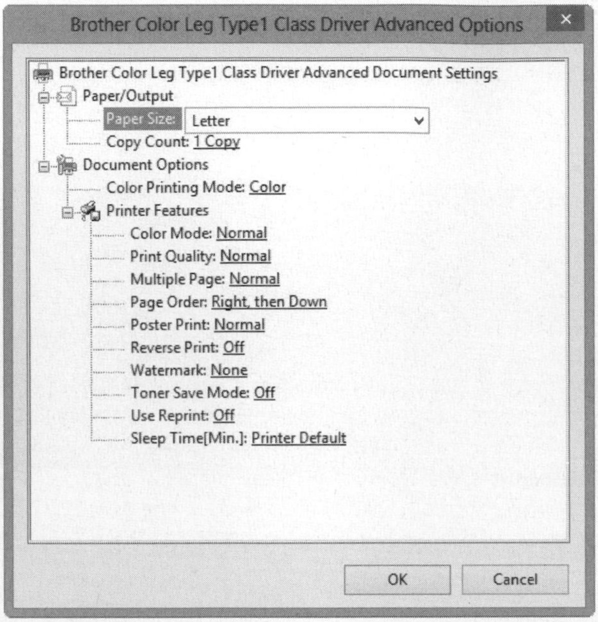

These settings affect how the printer behaves in all Windows-based programs, not just in PowerPoint, so you need to be careful not to change anything that you don't want globally changed. Here are some of the settings you may be able to change on your printer (not all of these are shown in Figure 17.2 and Figure 17.3):

- **Paper Size.** The default is Letter, but you can change to Legal, A4, or any of several other sizes.

- **Paper Source.** If your printer has more than one paper tray, you may be able to select Upper or Lower.

- **Media or Paper Type.** Some printers print at different resolutions or with different settings depending on the type of paper (for example, photo paper versus regular paper). You can choose the type of paper you are printing on.

- **Print Quality.** Some printers give you a choice of quality levels, such as Draft, Normal, and Best. Draft is the quickest; Best is the slowest and may use more ink.

- **Duplex or Print on Both Sides.** Some printers enable you to print on both sides of the paper. Some printers flip the paper over automatically but most prompt you to flip it over manually.

- **Orientation.** You can choose between Portrait and Landscape. It's not recommended that you change this setting here, though; make such changes in the Page Setup dialog box in PowerPoint instead. Otherwise, you may get the wrong orientation on a printout in other programs.

- **Page Order.** You can choose Front to Back or Back to Front. This determines the order in which the pages print.

- **Pages per Sheet.** The default is 1, but you can print smaller versions of several pages on a single sheet. This option is usually only available on PostScript printers.

- **Copies.** This sets the default number of copies that should print. Be careful; this number is a multiplier. If you set two copies here and then set two copies in the Print dialog box in PowerPoint, you end up with four copies.

- **Graphics Resolution.** If your printer has a range of resolutions available, you may be able to choose the resolution you want. For example, a laser printer might have you choose between 300 and 1,200 dots per inch (dpi); on an inkjet printer, choices are usually 360, 720, and 1,440 dpi. Achieving a resolution of 1,440 on an inkjet printer usually requires special glossy paper.

- **Graphic Dithering.** On some printers, you can set the type of dithering that makes up images. *Dithering* is a method of creating shadows (shades of gray) from black ink by using tiny crosshatch patterns. You may be able to choose between Coarse, Fine, and None.

- **Image Intensity.** On some printers, you can control the image appearance with a light/dark slide bar.

Some printers, notably inkjets, come with their own print-management software. If that's the case, you may have to run that print-management software separately from outside of PowerPoint for full control over the printer's settings. You can usually access such software from the Windows Start menu.

Using the Handout Master

Just as the slide master controls your slide layout, the handout master controls your handout layout. To view the handout master, as shown in Figure 17.4, click Handout Master on the View tab. Unlike the slide master and title master, you can have only one handout master layout per presentation.

You can do almost exactly the same things with the handout master that you can with the slide master. The following sections describe some of the common activities.

Setting the Number of Slides per Page

You can view the handout master with various numbers of slides per page to help you see how the layout will look when you print it. The settings you can change apply to all the layouts. For example, if you apply a header or footer or a page background for a three-slides-per-page layout, it also applies the four-slides-per-page layout as well as all the others. To choose the number of slides per page to display as you work with the handout master, click the Slides per Page button and then make your selection from its menu. See Figure 17.5.

17

FIGURE 17.4

The handout master lets you define the handout layout to be printed.

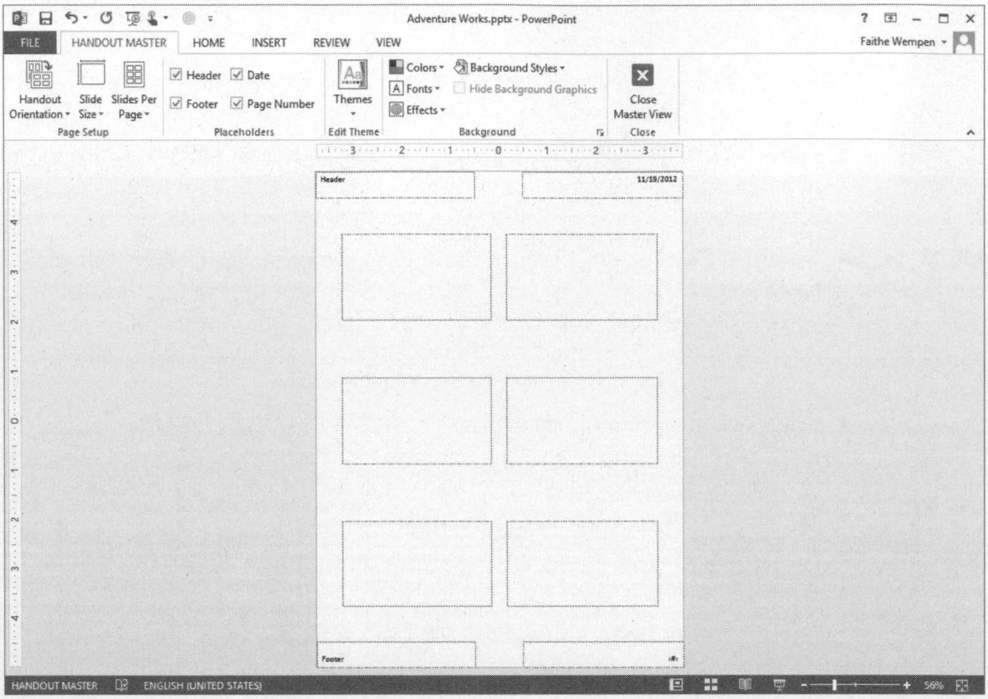

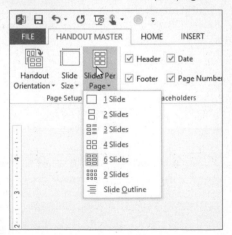

FIGURE 17.5

Choose a number of slides per page.

Using and Positioning Placeholders

The handout master has four placeholders by default: Header, Footer, Date, and Page Number, in the four corners of the handout respectively:

- **Header.** Appears in the upper-left corner and is a blank box into which you can type fixed text that will appear on each page of the printout.

- **Footer.** Same thing as Header but appears in the lower-left corner.

- **Date.** Appears in the upper-right corner and shows today's date by default.

- **Page Number.** Appears in the lower-right corner and shows a code for a page number, <#>. This will be replaced by an actual page number when you print.

In each placeholder box, you can type text (replacing, if desired, the Date and Page codes already there). You can also drag the placeholder boxes around on the layout.

There are two ways to remove the default placeholders from the layout. You select the placeholder box and press Delete, or you can clear the check box for that element on the Handout Master tab, as shown in Figure 17.6.

FIGURE 17.6

Turn on/off placeholder elements from the Handout Master tab.

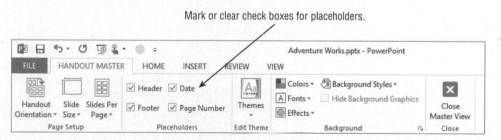

Mark or clear check boxes for placeholders.

> **NOTE**
>
> Because the header and footer are blank by default, there is no advantage to deleting these placeholders unless they have something in them you want to dispose of; having a blank box and having no box at all have the same result.

> **TIP**
>
> You can't move or resize the slide placeholder boxes on the handout master, nor can you change the handout master's margins. If you want to change the size of the slide boxes on the handout or change the margins of the page, consider exporting the handouts to Word and working on them there. See the section "Exporting Handouts or Notes Pages to Word" at the end of this chapter for more information.

Setting Handout and Slide Orientation

Orientation refers to the direction on the page the material runs. If the top of the paper is one of the narrow edges, it's called Portrait; if the top of the paper is a wide edge, it's Landscape. Figure 17.7 shows the difference in handout orientation. To change this setting, on the Handout Master tab, click Handout Orientation.

FIGURE 17.7

Portrait (left) and Landscape (right) handout orientation.

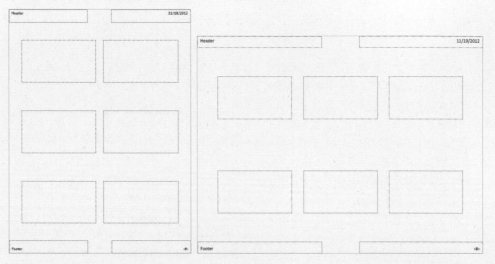

You can also set the slide size, either the Widescreen setting (16:9) or the Standard setting (4:3). PowerPoint 2013 defaults to Widescreen, both for the slides themselves and for the slide images on the handouts. To adjust this setting, on the Handout Master tab, click Slide Size and make your selection of Standard or Widescreen, or click Custom Slide Size to open the Slide Size dialog box and set a custom height and width. See Figure 17.8.

FIGURE 17.8

You can set any slide size and orientation combination in the Slide Size dialog box.

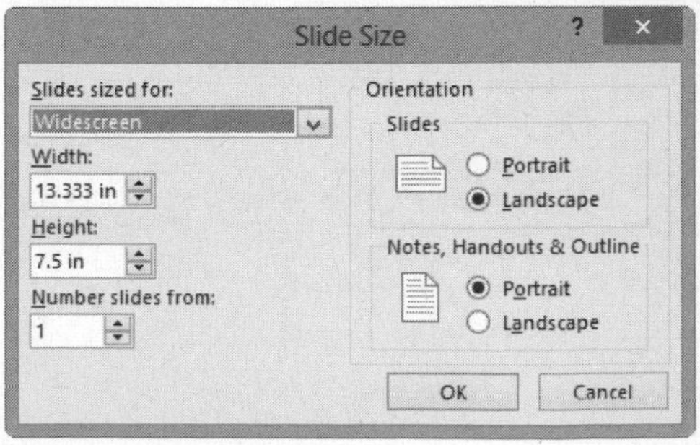

In the Slide Size dialog box, shown in Figure 17.8, you can also set a slide orientation. This is different from the orientation of the handout as a whole. The default slide orientation is landscape; setting the slide orientation to Portrait results in a layout like the one on the right in Figure 17.9. If you choose such a slide layout, PowerPoint prompts you to specify whether slide content should be sized to fit the new layout on the handouts or cropped.

FIGURE 17.9

Landscape (left) and Portrait (right) slide orientation.

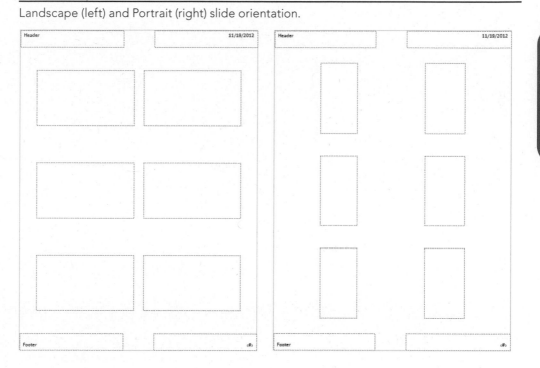

Formatting Handouts

You can manually format any text on a handout layout using the formatting controls on the Home tab, the same as with any other text. Such formatting affects only the text you select and only on the layout you're working with. You can also select the entire place-holder box and apply formatting.

You can also apply Colors, Fonts, and/or Effects schemes from the Edit Theme group, as shown in Figure 17.10, much as you can do for the presentation as a whole. The main difference is that you cannot select an overall theme from the Themes button; all the themes are unavailable from the list while in Handout Master view. The settings you apply here affect only the handouts, not the presentation as a whole.

FIGURE 17.10

Apply color, font, and/or effect schemes from the Edit Theme group.

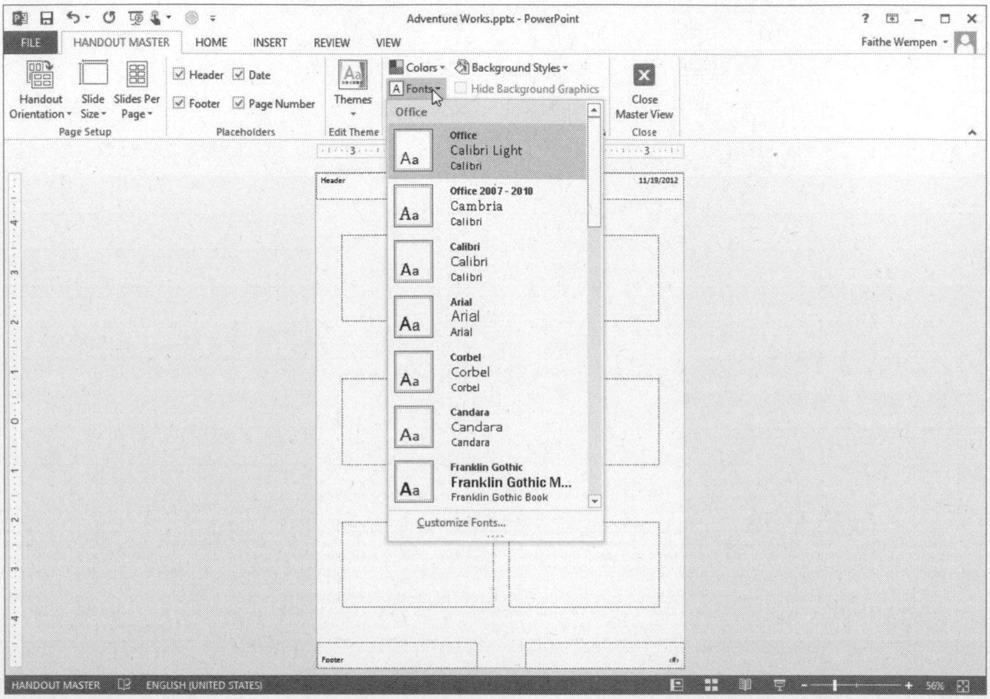

> **NOTE**
> You probably won't have much occasion to apply an Effects scheme to a handout layout because handouts do not usually have objects that use effects (i.e., drawn shapes, charts, or SmartArt diagrams).

Creating Speaker Notes

Speaker notes are like handouts, but for you. Only one printout format is available for them: the Notes Pages layout. It consists of the slide on the top half (the same size as in the two-slides-per-page handout) with the blank space below it for your notes to yourself.

Speaker notes printed in PowerPoint are better than traditional note cards for several reasons. For one thing, you can type your notes right into the computer and print them out on regular paper. There's no need to jam a note card into a typewriter and use messy correction fluid or erasers to make changes. The other benefit is that each notes page contains a picture of the slide, so it's not as easy to lose your place while speaking when compared to using traditional note cards.

Typing Speaker Notes

You can type your notes for a slide in Normal view (in the Notes pane) or in Notes Page view. The latter shows the page more or less as it will look when you print your notes pages; this can help if you need to gauge how much text will fit on the printed page.

To switch to Notes Page view, on the View tab click Notes Page as shown in Figure 17.11. Unlike with some of the other views, there is no shortcut button for this view in the bottom-right corner of the PowerPoint window. Once you're in Notes Page view, you can zoom and scroll just like in any other view to see more or less of the page at once. You can scroll further to move from slide to slide, or you can move from slide to slide in the traditional ways (the Page Up and Page Down keys on the keyboard or the Next Slide or Previous Slide buttons on-screen).

FIGURE 17.11

Notes Page view is one of the best ways to work with your speaker notes.

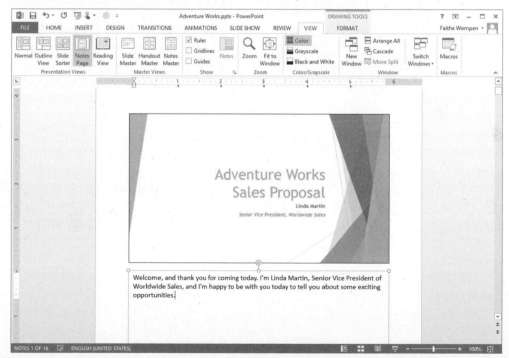

NOTE

Use the Zoom control to zoom in or out until you find the optimal view so that the text you type is large enough to be clear, but small enough so that you can see across the entire width of the note area. I find that 100 percent works well on my screen, but yours may vary.

Just type your notes in the Notes area, the same as you would type in any text box in PowerPoint. The lines in the paragraph wrap automatically. Press Enter to start a new paragraph. When you're done, move to the next slide.

Changing the Notes Page Layout

Just as you can edit your handout layouts, you can also edit your notes page layout. Just switch to its master and make your changes. Follow these steps:

1. **On the View tab, click Notes Master.**

2. **Edit the layout, as you have learned to edit other masters.** See Figure 17.12. This can include the following actions:

FIGURE 17.12

You can edit the layout of the notes pages in Notes Master view.

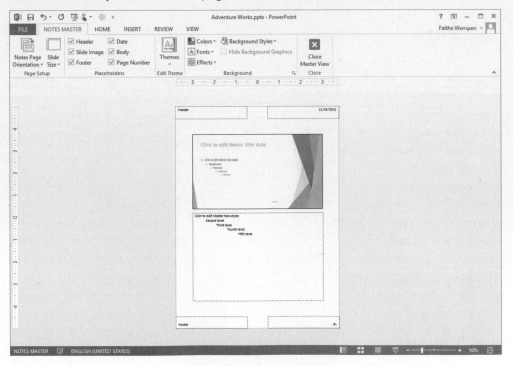

- Moving placeholders for the slide, the notes, or any of the header or footer elements
- Changing the font used for the text in any of those areas
- Resizing the placeholder for the slide graphic

- Resizing the Notes pane
- Adding clip art or other graphics to the background
- Adding a colored, textured, or patterned background to the notes page

3. **When you are finished, click the Close Master View button to return to Normal view.**

Printing Notes Pages

When you're ready to print your notes pages, follow these steps:

1. **Choose File ⇨ Print.** The Print controls appear.
2. **Click the button immediately below the Slides box, and choose Notes Pages as the type of layout to print.**
3. **Set any other options, just as you did when printing handouts earlier in the chapter.** (If you need to choose which printer to use or to set the options for that printer, see the section "Setting Printer-Specific Options" earlier in this chapter.) There are no special options for notes pages.
4. **Click OK.** The notes pages print.

CAUTION

If you print notes pages for hidden slides, you may want to arrange your stack after they're printed so that the hidden slides are at the bottom. That way you won't get confused when giving the presentation.

Printing an Outline

If text is the main part of your presentation, you might prefer to print an outline instead of mini-slides. You can use the outline for speaker notes, audience handouts, or both. To print the text from Outline view, follow these steps:

1. **View the outline in Normal or Outline view.**
2. **Choose File ⇨ Print.** The Print controls appear.
3. **Click the button immediately below the Slides text box, and choose Outline as the type of layout to print.**
4. **Set any other print options, as you learned in the section "Printing Handouts" earlier in the chapter.**
5. **Click OK.**

Be aware, however, that the outline will not contain text that you've typed in manually placed text boxes or any other non-text information, such as tables, charts, and so on.

Exporting Handouts or Notes Pages to Word

One of the drawbacks to PowerPoint is that the notes and handouts pages cannot be fully formatted. There's a lot you can't do with them—such as set margins or change the sizes of the slide images for handouts. To get around this, you might want to create your handouts in Microsoft Word. To send your presentation to Word, follow these steps:

1. **Choose File ⇨ Export ⇨ Create Handouts ⇨ Create Handouts.** The Send to Microsoft Office Word dialog box appears (Figure 17.13).

   FIGURE 17.13

   Choose a format for sending the presentation to Word.

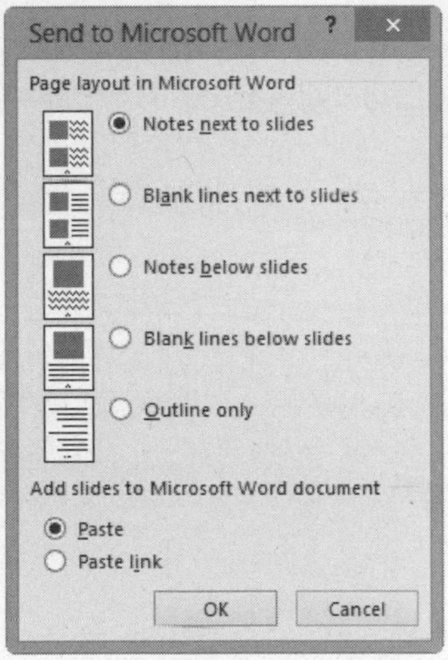

2. **Choose one of the formats shown in Figure 17.13.** You can send your presentation to Word in a variety of formats. Some formats are more appropriate for handouts, others for speaker notes. Table 17.2 gives some suggestions:

TABLE 17.2   Word Formats for Imported Text

For Handouts	For Speaker Notes
Blank Lines Next to Slides	Notes Next to Slides
Blank Lines Below Slides	Notes Below Slides
Outline Only	Outline Only

3. **(Optional) If you want to maintain a link between the PowerPoint file and the Word file, choose Paste Link.** Otherwise, leave Paste selected. If you maintain a

link, then the changes you make to the PowerPoint file are reflected in the Word file.

4. **Click OK.** Word opens and the slides appear in the format you chose. See Figure 17.14.

FIGURE 17.14

With the notes pages or handouts in Word, you can change the margins and other settings.

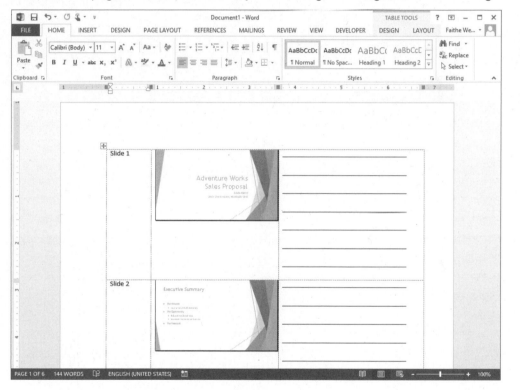

5. **Modify the formatting as desired, and then print from Word.**

6. **(Optional) Save your work in Word if you want to print the same pages again later.** (You may choose to resend to Word later, after making changes in PowerPoint instead.)

NOTE

The slides appear in Word in a table (if you chose a Next to Slides option) but without visible gridlines showing. You can resize (or even delete) the columns for each element by dragging the column dividers, just as you do in a table in PowerPoint.

Changing the Margins in Word

One benefit of exporting handouts to Word is being able to change the margins. In Word, on the Page Layout tab, click the Margins button, and choose a margin preset or choose Custom Margins.

However, note that changing the page margins does not resize the table. If you change the left margin, the table may start at a different place in relation to the left margin (because the table is left aligned), but if you want to increase the margins so that you can increase the table width, those are two separate activities.

You can also set internal margins in the cells in a table. To do so, on the Table Tools Layout tab, click Cell Margins.

Change the Table Alignment

The table itself has a default alignment in relationship to the page: Top Left. If you prefer the look of a centered table, you may want to switch this:

- To make the table horizontally centered on the page, select the table as a whole. To do this, click the square above and to the left of the table with the four-headed arrow in it. Then use the Center button on the Home tab (Paragraph group) to center it. Note that this does not center the text within the cells; this refers only to the table.

- To vertically center the table on the page, you need to set the vertical alignment for the document. To do so, on the Page Layout tab in Word, click the dialog box launcher in the Page Setup group, and on the Layout tab in the Page Setup dialog box, set the vertical alignment to Center.

Change Alignment within a Cell

To center the content within a cell horizontally, click in that cell, and then on the Table Tools Layout tab, click the Middle Center button. You can also choose any of the other buttons that are combinations of vertical and horizontal alignment. Figure 17.15 shows the nine available options, each of which is a unique combination of a vertical and a horizontal alignment.

FIGURE 17.15

Set table alignment from the Table Tools Layout tab.

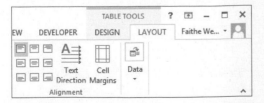

Resize Rows and Columns

To resize a column, drag the border between that column and the one to its right. When the mouse pointer is over a column border, it changes to a double-headed arrow with a line between the arrows. Alternatively you can specify an exact size by clicking in the column, and then on the Table Tools Layout tab, set a value in the Cell Size group. Do the same for row heights. For a better look at the gridlines, on the Table Tools Format tab, enable View Gridlines. These appear only on-screen; they will not print.

> **NOTE**
>
> You cannot resize a row or column to the point that its text content no longer fits. (And the lines for the audience to write on are made up of underline characters, which are considered text.) Therefore, you may need to resize the content or even delete some of it. For example, if you use a layout that includes blank lines, you'll get several blank lines in some of the cells. To make these cells narrower, you need to decrease the length of the lines first. To make these cells shorter, you may need to delete one or more of the lines.

Turn On/Off Cell Borders

By default, all borders are turned off for all cells in the table. You can turn them on in a variety of ways, but perhaps the easiest is to select one or more cells and then use the Borders button on the Table Tools Design tab. Choose the button that has no borders (all dotted lines) to turn all borders off again. See Figure 17.16.

> **NOTE**
>
> One thing to note about these borders is that whatever you choose applies to the selected range, not to the individual cells. For example, suppose you choose a range of cells that contains three rows and you apply a bottom border. The border would be applied only to the bottom of the third row of cells.

Apply a Background

To apply a background to the entire page, use the Page Color button on the Page Layout tab in Word. A palette of colors appears. The choices are much the same as in PowerPoint.

> **TIP**
>
> Word 2013 uses the same themes as PowerPoint. You can apply a theme to the document in Word to make it match the formatting of the presentation in PowerPoint.

To apply a background to only certain cells, select the cells, and then on the Table Tools Design tab, click the Shading button and select a color. This is a lot like applying a fill color in PowerPoint.

FIGURE 17.16

The Borders button has a drop-down list of border sides to turn on/off.

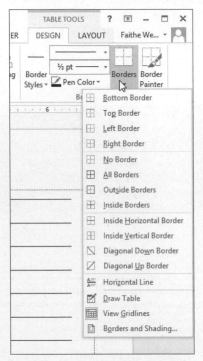

Resize the Graphics

Resizing the slide images is one of the most common reasons people export PowerPoint handouts to Word. Each image is resizable individually, so they need not necessarily be the same size (although it usually looks better if they are).

If you want to make the slides larger, you can first increase the column width for the column in which they reside. Then drag the selection handles on the slide thumbnail to resize.

> **NOTE**
> If you want to resize all of the slide images and you want them all to be the same size, set the table column width to the width you want for the images and then resize each picture so it's as large as it can be while still fitting in that column. Unfortunately you cannot resize multiple images as a batch.

Summary

In this chapter, you learned how to create a hard copy to support your presentation. You can now create a variety of handouts, and write and print out speaker notes for yourself. You also learned how to export handouts, notes pages, and outlines to Word, where you can use the full power of Word's formatting tools to create exactly the look you want.

In the next chapter, you take a look at the controls that PowerPoint offers for preparing for a live presentation. You learn how to create custom shows, work with hidden slides, and navigate through a presentation in Slide Show view.

17

Preparing for a Live Presentation

It's showtime! Well, actually I hope for your sake that it is *not* time for the show this very instant because things will go much more smoothly if you can practice using PowerPoint's slide-show controls before you have to go live.

Presenting the show can be as simple or as complex as you make it. At the most basic level, you can start the show, move through it slide by slide with simple mouse clicks or key presses, and then end the show. However, to take advantage of PowerPoint's extra slide-show features, you should spend a little time studying the following sections.

> **NOTE**
> The first part of this chapter assumes that you are showing your presentation on a PC that has PowerPoint 2013 installed; sections later in this chapter discuss other situations.

Starting and Ending a Show

To start a show, do any of the following:

- On the Slide Show tab, click either From Beginning or From Current Slide.
- Click the Slide Show View button in the bottom-right corner of the screen (to begin from the current slide).

- Press F5 (to begin from the beginning).
- Press Shift+F5 (to begin from the current slide).

Once the show is underway, you can control the movement from slide to slide as described in the section "Moving from Slide to Slide."

To end the show, do any of the following:

- Right-click and choose End Show.
- Press Esc, - (minus), or Ctrl+Break.

If you want to temporarily pause the show while you have a discussion, you can blank the screen by pressing W or , (comma) for a white screen or B or . (period) for a black screen. To resume the show, press any key.

TIP

If you set up the slide transitions to occur automatically at a certain time, you can stop or restart the show by pressing S or + (plus sign). However, this is more of an issue for self-running shows, which are discussed in Chapter 19, "Designing User-Interactive or Self-Running Presentations."

Using the On-Screen Show Controls

When you display a slide show, the mouse pointer and show controls are hidden. To make them appear, you can move the mouse. When you do this, very faint buttons, shown in Figure 18.1, appear in the bottom-left corner of the slide show and the mouse pointer also appears. PowerPoint calls this row of buttons the *popup toolbar*. The buttons on this toolbar are different from the ones in earlier versions of PowerPoint, and they offer many additional capabilities. From left to right, the buttons are as follows:

FIGURE 18.1

These buttons appear in the bottom-left corner of a slide in Slide Show view.

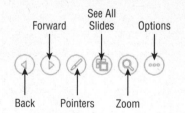

- **Back**, the leftmost button, takes you back to the previous slide or to the previous animation event if the present slide contains animation.
- **Forward** moves you to the next slide. Normally, you can just click to go to the next slide, but if you are using the pen (covered later in this chapter), then clicking it

causes it to draw rather than advance the presentation. In this situation, you can use the Forward button.

- **Pointers** opens a menu for controlling the appearance of the pen or pointer. (I discuss this feature later in this chapter.)

- **See All Slides** opens a slide-sorter-like view within Slide Show view, from which you can quickly select the slide you want to jump to by looking at thumbnails.

- **Zoom** enables you to zoom in on a portion of a slide and then zoom back out again.

- **Options** opens the menu shown in Figure 18.2. It contains a variety of commands for controlling the presentation, including setting arrow options and controlling display settings and Presenter view. You can also open this menu by right-clicking anywhere on the slide.

FIGURE 18.2

Click the Options button or right-click on the slide to open this menu.

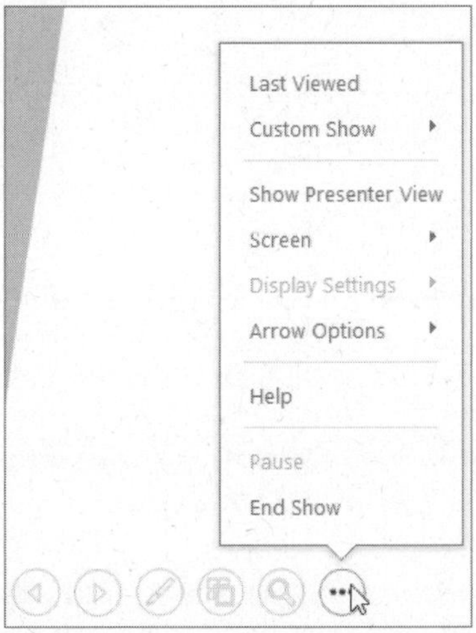

> **TIP**
>
> You can set up your show to move backward when you click the right-mouse button. Choose File ⇨ Options, click Advanced, and in the Slide Show section, deselect the Show Menu on Right Mouse Click check box. If you do that, you can't right-click to open the navigation menu though. The toolbar in the lower-left corner of Slide Show view can be disabled via File ⇨ Options ⇨ Advanced ⇨ Slide Show ⇨ Show Popup Toolbar.

> **NOTE**
>
> Because the menu that appears is identical whether you click the Options button or right-click anywhere on the slide, this chapter mentions only the right-click method when you need to choose something from this menu. However, keep in mind that you can also click the Options button on the popup toolbar if you prefer.

There are a lot of shortcut keys to remember when working in Slide Show view, and so PowerPoint provides a handy summary of these keys. To see them, right-click and choose Help, or press F1. The Slide Show Help dialog box appears (Figure 18.3). The dialog box has several tabbed pages; click a tab to browse for the shortcuts of interest to you. Click OK to close this dialog box when you are done.

FIGURE 18.3

The Slide Show Help dialog box provides a quick summary of the shortcut keys that are available during a presentation.

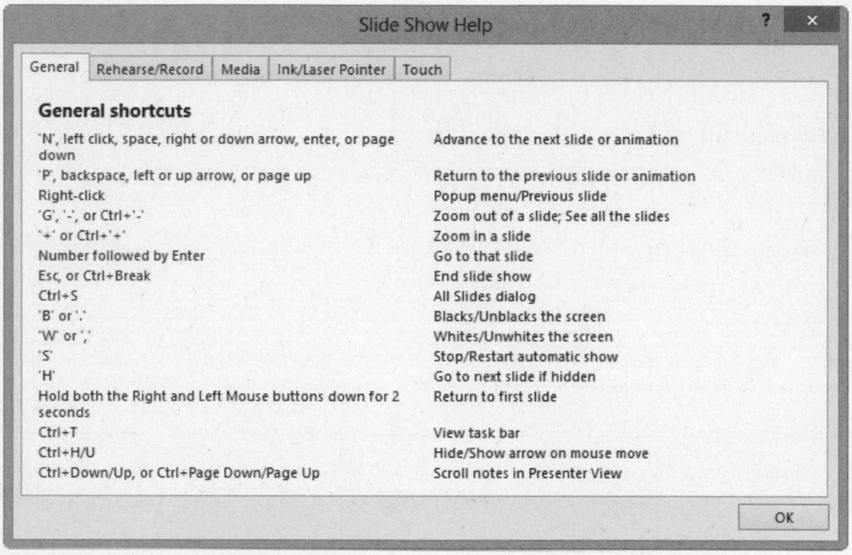

Moving from Slide to Slide

The simplest way to move through a presentation is to move to the next slide. To do so, you can use any of these methods:

- Press any of these keys: N, spacebar, right arrow, down arrow, Enter, or Page Down.
- Click the left mouse button.
- Right-click and choose Next.
- Click the right-pointing arrow button in the bottom-left corner of the slide.

If you have animated any elements on a slide, these methods advance the animation and do not necessarily move to the next slide. For example, if you have animated your bulleted list so that the bullets appear one at a time, then any of the actions in this list make the next bullet appear rather than making the next slide appear. Only after all of the objects on the current slide have displayed does PowerPoint advance to the next slide. If you need to immediately advance to the next slide, you can use the instructions in the next section, "Jumping to Specific Slides."

To back up to the previous slide, use any of these methods:

- Press any of these keys: P, Backspace, left arrow, up arrow, or Page Up.
- Click the left-pointing arrow button on the bottom-left corner of the slide.
- Right-click and choose Previous.

You can also go back to the last slide that you viewed. To do this, right-click and choose Last Viewed. Although you would think that the last slide viewed would be the same as the previous slide, this is not always the case. For example, if you jump around in the slide show — such as to a hidden slide — then the last slide viewed is not the previous slide in the show but the hidden slide that you have just viewed.

Jumping to Specific Slides

There are several ways to jump to a particular slide. One of the easiest ways is to use See All Slides to locate the slide from its thumbnail image. To do so, follow these steps:

1. **During the slide show, right-click to display the shortcut menu.**
2. **Select See All Slides.** Thumbnail images of the slides appear, as shown in Figure 18.4.

FIGURE 18.4

You can go to a specific slide using the See All Slides command on the menu.

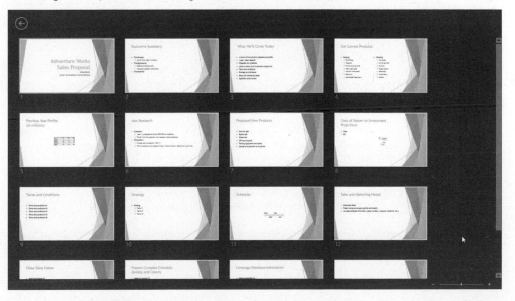

3. **Click the slide to which you want to jump.**

You can also jump to a certain slide by typing its number and pressing Enter. For example, to go to the third slide, you would type **3** and then press Enter. Another way is to press Ctrl+S to open an All Slides dialog box listing the titles of all of the slides in the presentation. You can click a slide to select it and then click Go To, as shown in Figure 18.5.

FIGURE 18.5

The All Slides dialog box lists the titles of all of the slides so that you can select the one you want to go to.

To jump back to the first slide in the presentation, hold down both the left and right mouse buttons for two seconds (or type **1** and press Enter).

Blanking the Screen

Sometimes during a live presentation there may be a delay. Whether it is a chatty audience member with a complicated question, a fire drill, or just an intermission, you will want to pause the show.

If you have the slides set for manual transition, then the slide you stopped on remains on the screen until you resume. However, you may not want this. For example, it may be distracting to the audience, especially if the pause is to allow someone to get up and speak in front of the screen. A solution is to turn the screen into a blank expanse of black or white. To do so, type W or a comma (for white), or type B or a period (for black). To return to the presentation, you can press the same key or press any key on the keyboard.

TIP

While the screen is completely black or white, you can draw on it with the pen tool so that it becomes a convenient "scratch pad." Annotations you make with the pen on the blank screen are not saved; when you resume the presentation, they are gone forever. (In contrast, you do have the opportunity to save any annotations you make on the slides themselves, as you will learn in the next section.)

Using the On-Screen Pen

Have you ever seen a coach in a locker room drawing out football plays on a chalkboard? Well, you can do the same thing in PowerPoint. You can have an impromptu discussion of concepts that are illustrated on slides and punctuate the discussion with your own circles, arrows, and lines. Perhaps during the discussion portion of your presentation, you may decide that one point on the slide is not important. In this case, you can use the pen to cross it out. Conversely, a certain point may become really important during a discussion and you want to emphasize it. In this case, you can circle it or underline it with the pen cursor.

You can choose your pen color as follows:

1. **Move the mouse to make the buttons appear.**

2. **Click the Pointers button (the one that looks like a pen).** A menu appears. Alternatively, you can right-click and then choose Pointer Options to see a similar menu. (The main difference is that on the right-click version, you have to select the Ink Color command for access to the ink color swatches.)

3. **Click the color you want, as shown in Figure 18.6.** (If you're using the right-click version of the menu, point to Ink Color first.)

FIGURE 18.6

You can select a pen type and an ink color for it.

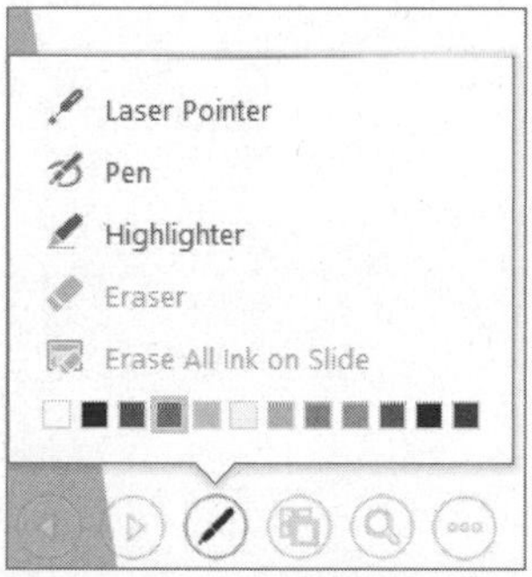

TIP

To change the default pen color for the show so you don't always have to manually select the color you want, click Set Up Show on the Slide Show tab. Then, in the Pen Color drop-down list, choose the color you want.

You can turn on the type of pen that you want, as follows:

1. **Click the Pointers button again.**

2. **Click the type of pen that you want:**
   - **Pen.** A thin solid line
   - **Highlighter.** A thick, semitransparent line

> **NOTE**
>
> The on-screen buttons in the slide show continue to work while you have a pen enabled, but you have to click them twice to activate them — once to tell PowerPoint to temporarily switch out of the Pen mode and then again to open the menu.

You can also turn on the default pen by pressing Ctrl+P and then return to the arrow again by pressing Ctrl+A or Esc.

After enabling a pen, just drag and draw on the slide to make your mark. You should practice drawing lines, arrows, and other shapes because it takes a while to master. Figure 18.7 shows an example of using the pen.

FIGURE 18.7

You can draw on the slide with the pen tools.

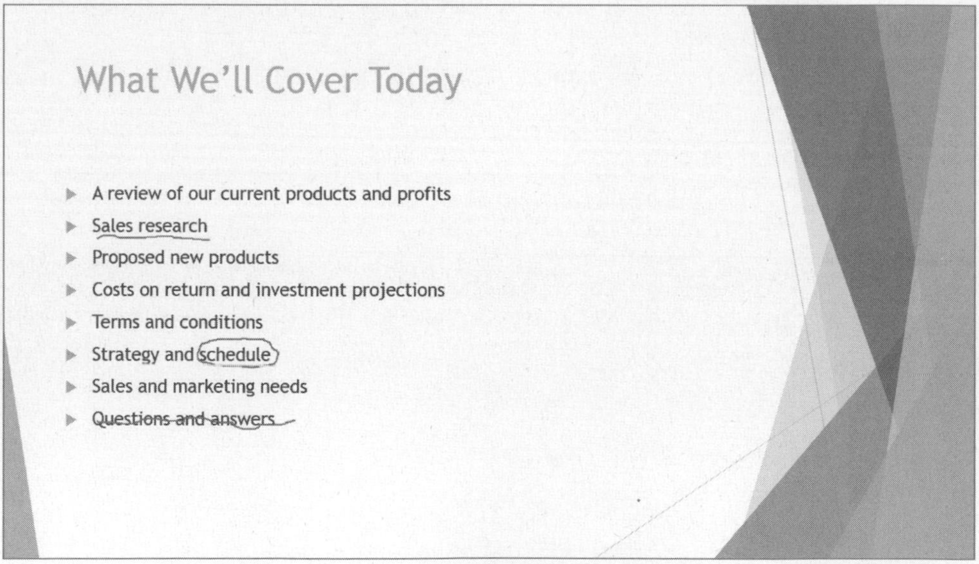

> **CAUTION**
>
> The on-screen pen is not very attractive. If you know in advance that you are going to emphasize certain points, you may prefer to build the emphasis into the presentation by making these points larger, bolder, or in different colors. You can also circle the points using an animated oval shape.

To erase your lines and try again, press E (for Erase), or open the Pointer menu (or right-click and choose Pointer Options) and choose Erase All Ink on Slide. To erase just a part of the ink, open the Pointer menu, choose Eraser, and then use the mouse pointer to erase individual lines.

> **NOTE**
>
> Unlike in some earlier versions of PowerPoint, drawings are not erased on a slide when you move to another slide.

When you exit Slide Show view after drawing on slides, a dialog box appears, asking whether you want to keep or discard your annotations. If you choose Keep, the annotations become drawn objects on the slides, which you can then move or delete, similar to a line drawn with the drawing tools.

The pen remains a pen when you advance from slide to slide. To change the pen back to a pointer again, open the Pointer menu and choose Arrow, press Ctrl+A, or press Esc.

Hiding Slides for Backup Use

You may not always want to show every slide that you have prepared. Sometimes it pays to prepare extra data in anticipation of a question that you think someone might ask or to hold back certain data unless someone specifically requests it.

By hiding a slide, you keep it filed in reserve, without making it a part of the main slide show. Then, at any time during the presentation when (or if) it becomes appropriate, you can display that slide. Hiding refers only to whether the slide is a part of the main presentation's flow; it has no effect in any other view.

> **TIP**
>
> If you have only a handful of slides to hide, go ahead and hide them. However, if you have a large group of related slides to hide, consider creating a custom show instead. Custom shows are covered later in this chapter.

Hiding and Unhiding Slides

Slide Sorter view is a good view from which to hide and unhide slides because an indicator appears below each slide to show whether it is hidden. This way, you can easily determine which slides are a part of the main presentation. In the slide thumbnail pane in Normal view, hidden slides appear ghosted out.

Follow these steps to hide a slide:

1. **Switch to Slide Sorter view.**
2. **Select the slide or slides that you want to hide.** Remember, to select more than one slide, hold down the Ctrl key as you click the ones that you want.
3. **Click the Hide Slide button on the Slide Show tab of the ribbon, or right-click one of the selected slides and choose Hide Slide from the shortcut menu.** A diagonal line crosses through the slide indicating that it is hidden. The slide's content also appears dimmed.

18

To unhide a slide, select the slide and click Hide Slide again. The slide's number returns to normal. You can also right-click a slide and choose Hide Slide again to toggle the hidden attribute off.

Showing a Hidden Slide during a Presentation

When you advance from one slide to the next during a show, hidden slides do not appear. (This is what being hidden is about, after all.) If you need to display one of the hidden slides, follow these steps:

1. **In Slide Show view, click the See All Slides button in the bottom-left corner of the screen, or right-click and choose See All Slides.**

   Thumbnails of the slides appear, and hidden slides appear dimmed and with a diagonal line drawn through their numbers, as in Figure 18.8.

FIGURE 18.8

Hidden slides appear dimmed.

Hidden slide

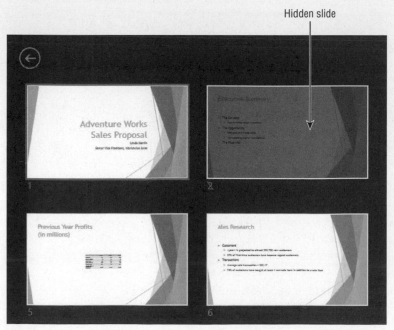

2. **Click the hidden slide to which you want to jump.**

Once you display a hidden slide, you can easily return to it later. When you move backward through the presentation (using the Backspace key, the left or up arrow key, or the on-screen Back button), any hidden slides that you displayed previously are included in the slides that PowerPoint scrolls back through. However, when you move forward through the presentation, the hidden slide does not reappear, regardless of when you viewed it previously. You can always jump back to it again using the preceding steps. You can also set up hyperlinks to go to, and leave, hidden slides.

Using Custom Shows

Many slide shows have a linear flow: First you show slide one, and then slide two, and so on, until you have completed the entire presentation. This format is suitable for situations where you are presenting clear-cut information with few variables, such as a presentation about a new insurance plan for a group of employees. However, when the situation becomes more complex, a single-path slide show may not suffice. This is especially true when you are presenting a persuasive message to decision makers; you want to anticipate their questions and their need for more information and have many backup slides, or even entire backup slide shows, that are prepared in case questions arise. Figure 18.9 shows a flow chart for this kind of presentation.

Another great use for custom shows is to set aside a group of slides for a specific audience. For example, you might need to present essentially the same information to employees at two different sites. In this case, you could create two custom shows within the main show and include in each show slides that they both have in common as well as slides that are appropriate for only one audience or the other. Figure 18.10 shows a flow chart for this kind of presentation.

FIGURE 18.9

You can use custom shows to hide related groups of backup slides.

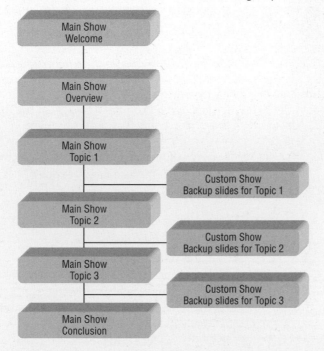

Notice in Figure 18.10 that although some of the slides in the two custom shows are the same, they repeat in each custom show rather than jumping back to the main presentation. This is because it is much easier to jump to the custom show once and stay there than it is to keep jumping into and out of the show.

Slides in a custom show remain a part of the main presentation. Placing a slide in a custom show does not exclude it from the regular presentation flow. However, you may decide that you no longer want to show the main presentation in its present form; you may just want to use it as a resource pool from which you can select slides for other custom shows. To learn how to set up PowerPoint so that a custom show rather than the main presentation starts when you enter Slide Show view, see the section "Using a Custom Show as the Main Presentation" later in this chapter.

Ideas for Using Custom Shows

Here are some ideas to start you thinking about how and why you might want to include some custom shows in your presentation files:

- **Avoiding duplication.** If you have several shows that use about 50 percent of the same slides and the other 50 percent are different ones, you can create all of the shows as custom shows within a single presentation file. This way, the presentations can share the 50 percent of the slides that they have in common.

- **Managing change.** By creating a single presentation file with custom shows, you make it easy to manage changes. If any changes occur in your company that affect any of the common slides, making the change once in your presentation file makes the change to each of the custom shows immediately.

- **Overcoming objections.** You can anticipate client objections to your sales pitch and prepare several custom shows, each of which addresses a particular objection. Then, whatever reason your potential customer gives for not buying your product, you have a counteractive argument at hand.

- **Covering your backside.** If you think that you may be asked for specific figures or other information during a speech, you can have this information ready in a custom show (or on a few simple hidden slides, if there is not a lot of information) to display if needed. No more going through the embarrassment of having to say, "I'm not sure, but let me get back to you on that."

FIGURE 18.10

You can create custom shows that allow you to use the same presentation for multiple audiences.

Creating Custom Shows

To create a custom show, first create all of the slides that should go into it. Start with all of the slides in the main presentation. Then follow these steps:

1. **On the Slide Show tab, click Custom Slide Show, and then click Custom Shows.** The Custom Shows dialog box opens.

> **NOTE**
>
> If no custom shows are defined yet, the Custom Shows command is the only item that appears on this menu. Otherwise, your existing custom shows appear on and can be run from the menu.

2. **Click New.** The Define Custom Show dialog box opens.

3. **Type a name for your custom show in the Slide Show Name text box, replacing the default name.**

4. **In the Slides in Presentation pane, click the check box for the first slide that you want to appear in the custom show.**

   You can select multiple slides before clicking Add in Step 5. However, be aware that if you do this, the slides move to the Slides in Custom Show pane in the order that they originally appeared. If you want them in a different order, copy each slide over separately, in the order that you want, or rearrange the order as described in step 7.

5. **Click Add to copy the slide to the Slides in Custom Show pane. See Figure 18.11.**

FIGURE 18.11

Use the Add button to copy slides from the main presentation into the custom show.

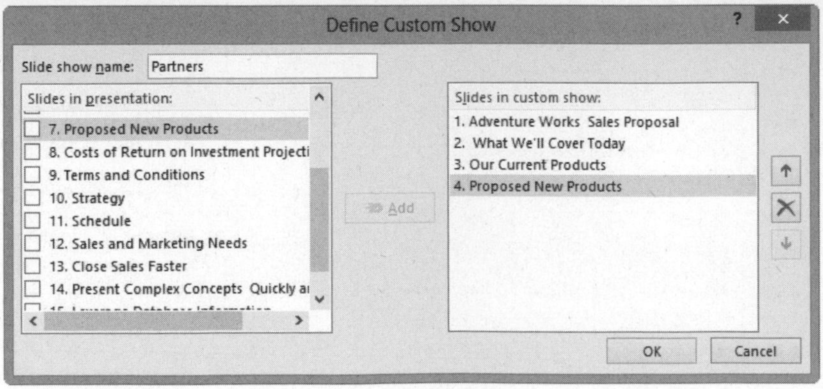

6. **If you need to select more slides, repeat steps 4 and 5 for each slide that you want to include in the custom show.**

7. **If you need to rearrange the slides in the custom show, click the slide that you want to move in the Slides in Custom Show pane and then click the up or down arrow button to change its position.**

8. **When you are finished building your custom show, click OK.** The new show appears in the Custom Shows dialog box.

9. **(Optional) To test your custom show, click the Show button.** Otherwise, click Close to close the Custom Shows dialog box.

Editing Custom Shows

You can manage your custom shows from the Custom Shows dialog box, the same place in which you created them. This includes editing, deleting, or making a copy of a show. To change which slides appear in a custom show, and in what order, follow these steps:

1. **On the Slide Show tab, click Custom Slide Show and then click Custom Shows.** The Custom Shows dialog box appears (Figure 18.12).

   FIGURE 18.12

   Select a custom show and then click the appropriate button to edit, copy, or delete it.

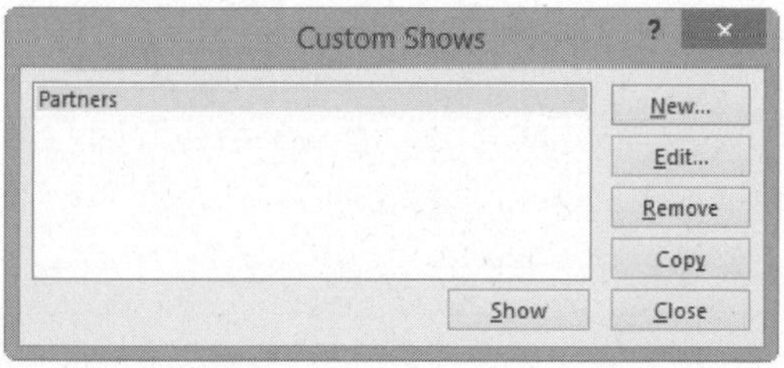

2. **If you have more than one custom show, click the one that you want to edit.**

3. **Click Edit.** The Define Custom Show dialog box reappears (Figure 18.11).

4. **Add or remove slides as needed.** To add a slide, select it in the left pane and click Add. To remove a slide, select it in the right pane and click Remove.

> **NOTE**
> Removing a slide from a custom show does not remove it from the overall presentation.

5. **Rearrange slides as needed with the up and down arrow buttons.**

6. **(Optional) You can change the custom show's name in the Slide Show Name text box.**

7. **Click OK.** PowerPoint saves your changes.

8. **Click Close to close the Custom Shows dialog box.**

Copying Custom Shows

A good way to create several similar custom shows is to create the first one and then copy it. You can then make small changes to the copies as necessary. To copy a custom show, follow these steps:

1. **On the Slide Show tab, click Custom Slide Show and then click Custom Shows.** The Custom Shows dialog box appears (Figure 18.12).

2. **If you have more than one custom show, select the show that you want to copy.**

3. **Click Copy.** A copy of the show appears in the dialog box. The filename includes the words *Copy of* so that you can distinguish it from the original.

4. **Edit the copy, as explained in the preceding section, to change its name and content.**

5. **When you are finished, click Close to close the Custom Shows dialog box.**

Deleting Custom Shows

It is not necessary to delete a custom show when you do not want it anymore; it does not do any harm remaining in your presentation. Because custom shows do not display unless you call for them, you can simply choose not to display it. However, if you want to make your presentation more orderly, you can delete a custom show that you no longer want. Follow these steps:

1. **On the Slide Show tab, click Custom Slide Show and then click Custom Shows.** The Custom Shows dialog box appears (Figure 18.12).

2. **Select the show that you want to delete.**

3. **Click Remove.** The show disappears from the list.

4. **Click Close to close the Custom Shows dialog box.**

Displaying a Custom Show

To start your presentation with a custom show, on the Slide Show tab, click Custom Slide Show and then click the name of the custom show on the drop-down menu. The custom show runs.

You can also call up the custom show at any time during your main presentation. There are two ways to do this: You can navigate to the custom show with PowerPoint's regular presentation controls, or you can create a hyperlink to the custom show on your slide.

Navigating to a Custom Show

During a presentation, you can jump to any of your custom shows by following these steps from Slide Show view:

1. **Click the Options button, or right-click to open the menu.**

2. **Choose Custom Show and then select the custom show that you want, as shown in Figure 18.13.** The custom show starts.

FIGURE 18.13

Choose the custom show that you want to jump to.

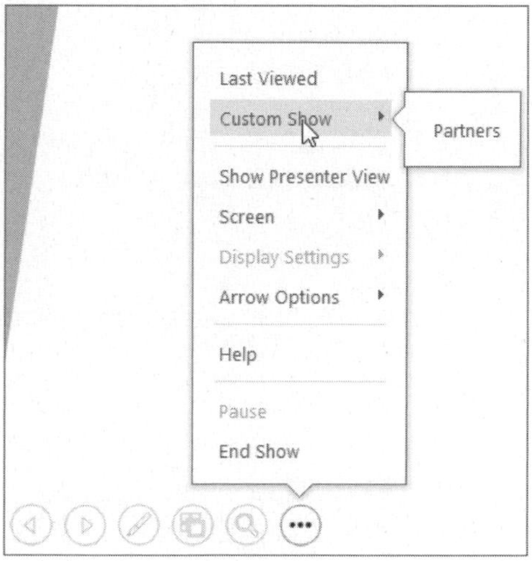

When you start a custom show, you are no longer in the main presentation. To verify this, open the shortcut menu again, choose Go to Slide, and check out the list of slides. This list shows only the slides that belong to the custom show.

Navigating Back to the Main Show

To return to the main show, follow these steps:

1. **Press Ctrl+S to open the All Slides dialog box.**
2. **Open the Show drop-down list and choose All Slides.**
3. **Select the slide that you want to go to.** You can choose from all of the slides in the entire presentation.
4. **Click Go To.**

TIP

To avoid having to press Ctrl+S to return to the main show, you can create a hyperlink or action button for a specific slide in your main show.

Creating a Hyperlink to a Custom Show

Although you learn a lot about hyperlinks in upcoming chapters, here is a preview. Hyperlinks are hot links that you place on your slides. When you click a hyperlink, you

559

jump the display to some other location. This is why they are called *hot*. A hyperlink can jump to an Internet location, a different spot in your presentation, an external file (such as a Word document), or just about anywhere else.

One way to gain quick access to your custom shows in a presentation is to create hyperlinks for them on certain key slides that act as jumping points. You can insert a text hyperlink into any text box, and its text becomes the marker that you click. For example, if you insert a hyperlink for a custom show called Radio Spots, then the hyperlink text could read Radio Spots. If you want to get fancier, you can select some existing text or an existing graphic object and then attach the hyperlink to it. For example, as shown in Figure 18.14, I have inserted a clip-art image of a radio and set it up to be a hyperlink to the custom show that provides details about the radio spots.

FIGURE 18.14

You can create hyperlinks on slides that display custom shows.

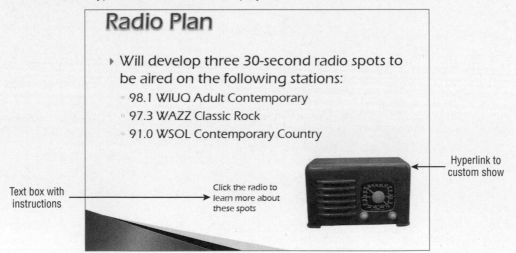

Follow these steps:

1. **If you are attaching the hyperlink to another object (such as the radio in Figure 18.14) or some text, then select the object or text.**

2. **On the Insert tab, click Hyperlink.** The Insert Hyperlink dialog box appears.

3. **Click the Place in This Document icon along the left side of the dialog box.**

4. **In the Select a Place in This Document pane, scroll down to the Custom Shows list.**

5. **Click the custom show that you want to jump to with this hyperlink, as shown in Figure 18.15.**

FIGURE 18.15

Choose one of your custom shows as the place to jump to when the user clicks the hyperlink.

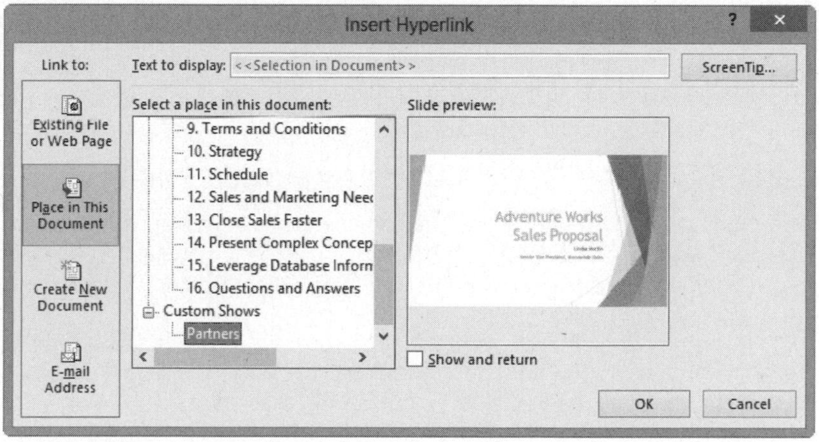

6. **(Optional) If you want to return to the same spot that you left in the main presentation after viewing this custom show, select the Show and Return check box.** If you do not select this option, the presentation will simply end when the custom show ends.

7. **(Optional) If you want to specify a ScreenTip for the hyperlink, click the ScreenTip button to create one.**

8. **Click OK.**

If you are using text for the hyperlink, the text now appears underlined and in a different color. This color is controlled by the color theme of your presentation (specifically the Hyperlink and Followed Hyperlink colors). If you are using a graphic, its appearance does not change. However, when you are in Slide Show view and you move the mouse pointer over the object, the pointer changes to a pointing hand, indicating that the object is a hyperlink.

TIP

If you do not want your linked text to be underlined or to change colors upon return, you can draw a rectangle with no border and 99 percent white fill over the top of the text and link to the rectangle instead. Because this shape is on top of the text, you click it instead of the text. Keep in mind that you should create your link before changing the border and fill of the shape to almost no color.

Another way to use hyperlinks for custom shows is to set up the first few slides generically for all audiences and then to branch off into one custom show or another, based on user input. The diagram in Figure 18.9 is an example of this type of presentation. After the first two slides, you could set up a "decision" slide that contains two hyperlinks — for example, one for video products and one for audio products. The user would then click the hyperlink they want.

> **TIP**
>
> You can also create hyperlinks to custom shows by using action buttons. Action buttons are a special type of drawn shape that is designed specifically for creating hyperlinks within a presentation.

Using a Custom Show as the Main Presentation

If you have a complete show contained in one of your custom shows, you may sometimes want to show it as the default presentation. To do this, you must tell PowerPoint that you want to bypass the main presentation and start with the custom show.

The easiest way to show a custom show is to select it from the Custom Slide Show drop-down menu on the Slide Show tab. However, you can also set up a custom show to be the default show for the presentation by following these steps:

1. **On the Slide Show tab, click Set Up Slide Show.** The Set Up Show dialog box appears.

2. **Click Custom Show, and then open the Custom Show drop-down list and choose the show that you want to use, as shown in Figure 18.16.**

FIGURE 18.16

Use the Set Up Show dialog box to control which of your custom shows runs when you start the show.

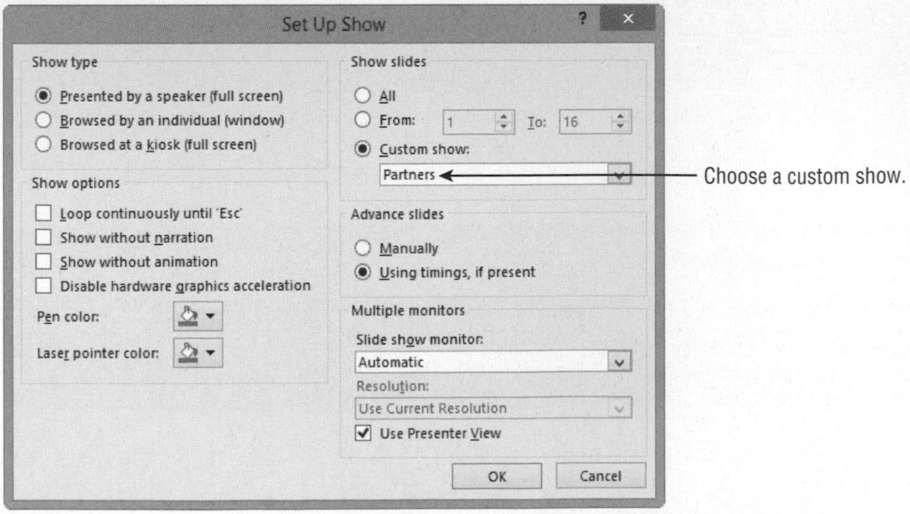

Choose a custom show.

3. **Click OK.** Now, when you start the show, the custom show runs.

Creating and Using Sections

When you have lots of slides in a presentation, you may find it helpful to organize them into sections for easier management in Normal or Slide Sorter view. You can then collapse or expand the sections to focus in on a subset of the slides, as shown in Figure 18.17.

FIGURE 18.17

Expand or collapse sections.

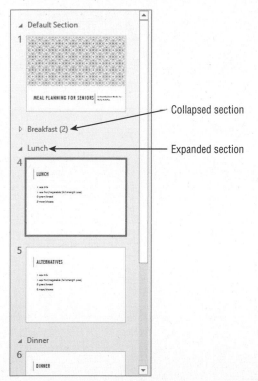

Collapsed section

Expanded section

Creating a Section Break

To divide your presentation into multiple sections, insert a section break between two slides. All the slides above the break are in one section, and all slides below the break are in another.

To insert a section break, follow these steps:

1. **In Normal view, in the Slides pane, click between two slides.** A horizontal line appears there.
2. **Right-click the horizontal line and choose Add Section.** A new section break is created.

You can also select the slide you want to use as the first slide in a section. Then choose Home ➪ Section ➪ Add Section to make it into a section heading.

Renaming a Section

Each section you create has a default generic name: Untitled Section. You will probably want to give the sections more meaningful names. To rename a section, follow these steps:

1. **Right-click the section name in the Slides pane.** A shortcut menu opens, as shown in Figure 18.18.

FIGURE 18.18

Right-clicking a section name opens a shortcut menu of commands.

2. **Click Rename Section.** The Rename Section dialog box opens.
3. **Type the new name.**
4. **Click Rename or press Enter.**

Instead of steps 1 and 2, you can choose Home ➪ Slides ➪ Section ➪ Rename Section.

Deleting a Section

There are several options when deleting a section:

- **Remove Section.** Deletes the section break but keeps the section's slides and places them in the previous section.
- **Remove Section & Slides.** Deletes the section break and all slides that were within that section.
- **Remove All Sections.** Deletes all section break lines but keeps all slides.

To do any of these, right-click the section name in the Slides pane and make your selection from the shortcut menu, as shown in Figure 18.18. You can also use the Section button's menu on the Home tab, but it does not contain the Remove Section & Slides option.

Reordering Sections

Sections can be useful for quickly reordering large blocks of slides. Place all the slides within a single section, and then move the section to move all the slides at once.

To move a section, use either of these techniques:

- Right-click the section bar and choose Move Section Up or Move Section Down. See Figure 18.18.
- Drag the section name up or down in the Slides pane. You might find this easier if you collapse the section, but it is not required.

> **CAUTION**
>
> If you select a section name and then issue the Cut or Delete command, all the slides within that section are removed but the section itself remains. The section itself is not included in the operation. Therefore, you cannot use the Cut and Paste commands (Ctrl+X and Ctrl+V) to move sections to different spots in the presentation.

Giving a Presentation on a Different Computer

The computer on which you create a presentation is usually not the same computer that you will use to show it. For example, you may be doing the bulk of your work on your desktop computer in your office in Los Angeles but you need to use your laptop computer to give the presentation in Phoenix.

One way to transfer a presentation to another computer is simply to copy the PowerPoint file (the file with the `.pptx` filename extension) using a flash drive or other removable media. However, this method is imperfect because it assumes that the other computer has all of the fonts, sounds, and other elements that you need for every part of the show. This can be a dangerous assumption. For example, suppose your presentation contains a link to some Excel data. If you do not also copy the Excel file, then you cannot update the data when you are on the road.

A better way to ensure that you are taking everything you need while traveling is to use the Package Presentation for CD feature in PowerPoint. This feature reads all of the linked files and associated objects and ensures that they are transferred along with the main presentation. You do not actually need to copy the presentation to a writeable CD, and you do not need a CD-R or CD-RW drive to use this feature. You can copy the presentation package anywhere you want, such as to a flash drive or a network location.

Copying a Presentation to CD

If you have a CD-R or CD-RW drive, then copying the presentation to CD is an attractive choice. It produces a self-running disc that contains all the presentation files and their needed linked files, plus a web page (HTML format) from which you can choose which presentation file to run. That web page also contains a hyperlink you can use to download the PowerPoint Viewer application if needed. (You need it only if PowerPoint itself is not installed on the PC on which you want to view the presentation.) Figure 18.19 shows a sample web page for accessing a package that contains two different presentations, for example.

FIGURE 18.19

The Package for CD command generates a CD containing all data files needed to show the presentation plus a browser-based interface like the one shown here.

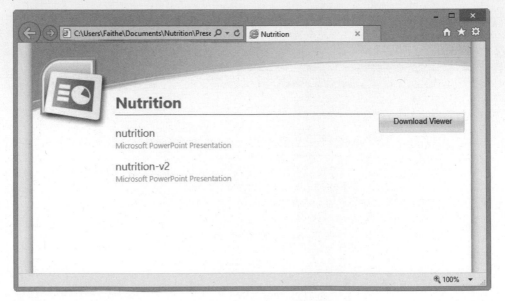

TIP

You can copy many presentation files onto a single CD, not just the currently active one, which is included by default. The only limit is the size of the disc (usually 650MB to 700MB).

Here is the basic procedure, which is elaborated on in the following sections:

1. **Place a blank CD-R or CD-RW disc in your writeable CD drive.**

2. **Make sure the presentation is exactly the way you want it.** If you are using a CD-R disc, keep in mind that this disc type is not rewriteable, and so you should ensure that the presentation is exactly as you want it.

3. **Choose File ⇨ Export ⇨ Package Presentation for CD ⇨ Package for CD.** The Package for CD dialog box opens (Figure 18.20).

FIGURE 18.20

Use the Package for CD feature to place all of the necessary files for the presentation on a CD.

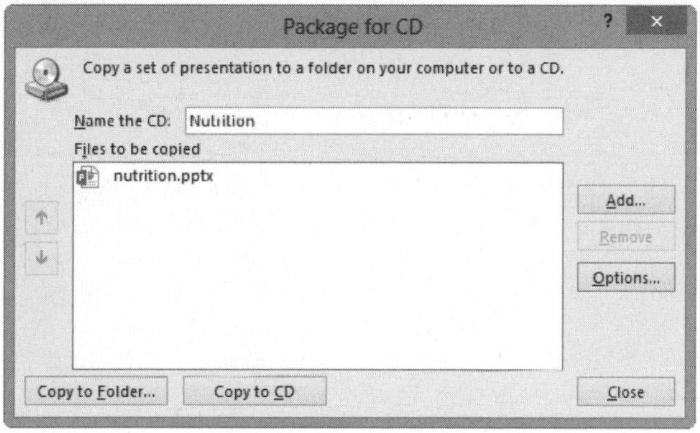

4. **Type a name for the CD; this is similar to adding a volume label for the disc.**

5. **(Optional) Add more files to the CD if you want.** See the next section, "Creating a CD Containing Multiple Presentation Files," for more details.

6. **(Optional) Set any options that you want.** See the section "Setting Copy Options" later in this chapter, for more details.

7. **Click Copy to CD.**

8. **If a warning appears asking if you want to include linked files in your package, click Yes.**

The CD-writing process may take several minutes, depending on the writing speed of your CD drive and the size of the presentation files that you are placing on it.

If a message appears that the package will not include comments, revisions, or ink annotations, click Continue. This message appears only if your presentation contains any of those things.

A message appears when the files are successfully copied to the CD asking whether you want to copy the same files to another CD.

9. **Click Yes or No.** If you choose No, then you must also click Close to close the Package for CD dialog box.

The resulting CD automatically plays the presentations when you insert it in any computer. You can also browse the CD's contents to open the PowerPoint Viewer separately and use it to play specific presentations.

CAUTION

File corruption can occur on a CD drive during the writing process. After burning a CD, test it thoroughly by running the complete presentation from CD before you rely on the CD copy as the version that you take with you while traveling.

Creating a CD Containing Multiple Presentation Files

By default, the active presentation is included on the CD, but you can also add others, up to the capacity of your disc. For example, if you have several versions of the same presentation for different audiences, a single CD can contain all of them. As you are preparing to copy the files using the Package for CD dialog box, shown in Figure 18.20, follow these steps to add more files:

1. **Click Add.** An Add dialog box opens, similar to the Open dialog box that you use to open PowerPoint files.

2. **Select the additional files that you want to include, and click Add to return to the Package for CD dialog box.** The list of files now appears as shown in Figure 18.21.

   You can select multiple files from the same location by holding down the Ctrl key as you click the ones you want. To include multiple files from different locations, repeat steps 1 and 2 for each location.

3. **(Optional) Rearrange the list by clicking a presentation and then clicking the up or down arrow buttons to the left of the list.**

4. **If you need to remove a presentation from the list, click it and then click Remove.**

5. **Continue making the CD as you normally would.**

FIGURE 18.21

When you specify multiple files for a CD, you can specify the order in which they should play.

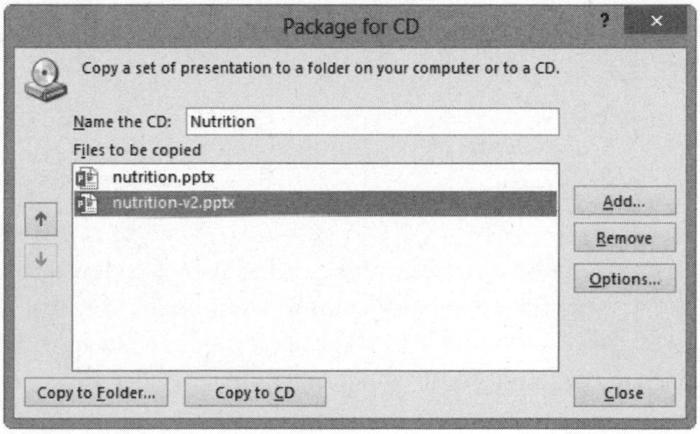

Setting Copy Options

The default copy options are suitable in most situations. However, you may sometimes want to modify them. To do this, open the Package Presentation for CD dialog box, and follow these steps:

1. **Click Options.** The Options dialog box opens (Figure 18.22).

   FIGURE 18.22

   You can set options for copying the presentations to CD.

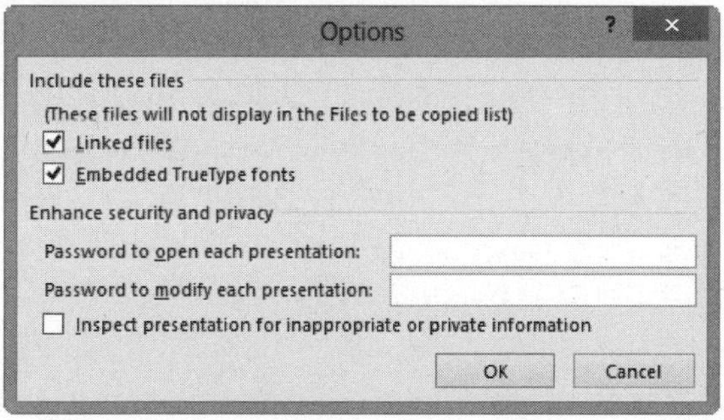

The Linked Files check box is selected by default; this option tells PowerPoint to include the full copies of all linked files. You can deselect this option if you want; a static copy of the linked data will remain in the presentation, but the link will not work. You should leave this option selected if you have sounds or multimedia files in your presentation that are linked rather than embedded.

The Embedded TrueType Fonts check box is also selected by default. If you are sure that the destination computer contains all of the fonts that are used in the presentation, then deselect this option. This makes the presentation file slightly smaller. Remember, not all fonts can be embedded; this depends on the level of embedding allowed by the font's manufacturer.

2. **If you want to add passwords for the presentations, do so in the Enhance Security and Privacy section.** There are separate text boxes for the password needed to open and the password needed to modify the presentation.

3. **Select the Inspect Presentations for Inappropriate or Private Information check box if you want to check the presentation for private information, such as your name or any comments.** The Document Inspector window opens. Select the types of content you want to check for and click Inspect.

4. **Click OK, and then write the CD as you normally would.**

Copying a Presentation to Other Locations

Although it is not well known, you can also use the Package Presentation for CD feature to copy presentation files and their associated support files to any location you want. For example, you can transfer files to another computer on a network or place them on a flash drive. To do so, follow these steps:

1. **In the Package for CD dialog box, set up the package exactly the way you want it, including all of the presentation files and options.** See the preceding sections for more information.

2. **Click Copy to Folder.** A Copy to Folder dialog box appears.

3. **Type a name for the new folder in the Name the Folder text box.**

4. **Type a path for the folder in the Choose Location text box.**

5. **Click OK.**

6. **If a warning appears about linked files, click Yes or No as appropriate.** PowerPoint copies the files to the location you specified.

7. **If a warning appears about comments or ink annotations, click Continue.**

8. **Click Close to close the Package for CD dialog box.**

 To make a DVD video of your presentation, see Chapter 20, "Preparing a Presentation for Mass Distribution."

Working with Audio-Visual Equipment

The first part of this chapter assumed that you were using a computer with a single monitor to show your presentation, but this may not always be the case. This part of the chapter looks at the entire range of audio-visual options from which you can choose. There are many models of projection equipment in conference rooms all across the world, but most of them fall into one of these categories:

- **Noncomputerized equipment.** This can include an overhead transparency viewer, a 35mm slide projector, or other older technology. You face two challenges if you need to work with this category of equipment: One challenge is figuring out how the equipment works because every model is different, and the other challenge is producing attractive versions of your slides to work with the older technology. There are companies that can produce 35mm slides from your PowerPoint files, or you can invest in a slide-making machine yourself. For transparencies, you simply print your slides on transparency film that is designed for your type of printer.

- **Single computer with a single monitor.** If there is a computer with a monitor in the meeting room, then you can run your presentation on that computer. You can do this with the Package Presentation for CD feature that is discussed in the preceding sections and then run the presentation directly from the CD, provided that PC has PowerPoint or the PowerPoint Viewer on it.

- **Single computer with a dual-monitor system.** On systems with dual monitors, one monitor is shown to the audience and the other is for your own use, via Presenter View. This is useful when you want to display your speaker notes on the monitor that the audience does not see. However, you might need to set up multi-monitor support in Windows so that you can view different displays on each monitor.

- **Projection system (LCD) or large monitor without a computer.** If the meeting room has a large monitor but no computer, you will need to bring your own laptop computer and connect it to the monitor. Most of these systems use a standard VGA plug and cable.

The following sections look at some of these options in more detail.

Presenting with Two Screens

If you have two monitors — either your laptop computer screen and an external monitor or two external monitors hooked up to the same computer — you can display the presentation on one of them and your own notes on the other one. This is a very handy setup! The details are covered in the next sections.

CAUTION

To use two screens, you need the full version of PowerPoint on your laptop, not just the PowerPoint Viewer. You also need compatible hardware. For example, your laptop must have an external VGA port and a built-in video card that supports DualView (a Windows feature) in your version of Windows. If you have a desktop computer, you must have two separate video cards or a video card with two separate video ports.

18

Configuring Display Hardware for Multi-Screen Viewing

First, you need to prepare your hardware. On a laptop computer, this means enabling both the built-in and the external monitor ports and connecting an external monitor. Some laptops toggle between internal, external, and dual monitors with an Fn key combination; refer to your laptop's documentation.

On a desktop computer, install a second video card and monitor, and then do the following to set them up in Windows:

1. **When Windows restarts after you install the second video card, right-click the Desktop and choose Screen Resolution.**

   A sample area displays two monitors. Figure 18.23 shows the Screen Resolution dialog box for Windows 7; the dialog boxes for other Windows versions are similar.

FIGURE 18.23

You must set up the second monitor in Windows before setting it up in PowerPoint.

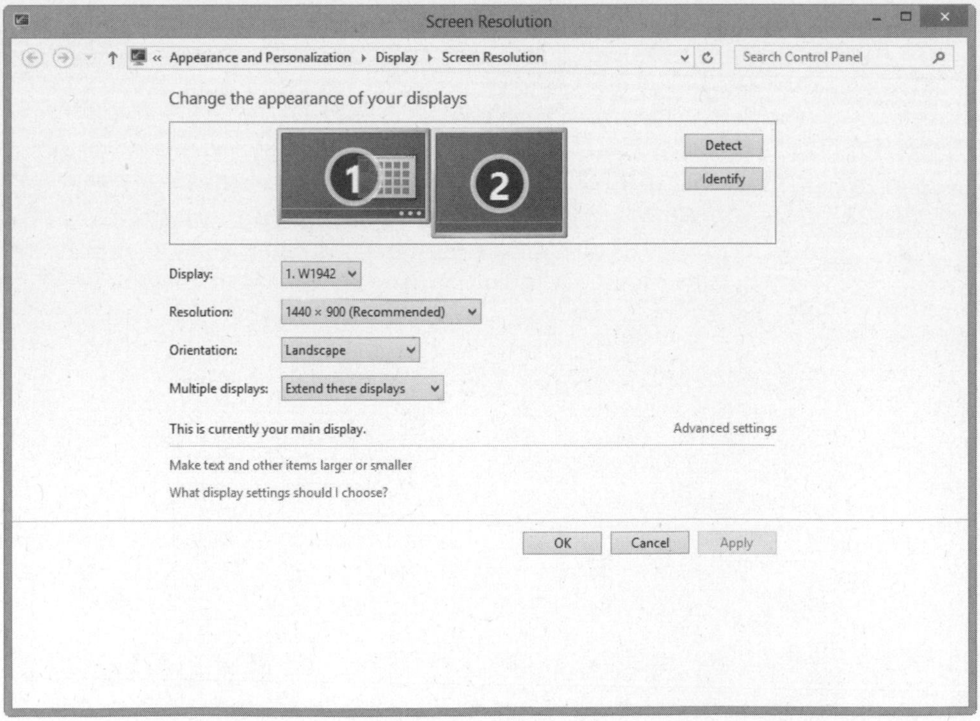

The monitor that you use most of the time should be monitor 1, and the other one should be monitor 2. To determine which is which, click Identify; large numbers appear briefly on each screen.

2. **If you need to swap the numbering of the monitors, click the one that should be the primary monitor and then select Make This My Main Display.** This option will be unavailable if the currently selected monitor is already set to be the primary one.

3. **Select the secondary monitor, and then select Extend These Displays from the Multiple Displays drop-down list.**

4. **(Optional) If the monitors are not arranged in the sample area in the way that they are physically positioned on your desk, drag the icons for the monitors to where you want them.**

5. **(Optional) Click a monitor in the sample area to adjust its display settings.**

6. **Click OK.** You are now ready to work with the two monitors in PowerPoint.

You can now drag items from your primary monitor to your secondary one! This can also be useful outside of PowerPoint. For example, you can have two applications open at once, each in its own monitor window.

Setting Up a Presentation for Two Screens

If you have two monitors available, and configured as described in the preceding section, you can use the following steps to help PowerPoint recognize and take advantage of these monitors:

1. **Open the presentation in PowerPoint.**

2. **On the Slide Show tab, click Set Up Slide Show.** The Set Up Show dialog box opens (Figure 18.24).

FIGURE 18.24

You can set up the show for multiple monitors in the Set Up Show dialog box.

18

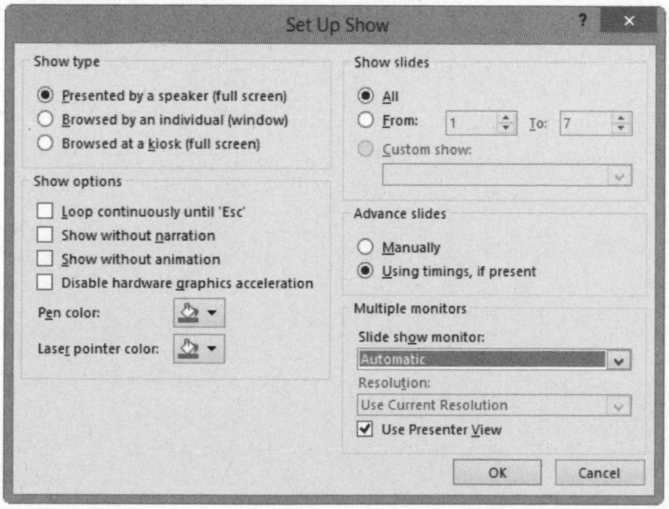

3. **In the Multiple Monitors section, open the Slide Show Monitor drop-down list and choose the monitor that the audience will see.** This list shows only Automatic and Primary Monitor if you do not have multiple monitors enabled (see the preceding section).

4. **Select the Use Presenter View check box.** This will give you a separate, very useful control panel on the other monitor during the show, as described in the next section.

5. **Click OK.** You are now ready to show the presentation using two separate displays — one for you and one for the audience.

Presenting with Two Screens Using Presenter View

Presenter View is a special view of the presentation that is available on systems with more than one monitor if you have enabled Presenter View, as described in the preceding section. This view provides many useful tools for managing the show behind the scenes, as shown in Figure 18.25. It appears automatically on the non-audience monitor when you enter Slide Show view.

TIP
New in PowerPoint 2013, you can experiment with Presenter View even if you don't have multiple monitors. While in Slide Show view, right-click anywhere and then choose Show Presenter View.

FIGURE 18.25

Presenter View provides tools for helping you manage your slide show from a second monitor.

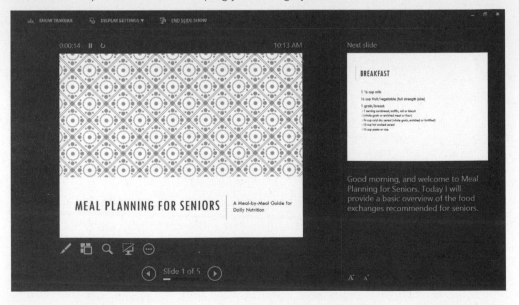

Here are some of the key features of Presenter View:

- The current slide (the one the audience is viewing) appears at the left. The next slide appears at the upper right.

- The speaker notes for each slide appear in the lower-right pane. You cannot edit them from here, however. Buttons for making the text larger or smaller appear below the speaker notes pane so you can adjust the font size.

- A time and duration display appears above the current slide. It tells you the current time and how long this slide has been displayed.

- Below the current slide are a series of icons that roughly correspond to the icons you see in Slide Show view in the lower-left corner. From left to right, they are as follows:

  - **Pen and Laser Pointer Tools.** Opens a menu from which you can choose a pen, laser pointer, highlighter, or arrow and choose the ink color. You can also erase any annotations you have made with the Eraser tool here.

  - **See All Slides.** Opens a page of thumbnail images of all the slides in the presentation so you can quickly jump to the one you want.

  - **Zoom.** Zooms in on a part of the slide.

  - **Black or Unblack Slide Show.** Toggles between showing the slide and showing a black screen.

  - **More Slide Show Options.** Opens a menu of additional control options. For example, you can hide Presenter view from here, show a black or white screen, show or hide ink markup, get help, or end the show.

- Forward and back arrows appear at the bottom of the screen; you can use these to move through the presentation.

- At the top of the screen are three buttons:

  - **Show Taskbar.** Shows or hides the Windows taskbar so you can switch out of Slide Show view to take care of some other task.

  - **Display Settings.** Opens a menu from which you can see which monitor is displaying Presenter View and which is displaying the full-screen show to the audience and switch them if you like.

  - **End Slide Show.** Exits from Slide Show view.

- The panes are adjustable by dragging the dividers between them, so you can have larger thumbnails, a smaller slide display, more or less room for notes, and so on.

Summary

In this chapter, you learned how to prepare for a big presentation. You now know how to package a presentation and move it to another computer, how to set up single and multi-screen audio-visual equipment to work with your laptop, and how to control a presentation on-screen using your computer. You also know how to jump to different slides, how to take notes during a meeting, and how to assign action items. You're all set! All you need now is a nice starched shirt and a shoeshine.

In the next chapter, you learn about designing presentations that are user-interactive or self-running. You can do this by creating easy-to-use action buttons for situations in which you cannot be there to press the buttons yourself.

CHAPTER 19

Designing User-Interactive or Self-Running Presentations

IN THIS CHAPTER

In the last few chapters, you've been learning how to build and present slide shows that support you as you speak to your audience directly. When you build such presentations, you design each slide to assist you, not duplicate your efforts. Slides designed for a live presentation typically do not contain a lot of detail; they function as pointers and reminders for the much more detailed live discussion or lecture taking place in the foreground.

When you build a self-running or user-interactive presentation, the focus is exactly the opposite. The slides are going out there all alone and must be capable of projecting the entire message all by themselves. Therefore, you want to create slides that contain much more information.

Another consideration is audience interest. When you speak to your audience live, the primary focus is on you and your words. The slides assist you, but the audience watches and listens primarily to you. Therefore, to keep the audience interested, you have to be interesting. If the slides are interesting, that's a nice bonus. With a self-running or user-interactive presentation, on the other hand, each slide must be fascinating. The animations and transitions that you learned about in Chapter 16 come in very handy in creating interest, as do sounds and videos, discussed in Chapter 14 and Chapter 15.

> **NOTE**
>
> Another name for a self-running presentation is a *kiosk* presentation. This name comes from the fact that many self-running informational presentations are located in little buildings, or kiosks, in public areas such as malls and convention centers.

Understanding User Interactivity

Letting the audience take control can be scary. If you aren't forcing people to go at a certain pace and view all the slides, what's to guarantee that they don't skim through quickly or quit halfway through?

Well, there are no guarantees. Even in a show with a live speaker, though, you can't control whether or not people pay attention. The best you can do is put together a compelling presentation and hope that people want to view it. The same applies to a user-interactive presentation. People are either going to watch and absorb it or they're not. There's no point in treating the audience like children. On the contrary, they will likely respond much better if you give them the options and let them decide what content they need.

Navigational controls are the main thing that separates user-interactive presentations from normal ones. You have to provide an idiot-proof way for people to move from slide to slide. Okay, technically, yes, they could use the same navigational controls that you use when presenting a show (see Chapter 18, "Preparing for a Live Presentation"), but those controls aren't always obvious. Moving forward is a no-brainer (click the mouse), but what about moving backward? Would you have guessed *P* for *Previous* if you hadn't already known? Probably not. And what if they want to end the show early? The first half of this chapter shows you various techniques for creating navigational controls.

Here are some ideas for ways to use navigational controls:

- **Web resource listings.** Include a slide that lists websites that users can visit for more information about various topics covered in your presentation. You can also include cross-references to those sites throughout the presentation at the bottom of pertinent slides.

- **Product information.** Create a basic presentation that describes your products, with For More Information buttons for each product. Then create hidden slides with the detailed information about each product and hyperlink those slides to the For More Information buttons. Don't forget to put a Return button on each hidden slide so that users can easily return to the main presentation.

- **Access to custom shows.** If you have created custom shows, set up action buttons or hyperlinks that jump the users to them on request.

- **Quizzes.** Create a presentation with a series of multiple-choice questions. Create custom action buttons for each answer. Depending on which answer the user clicks, set it up to jump to either a "Congratulations, you're right!" slide or a "Sorry, try again" slide. From each, include a Return button to go on with the quiz.

- **Troubleshooting information.** Ask the user a series of questions and include action buttons or hyperlinks for the answers. Set them up to jump to the slides that further narrow down the problem based on their answers until they finally arrive at a slide that explains the exact problem and proposes a solution.

- **Directories.** Include a company directory with e-mail hyperlinks for various people or departments so that anyone reading the presentation can easily make contact.

Besides navigational controls, the other big consideration with a user-interactive show is distribution. How will you distribute the presentation to your audience? Some of the methods you've already learned about in this book will serve you well here, such as packaging a presentation on CD (Chapter 18, "Preparing for a Live Presentation"). Or you may choose instead to set up a user kiosk in a public location, e-mail the presentation file to others, or make it available on the Web.

Navigational Control Basics

All navigational controls that you create on slides are, at their core, hyperlinks. You're probably familiar with these already from using the Web; they're underlined bits of text or specially enabled graphics that take you to a different site or page. In the case of your PowerPoint presentation, the hyperlinks take users to the next or previous slide, a hidden slide, a custom slide show, or perhaps some external source such as a website or data file.

Types of Navigational Controls

Even though they are all hyperlinks (so they all work the same underneath), the various types of navigational controls can look very different on the surface. You can have "bare" hyperlinks that show the actual address, hyperlinks with text that is different from the address, action button graphics, or graphics you create or import yourself. In addition, a navigational control can have pop-up helper text in a ScreenTip. Figure 19.1 shows several types of navigational controls on a sample slide.

19

FIGURE 19.1

A sampler of the various navigational control types available in PowerPoint

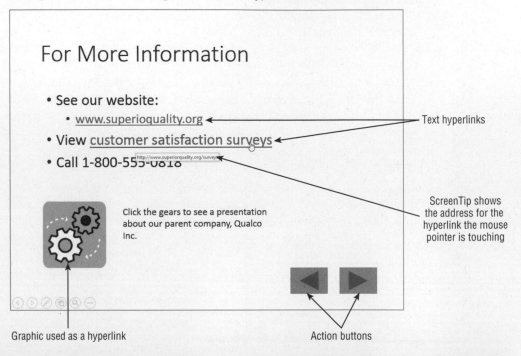

Text hyperlinks

ScreenTip shows
the address for the
hyperlink the mouse
pointer is touching

Graphic used as a hyperlink

Action buttons

> **NOTE**
>
> Most people associate the word *hyperlink* with the Internet. However, a hyperlink is simply a link to somewhere else;
> it does not necessarily refer to an Internet location. You can hyperlink to another slide in the same presentation, for
> example, or to a different presentation, or even to some unrelated data file in another application like Word or Excel.

Notice the directions at the bottom of Figure 19.1. This is necessary because it's not obvious
that the graphic is a hyperlink, and users would not normally think to try clicking on it.
Notice also the ScreenTip associated with the second text hyperlink. This is useful because
the text itself does not provide the address, and the user may want to know the address
before clicking the hyperlink. For example, if the PC does not have Internet access, the
user would not want to click a hyperlink that points to a web page.

The action buttons in the bottom-right corner in Figure 19.1 are typical of the action buttons that PowerPoint creates. They are just AutoShapes with preassigned action settings for
On Click. You can create your own, but the preset ones are awfully handy.

Evaluating Your Audience's Needs

Before you dive into building an interactive presentation, you must decide how the audience will navigate from slide to slide. There is no one best way; the right decision depends
on the audience's comfort level with computers and hyperlinks.

Consider these points:

- Is the audience technically savvy enough to know that they should press a key or click the mouse to advance the slide, or do you need to provide that instruction?
- Does your audience understand that the arrow action buttons mean Forward and Back, or do you need to explain that?
- Does your audience understand hyperlinks and web addresses? If they see underlined text, will they know that they can click it to jump elsewhere?
- Is it enough to include some instructions on a slide at the beginning of the show, or do you need to repeat the instructions on every slide?

Think about your audience's needs and come up with a plan. Here are some sample plans:

- **For a beginner audience.** Begin the presentation with an instructional slide explaining how to navigate. Place action buttons in the same place on each slide (using the slide master) to help them move backward and forward and include a Help button that they can click to get more detailed instructions.
- **For an intermediate audience.** Place action buttons on the same place on each slide along with a brief note on the first slide explaining their presence.
- **For an advanced audience.** Include other action buttons on the slide that allow the user to jump around freely in the presentation — go to the beginning, to the end, to a certain section, and so on. Advanced users understand and can take advantage of a more sophisticated navigation system.

In the next few sections, I show you how to create all of the types of navigational controls shown in Figure 19.1.

Creating Text Hyperlinks

Now that you know that hyperlinks are the key to user interactivity, you will want to add some to your presentation. You can start with text-based hyperlinks because they're the easiest. You can add either a bare hyperlink or a hyperlink with explanatory text.

Typing a Bare Hyperlink

The most basic kind of hyperlink is an Internet address, typed directly into a text box. When you enter text in any of the following formats, PowerPoint automatically converts it to a hyperlink:

- **Web addresses.** Anything that begins with http:// or www.
- **E-mail addresses.** Any string of characters with no spaces and an @ (ampersand) sign in the middle somewhere.
- **FTP addresses.** Anything that begins with ftp://.

You do not have to do anything special to create these hyperlinks; when you type them and press Enter or the spacebar, PowerPoint converts them to hyperlinks. You know the conversion has taken place because the text becomes underlined and a different color. (The exact color depends on the color scheme in use.)

Figure 19.2 shows some examples of these bare hyperlinks. I call them bare because you see what's underneath them — the actual address — right there on the surface. There is no friendly "click here" text that the link hides behind. For example, the text support@ microsoft.com is a hyperlink that sends e-mail to that address. In contrast, a link that reads "Click here to send e-mail to me" and contains the same hyperlink address is *not* bare, because you do not see the address directly.

FIGURE 19.2

Some examples of bare Internet hyperlinks.

- http://www.Microsoft.com/powerpoint
- http://www.wiley.com
- support@Microsoft.com
- ftp://ftp.wiley.com

> **NOTE**
>
> If PowerPoint does not automatically create hyperlinks, the feature may be disabled. Choose File ⇨ Options. Click Proofing, and then click AutoCorrect Options. Click the AutoFormat As You Type tab, and make sure the Internet and Network Paths with Hyperlinks check box is marked.

> **NOTE**
>
> FTP stands for File Transfer Protocol. It's a method of transferring files via the Internet. FTP used to be a totally separate system from the Web, but nowadays, web browsers have FTP download capabilities built in, so anyone who has a web browser can receive files via FTP.

Creating a Friendly Text Hyperlink

A *friendly* hyperlink is a hyperlink comprising text but not just the bare address. For example, in Figure 19.1, "Customer Satisfaction Surveys" is a text hyperlink. (*Friendly* is not an industry-standard technical term; it's just one I find convenient for discussion in this book.)

You can select already-entered text and make it a hyperlink, or you can enter new text.

NOTE

The steps for creating a hyperlink take you through the process generically; see the sections in "Choosing the Hyperlink Address" later in the chapter for specific information about various kinds of hyperlinks you can create.

Either way, follow these steps:

1. **To use existing text, select the text or its text box.** Otherwise, just position the insertion point where you want the hyperlink.

2. **On the Insert tab, click Hyperlink, or press Ctrl+K.** The Insert Hyperlink dialog box opens (Figure 19.3).

FIGURE 19.3

Insert a hyperlink by typing the text to display and choosing the URL or other location to jump to.

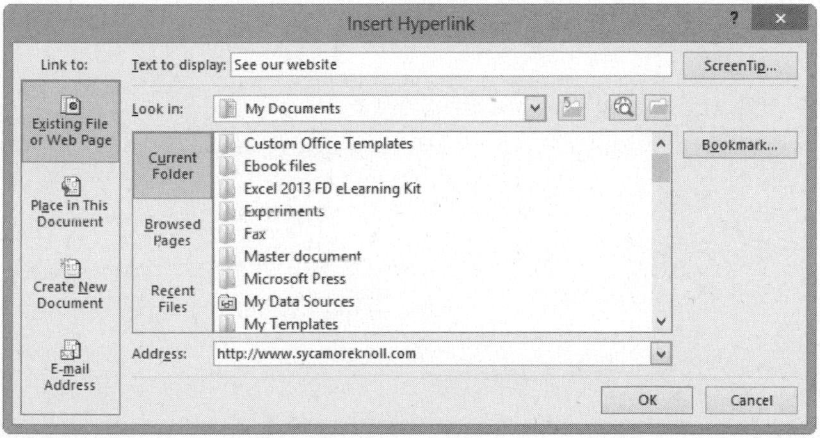

NOTE

If the Hyperlink button is not available on the Insert tab, check to make sure you have positioned the insertion point in a text box or selected some text.

3. **In the Text to Display field, type or edit the hyperlink text.** This text is what appears underlined on the slide. Any text you've selected appears in this field by default; changing the text here changes it on your slide as well.

4. **Enter the hyperlink or select it from one of the available lists.** (See the following section, "Choosing the Hyperlink Address," to learn about your options in this regard.)

19

5. **(Optional) If you want the ScreenTip to show something different when the user points the mouse at the hyperlink, click the ScreenTip button and enter the text for the ScreenTip.** The ScreenTip is text that pops up when you hover the mouse over the hyperlink. See Figure 19.4. The default ScreenTip for a hyperlink is its address (URL) or the file path if it is a file stored on a local disk.

FIGURE 19.4

Enter a custom ScreenTip if desired.

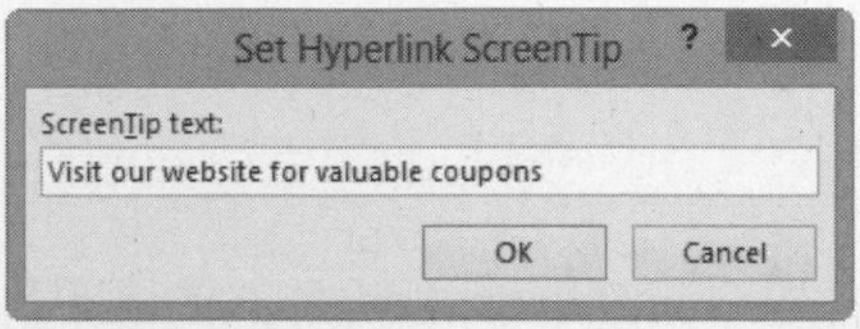

6. **Click OK to close the Set Hyperlink ScreenTip dialog box.**
7. **Click OK to accept the newly created hyperlink.**

> **TIP**
>
> Ideally the combination of the hyperlink text and the ScreenTip should provide both the actual address and some friendly explanation of it. If the bare address appears as the hyperlink text, use friendly text describing the link location as the ScreenTip. If the friendly text appears as the hyperlink text, use the actual address as the ScreenTip.

The options in step 4 for selecting the address were purposely glossed over because this is a rather complex topic. The various options are shown in the next sections.

Choosing the Hyperlink Address

You can use the Insert Hyperlink dialog box to create a hyperlink to any address that's accessible via the computer where the presentation will run. Although many people think of a hyperlink as an Internet address, it can actually be a link to any file, application, Internet location, or slide.

> **CAUTION**
>
> A hyperlink will not work if the person viewing the presentation does not have access to the needed files and programs or does not have the needed Internet or network connectivity. A hyperlink that works fine on your own PC might not work after the presentation has been transferred to the user's PC.

You can hyperlink to any of the following items:

- Other slides in the current presentation
- Slides in other presentations (if you provide access to those presentations)

- Documents created in other applications (if the user has those applications installed and those document files are available)

- Graphic files (if the user has access to an application that can display them)

- Internet web pages (if the user has an Internet connection and a web browser)

- E-mail addresses (if the user has an Internet connection and an e-mail program)

- FTP site addresses (if the user has an Internet connection and a web browser or an FTP program)

Creating a Link to a Slide in the Current Presentation

The most common kind of link is to another slide in the same presentation. There are many uses for this link type; for example, you can hide several backup slides that contain extra information. You can then create hyperlinks on certain key slides that allow the users to jump to one of those hidden slides to peruse the extra facts. To create a hyperlink to another slide, follow these steps:

1. **Start the hyperlink normally (on the Insert tab, click Hyperlink).**

2. **In the Insert Hyperlink dialog box, click Place in This Document.** The dialog box controls change to show a list of the slides in the presentation (see Figure 19.5).

FIGURE 19.5

Select the slide that the hyperlink should refer to.

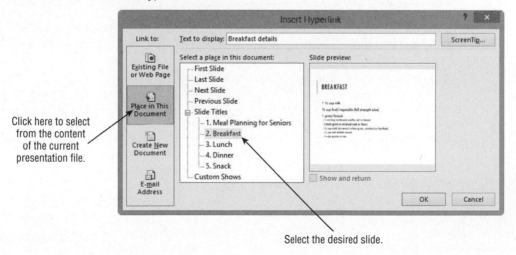

Click here to select from the content of the current presentation file.

Select the desired slide.

3. **Select the slide or custom show that you want.**

4. **Click OK.**

TIP

If you are choosing a custom show and you want the presentation to continue from the original spot after showing this custom show, mark the Show and Return check box (see Figure 19.5). This check box is not available for individual slides. For an individual slide, put a Return action button on it to return to the previously viewed slide. Hyperlinking to custom shows and using the Show and Return feature instead of linking to individual slides helps to avoid jumping to the next slide after the hyperlinked slide. See the section "Creating Your Own Action Buttons" later in this chapter.

Creating a Link to a Website or FTP Site

If you want to link to a website or FTP site, you can simply type the address directly into any text box. Alternatively, you can use the Insert Hyperlink command to create the link.

When the Insert Hyperlink dialog box is open, if you don't know the address you want to refer to, you can browse for it. Here's how:

1. **Leaving the Insert Hyperlink dialog box open, switch out of PowerPoint and back to Windows.**
2. **Open a web browser and navigate to the page to which you want to refer.**
3. **Switch back to PowerPoint.** The address is filled in for you in the Address box.
4. **Continue creating the hyperlink normally.**

TIP

You can also copy and paste a URL into the Address box, or choose a page from the Browsed Pages list.

Creating a Link to a File on Your Hard Disk or Network

You can also create a hyperlink to any file available on your PC's hard disk or on your local area network. This can be a PowerPoint file or a data file from any other program, such as a Word document or an Excel spreadsheet. Or, if you don't want to open a particular data file, you can hyperlink to the program file itself so that the other application simply opens.

For example, perhaps you have some detailed documentation for your product in Adobe Acrobat format (PDF). This type of document requires the Adobe Acrobat Reader. So you can create a hyperlink with the text "Click here to read the documentation" and link to the appropriate PDF file. When your audience member clicks that link, Adobe Acrobat Reader opens and the documentation displays.

CAUTION

Remember that not everyone has the same applications installed that you do. For example, although Adobe Acrobat Reader is free, many people don't have it installed yet. You might want to add another hyperlink or button to your slide that users can click to download a free viewer for the application's data from the Web if needed.

To link to a data file, start the hyperlink normally (on the Insert tab, click Hyperlink) and click Existing File or Web Page if that is not already selected. Then do one of the following:

- Click Current Folder to display a file management interface from which you can select any folder or drive on your system. You can open the Look In list and choose Computer to start from the top level of your drive/folder structure and then navigate to the location containing the file and select it. See Figure 19.6.

FIGURE 19.6

You can browse files on your hard disk by choosing Current Folder and then setting Look In to Computer.

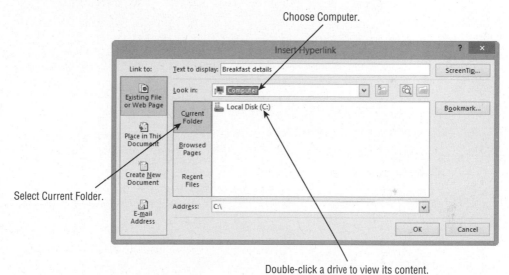

- Click Recent Files to display a list of the files you have recently opened on your PC (all types), and click the file you want from the list.

Complete the hyperlink normally from that point. You are not limited to only a folder on your local drives if you choose Current Folder; you can open the Look In list and choose My Network Places to browse the network. However, make sure the PC on which the presentation will be displayed will also have access to this same location.

Creating a Link to an Application for Creating a New Document

Perhaps you want the audience to be able to create a new document by clicking a hyperlink. For example, perhaps you would like them to be able to provide information about their experience with your Customer Service department. One way to do this is to let them create a new document using a program that they have on their system, such as a word processor.

To create a link that creates a new document in an application, start the hyperlink normally. Click the Create New Document button, and the controls in the Insert Hyperlink dialog box change to those shown in Figure 19.7.

FIGURE 19.7

You can create a new document with a hyperlink.

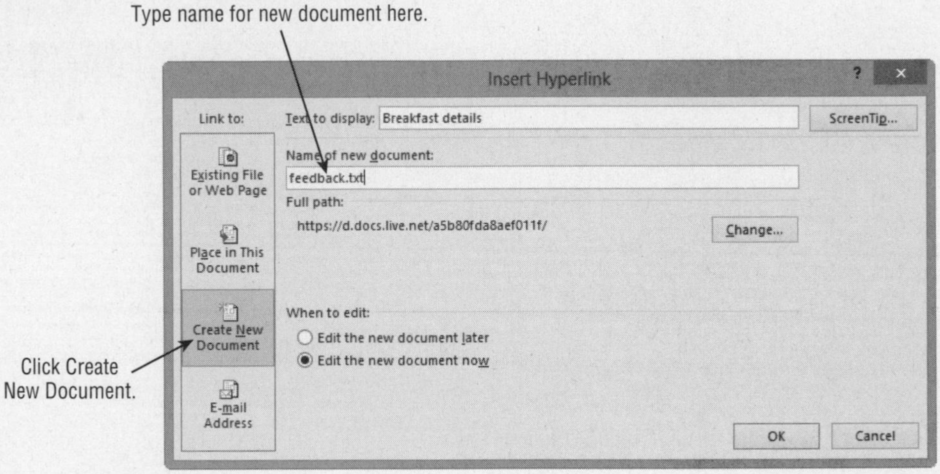

Type name for new document here.

Click Create New Document.

Enter the name of the new document that you want the user to create. The type of document created depends on the filename extension you include. For example, to create a Word document, use the .doc or .docx extension. See Table 19.1 for other filename extensions. If the path where it should be stored is not correct in the Full Path area, click the Change button. Navigate to the desired location, and click OK to return. Then click Edit the New Document Later and finish up normally.

The most important part about adding a link to create a new file is to make sure you use a filename extension that corresponds to a program that users have on the PCs where they will be viewing the presentation. When a program is installed, it registers its extension (the usually-three-character code after the period in a file's name) in the Windows Registry so that any data files with a name that includes the extension are associated with that program. For example, when you install Microsoft Word, it registers the extension `.docx` for itself, and PowerPoint registers `.pptx` for its own use. Table 19.1 lists some of the more common file types and their registered filename extensions on most PCs. Also make sure that the location you specify for the full path will always be accessible whenever the presentation is run.

TIP

If you need to hyperlink to an executable file but you do *not* need a new document (for example, to link to a program like Calculator), do not use Hyperlink on the Insert tab. Instead, click Action on the Insert tab and choose Run Program as the action. For the program to run, use the full path to the application, in quotation marks. Because you must enter the full path to each of these, the link will probably not work when the presentation is run on a different computer.

TABLE 19.1 Commonly Used Extensions for Popular Programs

Filename Extension	Associated Program
`.docx`, `.docm`, `.doc`	Microsoft Word, or WordPad if Word is not installed. Use for documents if you are not sure whether your audience has Word but you are sure they at least have Windows 95. The Word 2007 format is `.docx`, and `.docm` is the macro-enabled version of that. The format for Word 2003 and earlier is `.doc`.
`.txt`	Notepad, a plain text editor. Creates text files without any formatting. Not the first choice for documents unless you specifically need them to be without formatting.
`.rtf`	Rich Text format, a flexible, application-independent word processing format. It works in WordPad (the free word processor in Windows) and also in most other word processing programs, including Word and WordPerfect. This is a good choice if you don't know which word processing program is installed on the PC.
`.bmp`	Microsoft Paint (which comes free with Windows) or some other more sophisticated graphics program if one is installed.
`.mdb`	Microsoft Access, a database program.
`.mpp`	Microsoft Project, a project management program.
`.pptx` or `.ppt`	Microsoft PowerPoint (you know what that is!). The 2007 version is `.pptx`; the version for 2003 and earlier is `.ppt`.
`.xlsx`, `.xlsm`, `.xls`	Microsoft Excel, a spreadsheet program. The extensions `.xlsx` and `.xlsm` are the 2007 versions (non–macro enabled and macro enabled, respectively) and `.xls` is the 2003 and earlier version.

19

Creating a Link to an E-Mail Address

You can also create a link that opens the user's e-mail program and addresses an e-mail to a certain recipient. For example, perhaps you want users to e-mail feedback to you about how they liked your presentation or send you requests for more information about your product.

> **CAUTION**
>
> For an e-mail hyperlink to work, the person viewing the presentation must have an e-mail application installed on their PC and at least one e-mail account configured for sending e-mail. This isn't always a given, but it's probably more likely than betting that they have a certain application installed.

To create an e-mail hyperlink, either type the e-mail address directly into the text box on the slide (for a bare hyperlink) or start a hyperlink normally with the Hyperlink button on the Insert tab. Then click the E-mail Address button in the dialog box and fill in the e-mail address and an optional subject line. PowerPoint will automatically add `mailto:` in front of the address. Then complete the hyperlink normally. See Figure 19.8.

FIGURE 19.8

You can use a hyperlink to send e-mail.

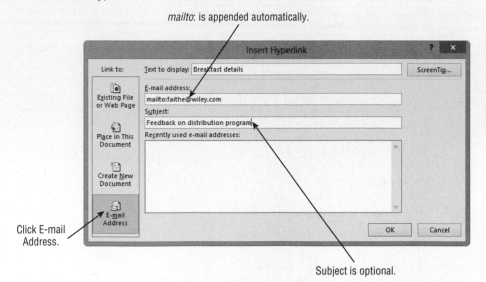

mailto: is appended automatically.

Click E-mail Address.

Subject is optional.

Editing or Removing a Hyperlink

If you need to change the displayed text for the hyperlink, simply edit it just as you do any text on a slide. Move the insertion point into it and press Backspace or Delete to remove characters, and then retype new ones.

If you need to change the address, or the ScreenTip, right-click the hyperlink and choose Edit Hyperlink. The Edit Hyperlink dialog box appears, which is identical to the Add Hyperlink dialog box except for the name. From there you can change any properties of the link, just as you did when you created it initially.

To remove a hyperlink, you can either delete the text completely (select it and press Delete) or just remove the hyperlink from the text, leaving the text intact. To do the latter, right-click the hyperlink and choose Remove Hyperlink.

Creating Graphical Hyperlinks

There are two ways to create a graphics-based hyperlink. Both involve skills that you have already learned in this chapter. Both work equally well, but you may find that you prefer one to the other. The Action Settings method is a little bit simpler, but the Insert Hyperlink method allows you to browse for web addresses more easily.

Creating a Graphical Hyperlink with Action Settings

A graphics-based hyperlink is really no more than a graphic with an action setting attached to it. You set it up just as you do with the action buttons (which you will learn more about later in this chapter), by following these steps:

1. **Place the graphic that you want to use for a hyperlink.**

2. **Click the graphic, and then on the Insert tab, click Action.** The Action Settings dialog box opens.

3. **Choose Hyperlink To.**

4. **Open the Hyperlink To drop-down list and choose URL.** The Hyperlink to URL dialog box opens.

5. **Type the URL to link to and click OK as shown in Figure 19.9.**

19

FIGURE 19.9

You can create a hyperlink via an action setting.

CAUTION

If you are using an e-mail address, type `mailto:` in front of the address you enter when creating the hyperlink. If you do not, PowerPoint will automatically add `http://` in front of it and the link will not work.

6. **Click OK in the Action Settings dialog box.**

Now the graphic functions just like an action button in the presentation; the audience can click it to jump to the specified location.

Creating a Graphical Hyperlink with Insert Hyperlink

If you would like to take advantage of the superior address-browsing capabilities of the Insert Hyperlink dialog box when setting up a graphical hyperlink, follow these steps instead of the preceding ones:

1. **Place the graphic that you want to use for a hyperlink.**

2. **Right-click it and choose Hyperlink, or choose Insert ➪ Links ➪ Hyperlink from the Ribbon.** The Insert Hyperlink dialog box appears.

3. **Choose the location, as you learned earlier in this chapter for text-based hyperlinks.** The only difference is that the Text to Display box is unavailable because there is no text. If you typed the text in a graphic, Text to Display is available.

4. **Click OK.**

Using Action Buttons

Action buttons, which you saw in Figure 19.1, enable your audience members to move from slide to slide in the presentation with a minimum of fuss. PowerPoint provides many preset action buttons that already have hyperlinks assigned to them, so all you have to do is place them on your slides.

The action buttons that come with PowerPoint are shown in Table 19.2 along with their preset hyperlinks. As you can see, some of them are all ready to go; others require you to specify the jump destination. Most of the buttons have a default action assigned to them, but you can change any of these as needed.

> **TIP**
>
> At first glance, there seems little reason to use action buttons that simply move the slide show forward and backward. After all, isn't it just as easy to use the keyboard's Page Up and Page Down keys or to click the left mouse button to advance to the next slide? Well, yes, but if you use Kiosk mode, described later in the chapter, you cannot move from slide to slide using any of the conventional keyboard or mouse methods. The only thing the mouse can do is click action buttons and hyperlinks.

TABLE 19.2 Action Buttons

Button	Name	Hyperlinks To
◀	Back or Previous	Previous slide in the presentation (not necessarily the last slide viewed; compare to Return).
▶	Forward or Next	Next slide in the presentation.
◀‖	Beginning	First slide in the presentation.
‖▶	End	Last slide in the presentation.
🏠	Home	First slide in the presentation. (Home is where you get started and it's a picture of a house; get it?)
ⓘ	Information	Nothing, by default, but you can point it to a slide or document containing information.

Continues

TABLE 19.2 *(continued)*

Button	Name	Hyperlinks To
	Return	Last slide viewed, regardless of normal order. This is useful to place on a hidden slide that the audience will jump to with another link (such as Help) to help them return to the main presentation when they are finished.
	Movie	Nothing, by default, but you can set it to play a movie that you specify.
	Document	Nothing, by default, but you can set it to open a file that you specify.
	Sound	Plays a sound that you specify. If you don't choose a sound, it plays the first sound on PowerPoint's list of standard sounds (Applause).
	Help	Nothing, by default, but you can point it toward a slide containing help or a help file from an application (usually has a `.hlp` filename extension but could also have a `.chm` or `.html` extension).
	None	Nothing, by default. You can add text or fills to the button to create custom buttons.

Placing an Action Button on a Slide

To place an action button, follow these steps:

1. **If you want to place the button on the slide master, display it (on the View tab, click Slide Master).** If you want to place the button on all layouts, click the top slide (the slide master itself). If you want only a certain layout to receive the buttons, click it.

> **TIP**
> Some action buttons are best placed on the slide master, such as Next and Previous; others, such as Return, are special-use buttons that are best placed on individual slides such as hidden slides.

2. **On the Insert or Home tab, click Shapes.** A palette of shapes appears; at the bottom of the palette are the action buttons, as shown in Figure 19.10.

FIGURE 19.10

Action buttons are shapes, inserted from the Shapes palette.

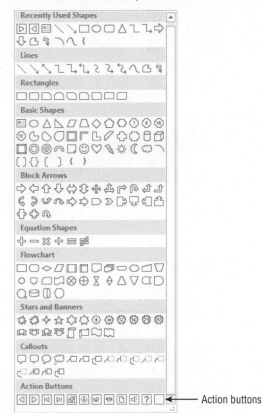

Action buttons

3. **Click the button that you want to place.** Your mouse pointer turns into a crosshair.

4. **To create a button of a specific size, drag on the slide (or slide master) where you want it to go.** Or, to create a button of a default size, simply click once where you want to place it. You can resize the button at any time later, the same as you can any object.

TIP

If you want to place several buttons, and you want them all to be the same size, place them at the default size to begin with. Then select them all, and resize them as a group. That way they will all be exactly the same size.

5. **The Action Settings dialog box appears.** Make sure the Mouse Click tab is on top, as shown in Figure 19.11.

FIGURE 19.11

Specify what should happen when you click the action button.

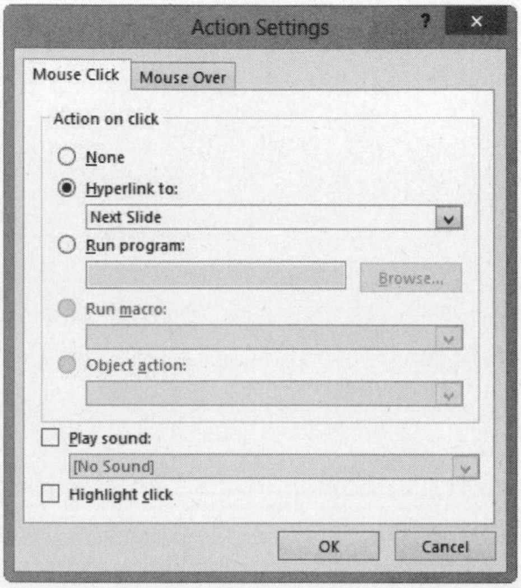

6. **Confirm or change the hyperlink set up there:**

   - If the action button should take the reader to a specific location, make sure the correct slide appears in the Hyperlink To box. Refer to Table 19.2 in the preceding section to see the default setting for each action button. Table 19.3 lists the choices you can make and what they do.

   - If the action button should run a program, choose Run Program and enter the program's name and path, or click Browse to locate it. For example, you could open the Calculator application from an action button. The executable file that runs it is `calc.exe`.

   - If the action button should play a sound, make sure the Play Sound check box is marked, and choose the correct sound from the Play Sound drop-down list (or pick a different sound file by choosing Other Sound).

7. **Click OK.** The button has been assigned the action you specified.

8. **Add more action buttons as desired by repeating these steps.**

9. **If you are working in Slide Master view, exit it by clicking the Close Master View button.**

10. **Test your action buttons in Slide Show view to make sure they jump where you want them to.**

To edit a button's action, right-click it and choose Hyperlink to reopen this dialog box at any time.

TABLE 19.3   Hyperlink to Choices in the Action Settings Dialog Box

Drop-Down Menu Choice	Result
Previous Slide Next Slide First Slide Last Slide Last Slide Viewed	These choices do just what their names say. These are the default actions assigned to certain buttons you learned about in Table 19.2.
End Show	Sets the button to stop the show or custom show when clicked.
Custom Show …	Opens a Link to Custom Show dialog box, where you can choose a custom show to jump to when the button is clicked.
Slide …	Opens a Hyperlink to Slide dialog box, where you can choose any slide in the current presentation to jump to when the button is clicked.
URL …	Opens a Hyperlink to URL dialog box, where you can enter a web address to jump to when the button is clicked.
Other PowerPoint Presentation …	Opens a Hyperlink to Other PowerPoint Presentation dialog box, where you can choose another PowerPoint presentation to display when the button is clicked.
Other File …	Opens a Hyperlink to Other File dialog box, where you can choose any file to open when the button is clicked. If the file requires a certain application, that application will open when needed. (To run another application without opening a specific file in it, use the Run Program option in the Action Settings dialog box instead of Hyperlink To.)

Adding Text to a Blank Action Button

The blank action button you saw in Table 19.2 can be very useful. You can place several of them on a slide and type text into them, creating your own set of buttons. To type text into a blank button, follow these steps:

1. **Place a blank action button on the slide (from the Shapes gallery).**
2. **Right-click the action button and choose Edit Text.** An insertion point appears in it. (You can also select the button and simply start typing.)

19

3. **Type your text, and then click away from the button when you are finished.** If you need to edit the text later, simply click the text to move the insertion point back into it, just as you do with any text box.

Formatting and Changing the Shape of an Action Button

You can format action buttons just as you can other shapes, as you learned to do in Chapter 9, "Drawing and Formatting Objects." You can apply borders, fills, and effects to them and apply Shape Style presets. You can also use WordArt styles or individual text formatting controls to format the text on them.

To make action buttons of different shapes, you can use the Change Shape button, as in the following steps:

1. **Select the action button(s) to change.**
2. **On the Drawing Tools Format tab, click Insert Shapes ⇨ Edit Shape ⇨ Change Shape.**
3. **Click a different shape.**

Figure 19.12 shows some examples of custom buttons you can create with your own text and some shape formatting.

FIGURE 19.12

You can create any of these sets of action buttons by typing and formatting text on blank buttons.

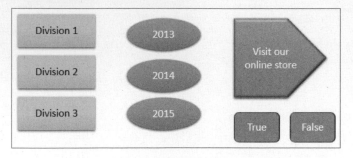

Creating Your Own Action Buttons

You can create an action button out of any object on your slide: a drawn shape, a piece of clip art, a photograph, a text box — anything. To do so, from the Insert tab just click Action. Then, set the On Click action to Hyperlink To, Run Program, or Play Sound, just as you did for the action buttons in the preceding sections.

Make sure you clearly label the object that you are using as an action button so that the users will know what they are getting when they click it. You can add text to the object directly (for example, with an AutoShape), or you can add a text box next to the button that explains its function. If you want to use a ScreenTip to label the item, use a hyperlink rather than an action setting.

Creating Self-Running Presentations

Self-running presentations are not exactly user interactive because the user does not participate in their running. The show runs at its own pace and the user sits (or stands) passively and observes it.

Not sure when you might use a self-running presentation in your daily life? Here are some ideas:

- **Trade shows.** A self-running presentation outlining your product or service can run continuously in your booth on equipment as simple as a laptop and an external monitor. People who might not feel comfortable talking to a salesperson may stop a few moments to watch a colorful, multimedia slide show.

- **Conventions.** Trying to provide hundreds of convention-goers with some basic information, such as session starting times or cocktail party locations? Set up an information booth in the convention center lobby to provide this information. The slide show can loop endlessly through three or four slides that contain meeting room locations, schedules, and other critical data.

- **In-store sales.** Retail stores can increase sales by strategically placing PC monitors in areas of the store where customers gather. For example, if there is a line where customers stand waiting for the next available register or clerk, you can show those waiting customers a few slides that describe the benefits of extended warranties or that detail the special sales of the week.

- **Waiting areas.** Auto repair shops and other places where customers wait for something to be done provide excellent sales opportunities. The customers don't have anything to do except sit and wait, so they will watch just about anything — including a slide presentation informing them of the other services that your shop provides.

The most important aspect of a self-running show is that it loops continuously until you stop it. This is important because there won't be anyone there to restart it each time it ends.

To set up the show to do just that, follow these steps:

1. **On the Slide Show tab, click Set Up Slide Show.** The Set Up Show dialog box opens.

2. **Mark the Loop Continuously until 'Esc' check box.** See Figure 19.13. Notice that the Loop Continuously until 'Esc' check box is set permanently to On whenever Browsed at a Kiosk is selected.

19

FIGURE 19.13

Tell PowerPoint that this show should loop continuously.

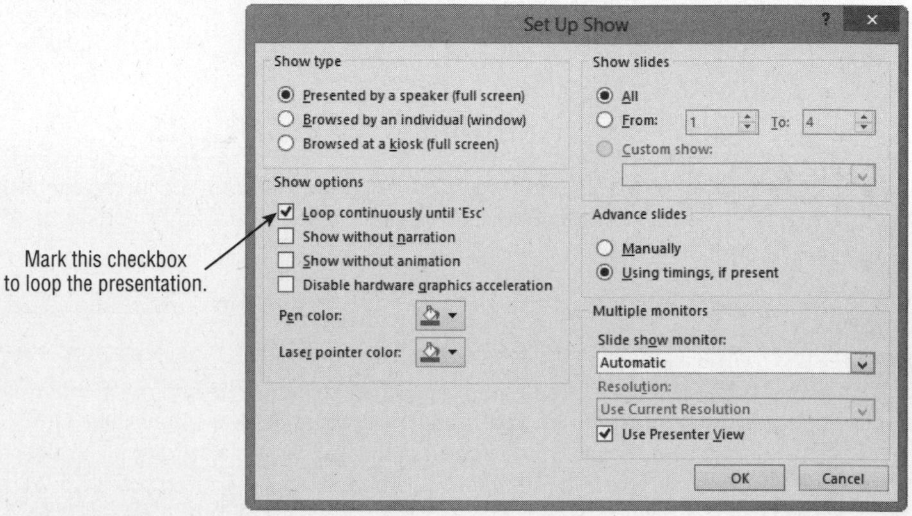

Mark this checkbox to loop the presentation.

3. **In the Advance Slides area, make sure the Using Timings, if Present option is selected.**

4. **Click OK.**

Timings refers to transition timings, which you learned about in Chapter 16, "Creating Animation Effects and Transitions," in the section "Assigning Transitions to Slides." Self-running presentations are good candidates for recorded voice-over narration, which you learned how to set up in Chapter 14, "Adding Sound Effects, Music, and Soundtracks."

Recording Narration and Timings

When creating a self-running presentation, you may want to record some voice-over narration to accompany all or some of the slides. That way, when people watch the presentation, they will hear your voice as if they were watching and listening to you in person.

To record narration, you will need a microphone that attaches to your computer, and your computer must have a microphone jack to plug it into.

In PowerPoint 2013 you can record not only narration but also animation and transition timings and laser pointer movements. Together all these recorded extras make the presentation file you distribute imitate more closely a live show.

The Laser Pointer option appears as a colored dot on-screen like a real laser pointer. To use it during Slide Show view, hold down the Ctrl key and click the mouse. To switch the mouse to a laser pointer without having to hold down Ctrl, click the Pointers button in the lower-left corner of the screen in Slide Show view and click Laser Pointer. To change the laser pointer's color, choose Slide Show ⇨ Set Up ⇨ Set Up Show and select a color from the Laser Pointer Color drop-down palette (see Figure 19.13). You cannot change the laser pointer color from the Pointers menu in Slide Show view.

Setting Up the Microphone

The first time you record narration, you will probably need to configure your microphone to make sure the volume level is set appropriately.

First, make sure the microphone is enabled. Here's how:

1. **Open the Control Panel in Windows.** In Windows 8, choose the Settings charm and then click Control Panel; in Windows 7, choose Control Panel from the Start menu.
2. **Click Hardware and Sound.**
3. **Under the Sound heading, click Manage Audio Devices.** The Sound dialog box opens.
4. **Click the Recording tab.** A list of available microphones appears here. (You might have only one.) See Figure 19.14.

FIGURE 19.14

Select the microphone you want to use, and make it the default device.

19

5. **If you have more than one microphone listed, make sure the one you want to use is set as the default device.** (Right-click it and choose Set as Default Device, or click it and then click Set Default. If it is already the default, the command is unavailable.)

6. **Select the microphone and then click Configure.** The Speech Recognition section of Control Panel opens.

7. **Click Set Up Microphone.** The Microphone Setup Wizard runs (Figure 19.15).

FIGURE 19.15

Work through the wizard to set up your microphone.

8. **Follow the prompts to complete your microphone setup.** The exact steps depend on the microphone type you chose (in the Sound dialog box, shown in Figure 19.15).

Recording the Presentation

When you record the presentation, you are recording several things at once: narration, transition and animation timing, and laser pointer movements.

You can do all your recording in a single pass, but if you flub the narration for a slide, keep going and don't start over because you can go back and rerecord the narration for a particular slide later.

Follow these steps to record the presentation:

1. **Plug the microphone into your Mic port on your computer, and test it to make sure it is working.**

2. **Choose Slide Show ⇨ Set Up ⇨ Record Slide Show.** (Click the top part of the button, not the arrow beneath it.) The Record Slide Show dialog box appears. It contains two check boxes:

   - Slide and Animation Timings
   - Narrations and Laser Pointer

3. **Leave both check marks selected (to record all of those things) and click Start Recording to begin the recording.**

   The presentation opens in Slide Show view, with a Recording floating toolbar in the upper-left corner, as shown in Figure 19.16.

FIGURE 19.16

Record both narration and timings in a single pass.

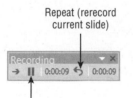

Repeat (rerecord
current slide)

Pause Recording

4. **Speak into the microphone to narrate the first slide.** When you are ready to move to the next slide, click the mouse.

   If you make a mistake on a slide, you can click the Repeat button (see Figure 19.16) to start that slide over. Alternatively, you can just go on to the next slide; you can rerecord the narration for individual slides later.

5. **Move slide by slide through the presentation until you have recorded all the narration.**

When you reach the last slide, the presentation switches to Slide Sorter view. Under each slide is information about what was recorded, as shown in Figure 19.17.

- **Star** indicates that there is a transition or animation effect.
- **Time** shows the total amount of time that slide will remain on-screen.
- **Speaker** indicates that there is recorded narration for that slide.

FIGURE 19.17

Recorded data appears below each slide.

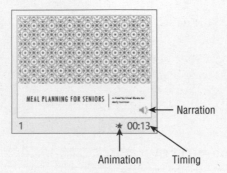

Rerecording Narration for Certain Slides

It's very hard to get all the narration recorded correctly in a single try! Most people have to go back and rerecord the narration for at least one slide. To rerecord narration for only part of the presentation, follow these steps:

1. **In Normal view, select the slide you want to rerecord.**
2. **Choose Slide Show ⇨ Record Slide Show ⇨ Start Recording from Current Slide.**
3. **Click Start Recording.**
4. **Record the narration for that slide.**
5. **Continue on to other slides by clicking through the presentation normally, or press Esc if you don't want to record narration for the next slides.**

Removing Narration

You can remove the narration either from individual slides or from the entire presentation:

- To remove narration from a single slide, select it and then choose Slide Show ⇨ Set Up ⇨ Record Slide Show ⇨ Clear ⇨ Clear Narration on Current Slide.
- To remove narration from all slides, choose Slide Show ⇨ Set Up ⇨ Record Slide Show ⇨ Clear ⇨ Clear Narrations on All Slides.

You can also delete the speaker icon from the lower-right corner of a slide to remove its narration.

Using Kiosk Mode

A kiosk is a self-serve booth or workstation where people can view something without supervision. You have probably seen information kiosks at malls, for example, where users can click or touch buttons on-screen to get information.

When providing a computer to operate unattended to the public, one major concern is that some prankster will come along and tamper with the system. You will learn about some ways to thwart that kind of tampering in the next section, "Setting Up a Secure System," but first let's look at one really basic thing you can do: Enable Kiosk mode.

When Kiosk mode is enabled, keyboard navigation is not possible (except for pressing Esc to exit Slide Show view), so users must employ the action buttons and hyperlinks on the slides for navigation. If you place a presentation in Kiosk mode and then hide the keyboard, users will only be able to view the content to which you have linked.

To enable Kiosk mode, follow these steps:

1. **On the Slide Show tab, click Set Up Slide Show.** The Set Up Show dialog box opens (see Figure 19.18).

FIGURE 19.18

Set up the slide show for Kiosk mode.

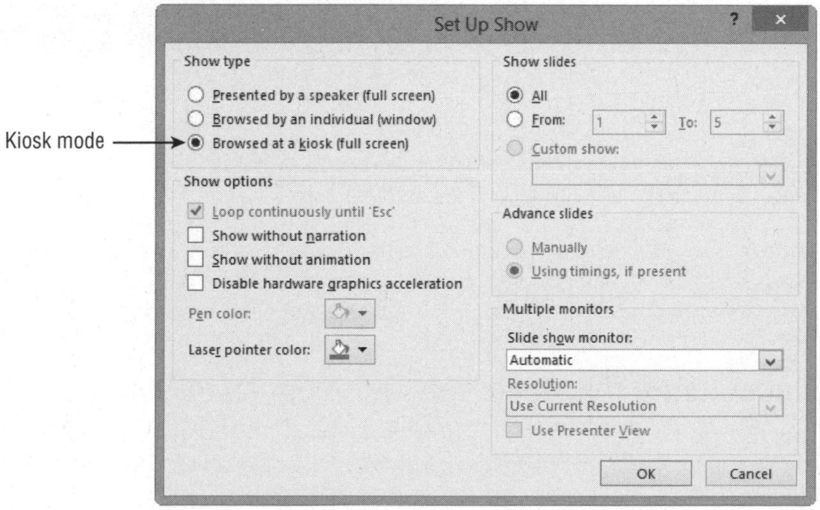

2. **In the Show Type area, click Browsed at a Kiosk (Full Screen).**

3. **Click OK.**

Setting Up a Secure System

Security is a definite concern in self-running presentations. Anytime you leave a computer unattended with the public, you run the risk of tampering and theft. At the very least, some guru geek will come along and experiment with your PC to see what you've got and whether they can do anything clever with it. At the worst, your entire computer setup could disappear entirely.

There are two levels of security involved in unattended presentation situations:

- The security of the physical hardware
- The security that the presentation will continue to run

Securing Your Hardware

For the most foolproof hardware security, get it out of sight. Hide everything except the monitor in a locked drawer, cabinet, or panel of the kiosk you are using, if possible. If you are at a trade show or convention where you don't have the luxury of a lockable system, at least put everything except the monitor under a table, and try to make sure that someone is attending the booth at all times.

> **CAUTION**
> Don't drape running computers with cloth or any other material that inhibits the airflow around them; doing so increases the risk of overheating.

In an unattended setting, the best way to protect your monitor from walking off is to place it behind a Plexiglas panel where nobody can touch it. Without such a barrier, you run the risk of some jokester turning off its power or turning down its contrast, and anyone who knows something about computers could walk right up and disconnect it and carry it away.

You can also buy various locking cables at computer stores and office supply centers. These cables lock down computer equipment to prevent it from being removed. They include steel cables with padlocks, metal locking brackets, and electronically controlled magnetic locks.

Making Sure the Presentation Continues to Run

I admit that I am guilty of disrupting other people's presentations. When I walk up to an unattended computer in a store, the first thing I do is abort whatever program is running and restart the system to check out its diagnostics and find out what kind of computer it is. It's a geek thing, but all geeks do it.

You will doubtless encounter such geeks wherever you set up your presentation, but especially at trade shows and conventions. (We geeks love trade shows and conventions.) Your mission is to prevent them from stopping your presentation.

The best way to prevent someone from tinkering with your presentation is to get the input devices out of sight. Hide the CPU (the main box of the computer), the keyboard, and the mouse. If the PC uses USB for keyboard and mouse, you can safely disconnect them while the computer is running; with older-style keyboard and mouse connectors, you can't because an error message appears when you do so that interferes with the show. If you must keep the keyboard or mouse connected, don't cover them with anything that might restrict the airflow or you might end up with an overheated PC. You can also set up the following security measures in your presentation file:

- On the Slide Show tab, click Set Up Slide Show and make sure you have chosen Browsed at a Kiosk. This disables the ability to advance the presentation on mouse click while the slide show is running. The only way to stop the show will be to use the keyboard. This works best for self-running shows where the slides advance automatically.

TIP

If you make the keyboard available for user navigation, the Esc key will also be available for stopping the program. A utility is available that disables the Esc key at www.mvps.org/skp/noesc.htm.

- Show the presentation using the PowerPoint Viewer program rather than PowerPoint itself. That way nobody can access PowerPoint and create a new presentation to show. For further security, remove the PowerPoint application completely from the PC on which the presentation is showing. The PowerPoint Viewer does not come with PowerPoint 2013, but it can be downloaded for free. Go to http://office.microsoft.com and search for PowerPoint Viewer. Set a startup password for your PC so that if people manage to reboot it, they won't get into your PC to tamper with its settings. This is usually set through the BIOS setup program. If you can't do that, set a Windows startup password for each of the user accounts. (Do that through User Accounts in Control Panel in Windows.)

- Assign a password to a PowerPoint file, as you learned in Chapter 2, "Creating and Saving Presentation Files," to prevent it from being opened, modified, or both. Although this will not prevent a running presentation from being stopped, it will at least prevent it from being altered or deleted. However, if it is already open, hackers will have full access to it, and if you set it to have a password only for modifications, a hacker could save it under a different name, make changes, and then run the changed version.

19

Summary

In this chapter, you learned the ins and outs of preparing a presentation that users can run interactively or that can run unattended without user interaction. You learned how to create action buttons and how to set up Kiosk mode and create a secure presentation system that can be left unattended. You can probably think of some uses for such shows, and even more may occur to you later. In the next chapter, you learn how to prepare a presentation — either a user-interactive one or a self-running one — for mass distribution on CD or over the Web.

Preparing a Presentation for Mass Distribution

W hen preparing a presentation that you will send out into the world, whether through e-mail, on CD, or on the Web, you never know what will happen to it or how people will end up viewing or even changing it. This can be a little unnerving!

In this chapter, you will learn how to protect your privacy by removing personal information from a PowerPoint file. You will also learn how to ensure that the presentation contains nothing that will be incompatible with an earlier version of PowerPoint. And you will learn how to distribute a presentation as a PDF file, on CD or DVD, or as a video clip on a web page or attached to an e-mail message.

Working with File Properties

The properties of a file include fixed attributes such as its creation date and size as well as properties that you can edit, such as the author name, keywords, subject, and comments. Some of these variable properties are also referred to as *metadata* — literally, data about data.

PowerPoint automatically saves some properties for you, such as the author name, and provides opportunities for you to save additional properties. Properties can be helpful when you are searching for a certain file or maintaining a presentation library, as discussed in Chapter 21, "Sharing and Collaborating." However, when you are distributing a presentation widely, you might prefer to remove some or all of its properties to preserve your privacy.

Changing a File's Properties

To add or change a file's properties, open the File menu. On the right side of the Info tab, click Properties. On the menu that appears, choose Show Document Panel.

You can then add, delete, or change the file's document properties, as shown in Figure 20.1. To close the Document Properties panel, click the X in its upper-right corner.

FIGURE 20.1

Use the Document Properties panel to assign or change document metadata.

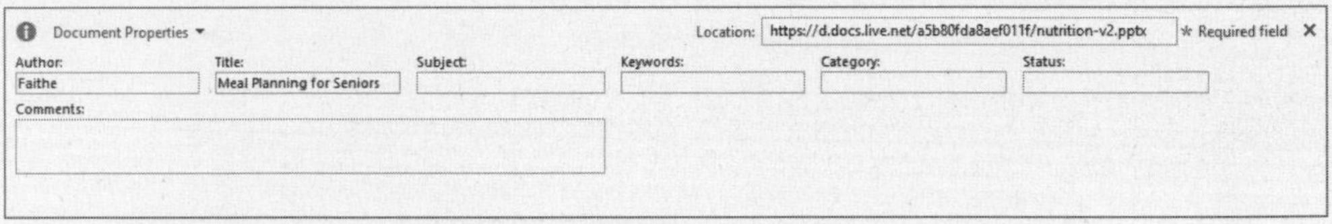

You can find the following properties in the Document Properties panel:

- **Author.** Filled in automatically from the username that you specified when you installed Office.
- **Title.** By default, the title is the first line of the document.
- **Subject, Keywords, Category, and Status.** By default, these fields are empty, but you can specify your own information and settings.

> **NOTE**
>
> The author's name is automatically added to each file that you create in PowerPoint based on the username that you specified when you installed Office. To change this name, choose File ⇨ Options, click General, and then change the entry in the User Name box.

You can also display a Properties dialog box for the file, in which you can set advanced properties. To do this, click the down arrow next to Document Properties on the Document Properties panel (Figure 20.1), and on the menu that opens, click Advanced Properties. Alternatively, you can open the File menu again and once again click Properties on the right side of the Info tab. On the menu that appears, choose Advanced Properties.

The Properties dialog box is the same dialog box that you would see if you right-clicked the file and then clicked Properties from outside of PowerPoint (that is, from File Explorer in Windows 8 or Windows Explorer in Windows 7). This dialog box contains the following tabs:

- **General.** Uneditable data about the file, such as its type, location, size, and operating system attributes — for example, read-only and hidden.

- **Summary.** A continuation of the Document Properties panel, with additional properties that you can specify or change, as shown in Figure 20.2.

FIGURE 20.2

The Summary tab of the Properties dialog box contains additional property fields.

- **Statistics.** Another page of uneditable data, this one relating to statistical analysis of the presentation, such as number of slides, number of words, number of revisions, and total editing time.

- **Contents.** Still more uneditable data. This data includes the fonts that are used, the theme, and the titles of the slides.

- **Custom.** A tab where you can set some of the less-common properties for the file.

You can define custom properties in the Custom tab. Custom properties are special-purpose fields that you can add when you need them. To set a custom property, follow these steps:

1. **In the Custom tab, click the property from the Name list that you want to use.**

2. **Open the Type drop-down list and select the type of data that it should hold.** The default is Text, which accepts any input.

3. **In the Value field, type the desired value for this property.**

4. **Click Add to add the property, type, and value to the Properties list, as shown in Figure 20.3.**

FIGURE 20.3

Set a custom property in the Custom tab.

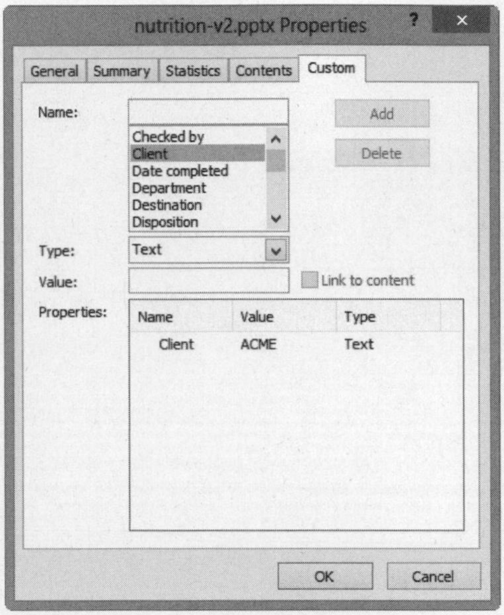

5. **Repeat steps 1 to 4 to add more custom properties, if needed; then click OK.**

Removing Personal Information from a File

Before you distribute a PowerPoint file, you might want to remove some of the properties from it that contain sensitive information. For example, if you have entered confidential information about a client in the Comments property, you may not want the client or others to see it.

If you can remember all of the properties that you set for the file, then you can go back in and remove them manually, as you learned in the preceding section. However, it is much easier to use the Document Inspector feature in PowerPoint to remove personal information from the file. Follow these steps:

1. **If you have made any changes to the presentation since it was last saved, save it again.**

2. **Choose File ⇨ Info ⇨ Check for Issues ⇨ Inspect Document.** The Document Inspector dialog box opens (Figure 20.4).

FIGURE 20.4

Inspect the presentation for information that you might want to remove.

3. **Select or deselect the check boxes for the various types of information that you want to look for.** The personal information contained in properties falls under the Document Properties and Personal Information category.

4. **Click Inspect.**

5. **Review the inspection results.** Categories in which items have been found display their findings; categories in which no items have been found appear with check marks, as shown in Figure 20.5.

6. **For each category that you want to clear, click Remove All.**

7. **When you are finished, click Reinspect to check the document again, or click Close to end the process.**

CAUTION

Be careful that you don't remove hidden objects you want to keep or strip all the speaker notes out of a presentation unintentionally. One way to ensure that you don't do this is to perform the inspection on a copy of the presentation, not the original.

20

FIGURE 20.5

View the inspection results.

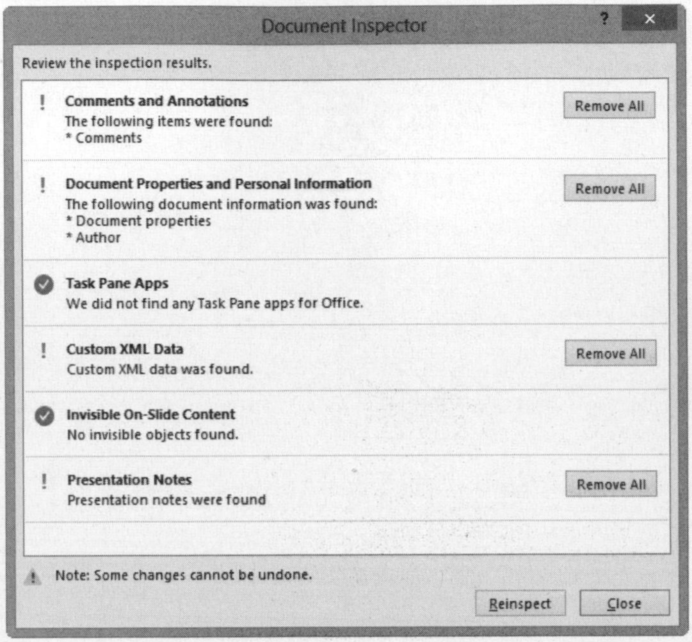

Checking for Compatibility and Usability

Before you send your presentation off to a remote audience, think about what their needs might be. Do they have an earlier version of PowerPoint than you do? Do some of them have disabilities that might make it difficult for them to view your presentation? In the following sections, you'll learn about some features that can help you make your presentation more accessible to a wider audience without very much extra work on your part.

Assessing Prior-Version Compatibility

If you plan to share your presentation with people who have earlier versions of PowerPoint, you need to send it to them in a format that they can display and edit. The "display" part is actually easier than the "edit" part because, generally speaking, when you convert a modern PowerPoint file to PowerPoint 97-2003 format, it retains most of its original appearance, from a Slide Show view perspective. However, editing some of the content in the presentation is a different matter. When an object that's available only in PowerPoint 2007 and higher, such as a SmartArt diagram or chart, is saved in 97-2003 format, PowerPoint converts it to a graphic. It looks the same as it always did, but you cannot edit the object in an earlier version as the type of content that it actually is.

If you plan to share a presentation file with someone who will need to edit it, it is a good idea to run the Compatibility Checker to find out exactly which parts of the presentation may cause a problem. To run the Compatibility Checker, follow these steps:

1. **Choose File ➪ Info ➪ Check for Issues ➪ Check Compatibility.** The Microsoft PowerPoint Compatibility Checker dialog box appears (Figure 20.6).

FIGURE 20.6

Find out about potential problems that may occur when sharing the file in PowerPoint 97-2003 format.

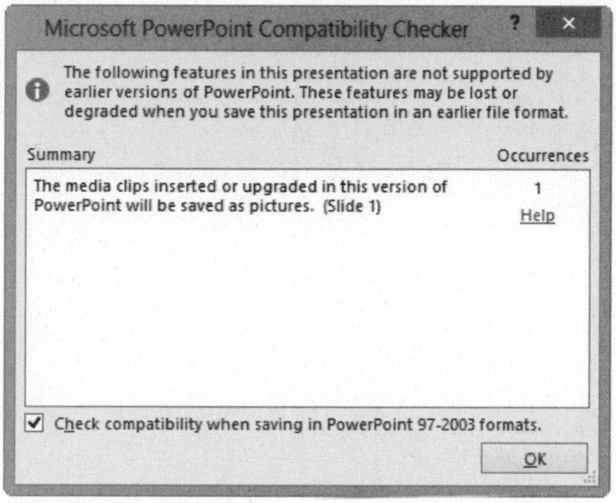

2. **Read the summary information that appears.** If you do not understand one of the messages, click its Help link to open a help document that explains it.

3. **(Optional) To specify whether this check runs automatically when you save in PowerPoint 97-2003 format, select or deselect the Check Compatibility When Saving in PowerPoint 97-2003 Formats check box.**

4. **Click OK.**

NOTE

Embedded video in a presentation will play in PowerPoint 2007, even though PowerPoint 2007 does not support inserting and modifying embedded video. Embedded video will not play in PowerPoint 2003. If you save a presentation containing embedded video in PowerPoint 97-2003 format, the video clips are saved as pictures.

Checking Accessibility

Accessibility refers to the ease with which someone using assistive technology is able to navigate and use your data files. For example, if someone has a visual impairment, how easy will it be for them to understand images on the slides? If someone cannot hear, will they miss out on important points in your presentation that are audio-only?

20

To check accessibility, follow these steps:

1. **Choose File ➪ Info ➪ Check for Issues ➪ Check Accessibility.** The Accessibility Checker task pane appears (Figure 20.7).

FIGURE 20.7

Find out about potential problems that may occur when people using assistive technology view your presentation.

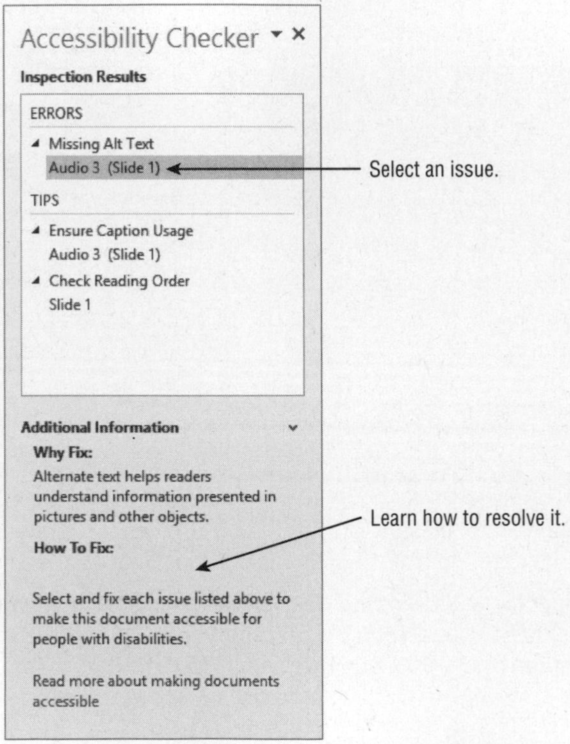

2. **Click one of the problems found, and view the suggestion at the bottom of the pane.** Implement the suggestion if desired by following its steps.

3. **Repeat step 2 for each problem found.**

> **NOTE**
>
> Persons who work for or are funded by the American Federal Government are required to make all files accessible by law under Section 508 of the Rehabilitation Act. See `http://www.section508.gov` for details. Check out the STAMP add-in for PowerPoint that captions audio and video at `http://www.microsoft.com/enable/products/office2010`. Also at that site you can learn about a DAISY add-in that exports content to Word and uses DAISY for people using a screen reader.

Compressing Media

A presentation that contains large video and sound files can take up a lot of disk space. If you have plenty of room on the disk you will be using to transport the presentation, great. But if you will be distributing the presentation in a situation where size is limited, such as via an e-mail attachment, you might want to consider compressing the media.

Compressing media decreases its quality so that it takes up less space. Sounds may be less crisp, and videos may lose sharpness in both picture and sound. It's a trade-off, therefore, between size and quality. Each situation will be different in determining the appropriate balance.

To compress media, follow these steps:

1. **(Optional) Make a backup copy of your presentation file in case you don't like the decreased quality of the clips after compression and want to revert to your original version.**

2. **Choose File ⇨ Compress Media.** (If that command doesn't appear on the Info tab, you don't have any compressible media in your presentation.)

3. **Choose a quality level: Presentation Quality, Internet Quality, or Low Quality.** See Figure 20.8.

   A Compress Media dialog box appears showing the compression progress.

FIGURE 20.8

Choose a quality level appropriate for the distribution method you will use.

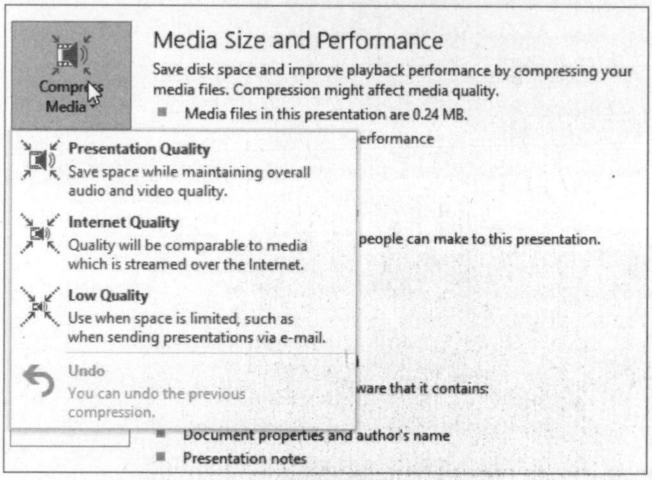

4. **Wait until the process is complete.**
5. **Click Close.**

Limiting User Access to a Presentation

There are several ways of locking down a presentation, with varying degrees of security and effectiveness. The following sections explain the most common methods.

Finalizing a Presentation

When the presentation is completely finished, you may want to mark it as finalized.

Finalizing a presentation doesn't provide any "security," per se, because it is easy to override. However, it prevents users from inadvertently making additional changes to it, and so it gives you some measure of protection against unexpected modifications that can distort your message. It can also serve as a warning; if a finalized presentation has been changed, you can tell by checking to see if its finalized status is still enabled.

To mark a presentation as final, follow these steps:

1. **Choose File ➪ Info ➪ Protect Presentation ➪ Mark as Final.** A message appears that the presentation will be marked as final and then saved.

2. **Click OK.** A message appears, explaining that the presentation has been marked as final and that editing has been turned off for it, as shown in Figure 20.9.

FIGURE 20.9

This message appears after you mark a document as final.

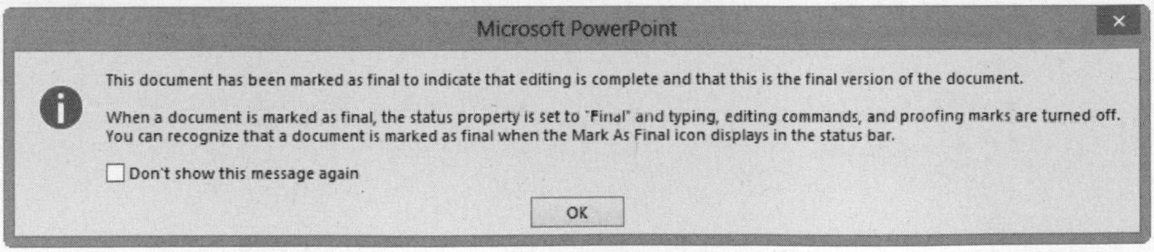

When you mark a document as final, an icon appears in the status bar to indicate that it is final, and the presentation becomes uneditable. [Read-Only] appears in the title bar, and an information bar appears below the Ribbon (which is collapsed) letting you know that document is marked as final. An Edit Anyway button appears there; if you change your mind about the presentation and need to edit it, you can click Edit Anyway to easily turn off this attribute and edit it again, or choose File ➪ Info ➪ Protect Presentation ➪ Mark as Final again to toggle off the Finalized status.

Encrypting a File with a Password

You can prevent unauthorized access to a PowerPoint file by assigning a password to it. Without the password, nobody can open the file. To assign a password, follow these steps:

1. **Choose File ➪ Info ➪ Protect Presentation ➪ Encrypt with Password.** The Encrypt Document dialog box opens.

2. **Type a password in the Password text box and click OK.** A Confirm Password dialog box appears.

3. **Retype the same password that you typed in step 2 and click OK.**

When anyone attempts to open the file in the future, a password prompt will appear. They must enter the password and click OK to continue.

To remove a password, returning the document to its original unencrypted status, follow these steps:

1. **Choose File ➪ Info ➪ Protect Presentation ➪ Encrypt Document.** The Encrypt Document dialog box opens.

2. **Delete the contents of the Password text box.**

3. **Click OK.**

> **CAUTION**
>
> Notice that you do not have to know the password to remove it if the file is already open. Do not leave encrypted presentations open on your computer when you step away from your desk if security is an issue.

Restricting Access

If you have access to a Digital Rights Management (DRM) service, you may be able to grant people access to your presentation while removing their ability to edit, copy, or print it. To check this out, choose File ➪ Info ➪ Protect Presentation ➪ Restrict Access ➪ Connect to Digital Rights Management Servers and Get Templates. Then follow the prompts to connect to the DRM server for your network. If you aren't on a network that supports this, you won't be able to use this feature. Check with your company's network administrator to find out if DRM is available.

Adding a Digital Signature

A digital signature enables you to "sign" a document on your computer — for example, to approve a draft. To sign a document, choose File ➪ Info ➪ Protect Presentation ➪ Restrict Access ➪ Add a Digital Signature. If you do not yet have a digital ID set up on your PC, a prompt appears asking if you want to get one. Click Yes, and on the web page that appears, review the options for digital signatures and sign up with one of the companies. (A charge applies.)

Creating a PDF or XPS Version of a Presentation

PDF is a very common format for distributing documents in read-only format. The acronym stands for *Page Description Format*; it's a proprietary format owned by Adobe. XPS is the

20

Microsoft version. Both PDF and XPS formats create static copies of your slides that anyone with an appropriate reader can view. For PDF, the Adobe Reader program is available from www.adobe.com. Windows Vista and higher, comes with a free XPS reader, and an XPS reader is available for other operating systems from www.microsoft.com.

When you save your presentation in PDF or XPS format, the resulting document consists of each of the slides arranged in the order in which they originally appear in the presentation. No animations or transitions are present, and links to audio and video clips do not function.

To publish as PDF or XPS, follow these steps:

1. **Choose File ➪ Export ➪ Create PDF/XPS Document ➪ Create PDF/XPS.** The Publish as PDF or XPS dialog box opens. See Figure 20.10.

FIGURE 20.10

Save in PDF or XPS format.

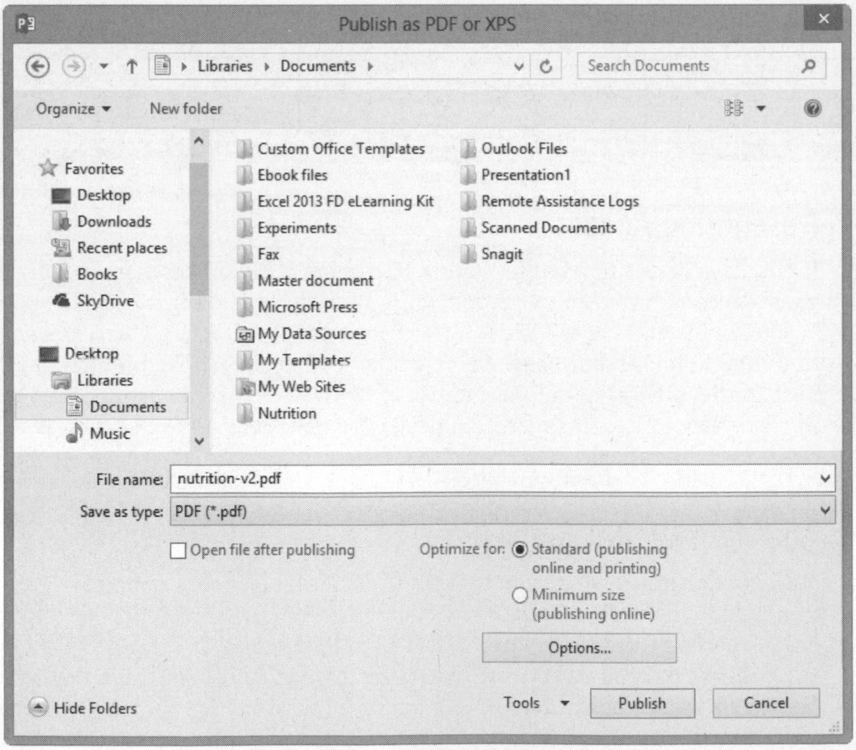

CAUTION

Instead of step 1 you could choose File ➪ Save As.

2. **Navigate to the location where you want to save.**

3. **Open the Save as Type drop-down list and choose PDF or XPS, as desired.**

4. **Type a filename in the File Name box if you do not want to use the same name as the presentation file itself.**

5. **In the Optimize For section, choose Standard or Minimum Size, depending on the intended use for the file.** Standard maintains the quality of the graphics; Minimum Size compresses them.

6. **(Optional) Click Options to open the Options dialog box, from which you can make the following choices (and then click OK to return):**

   - **Range.** You can choose which slides to publish (the default is all of them).

   - **Publish What.** You can choose whether to publish slides, handouts, notes pages, or Outline view.

   - **Include Non-Printing Information.** You can choose whether or not to include document properties and document structure tags for accessibility.

7. **Click Publish.** The document is created.

Converting a Presentation to a Video File

Another way to distribute a presentation is to make a video of it. Viewers can see the presentation exactly as you intended, including narration, animations, and specific timings between slides, and they don't need PowerPoint to do so. All they need is an application capable of playing back video clips (which nearly all operating systems have).

You can output your presentation as either an MPEG-4 video or Windows Media Video (WMV) video clip. These formats will play in almost any digital video player software, such as Windows Media Player, and can be distributed via e-mail, on disk, or on a website.

To save a presentation as a video, follow these steps:

1. **Be sure that you have finalized your presentation, including all text changes, animation, and narration.**

2. **Choose File ⇨ Export ⇨ Create a Video.** Options appear to configure the video settings, as shown in Figure 20.11.

3. **Click Computer & HD Displays, opening a menu of sizes.** Then click the one that is most appropriate for your distribution method. (If you are going to distribute on computer, leave it at the default setting.)

4. **Confirm whether you want to use the timings and narrations you recorded.** The default is Use Recorded Timings and Narrations. If you leave that selected, PowerPoint will use them for any slides that have them; for any slides that are not set to automatically advance, the default timing will be used.

20

FIGURE 20.11

Choose the video clip dimensions and the timing between slides.

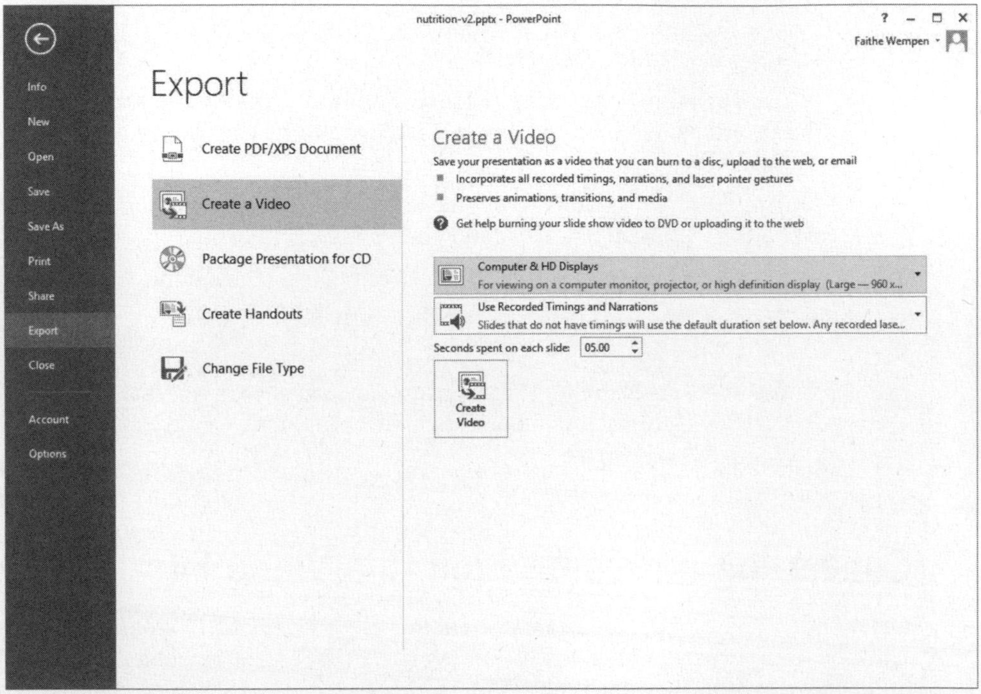

5. **In the Seconds Spent on Each Slide box, enter the number of seconds to use for the default timing.**

6. **Click Create Video.** The Save As dialog box opens.

7. **Type a name for the video clip in the File Name box.**

8. **Open the Save as Type drop-down list and select the desired format.**

9. **Click Save.**

10. **Wait while the video is created.** A progress bar shows on the status bar in PowerPoint.

    The presentation will run and be recorded in real time, so it takes as long to record as the presentation would take to be shown. (You can't watch it as it's recording; it happens behind the scenes.)

Making a DVD Movie of a Presentation

If you have Windows 7, you have access to Windows DVD Maker, and you can use it to turn your presentation video (made in the preceding section) into a DVD that people with ordinary noncomputer DVD players can watch on their TV sets. (People can watch them on their computers too, if the computers have DVD movie players installed.)

> **NOTE**
>
> Windows DVD Maker is not included in Windows 8. If you have Windows 8, you will need to use a third-party DVD burning software instead.

The following are the steps for Windows DVD Maker. You can use any DVD creation software you like, but you'll need to consult the Help system in that program for the steps to take.

Here are the steps for Windows DVD Maker:

1. **In Windows 7, choose Start ➪ All Programs ➪ Windows DVD Maker.**
2. **Click Choose Photos and Videos.** (This step may not be necessary; it depends on whether you have turned off the Welcome screen or not.)
3. **Click Add Items.** The Add Items to DVD dialog box opens.
4. **Select the video you made of your PowerPoint presentation.** (See the preceding section.)
5. **Click Add.**
6. **Click Next.**
7. **(Optional) Change any options as desired in the application.**
8. **Click Burn, and follow the prompts to complete the process.**

Presenting Online

Presenting online (which was called presentation broadcasting in earlier PowerPoint versions) enables you to show your presentation in real time via a network. This makes it possible for people to attend a live show when they cannot be there in person. It uses the Office Presentation Service, a free service that Microsoft makes available to PowerPoint users. You need a Windows Live ID, which is also free.

Before it's time to broadcast your presentation "for real," you will probably want to do a practice run to make sure you understand the broadcasting feature.

Follow these steps:

1. **Choose Slide Show ➪ Start Slide Show ➪ Present Online ➪ Office Presentation Service.** The Present Online dialog box opens. See Figure 20.12.
2. **If desired, mark the Enable Remote Viewers to Download the Presentation check box.**
3. **If there are any warnings in the dialog box, as in Figure 20.12, click their hyperlinks to resolve the issues.** For example, in Figure 20.12, you could click

20

Optimize Media. If you follow one of these hyperlinks, repeat steps 1 and 2 to return to this spot after you are finished.

FIGURE 20.12

Choose whether remote viewers can download the presentation, and then connect to a server.

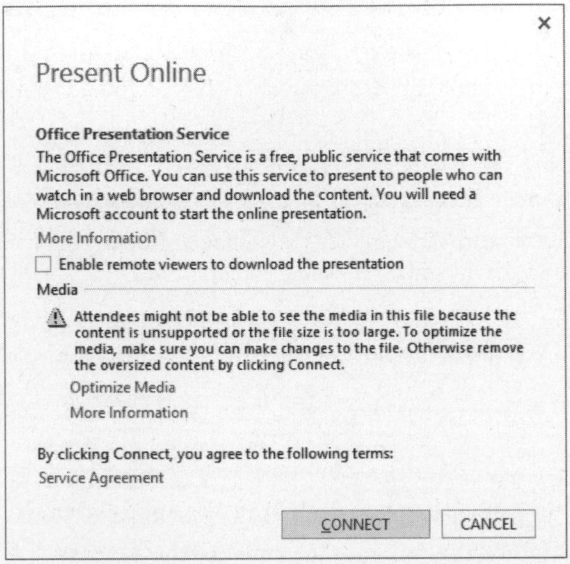

4. **Click Connect.** You are connected to the broadcast server. (You may be prompted for your Windows Live ID; sign in if prompted.) A link appears for participants to use to see the broadcast.

5. **Copy this link to the Clipboard (click Copy Link, or select it and press Ctrl+C) and then paste it into an e-mail, instant message, or other medium through which you want to share it with others.** You can click Send in E-Mail to automatically start a new e-mail containing the link.

6. **Click Start Presentation.** The show begins in Slide Show view on your PC.

7. **Show the presentation as you would normally.** When you are finished, Normal view reappears.

8. **On the Present Online tab on the Ribbon, click End Online Presentation.**

9. **At the confirmation box, click End Online Presentation.**

As you are broadcasting, a Present Online tab appears in Normal view. (You can return to Normal view at any time to work with it.) There you'll find the following options, as shown in Figure 20.13:

- **Use Presenter View.** If you have more than one monitor, you can choose to use Presenter view on one of them by marking this check box.

FIGURE 20.13

Use the Present Online tab to set options for your broadcast.

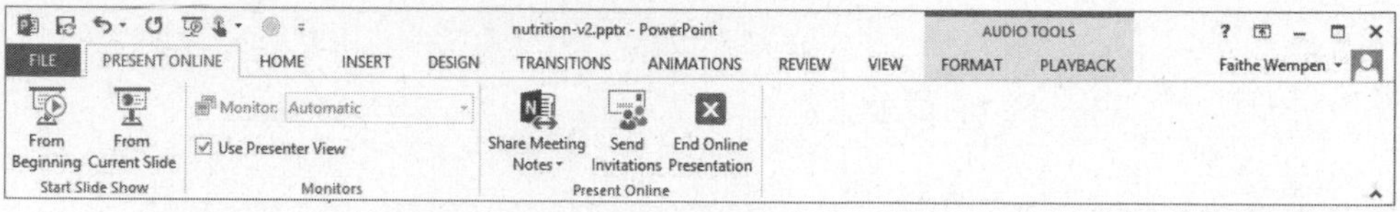

- **Share Meeting Notes.** When you click Share Meeting Notes, a Choose Notes to Share with Meeting dialog box opens. Click the New Notebook button, and OneNote appears. Use it to create a new notebook, and then close OneNote and return to PowerPoint. In the Choose Notes to Share with Meeting dialog box, click the plus sign next to the new notebook to view its sections; click New Section 1 to select it. Then click the OK button to close the dialog box. The notebook opens in OneNote; you can switch back and forth between this notebook and PowerPoint as the presentation progresses.

- **Send Invitations.** Use this command to reopen the dialog box containing the link to the presentation URL, in case you need to send it to anyone else.

Working with the PowerPoint Viewer

The PowerPoint Viewer is a utility that shows PowerPoint presentations but cannot edit them. It is similar to being permanently in Slide Show view. If the computer on which you will show the presentation does not have PowerPoint installed and you want to distribute the presentation in PowerPoint format, you will need to also distribute PowerPoint Viewer so the audience can view the presentation.

Downloading the PowerPoint Viewer

When you package a presentation on CD, the resulting disc includes a PresentationPackage.html page, which opens automatically when the disc is inserted. On this page is a link to download the PowerPoint Viewer from the Microsoft website, as shown in Figure 20.14. Click the link and then follow the prompts.

You don't have to do this on a PC that already has PowerPoint installed on it, but you may want to anyway, just so you can understand the Viewer's interface, which you'll be asking your audience to use.

Playing a Presentation with the PowerPoint Viewer

When you insert a presentation CD on a system that has either PowerPoint or the PowerPoint Viewer installed, all you have to do is select the presentation's link on the CD's navigation page; it opens in whichever of those programs you have.

20

FIGURE 20.14

Open `PresentationPackage.html` and click the Download Viewer button.

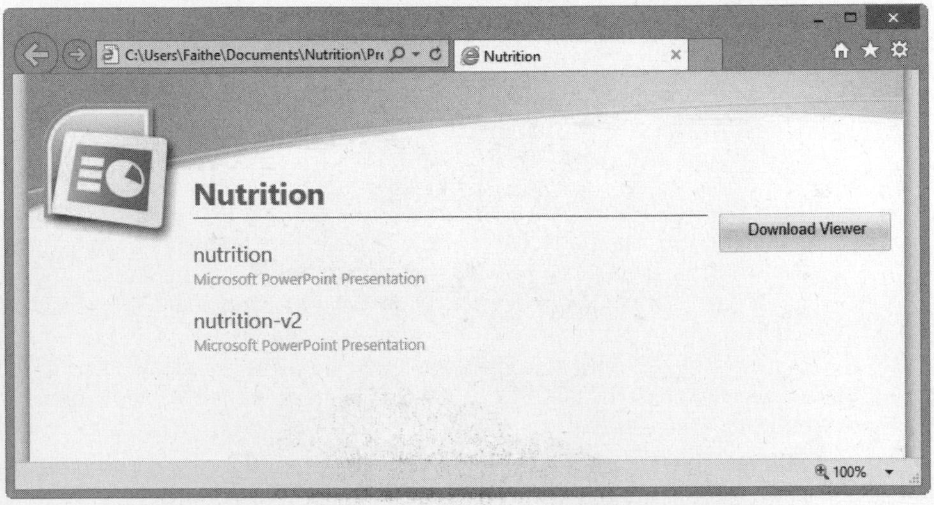

You can also manually start up the PowerPoint Viewer and then manually load a presentation file. Here's how to do that:

1. **In Windows 7, choose Start ➪ All Programs ➪ Microsoft Office PowerPoint Viewer 2007.** Or, in Windows 8, from the Start screen, type **powerpoint**, and then click Microsoft Office PowerPoint Viewer 2007. (The first time you run it, you have to click Accept to accept the license agreement.)

   A Microsoft Office PowerPoint Viewer window opens, which is very much like the Open dialog box in PowerPoint.

2. **Select the presentation you want to view.** (Navigate to the CD if needed.)

3. **Click Open.** The presentation opens.

You can click to move to the next slide or press Backspace or the right arrow key to move backward; the presentation tools do not appear in the lower-left corner as they do in the full version of PowerPoint. However, you can right-click to open a menu that provides basic controls, such as moving between slides, printing, and ending the show.

Summary

In this chapter, you learned how to prepare a presentation for mass distribution through e-mail or the Internet and how to prepare a presentation for these distribution methods by removing personal information and setting properties. You also learned how to save a presentation as a video and to make a DVD movie of the presentation.

Sharing and Collaborating

IN THIS CHAPTER

In many organizations, creating an important presentation is a collaborative project, with several people providing input on a draft. There are several ways to share a draft presentation with others; you can post a presentation to a server, distribute one via e-mail, or post a draft on a document management server. You can also create a slide library on a SharePoint server or on a shared drive (such as on your company's network) and make individual slides available for reuse.

In this chapter, you'll learn how to use PowerPoint's collaborative tools, such as comments, and how to share and distribute presentations and individual slides in a variety of ways.

Working with Comments

Comments are like sticky notes that you can attach to various spots in a presentation, just as you would attach notes to a paper copy. With comments, multiple reviewers can offer suggestions without changing the actual presentation.

Adding Comments

As you review a presentation, you can insert comments pertaining to a slide as a whole or to an individual object on that slide. To add a comment, follow these steps:

1. **Display the slide on which you want to place the comment.** If you want to attach the comment to a specific object, select it.

2. **On the Review tab, click New Comment.** The Comments task pane opens, and a new comment appears. The icon appears on the slide, and a text box in which you can type the comment appears in the Comments pane.

   If you did not choose a specific object in step 1, the comment icon is placed in the top-left corner of the slide. Otherwise, a comment icon is placed adjacent to the object you selected.

3. **Type the comment into the box provided, as shown in Figure 21.1.**

FIGURE 21.1

Type a comment in the text box in the Comments pane.

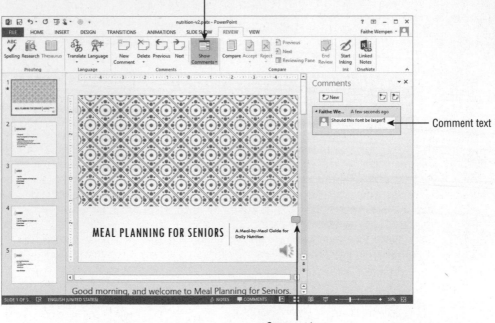

Click here to show or hide the Comments pane.

Comment text

Comment icon

4. **Close the task pane, or leave it open if you are going to be creating more comments.**

Editing and Deleting Comments

Here's how to manage existing comments:

- To view a comment at any time, click the comment icon on the slide, and the Comments pane reopens.

- To delete a comment, point to the comment in the Comments pane so that an *X* appears in the upper-right corner. See Figure 21.2. Then click the *X* to delete the comment. Alternatively, you can right-click the comment icon on the slide and choose Delete Comment.

FIGURE 21.2

To delete a comment, point to it, and then click the *X* in the corner.

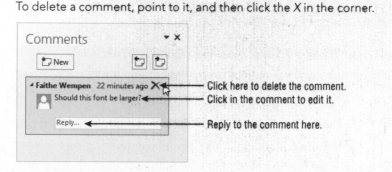

The only places you can't add comments are to the slide masters and layouts. If you want to mark something up for a master or layout, you need to build a slide from that master or layout and then add the comment.

TIP

You do not have to delete the comments to hide them. Instead, you can click the Show Comments button on the Review tab and then click Show Markup to toggle the comments on/off. Comments do not show in Slide Show view.

- To reply to a comment, click in the Reply text box under the main comment, as shown in Figure 21.2.
- To edit the original comment, click the comment text in the task pane; the insertion point moves into it so you can edit it.

The only places you can't add comments are to the slide masters and layouts. If you want to mark something up for a master or layout, you need to build a slide from that master or layout and then add the comment.

NOTE

If you have a tablet or touchscreen, you might want to comment on a document using the Ink feature, which enables you to write directly on the slide with a stylus on your touchscreen. To use this feature, choose Review ➪ Ink ➪ Start Inking.

Printing Comments

To print comments, choose File ➪ Print and then click Full Page Slides, which displays a menu. At the bottom of that menu, make sure that the Print Comments and Ink Markup option is marked, as shown in Figure 21.3. The comments print on a separate page.

FIGURE 21.3

Make sure the Print Comments and Ink Markup option is selected to see the comments in print.

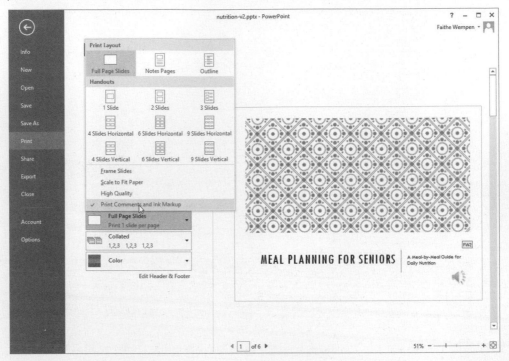

Reviewing Comments

After everyone has had a chance to comment on a draft presentation, you will want to review those comments and probably delete some or all of them.

To move from one comment to the next in the presentation, use the Previous and Next buttons on the Comments task pane or on the Review tab. The comments appear in the Comments task pane (so that you can read them). To edit one, click it to move the insertion point into it and then make your changes.

Comparing and Merging Presentations

You can compare two versions of the same presentation and see the differences between them marked as revisions. You can then accept or reject each revision. This is very helpful when multiple people are making changes to separate copies of a presentation and then someone has to go back through all the copies and merge all the changes into a single cohesive copy.

To use this feature, first ensure that you have two PowerPoint files that contain essentially the same presentation (but with some changes made to one copy). Let's call them presentation A and presentation B for the sake of this discussion. Decide which one you want to be the *original* and which one you want to be the *revision*. Open the original one in PowerPoint, and then do the following:

1. **Choose Review ⇨ Compare.** The Choose File to Merge with Current Presentation dialog box opens.

2. **Select the other version of the presentation and click Merge.** The Revisions pane opens and shows the first change in the presentation, as shown in Figure 21.4. If there are also new comments in the file, they appear in the Revisions pane with a sticky-note icon.

   The little notepad-and-pencil icon (revision icon) on the slide in Figure 21.4 represents one of the changes listed in the Revisions pane. You can click that icon to see a pop-up explaining the change, as shown in Figure 21.4.

FIGURE 21.4

See the revisions made to the current slide.

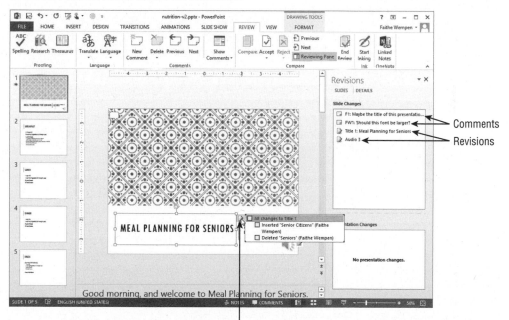

Click the revision icon to open menu.

Each change can be individually accepted. Notice in Figure 21.4 the check boxes next to each change listed in the pop-up; you can accept a change by clicking its check box to mark it there. You can also accept a change by choosing Review ⇨ Compare ⇨ Accept. (Click the face of the Accept button, not the arrow beneath it.)

The Reject button works only after a change has been accepted. To reject the change, accept it and then choose Review ➪ Compare ➪ Reject.

To accept all the changes on the current slide, click the arrow under the Accept button to display its menu, and then choose Accept All Changes to This Slide. You can do the same thing with the Reject button to reject all changes to the current slide.

To accept all the changes to the entire presentation, click that same arrow and choose Accept All Changes to the Presentation. Again, you can do the same thing with the Reject button to reject all changes to the presentation.

Use the Previous and Next buttons in the Compare group of the Review tab to move between changes. (Don't confuse these with the Previous and Next buttons in the Comments group, which are for comments only.) When you are finished, choose Review ➪ Compare ➪ End Review. Any unaccepted changes will be discarded, so do not end the review until you are finished reviewing each change.

Sharing Your Presentation File on a LAN

If your PC is on a network, you can share a presentation file with others by placing it in a location that other network users can access. You can save it to a centrally accessible network drive, such as a file server, or you can make a folder on your own hard disk network accessible.

Saving to a Network Drive

To save to a network drive that others also have access to, navigate to that location in the Save As dialog box. Start by choosing Network in the navigation pane at the left side of the Save As dialog box and then browse to the desired location.

Sharing a Folder on the Network

You can also make your own hard disk's folders available for others to access on your network. The process of doing that depends on the version of Windows you have and on whether or not you are using a HomeGroup (a special type of peer-to-peer workgroup specifically for Windows 7 and 8 computers).

Folder Sharing with a HomeGroup

A HomeGroup is a small network for situations where there is no file server, as in a home. If all the PCs in your network use Windows 7 or 8, you can use a HomeGroup to share files, folders, and printers.

If you have a HomeGroup set up, follow these steps to share a folder on it:

1. **Open a File Explorer window in Windows 8 or a Windows Explorer window in Windows 7 and locate the folder you want to share.**

2. **Right-click the folder and choose one of these (see Figure 21.5):**

   - Share With ⇨ HomeGroup (Read) in Windows 7, or Share With ⇨ HomeGroup (View) in Windows 8

   - Share With ⇨ HomeGroup (Read/Write) in Windows 7, or Share With ⇨ HomeGroup (View and Edit) in Windows 8

FIGURE 21.5

Share with the HomeGroup.

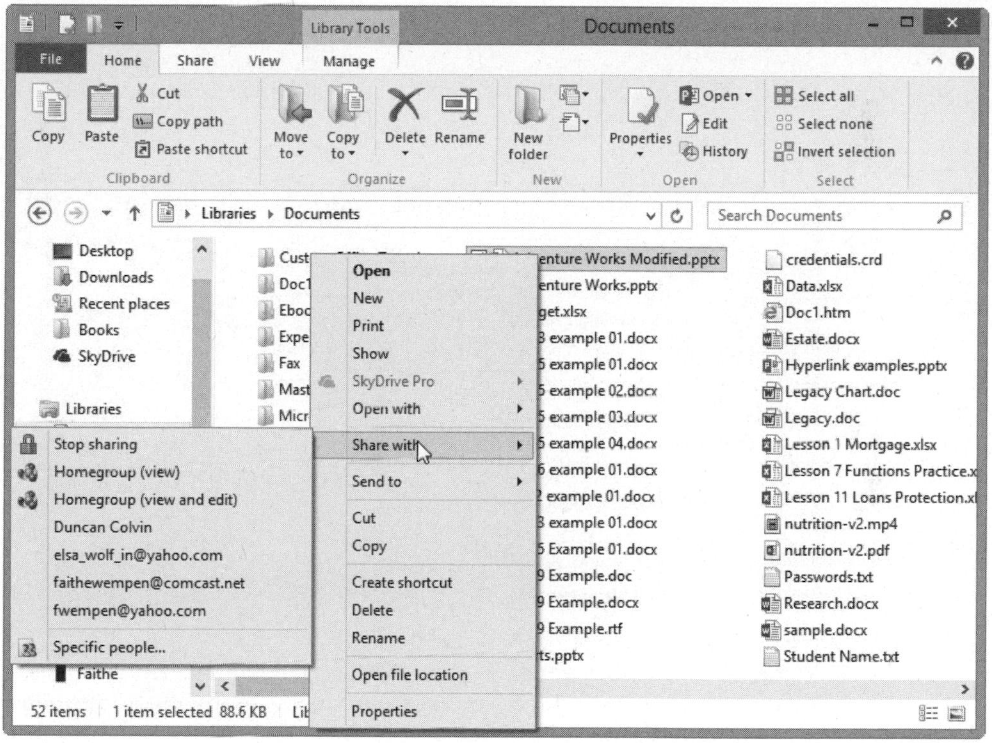

Everyone in your HomeGroup will have the same rights to the folder. If you want to specify that only certain people have certain rights, see the following section.

Folder Sharing without a HomeGroup

If you don't use a HomeGroup, follow these steps to share the folder with all other users who have network access to your hard disk:

1. **Open a File Explorer or Windows Explorer window and locate the folder you want to share.**

2. **Right-click the folder and choose Share With ⇨ Specific People.** The File Sharing dialog box opens.

3. **Do any of the following:**

   - To share with a particular user who has a user account and password, enter that user's name and click Add.

   - To share with everyone, type **Everyone** (or select Everyone from the drop-down list) and click Add, as shown in Figure 21.6.

FIGURE 21.6

Share the folder with everyone by adding the Everyone group to the sharing list.

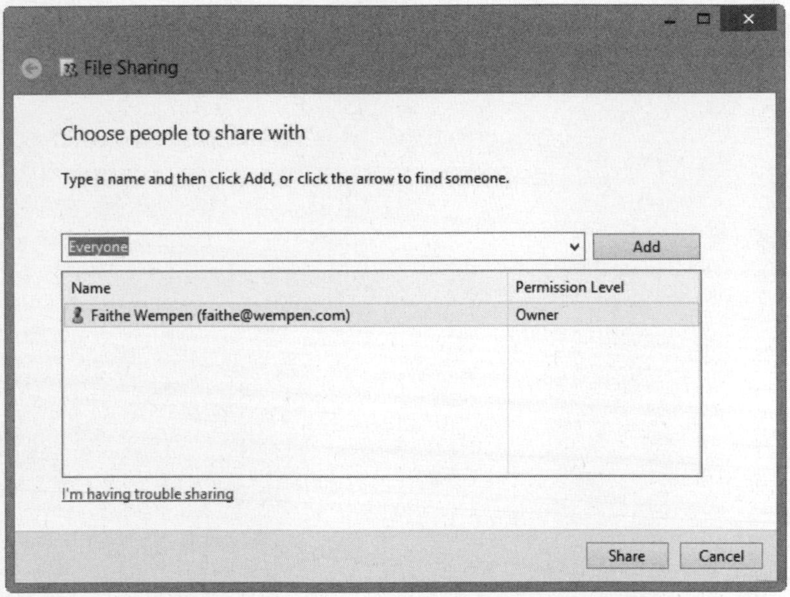

4. **If you want to give the user(s) that you just added Read/Write access, click Read on the row just added (for example, the Everyone row) and choose Read/Write from the menu that appears.** See Figure 21.7.

5. **Click Share.**

6. **Click Done.**

Sending a Presentation via E-Mail

You can e-mail a presentation file to others directly from within PowerPoint using your default e-mail program, such as Outlook, Windows Mail, or Outlook Express. Recipients get the presentation as an e-mail attachment, which they can then open in their own copies of PowerPoint.

FIGURE 21.7

Set Read/Write access if desired.

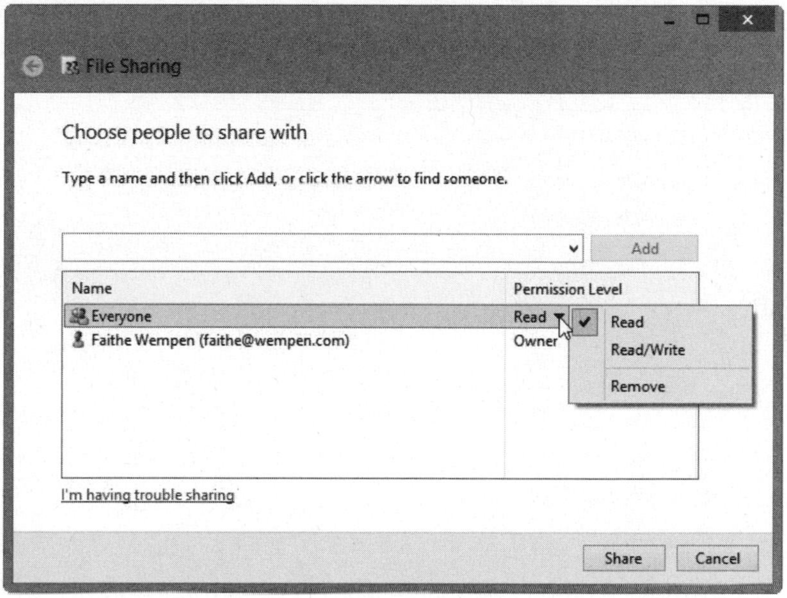

To e-mail a presentation from within PowerPoint, follow these steps:

1. **From an open presentation, choose File ⇨ Share ⇨ E-mail ⇨ Send as Attachment.** A new e-mail message opens in your default e-mail application with the presentation set as an attachment, as shown in Figure 21.8.

2. **Type or select the e-mail addresses for the recipients.** The exact procedure depends on the e-mail application you are using.

3. **The default entry in the Subject line is the PowerPoint file's name; change it if desired.**

4. **If desired, in the body section of the e-mail, type a note telling the recipients what you have attached and what you want them to do with the presentation.**

5. **Click Send.**

Sharing a Presentation on Your SkyDrive

As you learned back in Chapter 2, "Creating and Saving Presentation Files," SkyDrive is a free online repository where you can save files that you want to make available—either to yourself or to others—from within PowerPoint, from File Explorer (Windows 8) or Windows Explorer (Windows 7), or via a web interface, from anywhere that Internet access is available. This is a great feature because it eliminates the need to carry around a disk or flash drive with your presentation on it. Just log into the Internet and there it is! You'll learn much more about SkyDrive in Appendix B, "Essential SkyDrive Skills."

FIGURE 21.8

PowerPoint helps you e-mail presentations easily.

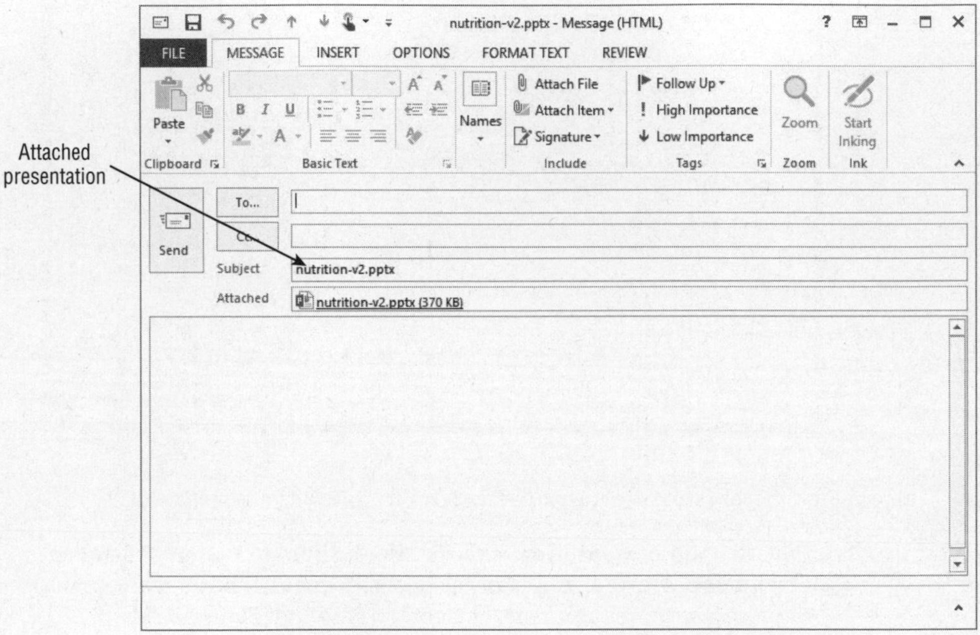

You can easily share your SkyDrive files with other people. There are a variety of ways to do so. You can send e-mail, post a link to Facebook, or create a hyperlink that you can then share with others any way you like (such as pasting it into the HTML for a web page or pasting it into an instant messaging program).

The following sections assume that your presentation file is already stored on your SkyDrive. If it isn't, save it there, as you learned in Chapter 2.

Inviting People to View Your Shared Presentation

For other people to view files on your SkyDrive, they need a hyperlink that provides the location. You can send such a hyperlink to people via e-mail from within PowerPoint. (You can also do it from outside of PowerPoint, as explained in Appendix B.)

To send an e-mail invitation, follow these steps:

1. **Choose File ⇨ Share ⇨ Invite People.** Controls appear for composing an e-mail message.
2. **In the Type Names or E-Mail Addresses box, type the e-mail address(es).**
3. **By default, the link sent allows the recipient to edit the file.** If you do not want them to be able to, open the Can Edit drop-down list and choose Can View. See Figure 21.9.

FIGURE 21.9

Send an e-mail invitation to view your presentation on your SkyDrive.

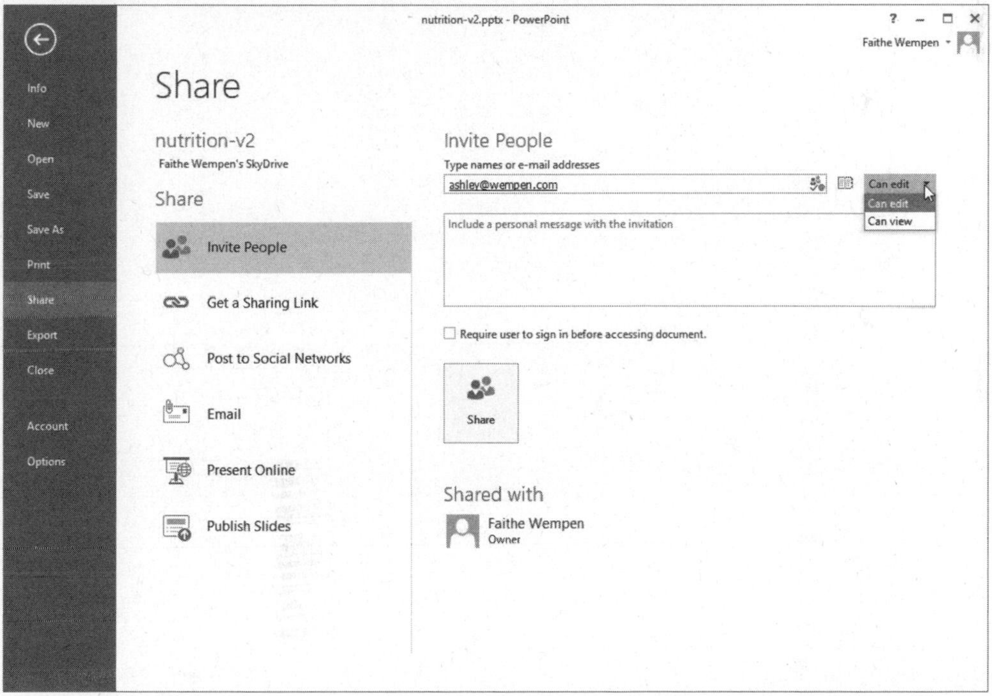

4. **If desired, enter a personal message to include with the invitation.**
5. **If desired, mark the Require User to Sign In Before Accessing Document check box.** If you mark this check box, only people with a Microsoft account will be able to see your file.
6. **Click Share.** The e-mail is sent.

Getting a Sharing Link

You don't have to send a link to the file via e-mail; you can distribute it any way you like (such as via instant messaging, for example). To generate a hyperlink to your file that you can then paste into any application, follow these steps:

1. **Choose File ⇨ Share ⇨ Get a Sharing Link.** Controls appear for generating links.

   If you don't see the Get a Sharing Link command, you probably haven't saved the file to your SkyDrive.

2. **Click the Create Link button next to either View Link or Edit Link, depending on the permission you want to grant.** See Figure 21.10.

FIGURE 21.10

Choose to create a link for viewing or editing.

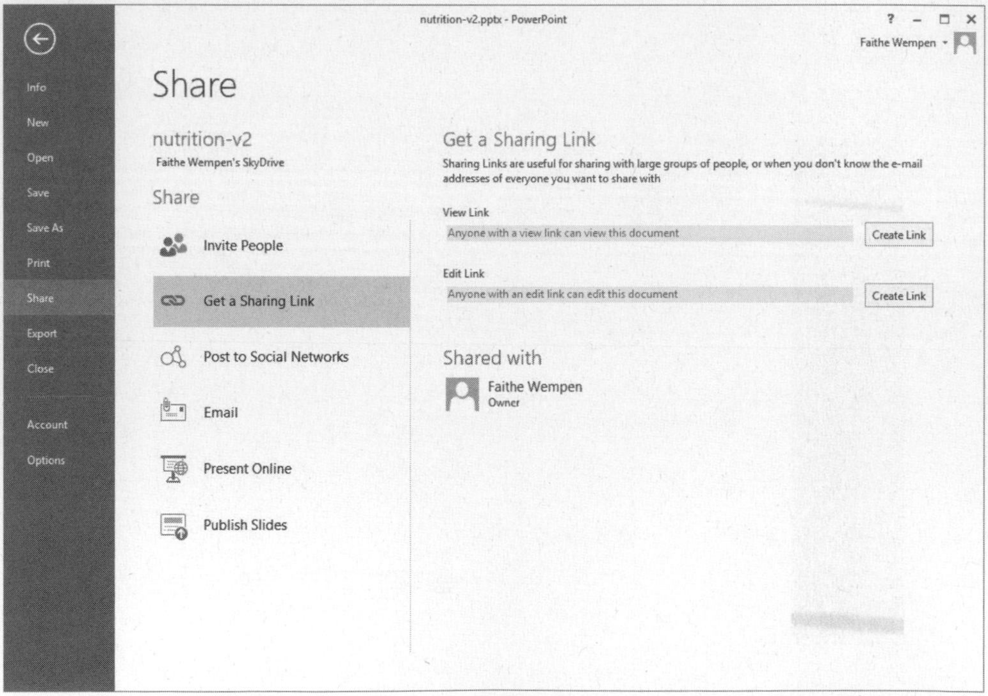

If you later want to stop sharing this file, return here and click Disable Link to turn that link off.

3. **Click the hyperlink to select it, and then press Ctrl+C to copy it to the Clipboard.**

4. **Click in the application where you want to paste it and press Ctrl+V.**

5. **Return to PowerPoint and press Esc to close Backstage view when you're finished.**

Posting Your Presentation to Facebook

If you use Facebook to distribute your work in PowerPoint (such as for a marketing campaign), you can post your link directly to the site from PowerPoint. Note that this procedure posts a link and not a copy of the original file.

Follow these steps to post:

1. **Choose File ➪ Share ➪ Post to Social Networks.** Controls appear for posting a message on Facebook. See Figure 21.11.

FIGURE 21.11

Share a link to your presentation on Facebook.

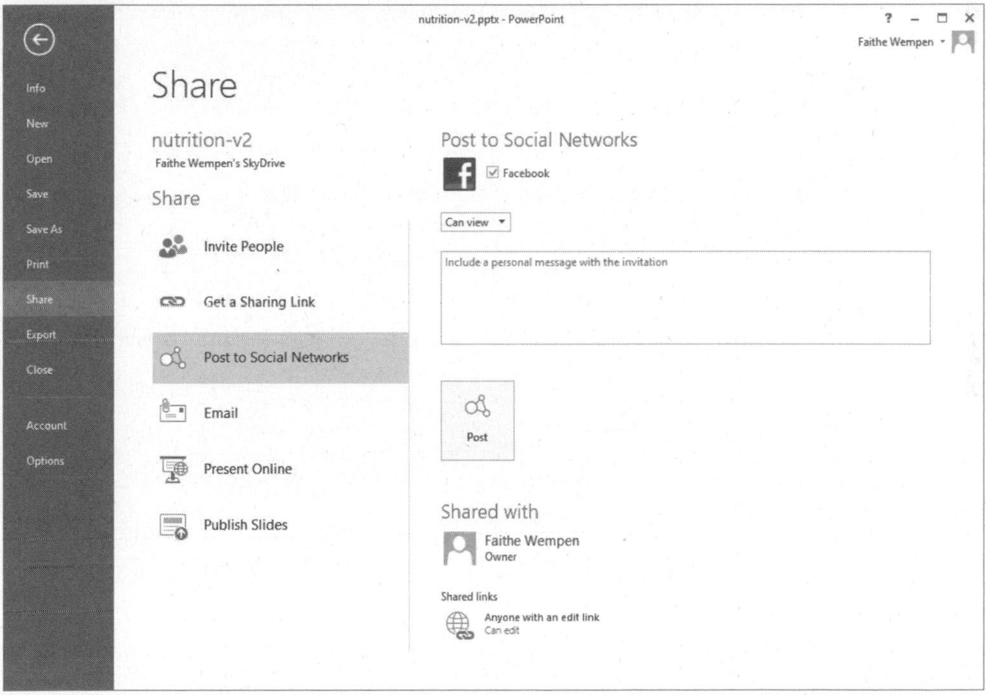

If you don't see the Post to Social Networks command, you probably haven't saved the file to your SkyDrive.

2. **If you want others to be able to edit your presentation, open the Can View drop-down list and click Can Edit.**

3. **(Optional) Type a message to include with the posting.**

4. **Click Post.**

Sharing a Presentation via Office 365 SharePoint

If you have access to a SharePoint server via Office 365, you can use it to share your work with others. This works in much the same way as a SkyDrive share, which you learned about earlier in this chapter. Whereas SkyDrive is designed primarily for individual users, SharePoint sites are designed for corporate/business users.

First, add the SharePoint site to your list of Save As places. To do so, follow these steps:

1. **Click File > Save As, and then click Add a Place.**
2. **Click Office 365 SharePoint.**
3. **Click Sign In.**
4. **Sign in with your user name and password.** The site is added to your Save As list of places.

From that point, you can save your presentation to the new SharePoint place, and then share it with others. Follow these steps to do so:

1. **Click File > Save As, and then under the Save As heading, click your SharePoint document library.**
2. **Click Browse to open the Save As dialog box.** The site content appears. Browse to the folder in which you want to save the presentation file.
3. **Click Save.** The presentation is saved to the specified location.

Next, you will want to share your presentation with other people. To let them know it is available, follow these steps:

1. **Click File > Share > Invite People.**
2. **Enter the email addresses of the people with whom you want to share.**
3. **Choose Can Edit or Can View, depending on the permissions you want to assign.**
4. **Enter a message in the box below the address line, and then click Share.**

To stop sharing the presentation, choose File > Share, and under Shared With, right-click the person with whom you want to stop sharing and click Remove User.

Managing Simultaneous Edits

When you save to a cloud-based storage location such as SkyDrive or Office 365 SharePoint, multiple people can work on a presentation simultaneously, provided they all have PowerPoint 2010 or later, or are using the latest release of the PowerPoint Web App.

Here's how it works:

1. **Create a draft of the presentation and save it to a shared location**. If needed, give permission to edit it to the people with whom you will collaborate.

2. **Open and start working on the presentation**. It's as easy as that! When other people are working on the presentation, you'll see a Co-authoring icon in the status bar telling you how many people are working on it.

3. **Save your work when you are finished editing by choosing File > Save.**

   If you were the only one working on the presentation, the process ends here; it's just like any other save. However, if others were also editing the presentation, a notification appears that updates are available. Continue the process by following these steps:

4. **Click the Updates Available indicator on the status bar to merge the changes.** Unless your edits conflict, they merge automatically, and you're done.

   If someone else made a change that conflicts with some edit you made, a message appears. If that happens, click the Resolve Conflicts button.

5. **A message appears that PowerPoint has refreshed your presentation with changes made by other authors.** Click OK to accept that.

6. **On the Merge tab, click Show Changes.**

7. **Do one of the following**:

   - To view conflicting updates only, click Show Only Conflicts.
   - To view all changes, click Show All Changes.

8. **To accept a conflicting change, click the box next to the change.** Or, to reject a conflicting change, do nothing to it. Ignored changes are the same as rejected changes.

9. **When you are done reviewing changes, click Close Merge View.** All changes are applied and uploaded to the server, and all change indicators disappear.

Sharing Slides with a SharePoint Slide Library

Often people who work at the same company can benefit from sharing slides with one another. For example, a product manager might have slides that describe his product, and a sales or marketing person in the company could save a great deal of time by copying such slides instead of re-creating them from scratch. However, it can be time consuming to wade through large presentations to find a single slide that could be of benefit.

A *slide library* is a specialized type of document library that stores individual slides rather than entire presentations. A slide library enables users to publish individual slides that they think might be of interest to others in their organization. For example, with a slide library, product managers could post two or three slides about their products and an executive or salesperson could easily browse these and choose the ones needed for a presentation to a particular client.

> **CAUTION**
>
> If a slide contains links to other content, such as videos or sounds, that linked content is not included in the slide library.

You can check out slides from a slide library and attach an approval process and tasks to them. In addition, you can tag each slide in several ways and search the slide libraries for just the slides you need.

The following sections assume that you already have a SharePoint slide library available to you. If that's not the case, contact the IT department at your company to find out how to get a SharePoint slide library set up for your department or project.

Placing Slides into a Slide Library from PowerPoint

If the presentation is already open in PowerPoint, it's a natural next step to publish slides directly from within PowerPoint to the slide library. This process also works to publish slides to a local slide library folder (not on a SharePoint server). You or your coworkers who have access to the drive can then reuse slides.

To store slides in a slide library from within PowerPoint, follow these steps:

1. **Open your presentation and choose File ⇨ Share ⇨ Publish Slides ⇨ Publish Slides.** The Publish Slides dialog box opens (Figure 21.12).

FIGURE 21.12

Publish slides to a slide library from within PowerPoint.

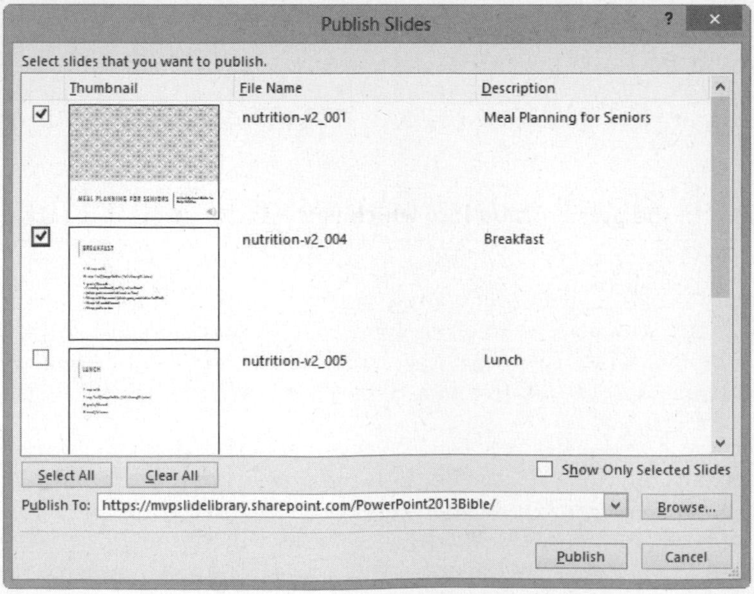

2. **Mark the check box for each slide that you want to publish, or click the Select All button to add all of the slides to the library.**

   Can't see all of the slides? Use the scroll bar on the right to move down through the slides.

3. **(Optional) Change the filename and/or description for a slide if desired.** The text in the File Name and Description columns is editable; just click in it and type.

4. **Type the path to your slide library in the Publish To field.**

   If you already have your SharePoint slide library open in your web browser, the easiest way to get the path to your slide library is to copy it from your browser. Select the beginning of the path. (Don't select from the /Forms part on.) Or if the slide library is locally accessible, click Browse to browse for it.

> **NOTE**
>
> If you don't have access to the desired slide library right now, click Browse, and in the Select a Slide Library dialog box, create a new folder to serve as a temporary slide library. Then select that folder and click Select. This results in a new pointer placed in `C:\Users\`*`username`*`\Roaming\Microsoft\PowerPoint\My Slide Libraries`. You can then upload this folder to the slide library on the SharePoint server when it is available. However, you won't be able to insert slides from this folder into your presentation as if it were a slide library (see the next section) until it has been published to SharePoint.

5. **Click the Publish button to publish the slides to the library.** (You may be prompted for a username and password for the server.)

6. **Wait for the slides to be uploaded to the slide library.** A progress bar appears in the status bar as the upload is happening.

Pulling Slides from the Library to PowerPoint

Once you have slides in your library, you will work with them primarily from within PowerPoint. You can quickly pull individual slides into presentations using the following steps:

1. **Open the presentation into which you want to insert one or more slides.**

2. **On the Home tab in the Ribbon, click the down arrow under the New Slides button and select Reuse Slides.**

3. **In the task pane that appears to the right, type the URL of your slide library in the Insert Slide From text box, or select it from the text box's drop-down list.**
   If you paste the URL from your browser, remove everything after the slide library name.

> **NOTE**
>
> You can create a temporary library file on your local hard drive in which to save files to be published. However, you can't access that local folder as if it were a real slide library.

4. **Click the arrow button to the right of the drop-down list to open your slide library.** A thumbnail list of slides will appear in the task pane. See Figure 21.13.

FIGURE 21.13

Use the slides stored in a slide library.

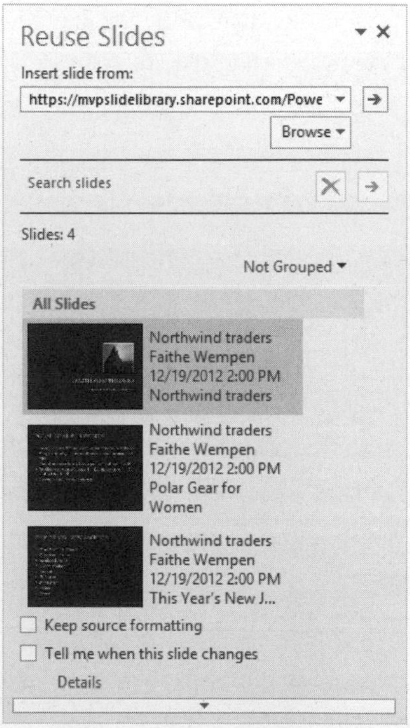

5. **(Optional) To keep the source formatting for the slide(s), mark the Keep Source Formatting check box.** Otherwise, the content of the slides inserted will adjust to the destination presentation's master slide settings.

6. **(Optional) Mark the check box labeled Tell Me When the Slide Changes.** This ensures that if someone else changes this slide and checks it into the library, you will be notified.

7. **Click a slide to add it to the presentation.** Repeat for each slide you want to add.

> **TIP**
>
> To best see all of the slides, you might want to widen and/or undock the task pane. To undock it, click the blue bar at the top of the task pane and drag it toward the middle of the screen. Drag the edge of the task pane to widen it.

TIP

If your library is very large and you want to search for slides that match a certain criteria, type the criteria (such as a keyword) in the Search box. This works only if your server supports Search. You can also change how the slides are grouped, to find specific slides, using the drop-down above the slides.

    8. **Close the task pane.**

Summary

In this chapter, you learned how to share presentations and your slides with other users. You can make comments to a presentation and compare and combine changes made by multiple users. You can share full presentation files using a LAN drive and e-mail, SkyDrive, and a SharePoint slide library. In the next chapter, you will learn how to customize PowerPoint and automate its use with macros.

Customizing PowerPoint

IN THIS CHAPTER

Setting program defaults

Configuring the Trust Center

Customizing the Ribbon

Customizing the Quick Access Toolbar

Managing add-ins

Customizing the status bar

A lthough PowerPoint works great right out of the box, it can work even better for you with a few tweaks. You can change program defaults and customize the Quick Access Toolbar and Ribbon to make PowerPoint your own.

Setting Program Defaults

PowerPoint contains a large assortment of customizable program settings. Some make purely cosmetic changes to the interface, whereas others enable or disable timesaving or safety features.

You can access most options by selecting File ➪ Options and working in the PowerPoint Options dialog box. Click a category in the PowerPoint Options dialog box along the left side, and then set the options that you want. Table 22.1 lists all of the options, divided by category (or most of them, anyway; depending on the language, you may have a few extra options or be missing a few).

TABLE 22.1 PowerPoint Options

Section	Option	Description
Category: General		
User Interface options	Show Mini Toolbar on selection	Shows or hides the floating mini toolbar when you select text.
	Enable Live Preview	Shows a preview of a setting when you move your mouse pointer over it in a gallery. For example, if you hover over a different theme on the Design tab, the slide shows it in the background, behind the open menu.
	ScreenTip style	Determines how detailed the ScreenTips are when you hover the mouse pointer over a command or button.
Personalize your copy of Microsoft Office	User Name	Your name appears here; changing this name affects the username that is associated with comments and file properties.
	Initials	Same as the username, except that it uses only your initials; for example, your initials appear on comments.
	Always use these values regardless of sign in to Office	When this check box is marked, the username and initials will not change when a different user signs in.
	Office Background	Determines the design (if any) that will appear in the title bar.
	Office Theme	Determines the color of the Ribbon and background (White, Light Gray, or Dark Gray).
Start Up Options	Choose the extensions you want PowerPoint to open by Default	Click the Default Programs button to open the section of the Windows Control Panel that enables you to set filename extensions.
	Tell me if Microsoft PowerPoint isn't the default program for viewing and editing presentations	When this check box is marked, PowerPoint performs this check each time at startup.
	Show the Start screen when this application starts	If you don't like the Start screen in PowerPoint, deselect this check box to start up with a blank presentation.

Section	Option	Description
Category: Proofing		
AutoCorrect options	Change how PowerPoint corrects and formats text as you type	Click the AutoCorrect Options button here to access and configure AutoCorrect, as described in Chapter 7.
When correcting spelling in Microsoft Office programs	Ignore words in UPPERCASE	Use these check boxes to adjust the spelling check, as described in Chapter 7. The options here affect all Office applications.
	Ignore words that contain numbers	
	Ignore Internet and file addresses	
	Flag repeated words	
	Enforce accented uppercase in French	
	Suggest from main dictionary only	
	Custom Dictionaries	
	French modes	
	Spanish modes	
When correcting spelling in PowerPoint	Check spelling as you type	Use these check boxes to adjust the spelling check, as described in Chapter 7. The options here affect only PowerPoint.
	Hide spelling and grammar errors	When this option is enabled, potential spelling and grammar errors on slides are not marked.
	Check grammar with spelling	When this option is enabled, performs a grammar check as well as a spelling check.
	Recheck Document	Reruns the spelling and grammar check.
Category: Save		
Save presentations	Save files in this format	Sets the default file format for new presentations.
	Save AutoRecover information every *XX* minutes	Enables PowerPoint to AutoSave your changes so that PowerPoint may be able to restore them in the event of a system crash.

Continues

TABLE 22.1   *(continued)*

Section	Option	Description
	Keep the last autosaved version if I close without saving	Helps prevent data loss through user error by retaining an Auto Recover version of any work that you don't save as you close the program.
	AutoRecover file location	Sets the location where PowerPoint saves the AutoRecover temporary files.
	Don't show the Backstage when opening or saving files	Clear this check box if you want the Save As or Open dialog box to appear immediately when you select the respective command (as it did in earlier PowerPoint versions).
	Show additional places for saving, even if sign-in may be required	Includes all available places for saving.
	Save to Computer by default	Mark this check box if you want your local hard disk rather than SkyDrive to be the default save location.
	Local default file location	Sets the location that appears by default in the Save As dialog box.
	Default personal templates location	Sets the location of personal templates (that is, templates you create or acquire yourself).
Offline editing options for document management server files	Save checked-out files to	When you check out a file from a document server, this option allows you to specify whether the draft is stored locally or back to the Web.
	Server drafts location	When you check out a file from a document server and you choose to save a local copy, this option determines the location of that local copy.
File merge options for shared document management server files	Show detailed merge changes when a merge occurs	Provides additional information about the changes made during a merge operation where two versions of a presentation are being synchronized.
Preserve fidelity when sharing this presentation	Embed fonts in the file	Packages the fonts with the presentation file so that when the presentation is shown on a computer that does not have these fonts, it still displays correctly.

Section	Option	Description
Category: Language		
Choose editing languages	Add additional editing languages	Enables you to add other languages in which you may be editing content for access to their spelling, grammar, currency, and other settings.
Choose display and help languages	Set the language priority for the buttons, tabs, and Help	Use the arrow buttons to move languages up or down on the priority list. The language at the top of the list is the default.
	View display languages installed for each Microsoft Office program	Click here to see a table listing all the language packs installed for each Office application on your system.
Choose ScreenTip language	Set your ScreenTip language	Select the desired language from the drop-down list, if you have more than one language installed.
Category: Advanced		
Editing options	When selecting, automatically select entire word	Extends the selection to entire words when you drag to select.
	Allow text to be dragged and dropped	Enables drag-and-drop moving and copying.
	Automatically switch keyboard to match language of surrounding text	Switches the keyboard layout for the language you are working with.
	Do not automatically hyperlink screenshot	Specifies whether screenshots should be live hyperlinks.
	Maximum number of undos	Sets the number of undo operations.
Cut, copy, and paste	Use smart cut and paste	Automatically adjusts sentence and word spacing and table formatting as well as other formatting details.
	Show Paste Options buttons when content is pasted	If this option is enabled, then when you paste, an icon appears that opens a menu where you can specify paste options.
Image Size and Quality	Discard editing data	Saves disk space by not saving information about the original picture when you are applying a transformation or other effect.
	Do not compress images in file	Does not allow images to be compressed, to keep them at maximum quality.

Continues

651

TABLE 22.1   *(continued)*

Section	Option	Description
	Set default target output to	Sets a quality level, in pixels per inch (ppi), for image compression. The default 220 is good for print; 150 or 96 would be appropriate for on-screen shows.
Chart	Properties follow chart data point for all new presentations	When this option is enabled, custom formatting and data labels follow the data points as they are moved or changed in the chart.
	Current presentation	Enables you to choose which presentation is considered the current one (for the next option).
	Properties follow chart data point for current presentation	Sets the behavior of custom formatting and data labels for the current presentation (as set above).
Display	Show this number of Recent Presentations	Controls the number of presentations that appear in the Recent section of the File ⇨ Open menu.
	Quickly access this number of Recent Presentations	When enabled, activates a Recent Presentations list in the Quick Access Toolbar and sets the number of presentations that appear on that list.
	Show this number of unpinned Recent Folders	Sets the number of recent folders that appear as shortcuts when you are saving or opening files from Backstage view.
	Show shortcut keys in ScreenTips	Includes shortcut keys when you move your mouse over a command or button.
	Show vertical ruler	Includes the vertical ruler when the ruler is enabled (from the View tab).
	Disable hardware graphics acceleration	Prevents the video card from using its graphics acceleration features. You can turn this on to troubleshoot problems with the display, but it may decrease display performance.
	Disable Slide Show hardware graphics acceleration	Same as the preceding option except only for Slide Show view. You might want this set differently than when editing the presentation.

Section	Option	Description
	Automatically extend display when presenting on a laptop or tablet	When enabled, sets the Windows display mode to extend the Desktop on additional monitors rather than mirroring the same content on each.
	Open all documents using this view	Chooses the default view with which to open presentations.
Slide Show	Show menu on right-mouse click	Enables the right-click menu in Slide Show view.
	Show popup toolbar	Enables the pop-up toolbar (lower-left corner of the screen) in Slide Show view.
	Prompt to keep ink annotations when exiting	When you're exiting from Slide Show view after using ink annotations, this option asks whether you want to save them.
	End with black slide	Displays a black screen after the final slide (otherwise, it returns to Normal view).
Print	Print in background	Enables print spooling, so that PowerPoint is freed up faster to continue working.
	Print TrueType fonts as graphics	Sends TrueType fonts to the printer as graphics rather than as fonts.
	Print inserted objects at printer resolution	When an object has a different resolution than the printer, this changes the object to match the printer resolution.
	High quality	Enables high-quality printing, including minor improvements such as printing text shadows.
	Align transparent graphics at printer resolution	The presence of this option is actually a bug in the software; it does nothing.
When printing this document	Use the most recently used print settings OR Use the following print settings	Selects whether to remember print settings or to use settings that you specify.
General	Provide feedback with sound	Enables sound with visual notifications, such as alerts when a process is complete.
	Show add-in user interface errors	Turns on error messages received from add-ins.

Continues

TABLE 22.1   *(continued)*

Section	Option	Description
Category: Customize Ribbon		
Customize the Ribbon	Customize the Ribbon	Customizes the Ribbon, as explained later in this chapter.
Category: Quick Access Toolbar		
Customize the Quick Access Toolbar	Customize the Quick Access Toolbar	Customizes the Quick Access Toolbar, as explained later in this chapter.
Category: Add-Ins		
Add-Ins	(List)	Displays the installed add-ins. Add-ins are explained later in this chapter.
	Manage	Selects an add-in category. You can then click Go to manage this category.
Category: Trust Center		
Microsoft PowerPoint Trust Center	Trust Center Settings	Opens the Trust Center dialog box, explained later in this chapter.

Configuring the Trust Center

The Trust Center is a separate dialog box from the main PowerPoint options; it contains categories for controlling the permissions that users, programs, and Internet sites have to access your computer through PowerPoint. After clicking the Trust Center category in the PowerPoint Options dialog box, you can click the Trust Center Settings button to access it.

Setting Up Trusted Locations

A *trusted location* is a location that you verify to be threat-free. When a presentation file is stored in a trusted location, PowerPoint allows macros to run without the usual safeguards (discussed later in this chapter). To allow free access to your macros in a presentation file, you should store it in a trusted location.

The following folders are trusted by default:

- `Users\`*username*`\AppData\Roaming\Microsoft\Templates`
- `Users\`*username*`\AppData\Roaming\Microsoft\Addins`
- `Program Files\Microsoft Office\Templates`
- `Program Files\Microsoft Office\Document Themes 15`

You can also add more trusted locations. For example, you may want to trust a folder in which you store your presentation files for a certain client.

To add a trusted location, follow these steps:

1. **Choose File ⇨ Options.**
2. **Click Trust Center, and click the Trust Center Settings button.**
3. **Click Trusted Locations.** A list of currently trusted locations appears, as shown in Figure 22.1.

FIGURE 22.1

You can set up new trusted locations in the Trust Center dialog box.

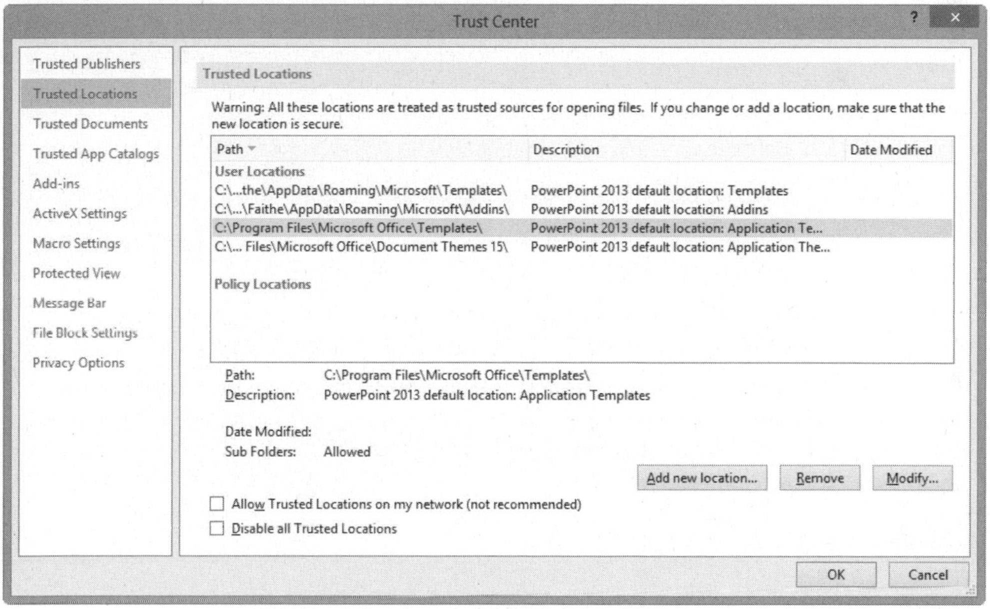

4. **Click Add New Location.**
5. **Click the Browse button, and browse to the location you want.** If you want, select the Subfolders of This Location Are Also Trusted check box.
6. **Click OK.**
7. **Click OK to close the Trust Center dialog box.**
8. **Click OK to close the PowerPoint Options dialog box.**

Figure 22.1 shows other settings and buttons that you can also select:

■ **Allow Trusted Locations on My Network.** Enables you to add trusted locations that exist other than on your local computer.

- **Disable All Trusted Locations.** This setting does just what its name says. You will learn more about trusted publishers in the next section.
- **Remove.** Removes a trusted location from the list. (There is no confirmation; it is removed immediately.)
- **Modify.** Opens the Trusted Location dialog box for a location so that you can change its path or options.

Working with Trusted Publishers

Another way to trust a macro is to verify that it comes from a trusted publisher. The macro settings (covered in a later section) enable you to specify what should happen when a macro from a trusted publisher wants to run outside of a trusted location.

When you open a presentation that includes one or more signed macros, PowerPoint asks you whether or not you want to trust macros from that signer. Information about the signer's certificate appears, including the name, the issuing authority, and the valid dates. If you choose Yes, then this signer is added to your Trusted Publishers list. If you have not yet added a signer to the Trusted Publishers list, the list will be blank in the Trust Center dialog box.

If you have a trusted publisher on your list, you can select it and then click View to view its information or click Remove to remove it from the Trusted Publishers list.

Trusted Documents and Protected View Settings

When you open a presentation that is not from a trusted location or trusted publisher, it opens in an uneditable mode; you must click Enable Content on the information bar that appears across the top of the window to trust that document (see Figure 22.2) or choose File ➪ Info ➪ Enable Editing.

FIGURE 22.2

A warning appears when you access a file that originated from outside your trusted locations.

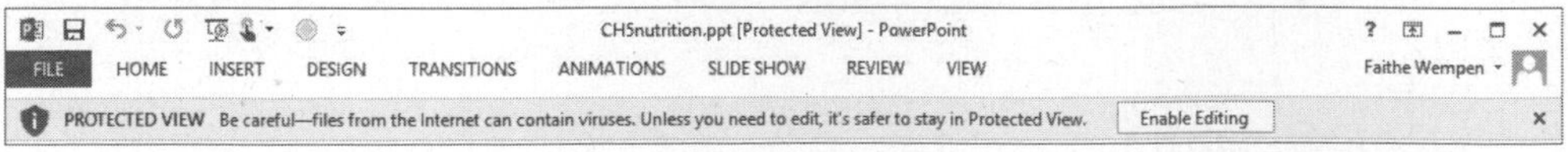

The Trust Center has several settings for managing the process of trusting a document (or not). First, in the Trusted Documents category, you can set these options:

- **Allow Documents on a Network to Be Trusted.** If you clear this check box, documents that originate from a source other than your own computer will not be editable.
- **Disable Trusted Documents.** If you mark this check box, it completely disables the ability to trust any documents, whether on a network or your own PC.

In the Protected View category, you can then fine-tune the criteria for a document being protected:

- **Enable Protected View for Files Originating from the Internet.** This includes presentations you download from websites.

- **Enable Protected View for Files Located in Potentially Unsafe Locations.** This includes presentations stored on your local hard disk but not in locations marked as Trusted (see "Setting Up Trusted Locations" earlier in this chapter).

- **Enable Protected View for Outlook Attachments.** This includes any presentations that you have received as e-mail attachments in Outlook.

Add-Ins

You will learn about managing add-ins later in this chapter; they extend PowerPoint's functionality by integrating mini-programs written by third-party individuals or companies not affiliated with Microsoft. Add-ins can often dramatically extend the capabilities of an application by adding new tabs on the Ribbon, new buttons, and more. Because they connect with the application at a fairly low level, they can be devastating if they contain viruses. (It is not common for add-ins to contain viruses, but you never know what could happen.)

In the Add-Ins section of the Trust Center, you can specify the criteria for add-ins being able to run:

- **Require Application Add-Ins to Be Signed by Trusted Publisher.** Prevents unsigned add-ins from being installed. Trusted publishers are defined and configured in the Trusted Publishers section, discussed earlier in this chapter.

- **Disable Notification for Unsigned Add-Ins.** Prevents a warning from appearing when an add-in is disabled because it is not signed. This is applicable only if the preceding option is selected.

- **Disable All Application Add-Ins.** Prevents all add-ins from running, regardless of the signed or unsigned status.

ActiveX Settings

ActiveX controls are somewhat like add-ins or macros; they are more commonly used on web pages, but sometimes PowerPoint files (or other Office files) contain them as well. They extend the functionality of the program in some way.

In the ActiveX Settings for All Office Applications section, you can choose a level of permission for ActiveX controls, ranging from disabling all of them to enabling all of them. See Figure 22.3.

FIGURE 22.3

Specify what level of permission ActiveX controls should have.

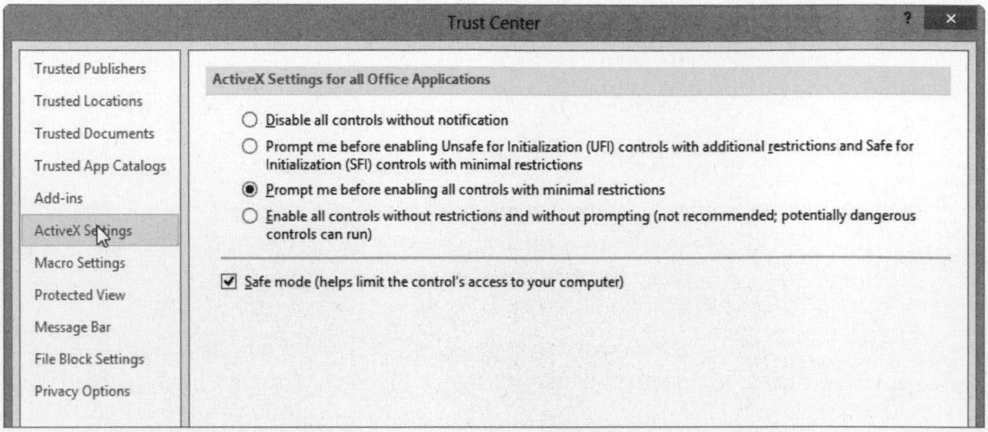

Macro Settings

Macro settings apply only to macros that are stored in presentations that are not in trusted locations. These settings determine whether or not the macro should run and whether you should receive notification, as shown in Figure 22.4.

FIGURE 22.4

You can specify what should happen when a presentation outside a trusted location tries to run a macro.

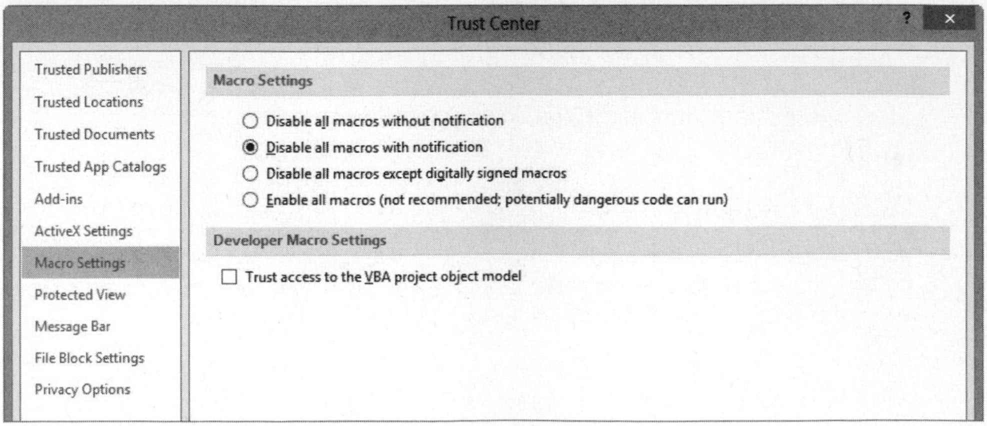

Message Bar

By default, when content is blocked, a message bar appears between the Ribbon and the presentation to let you know what has happened. You can enable or disable the appearance of this message bar.

File Block Settings

In this area of the Trust Center, you can prevent certain file types from being opened or saved via PowerPoint. If you place a check mark in the Open column for a certain file type, PowerPoint either prevents it from opening at all or opens it in Protected view, depending on the Open Behavior for Selected File Types setting (at the bottom of the dialog box). If you place a check mark in the Save column, PowerPoint will prevent the file from being saved. See Figure 22.5.

FIGURE 22.5

You can block certain file types from being saved or opened or force them to be opened in Protected view.

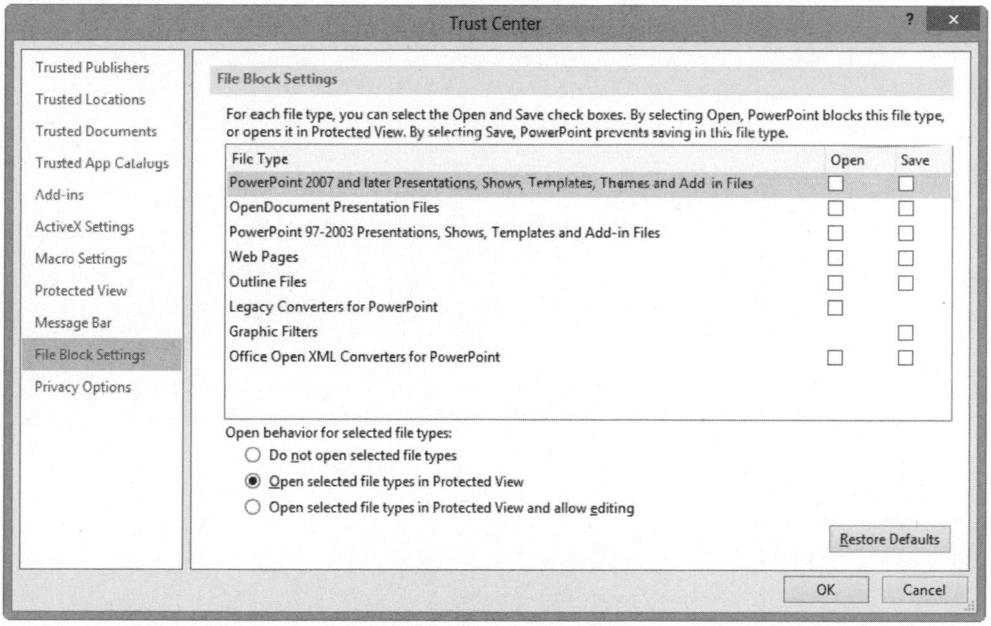

Privacy Options

It is usually safe to connect to the Internet to download content such as clip art and templates and to send feedback to Microsoft about errors and usage. However, some people are concerned about security and prefer to control their computer's connection to outside sources such as the Internet. (Yes, I know, just because you are paranoid does not mean that someone is not out to get you.) In the Privacy Options category, you can find a set of check boxes you can use to specify what connectivity to allow.

Customizing the Ribbon

You can customize any part of the Ribbon in PowerPoint 2013. You can even create your own new tabs, making it possible to consolidate the commands you use most often on a single tab for greater efficiency.

Minimizing the Ribbon

If you aren't using the Ribbon at the moment, you can hide it to get extra space on the screen to see more text at once. There are several ways to do this:

- Right-click any button on either the Ribbon or the Quick Access Toolbar and choose Collapse the Ribbon.
- Click the up-pointing arrow on the far right end of the Ribbon.
- Press Ctrl+F1.

To redisplay it again, do any of the following:

- Right-click any button on the Quick Access Toolbar and choose Collapse the Ribbon to toggle the option off.
- Click any tab to display the Ribbon temporarily, and then click the pushpin icon on the far right end of the Ribbon.
- Press Ctrl+F1.

Displaying or Hiding Ribbon Tabs

If there are certain tabs you never use, you might want to hide them. (You can always change your mind later and redisplay them.)

To choose which tabs display, follow these steps:

1. **Right-click any button on the Ribbon and choose Customize the Ribbon.** The PowerPoint Options dialog box opens with the Customize Ribbon tab displayed.
2. **Mark or clear the check boxes as needed for each Ribbon tab listed in the right pane.** See Figure 22.6.
3. **Click OK.**

Some of the tabs listed in Figure 22.6 are not displayed all the time. For example, the Slide Master tab appears only when you are working in Slide Master view. If you disable one of these tabs and then perform an action that would normally make that tab appear, it won't appear. This can be perplexing to someone else using your computer who doesn't know you've hidden it — or even to yourself if you forgot you did.

FIGURE 22.6

You can turn certain tabs on or off.

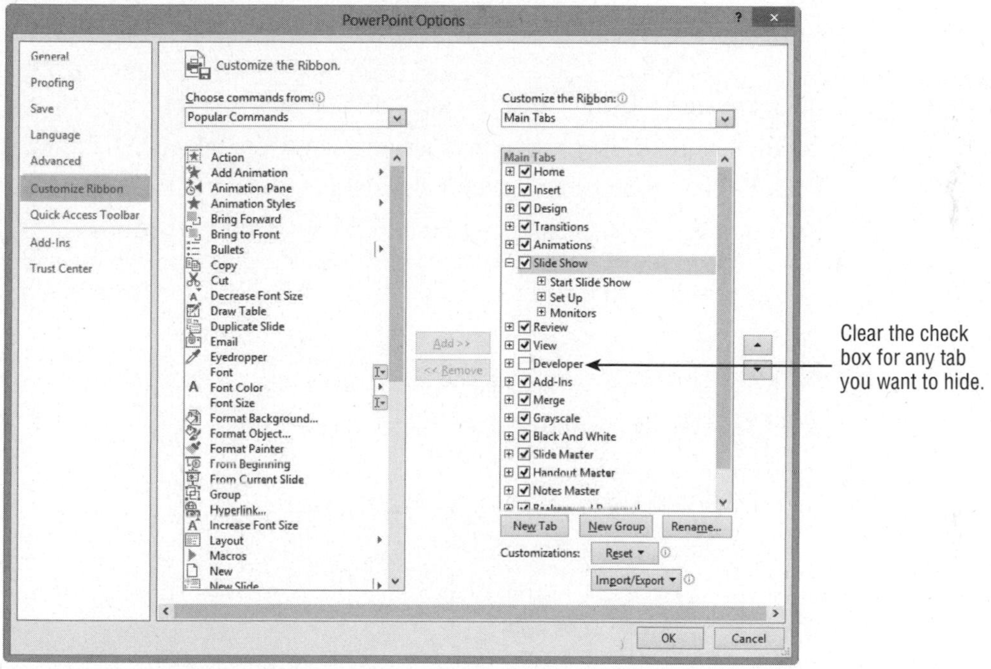

Clear the check box for any tab you want to hide.

Creating or Deleting a Tab or a Custom Group

You can add any command to any tab as long as it is in a custom group (that is, a user-created group). Therefore, you have to create the custom group first, before you can start customizing an existing tab. If desired, you can create a whole new tab first and then create your custom groups on that new tab.

Creating a Custom Tab

To create your own tab, follow these steps:

1. **Right-click any button on the Ribbon and choose Customize the Ribbon.** The PowerPoint Options dialog box opens with the Customize Ribbon tab displayed.

2. **On the Main Tabs list (right side of dialog box), click the existing tab that the new one should appear after (that is, to the right of).**

3. **Click New Tab.** A new tab appears on the list called New Tab (Custom). By default, it has one group in it: New Group (Custom). See Figure 22.7.

FIGURE 22.7

When you create a custom tab, a custom group is automatically created in it.

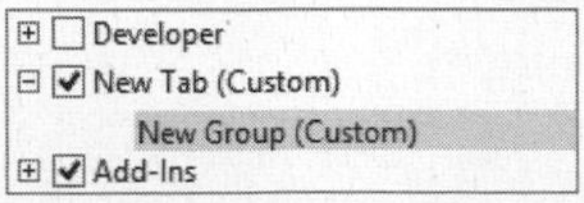

4. **Click the new tab, and click the Rename button.**
5. **In the Rename dialog box, type a new name for the tab and click OK.**
6. **Click the new group within that new tab, and rename it the same way.**

The dialog box for renaming a group is different from that for renaming a tab; it contains icons as well as a text box, as shown in Figure 22.8. An icon appears when a group is collapsed (for example, when the PowerPoint window is not wide enough to show it).

FIGURE 22.8

When renaming a group, you can also choose its icon.

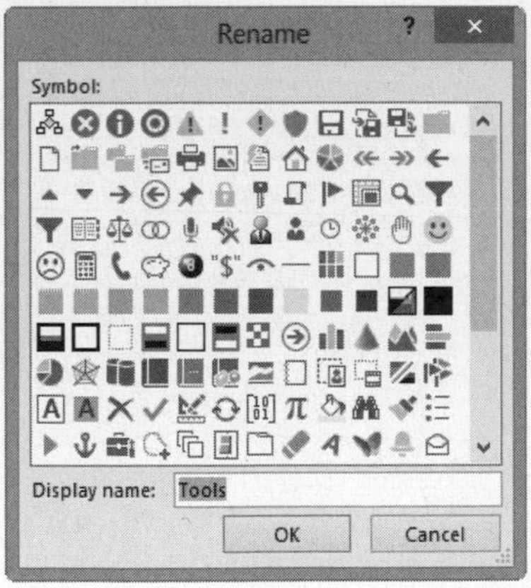

7. **Click OK to close the dialog box, or leave it open for more editing.**

Creating a Custom Group

As you just saw, when you create a new tab, you also get a group with it automatically. You can add more groups to your new tab, and you can also add groups to existing tabs.

Here's how to create a custom group on an existing tab:

1. **If the PowerPoint Options dialog box is not already open, right-click any button on the Ribbon and choose Customize the Ribbon.**
2. **Click the tab on which you want to create the new group.**

3. **Click New Group.** A new group is added to that tab, with the name New Group (Custom).

   All custom groups have the same name by default; PowerPoint does not number them or give them sequential names.

4. **(Optional) Rename the group:**

   a. Click Rename.

   b. Type a new name for the group.

   c. Click an icon for the group. (This icon will appear if the group is collapsed because of inadequate window width to display it.) See Figure 22.8.

   d. Click OK.

5. **Click OK to close the dialog box, or leave it open for more editing.**

Adding or Removing Commands

You can't remove the standard commands on any of the built-in tabs; only the groups and commands you have placed yourself can be modified.

> **NOTE**
>
> Before you add a command to the Ribbon, consider whether it might be better to add it to the Quick Access Toolbar instead (covered later in this chapter). The Quick Access Toolbar is always available, regardless of which tab is displayed. This can save you a step in executing the command because you never have to change tabs to get to it.

Adding a Command

To add a command, follow these steps:

1. **Select the custom group to which you want to add the command.** (Remember, you can't add commands to built-in groups.)

2. **On the list at the left, select the command to add.**

   You may wish to narrow down the list of commands by making a selection from the drop-down list first. For example, you could choose Commands Not on the Ribbon to exclude commands that are already on other tabs.

3. **Click the Add button.** The command appears under the group name on the left side of the window.

4. **Click OK to close the dialog box, or leave it open for more editing.**

Removing a Command

To remove a command, follow these steps:

1. **Right-click the command you want to remove.**

2. **Click Remove.**

Alternately, you can click the Remove button to the left of the tabs list.

The command is removed from the custom group but is still available on the list on the left so that you can add it later to some other group or tab.

Renaming or Reordering Tabs

You can change the entire look of the Ribbon by renaming and/or reordering its tabs.

Any tab can be renamed, even the built-in ones. Just right-click it and choose Rename, or click the Rename button and then type the new name. PowerPoint does not check whether each name is unique, so you can name them all the same thing if you like. (That wouldn't be very useful, though.)

To move a tab or group, right-click it and then click Move Up or Move Down, or use the Move Up or Move Down button.

Resetting Customizations

It's easy to get carried away with customizing PowerPoint and end up with an interface you barely recognize. If this happens, reset the Ribbon to its original state and start over.

To reset only one tab, do the following:

1. **If the PowerPoint Options dialog box is not already open, right-click any button on the Ribbon and choose Customize Ribbon.**
2. **Click the Reset button.** A menu opens.
3. **Click Reset Only Selected Ribbon Tab.**
4. **Click OK to close the dialog box, or leave it open for further editing.**

To reset all customization, including any custom shortcut keys and the Quick Access Toolbar, do the following:

1. **If the PowerPoint Options dialog box is not already open, right-click any button on the Ribbon and choose Customize Ribbon.**
2. **Click the Reset button.** A menu opens.
3. **Click Reset All Customizations.**
4. **Click OK to close the dialog box, or leave it open for further editing.**

Importing and Exporting Customization Settings

After you get the Ribbon and other program options just the way you like them, what happens if you need to switch to a different computer? The good news is you don't have to recustomize everything; you can export your customization settings to a file. Then you can transfer that file to the other PC and import the customization settings there.

Exporting Customization

To export your customization settings, follow these steps:

1. **If the PowerPoint Options dialog box is not already open, right-click any button on the Ribbon and choose Customize Ribbon.**

2. **Click the Import/Export button.** A menu opens.

3. **Click Export All Customizations.** The File Save dialog box opens.

4. **(Optional) Change the filename and location if desired.** You might save the file to a USB flash drive, for example, or a network location that is accessible on both PCs.

5. **Click Save.**

6. **Click OK to close the PowerPoint Options dialog box.**

Importing Customization

User interface configuration files like the one you just saved in the preceding section can be imported into PowerPoint 2013 on any other PC. Importing will wipe out any customization settings on the other PC, so before you do this, make sure there are no customizations that you want to keep and you can't reproduce. Make sure that the PC receiving the customization settings can access the file where you stored the settings. Then follow these steps to import:

1. **If the PowerPoint Options dialog box is not already open, right-click any button on the Ribbon and choose Customize Ribbon.**

2. **Click the Import/Export button.** A menu opens.

3. **Click Import Customization File.**

4. **Select the customization file and click Open.**

5. **A confirmation box appears; click Yes.**

6. **Click OK to close the PowerPoint Options dialog box.**

Customizing the Quick Access Toolbar

The Quick Access Toolbar, or QAT, is the row of buttons above the File button, in the upper-left corner of the PowerPoint window. It contains a few buttons by default, such as Save, Undo, and Redo, and you can add others to it. For example, I use Format Painter a lot, but every time I need it, I don't want to have to click the Home tab. By adding Format Painter to the QAT, I make it available all of the time, and I don't have to remember which tab it is on.

Adding Common Commands

PowerPoint maintains a short list of popular commands that you can quickly turn on or off on the QAT. To do so, click the down arrow at the right end of the QAT and then select a command from the menu to toggle it on or off. See Figure 22.9.

FIGURE 22.9

Certain commands can be toggled on or off on the QAT via its menu.

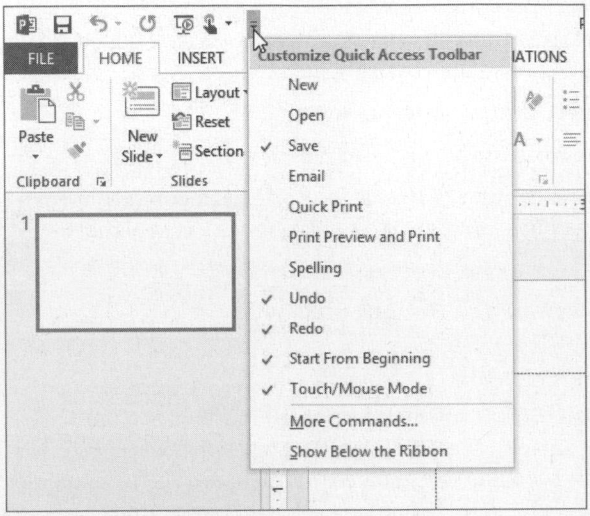

Adding Already-Available Commands to the QAT

If the command is already available on a tab or menu, then adding it to the QAT is easy. Just right-click it and choose Add to Quick Access Toolbar. You can use this method to combine all of your most-used commands and buttons in a single location so that you do not have to switch among the tabs as frequently.

However, in order for you to use this method, the command already has to be available somewhere within PowerPoint's Ribbon or Office menu. As a result, you cannot use this method to add capabilities to PowerPoint that it does not already have by default.

Removing Commands from the QAT

To remove a command from the QAT, right-click it on the QAT and choose Remove from Quick Access Toolbar. If you want to add it again later, you can use the method in the preceding section if the command exists on a tab or menu. You can use the method in the following section if it does not or if you cannot seem to find it on any of the tabs or menus.

Adding Other Commands to the QAT

Besides the standard set of commands, PowerPoint also contains a secret list of extra commands and capabilities. Most of these are old features from previous versions of PowerPoint that Microsoft is phasing out or features for which there was no room on the Ribbon. For example, the Nudge commands are not on the main Ribbon by default (Nudge Left, Nudge Right, and so on).

To add a command to the QAT, follow these steps:

1. **Right-click the QAT and choose Customize Quick Access Toolbar.**

2. **Open the Customize Quick Access Toolbar drop-down list (on the right), and choose For All Documents, or choose a particular presentation name from the list.** You can only customize for either one presentation or for all presentations. If you're customizing for one presentation, that presentation must be open.

3. **Open the Choose Commands From drop-down list and select a category.** There are categories for every tab as well as some extra ones at the top of the list:

   - **Popular.** A selection of the most commonly used commands.

   - **Commands Not in the Ribbon.** The collection of commands that do not have Ribbon or Office menu equivalents; this is where you will find the hidden goodies.

   - **All Commands.** A complete list of all commands; use this list when you think a command is already available on a tab but you do not know which one.

   - **Macros.** Any macros stored in the current presentation or template appear here.

4. **Select a command from the list, and click the Add>> button to move it to the Customize Quick Access Toolbar list, as shown in Figure 22.10.**

5. **Add any other commands that you want.**

6. **(Optional) Perform any of the following tasks, if necessary:**

   - To reset the QAT, click Reset.

   - To modify a macro after adding it to the QAT, select it and click Modify.

   - To change the order in which buttons appear on the QAT, select a button and click the Up or Down arrow button to the right of the listing.

7. **Click OK to accept the changes.**

Managing Add-Ins

Add-ins are extra features that you can install for PowerPoint that extend its capabilities in some way. You can add, remove, or temporarily enable/disable the various add-ins in PowerPoint to control how it behaves.

One of the most powerful types of add-ins is a Component Object Model (COM) add-in. COM add-ins are supplemental programs that extend PowerPoint's capabilities by adding custom commands or features. COM add-ins can come from Microsoft or from third-party sources. They usually have a `.dll` or `.exe` filename extension and are written in a programming language such as Visual Basic or C++. For example, if you have Adobe Acrobat installed on your system, you might have PDF Maker add-ins that help you create PDF files from Office content.

FIGURE 22.10

You can add commands to the Quick Access Toolbar.

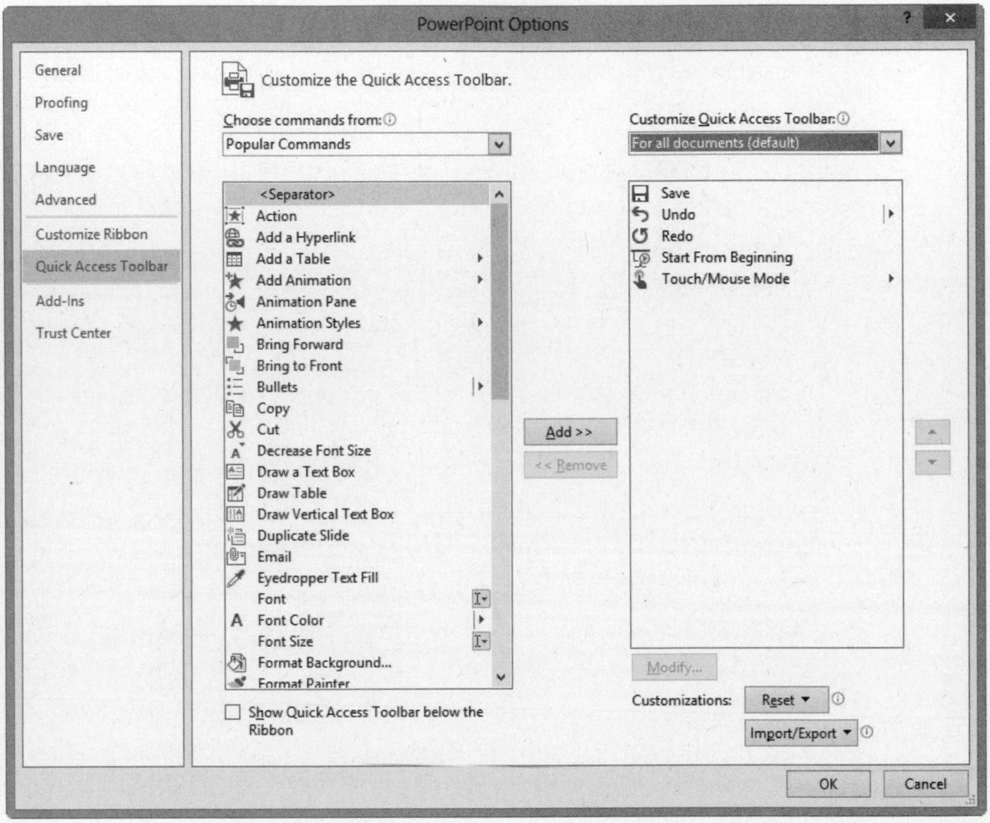

To view installed add-ins, follow these steps:

1. **Choose File ⇨ Options.**
2. **Click Add-Ins.** A list of installed add-ins appears (see Figure 22.11).

An installed add-in can be either enabled or disabled. Having the option of disabling an add-in rather than removing it entirely is handy because it allows you to turn one off temporarily without losing it. Disabling add-ins is also helpful for troubleshooting. If you are not sure what add-in is causing PowerPoint to crash, you can disable them all and then enable them one at a time until you find the problem.

To disable or remove an add-in, you need to know what type it is because the steps are different for the various types. To determine a type, look in the Type column.

Based on the type, open the Manage drop-down list at the bottom of the dialog box and select the desired add-in type. Then click Go to open a dialog box interface specifically for that type of add-in.

FIGURE 22.11

See a list of installed add-ins here.

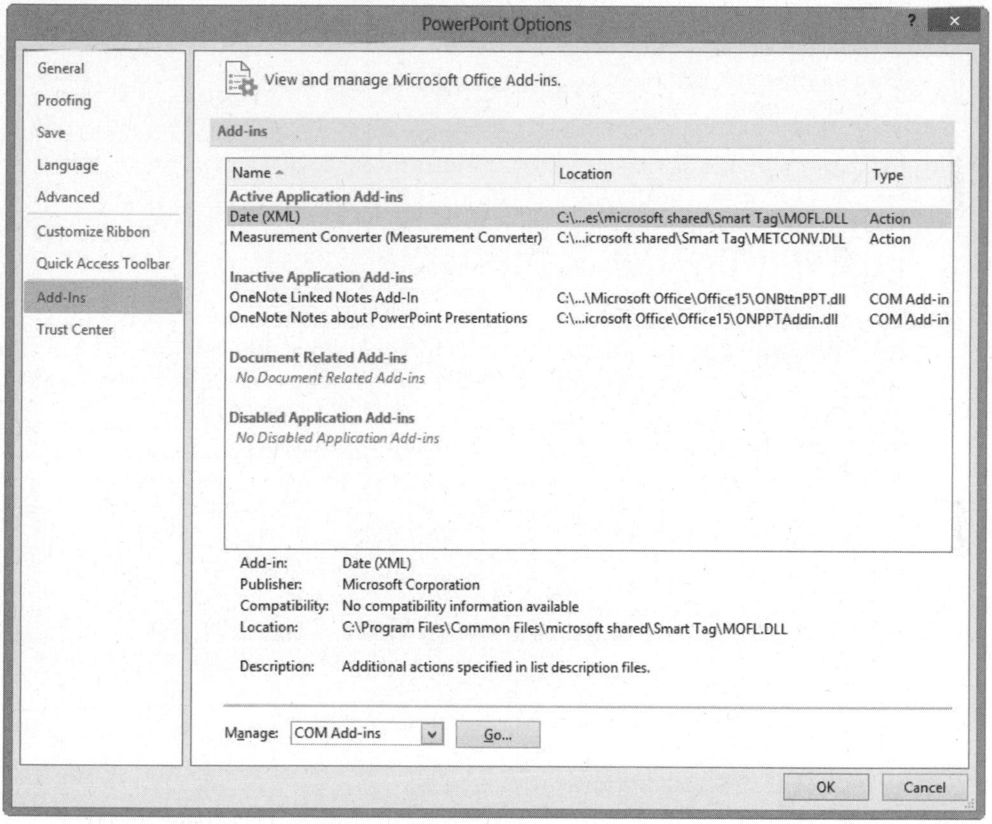

Enabling/Disabling COM Add-Ins

Choose COM Add-Ins in the Manage drop-down list and click Go to display the COM Add-Ins dialog box. It lists the available COM add-ins; you can select one and click Remove, or you can change its load behavior. You can also click Add to add more COM add-ins, although most COM add-ins come with their own setup programs that do that part for you.

Enabling Actions

Choose Actions in the Manage drop-down list and click Go to display the AutoCorrect dialog box with the Actions tab selected. From here, you can click More Actions to add additional actions to PowerPoint, or click an existing action on the Available Actions list and then click Properties to configure it.

Enabling/Disabling PowerPoint Add-Ins

PowerPoint add-ins, which are usually written by a third party, are specific to PowerPoint (not generic to all Office apps, as Actions are).

From the Manage drop-down list, choose PowerPoint Add-Ins, and click Go. The Add-Ins dialog box opens. Add, remove, or enable/disable each add-in as desired.

Customizing the Status Bar

The status bar is the bar across the bottom of the PowerPoint window, where the Zoom slider and view buttons appear. You can customize what appears there by right-clicking the status bar and marking or clearing the check boxes on the menu that appears. See Figure 22.12.

FIGURE 22.12

Right-click the status bar and choose commands to display or hide on it.

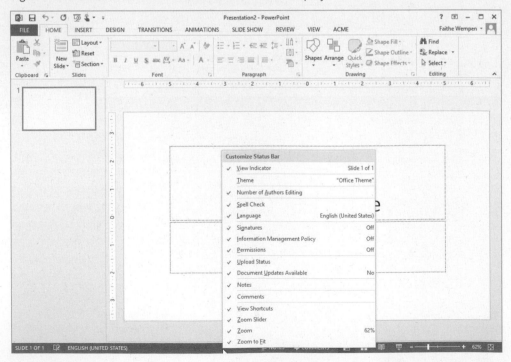

Summary

In this final chapter of the book, you learned how to customize PowerPoint in a variety of ways. You learned how to set program defaults, configure the Trust Center, customize the Ribbon and Quick Access Toolbar, and manage add-ins.

Congratulations on completing your PowerPoint education! I hope you have found this book interesting and useful and will continue learning about PowerPoint on your own.

22

Part IV

Project Labs

IN THIS PART

Presenting Content without Bulleted Lists

IN THIS LAB

Using shapes as text boxes

Converting bulleted lists to SmartArt

I n this lab, you have the opportunity to practice several ways of serving up content that's free from the traditional bulleted-list structure.

You are creating slides for a computer technology teacher to use in a class on PC hardware. The lecture she is preparing for involves safety issues when working on a PC.

Please visit www.wiley.com/go/powerpoint2013bible to download the files you need for the project labs.

Lab 1A: Using Shapes as Text Boxes

In this lab session, you create a set of starbursts and use them as text boxes.

Level of difficulty: Moderate

Time to complete: 10 to 20 minutes

1. **Open the file Lab1A.pptx from the Labs folder on the book's companion website and save it as MyLab1A.pptx.**

2. **Insert a new slide that uses the Title Only layout.**

    a. On the Home tab, click the down arrow below New Slide.

    b. Click Title Only.

    c. In the title box, type **Protect Yourself from Hazards**.

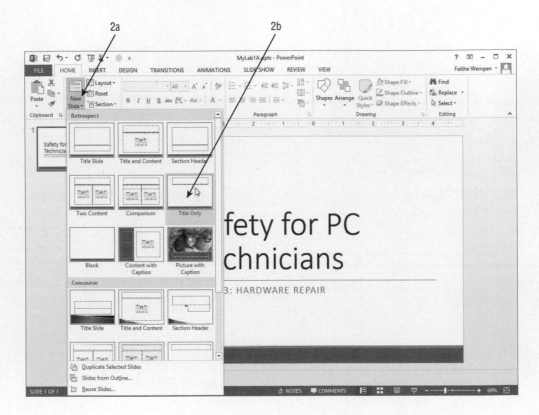

3. **Draw an Explosion shape on the slide.**

   a. On the Insert tab, open the Shapes gallery and choose Explosion 1 from the Stars and Banners section.

   b. Drag on the slide to create the shape (any size).

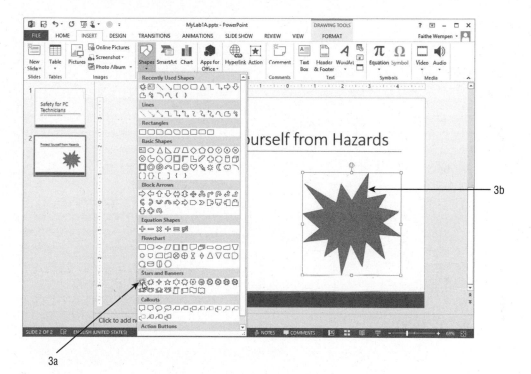

4. **Apply a white, orange, and red path gradient to the shape.**

   a. Click the shape to select it.

   b. On the Drawing Tools Format tab, open the Shape Fill button's menu and select Gradient ⇨ More Gradients.

   c. In the task pane, click Gradient Fill.

   d. Set Type to Path.

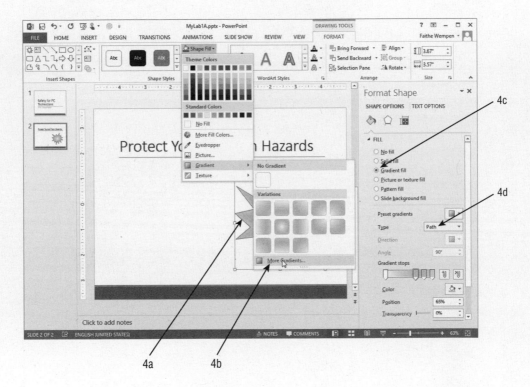

e. In the Gradient Stops section, open the Color button's menu and choose white.

f. Click the second stop position marker from the left on the gradient line and drag it to 65%.

TIP
Alternatively, you can set Position to 65% instead of dragging the marker.

g. Open the Color button's menu and choose the bright-orange Standard color.

h. Click the third stop position marker from the left on the gradient line.

i. Click the Remove Gradient Stop button.

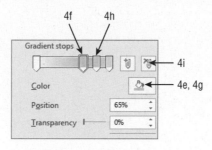

j. Click the rightmost stop position marker on the gradient line.

k. Open the Color button's menu and choose the bright-red Standard color.

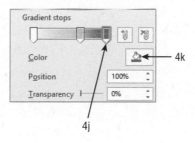

5. **Remove the shape's outline.**

   a. At the bottom of the task pane, click the Line heading to expand the Line options.

   b. If needed, scroll down in the task pane so the Line options become visible.

   c. Click No Line.

   d. Close the task pane.

6. **Size the shape to 3"× 3" and position it below the word *Hazards*.**

   a. Click the shape to select it if it is not already selected.

   b. On the Drawing Tools Format tab, in the Size group, set the Height and Width values to 3" each.

   c. Drag the shape so that it is about 1/2 inch below the word *Hazards* and centered beneath it horizontally.

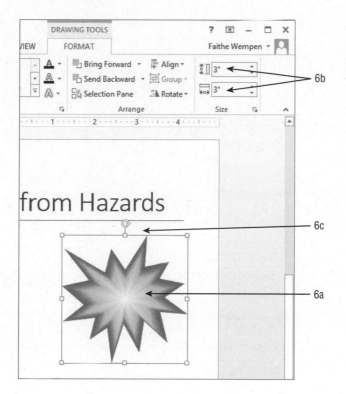

7. **Create a copy of the shape, and flip it horizontally.**

   a. Hold down the Ctrl key and drag the shape to the left, creating a copy next to the original. (Optional: You can hold down Shift to maintain horizontal position.)

   b. On the Drawing Tools Format tab, click Rotate, and click Flip Horizontal.

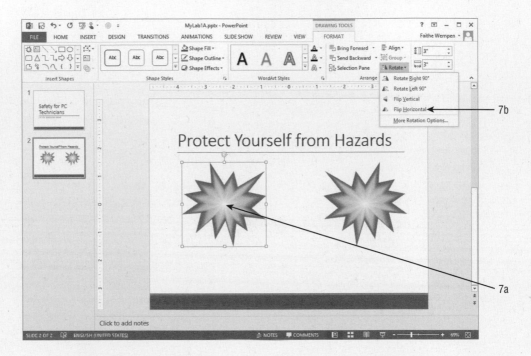

8. **Modify the gradient for the copy so that it uses bright yellow instead of red.**

   a. Select the copy you just made.

   b. Open the Shape Fill button's menu and choose Gradient ⇨ More Gradients.

   c. Click the marker at the 100% position on the gradient scale.

   d. Open the Color button's menu and choose the bright-yellow Standard color.

   e. Close the task pane.

8a

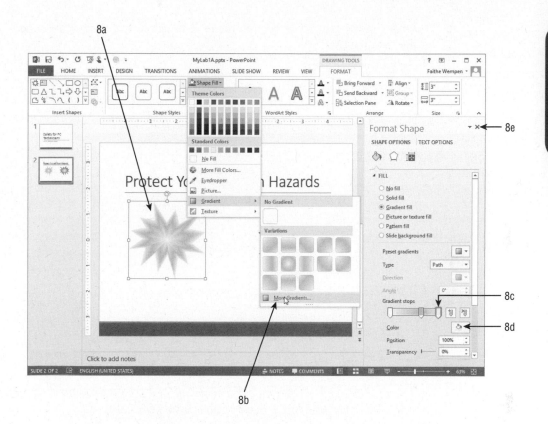

8e

8c

8d

8b

1

9. **Move the yellow shape so that it barely overlaps the red shape.**

   a. Select the yellow shape.

   b. Drag the yellow shape to the right until the tips of its points barely overlap the tips of the red shape's points.

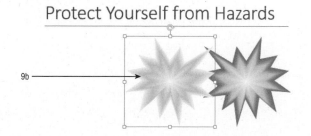

9b

10. **Create a copy of the red shape, and place it to the left of the yellow shape, barely overlapping it.**

    a. Select the red shape.

    b. Hold down the Ctrl key and drag the red shape to the left, releasing the mouse button when the new shape barely overlaps the yellow shape.

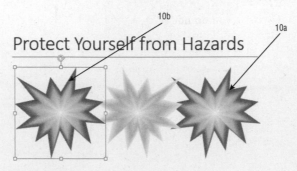

11. **In the red shape on the left, type** Watch for protruding wires **and change the text color to black.**

    a. Click the left shape.

    b. Type **Watch for protruding wires**. The text appears in white.

    c. Select the text you just typed.

    d. On the Drawing Tools Format tab, in the WordArt Styles group, click Text Fill and change the text to the black swatch in the color theme.

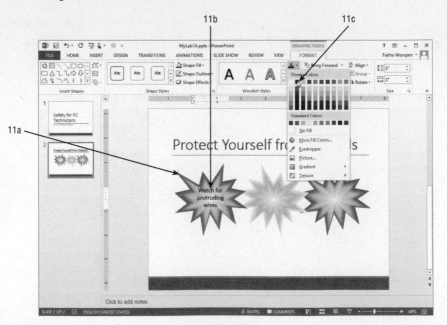

12. **In the yellow shape (center), type** Don't wear dangling jewelry **and change the text color to black.**

13. **In the red shape on the right, type** Inner edges of cases may be sharp **and change the text color to black.**

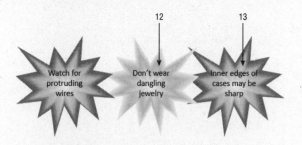

14. **Apply animation so that each shape pinwheels in individually when you click the mouse.**

    a. Select the red shape on the left.

    b. On the Animations tab, click Add Animation.

    c. Click More Entrance Effects.

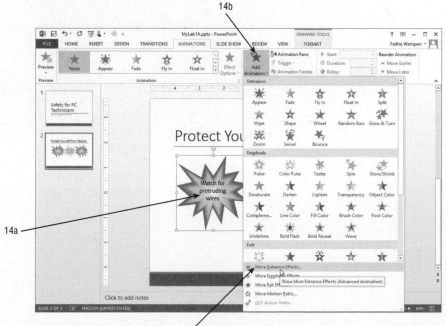

d. In the Add Entrance Effect dialog box, choose Pinwheel.

e. Click OK.

15. **Use the Animation Painter to apply the same pinwheel entrance effect to the other two shapes (individually).**

a. Select the left shape.

b. On the Animations tab, click Animation Painter.

c. Click the center shape.

d. Click Animation Painter again.

e. Click the right shape.

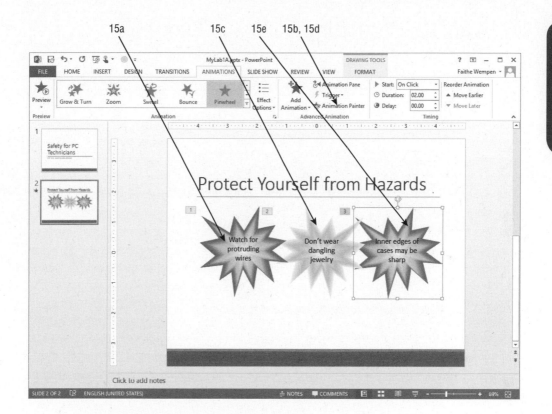

16. **Check the animation in Slide Show view.**

    a. Click the Slide Show View button in the status bar.

    b. Click the mouse and watch the first shape appear. Repeat for each shape.

    c. Press Esc to return to Normal view.

17. **Save your work and close the presentation file.**

    You should have saved the file in step 1 as MyLab1A.pptx, so you can simply resave with the Save button on the Quick Access Toolbar.

Lab 1B: Converting Bullets to SmartArt

If a presentation is already set up using bulleted lists, you might not want to take the time to retype them in shapes. You can easily convert a bulleted list to SmartArt in PowerPoint, making the list appear more graphical and interesting. In this exercise, you create a bulleted list and then convert it to SmartArt.

Level of difficulty: Easy

Time to complete: 5 to 10 minutes

1. **Open the file** `Lab1B.pptx` **from the Labs folder on the book's companion website and save it as** `MyLab1B.pptx`.

2. **Convert the content on slide #2 to SmartArt.**

   a. Display slide #2 (Electrostatic Discharge).

   b. Right-click the content (text) placeholder and choose Convert to SmartArt.

   c. Click the Vertical Bullet List type (leftmost on the top row).

   The list is converted to a SmartArt diagram.

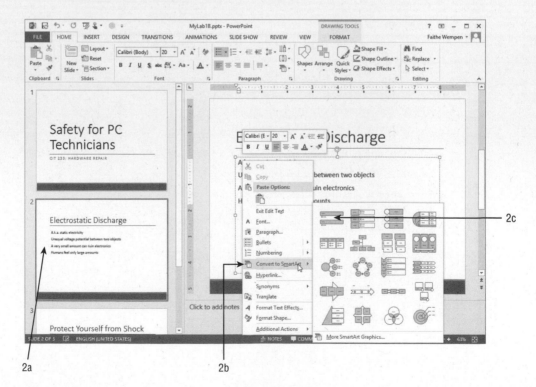

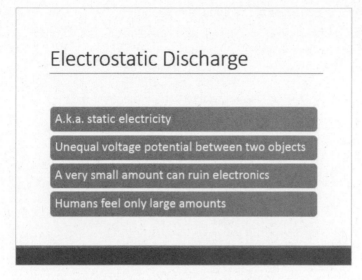

3. **Convert the content on slide #3 to SmartArt.**

   a. Display slide #3 (Protect Yourself from Shock).

   b. Right-click the slide content (the bulleted list) and choose Convert to SmartArt.

   c. Click the Vertical Block List type (second from the left on the top row).

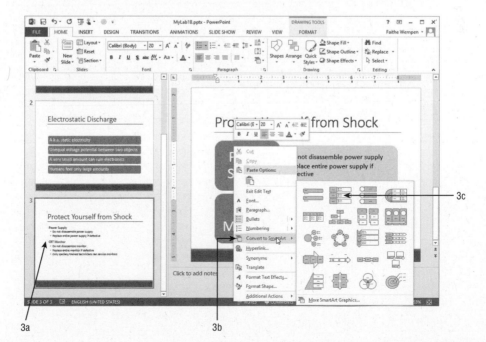

4. **Apply a Quick Style to the SmartArt on slide #3.**

    a. On the SmartArt Tools Design tab, open the SmartArt Styles gallery and click the second 3-D style.

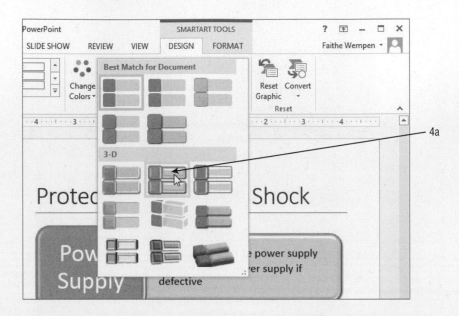

5. **Change the colors for the SmartArt on slide #3 to Colorful – Accent Colors.**

    a. On the SmartArt Tools Design tab, click Change Colors and click the first color set in the Colorful section.

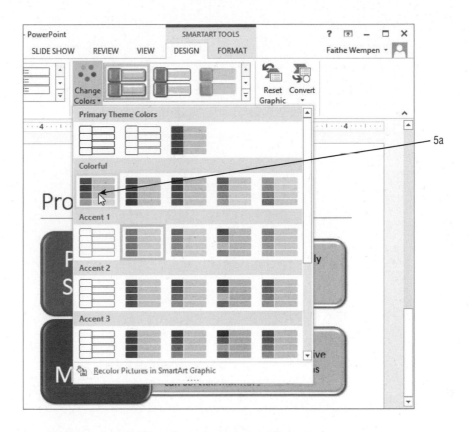

6. **Save your work and close the presentation file.**

You should have saved the file in step 1 as MyLab1B.pptx, so you can simply resave with the Save button on the Quick Access Toolbar.

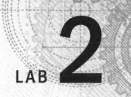
Adding Sound and Movement to a Presentation

IN THIS LAB

Applying custom animations

Assigning transitions to slides

Adding a musical soundtrack from a file

I n an ideal world, you'd have great video equipment to create live-action movies for your audiences, but that's not always the case. Often you're stuck with a bunch of static images, and you need to make them as lively and animated as possible within the confines of PowerPoint.

In this lab, you animate a presentation for Spice Meadow Shelties, a small kennel that breeds pure-bred Shetland sheepdogs. The graphics and text are already in place. Your job is to apply animations and transitions to make the presentation more interesting and appealing.

Please visit www.wiley.com/go/powerpoint2013bible to download the files you need for the project labs.

Lab 2A: Fading Text and Graphics In and Out

In this lab session, you add some text to a slide. You then animate it and the photos so that the first set fades in and out and then the other set fades in. Even though the text and pictures seem to overlap in Normal view, they appear at different times in Slide Show view so there is no conflict.

Level of difficulty: Moderate

Time to complete: 15 to 30 minutes

1. **Open the file** `Lab2A.pptx` **and save it as** `MyLab2A.pptx`.
2. **On the Animations tab, click Animation Pane to open the Animation pane.**

3. **On slide #2, set up the Champion Sires text box to appear by fading in when the slide first appears.**

   a. Select the text box on the left (Champion Sires).

   b. Choose Animations ⇨ Advanced Animations ⇨ Add Animation ⇨ More Entrance Effects.

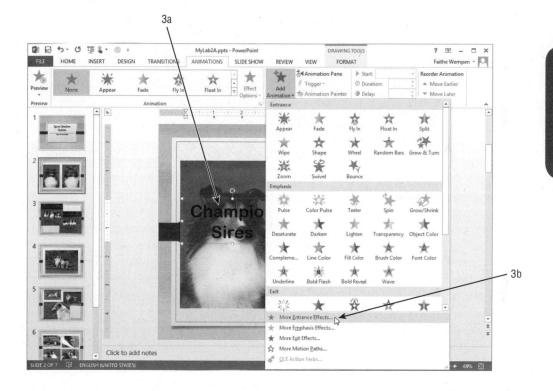

c. In the Add Entrance Effect dialog box, choose Fade.

d. Click OK.

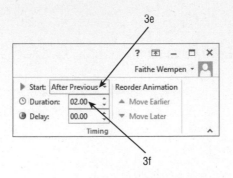

e. Open the Start drop-down list and choose After Previous.

f. In the Duration box, click the Up increment arrow until the value is 2 seconds.

4. **Set up the picture on the right to appear by fading in simultaneously with the text that you animated in step 3.**

a. Select the picture on the right (not the text box).

b. Choose Add Animation ⇨ Fade. (Notice that Fade is on the top-level list because you recently used it. It might have already been in step 3, but it was good to learn the other technique.)

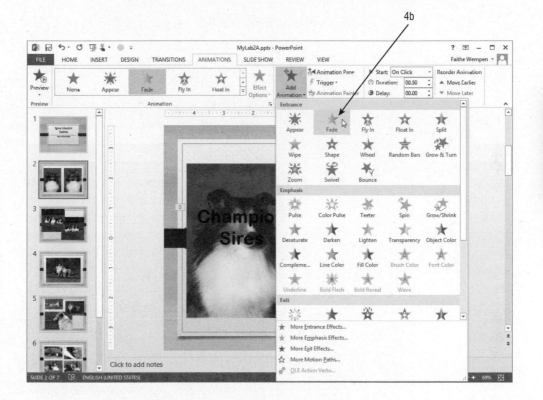

c. Open the Start drop-down list on the Animations tab of the Ribbon and choose With Previous.

d. In the Duration box, click the Up increment arrow until the value is 2 seconds.

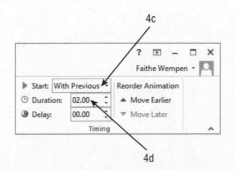

5. **Repeat steps 3 and 4, but this time set up exit effects instead of entrance effects.**

   a. Create an exit effect for the left text box set to occur After Previous. Set the duration for 2 seconds.

   b. Create an exit effect for the right picture set to occur With Previous. Set the duration for 2 seconds.

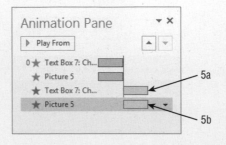

6. **Create a delay of 5 seconds between the text box's entrance and its exit.**

   a. Select the exit animation for the text box in the Animation pane.

   b. Open its menu and choose Timing.

c. Enter **5** in the Delay box.

d. Click OK.

NOTE

You could have simply typed a number in the Delay box on the Animations tab of the Ribbon instead of following steps 6a through 6d, but it's useful to know both methods. You will use the simpler method later in this lab.

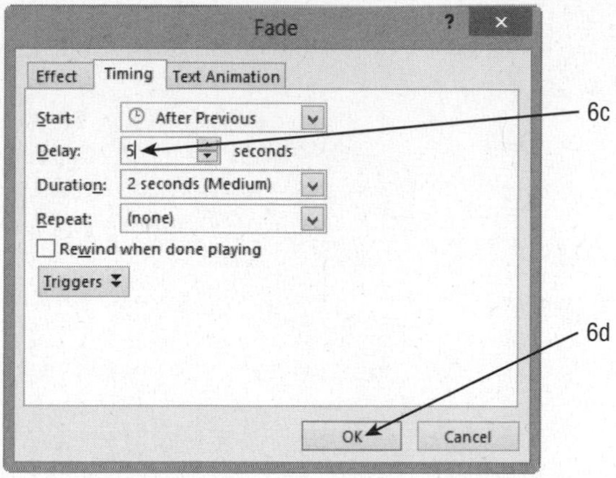

---

7. **Repeat step 6 for the exit animation for the right picture.**

8. **Create a Fade entrance effect for the opposite text box (the one on the right) that occurs After Previous.** Set the duration to 2 seconds. Refer to step 3.

9. **Create a Fade entrance effect for the opposite picture (the one on the left) that occurs With Previous.** Set the duration to 2 seconds. Refer to step 4.

10. **Preview the slide's animation and check your work.**

  a. Click the Slide Show View button.

  b. If you did the animation correctly, the Champion Sires text and the right photo will appear first, fading in.

  c. They will pause for 5 seconds, fade out, and then the opposite text and picture will fade in. They will remain on the screen until you click to move to the next slide.

10b

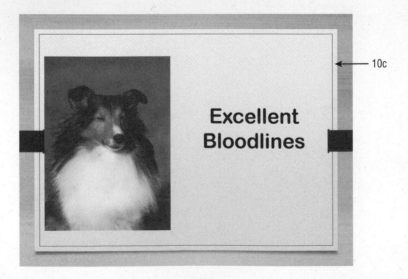
10c

11. **Press Esc to exit Slide Show view.**

12. **Save your work.**

Lab 2B: Replacing One Picture with Another

In this lab session, you place one photo on top of another and animate the top one so that it disappears, revealing the one underneath, after a delay.

Level of difficulty: Moderate

Time to complete: 10 to 15 minutes

1. **Open the presentation file if it is not already open.**

   Start in your completed file from the previous project (MyLab2A.pptx), or open Lab2B.pptx from the Labs folder if you did not do the previous lab.

2. **Save the file as MyLab2B.pptx.**

3. **Display slide #3, and arrange the pictures so that they are stacked one on top of the other.**

   a. Click slide #3 in the Slides pane.

   b. Drag the pictures so that they are both in the same spot in the center of the slide. Only the top one (where all three dogs are sitting up) should be visible.

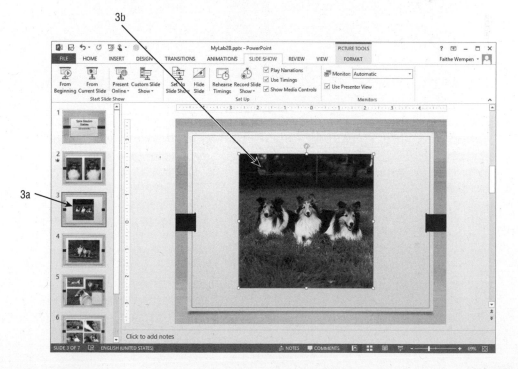

4. **Add a Checkerboard exit animation to the top picture so that it goes away after being displayed for 6 seconds.**

   a. Click the top picture to select it.

   b. Choose Animations ⇨ Advanced Animations ⇨ Add Animation ⇨ More Exit Effects.

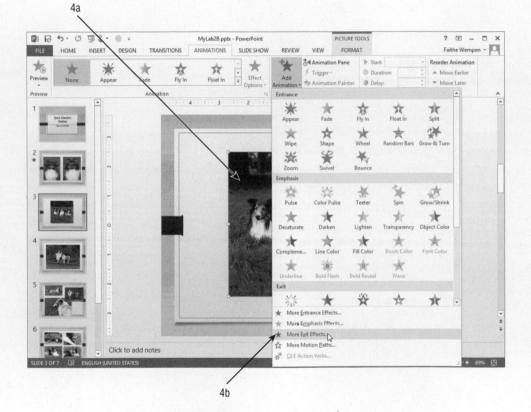

   c. In the Add Exit Effect dialog box, choose Checkerboard.

   d. Click OK.

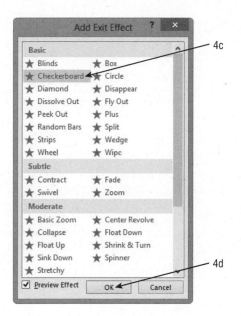

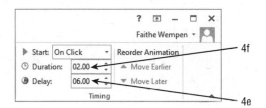

e. On the Animations tab, enter **6** in the Delay box by clicking the up increment arrow until it reads 06:00.

f. Enter 2 seconds in the Duration box by clicking the up increment arrow until it reads 02:00.

5. **Preview the slide's animation and check your work.**

   a. Click the Slide Show View button. Then click the mouse once to get the animation started. If you did the animation correctly, the top picture displays when the slide appears, and after 6 seconds, it will checkerboard into the picture beneath it.

   b. Press Esc to return to PowerPoint.

6. **Save your work.**

Lab 2C: Zooming In on a Picture

In this lab session, you make a picture grow so that it looks like the camera is zooming in on it.

Level of difficulty: Easy

Time to complete: 5 minutes

1. **Open the presentation file if it is not already open.**

   Start in your completed file from the previous project (`MyLab2B.pptx`), or open `Lab2C.pptx` from the Labs folder if you did not do the previous lab.

2. **Save the file as `MyLab2C.pptx`.**

3. **On slide #4, set an emphasis animation for the picture to Grow.**

   a. Click the picture to select it.

   b. Choose Animations ⇨ Advanced Animation ⇨ Add Animation ⇨ Grow/Shrink.

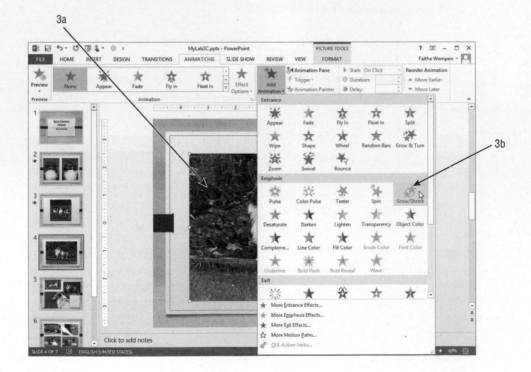

4. **Set the animation to occur after 5 seconds.**

   a. On the Animations tab, open the Start drop-down list and choose After Previous.

   b. Set Duration to 5 seconds.

   c. Set Delay to 2 seconds.

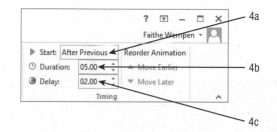

5. **Preview the slide's animation and check your work.**

   a. Click the Slide Show View button. If you did the animation correctly, the picture will begin a slow zoom in after 2 seconds.

   b. Press Esc to return to PowerPoint.

6. **Save your work.**

Lab 2D: More Animation Practice

In this lab session, you complete the animations for the rest of the presentation. This project is more challenging, not because of the animations per se, but because less-detailed instructions are provided here. You will need to determine how to accomplish each animation on your own.

Level of difficulty: Challenging

Time to complete: 15 to 30 minutes

1. **Open the presentation file if it is not already open, and save it as `MyLab2D` `.pptx`.**

   Start in your completed file from the previous project (`MyLab2C.pptx`), or open `Lab2D.pptx` from the Labs folder if you did not do the previous lab.

2. **Add a text box to slide #4, near the bottom of the picture, with the following text:** Puppies raised with adult dogs are better socialized.

   Make the text center-aligned, Arial Rounded Bold MT font, 24 point, and white.

3. **Animate the text box you just added so that it appears after the picture's Grow effect has taken place and 2 seconds later it changes color to bright yellow with a Brush Color effect.**

TIP

Hint: Apply two separate animations to the text: an entrance with an Appear effect and an emphasis with a Brush Color effect. To change the brush color, you need to display the Animation pane and then right-click the animation and choose Effect Options.

4. **On slide #5, animate each of the pictures to appear using the Dissolve In animation, in the order specified in the following illustration, with a 2-second delay between them.** Set the animation (duration) for each of them to 1 second.

5. **On slide #6, use the Align commands to more precisely align all four pictures.**

To do this, first align the tops of the top two pictures, and then align the tops of the bottom two pictures.

Next align the two left pictures at the left side and then the two right pictures at the right side, if they are not already aligned.

6. **Animate the pictures on slide #6 so that the top two pictures appear (simultaneously) first using the Diamond entrance effect, then there's a 3-second delay, and then the other two pictures appear simultaneously using the same effect.**

7. **On slide #7, adjust the positions of the pictures as needed to make their edges align with the white part of the background on the slide on the background.**

8. **Animate the top-left picture to fade out after 6 seconds, and make the bottom-right picture fade in as the top-left picture is fading out.** Set the duration of both animations to 3 seconds.

9. **View the entire presentation in Slide Show view to check your work.**

10. **Return to PowerPoint and save your work.**

First, these two…

…then, these two

Lab 2E: Using Transitions and Soundtracks

In this project, you set up each slide to automatically advance after 15 seconds, and you specify a transition effect. You also add a MIDI-based soundtrack to the presentation that will loop continuously as long as the presentation is playing.

Level of difficulty: Easy

Time to complete: 5 to 10 minutes

1. **Open the presentation file if it is not already open, and save it as `MyLab2E`** **`.pptx`.**

   Start in your completed file from the previous project (`MyLab2D.pptx`), or open `Lab2E.pptx` from the Labs folder if you did not do the previous lab.

2. **Set all slides to the Fade Smoothly transition automatically after 15 seconds.**

   a. On the Transitions tab, in the Transition to This Slide group, open the gallery and choose Fade.

   b. Set Duration to 00:02.

   c. Click the After check box and enter **00:15**.

   d. Click Apply to All.

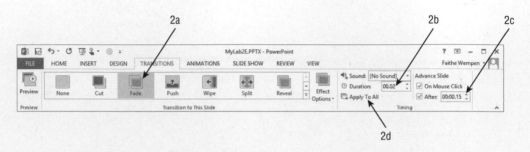

3. **Locate a classical music clip and insert it on the slide as an icon.**

   a. Display slide #1.

   b. Choose Insert ➪ Media ➪ Audio ➪ Online Audio.

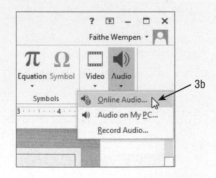

   c. Click in the text box and type **classical**.

   d. Click Search.

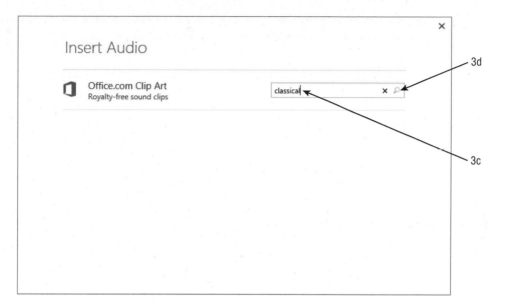

e. Click one of the found clips.

f. Click Insert.

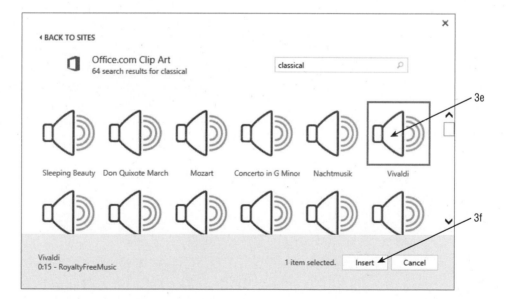

4. **Set the clip up to play automatically when the slide appears and to continue playing until the presentation is over.**

   a. Make sure the audio icon is selected.

   b. On the Audio Tools Playback tab, click the Play in Background button.

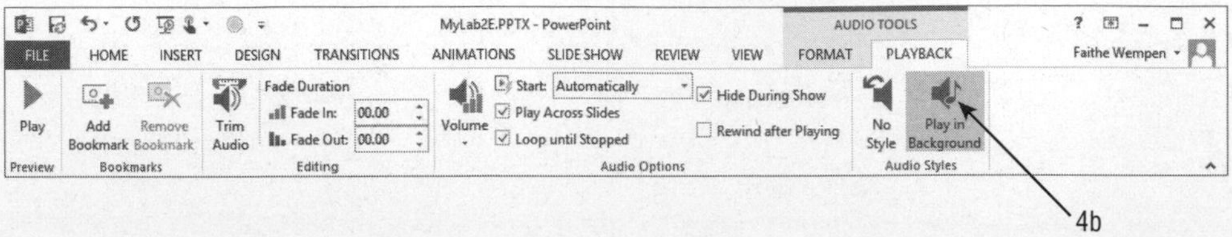

4b

5. **Watch the entire presentation in Slide Show view, without clicking, to check the transitions, animation, and music.** Then adjust any transition timings that might seem awkward to you.

6. **Save your work.**

Creating a Menu-Based Navigation System

IN THIS LAB

Making room for a navigation bar

Creating a navigation bar

Creating a graphical navigation system

When you create user-interactive presentations that contain many slides, it is considered courteous to provide your audience with a navigation system so that they can browse through the presentation without having to view every single slide. Menu systems can be as simple or as complex as you like and can be integrated into the slide design.

In this project lab, you learn how to create a navigation system in a presentation that is designed to teach computer technicians about safety issues for working on PCs. You modify the presentation's layout and design to make room for a menu system, and then you create navigational hyperlinks on the slide master.

Please visit www.wiley.com/go/powerpoint2013bible to download the files you need for the project labs.

Lab 3A: Making Room for a Navigation Bar

In this lab session, you start with a plain-looking presentation and modify its slide master to make room for a menu system on the left side of the slide.

This lab session includes some cleanup work on a "messy" PowerPoint file that is missing a layout needed for some of the slides. This session simulates the type of cleanup situations you might run into in everyday work on older presentation files.

Level of difficulty: Moderate

Time to complete: 15 to 30 minutes

1. **Open the file Lab03A.pptx and save it as MyLab03A.pptx.**
2. **Display the slide master.** To do so, choose View ⇨ Master Views ⇨ Slide Master.

3. **On the top-level slide master, draw a rectangle that covers the entire slide vertically and stops at the 3" mark on the ruler.**
   a. Click the slide master at the top of the left pane.
   b. Choose Insert ⇨ Illustrations ⇨ Shapes.
   c. Click a rectangle.

   d. Click and drag on the slide to draw a rectangle that covers 2" at the left of the slide.

4. **Bring the text boxes to the front so that the rectangle overlaps.**

   a. Click the Title placeholder box.

   b. Hold down the Shift key and click the Content placeholder box.

   c. Hold down the Shift key and click the Date placeholder box.

   d. Click the Drawing Tools Format tab.

   e. In the Arrange group, open the Bring Forward button's drop-down list and choose Bring to Front.

5. **Change the color of the rectangle to a dark-blue shade from the second column of the color palette.**

   a. Select the rectangle.

   b. Choose Drawing Tools Format ➪ Shape Styles ➪ Shape Fill.

   c. Click the second square from the bottom in the second column in the Theme Colors section.

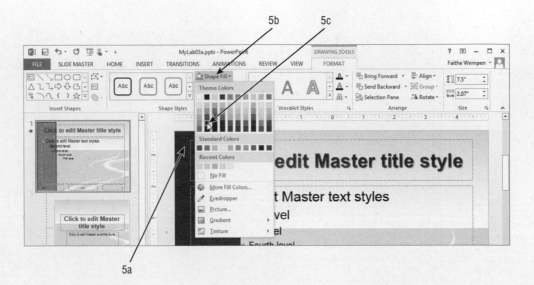

6. **Move the left borders of the title and content placeholder boxes to the right so that they do not overlap the rectangle.**

   a. Make sure the main slide master (top slide) is selected.

   b. Click the Title placeholder.

   c. Hold down the Shift key and click the content placeholder.

   d. Drag the left border of the placeholders to align with the 3″ mark on the horizontal ruler.

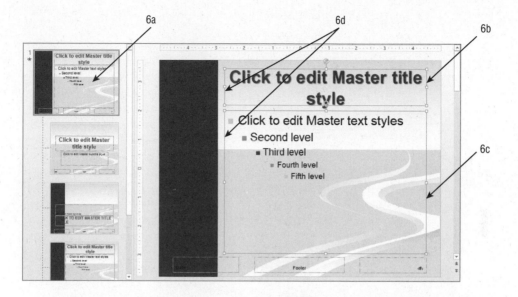

7. **Repeat step 6 for the individual slide layouts that were not affected by step 6.**

   a. Select the Section Header Layout master (the second slide layout in the list).

   b. Select the Title and text placeholders.

   c. Drag the left border to the right to the 3" mark on the horizontal ruler.

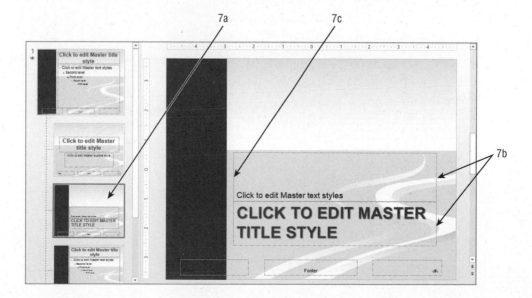

d. Select the Title, Text, and Content layout (bottom slide layout).

e. Select both content placeholders.

f. Drag the left border of the left content placeholder to the right, to align with the 3" mark on the horizontal ruler. Both placeholder boxes shrink an equal amount horizontally.

g. Click away from the selection to deselect it.

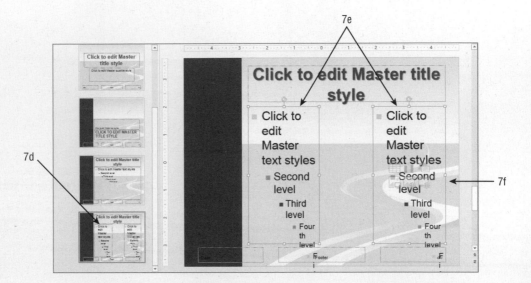

h. Click the left placeholder to select it.

i. Drag the right border of the left placeholder to the 0.75" mark on the ruler.

j. Click the right placeholder to select it.

k. Drag the left border of the right placeholder to the 1" mark on the ruler.

7h 7i

7j

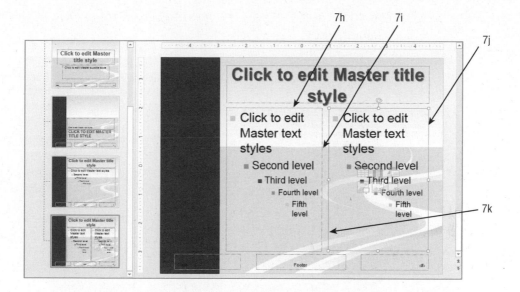

7k

8. **Exit from Slide Master view and clean up the presentation so that all slides use valid layouts and no content overflows or overlaps.**

   a. Click Close Master View.

8a

3

b. On slide #2, click inside the text box and then click the AutoFit Options button.

c. Click AutoFit Text to Placeholder.

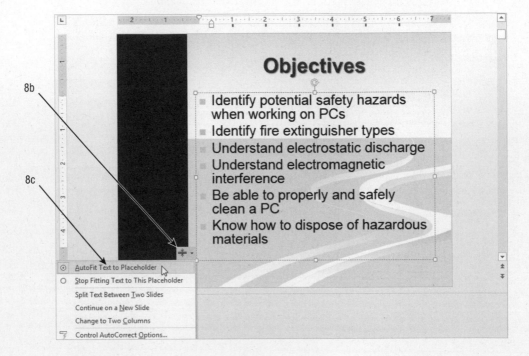

d. Select slides 4 and 5.

e. Choose Home ➪ Slides ➪ Layout.

f. Click Title and Text.

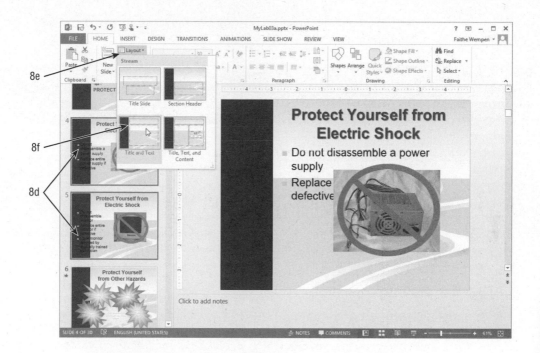

g. On slides 4 and 5, resize and reposition the graphics so that they do not overlap with the text.

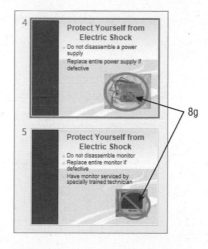

h. Repeat steps 8e through 8g for slides 11, 21, 23, 25, 27, and 29, and repeat steps 8b and 8c for slide 22.

i. On slide 23, reapply numbered list formatting using Home ➪ Paragraph ➪ Numbering.

> **NOTE**
> Slide #25 has an unusual layout. Only the first bullet is in a placeholder box; the other one is in a manual text box. Adjust as needed.

9. **Save your work.**

Lab 3B: Creating a Navigation Bar

In this lab session, you start with a presentation that has an area cleared for a navigation bar (from Lab 3A) and you create hyperlinks on the slide master that link to the section titles within the presentation.

Level of difficulty: Moderate

Time to complete: 15 to 20 minutes

1. **Open the presentation file if it is not already open.** Start in your completed file from the previous project (MyLab03A.pptx), or open Lab03B.pptx from the Labs folder if you did not do the previous lab.

2. **Save the file as MyLab03B.pptx.**

3. **Display the slide master and create a text box on top of the blue rectangle.**

   a. Choose View ➪ Master Views ➪ Slide Master.

   b. Click the top-level slide master.

   c. Choose Insert ➪ Text ➪ Text Box.

   d. Drag to create a text box near the top of the blue rectangle. (Alternately, you can create the text box elsewhere on the slide and then drag it onto the blue rectangle.)

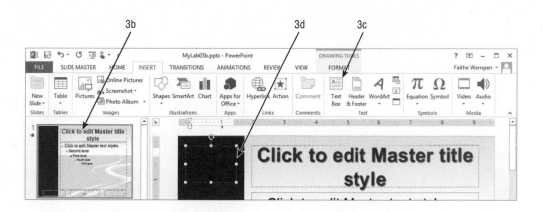

4. **Type the names of the section titles from the presentation in white, into the new text box.**

   a. Click in the new text box. If the insertion point does not appear, right-click the text box and choose Edit Text to make it appear there.

   b. Choose Home ➪ Font ➪ Font Color and click the white square in the Theme Colors section.

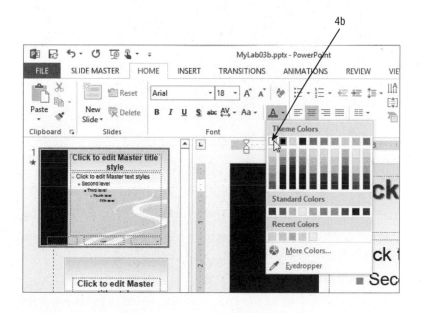

   c. Type the following list into the text box:

   Protect Yourself

   Avoid ESD

Avoid EMI

Protect the PC

Clean the PC

Work Safely with Hazardous Materials

d. With the insertion point inside the text box, press Ctrl+A to select all of the text in it.

e. Click the dialog box launcher in the Paragraph group on the Home tab. The Paragraph dialog box appears.

f. In the Spacing section, set the Before value to 12 pt.

g. Click OK.

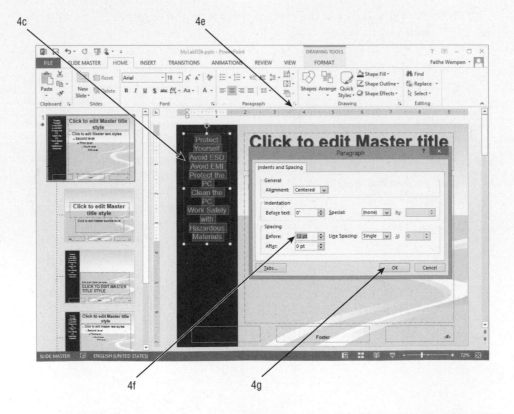

5. **Hyperlink each of the section titles you just typed to the corresponding slide.**

a. In the text box, select Protect Yourself.

b. On the Insert tab, click Hyperlink. The Insert Hyperlink dialog box appears.

c. Click Place in This Document.

d. On the Slide Titles list, click Protect Yourself (slide #3).

e. Click OK.

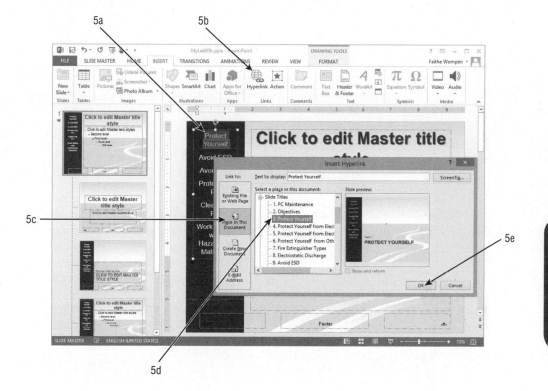

f. Repeat steps 5a through 5e for each of the other section title slides:

Avoid ESD: Slide #8

Avoid EMI: Slide #13

Protect the PC: Slide #16

Clean the PC: Slide #19

Work Safely with Hazardous Materials: Slide #28

6. **Exit from Slide Master view.** Choose Slide Master ➪ Close ➪ Close Master View.

7. **Try out the presentation in Slide Show view and click each of the links to make sure they work.**

8. **Save your work.**

Lab 3C: Creating a Graphical Navigation System

In this lab session, you learn how to create a navigation bar similar to the one in Lab 3B except you use shapes for buttons instead of text-based hyperlinks.

Level of difficulty: Moderate

Time to complete: 20 minutes

1. **Open the presentation file if it is not already open.** Start in your completed file from the previous project (MyLab03B.pptx), or open Lab03C.pptx from the Labs folder if you did not do the previous lab.

2. **Save the file as MyLab03C.pptx.**

3. **Display the slide master.**

   a. Choose View ⇨ Master Views ⇨ Slide Master.

   b. Click the slide master (topmost slide).

4. **Replace the text** *Protect Yourself* **with a rectangle containing that text.**

   a. Move the text box down 1" to make room above it for the rectangle.

   b. On the Insert tab, click Shapes, and click a rounded rectangle.

   c. Draw a rectangle above the text box.

d. Select the *Protect Yourself* text in the text box and press Ctrl+X to cut it to the Clipboard.

e. Click the rectangle and press Ctrl+V to paste the text into it.

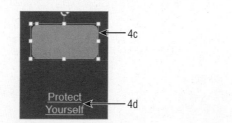

5. **Repeat step 4 for each of the other text hyperlinks to create the rest of the buttons.**

a. Move the text box lower as needed to make room for the buttons.

b. As needed, increase the height of the button or buttons to make all of the text fit.

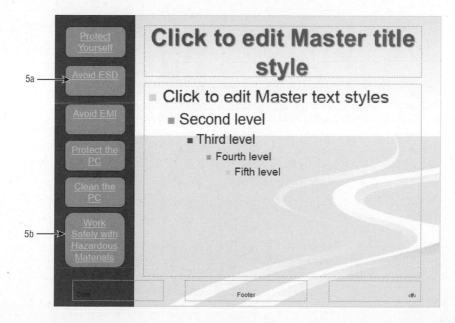

6. **Modify the current color theme so that hyperlinks (both followed and unfollowed) are white.**

   a. Choose Slide Master ⇨ Background ⇨ Colors ⇨ Customize Colors.

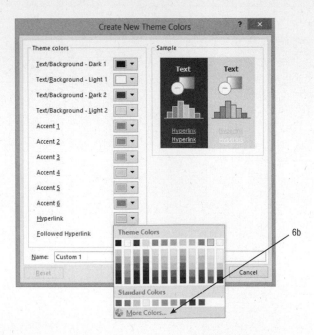

   b. Open the Hyperlink button's palette and choose More Colors.

c. In the Colors dialog box, click a white hexagon.

d. Click OK.

e. Repeat steps 6b through 6d for the Followed Hyperlink button.

f. Click Save.

7. **Format the buttons to make them more attractive.**

   a. Select all of the buttons. Hold down the Ctrl key as you click each one.

   b. Choose Drawing Tools Format ⇨ Shape Styles ⇨ Shape Effects ⇨ Shadow, and click the first Shadow setting (top left) in the Outer section.

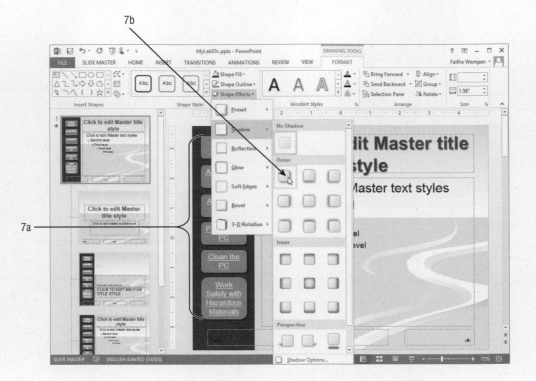

c. Open the Shape Effects menu, click Bevel, and click the first bevel style (top left).

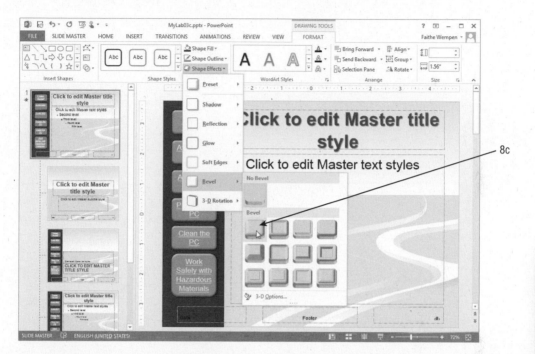

8. **Save your work.**

8c

TIP

If you prefer buttons that do not have the text underlined, you can set them up differently. Instead of using the existing hyperlink text, remove the hyperlink from the text to make it ordinary text typed in a shape, and then select the entire button and reapply the hyperlink to make the whole button a graphical hyperlink.

3

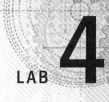

Creating a Classroom Game

IN THIS LAB

Making the game board

Creating the question slides

Creating the answer slides

Linking up the game board

PowerPoint's ability to hyperlink between slides and hide slides until they are needed makes it a natural choice for creating multiple-choice quizzes and games. You can create a slide with a question on it and then create hidden slides for each of the possible answers. Then, depending on which answer the user clicks, a different hidden slide appears indicating whether the answer was right or wrong.

In this project lab, you learn how to create a simple game to use in a classroom setting that tests students' understanding of the informational presentation you worked with in Lab 3.

Please visit www.wiley.com/go/powerpoint2013bible to download the files you need for the project labs.

Lab 4A: Making the Game Board

In this lab session, you create the basic game board by drawing a set of shapes and arranging them in relation to one another.

Level of difficulty: Moderate

Time to complete: 15 to 30 minutes

1. **Start a new blank presentation and save it as MyLab04A.pptx.**

2. **Change the layout of the slide to Blank.**

   a. Choose Home ➪ Slides ➪ Layout.

   b. Click Blank.

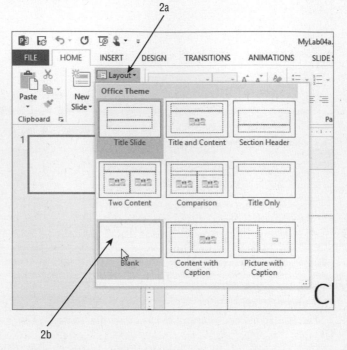

3. **Draw a rounded rectangle on the slide that is 0.75" high and 2" wide.**

   a. Choose Home ➪ Drawing ➪ Shapes (or Insert ➪ Illustrations ➪ Shapes), and click the rounded rectangle.

b. Drag on the slide, near the top-left corner, to create the shape.

c. On the Drawing Tools Format tab, click in the Height box and type **0.75"**.

d. Click in the Width box and type **2"**.

4. **Apply a dark-blue Shape Style to the shape.** On the Drawing Tools Format tab, open the Shape Styles gallery and click the bottommost dark-blue style.

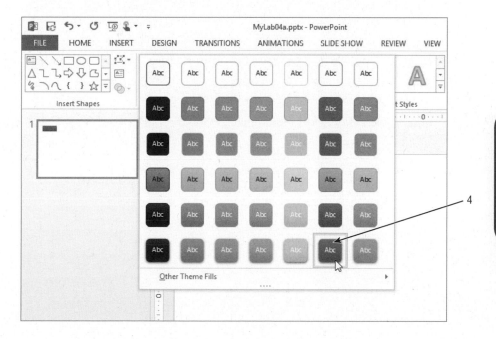

5. **Copy the shape, and paste it three times.** Then arrange the copies side by side horizontally across the top of the slide and distribute them evenly.

   a. Select the blue shape.

   b. Hold down Shift+Ctrl and drag it to the right to create a copy. Repeat two more times so that you have a total of four shapes. Watch for the arrow guides to help you create consistent spacing between the shapes and Smart Guides to align the shapes with each other.

   c. Select all four shapes by holding down the Ctrl key and clicking each one.

   d. Choose Drawing Tools Format ⇨ Arrange ⇨ Align ⇨ Align to Slide.

   e. Choose Drawing Tools Format ⇨ Arrange ⇨ Align ⇨ Distribute Horizontally.

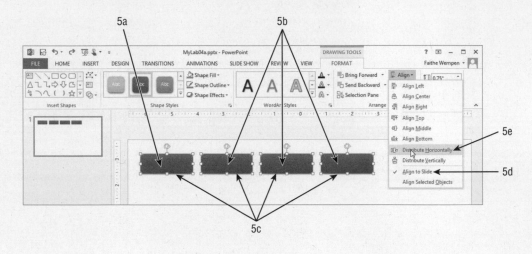

6. **Copy the four shapes four times, and place the copies under the originals to form columns.**

   a. Select all four blue shapes if they are not already selected.

   b. Hold down Shift+Ctrl and drag downward to create a copy below the originals.

   c. Repeat step 6b three more times to create three more rows of buttons.

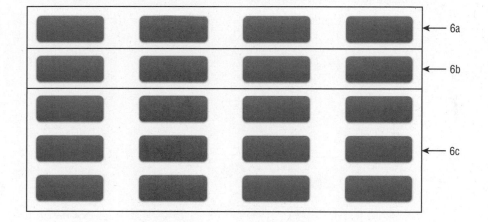

7. **Use Align and Distribute to make sure the grid of buttons is evenly spaced.**

   a. Select all of the shapes in the first column.

   b. Choose Drawing Tools Format ⇨ Arrange ⇨ Align ⇨ Align to Slide if it is not already selected.

   c. Choose Drawing Tools Format ⇨ Arrange ⇨ Align ⇨ Distribute Vertically.

   d. Repeat steps 7a and 7c for each column.

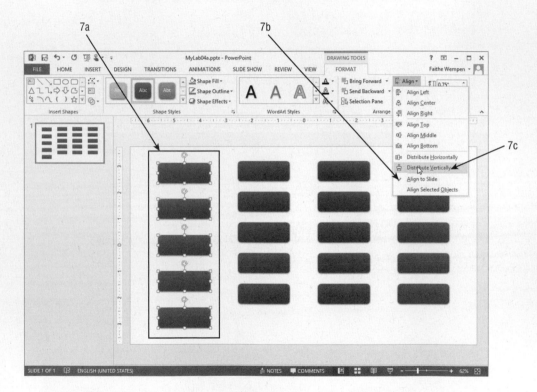

8. **Change the color of all of the rows except the first one to green.**

   a. Select all of the shapes in each row except the first one.

   b. On the Drawing Tools Format tab, click the green sample in the Shape Styles gallery. (Its full name is Intense Effect – Green, Accent 6.)

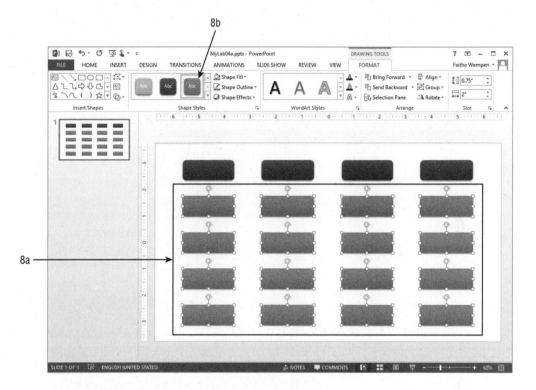

9. **Type the following text into the top row of shapes.**

   a. Select the leftmost blue shape and type **Safety**.

   b. Select the second blue shape and type **ESD**.

   c. Select the third blue shape and type **EMI**.

   d. Select the fourth blue shape and type **Cleaning**.

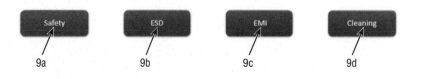

10. **Type 10, 20, 30, and 40 in each column.**

   a. In the topmost, leftmost green shape, type **10**.

   b. Select the 10 you just typed and press Ctrl+C to copy it.

   c. Select the next shape in that row and press Ctrl+V. Repeat two more times so that all of the shapes in the first green row have 10 in them.

   d. Repeat the process to put **20** in the next row, **30** in the next, and then **40** in the bottom row.

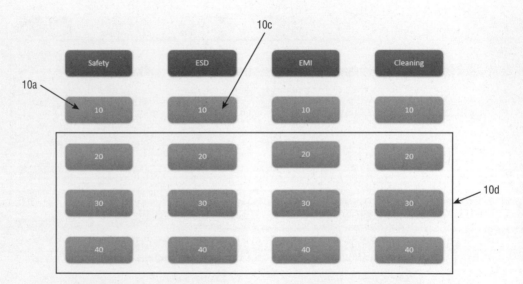

11. **Save your work.**

Lab 4B: Creating the Question Slides

In this lab session, you generate slides containing the questions that the game board created in Lab 4A will link to. Because the game board is large, you'll do just one slide step-by-step here, and then you can create the rest of the slides on your own.

Level of difficulty: Easy

Time to complete: 15 to 20 minutes

1. **Open the presentation file if it is not already open.** Start in your completed file from the previous project (MyLab04A.pptx), or open Lab04B.pptx if you did not do the previous lab.

2. **Save the file as** `MyLab04B.pptx`.

3. **Create a new blank slide using the Title and Content layout after the first one.**

   a. On the Home tab, click the text at the bottom of the New Slide button to open the menu.

   b. Click Title and Content.

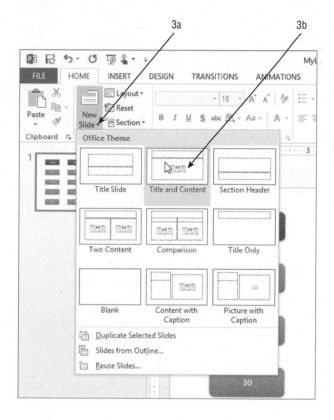

4. **For the new slide's title, type the following:**

   Safety for 10 Points

5. **For the new slide's body, type the following:**

   True or false: you should wear long sleeves when working on a PC.

4

5

Safety for 10 Points

- True or false: you should wear long sleeves when working on a PC.

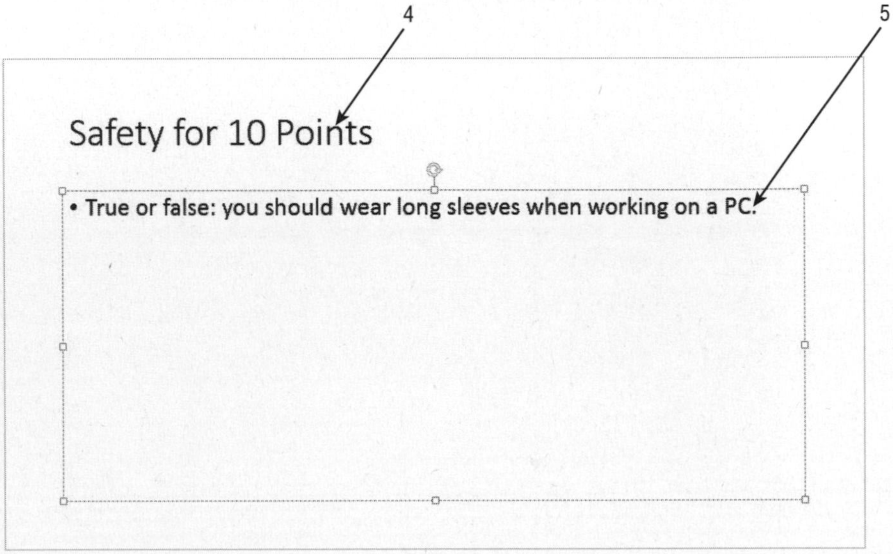

6. **Add True and False buttons below the question.**

   a. Display slide #1, and select any of the green shapes.

   b. Press Ctrl+C to copy the shape.

   c. Display slide #2.

   d. Press Ctrl+V to paste the shape.

   e. Edit the text on the shape to read **True**.

   f. Hold down the Ctrl key and drag the True shape to create a copy of it. Hold down Shift to keep the copy aligned.

   g. Edit the text on the new shape to read **False**.

   h. Arrange the shapes side by side under the question text.

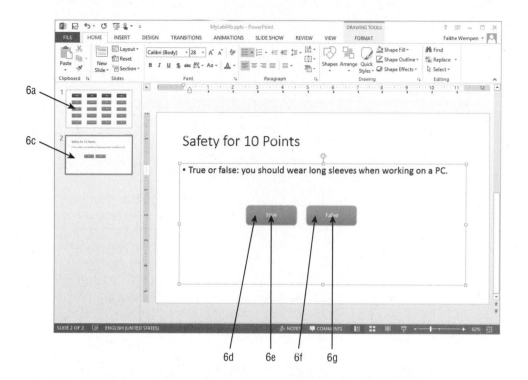

6a
6c
6d 6e 6f 6g

7. **Create additional slides for the other questions by copying the slide you just created and modifying its text.** Refer to the following table for the question text to use. (If you do not want to do all of that typing, see the solution file MyLab04B.pptx provided on the book's companion website.)

Question Number	Question Text
Safety 20	True or false: you should replace the entire power supply if it is defective, not try to repair it.
Safety 30	True or false: monitors must be serviced by specially trained technicians.
Safety 40	True or false: a Class A fire extinguisher is best for electrical fires.
ESD 10	True or false: ESD stands for Electrostatic Discharge.
ESD 20	True or false: a circuit board can be ruined by ESD that is too weak for a human to feel.
ESD 30	True or false: to minimize ESD, work in a room with very low humidity (0% to 30%).
ESD 40	True or false: rubber-soled shoes are best for avoiding ESD.
EMI 10	True or false: EMI stands for Electrostatic Issues.

Continues

continued

EMI 20	True or false: EMI is a magnetic field generated by electricity passing through a cable.
EMI 30	True or false: shielded cables can prevent problems caused by EMI.
EMI 40	True or false: longer cables are more susceptible to EMI.
Cleaning 10	True or false: you should not use regular glass cleaner on a monitor screen.
Cleaning 20	True or false: the best way to clean a circuit board is with soapy water.
Cleaning 30	True or false: to clean the print heads on an inkjet printer, run the printer's self-cleaning utility.
Cleaning 40	True or false: you should use alcohol to clean the corona wires in a laser printer.

8. **Hide all of the slides except the game board.**

   a. From Slide Sorter view, select all slides except slide #1.

   b. On the Slide Show tab, click Hide Slide.

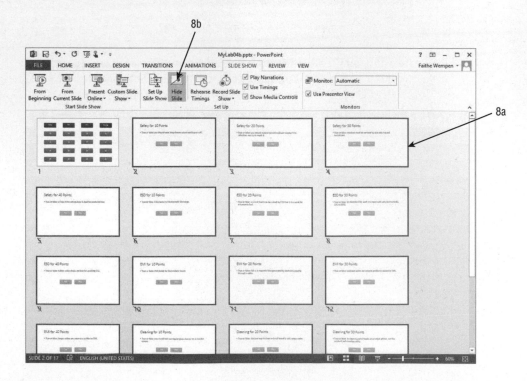

9. (Recommended) To prevent the presentation from advancing when you click anything other than the buttons, on the Transitions tab, clear the On Mouse Click check box and then click Apply to All.

10. Save your work.

Lab 4C: Creating the Answer Slides

In this lab session, you create slides that tell the players whether or not their answers are correct, and you will link each of the True and False buttons from Lab 4B to one of those slides or the other.

Level of difficulty: Moderate

Time to complete: 20 minutes

1. **Open the presentation file if it is not already open.** Start in your completed file from the previous project (MyLab04B.pptx), or open Lab04C.pptx from the Labs folder if you did not do the previous lab.

2. **Save the file as MyLab04C.pptx.**

3. **Create a slide to display when the player answers correctly.**

   a. Switch to Normal view if not already there.

   b. Create a new slide with the Title and Content layout after the existing slides in the presentation.

   c. For the slide title, type **You Are Correct!**

   d. For the slide body text, type **Congratulations, that is the correct answer.**

   e. Remove the bullet from the body text.

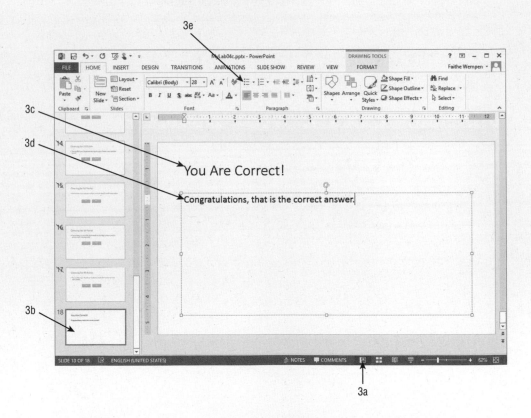

4. **Add a Return button on the slide, and set it to return to the game board.**

   a. Copy and paste any blue button from the game board slide onto the You Are Correct slide, in a position of your choice.

b. Edit the text on the button to read **Return**.

c. Select the Return button.

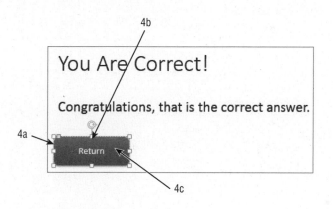

d. Choose Insert ⇨ Links ⇨ Action.

e. Click Hyperlink To.

f. Open the drop-down list and choose First Slide.

g. Click OK.

5. **Copy the You Are Correct! slide.**

    a. In the Slides pane, right-click the You Are Correct! slide.

    b. Choose Duplicate Slide.

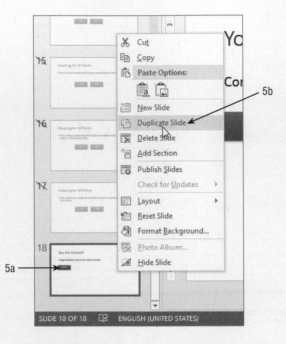

6. **Change the text on the copy of the You Are Correct! slide to reflect that the player has answered incorrectly.**

    a. Change the slide title text to **You Are Incorrect**.

    b. Change the slide body text to **Sorry, you answered incorrectly.**

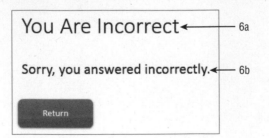

7. **Hide the two slides you just created.**

   a. From Slide Sorter view, select the two new slides.

   b. On the Slide Show tab, click Hide Slide.

8. **Save your work.**

Lab 4D: Linking Up the Game Board

In this lab session, you finish the game board built in Labs 4A through 4C by creating hyperlinks from the game board to the question slides and from the True and False buttons on each question slide to the result slides you created in Lab 4C.

Level of difficulty: Moderate

Time to complete: 30 minutes or more

1. **Open the presentation file if it is not already open.** Start in your completed file from the previous project (MyLab04C.pptx), or open Lab04D.pptx from the Labs folder if you did not do the previous lab.

2. **Save the file as MyLab04D.pptx.**

3. **Create a hyperlink between the leftmost 10 button on the game board to the Safety for 10 Points slide.**

   a. On the game board, select the 10 button in the Safety column. (Select the button itself, not the text on the button.)

   b. Choose Insert ➪ Links ➪ Hyperlink.

   c. Click Place in This Document.

   d. Click Safety for 10 Points.

   e. Click OK.

4

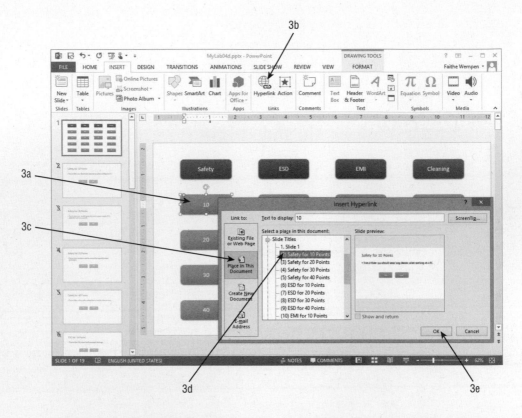

4. **Repeat the process in step 3 to create links from each of the other buttons on the game board to its corresponding question.**

5. **On slide #2 (Safety for 10 points), hyperlink from the True button to the You Are Incorrect slide.**

   a. On slide #2, select the True button.

   b. Choose Insert ⇨ Links ⇨ Hyperlink.

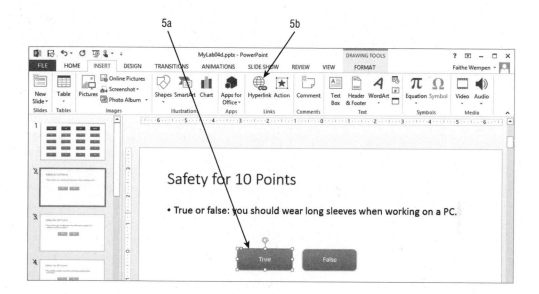

c. Click Place in This Document.

d. Click slide #19, You Are Incorrect.

e. Click OK.

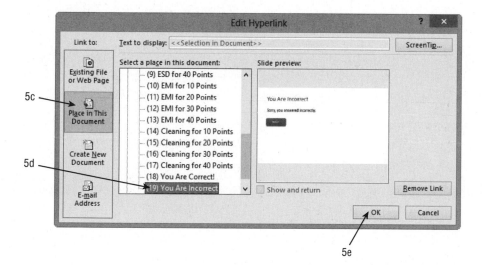

6. **Repeat step 6 for the False button, linking it to the You Are Correct slide.**

7. **Assign hyperlinks to the True and False buttons on all of the other question slides the same way.** Refer to the following table for the correct answers.

Question Number	Correct Answer
Safety 20	True
Safety 30	True
Safety 40	False
ESD 10	True
ESD 20	True
ESD 30	False
ESD 40	True
EMI 10	False
EMI 20	True
EMI 30	True
EMI 40	False
Cleaning 10	True
Cleaning 20	False
Cleaning 30	True
Cleaning 40	True

8. **Display the game board in Slide Show view and try out the game to make sure that all of the buttons have been programmed correctly.**

9. **Save your work.**

TIP

If you were going to set this game up on a self-running kiosk, you would want to put it into Kiosk mode so that clicking on the slide itself does not advance the presentation. To do so, choose Slide Show ⇨ Set Up ⇨ Set Up Slide Show and choose Browsed at a Kiosk (Full Screen).

What Makes a Great Presentation?

IN THIS APPENDIX

Qualities of an effective presentation

Developing your presentation action plan

Choosing and arranging the room

Choosing your attire

Keeping the audience interested

Managing stage fright

Wow! *What a great presentation*! That's what you want your audience to come away thinking, right?

Most people won't be nit-picky enough to pinpoint exactly what they loved about the experience. Nobody is likely to say, "Weren't the colors in that pie chart on slide 43 artfully chosen?" or "Did you see his tie? I wonder where I can buy one just like it." Instead, you'll leave your audience with an overall impression that they gather from a host of little details, from the color scheme on your slides to the anecdotes and jokes you tell.

You can turn off your computer for this appendix because you won't need it to follow along. I'll present some strategies for planning the best presentation ever. I'll provide an 11-point action plan for building your presentation file and address some of the "soft" topics that can make or break a show, such as how to arrange a room, what to wear, where to stand, and more.

Qualities of an Effective Presentation

What separates an effective presentation from an ineffective one? No, it's not just a gut feeling; there are proven attributes for which you can strive. The rest of this chapter elaborates on these points, but here's a quick overview of what to work on.

An effective presentation has the following characteristics:

- It's designed and formatted appropriately for the audience and the medium.
- It's tightly focused on its subject, with extraneous facts trimmed away or hidden for backup use.
- It uses the right PowerPoint theme, with colors and fonts chosen to reinforce the message of the presentation.
- It includes the right amount of text on each slide, without overcrowding.
- It uses artwork purposefully to convey information and create an overall visual impression.
- It uses charts rather than raw columns of numbers to present financial or numeric information.
- It employs sound and video to create interest where needed but does not allow the effects to dominate the show.
- It uses animations and transitions if appropriate for the audience and message but does not allow them to dominate.
- It includes handouts for the audience that contain the information they will want to take with them.
- It leaves time at the end for a question-and-answer session so the audience members can clarify any points they were confused about.

Now that you know what the goal is, how do you get there? You need a precise, step-by-step action plan for developing a presentation that has these qualities.

Developing Your Presentation Action Plan

Can you guess what the single biggest problem is when most people use PowerPoint? Here's a hint: It's not a problem with the software at all. It's that they don't think things through carefully before they create their presentation, and then they have to go back and make major modifications later. You've probably heard the saying "If you don't have time to do it right, how are you going to find time to do it over?" This sentiment is certainly applicable to creating presentations.

In the following sections, I outline a strategy for creating the appropriate PowerPoint presentation right from the start. By considering the issues addressed here, you can avoid making false assumptions about your audience and their needs and so avoid creating a beautiful presentation with some horrible flaw that makes it unusable. By spending a half hour or so in this chapter, you can save yourself literally days in rework later.

Step 1: Identifying Your Audience and Purpose

Before you can think about the presentation you need to create, you must think of your audience. As you probably already know from real-life experience, different audiences respond to different presentation types. For example, a sales pitch to a client requires a very different approach than an informational briefing to your coworkers. Ask yourself these questions:

- **How many people will be attending the presentation?** The attendance makes a difference because the larger the group, the larger your screen needs to be so that everyone can see. If you don't have access to a large screen, you have to make the lettering and charts big and chunky so that everyone can read your presentation.

- **What is the average age of the attendees?** Although it's difficult to generalize about people, it's especially important to keep your presentation light and entertaining when you're presenting to a very young audience (teens and children). Generally speaking, the older the audience, the more authoritative you need to be.

- **What role will the audience take in relation to the topic?** If you are rolling out a new product or system, the managerial staff will likely want a general overview of it, but the line workers who will actually be operating the product need a lot of details. Generally speaking, the higher the level of managers, the more removed they will be from the action and the fewer details of operation they need.

- **How well does the audience already know the topic?** If you are presenting to a group that knows nothing about your topic, you want to keep things basic and make sure that you define all of the unfamiliar terms. In contrast, with a group of experts, you are likely to have many follow-up questions after the main presentation, and so you should plan on having some hidden backup slides ready in anticipation of those questions. See Chapter 18, "Preparing for a Live Presentation," for more on hiding slides for backup use.

- **Does the audience care about the topic?** If the topic is personally important to the attendees (such as information on their insurance benefits or vacation schedule), they will likely pay attention even if your presentation is plain and straightforward. However, if you must win them over, you need to spend more time on the bells and whistles.

- **Are the attendees prejudiced either positively or negatively toward the topic?** Keep in mind that the audience's preconceived ideas can make the difference between success and failure in some presentations. For example, knowing that a client hates sales pitches can help you to tailor your own presentation to be out of the ordinary.

- **Are the attendees in a hurry?** Do your attendees have all afternoon to listen to you, or do they need to get back to their regular jobs? Nothing is more frustrating

A

than sitting through a leisurely presentation when you're watching precious minutes tick away. Know your audience's schedule and their preference for quick versus thorough coverage.

Next, think about what you want the outcome of the presentation to be. Although you might want more than one outcome, you should try to identify the primary one as your main goal. The following outcomes are among those to consider:

- **Audience feels good about the topic.** Some presentations are strictly cheerleading sessions, designed to sway the audience's opinion. Don't discount this objective — it's a perfectly legitimate reason to make a presentation! For example, suppose a new management staff has taken over a factory. The new management team might want to reassure the workers that everything is going to be okay. A feelgood, *Welcome to the Team* presentation, complete with gimmicks such as company T-shirts or hats, can go a long way in this regard.

- **Audience is informed.** Sometimes you need to convey information to a group of people, and no decision is involved on their part. For example, suppose your company has switched insurance carriers and you want to let all of the employees know about their new benefits. An informational presentation can cover most of the common questions and save your human resources people a lot of time in answering the same questions over and over.

- **Audience members make individual decisions.** This presentation is a kind of sales pitch in which you are pitching an idea or product to a group, but each person says yes or no individually. For example, suppose you are selling timeshare vacation condos. You may give a presentation to a group of 100 people in an attempt to sell your package to at least a few members of the group.

  This presentation type can also have an informational flavor; you are informing people about their choices without pushing one choice or the other. For example, if your employees have a choice of health plans, you might present the pros and cons of each plan and then leave it to each employee to make a selection.

- **Audience makes a group decision.** This is the kind of presentation that scares a lot of people. You face a group of people who will confer and make a single decision based on the information you present. Most sales pitches fall into this category. For example, you might be explaining your product to a group of managers to try to get their company to buy it.

Think about these factors carefully and try to come up with a single statement that summarizes your audience and purpose. Here are some examples:

- *I am presenting to 100 factory workers to explain their new health insurance choices and teach them how to fill out the necessary forms.*

- *I am presenting to a group of 6 to 10 mid-level managers, trying to get them to decide as a group to buy my product.*

- *I am presenting to a group of 20 professors to convince at least some of them to use my company's textbooks in their classes.*
- *I am presenting to individual Internet users to explain how my company's service works.*

Let's take that first example. Figure A.1 shows some notes that a presenter might make when preparing to explain information about employee benefits enrollment to a group of factory workers. Jot down your own notes before moving to step 2.

FIGURE A.1

Make notes about your presentation's purpose and audience.

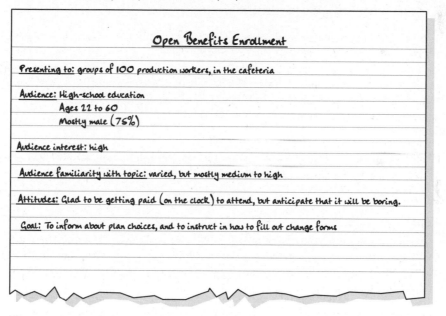

> ## Open Benefits Enrollment
>
> Presenting to: groups of 100 production workers, in the cafeteria
>
> Audience: High-school education
> Ages 22 to 60
> Mostly male (75%)
>
> Audience interest: high
>
> Audience familiarity with topic: varied, but mostly medium to high
>
> Attitudes: Glad to be getting paid (on the clock) to attend, but anticipate that it will be boring.
>
> Goal: To inform about plan choices, and to instruct in how to fill out change forms

Step 2: Choosing Your Presentation Method

You essentially have three ways to present your presentation to your audience, and you need to pick the way that you're going to use up front. These methods include speaker-led, self-running, and user-interactive. Within each of those three broad categories, you have some additional choices. Before you start creating the presentation in PowerPoint, you should know which method you are going to use because it makes a big difference in the text and other objects that you put on the slides.

A

Speaker-Led Presentations

The speaker-led presentation is the traditional type of presentation: You stand up in front of a live audience (or one connected through teleconferencing) and give a speech. The slides that you create in PowerPoint become your support materials. The primary message comes from you, and the slides and handouts are just helpers.

With this kind of presentation, your slides don't have to tell the whole story. Each slide can contain just a few main points, and you can flesh out each point in your discussion. In fact, this kind of presentation works best when your slides don't contain a lot of information because people pay more attention to you, the speaker, if they're not trying to read at the same time. For example, instead of listing the top five reasons to switch to your service, you might have a slide that just reads *Why Switch? Five Reasons*. The audience has to listen to you to find out what the reasons are.

This kind of presentation also requires some special planning. For example, do you want to send each audience member home with handouts? If so, you need to prepare them. They may or may not be identical to your PowerPoint slides; that's up to you. You also need to learn how to handle PowerPoint's presentation controls. It can be really embarrassing to be fiddling with the computer controls in the middle of a speech, and so you should *practice, practice, practice* ahead of time.

Handouts and other support materials (such as cards for speaker notes) are covered in Chapter 17, "Creating Support Materials." For more on PowerPoint presentation controls, see Chapter 18, "Preparing for a Live Presentation."

Self-Running Presentations

With a self-running presentation, all of the rules change. Instead of using the slides as teasers or support materials, you must make the slides carry the entire show. All of the information must be right there because you won't be looking over the audience's shoulders with helpful narration.

In general, self-running presentations are presented to individuals or very small groups. For example, you might set up a kiosk in a busy lobby or a booth at a trade show and have a brief but constantly running presentation of perhaps five slides that explains your product or service.

Because there is no dynamic human being keeping the audience's attention, self-running presentations must include attention-getting features. Sounds, video clips, interesting transitions, and prerecorded narratives are all good ways to attract viewers.

You must also consider the timing in a self-running presentation. Because there is no way for a viewer to tell the presentation, "Okay, I'm done reading this slide; bring on the next one," you must carefully plan how long each slide will remain on-screen. This kind of timing requires some practice!

Part II explains how to use sounds, videos, and other moving objects in a presentation to add interest. Chapter 19, "Designing User-Interactive or Self-Running Presentations," deals with timing issues that are associated with a self-running presentation as well as how to record voice-over narration.

User-Interactive Presentations

A user-interactive presentation is like a self-running presentation except that the viewer has some input. Rather than standing passively by, the viewer can tell PowerPoint when to advance a slide. Depending on the presentation's setup, viewers may also be able to move around in the presentation (perhaps to skip over topics that do not interest them) and request more information. This type of presentation is typically addressed to a single user at a time, rather than a group, and is usually distributed over the Internet, on a company intranet, or via CD.

The user runs the presentation using either PowerPoint or a free program called PowerPoint Viewer that you can provide for download.

Chapter 19 explains how to place action buttons on slides so that the viewer can control the action. Chapter 20 covers some of the issues involved in preparing a presentation for mass distribution.

Step 3: Choosing Your Delivery Method

Whereas the presentation method is the general conceptual way that the audience interacts with the information, the delivery method is the way that you *deliver* that interaction. There's a subtle but important difference. For example, suppose that you have decided to use a speaker-led presentation method. That's the big picture, but how will you deliver it? Will you present from a computer or use 35mm slides or overhead transparencies or just plain old handouts? All of these methods fall under the big umbrella of "speaker-led."

PowerPoint gives you a lot of options for your delivery method. Some of these options are more appropriate for speaker-led shows, while others can be used for any presentation method. Here are some of the choices:

- **PowerPoint presentation as a live show.** You can use PowerPoint's Slide Show view to play the slides on a computer screen. If necessary, you can also hook up a large, external monitor to the PC so that the audience can see it better. This setup requires that PowerPoint be installed on the computer at the presentation site. This method works for speaker-led, self-running, or user-interactive shows.

- **PDF or XPS file.** You can save your presentation in PDF or XPS format and then distribute that file in any way you like. You could make it available for download from a website, for example, or send it to people via e-mail. However, you lose the animation effects, the narration, the timings, and the music.

A

- **Video.** You can save the presentation as a video and then distribute the video. Unlike with PDF/XPS, you don't lose any of the audiovisual effects; the audience sees the show just as you created it, and they don't need PowerPoint to see it. (They do, however, need a player that can handle the video format in which you are distributing the video.)

- **Presentation on CD.** You can create a CD that contains the presentation. The presentation starts automatically when the viewer inserts the CD into a PC. This method is most useful for self-running or user-interactive shows.

- **Broadcast.** You can broadcast your presentation on the Internet so that others can view it on their own computers in real time. Presentation broadcasting has been improved in PowerPoint 2013 and is covered in Chapter 20, "Preparing a Presentation for Mass Distribution."

- **Overhead transparencies.** This is a very old and low-tech method, but it's still an option. You can create overhead transparencies, which are just clear sheets, on most printers. During your presentation, you place them on an overhead projector one at a time.

> **CAUTION**
> Be careful that the transparencies that you buy are designed for your printer! For example, inkjet transparencies will melt in a laser printer.

- **35mm slides.** Again, a very old technology, but still available if needed. 35mm slides look good and transport well in carousels, but you lose all your special effects, such as animation and sounds.

- **Paper.** If there is no projection media available, then your last resort is to distribute your slides to the audience on paper. If you give them handouts, these handouts should be a supplement to an on-screen show and not the main show themselves.

Chapter 17 covers printing. See Chapter 19 for more on self-running presentations.

Step 4: Choosing a Theme That Matches Your Medium

PowerPoint comes with so many themes and templates that you're sure to find one that is appropriate for your situation. A *theme* is a set of design settings: background, fonts, colors, and graphic effects. PowerPoint 2013 has many built-in themes that are available in every presentation, and you can also create your own themes and use themes that others have created and stored in theme files.

A *template* is a full-fledged PowerPoint file that has been designated as a sample from which you can create new presentations. It contains everything that a presentation requires, including sample slides. A template can also contain multiple themes that are piggybacked onto slide masters within the template. When you start a new presentation, you do so from a template, and you inherit any themes and sample slides in that template in addition to having the built-in themes available.

> **TIP**
>
> You aren't stuck with the color scheme or design that comes with a particular theme or template. As you learn in Chapter 4, "Working with Layouts, Themes, and Masters," you can apply different color, font, and effects themes separately from the overall theme.

What's the best theme to use? What are the best colors? It all depends on the situation and on your presentation medium.

If you are lucky enough to have access to a computer-based presentation system, you can show your slides on a PC monitor or TV screen. Some large meeting facilities have projectors that let you project the image onto very large screens.

Here are some formatting guidelines for presenting on a computer screen:

- **Fonts.** The image on a computer screen is usually nice and sharp, and so you can use any font. However, you should first test your presentation on the computer and projector from which you'll be presenting because some fonts may look more jagged than others. If you are presenting to a large group on a small screen, make sure you keep all of the lettering rather large. Also make sure the font is available on the presentation computer; if it's not there, your text and bullets may not look the way you anticipated.

- **Text color.** Go for contrast. Both dark text on a light background and light text on a dark background work well.

- **Background color.** A dark background such as dark blue, green, or purple is a good choice if the room is not too dark. Light backgrounds can add ambient light to the room, which can sometimes be helpful. You are also free to use gradients, shading, patterns, pictures, and other special backgrounds because all of these elements display nicely on most monitors.

- **Content.** You can go all out with your content. Not only can you include both text and graphics, you can also include animations, transitions, sounds, and videos.

If you are showing the presentation on a large screen, the following suggestions may be helpful:

- **Fonts.** You can use almost any readable font. If your audience will sit far away from the screen, stick with plain fonts such as Arial and Calibri for the body text.

- **Text color.** Go for contrast. Try light text on a dark background. My personal favorite for large-format screens is bright yellow text on a navy blue background.

A

- **Background color.** Keep it dark — but not black. Light colors make the screen too bright. Dark blues, greens, and purples are all good choices. Stick with solid backgrounds to compensate for any image distortion that occurs on-screen. You should avoid patterned, shaded, or clip art backgrounds.
- **Content.** You can use any combination of text and graphics with success, but it has to be static. Animations and transitions don't work with 35mm slides. For example, if you have a bulleted list, don't build the bulleted list one bullet at a time from slide to slide. It looks awkward.

Using a noncomputerized overhead projector, like the one your teacher may have had in grade school (if you're middle-aged or older), is never anyone's first choice. However, sometimes it may be all that is available. An overhead projector image is medium sized (probably about 36" × 36"), but often of poor quality. You will probably be fighting with room lighting, and so your slides may appear washed out. Here are some tips for preparing slides that you will be showing with overhead projectors:

- **Fonts.** For headings, choose chunky block fonts, such as Arial Black, that can stand up to a certain amount of image distortion. For small type, choose clear, easy-to-read fonts such as Arial or Calibri.
- **Text color.** Black letters on a light background stand out well. Avoid semi-dark lettering, such as medium blue, because it easily washes out under an overhead projector's powerful light.
- **Background color.** Avoid dark backgrounds. You probably will not position each slide perfectly on the overhead projector, and the white space around the edges is distracting if your transparencies have a dark background. Consider using a simple white background when you know that you're going to be using transparencies — and *especially* when you want to write on the transparencies.
- **Content.** Keep it simple. Overheads are best when they are text heavy, without a lot of fancy extras or clip art. The overhead projector is an old technology, and slides that are too dressy seem pretentious.

Step 5: Developing the Content

Your slides should say to the audience, "I had you in mind when I created this." They should also say, "Relax; I'm a professional, and I know what I'm doing." Good-looking, appropriate slides can give the audience a sense of security and can lend authority to your message. On the other hand, poorly done or inconsistent slides can tell the audience, "I just slapped this thing together at the last minute." They might even say, "I don't really know what I'm doing."

Only after you have made all of the decisions in steps 1 through 4 can you start developing your content in a real PowerPoint presentation. Now comes the work of writing the text for each slide, which most people prefer to do in Normal view. Type the text on the outline or on the text placeholder on the slide itself, and you're ready to roll.

Developing your content may include more than just typing text. For example, your content may include charts (created in PowerPoint or imported from another program such as Excel), pictures, and other elements.

Avoiding Information Overload

When presenting, you want to give the audience exactly the information they need and no more. You don't want them to leave clutching their heads and saying, "Wow! That was too much to absorb!" or "What a waste of time!" You may have a great deal of information that you need to convey to the audience in a very short time. To ensure that they absorb it all without feeling overwhelmed, here are a few ideas:

- **Before you give your presentation, analyze it closely to make sure that you cover only the essential topics.** By trimming some nonessential topics, you make more room to cover the important themes in enough detail.

- **Don't try to cram every detail onto your slides.** Use the slides for general talking points, and then fill in the discussion with your speech.

- **Use SmartArt to replace bullets.** As you learn in Chapter 10, you can easily use the SmartArt diagrams in PowerPoint in place of a plain bulleted list to make the information more memorable and easier to understand.

- **Provide detailed handouts that elaborate on your slides.** Ensure that the audience receives them at the beginning of the presentation. Then, refer to the handouts throughout the presentation, letting the audience know that they can read all of the details later.

- **Summarize at the end of the presentation with a few simple slides.** These should contain bullet points that outline what the audience should have learned. You might even want to use interim summary slides throughout a complex presentation.

Chapter 3 guides you through the process of creating slides and text boxes. You learn about graphical content in Part II of this book. In Lab 1, you learn how to present content without bulleted lists.

Step 6: Creating the Visual Image

The term *visual image* refers to the overall impression that the audience gets from watching the presentation. You can create a polished, professional impression by making small tweaks to your presentation after you have decided on the content.

You can enhance the visual image by making minor adjustments to the slide's design. For example, you can give a dark slide a warmer feel by using bright yellow instead of white for lettering. Repositioning a company logo and making it larger may make the headings look less lonely. You can use WordArt effects to dress up some text and make it look more

A

graphical. A product picture is more attractive in a larger size or with a different-colored matte around it. It takes practice and experience to add these little touches successfully.

Audiences like consistency. They like visual elements that they can rely on, such as a repeated company logo on every slide, accurate page numbering on handouts, and the title appearing in exactly the same spot on every slide. You can create a consistent visual image by enforcing these rules in your presentation development. It's easier than you might think because PowerPoint provides a slide master specifically for images and text that should appear on each slide.

 You'll work with slide masters and learn more about the benefits of consistency in Chapter 4.

Step 7: Adding Multimedia Effects

If you're creating a self-running presentation, multimedia effects are extremely important for developing audience interest. Flashy videos and soundtracks can make even the most boring topic fun to hear about, especially for young audiences. How about a trumpet announcing the arrival of your new product on the market or a video of your CEO explaining the reasoning behind the recent merger?

> **CAUTION**
>
> Even if you are going to be speaking live, you still might want to incorporate some multimedia elements into your show. However, be careful not to let them outshine you or appear gratuitous. Be aware of your audience (see step 1), and remember that older and higher-level managers want less flash and more substance.

All kinds of presentations can benefit from slide animations and transitions. *Animations* are simple movements of the objects on a slide. For example, you can make the bullet points on a list fly onto the page one at a time and discuss each one on its own. When the next bullet flies in, the previous ones can turn a different color so that the current one stands out. You might also animate a picture of a car so that it appears to "drive onto" the slide, accompanied by the sound of an engine revving. You can also animate charts by making data series appear one at a time so that it looks like the chart is building. *Transitions* are animated effects for moving from slide to slide. The most basic and boring transition is to simply remove one slide from the screen and replace it with another. However, you can also use many alternative effects such as zooming the new slide in; sliding it from the top, bottom, left, or right; or creating a fade-in transition effect.

 Chapters 14 and 15 deal with the mechanics of placing sound and video clips into a presentation and controlling when and how they play. You can learn about animations and transitions in Chapter 16.

Step 8: Creating the Handouts and Notes

This step is applicable only to speaker-led presentations. With a live audience, you may want to provide handouts so that they can follow along. Handouts can be verbatim copies of your slides or abbreviated versions with only the most basic information included as a memory jogger. Handouts can be either black and white or in color, and PowerPoint provides several handout formats. For example, you can print from one to nine slides per page or export the slides to a Word document with or without lines so the audience can write additional notes.

> **TIP**
>
> A continual debate rages in the professional speakers' community over when to give out handouts. Some people feel that if you distribute handouts beforehand, people will read them and then not listen to the presentation. Others feel that if you distribute handouts after the presentation, people will frantically try to take their own notes during the presentation or will not follow the ideas as easily. There's no real right or wrong answer, it seems, and so you should distribute them whenever it makes the most sense for your situation.

As the speaker, you may need your own special set of handouts with your own notes that the audience should not see. PowerPoint calls these notes pages, and there is a special view for creating them. (You can also enter notes directly into the Notes pane in Normal view.)

Notes are covered, along with handouts, in Chapter 17, which also guides you through selecting the appropriate size and format for your handouts as well as working with your printer to get the best results.

Step 9: Rehearsing the Presentation

No matter which type of presentation you are creating (speaker led, self-running, or user interactive), you need to rehearse it. However, the goals for rehearsing are different for each type.

Rehearsing a Live Presentation

When you rehearse a live presentation, you check the presentation slides to ensure that they are complete, accurate, and in the right order. You may need to rearrange them and hide some of them for backup-only use.

You should also rehearse using PowerPoint's presentation tools in Presenter view, which displays each slide on a monitor and lets you move from slide to slide, take notes, assign action items, and even draw directly on a slide. Make sure you know how to back up, how to jump to the beginning or end, and how to display one of your backup slides.

A

You can learn about presentation navigation skills in Chapter 18.

Rehearsing a Self-Running Presentation

With a speaker-led presentation, the presenter can fix any glitches that pop up or explain away any errors. With a self-running presentation, you don't have that luxury. The presentation itself is your emissary. Therefore, you must go over it repeatedly, checking it many times to make sure that it is perfect before distributing it. Nothing is worse than a self-running presentation that doesn't run or one that contains an embarrassing error.

The most important feature in a self-running presentation is *timing*. You must make the presentation pause for the correct amount of time so that the audience can read the text on each slide. The pause must be long enough so that even slow readers can catch it all but short enough so that fast readers do not become bored. You can now see how difficult this can be to make perfect.

PowerPoint has a Rehearse Timings feature that is designed to help you with this task. It lets you show the slides and advance them manually after the correct amount of time has passed. The Rehearse Timings feature records how much time you spend on each slide and gives you a report so that you can modify the timing if necessary. For example, you may be working on a presentation that is supposed to last 10 minutes, but with your timings, it comes out to only 9 minutes. You can add additional time for each slide to stretch it out to last the full 10 minutes. You may also want to record voice-over narration for your presentation. You can also rehearse this, to make sure the voice matches the slide that it is supposed to describe (which is absolutely crucial, as you can imagine!).

Rehearsing a User-Interactive Presentation

In a user-interactive presentation, you provide the readers with on-screen buttons that they can click to move through the presentation, so timing is not an issue. The crucial factor with a user-interactive presentation is link accuracy. Each button on each slide is a link. When your readers click a button for the next slide, it must take them to the next slide and not to somewhere else. And if you include a hyperlink to a web address on the Internet, when the readers click it, the web browser should open and that page should appear. If the hyperlink contains a typo and the readers see File Not Found instead of the web page, the error reflects poorly on you. Chapter 20 covers creating and inserting these links.

Step 10: Giving the Presentation

For a user-interactive or self-running presentation, giving the presentation is somewhat anticlimactic. You just make it available and the users watch it. Yawn.

However, for a speaker-led presentation, giving the speech is the highlight, the pinnacle, of the process. If you've done a good job rehearsing, you are already familiar with PowerPoint's presentation controls. You should be prepared to back up, to skip ahead, to answer questions by displaying hidden slides, or to pause the whole thing (and black out the screen) so that you can hold a tangential discussion.

 Chapter 18 covers all of the situations in which you would use PowerPoint's presentation controls in case you need to review them.

What remains now? Nothing, except for setting up the room and overcoming your stage fright. Later in this chapter, you'll get some tips about using a meeting room most effectively and being a dynamic speaker. Check them out — and then go get 'em!

If you are planning to distribute your presentation through the Internet, you have a big decision to make. You can distribute the presentation in its native PowerPoint format and preserve all of its more exciting features, such as animations and videos. However, not everyone on the Internet owns a copy of PowerPoint, and so you are limiting your audience.

Another option is to save the presentation in PDF or XPS format. These are similar formats; PDF format is owned by Adobe, and XPS format is owned by Microsoft. Viewers need Adobe Reader (free from www.adobe.com) or Microsoft XPS Reader (comes with Windows Vista and later or free from www.microsoft.com). This converts the slides to a series of static pages with no multimedia effects, but everyone can view it, provided they have or download the appropriate viewer.

You could also save the presentation as a series of graphic files, in any of several popular formats (GIF, JPEG, PNG, or TIFF). With this method, you not only lose all multimedia capability, you also lose a sense of continuity because the viewer must load and view each slide individually in the correct order.

Finally, you can save the presentation as a video (movie) clip and make that available online. PowerPoint 2013 provides a very easy-to-use interface for making videos in the MPEG-4 and Windows Media Video (WMV) formats. You lose none of the effects, but the audience is at your mercy in terms of timing; they can't flip quickly through the slides to skim them. They can jump to spots in the video using the video player, but jumping from slide to slide is iffy, especially if the amount of time spent on each slide is inconsistent.

 You learn more about preparing a presentation for the Internet in Chapter 20. For more on saving a movie clip and making it available online, see Chapter 15.

A

Step 11: Assessing Your Success and Refining Your Work

If giving a presentation is a one-time thing for you — great. It's over, and you never have to think about it again. However, it is more likely that you will have to give another presentation someday, somewhere, and so you shouldn't drive the experience out of your mind just yet. Perhaps you learned something that might be useful to you later. Immediately after the presentation, while it is still fresh in your mind, jot down your responses to the following questions. Then keep them on file to refer to later, the next time you have to do a presentation!

- Did the colors and design of the slides seem appropriate?
- Could everyone in the audience read the slides easily?
- Did the audience look mostly at you, at the screen, or at the handouts? Was that what you intended?
- Did the audience take notes as you were speaking? If so, did you give them handouts with note-taking lines to write on?
- Was the length of the presentation appropriate? Did the audience become bored or restless at any point?
- Were there any slides that you wished you had prepared but didn't?
- Were there any slides that you would omit if you were doing it over?
- Did your speaker notes give you enough help that you could speak with authority?
- Did the transitions and animations add to the entertainment value, or were they distracting or corny?
- Did the sound and video clips play with adequate quality? Were they appropriate and useful?

Choosing and Arranging the Room

Are you giving a live presentation? The choice of room — and its arrangement — can make a big difference in your success. If you have any say in it, make sure that you get an appropriate size room for the presentation. For example, a room that is too small makes people feel uncomfortable and seems crowded, whereas a room that is too large can create a false formality and distance that can cause people to lose focus. You also don't want to have to shout to be heard.

> **CAUTION**
> To avoid having to shout during your presentation, make sure there is a working sound system, with a microphone and amplifier available, if necessary. If possible, check this detail a few days ahead of time to avoid scrambling for one at the last minute.

Next, make sure that tables and chairs are set up appropriately. Figure A.2 through Figure A.5 illustrate several setups, each of which is appropriate for a certain kind of presentation:

- For a classroom setting where the audience will take a lot of notes, give them something to write on, as shown in Figure A.2. This arrangement works well when the audience will be listening to and interacting with you but not with one another.

FIGURE A.2

In a classroom arrangement, each audience member has plenty of room to write and work.

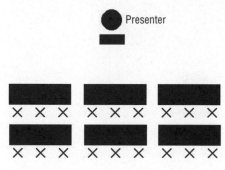

- If the audience is not expected to take notes while you are giving the speech, consider an auditorium setup, as shown in Figure A.3. This arrangement is also good for fitting a lot of people into a small room. (This is also known as theater-style seating.)

FIGURE A.3

An auditorium setup (or theater-style seating) fits a lot of people into a small space; it's great for large company meetings.

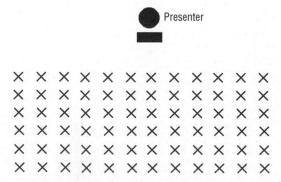

A

- If you want the audience to interact in small groups, you should set up groups so that people can see each other and still see you. Figure A.4 shows a small-group arrangement.

FIGURE A.4

Having small groups clustered around tables encourages discussion and works well for presentations that incorporate hands-on activities.

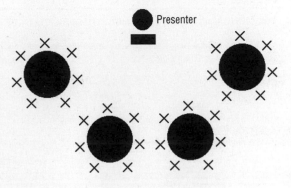

- To make it easier for the entire group to interact with one another as a whole, use a U-shaped setup, as shown in Figure A.5.

FIGURE A.5

Arrange the room in a U shape if you want participants to have discussions as a large group.

Choosing Your Attire

The outfit that you choose for the presentation should depend on the expectations of the audience and the message that you want to send to them. Before you decide what to wear, ask yourself, "What will the audience be wearing?" Choose one of these classifications:

- **Very informal.** Jeans, shorts, T-shirts
- **Informal.** Nice jeans, polo shirts
- **Business casual.** Dress slacks and oxfords, with or without a tie, for men; dress slacks or a skirt and a dressy, casual shirt (sweater, silk blouse, vest) for women
- **Business.** Dress slacks and a shirt and tie, with or without a jacket, for men; dress or skirt (blazer optional) for women
- **Business formal.** Suit and tie for men; suit or conservative dress for women

Now, shape your own choice of attire, depending on the impression that you want to convey. To convey authority, dress one level above your audience. Use this attire any time your audience does not know who you are and when you need to establish yourself as the leader or the expert. (Most teachers fall into this category.) For example, if the audience is dressed informally, men should wear a dress shirt and tie and women should wear a skirt and sweater. (If you're female and will be seated on a stage, you might want to wear pants or a very long skirt.) However, you should not dress more than two levels above your audience because it makes them feel intimidated. For example, if you are presenting to factory workers who are dressed in very informal clothing, you should not wear a business suit.

To convey teamwork and approachability, dress at the same level as the audience, or slightly (no more than one level) above. For example, if you are a CEO visiting a factory that you manage, the workers already recognize your authority — you don't have to prove it. Instead, you want to appear approachable, and so if they are wearing informal clothing, you might wear dress slacks and a dress shirt (but no tie) if you're a man or slacks and a sweater if you're a woman.

Avoid dressing below the audience's level. This is almost never a good idea. If you do not know what the audience will be wearing, err on the side of formality. It is better to look a little stiff than it is to look less professional than your audience.

Keeping the Audience Interested

There are no miracle cures here — some people are naturally better, more interesting speakers than others. However, there are definite steps that all speakers can take to stack the odds in their favor when it comes to giving a successful live presentation.

A

Speech Techniques

Here are some strategies for improving your speaking style:

- **Plant your feet firmly; don't pace.** Pacing makes you appear nervous, and people have to constantly follow you with their eyes. However, you should keep your upper body mobile and should not be afraid to use arm gestures.

- **Use gestures to support your voice.** If you are talking about three different points, then hold up fingers to illustrate one, two, and three points. If you are talking about bringing things together, bring your hands together in front of you to illustrate. Don't freeze your hands at your sides.

- **Don't memorize your speech.** If someone asks a question, it will throw you off and you'll forget where you were.

- **Conversely, don't read the speech word for word from your notes.** Notes should contain keywords and facts but not the actual words that you will say.

- **Don't talk with your face in your notes.** Make eye contact with an audience member before you begin speaking.

- **Pick a few people in the audience, in different places in the room, and make direct eye contact with each of them, in turn, as you speak.** Talk directly to a single person for the duration of the point that you are making and then move on. Also, don't forget to smile!

- **Don't be afraid to pause.** Speaking slowly, with pauses to look at your notes, is much more preferable than rushing through the presentation. Keep in mind that pauses that might seem very long to you really aren't.

- **Don't stare at or read your slides.** Focus your attention on your audience, and pay as little attention to the support materials as possible while you speak. You want to engage directly with your audience to deliver your message in your own words.

- **Emphasize verbs and action words in your presentation.** Remember that the verb is the most powerful element in the sentence.

Content Tips

Consider these content techniques:

- If the audience is not in a hurry and you are not rushed for time in your presentation, start with some kind of icebreaker, like an anecdote or joke.

CAUTION

Be careful with humor. Analyze the joke that you plan to tell from all angles, making very sure that it does not include offensive references to race, ethnic group, gender, sexual orientation, or class of workers. It is *much* worse to tell a joke that hurts someone's feelings — even one person — than it is to tell none at all.

- Include the audience in interactive exercises that help to firm up their understanding of the topic.

- Ask questions to see whether the audience understood you, and give out small prizes to the people who give correct answers. Nothing energizes an audience into participation more than prizes, even if they are cheap giveaways like key chains and bandannas.

- If possible, split the presentation into two or more sessions, with a short break and question-and-answer period between each session.

- During the Q&A portion, turn off the slide projector, overhead, or computer screen so that people focus on you and on the question, not on the previous slide. If turning off the equipment isn't practical, consider inserting a simple Q&A Session title slide or a blank slide that displays during the Q&A, or press the B key (for a black screen) or the W key (for a white screen).

Managing Stage Fright

Even if you're comfortable with the PowerPoint slides that you've created, you still might be a little nervous about the actual speech that you're going to give. This is normal. In fact, a study from a few years ago showed that public speaking is the number-one fear among businesspeople. Fear of death came in second. That should tell you something.

It's okay to be a little bit nervous because it gives you extra energy and an edge that can actually make your presentation better. However, if you're too nervous, it can make you seem less credible.

One way to overcome stage fright is to stop focusing on yourself and instead focus on your audience. Ask yourself what the audience needs and how you are going to supply that need. Become their caretaker. Dedicate yourself to making the audience understand you. The more you think of others, the less you think of yourself.

Summary

Although this appendix had little to do with PowerPoint *per se*, it focused on making successful presentations using your PowerPoint slides as a tool. The information that you learned here can help beginning presenters look more experienced and more experienced presenters polish their skills to perfection.

A

Essential SkyDrive Skills

IN THIS APPENDIX

Understanding Your SkyDrive Interface Options

Managing Files on Your SkyDrive

SkyDrive is a Microsoft-owned cloud-based storage space. Each user has their own storage area, where they can store private files, share files with certain specific others, or make files publicly available. A certain amount of storage space is free, and you can pay if you want more than what's provided. (The amount of storage space available depends on when you signed up for your account and what type of account you have.)

As you've seen in your work with PowerPoint throughout this book, your SkyDrive is your default save location for PowerPoint and other Office apps. Using SkyDrive as your main document storage area has these consequences:

- You can access your files from any computer, whether or not it has PowerPoint installed on it.

- You can share your work with other people without having to send them separate copies of it.

- Your files are available only when Internet access is available. However, you can get around that by installing the SkyDrive for Windows app on your PC, which automatically mirrors the content of your SkyDrive on your PC and keeps the copy in sync with the SkyDrive's actual content.

There are several ways of accessing your SkyDrive. This appendix covers the four major ways:

- Access your SkyDrive space on the Web via www.skydrive.com.
- Use the SkyDrive for Windows desktop app.
- Use the SkyDrive links within PowerPoint when saving or opening files.
- Use the Windows 8 SkyDrive app on a PC or tablet that has Windows 8 installed.

Understanding Your SkyDrive Interface Options

The following sections explain the four methods of accessing your SkyDrive.

Signing into the SkyDrive Web Interface

Some SkyDrive management activities can be performed only via the SkyDrive web interface, so you should know how to access it. To get started, point your browser to www.skydrive.com. (The page will redirect to the server where Microsoft is hosting SkyDrive at the moment. As of this writing it is https://skydrive.live.com, but by the time you read this, it may have changed.)

If you already have a Microsoft account and your computer is set up to automatically sign you into it, your SkyDrive's content appears automatically. Figure B.1 shows an example, but you may have different files and folders than shown. From this interface you can click folders and files to open them or use the buttons on the toolbar at the top of the window to perform other actions. I'll tell you more about those actions later in this appendix.

FIGURE B.1

The SkyDrive web interface

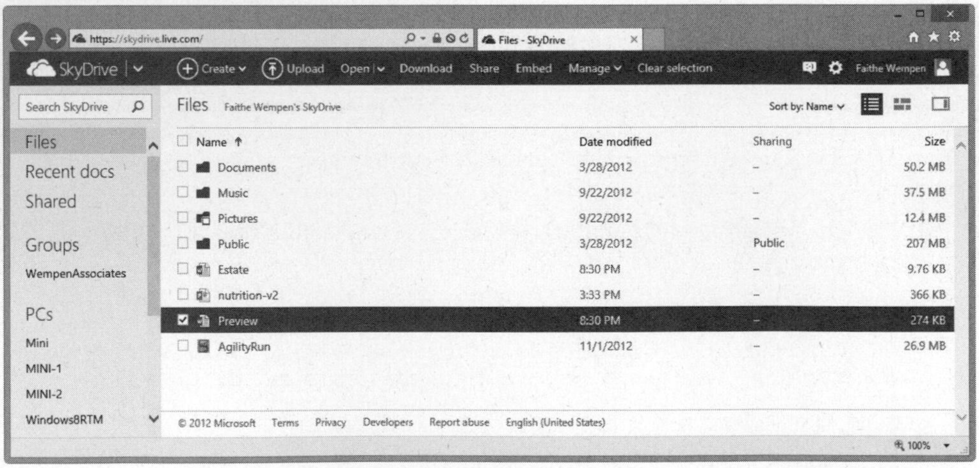

Installing and Using SkyDrive for Windows

To get around the drawback of not being able to access your SkyDrive files offline, and to make managing SkyDrive files as easy as managing your local files, install the SkyDrive for Windows app on your PC.

The SkyDrive for Windows app automatically mirrors the content of your SkyDrive on your PC and keeps the copy in sync with the SkyDrive's actual content. When you are not connected to the Internet, it allows you to work on local copies of your files, and then it automatically uploads the updates to your SkyDrive the next time Internet connectivity is available. The SkyDrive for Windows app also places a shortcut to your locally mirrored copies of your SkyDrive content on the Favorites list in File Explorer (or Windows Explorer), so you can easily access them with one click.

To get SkyDrive for Windows, open the SkyDrive web interface, as described in the preceding section, and then in the navigation pane at the left, click the Get SkyDrive Apps hyperlink. From there, find and follow the link for the Windows desktop apps. Click Download Now and follow the prompts to complete the installation. (I'm being intentionally vague about the steps here because by the time you read this, they may have changed; Microsoft updates its websites frequently.)

After SkyDrive for Windows has been installed, you'll see a SkyDrive shortcut in the Favorites list in File Explorer (Windows 8) or Windows Explorer (Windows 7). This shortcut points to a folder on your hard drive: C:\Users*username*\SkyDrive. This folder is a staging area for your online SkyDrive and is automatically synchronized with it. Figure B.2 shows my SkyDrive folder on my hard drive, for example. Notice that each icon has a green check mark on it, indicating that it has been synchronized. In other words the copies on my SkyDrive are identical to these copies on my local machine. When the copies are out of sync because an update hasn't occurred yet, a pair of blue arrows appears on the icon to indicate a sync is scheduled or in progress. If there is a problem with a sync (such as Internet unavailability), a red *x* symbol appears on the icon to indicate that.

FIGURE B.2

The SkyDrive for Windows desktop application has been installed and operates within File Manager.

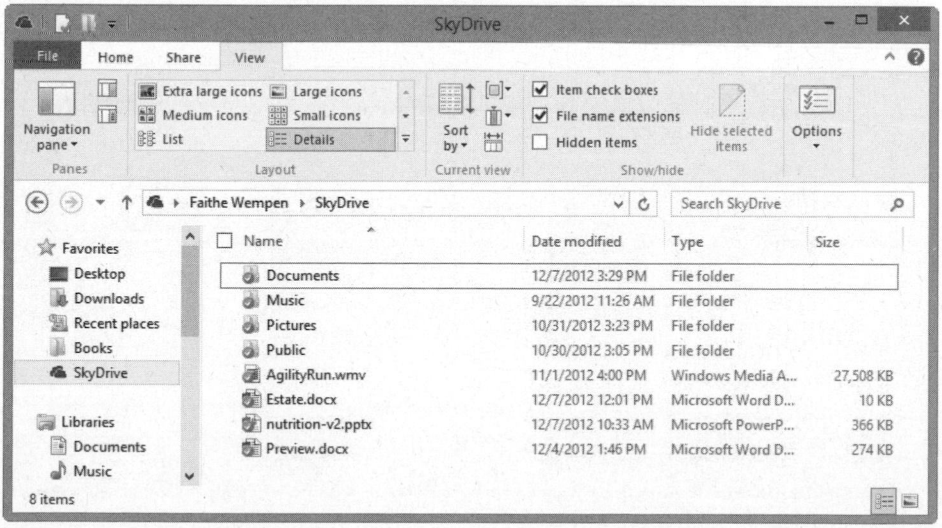

B

Managing SkyDrive Files Within PowerPoint

As you saw in Chapter 2, "Creating and Saving Presentation Files," you can save and open files on your SkyDrive from within PowerPoint. When you choose Save As from the File menu, the default save location is your SkyDrive. You can click Browse to browse your SkyDrive's content, or you can click one of the folder names under Recent Folders to access one of the folders within your SkyDrive.

Using the Windows 8 SkyDrive App

If you are running Windows 8, you can access the Windows 8 SkyDrive app from the Start screen. It's a tablet-style app optimized for touchscreens, like the other new Windows 8–style applications. Access it from the SkyDrive tile on the Start screen.

Within the SkyDrive app you will see your folders listed to the left, with picture previews of the folders' content if available. To the right of the folders, you'll see tiles for any files that are stored at the top level of your SkyDrive's organizational system, not in any particular folder. Right-click to open a command bar at the bottom of the screen, and choose commands from it to work with your content. Figure B.3 shows the command bar open. Using the commands on the command bar, you can do all the basic file management tasks from the Windows 8 SkyDrive app, such as uploading and downloading, creating new folders, deleting, renaming, and moving. (Those latter three commands are on a submenu when you choose Manage.)

FIGURE B.3

The Windows 8 SkyDrive app

When you click a file or folder, it opens. If it's a file, it opens in its default program. To choose some other program in which to open the file, click Open With on the command bar, and then select the desired app from the menu that appears.

Managing Files on Your SkyDrive

In the following sections, you'll learn how to perform basic file management activities on your SkyDrive, including uploading and downloading, copy, moving, deleting, and renaming files.

Uploading a File

Uploading means transferring a file from your local hard drive, or some other local location, to your SkyDrive. The procedure for placing a file on your SkyDrive depends on which interface you are using. Table B.1 summarizes the steps by interface type.

TABLE B.1   **Uploading to Your SkyDrive**

Interface Type	Steps
Web interface	1. Display the folder in which you want to place the file.
	2. Click the Upload button in the toolbar.
	3. Select the file to upload.
	4. Click Open.
SkyDrive for Windows	1. In File Explorer (Windows Explorer), select the file.
	2. Press Ctrl+C to copy the file to the Clipboard.
	3. In the Favorites bar, click SkyDrive.
	4. Navigate to the desired folder on your SkyDrive.
	5. Press Ctrl+V to paste the file.
PowerPoint 2013	1. Choose File ➪ Save As.
	2. Click Browse.
	3. Navigate to the desired folder on your SkyDrive.
	4. Type a filename in the File Name box.
	5. Click OK.
Windows 8 SkyDrive app	1. Display the folder in which you want to place the file.
	2. Right-click or swipe up from the bottom to display the command bar.
	3. Click Upload.
	4. Select the file to upload.
	5. Click Add to SkyDrive.

B

Downloading a File from Your SkyDrive

Downloading means copying a file from your SkyDrive to a local drive, such as your hard drive. Table B.2 summarizes the steps by interface type.

TABLE B.2   Downloading from Your SkyDrive

Interface Type	Steps
Web interface	1. Click the check mark next to a file's name to select it.
	2. Click the Download button in the toolbar.
	3. If prompted by your browser to open or save, click Save.
	4. If prompted for a save location, choose it and click Save. (Some browsers do not prompt for a save location; they save all downloads to a default location.)
SkyDrive for Windows	1. In File Explorer (Windows Explorer), click SkyDrive in the Favorites list.
	2. Select the file to be downloaded.
	3. Press Ctrl+C to copy the file to the Clipboard.
	4. Navigate to a local folder location.
	5. Press Ctrl+V to paste the file.
PowerPoint 2013	1. Choose File ➪ Open.
	2. Click Browse.
	3. Select the file on your SkyDrive.
	4. Click Open.
	5. Choose File ➪ Save As.
	6. Click Computer, and then click Browse.
	7. Navigate to a local folder location.
	8. Click OK.
Windows 8 SkyDrive app	1. Right-click the file to select it, or on a touchscreen, press and hold on the file.
	2. Click Download.
	3. Navigate to a local folder location.
	4. Click Choose This Folder.
	5. Click OK.

Renaming a File or Folder

One way to rename a file is to save it with a different name and then delete the original. However, it's much easier to directly rename a file with the Rename command. Table B.3 summarizes the steps for renaming a file or folder on your SkyDrive.

TABLE B.3 Renaming a File or Folder on Your SkyDrive

Interface Type	Steps
Web interface	1. Click the check mark next to a file's name to select it.
	2. Click the Manage button on the toolbar.
	3. Click Rename.
	4. Type the new name and press Enter.
SkyDrive for Windows	1. In File Explorer (Windows Explorer), click the file you want to rename.
	2. Click Home ⇨ Rename.
	3. Type the new name and press Enter.
PowerPoint 2013	1. Choose File ⇨ Open.
	2. Click Browse.
	3. Right-click the file on your SkyDrive.
	4. Choose Rename.
	5. Type the new name and press Enter.
Windows 8 SkyDrive app	1. Right-click the file to select it.
	2. Click Manage.
	3. Click Rename.
	4. Type the new name and press Enter.

Moving or Copying a File or Folder

Moving and *copying*, in the context of this section, refer to moving or copying within the SkyDrive itself, from one folder to another, and not into or out of the SkyDrive (which would be considered uploading or downloading, respectively, and which were covered earlier in this chapter). Table B.4 explains how to move and copy files or folders on your SkyDrive.

TABLE B.4 Moving or Copying Files or Folders on Your SkyDrive

Interface Type	Moving	Copying
Web interface	1. Click the check mark next to the name of a file or folder to select it. 2. Click the Manage button on the toolbar. 3. Click Move To. 4. Click the desired folder in the dialog box. 5. Click Move.	1. Click the check mark next to the name of a file or folder to select it. 2. Click the Manage button on the toolbar. 3. Click Copy To. 4. Click the desired folder in the dialog box. 5. Click Copy.
SkyDrive for Windows	1. In File Explorer (Windows Explorer), click the file or folder you want to move. 2. Press Ctrl+X or choose Home ⇨ Cut. 3. Navigate to the folder to which you want to move the file or folder. 4. Press Ctrl+V or choose Home ⇨ Paste.	1. In File Explorer (Windows Explorer), click the file or folder you want to move. 2. Press Ctrl+C or choose Home ⇨ Copy. 3. Navigate to the folder to which you want to copy the file or folder. 4. Press Ctrl+V or choose Home ⇨ Paste.
PowerPoint 2013	1. Choose File ⇨ Open. 2. Click Browse. 3. Right-click the file or folder on your SkyDrive and click Cut, or press Ctrl+X. 4. Navigate to the folder to which you want to move the file. 5. Right-click an empty area and choose Paste, or press Ctrl+V.	1. Choose File ⇨ Open. 2. Click Browse. 3. Right-click the file or folder on your SkyDrive and click Copy, or press Ctrl+C. 4. Navigate to the folder to which you want to copy the file or folder. 5. Right-click an empty area and choose Paste, or press Ctrl+V.
Windows 8 SkyDrive app	1. Right-click the file or folder to select it. 2. Click Manage. 3. Click Move. 4. Navigate to the folder to which you want to move the file or folder. 5. Click Move Here.	Not applicable; you can't copy files or folders in this app.

Deleting a File or Folder

Deleting a file or folder removes it. A Recycle Bin is available for retrieving deleted files on your SkyDrive, but it is accessible only from the web interface.

Table B.5 summarizes the steps for deleting and restoring files and folders on your SkyDrive.

TABLE B.5   Deleting and Restoring a File or Folder on Your SkyDrive

Interface Type	Deleting	Restoring a Deleted File
Web interface	1. Click the check mark next to the name of a file or folder to select it. 2. Click the Manage button. 3. Click Delete.	1. Click Recycle Bin at the bottom of the navigation pane at the left. 2. Click the check mark next to the name of a file or folder to select it. 3. Click Restore.
SkyDrive for Windows	1. In File Explorer (Windows Explorer), click the file or folder you want to delete. 2. Press the Delete key, or choose Home ⇨ Delete.	1. Open the Recycle Bin from your Windows Desktop. 2. Click the file to restore. 3. Click Restore the Selected Items.
PowerPoint 2013	1. Choose File ⇨ Open. 2. Click Browse. 3. Click the file or folder on your SkyDrive. 4. Press the Delete key.	To immediately restore a deletion, press Ctrl+Z. Otherwise, use the web interface or SkyDrive for Windows to restore the file.
Windows 8 SkyDrive app	1. Right-click the file or folder to select it. 2. Click Manage. 3. Click Delete. 4. Click Delete to confirm.	Not applicable; you can't restore files or folders in this app.

Sharing SkyDrive Files

You can easily share your SkyDrive files with other people. There are a variety of ways to do so. You can send email, post a link to Facebook, or create a hyperlink that you can then

B

share with others any way you like (such as pasting it into the HTML for a web page or pasting it into an instant messaging program).

Sharing is configured primarily through the web interface; the other interfaces aren't designed for doing it. However, in some cases you can access a command in another interface that will automatically open the web interface and start the sharing process. Table B.6 summarizes the methods of sharing.

TABLE B.6   Sharing a File on Your SkyDrive

Interface Type	Sharing Via Email	Getting a Share Link
Web interface	1. Click the check mark next to the name of a file or folder to select it. 2. Click the Share button. 3. Click Send Email. 4. In the To box, type the email address of the recipient. 5. Type a personal message (optional). 6. Mark or clear the Recipients Can Edit check box as desired. 7. Mark or clear the Require Everyone Who Accesses This to Sign In check box as desired. Note: If you mark the check box in step 7, only people with a Microsoft account will have access. 8. Click Share.	1. Click the check mark next to the name of a file or folder to select it. 2. Click the Share button. 3. Click Get a Link. 4. Click the Create button in either the View Only or View and Edit section. Or you can click the Make Public button. 5. Press Ctrl+C to copy the code. 6. Click Done. 7. Click in the application in which you want to share the link, and press Ctrl+V to paste it there.
SkyDrive for Windows	1. In File Explorer (Windows Explorer), right-click the file or folder you want to share, point to SkyDrive, and click Share. The web interface opens. 2. Go to step 3 in the procedure for the web interface above.	1. In File Explorer (Windows Explorer), right-click the file or folder you want to share, point to SkyDrive, and click Share. The web interface opens. 2. Go to step 3 in the procedure for the web interface above.

Interface Type	Sharing Via Email	Getting a Share Link
PowerPoint 2013	1. Choose File ⇨ Open.	1. Choose File ⇨ Open.
	2. Click Browse.	2. Click Browse.
	3. Right-click the file or folder on your SkyDrive that you want to share, point to SkyDrive, and click Share. The web interface opens.	3. Right-click the file or folder on your SkyDrive that you want to share, point to SkyDrive, and click Share. The web interface opens.
	4. Go to step 3 in the procedure for the web interface above.	4. Go to step 3 in the procedure for the web interface above.
Windows 8 SkyDrive app	Not applicable; you can't share files or folders in this app.	Not applicable; you can't share files or folders in this app.

B

Index

Index

S